A SOCIAL H
WESTERN POLITICAL THOUGHT

Ellen Meiksins Wood (1942–2016), for many years professor of political science at York University, Toronto, was the author of many books, including *Democracy against Capitalism*, *The Pristine Culture of Capitalism*, *The Origin of Capitalism*, and *Peasant-Citizen and Slave*.

A SOCIAL HISTORY
OF WESTERN
POLITICAL THOUGHT

ELLEN MEIKSINS WOOD

VERSO

London • New York

First published as one volume by Verso 2022
*Citizens to Lords: A Social History of Western Political Thought from
Antiquity to the Middle Ages* first published by Verso 2008
*Liberty and Property: A Social History of Western Political Thought
from Renaissance to Enlightenment* first published by Verso 2012
© Ellen Meiksins Wood 2022

1 3 5 7 9 10 8 6 4 2

Verso
UK: 6 Meard Street, London W1F 0EG
US: 388 Atlantic Avenue, Brooklyn, NY 11217
versobooks.com

Verso is the imprint of New Left Books

ISBN-13: 978-1-83976-609-1
ISBN-13: 978-1-83976-610-7 (UK EBK)
ISBN-13: 978-1-83976-611-4 (US EBK)

British Library Cataloguing in Publication Data
A catalogue record for this book is available from the British Library

Library of Congress Cataloging-in-Publication Data
A catalog record for this book is available from the Library of Congress

Typeset in Sabon MT by Hewer UK Ltd, Edinburgh
Printed and bound by CPI Group (UK) Ltd, Croydon CR0 4YY

CONTENTS

PART I.

CITIZENS TO LORDS:
ANTIQUITY TO THE MIDDLE AGES

ACKNOWLEDGEMENTS

As so often before, I am particularly grateful to George Comninel, who read the whole manuscript and made his customarily generous and insightful suggestions. My thanks also to Paul Cartledge, Janet Coleman and Gordon Schochet, who read parts of the manuscript and made useful comments but cannot, of course, be held responsible for any failures on my part to take good advice. Perry Anderson kindly agreed to my last-minute request for a quick reading of the whole text and made some very helpful suggestions. And special thanks to Ed Broadbent, who brilliantly played the role of every writer's dream audience, the intelligent general reader. I owe a great deal to his keenly critical eye, together with his unfailing support and encouragement.

My greatest debt is to Neal Wood. Many years ago, we decided that one day we would write a social history of political theory together. Somehow we never got around to it. There were always other projects to embark on and complete. Yet when, after his death, I set out to do it on my own, he remained in a sense the co-author. It was he who first introduced me to the history of political thought; it was he who coined the phrase, the 'social history of political theory'; and this project would have been inconceivable without his rich body of work in the field and his example of scholarly integrity combined with passionate engagement.

1

THE SOCIAL HISTORY
OF POLITICAL THEORY

What is Political Theory?

Every complex civilization with a state and organized leadership is
bound to generate reflection on the relations between leader and led,
rulers and subjects, command and obedience. Whether it takes the
form of systematic philosophy, poetry, parable or proverb, in oral
traditions or in the written word, we can call it political thought. But
the subject of this book is one very particular mode of political thinking
that emerged in the very particular historical conditions of ancient
Greece and developed over two millennia in what we now call Europe
and its colonial outposts.[1]

For better or worse, the Greeks invented their own distinctive mode
of political *theory*, a systematic and analytical interrogation of political
principles, full of laboriously constructed definitions and adversarial
argumentation, applying critical reason to questioning the very
foundations and legitimacy of traditional moral rules and the principles
of political right. While there have been many other ways of thinking
about politics in the Western world, what we think of as the classics

---

1   'Political' thought, in any of its forms, assumes the existence of political organization. For the purposes of this book, I shall call that form of organization the 'state',
defining it broadly enough to encompass a wide variety of forms, from the polis and
the ancient bureaucratic kingdom to the modern nation state – although throughout
this book, we shall often have occasion to take note of the differences among various
types of state. The state, then, is a 'complex of institutions by means of which the
power of the society is organized on a basis superior to kinship' – an organization of
power that entails a claim 'to paramountcy in the application of naked force to social
problems' and consists of 'formal, specialized instruments of coercion' (Morton Fried,
The Evolution of Political Society, New York: Random House, 1968, pp. 229–30). The
state embraces less inclusive institutions – households, clans, kinship groups, etc. –
and performs common social functions that such institutions cannot carry out.

of Western political thought, ancient and modern, belong to the tradition of political *theory* established by the Greeks.

Other ancient civilizations in many ways more advanced than the Greeks – in everything from agricultural techniques to commerce, navigation, and every conceivable craft or high art – produced vast literatures on every human practice, as well as speculations about the origins of life and the formation of the universe. But, in general, the political order was not treated as an object of systematic critical speculation.

We can, for example, contrast the ancient Greek mode of political speculation about principles of political order with the philosophy of ethical precept, aphorism, advice and example produced by the far more complex and advanced civilization of China, which had its own rich and varied tradition of political thought. Confucian philosophy, for instance, takes the form of aphorisms on appropriate conduct, proverbial sayings and exemplary anecdotes, conveying its political lessons not by means of argumentation but by subtle allusions with complex layers of meaning. Another civilization more advanced than classical Greece, India, produced a Hindu tradition of political thought lacking the kind of analytical and theoretical speculation that characterized Indian works of moral philosophy, logic and epistemology, expressing its commitment to existing political arrangements in didactic form without systematic argumentation. We can also contrast classical political philosophy to the earlier Homeric poetry of heroic ideals, models and examples or even to the political poetry of Solon, on the eve of the classical polis.

The tradition of political theory as we know it in the West can be traced back to ancient Greek philosophers – notably, Protagoras, Socrates, Plato and Aristotle – and it has produced a series of 'canonical' thinkers whose names have become familiar even to those who have never read their work: St Augustine, St Thomas Aquinas, Machiavelli, Hobbes, Locke, Rousseau, Hegel, Mill, and so on. The writings of these thinkers are extremely varied, but they do have certain things in common. Although they often analyze the state as it is, their principal enterprise is criticism and prescription. They all have some conception of what constitutes the right and proper ordering of society and government. What is conceived as 'right' is often based on some conception of justice and the morally good life, but it may also derive from practical reflections about what is required to maintain peace, security and material well-being.

Some political theorists offer blueprints for an ideally just state. Others specify reforms of existing government and proposals for guiding public policy. For all of them, the central questions have to do with who should govern and how, or what form of government is best; and they generally agree that it is not enough to ask and answer questions about the best form of government: we must also critically explore the grounds on which such judgments are made. Underlying such questions is always some conception of human nature, those qualities in human beings that must be nurtured or controlled in order to achieve a right and proper social order. Political theorists have outlined their human ideals and asked what kind of social and political arrangements are required to realize this vision of humanity. And when questions such as these are asked, others may not be far off: why and under what conditions ought we to obey those who govern us, and are we ever entitled to disobey or rebel?

These may seem obvious questions, but the very idea of asking them, the very idea that the principles of government or the obligation to obey authority are proper subjects for systematic reflection and the application of critical reason, cannot be taken for granted. Political theory represents as important a cultural milestone as does systematic philosophical or scientific reflection on the nature of matter, the earth and heavenly bodies. If anything, the invention of political theory is harder to explain than is the emergence of natural philosophy and science.

In what follows, we shall explore the historical conditions in which political theory was invented and how it developed in specific historical contexts, always keeping in mind that the classics of political theory were written in response to particular historical circumstances. The periods of greatest creativity in political theory have tended to be those historical moments when social and political conflict has erupted in particularly urgent ways, with far-reaching consequences; but even in calmer times, the questions addressed by political theorists have presented themselves in historically specific ways.

This means several things. Political theorists may speak to us through the centuries. As commentators on the human condition, they may have something to say for all times. But they are, like all human beings, historical creatures; and we shall have a much richer under-standing of what they have to say, and even how it might shed light on our own historical moment, when we have some idea of why they said it, to whom they said it, with whom they were debating (explicitly or implicitly), how their immediate world looked to them, and what they believed should be changed or preserved. This is not simply a matter of biographical detail or even historical 'background'. To

understand what political theorists are saying requires knowing what
questions they are trying to answer, and those questions confront them
not simply as philosophical abstractions but as specific problems posed
by specific historical conditions, in the context of specific practical
activities, social relations, pressing issues, grievances and conflicts.

The History of Political Theory

This understanding of political theory as a historical product has not
always prevailed among scholars who write about the history of political
thought; and it probably still needs to be justified, not least against the
charge that by historicizing the great works of political theory we
demean and trivialize them, denying them any meaning and significance
beyond their own historical moment. I shall try to explain and defend
my reasons for proceeding as I do, but that requires, first, a sketch of
how the history of political thought has been studied in the recent past.

In the 1960s and 70s, at a time of revival for the study of political
theory, academic specialists used to debate endlessly about the nature
and fate of their discipline. But in general political theorists, especially
in American universities, were expected to embrace the division of
political studies into the 'empirical' and the 'normative'. In one camp
was the *real* political science, claiming to deal scientifically with the
facts of political life as they are, and in the other was 'theory', confined
to the ivory tower of political philosophy and reflecting not on what
is but on what *ought to be*.

This barren division of the discipline undoubtedly owed much to
the culture of the Cold War, which generally encouraged the withdrawal
of academics from trenchant social criticism. At any rate, political
science lost much of its critical edge. The object of study for this so-
called 'science' was not creative human action but rather political
'behaviour', which could, it was claimed, be comprehended by quantitative methods appropriate to the involuntary motions of material
bodies, atoms or plants.

This view of political science was certainly challenged by some
political theorists, notably Sheldon Wolin, whose *Politics and Vision*
eloquently asserted the importance of creative vision in political analysis.[2]
But at least for a time, many political theorists seemed happy enough

---

2 *Politics and Vision: Continuity and Innovation in Western Political Thought* was
first published in 1960. The most recent expanded edition was published by Princeton
University Press in 2006.

to accept the place assigned to them by the ultra-empiricist 'behaviouralists' then dominant in US political science departments. It seemed especially congenial to the disciples of Leo Strauss, who formed an unholy alliance with the behaviouralists, each faction agreeing to respect the inviolability of the other's territory.[3] The empiricists would leave the philosophers in peace to spin their intricate conceptual webs, while the 'normative' theorists would never cast a critical eye at their empirical colleagues' political analysis. The Straussian attack on 'historicism' was directed against other theorists, in self-proclaimed defence of universal and absolute truths against the relativism of modernity; and, although they would later emerge as influential ideologues of neoconservatism and as something like philosophical mentors to the regime of George W. Bush, Straussian political theorists of an earlier generation were on the whole content to pursue their reactionary and antimodernist (if not antidemocratic) political agenda on the philosophical plane – except when they ventured completely outside the walls of the academy to write speeches for right-wing politicians. Their 'empiricist' colleagues seem to have understood that Straussians, with their esoteric, even cabalistic philosophical preoccupations, represented no challenge to the shallowness and vacuity of 'empirical' political science.

---

3 This is not the place to engage in the debate about Leo Strauss's own political views. The issue here is his approach to the study of political theory. Born in Germany in 1899, Strauss emigrated to the US in 1937 and, especially after his appointment to the faculty at the University of Chicago in 1949, exerted a great influence on the study of political theory in North America, producing a school of interpretation which would be carried on by his disciples and their students. The Straussian approach to political theory begins from the premise that political philosophers, who are concerned with truth and knowledge rather than mere opinion, have been compelled throughout the history of the canon to disguise their ideas, in order not to be persecuted as subversives. They have therefore, according to Straussians, adopted an 'esoteric' mode of writing, which obliges scholarly interpreters to read between the lines. This compulsion, the Straussians seem to suggest, has been aggravated by the onset of modernity, and particularly mass democracy, which (whatever other virtues they may or may not have) are inevitably dominated by opinion and, apparently, hostility to truth and knowledge. Straussians regard themselves as a privileged and exclusive fraternity in their access to the true meaning of political philosophy, taking enormous liberties of interpretation, which stray from the literal text in ways few other scholars would allow themselves. This approach tends, needless to say, to limit the possibilities of debate between Straussians and those outside the fraternity, since other interpretations of texts can be ruled out *a priori* as blind to hidden 'esoteric' meanings. However much Straussians may have denigrated 'empirical' political science, their method has reinforced the enclosure of 'normative' political theory in its own solipsistic domain.

Yet Straussians were not alone in accepting the neat division between empirical and normative, or between theory and practice. At least, there was a widespread view that grubbing around in the realities of politics, while all right for some, was not what political theorists should do. The groundbreaking work of the Canadian political theorist, C.B. Macpherson, who had introduced a different approach to the study of political theory by situating seventeenth-century English thinkers in the historical context of what he called a 'possessive market society', proved to be little more than a detour from the mainstream of Anglo-American scholarship.[4] Scholars who studied and taught the history of political thought, the 'classics' of the Western 'canon', did not always subscribe to the Straussian variety of anti-historicism; but they were often even more averse to history. Many treated the 'greats' as pure minds floating free above the political fray; and any attempt to plant these thinkers on firm historical ground, any attempt to treat them as living and breathing historical beings passionately engaged in the politics of their own time and place, would be dismissed as trivialization, demeaning great men and reducing them to mere publicists, pamphleteers and propagandists.[5]

What distinguished real political philosophy from simple 'ideology', according to this view, was that it rose above political struggle and partisanship. It tackled universal and perennial problems, seeking principles of social order and human development valid for all human beings in all times and places. The questions raised by true political philosophers are, it was argued, intrinsically transhistorical: what does it mean to be truly human? What kind of society permits the full development of that humanity? What are the universal principles of right order for individuals and societies?

It seems not to have occurred to proponents of this view that even such 'universal' questions could be asked and answered in ways that served certain immediate political interests rather than others, or that these questions and answers might even be intended as passionately partisan. For instance, the human ideals espoused by philosophers can tell us much about their social and political commitments and where

---

4 *The Political Theory of Possessive Individualism: Hobbes to Locke*, was published by Oxford University Press in 1962, but Macpherson had already published articles in the 1950s applying his contextual approach. Although I have disagreements with him and regard his ideal-type 'possessive market society' as a rather ahistorical abstraction, there can be little doubt that he broke important new ground.

5 See, for instance, Dante Germino, *Beyond Ideology: The Revival of Political Theory* (New York: Harper and Row, 1967).

they stand in the conflicts of their day. The failure to acknowledge this meant that these scholars saw little benefit in trying to understand the classics by situating them in their author's time and place. The contextualization of political thought or the 'sociology of knowledge' might tell us something about the ideas and motivations of lesser mortals and ideologues, but it could tell us nothing worth knowing about a great philosopher, a genius like Plato.

This almost naïve ahistoricism was bound to produce a reaction, and a very different school of thought emerged, which has since overtaken its rivals. What has come to be called the Cambridge School appears, at least on the face of it, to go to the other extreme by radically historicizing the works, great and small, of political theory and denying them any wider meaning beyond the very local moment of their creation. The most effective exponent of this approach, Quentin Skinner, in the introduction to his classic text, *The Foundations of Modern Political Thought*, gives an account of his method that seems directly antithetical to the dichotomies on which the ahistorical approach was based, against the sharp distinction between political philosophy and ideology and the facile opposition of 'empirical' to 'normative'. In fact, argues Skinner, we can best understand the history of political theory by treating it essentially as the history of ideologies, and this requires a detailed contextualization. 'For I take it that political life itself sets the main problems for the political theorist, causing a certain range of issues to appear problematic, and a corresponding range of questions to become the leading subjects of debate.'[6]

The principal benefit of this approach, Skinner writes, is that it equips us 'with a way of gaining greater insight into its author's meaning than we can ever hope to achieve simply from reading the text itself "over and over again" as the exponents of the "textualist" approach have characteristically proposed.'[7] But there is also another advantage:

> It will now be evident why I wish to maintain that, if the history of political theory were to be written essentially as a history of ideologies, one outcome might be a clearer understanding of the links between political theory and practice. For it now appears that, in recovering the terms of the normative vocabulary available to any

6 Quentin Skinner, *The Foundations of Modern Political Thought, Volume I: The Renaissance* (Cambridge: Cambridge University Press, 1978), p. xi.

7 *Ibid.*, p. xiii.

given agent for the description of his political behaviour, we are at the same time indicating one of the constraints upon his behaviour itself. This suggests that, in order to explain why such an agent acts as he does, we are bound to make some reference to this vocabulary, since it evidently figures as one of the determinants of his action. This in turn suggests that, if we were to focus our histories on the study of these vocabularies, we might be able to illustrate the exact ways in which the explanation of political behaviour depends upon the study of political thought.

Skinner then proceeded to construct a history of Western political thought in the Renaissance and the age of Reformation, especially the notion of the *state* as it acquired its modern meaning, by exploring the political vocabularies available to political thinkers and actors and the specific sets of questions that history had put on their agenda. His main strategy, here as elsewhere in his work, was to cast his net more widely than historians of political thought have customarily done, considering not just the leading theorists but, as he put it, 'the more general social and intellectual matrix out of which their works arose'.[8] He looked not only at the work of the greats but also at more 'ephemeral contemporary contributions to social and political thought', as a means of gaining access to the available vocabularies and the prevailing assumptions about political society that were shaping debate in specific times and places.

Skinner's approach has certain very clear strengths; and other members of the Cambridge School have also applied these principles, often very effectively, to the analysis of specific thinkers or 'traditions of discourse', especially those of early modern England. The proposition that the political questions addressed by political theorists, including the great ones, are thrown up by real political life and are shaped by the historical conditions in which they arise seems hardly more *nor* less than good common sense.

But much depends on what the Cambridge School regards as a relevant *context,* and it soon becomes clear that contextualization has a different meaning than might be inferred from Skinner's reference to the 'social and intellectual matrix'. It turns out that the 'social' matrix has little to do with 'society', the economy, or even the polity. The social context is itself intellectual, or at least the 'social' is defined by, and only by, existing vocabularies. The 'political life' that sets the agenda for theory is essentially a language game. In the end, to contex-

---

8 *Ibid.*, p. x.

tualize a text is to situate it among other texts, among a range of vocabularies, discourses and ideological paradigms at various levels of formality, from the classics of political thought down to ephemeral screeds or political speeches. What emerges from Skinner's assault on purely textual histories or the abstract history of ideas is yet another kind of textual history, yet another history of ideas – certainly more sophisticated and comprehensive than what went before, but hardly less limited to disembodied texts.

A catalogue of what is missing from Skinner's comprehensive history of political ideas from 1300 to 1600 reveals quite starkly the limits of his 'contexts'. Skinner is dealing with a period marked by major social and economic developments, which loomed very large in the theory and practice of European political thinkers and actors. Yet there is in his book no substantive consideration of agriculture, the aristocracy and peasantry, land distribution and tenure, the social division of labour, social protest and conflict, population, urbanization, trade, commerce, manufacture, and the burgher class.[9]

It is true that the other major founding figure of the Cambridge School, J.G.A. Pocock, is, on the face of it, more interested in economic developments and what appear to be material factors, like the 'discovery' (in Pocock's words) of capital and the emergence of 'commercial society' in eighteenth-century Britain. Yet his account of this 'sudden and traumatic discovery' is, in its way, even more divorced from historical processes than Skinner's account of the state.[10] The critical moment for Pocock is the foundation of the Bank of England, which, he argues, brought about a complete transformation of property, the transformation of its structure and morality, with 'spectacular abruptness' in the mid-1690s; and it was accompanied by sudden changes in the psychology of politics. But in this argument, the Bank of England, and indeed commercial society, seem to have no history at all. They suddenly emerge full-grown, as if the transformations of property and social relations in the sixteenth and seventeenth centuries and the formation of English agrarian capitalism, or the distinctively English banking system associated with the development of capitalist property which preceded the foundation of the national bank, had no bearing on their consolidation in the commercial capitalism of the eighteenth century.

---

9 See Neal Wood, *John Locke and Agrarian Capitalism* (Berkeley and Los Angeles: University of California Press, 1984) p. 11.

10 J.G.A. Pocock, *Virtue, Commerce, and History* (Cambridge: Cambridge University Press, 1985), p. 108. An elaboration of this argument on Pocock and 'commercial society' will have to await another volume devoted to the relevant period.

Such a strikingly ahistorical account is possible only because, for Pocock perhaps even more than for Skinner, history has little to do with social processes, and historical transformations are manifest only as visible shifts in the languages of politics. Changes in discourse that represent the culmination and consolidation of a social transformation are presented as its origin and cause.

So, what purports to be the *history* of political thought, for both Pocock and Skinner, is curiously ahistorical, not only in its failure to grapple with what on any reckoning were decisive historical developments in the relevant periods but also in its lack of *process*. Characteristically, history for the Cambridge School is a series of disconnected, very local and particular episodes, such as specific political controversies in specific times and places, which have no apparent relation to more inclusive social developments or to any historical process, large or small.[11]

This emphasis on the local and particular does not, however, preclude consideration of larger spans of time and space. The 'traditions of discourse' that are the stuff of the Cambridge School embrace long periods, sometimes whole centuries or even more. A tradition may cross national boundaries and even continents. It may be a particular literary genre fairly limited in time and geographic scope, like the 'mirror-for-princes' literature, which Skinner very effectively explores to analyze the work of Machiavelli; or, notably in the case of John Pocock, it may be the discourse of 'commercial society' which characterized the eighteenth century, or the tradition of 'civic humanism', which had a longer life and a wider scope. But whatever its duration or spatial reach, the tradition of discourse plays a role in analyzing political theory hardly different from the role played by particular episodes (which are themselves an interplay of discourses), like the Engagement Controversy in which Skinner situates Hobbes, or the Exclusion Crisis which others have invoked in the analysis of Locke. In both cases, contexts are texts; and at neither end of the Cambridge historical spectrum, from the very local episode to the long and widespread tradition of discourse, do we see any sign of historical movement, any sense of the dynamic connection between one historical moment and another or between the political episode and the social

---

11 For a critical discussion of Skinner's 'atomized' and 'episodic' treatment of history, see Cary Nederman, 'Quentin Skinner's State: Historical Method and Traditions of Discourse', *Canadian Journal of Political Science*, Vol. 18, No. 2, June 1985, pp. 339–52.

processes that underlie it. In effect, long historical processes are themselves converted into momentary political episodes.

In its conception of history, the Cambridge School has something essential in common with more fashionable 'postmodernist' trends. Discourse is for both the constitutive, indeed the only, practice of social life; and history is dissolved into contingency. Both respond to 'grand narratives' not by critically examining their virtues and vices but by discarding historical processes altogether.

The Social History of Political Theory

The 'social history of political theory', which is the subject of this book, starts from the premise that the great political thinkers of the past were passionately engaged in the issues of their time and place.[12] This was so even when they addressed these issues from an elevated philosophical vantage point, in conversation with other philosophers in other times and places, and even, or especially, when they sought to translate their reflections into universal and timeless principles. Often their engagements took the form of partisan adherence to a specific and identifiable political cause, or even fairly transparent expressions of particular interests, the interests of a particular party or class. But their ideological commitments could also be expressed in a larger vision of the good society and human ideals.

At the same time, the great political thinkers are not party hacks or propagandists. Political theory is certainly an exercise in persuasion, but its tools are reasoned discourse and argumentation, in a genuine search for some kind of truth. Yet if the 'greats' are different from lesser political thinkers and actors, they are no less human and no less steeped in history. When Plato explored the concept of justice in the *Republic*, or when he outlined the different levels of knowledge, he was certainly opening large philosophical questions and he was certainly in search of universal and transcendent truths. But his questions, no less than his answers, were (as I shall argue in a subsequent chapter) driven by his critical engagement with Athenian democracy.

To acknowledge the humanity and historic engagement of political thinkers is surely not to demean them or deny them their greatness. In any case, without subjecting ideas to critical historical scrutiny, it

---

12 For a discussion of the term 'social history of political theory', see Neal Wood, 'The Social History of Political Theory', *Political Theory*, Vol. 6 No. 3, August 1978, pp. 345–67.

is impossible to assess their claims to universality or transcendent truth. The intention here is certainly to explore the ideas of the most important political thinkers; but these thinkers will always be treated as living and engaged human beings, immersed not only in the rich intellectual heritage of received ideas bequeathed by their philosophical predecessors, nor simply against the background of the available vocabularies specific to their time and place, but also in the context of the social and political processes that shaped their immediate world.

This social history of political theory, in its conception of historical contexts, proceeds from certain fundamental premises, which belong to the tradition of 'historical materialism': human beings enter into relations with each other and with nature to guarantee their own survival and social reproduction. To understand the social practices and cultural products of any time and place, we need to know something about those conditions of survival and social reproduction, something about the specific ways in which people gain access to the material conditions of life, about how some people gain access to the labour of others, about the relations between people who produce and those who appropriate what others produce, about the forms of property that emerge from these social relations, and about how these relations are expressed in political domination, as well as resistance and struggle.

This is certainly not to say that a theorist's ideas can be predicted or 'read off' from his or her social position or class. The point is simply that the questions confronting any political thinker, however eternal and universal those questions may seem, are posed to them in specific historical forms. The Cambridge School agrees that, in order to understand the answers offered by political theorists, we must know something about the questions they are trying to answer and that different historical settings pose different sets of questions. But, for the social history of political theory, these questions are posed not only by explicit political controversies, and not only at the level of philosophy or high politics, but also by the social pressures and tensions that shape human interactions outside the political arena and beyond the world of texts.

This approach differs from that of the Cambridge School both in the scope of what is regarded as a 'context' and in the effort to apprehend historical *processes*. Ideological episodes like the Engagement Controversy or the Exclusion Crisis may tell us something about a thinker like Hobbes or Locke; but unless we explore how these thinkers situated themselves in the larger historical processes that were shaping their world, it is hard to see how we are to distinguish the great theorists from ephemeral publicists.

Long-term developments in social relations, property forms and state-formation do episodically erupt into specific political-ideological controversies; and it is undoubtedly true that political theory tends to flourish at moments like this, when history intrudes most dramatically into the dialogue among texts or traditions of discourse. But a major thinker like John Locke, while he was certainly responding to specific and momentary political controversies, was raising larger fundamental questions about social relations, property and the state generated by larger social transformations and structural tensions – in particular, developments that we associate with the 'rise of capitalism'. Locke did not, needless to say, know that he was observing the development of what we call capitalism; but he was dealing with problems posed by its characteristic transformations of property, class relations and the state. To divorce him from this larger social context is to impoverish his work and its capacity to illuminate its own historical moment, let alone the 'human condition' in general.

If different historical experiences give rise to different sets of problems, it follows that these divergences will also be observable in various 'traditions of discourse'. It is not, for instance, enough to talk about a Western or European historical experience, defined by a common cultural and philosophical inheritance. We must also look for differences among the various patterns of property relations and the various processes of state-formation that distinguished one European society from another and produced different patterns of theoretical interrogation, different sets of questions for political thinkers to address.

The diversity of 'discourses' does not simply express personal or even national idiosyncrasies of intellectual style among political philosophers engaged in dialogue with one another across geographical and chronological boundaries. To the extent that political philosophers are indeed reflecting not only upon philosophical traditions but upon the problems set by political life, their 'discourses' are diverse in large part because the political problems they confront are diverse. The problem of the state, for instance, has presented itself historically in different guises even to such close neighbours as the English and the French.[13]

Even the 'perennial questions' have appeared in various shapes. What appears as a salient issue will vary according to the nature of the

---

13 I have discussed these differences at some length in *The Pristine Culture of Capitalism: A Historical Essay on Old Regimes and Modern States* (London: Verso, 1992).

principal contenders, the competing social forces at work, the conflict-ing interests at stake. The configuration of problems arising from a struggle such as the one in early modern England between 'improving' landlords and commoners dependent on the preservation of common and waste land will differ from those at issue in France among peasants, seigneurs, and a tax-hungry state. Even within the same historical or national configuration, what appears as a problem to the commoner or peasant will not necessarily appear so to the gentleman-farmer, the seigneur, or the royal office-holder. We need not reduce the great political thinkers to 'prize-fighters' for this or that social interest in order to acknowledge the importance of identifying the particular constellation of problems that history has presented to them, or to recognize that the 'dialogue' in which they are engaged is not simply a timeless debate with rootless philosophers but an engagement with living historical actors, both those who dominate and those who resist.

To say this is not to claim that political theorists from another time and place have nothing to say to our own. There is no inverse relation between historical contextualization and 'relevance'. On the contrary, historical contextualization is an essential condition for learning from the 'classics', not simply because it allows a better understanding of a thinker's meaning and intention, but also because it is in the context of history that theory emerges from the realm of pure abstraction and enters the world of human practice and social interaction.

There are, of course, commonalities of experience we share with our predecessors just by virtue of being human, and there are innumerable practices learned by humanity over the centuries in which we engage as our ancestors did. These common experiences mean that much of what great thinkers of the past have to say is readily accessible to us. But if the classics of political theory are to yield fruitful lessons, it is not enough to acknowledge these commonalities of human and historical experience or to mine the classics for certain abstract universal principles. To historicize is to humanize, and to detach ideas from their own material and practical setting is to lose our points of human contact with them.

There is a way, all too common, of studying the history of political theory which detaches it from the urgent human issues to which it is addressed. To think about the *politics* in political theory is, at the very least, to consider and make judgments about what it would mean to translate particular principles into actual social relationships and political arrangements. If one of the functions of political theory is to sharpen our perceptions and conceptual instruments for thinking about politics in our own time and place, that purpose is defeated by emptying historical political theories of their own political meaning.

Some years ago, for instance, I encountered an argument about Aristotle's theory of natural slavery, which seemed to me to illustrate the shortcomings of an ahistorical approach.[14] We should not, the argument went, treat the theory of natural slavery as a comment on a historically actual social condition, the relation between slaves and masters as it existed in the ancient world, because to do so is to deprive it of any significance beyond the socio-economic circumstances of its own time and place. Instead, we should recognize it as a philosophical metaphor for the universal human condition in the abstract. Yet to deny that Aristotle was defending a real social practice, the enslavement of real human beings, or to suggest that we have more to learn about the human condition by refusing to confront his theory of slavery in its concrete historical meaning, seems a peculiar way of sensitizing us to the realities of social life and politics, or indeed the human condition, in our own time or any other.

There is also another way in which the contextual analysis of political

---

14 Arlene Saxonhouse, in a review of M.I. Finley's *Ancient Slavery and Modern Ideology*, writes dismissively of his approach as a 'social historian', which, apparently, can tell us a few unsurprising things about the predispositions of writers on slavery but cannot illuminate the deeper meaning of philosophical reflections such as those of Aristotle. 'Aristotle's reflections on the nature of slavery,' she writes, 'move us beyond a particular slave and a particular master. Instead, the slave's subordination to the master reflects our own subordination to nature. Slavery is not only the degraded position of one without control over his or her labour. It is the condition of all humans vis-à-vis nature. The master and the slave is not a relationship limited to the slave societies of the ancient and modern world to which Finley refers. The master and slave are perennial states which Aristotle exhorts us to understand so that we may understand our own place within society and within nature. Finley, the social historian, turns our attention to the specifics of a time and a place, and that is why, though he notes the importance of the study of American slavery to American society today, he does not explain the relevance of ancient slavery. For that we must turn to the ancient philosopher' (*Political Theory*, Vol. 9, No. 4, November 1981, p. 579). It is undeniable that Aristotle situates slavery in his all-embracing philosophical reflections on nature in general; but it seems perverse to deny that he is, in the process, reflecting on the very specific condition of slavery as he knew it in the Greek world. It might perhaps be possible to deny that Aristotle intends to *justify* slavery by treating it as a manifestation of humanity's general subordination to nature (though we may be inclined, on the contrary, to think that this naturalization of slavery serves precisely as justification). But there is, in any case, something rather troubling about the view that a 'philosophical' interpretation of Aristotle, which detaches his discussion of slavery from the concrete realities of the master–slave relation in historical time and space, tells us more about 'the relevance of ancient slavery' (or, indeed, Aristotle's views about it) than does mere 'social history', which treats the philosopher's reflections as, precisely, reflections on ancient slavery, not as a metaphor but as an all-too-concrete historical reality.

theory can illuminate our own historical moment. If we abstract a political theory from its historical context, we in effect assimilate it to our own. Understanding a theory historically allows us to look at our own historical condition from a critical distance, from the vantage point of other times and other ideas. It also allows us to observe how certain assumptions, which we may now accept uncritically, came into being and how they were challenged in their formative years. Reading political theory in this way, we may be less tempted to take for granted the dominant ideas and assumptions of our own time and place.

This benefit may not be so readily available to contextual approaches in which historical processes are replaced by disconnected episodes and traditions of discourse. The Cambridge mode of contextualization encourages us to believe that the old political thinkers have little to say in our own time and place. It invites us to think that there is nothing to learn from them, because their historical experiences have no apparent connection to our own. To discover what there is to learn from the history of political theory requires us to place ourselves on the continuum of history, where we are joined to our predecessors not only by the continuities we share but by the processes of change that intervene between us, bringing us from there to here.

The intention of this study, then, is not only to illuminate some classic texts and the conditions in which they were created but also to explain by example a distinctive approach to contextual interpretation. Its subject matter will be not only texts, nor discursive paradigms, but the social relations that made them possible and posed the particular questions addressed by political theorists. This kind of contextual reading also requires us to do something more than follow the line of descent from one political thinker to the next. It invites us to explore how certain fundamental social relations set the parameters of human creativity, not only in political theory but in other modes of discourse that form part of the historical setting and the cultural climate within which political theories emerged – such as, say, Greek tragedy, the Roman law or Christian theology.

While I try to strike a balance between contextual analysis and interpretation of the major texts, some readers may think that this way of proceeding places too much emphasis on grand structural themes at the expense of a more exhaustive textual reading. But the approach being proposed in this book is best understood not as in any way excluding or slighting close textual analysis but, on the contrary, as a way of shedding light on texts, which others can put to the test by more minute and detailed reading.

The Origin of Political Theory

Scholars have offered various explanations for the emergence of political theory in ancient Greece. There will be more in the next chapter about the specific historical conditions that produced, especially in Athens, the kind of confidence in human agency that is a necessary condition of political theory. In this chapter, we shall confine ourselves to the general conditions that marked the Greeks out from other ancient civilizations and set the agenda for political theory.

The most vital factor undoubtedly was the development, perhaps by the late eighth century BC, of the unique Greek state, the polis, which sometimes evolved into self-governing democracies, as in Athens from the early fifth to the late fourth century. This type of state differed sharply from the large imperial states that characterized other 'high' civilizations, and from states that preceded the polis in Greece, the Minoan and Mycenean kingdoms. In place of an elaborate bureaucratic apparatus, the polis was characterized by a fairly simple state administration (if we can even call it a 'state' at all) and a self-governing civic community, in which the principal political relations were not between rulers and subjects but among *citizens* – whether the citizen body was more inclusive, as in Athenian democracy, or less so, as in Sparta or the city-states of Crete. Politics, in the sense we have come to understand the word, implying contestation and debate among diverse interests, replaced rule or administration as the principal object of political discourse. These factors were, of course, more prominent in democracies, and Athens in particular, than in the oligarchic polis.

It is also significant that by the end of the fifth century, Greece was becoming a literate culture, in unprecedented ways and to an unprecedented degree. Although we should not overestimate its extent, a kind of popular literacy, especially in the democracy, replaced what some scholars have called craft literacy, in which reading and writing were specialized skills practised only, or largely, by professionals or scribes. What happened in Greece, and especially in Athens, has been described as the democratization of writing.

Popular rule, which required widespread and searching discussion of pressing social and political issues, and which provided new opportunities for political leadership and influence, when coupled with economic prosperity, brought an increasing demand for schooling and teaching. An economically vital, democratic and relatively free culture with a growing means of written expression and exact argumentation, and an increasing audience for such discourse, created an atmosphere favourable to the birth and early thriving of political theory, a powerful and ingenious mode of self-examination and reflection that continues to the present.

But we need to look more closely at the polis, and especially the democracy, to understand why this new mode of political thinking took the form that it did, and why it raised certain kinds of questions that had not been raised before, which would thereafter set the agenda for the long tradition of Western political theory. There will be more in the next chapter about Athenian society and politics, as the specific context in which the Greek classics were written. For our purposes here, a few general points need to be highlighted about the conditions in which political theory originated.

The polis represented not only a distinctive political form but a unique organization of social relations. The state in other high civilizations typically embodied a relation between rulers and subjects that was at the same time a relation between appropriators and producers. The Chinese philosopher, Mencius, once wrote that 'Those who are ruled produce food; those who rule are fed. That this is right is universally recognized everywhere under Heaven.' This principle nicely sums up the essence of the relation between rulers and producers which characterized the most advanced ancient civilizations.

In these ancient states, there was a sharp demarcation between production and politics, in the sense that direct producers had no political role, as rulers or even as citizens. The state was organized to control subject labour, and it was above all through the state that some people appropriated the labour of others or its products. Office in the state was likely to be the primary means of acquiring great wealth. Even where private property in land was fairly well developed, state office was likely to be the source of large property, while small property generally carried with it obligations to the state in the form of tax, tribute or labour service. It remained true of China, for instance, throughout its long imperial history that large property and great wealth were associated with office, and the imperial state did everything possible – if not always successfully – to maintain that connection and to impede the autonomous development of powerful propertied classes.

The ancient 'bureaucratic' state, then, constituted a ruling body superimposed upon and appropriating from subject communities of direct producers, above all peasants. Although such a form had existed in Greece, both there and in Rome a new form of political organization emerged which combined landlords and peasants in one civic and military community. While others, notably the Phoenicians and Carthaginians, may have lived in city-states in some ways comparable to the Greek polis or the Roman Republic, the very idea of a civic community and citizenship, as distinct from the principles of rule by a superimposed state apparatus, derive from the Greeks and the Romans. The idea of a *peasant*-citizen was even further removed from the experience of other ancient states. The role of slavery in Greece and Rome will be discussed in subsequent chapters; but, for the moment, it is important to acknowledge the distinctive political role of producing classes, peasants and craftsmen, and their unique relation to the state. In the Greek polis and the Roman Republic, appropriators and producers in the citizen body confronted one another directly as individuals and as classes, as landlords and peasants, not primarily as rulers and subjects. Private property developed more autonomously and completely, separating itself more thoroughly from the state. A new and distinctive dynamic of property and class relations was differentiated out from the traditional relations of (appropriating) state and (producing) subjects.

The special characteristics of these states are reflected in the classics of ancient political thought. When Plato, for example, attacked the democratic polis of Athens, he did so by opposing to it a state-form that departed radically from precisely those features most unique and specific to the Greek polis and which bore a striking resemblance in principle to certain non-Greek states. In the *Republic*, Plato proposes a community of rulers superimposed upon a ruled community of producers, primarily peasants, a state in which producers are individually 'free' and in possession of property, not dependent on wealthier private proprietors; but, although the rulers own no private property, producers are collectively subject to the ruling community and compelled to transfer surplus labour to their non-producing masters. Political and military functions belong exclusively to the ruling class, according to the traditional separation of military and farming classes, which Plato and Aristotle both admired. In other words, those who are ruled produce food, and those who rule are fed. Plato no doubt drew inspiration from the Greek states that most closely adhered to these principles – notably Sparta and the city-states of Crete; but it is likely that the model he had more specifically in mind was Egypt – or, at least, Egypt as the Greeks, sometimes inaccurately, understood it.

Other classical writers defended the supremacy of the dominant classes in less radical and more specifically Greco-Roman ways. In particular, the doctrine of the 'mixed constitution' – which appears in Plato's *Laws* and figures prominently in the writings of Aristotle, Polybius, and Cicero – reflects a uniquely Greek and Roman reality and the special problems faced by a dominant class of private proprietors in a state

that incorporates rich and poor, appropriators and producers, landlords
and peasants, into a single civic and military community. The idea of
the mixed constitution proceeded from the Greco-Roman classification
of constitutions – in particular, the distinction among government by
the many, the few, or only one: democracy, oligarchy, monarchy. A
constitution could be 'mixed' in the sense that it adopted certain
elements of each. More particularly, rich and poor could be respectively
represented by 'oligarchic' and 'democratic' elements; and the predominance of the rich could be achieved not by drawing a clear and rigid
division between a ruling apparatus and subject producers, or between
military and farming classes, but by tilting the constitutional balance
towards oligarchic elements.

In both theory and practice, then, a specific dynamic of *property* and
class relations, distinct from the relations between rulers and subjects,
was woven directly into the fabric of Greek and Roman politics. These
relations generated a distinctive array of practical problems and theoretical issues, especially in the democratic polis. There were, of course,
distinctive problems of social order in a society, like Athens, that lacked
an unequivocally dominant ruling stratum whose economic power and
political supremacy were coextensive and inseparable, a society where
economic and political hierarchies did not coincide and political
relations were less between rulers and subjects than among citizens.
These political relations were played out in assemblies and juries, in
constant debate, which demanded new rhetorical skills and modes of
argumentation. Nothing could be taken for granted; and, not surprisingly, this was a highly litigious society, in which political discourse
derived much of its method and substance from legal disputation, with
all its predilection for hairsplitting controversy.

Greek political theorists were self-conscious about the uniqueness
of their specific form of state, and they inevitably explored the nature
of the polis and what distinguished it from others. They raised questions
about the origin and purpose of the state. Having effectively invented
a new identity, the civic identity of citizenship, they posed questions
about the meaning of citizenship, who should enjoy political rights
and whether any division between rulers and ruled existed by nature.
They confronted the tension between the levelling identity of citizenship
and the hierarchical principles of noble birth or wealth. Questions
about law and the rule of law; about the difference between political
organization based on violence or coercion and a civic community
based on deliberation or persuasion; about human nature and its
suitability (or otherwise) for political life – all of these questions were
thrown up by the everyday realities of life in the polis.

In the absence of a ruling class whose ethical standards were accepted by the whole community as its governing principles, it was no longer possible to assume the eternity and inviolability of traditional norms. They were inevitably subjected to theoretical scrutiny and challenge. Defenders of traditional hierarchies were obliged to respond not by repeating old proverbs or reciting epics of aristocratic hero-kings but by constructing theoretical arguments to meet theoretical challenges. Questions arose about the origin of moral and political principles and what makes them binding. From the same political realities emerged the humanistic principle that 'man is the measure of all things', with all the new questions that this principle entailed. So, for instance, the Sophists (Greek philosophers and teachers who will be discussed in the next chapter) asked whether moral and political principles exist by nature or merely by custom – a question that could be answered in various ways, some congenial to democracy, others in support of oligarchy; and when Plato expressed his opposition to democracy, he could not rely on invoking the gods or time-honoured custom but was obliged to make his case by means of philosophic reason, to construct a definition of justice and the good life that seemed to rule out democracy.

Political Theory in History: An Overview

Born in the polis, this new mode of political thought would survive the polis and continue to set the theoretical agenda in later centuries, when very different forms of state prevailed. This longevity has not been simply a matter of tenacious intellectual legacies. The Western tradition of political theory has developed on the foundations estab-lished in ancient Greece because certain issues have remained at the centre of European political life. In varying forms, the autonomy of private property, its relative independence from the state, and the tension between these foci of social power have continued to shape the political agenda. On the one hand, appropriating classes have needed the state to maintain order, conditions for appropriation and control over producing classes. On the other hand, they have found the state a burdensome nuisance and a competitor for surplus labour.

With a wary eye on the state, the dominant appropriating classes have always had to turn their attention to their relations with subor-dinate producing classes. Indeed, their need for the state has been largely determined by those difficult relations. In particular, throughout most of Western history, peasants fed, clothed, and housed the lordly minority by means of surplus labour extracted by payment of rents, fees, or tributes. Yet, though the aristocratic state depended on peasants and though lords were always alive to the threat of resistance, the politically voiceless classes play little overt role in the classics of Western political theory. Their silent presence tends to be visible only in the great theoretical efforts devoted to justifying social and political hierarchies.

The relation between appropriating and producing classes was to change fundamentally with the advent of capitalism, but the history of Western political theory continued to be in large part the history of tensions between property and state, appropriators and producers. In general, the Western tradition of political theory has been 'history from above', essentially reflection on the existing state and the need for its preservation or change written from the perspective of a member or client of the ruling classes. Yet it should be obvious that this 'history from above' cannot be understood without relating it to what can be learned about the 'history from below'. The complex three-way relation between the state, propertied classes and producers, perhaps more than anything else, sets the Western political tradition apart from others.

There is nothing unique to the West, of course, about societies in which dominant groups appropriate what others produce. But there is something distinctive about the ways in which the tensions between them have shaped political life and theory in the West. This may be precisely because the relations between appropriators and producers have never, since classical antiquity, been synonymous with the relation between rulers and subjects. To be sure, the peasant-citizen would not survive the Roman Empire, and many centuries would pass before anything comparable to the ancient Athenian idea of democratic citizenship would re-emerge in Europe. Feudal and early modern Europe would, in its own way, even approximate the old division between rulers and producers, as labouring classes were excluded from active political rights and the power to appropriate was typically associated with the possession of 'extra-economic' power, political, judicial or military. But even then, the relation between rulers and producers was never unambiguous, because appropriating classes confronted their labouring compatriots not, in the first instance, as a collective power organized in the state but in a more directly personal relation as individual proprietors, in rivalry with other proprietors and even with the state.

The autonomy of property and the contradictory relations between ruling class and state meant that propertied classes in the West always had to fight on two fronts. While they would have happily subscribed to Mencius's principle about those who rule and those who feed them, they could never take for granted such a neat division between rulers and producers, because there was a much clearer division than existed elsewhere between property and state.

Although the foundations of Western political theory established in ancient Greece proved to be remarkably resilient, there have, of course, been many changes and additions to its theoretical agenda, in keeping with changing historical conditions, which will be explored in the following chapters. The Romans, perhaps because their aristocratic republic did not confront challenges like those of the Athenian democracy, did not produce a tradition of political theory as fruitful as the Greek. But they did introduce other social and political innovations, especially the Roman law, which would have major implications for the development of political theory. The empire also gave rise to Christianity, which became the imperial religion, with all its cultural consequences.

It is particularly significant that the Romans began to delineate a sharp distinction between public and private, even, perhaps, between state and society. Above all, the opposition between property and state as two distinct foci of power, which has been a constant theme throughout the history of Western political theory, was for the first time formally acknowledged by the Romans in their distinction between *imperium* and *dominium,* power conceived as the right to command and power in the form of ownership. This did not preclude the view – expressed already by Cicero in *On Duties (De Officiis)* – that the purpose of the state was to protect private property or the conviction that the state came into being for that reason. On the contrary, the partnership of state and private property, which would continue to be a central theme of Western political theory, presupposes the separation, and the tensions, between them.

The tension between these two forms of power, which was intensified in theory and practice as republic gave way to empire, would, as we shall see, play a large part in the fall of the Roman Empire. With the rise of feudalism, that tension was resolved on the side of *dominium,* as the state was virtually dissolved into individual property. In contrast to the ancient division between rulers and producers, in which the state was the dominant instrument of appropriation, the feudal state scarcely had an autonomous existence apart from the hierarchical chain of individual, if conditional, property and personal lordship. Instead of a centralized public authority, the feudal state was a network of 'parcellized sovereignties', governed by a complex hierarchy of social relations and competing jurisdictions, in the hands not only of lords and kings, but also of various autonomous corporations, to say nothing of Holy Roman emperors and popes.[15] Feudal relations – between king and lords, between lords and vassals, between lords and peasants – were both a political/military relation and a form of property. Feudal lordship meant command of property, together with control of legally dependent labour; and, at the same time, it was a piece of the state, a fragment of political and military *imperium*.

The feudal resolution of the tension between property and state could not last forever. In their relations with the peasantry, lords would inevitably turn to the state for support; and parcellized sovereignty, in turn, gave way, yet again, to state centralization. The new form of state that would emerge in the late Middle Ages and develop in the early modern period would forever be marked by the underlying conflict between monarchy and lordship – until capitalism completely transformed the relation between politics and property.

At each stage in this history of political practice, there were corresponding changes in theory and variations on old themes to accommodate new social tensions and political arrangements. The contradictory relations between property and state acquired new complexities, giving rise to new ideas about relations between monarchs and lords, the origins and scope of monarchical power, constitutional limits on state power, the autonomous powers of various corporate entities, conceptions of sovereignty, the nature of obligation and the right to resist. Developments in Christianity and the rise of the Church as an independent power introduced yet more complications, raising new questions about relations between divine and civil law and about the challenge posed by the Church to secular authority. Finally, the advent of capitalism brought its own conceptual transformations, in new ideas of property and state, together with new conceptions of 'public' and 'private', political and economic, state and 'society', and a resurrection of 'democracy', not in its ancient Greek form but in a new and distinctively capitalist meaning, which no longer represented a fundamental challenge to dominant classes.

Throughout this 'Western' history, there were also, as we shall see,

---

15 On the concept of 'parcellized sovereignty', see Perry Anderson, *Passages from Antiquity to Feudalism* (London: Verso, 1974), pp. 148ff. English feudalism, as we shall see, represented a partial exception. All property was legally defined as 'feudal' and conditional; but the Anglo-Saxon state was already relatively unified, and the Normans would consolidate that unity, so that 'parcellized sovereignty' never existed in England to the extent that it did on the Continent. The distinctive development of English capitalism was not unrelated to this distinctive 'feudalism'. But more on this later.

significant theoretical variations among diverse European states, not just because of linguistic and cultural differences but because social and political relations varied too. Not only were there several European feudalisms, but the dissolution of feudalism gave rise to several different transformations, producing forms as diverse as the city-states of Italy, the principalities of Germany, the absolutist state of France, and the commercial republics of the Netherlands, while the so-called 'transition from feudalism to capitalism' occurred only in England. For all the commonalities of European culture, and all the shared social issues that continued to make the Western tradition of political theory a fruitful common legacy, each of these transformations produced its own characteristic 'traditions of discourse'.

One further point is worth making. The ambiguous relation between ruling class and state gave Western political theory certain unique characteristics. Even while propertied classes could never ignore the threat from below, and even while they depended on the state to sustain their property and economic power, the tensions in their relations with the state placed a special premium on their own autonomous powers, their rights against the state, and also on conceptions of liberty – which were often indistinguishable from notions of aristocratic privilege asserted against the state. So challenges to authority could come from two directions: from resistance by subordinate classes to oppression by their overlords, and from the overlords themselves as they faced intrusions by the state. This helped to keep alive the habit of interrogating the most basic principles of authority, legitimacy and the obligation to obey, even at moments when social and political hierarchies were at their most rigid.

The Canon

A final introductory word needs to be said about why we should concern ourselves with the classics of Western political theory at all. Why select a few 'classic' works or 'great books', written by 'Dead White Males', largely confined to Western Europe and its cultural offshoots? Is it not true that, with very few exceptions, the 'canon' neglects the life experience of most of the world's population, the male domination of women, the oppression of racial and national minorities, the endemic violence in social relations, the whole history of colonialism and imperialism – when it does not actively support such domination and oppression?

For that matter, is it even meaningful to talk about the 'Western' tradition at all? The days are long gone when courses on 'Western

Civilization' were taken for granted, particularly in US universities, as a necessary introduction to higher education. Even the division between 'East' and 'West' is now recognized as problematic. What, for instance, does it mean to identify ancient Greek culture as belonging to the 'Western' tradition? 'East' versus 'West' is an artificial historical construct, and even 'Europe' is a concept that emerged fairly late. It is even more artificial to detach ancient Greece from, say, Egypt or Persia, as if the Greeks were always 'European', living a separate history, and not part of a larger Mediterranean and 'Eastern' world. Besides, the 'East' is even more diverse than Europe or the 'West', so there is no justification for treating it as some kind of residual category, encompassing everything not 'Western' or 'European'. And even if we accept the 'West' as a kind of shorthand, without lumping together the rest of the world as an undifferentiated 'other', which Western tradition are we talking about? Are there not, for instance, working class traditions as well as ruling class ideologies?

Let me offer at least a partial reply to these important doubts. First, for the purposes of this study, the main justification for using the shorthand 'Western' political theory has to do with the particularities of political life, since classical antiquity, within the geographic area we now call Europe. For all its internal diversity – which should be evident throughout this work – this 'Western' world has been marked by certain social and political peculiarities, which have been briefly outlined in this chapter and which have produced certain distinctive patterns of political thinking. The justification for treating ancient Greece and Rome as part of this 'tradition' is simply that we can trace the 'West's' political divergence back to Greco-Roman antiquity, and with it the development of political theory.[16]

The classic texts of political theory considered in this book, then, focus upon the Western state. Generally conceived by powerful minds and often written by first-rate literary stylists, they give us unparalleled access to the West's political history; and whether we like it or not, these works have indelibly stamped our modern culture and the world today. They have, in general, been the ruling ideas of ruling classes; and this also means, of course, that the imperial powers which have spread their tentacles throughout the world have taken these ideas with

---

16 See Paul Cartlege, *The Greeks* (Oxford: Oxford University Press, 2nd edn, 2002) for a masterful illustration of how our own political and cultural self-understanding can benefit from recognizing both the historical specificity of the Greeks and the continuities between them and us, both their 'otherness' and what we owe to them.

them. The spread of the West's ruling ideas, it must be said, has had its benefits, but they have also been invoked to justify colonial oppression. For better or worse, they have, in various ways, governed the world.

It is also true that, since classical antiquity, the Western state has been marked by a systemic inequality and domination of the many by a few. This reality, too, is reflected in the canon, since the voices we hear tend to be those of the ruling classes, propertied men (it is indeed men) and those who speak for them. Although we occasionally hear dissent from below, the peasants who have made up the majority of the population throughout most of the relevant history are largely silent. Yet this silence is not a reason for neglecting the voices of the masters. On the contrary, they are often our best access to the voiceless majority, to their grievances and the challenges they posed to those who dominated and exploited them. We are able, of course, to learn a great deal more when we can also listen directly to the words of those who opposed and resisted; but even when those words are unavailable, a careful and contextual reading of the canonical texts will tell us much about what dominant classes expected from their subordinates as well as what they feared from them.

This study works from the premise that it is wrong to treat the canon uncritically and to take its dominance for granted. It is equally wrong to write out of history identities and cultures not represented in canonical texts. But it is also a mistake to pretend that nothing like the canon exists or that the dominance of ruling ideas is not a major fact of history. The important thing is to recognize that this fact does indeed have a history. This means, among other things, trying to understand the conditions in which this canonical tradition emerged and developed, the social relations and struggles that shaped it. Without that kind of historical understanding, we cannot learn whatever universal lessons the classics may still have for us, but nor are we in any position to dismiss them as having nothing to teach us at all.

2

THE ANCIENT GREEK POLIS

The Invention of Politics

In his play, *The Suppliant Women*, Euripides interrupts the action with a short political debate between a herald from despotic Thebes and the legendary Athenian hero, Theseus. The Theban boasts that his city is ruled by only one man, not by a fickle mob, the mass of poor and common people who are unable to make sound political judgments because they cannot turn their minds away from labour. Theseus replies by singing the praises of democracy. In a truly free city, he insists, the laws are common to all, equal justice is available to rich and poor alike, anyone who has something useful to say has the right to speak before the public, and the labours of a free citizen are not wasted 'merely to add to the tyrant's substance by one's toil'.

This brief dramatic interlude may do little to advance the action of the play, but it nicely sums up the issues at stake in Athenian political theory. It also tells us much about the polis and the social conditions that gave rise to political theory. Contained in the conception of freedom exalted by Theseus are certain basic principles that the Athenians, and other Greeks, regarded as uniquely theirs, defining the essence of their distinctive state. The Greek word for freedom, *eleutheria*, and, for that matter, even the more restricted and elitist Latin *libertas* – in reference to both individuals and states – have no precise equivalent in any ancient language of the Near East or Asia, for instance in Babylonian or classical Chinese; nor can the Greek and Roman notions of a 'free man' be translated into those languages.[1] In Greek, these concepts appear again and again, in everything from historical writing to drama, as the defining characteristics of Athens.

---

1 See M.I. Finley, *The Ancient Economy* (Berkeley and Los Angeles: University of California Press, 1973), p. 28.

So, for instance, when the historian Herodotus offers his explanation for the Athenian defeat of Persia, he attributes their strength to the fact that they had shaken off the yoke of tyranny. When they were living under tyrannical oppression, 'they let themselves be beaten, since they worked for a master . . .' [2] Now that they were free, they had become 'the first of all'. Similarly, the tragedian, Aeschylus, in *The Persians*, tells us that – in contrast to subjects of the Persian king, Xerxes – to be an Athenian citizen is to be masterless, a servant to no mortal man.

It would, of course, be possible to attribute the Greeks' clear delineation of 'freedom' to the prevalence of chattel slavery, which entailed an unusually sharp conceptual and legal distinction between freedom and bondage. The growth of slavery certainly did clarify and sharpen the distinction. But the distinctive Greek conception of autonomy and self-sufficiency owes its origin to something else, and the uncompromising definition of servitude is a consequence of that conception more than its cause.

The distinguished medieval historian, Rodney Hilton, once remarked that 'the concept of the freeman, owing no obligation, not even deference, to an overlord is one of the most important if intangible legacies of medieval peasants to the modern world.'[3] If Hilton was right to trace this concept to the peasantry, he was surely wrong not to give the credit for it to the ancient Greeks. It was the liberation of Greek peasants from any form of servitude or tribute to lord or state, unlike their counterparts elsewhere, that produced a new conception of freedom and the free man. This conception was increasingly associated with democracy – so much so that an anti-democrat like Plato (who, as we shall see, thought that anyone engaged in necessary labour should be legally or politically dependent) sought to subvert the concept of *eleutheria* by equating it with licence. At the same time, the liberation of the peasantry wiped out a whole spectrum of dependence and left behind the stark dichotomy of freedom and slavery, the one an attribute of citizens, the other a condition to which no citizen could be reduced.

Although a leisurely life was no doubt a cultural ideal, the Greek conception of *eleutheria* has at its heart a freedom from the necessity to work for another – not freedom *from* labour but the freedom *of* labour. This applies not only to the masterless individual but also to

2 V. Herodotus, *The Persian Wars*, transl. George Rawlinson (New York: Modern Library [Random House], 1947), V.78.

3 Rodney Hilton, *Bond Men Made Free: Medieval Peasant Movements and the English Rising of 1381* (London: Temple Smith, 1973), p. 235.

the polis governed by a citizen body and one that owes no tribute to another state. In its emphasis on autonomous labour and self-sufficiency, this concept of freedom reflects the unique reality of a state in which producers were citizens, a state in which a civic community that combined appropriating and producing classes ruled out relations of lordship and dependence between them, whether as masters and servants or as rulers and subjects. That civic community, which was most highly developed in democratic Athens, was the decisive condition for the emergence of Greek political theory.

In the previous chapter, we outlined some of the ways in which the polis, and especially the democracy, generated a new mode of thinking, a systematic application of critical reason to interrogate the very foundations of political right. This mode of thinking was, it was suggested, rooted in a new kind of practice, which had less to do with relations between rulers and subjects than with transactions and conflicts among citizens, united in their civic identity yet still divided by class. The self-governing civic community and the practice of politics – action in the public sphere of the polis, a community of citizens – reached its apogee in democratic Athens, which was also home to the classic tradition of Greek political theory.

The Rise of the Democracy

The evolution of the democracy can be traced by following the development of the civic or political principle, the notion of citizenship and the gradual elevation of the polis, civic law and civic identity at the expense of traditional principles of kinship, household, birth and blood. To put it another way, the processes of politicization and democratization went hand in hand, and the most democratic polis was the one in which the political principle was most completely developed. The historic events commonly identified as the milestones in Athenian political development can all be understood in these terms. In each case, the strengthening of the political principle at the same time represented an advance in popular power and a reconfiguration of relations between classes.

Archaeology and the decipherment of Linear B, the script that preceded the Greek alphabet, have revealed much about the states that existed in Greece before the emergence of the polis. They were, as has already been suggested, analogous to other ancient states, albeit on a smaller scale, in which a bureaucratic power at the centre controlled land and labour, appropriating tax or tribute from subordinate peasant communities. Little is known about how this state-form disappeared or what intervened between its demise and the rise of the polis. Much of what is known about Greek society on the eve of the polis depends on the Homeric epics, which certainly do not describe the Mycenean civilization that is supposed to be their theme. Invoking myths and legends from an earlier time, they depict a social structure and social values of a later age. The Homeric poems may not exactly describe any society that ever existed in Greece; but, in general outline, they remain our best source of information about the aristocratic society that preceded the polis, a society already coming to an end when the poet(s) memorialized it. The epics at least allow us some access to the social and political arrangements that gave way to the polis.

The principal social and economic unit of 'Homeric' society is the *oikos*, the household, and especially the aristocratic household, dominated by a lord who is surrounded by his kin and retainers and supported by the labour of dependents. There is scarcely any 'public' sphere: duties and rights are primarily to household, kin and friends; and various social functions, such as the disposal of property and the punishment of crime, are dictated by the customary rules of kinship, while jurisdiction, such as it is, belongs exclusively to lords.

Yet when the epics were written, household and kinship ties were already being displaced by different principles. There were ties of territoriality, around an urban centre, while the bonds and conflicts of class were at work in relations between master and servant, or lord and peasant, and in the class alliances of lordship. 'Homeric' lords had become an aristocracy of property, bound together by common interests as appropriators, though often in vicious rivalry with one another, and increasingly isolated from their producing compatriots.

The aristocracy used its non-economic powers, especially its judicial functions, to appropriate the labour of subordinate producers. In that respect, it still had something in common with the ancient bureaucratic state, in which the state and state office were the principal means of appropriation. The status of lords may even have been a remnant of the old bureaucratic state and its system of state-controlled appropriation. But the critical difference is that there was, in post-Mycenean Greece, effectively no state, no powerful apparatus of rule to sustain the power of appropriators over producers. Property was held by individuals and households, and the aristocracy of property had to face its subordinates not as a well organized ruling force but as a fairly loose collection of such individuals and households, often engaged in fierce conflict with each other, and distinguished from their non-aristocratic compatriots less by superior power than by superior property and noble birth. Their relations with peasant producers were further complicated by the community's growing military reliance on the peasantry.

By the time we reach the first relatively well-documented moment in the evolution of Athenian democracy, the reforms of Solon, the conflict between lords and peasants had decisively come to the fore. Although Aristotle, in his account of the Solonian reforms, is no doubt exaggerating when he says that, at the time, all the poor were serfs to the wealthy few, there can be little doubt that dependence of one kind or another was very common. There was widespread unrest, which the aristocracy was in no position to quell by sheer force. Instead, there was an effort to settle the conflict between peasants and lords by means of a new political dispensation.

Whatever Solon's motivations may have been, the significant point for us here is *how* he sought to placate the unruly peasantry. He eliminated various forms of dependence which allowed Attic peasants to be exploited by their aristocratic compatriots. He abolished debt-bondage and prohibited loans on the security of the person, which could issue in slavery in case of default; and, by instituting his famous *seisachtheia*, the 'shaking off of burdens', he abolished the status of the *hektemoroi*, peasants whose land, and some portion of their labour, was held in bondage to landlords.[4] In other words, he eliminated various forms of 'extra-economic' appropriation through the medium of political power or personal dependence.

The effects of these reforms, liberating the peasantry from dependence and extra-economic exploitation, were enhanced by strengthening the civic community, extending political rights and elevating the individual citizen at the expense of traditional principles of kinship, birth and blood. Although citizens would still be classified into stratified categories, the old division among artisans, farmers and the aristocracy of well-born clans would no longer be politically significant and would be replaced by more quantitative criteria of wealth, based on an already existing system of military classification. While the former governing council, the Areopagus, was still confined to the two richest classes, the third class was given access to a new Council of 400, to act as a counterweight. The poorest military category, the *thetes*, was apparently admitted for the first time to the assembly, which became increasingly important as the power of the aristocratic council declined.

---

4 Hektemorage used to be understood as a consequence of default on a mortgage or loan, but it is now more commonly thought to be an old-established dependent condition in which, whether as serfs or clients, peasants were bound to a lord.

Solon also reformed the judicial system, creating a new people's court, to which all citizens had access. Any citizen could have his case transferred to this court, taking it out of the reach of aristocratic judgment and weakening the aristocracy's monopoly of jurisdiction. Traditionally, kinship groups had always had the initiative in avenging crimes against their members, according to age-old customs of blood vengeance. Now, any citizen could bring charges against anyone else on behalf of any member of the community. Crime was now defined as a wrong committed against a member of the civic community, not necessarily a kinsman; and the individual Athenian had the initiative as *citizen*, while the civic community, in the form of citizens' courts, had jurisdiction.

In various ways, then, Solon weakened the political role of noble birth and blood, kinship and clan, while strengthening the community of citizens. It is too much to say that his reforms were democratic; but they did have the effect of weakening the aristocracy, which was increasingly incorporated into the civic community and subject to the jurisdiction of the polis. Impersonal principles of law and citizenship were taking precedence over the personal rule of kings or lords. The new civic relationship between aristocracy and peasants, together with other labouring citizens, meant that the Athenians had moved decisively away from the old division between rulers and producers. The state, in the form of the polis, was becoming not a primary means of appropriation from direct producers but, on the contrary, a means of protecting citizen producers from appropriating classes.

The polis also created a new arena for aristocratic rivalries. Solon's reforms certainly did not end the influence of noble families, nor did they diminish the ferocity of intra-class rivalry. Athens would long continue to be plagued by aristocratic infighting, even to the point of virtual civil war, sometimes with help from Sparta for one or another of the contenders. But it was becoming harder for landlords to contend for power just among themselves. They now had to conduct their competition within the community of citizens, and this meant that they could advance their positions by gaining support from the common people, the *demos*. The paradoxical effect was that the civic community and the political principle were further strengthened by aristocratic rivalry. Although there has been much dispute about the 'tyrants' who followed Solon, who they were and what they represented, the most likely explanation is that they were a product of just such competition among Athenian aristocrats;[5] and the general

---

5 The Greek word, *tyrannos*, referred not necessarily to an evil or autocratic ruler but simply to a leader and sole ruler who had not been lawfully established.

tendency of their regime was, again, to strengthen the polis against traditional principles – for instance, building on what might be called 'national' as against local loyalties, by such means as a national coinage, festivals and cults, including the cult of the goddess Athena, patron of the polis.

After the expulsion of the last tyrant by Sparta, there followed, in 510–508 BC, a period of particularly violent struggle, in which the principal contenders were Isagoras and Cleisthenes, both representing noble families. When Cleisthenes prevailed, at least temporarily, he instituted reforms that would later be regarded as the true foundation of democracy. In a sense, he was simply following the logic established by Solon and the tyrants. His reforms, in 508(?) BC, further weakened the traditional authority of the aristocracy, their power over their own neighbourhoods and over smaller farmers in their area. Like his predecessors, he accomplished this by elevating the polis and the whole community of citizens over old forms of authority and old loyalties, submitting local and regional power to the all-embracing authority of the polis.

But what was most distinctive about this moment in the history of Athens was that the demos had become a truly central factor in the political struggle. By now, the people were a conscious and vocal political force. Cleisthenes did not create this force, but he had the strategic sense to mobilize it in his favour. Whether he was himself a true democrat or simply another scion of a noble clan seeking to enhance the position of his own aristocratic family, his appeal to the demos was direct and unambiguous. Herodotus writes that, when Cleisthenes found himself weaker than Isagoras, he made the demos his *hetairoi* – a word difficult to translate but suggesting comrades or partners. It also suggests the associations, friendship groups or clubs, the *hetaireiai*, which formed the power base of the aristocrat in Athens.[6] The demos, in other words, had replaced friends and kin of aristocrats as the

---

6 Paul Cartledge, who prefers to translate this passage from Herodotus to read that Cleisthenes 'hetairized [the demos] to himself', has argued that this is a tendentious formulation on the part of the historian ('Democracy, Origins of: Contribution to a Debate', in Kurt Raaflaub et al., *Origins of Democracy in Ancient Greece*, Berkeley and Los Angeles: University of California Press, 2007, pp. 155–69). Cleisthenes could not, of course, have literally included the demos collectively in his *hetaireia* (if, indeed, he had one). The effect of Herodotus's formulation, which makes the demos little more than a pawn of its aristocratic leader, is to deny its revolutionary force; and the passage, Cartledge suggests, represents the historian (or his aristocratic source) using traditional aristocratic (and hence antidemocratic) language to describe, and traduce, a revolutionary transformation of consciousness that had led to political revolution in practice.

source of political power. When Cleisthenes's enemy, Isagoras, drove him out, with the help of Sparta under its leader, Cleomenes, the demos rose in revolt, erupting into the political arena in an unprecedented way, as a conscious political force acting in its own right and in defence of its own interests.

Whatever his intentions, the result of Cleisthenes's reforms was the establishment of an institutional framework that was to govern Athenian democracy from then on, with only a few modifications. He changed the whole organization of the polis by removing the political functions of the four tribes, dominated by the aristocracy, which had been the traditional basis of political organization – for instance, in the conduct of elections – and replaced them with ten new tribes based on complex and artificial geographic criteria. More significantly, he subdivided the tribes into *demes*, generally (but perhaps not always) based on existing villages, and made them the foundation of the democracy, its fundamental constituent unit and the locale of citizenship. The new divisions cut across tribal and class ties and elevated locality over kinship, establishing and strengthening new bonds, new loyalties specific to the polis, the community of citizens.

Cleisthenes also effected other major reforms, introducing measures designed to create some kind of counterbalance to institutions still dominated by the aristocracy, such as the Areopagus, which continued to have a monopoly of jurisdiction in crimes against the state and in controlling magistrates. In particular, he gave the Assembly a new legislative role. But it was the institution of the demes perhaps more than any other institutional reform that vested power in the demos. It was in the deme that the peasant-citizen was truly born. Democratic politics began in the deme, where ordinary citizens dealt with the immediate and local matters that most directly affected their daily lives, and the democratic polis at the centre was constructed on this foundation. It was here that the traditional barrier between producing peasant village and appropriating central state was most completely broken down; and the new relation between producing classes and the state extended to other labouring citizens too.

Nothing symbolizes more neatly the effect of Cleisthenes's reforms than the fact that Athenian citizens were thereafter to be identified not by their patronymic or clan name but by their *demotikon*, the name of the deme in which their citizenship was rooted – an identification not surprisingly resisted by the aristocracy, which clung to the old identity of blood and noble birth. To be sure, the aristocracy continued to hold positions of power and influence, and Cleisthenes may or may not have intended to establish true popular sovereignty.

But his reforms did advance the power of the people. Cleisthenes himself seems to have described the new political order as *isonomia*, literally equality of law, which had to do not simply with equal rights of citizenship but with a more even balance among the various organs of government, giving the popular assembly a more active legislative role than ever before. Although the demos, who elected magistrates, would not achieve full sovereign control as long as the Areopagus retained its dominant role in enforcing state decisions and holding magistrates to account, the new legislative role that Cleisthenes gave to the Assembly was a major enhancement of popular power.

There were also other more intangible effects of Cleisthenes's reforms. We shall have more to say later about developments in the concepts of law, justice and equality; but it is worth mentioning here that Cleisthenes has been credited with a significant change in Greek political vocabulary, the application of the word *nomos*, instead of the traditional *thesmos*, to designate statutory law.[7] What is significant about this change is that, while *thesmos* implies the imposition of law from above and has a distinctly religious flavour, *nomos* – a word that suggests something held in common, whether pasture or custom – implies a law to which there is common agreement, something that people who are subject to it themselves regard as a binding norm. The application of *nomos* to statute became common usage in Athens, which had thereby adopted 'the most democratic word for "law" in any language.'[8]

Was the Democracy Democratic?

After Cleisthenes, popular power continued to evolve, with the Areopagus losing its exclusive jurisdiction in political cases, with popular juries playing an ever greater role (pay for attendance was introduced in the 450s under Pericles), and the Assembly gaining strength (though pay for attendance was introduced only in the late 390s). Since much of what we might regard as political business was dealt with in Athens by means of judicial proceedings, the power of popular juries was particularly important, and Aristotle – or whoever wrote the *Constitution of Athens* commonly attributed to him – would later describe it as one of the three most democratic features of the Athenian polis.

---

7 Martin Ostwald, *Nomos and the Beginnings of Athenian Democracy* (Oxford: Clarendon Press, 1969), p. 55.
8 *Ibid.*, p. 160.

Athens's victory over Persia in the Battle of Marathon in 490 BC or, more especially, the naval victory at Salamis in 480 ushered in the golden age of the democracy, a new age of democratic self-confidence. When the historian Thucydides a few decades later depicted the most famous democratic leader, Pericles, he was able to put into his mouth a glowing account of democracy in his famous Funeral Oration. For all its rose-tinted prose, this speech tells us much about the realities, and even more about the aspirations, of Athenian political life. Pericles, himself an aristocrat, tells us that Athens is called a democracy

> because its administration is in the hands, not of the few, but of the many; yet while as regards the law all men are on an equality for the settlement of their private disputes, yet . . . it is as each man is in any way distinguished that he is preferred to public honours, not because he belongs to a particular class, but because of personal merits; nor, again, on the ground of poverty is a man barred from a public career by obscurity of rank if he but has it in him to do the state a service . . . and we Athenians decide public questions for ourselves or at least endeavour to arrive at a sound understanding of them, in the belief that it is not debate that is a hindrance to action, but rather not to be instructed by debate before the time comes for action.[9]

And indeed the Assembly, which all citizens were entitled to attend, deliberated and decided on every kind of public question, while legal cases were commonly tried in popular courts. The council which set the agenda for the Assembly was now chosen by lot annually from among all citizens. Although election was regarded as an oligarchic practice, it was used for some positions, typically military and financial, which required a specialized skill. But in general public offices, which tended to be ad hoc, were not treated as specialized professional employments; and many officials were chosen by lot. In principle, then, and to a great extent in practice, all citizens could be involved in all government functions – executive, legislative and judicial. To be sure, aristocrats like Pericles (who reached his influential position in the democracy as a military leader chosen by the people) still enjoyed great influence, while wealthy and well-born citizens probably still had disproportionate weight in the assembly. Yet (as anti-democrats like

---

9 Thucydides, *The Peloponnesian War*, II.XXXVII.1 and XL.2–3, Loeb Classical Library translation.

Plato make very clear) we should not underestimate the day-to-day role of popular power in juries and assemblies, nor the significance of democratic practices like sortition (selection by lot) for various public positions.

Nevertheless, even taking into account the historically unprecedented, and in many ways still unequalled, power of the Athenian people, we must pause here to ask whether, or in what sense, it is appropriate to call the Athenian polis a democracy. After all, this was a society in which slavery played a major role, and in which women had no political rights. In fact, the evolution of democracy increased the role of slavery and in some ways diminished the status of women, especially in respect to the disposition of property. It can hardly be denied that the imperatives of preserving property had a great deal to do with restrictions on the freedom of women, and it is difficult to avoid the conclusion that the position of smallholders, the peasant-citizens of Athens, generated particularly strong pressures for the conservation of family property. It is even more obvious that the liberation of the peasantry and its unavailability as dependent labour created new incentives for enslavement of non-Greeks. So, while slavery was relatively unimportant in the days of Solon, in the golden age of the democracy, according to some estimates, there may have been as many as 110,000 slaves out of a total Attic population of 310,000, of which 172,000 were free citizens and their families (the number of citizens with full political rights would then have been somewhere in the region of 30,000), with another 28,500 metics or resident aliens, free but without political rights.[10]

Athens was a democracy in the sense – and only in the sense – that the Greeks understood the term, which they themselves invented. It had to do with the power of the demos, not only as a political category but as a social one: the poor and common people. Aristotle defined

---

10 These estimates come from an article on 'Population (Greek)' by A.W. Gomme and R.J. Hopper in the *Oxford Classical Dictionary* (1970). I am not offering this estimate as in any way decisive. There are other, different estimates, some of which suggest a far smaller slave population. The point for our purposes here is that the argument about Athenian democracy can be persuasive only if it can confront even large numbers of slaves. The role of slaves in the Athenian economy is just as controversial. This is not the place to deal with this matter, which is discussed in detail in Ellen Meiksins Wood, *Peasant-Citizen and Slave: The Foundations of Athenian Democracy* (London: Verso, 1988), especially Ch. 2 and Appendix 1. The essential point is that slavery did not free Athenians from labour and that the majority of the citizen body worked for a livelihood.

democracy as a constitution in which 'the free-born and poor control the government – being at the same time a majority', and distinguished it from oligarchy, in which 'the rich and better-born control the government – being at the same time a minority'. The social criteria – poverty in one case, wealth and high birth in the other – play a central role in these definitions and even in the end outweigh the numerical criterion. This notion of democracy as a form of class rule – rule by the poor – certainly reflected the views of those who opposed it, who may even have invented the word as a term of abuse; but supporters of the democracy, even moderates like Pericles, regarded the political position of the poor as essential to the definition of democracy.

The enemies of the democracy hated it above all because it gave political power to working people and the poor. It can even be said that the main issue dividing democrats from anti-democrats – as it divided Theseus and the Theban herald in *The Suppliant Women* – was whether the labouring multitude, the *banausic* or menial classes, should have political rights, whether such people are able to make political judgments. This is a recurring theme not only in ancient Greece, where it emerges very clearly in Plato's philosophy, but in debates about democracy throughout most of Western history.

The question raised by critics of democracy is not only whether people who have to work for a living have time for political reflection, but also whether those who are bound to the necessity of working in order to survive can be free enough in mind and spirit to make political judgments. For Athenian democrats, the answer is, of course, in the affirmative. For them, one of the main principles of democracy, as we saw in Theseus's speech, was the capacity and the right of such people to make political judgments and speak about them in public assemblies. The Athenians even had a word for it, *isegoria*, which means not just freedom of speech in the sense we understand it in modern democracies but rather *equality* of public speech. This may, in fact, be the most distinctive idea to come out of the democracy, and it has no parallel in our own political vocabulary. Freedom of speech as we know it has to do with the absence of interference with our right to speak. Equality of speech as the Athenians understood it had to do with the ideal of active political participation by poor and working people.

We can judge the significance of the Athenian definition only by comparing it to democracy as we understand it today. While we have to recognize the severe limitations of Athenian democracy, there are also ways in which it far exceeds our own. This is true of procedures such as sortition or direct democracy, with ordinary citizens, and not just representatives, making decisions in assemblies and juries. But even more important is the effect of democracy on relations between classes. It is true that modern democracy, like the ancient, is a system in which people are citizens regardless of status or class. But if class makes no (legal) difference to citizenship in either case, in modern democracy the reverse is also true: citizenship makes little difference to class. This was not and could not be so in ancient Greece, where political rights had far-reaching effects on the relations between rich and poor.

We have already encountered the peasant-citizen, whose political rights had wider implications. Peasants have been the predominant producing classes throughout much of history, and an essential feature of their condition has been the obligation to forfeit part of their labour to someone who wields superior force. Peasants have been in possession of land, either as owners or as tenants; but they have had to transfer surplus labour to landlords and states, in the form of labour services, rents or taxes. The appropriating classes which have made these claims on them have been able to do so because they have possessed not only land but privileged access to coercive military, political and judicial power. They have possessed what has been called 'politically constituted property'.[11] The military and political powers of lordship in feudal Europe, for instance, were at the same time the power to extract surpluses from peasants. If feudal lords and serfs had been politically and juridically equal, they would not, by definition, have been lords and serfs, and there would have been no feudalism.

This type of relationship, and even patronage (such as would exist in Rome), was absent in democratic Athens. Its absence certainly had the effect of encouraging the enslavement of non-Greeks. But it is, again, important to keep in mind that the majority of Athenian citizens worked for a living, mainly as farmers or craftsmen, and that citizenship in Athens precluded a whole range of legally and politically dependent conditions which throughout history have compelled direct producers to forfeit surplus labour to their masters and rulers. This is not to say that the rich in Athens had no advantages over the poor – though the gap between rich and poor was very much narrower in Athens than in ancient Rome. The point is rather that the possession of political

---

11 The phrase 'politically constituted forms of property' was originally proposed by Robert Brenner, who used it for the first time (probably) in the Postscript to his book, *Merchants and Revolution: Commercial Change, Political Conflict, and London's Overseas Traders, 1550–1653* (Princeton: Princeton University Press, 1993), p. 652.

rights made an enormous difference, because it affected how, and even whether, the rich could exploit the poor.

Here lies the great difference between ancient and modern democracy. Today, there is a system of appropriation that does not depend on legal inequalities or the inequality of political rights. It is the system we call capitalism, a system in which appropriating and producing classes can be free and equal under the law, where the relation between them is supposed to be a contractual agreement between free and equal individuals, and where even universal suffrage is possible without fundamentally affecting the economic powers of capital. The power of exploitation in capitalism can coexist with liberal democracy, which would have been impossible in any system where exploitation depended on a monopoly of political rights. The reason this is possible is that capitalism has created new, purely *economic* compulsions: the propertylessness of workers – or, more precisely, their lack of property in the means of production, the means of labour itself – which compels them to sell their labour power in exchange for a wage simply in order to gain access to the means of labour and to obtain the means of subsistence; and also the compulsions of the market, which regulate the economy and enforce certain imperatives of competition and profit-maximization.

So, both capital and labour can have democratic rights in the political sphere without completely transforming the relation between them in a separate economic sphere. In fact, it is only in capitalism that there *is* a separate economic sphere, with its own imperatives, and so it is only in capitalism that democracy *can* be confined to a separate political domain. It is also only in capitalism that so much of human life has been put outside the reach of democratic accountability, regulated instead by market imperatives and the requirements of profit, the commodification that affects all aspects of life, not just in the workplace but everywhere. Citizenship today, in the conditions of capitalism, may be more inclusive, but it simply cannot mean as much to ordinary citizens as it meant to Athenian peasants and craftsmen – even in the more benign forms of capitalism which have moderated the effects of market imperatives. Athenian democracy had many great short-comings, but in this respect, it went beyond our own.

In one other respect, Athenian democracy was no less imperfect than is today's most powerful democracy. The commitment to civic freedom and equality among citizens at home did not extend to relations with other states. Athens increasingly exploited its growing power to impose imperial hegemony on allied city-states, largely for the purpose of extracting tribute from them. The Athenian empire was, to be sure, shaped and limited by the democracy at home. Imperial expansion was not driven by the interests of a landed aristocracy, and the Athenians often displaced local oligarchies in dependent city-states, establishing democracies friendly to Athens. Nor, while commercial interests were certainly at work, was the Athenian empire a mercantile project. The imperial mission was, in the first instance, to compensate for domestic agricultural deficiencies in order to ensure the food supply by controlling sea routes for the import of grain. This project was certainly a costly one, requiring ever-increasing revenues from tribute to maintain the Athenian navy; but the social property relations underlying the democracy ensured that Athens never established a territorial empire, as the Romans would do. While Roman peasant soldiers, as we shall see, would be subject to years of service far away from home, leaving their properties vulnerable to expropriation by aristocratic landowners, Athenian military ventures were strictly limited by agricultural cycles and the needs of free peasant soldiers returning home to work their farms. Yet however limited their imperial objectives may have been, the Athenians could be spectacularly brutal in pursuit of their aims; and nothing in their democratic culture precluded such brutality.

The two faces of Athenian democracy would be eloquently captured by the historian, Thucydides, in two of the most famous passages in his *History of the Peloponnesian War*. In Pericles's Funeral Oration, the historian puts in the mouth of the great democratic leader a speech extolling, among other things, the virtues of civic equality. In Athens, Pericles suggests, inequalities between rich and poor, the strong and the weak, are tempered by law and democratic citizenship. In the Melian Dialogue, the Athenians, in debate with a recalcitrant city-state that refuses the status of tributary ally, are made to express with unadorned ruthlessness the imperial principle that 'right, as the world goes, is only in question between equals in power, while the strong do what they can and the weak suffer what they must.'

The Evolution of Political Theory

Political theory has been defined here as the systematic application of critical reason to interrogate political principles, raising questions not only about good and bad forms of government but even about the grounds on which we make such judgments. It asks the most fundamental questions about the source and justification of moral and political standards. Do standards of justice, for instance, exist by nature, or are they simply human conventions? In either case, what, if anything, makes them binding? Are the differences between rulers and subjects, masters and slaves, based on natural inequalities, or have human beings who are naturally equal become unequal as a result of human practices and customs? These moral and political questions have inevitably raised even more fundamental issues. In fact, the tradition of Western philosophy emerged in ancient Greece in large part out of debates that were in the first instance political. In Athens, political debate opened up a whole range of philosophical questions discussed ever since by Western philosophers: not only ethical questions about the standards of good and bad but questions about the nature and foundations of knowledge, about the relation between knowledge and morality, about human nature, and the relation between human beings and the natural order or the divine.

It is easy to take these forms of thought for granted as emerging more or less naturally out of the human condition and the perennial problems humanity faces in its efforts to cope with its social and natural universe. We seldom stop to consider the very specific historical preconditions, intellectual and social, that made it possible to think in these critical terms. But it is worth asking what kinds of intellectual assumptions we must make in order systematically to raise questions about the foundations of good government, standards of justice, or the obligation to obey authority; and it is also worth asking what social conditions have given rise to such assumptions.

In order to question existing arrangements, there must, at the minimum, be some belief in humanity's ability to control its own circumstances, some sense of the separation of human beings from an unchangeable natural order, and of the social from the natural realm. There must be, to put it another way, a conception of *human* history instead of simply natural history or supernatural myth, an idea that history involves conscious human effort to solve human problems, that there is a possibility of deliberate change in accordance with conscious human goals, and that human reason is a formative, creative principle, to some extent capable of transcending the predetermined and inexorable cycle of natural necessity or divinely ordained destiny. Such a view of humanity's place in the world tends to be associated with some direct experience of social change and mobility, some practical distance from the inexorable cycles of nature, which is most likely to come with urban civilization, a well-developed realm of human experience outside the cycles and necessities of nature.

These conditions were present in all the 'high' civilizations of the ancient world and gave rise to rich and varied cultural legacies. But nowhere else had the emphasis on human agency taken centre stage in intellectual life, as it would do in Greece. The two most characteristic products of that distinctive legacy are history as practised by the Greek historians, notably Herodotus and Thucydides, and political theory, in the sense intended here. What distinguished Greece, and especially democratic Athens, from other complex civilizations was the degree to which the prevailing order, especially traditional hierarchies, had been challenged in practice; and conflict or debate about social arrangements was a normal, even institutionalized, part of everyday life. It was in this context that Athenians were faced, in new and unprecedented ways, with moral and political responsibility for shaping their own circumstances. Debate was the operative principle of the Athenian state, and the citizen majority had a deep-seated interest in preserving it. This was so because, and to the extent that, politics in Athens was not about sustaining the rule of a dominant power but about managing the relation between 'mass' and 'elite', with the public institutions of the state acting less as an instrument of rule for the propertied elite than as a counterweight against it, and with the common people in the role of political actors, not simply the object of rule. Reflection on the state was from the start shaped by that relation and by the tensions it inevitably generated.

To get a sense of how Greek political theory came into being, it is useful, again, to consider it against the background of the Homeric epics, the last major expression of ostensibly unchallenged aristocratic rule, at the very moment of its passing. When the epics were written down, whether by Homer himself or by someone else recording an oral tradition, traditional modes of transmitting cultural knowledge and values were no longer adequate, and conditions were emerging that required other forms of discourse, placing new demands on writing. In that respect, Homer was a transitional figure, both in the development of Greek literacy, as a poet still obviously steeped in the oral tradition but whose work was set down in writing, and as the poet of a dying aristocracy, no longer safe in its dominance, no longer able to take obedience for granted, and increasingly beleaguered by a challenge from below. Perhaps the very act of writing down the epics acknowledges the passing of the social order they describe (or the passing of a social order something like the one they have invented) and the need to preserve its principles in a form less ephemeral than oral recitation; but there is no evidence in the substance of the epics, in which the lower classes are scarcely visible, that aristocratic values now require a more robust and systematic defence than songs in praise of hero-nobles.

What happens to the concept of *dikē*, the Greek word for justice, is a telling illustration. In Homer, there is no real conception of justice as an ethical norm. The word *dikē* appears in *The Odyssey* several times but largely as a morally neutral term, describing a characteristic behaviour or disposition, or something like 'the way of things'. So, for example, the *dikē* of bodies in death is that flesh and bone no longer hold together, or the *dikē* of a dog is that it fawns on its master, or a serf does best when his *dikē* is to fear his lord. There are one or two usages that have a somewhat more normative connotation. On his return to Ithaca from the Trojan War, a still unrecognized Odysseus comes upon his father, Laertes, digging in the vineyard like a peasant or slave. Odysseus tells him that he looks more like a man of royal blood, the kind whose *dikē* is to sleep on a soft bed after he has bathed and dined. This could simply refer to the typical lordly way of life, but *dikē* here may also have about it the sense of a due right. Perhaps the closest Homer comes to a moral norm of justice appears in a passage suggesting that the gods do not like foul play but respect *dikē* and upright deeds, the *right* way. Yet even here, *dikē* does not refer to an ethical standard of justice so much as correct and proper behaviour, especially the behaviour of true nobles, in contrast to the intrusive rudeness of Penelope's suitors who, in their confidence that her husband, Odysseus, will never return to punish them, are breaking all the rules of decency.

Homeric usage, then, idealizes a society in which the way of things has not been subjected to serious challenge. *Dikē* does not appear as a standard of justice against which the prevailing order can and should be judged. But a very different meaning of *dikē* already appears in the work of Homer's near, if not exact, contemporary, Hesiod; and it is surely significant that the poet in this case is speaking not for nobles but for peasants. Himself a 'middling' farmer in Boeotia, Hesiod is no radical; yet his poem, *Works and Days,* is not only a compendium of farming information and moral advice but also a long poetic grumble about the lot of hard-working farmers and the injustices perpetrated against them by greedy lords. In this context, *dikē* appears in the figure of a goddess who sits at the right hand of Zeus. Hesiod tells us that she watches and judges 'gift-eating' or 'bribe-swallowing' lords who use their judicial prerogatives to exploit the peasantry by means of 'crooked' judgments. *Dikē*, Hesiod warns, will make sure that the crooked lords get their come-uppance. The poet, to be sure, is not calling for a peasant revolt, but he is certainly doing something of great conceptual significance. He is proposing a concept of justice that stands apart from the jurisdiction of the lords, a standard against which they and their judgments can and must themselves be judged.

It could hardly be more different from Homer's customary and unchallenged aristocratic way of things.

The difference between Homer and Hesiod is social no less than conceptual, the one idealizing an unchallenged dominant class whose values and judgments pass for universal norms, the other speaking for a divided community in which social norms, and the authority of dominant classes, are acknowledged objects of conflict. The issues raised here by poetry would become the subject of complex and abstract debates, for which writing would increasingly become the favoured medium, reaching fruition in the philosophical discourse of the fifth and fourth centuries BC, especially in democratic Athens. The kind of systematic enquiry that the Greeks had already applied to the natural order would be extended to moral rules and political arrangements. *Dikē* would pass from the poetry of Homer and Hesiod to the elaborate philosophical speculations of Plato on justice or *dikaiosune* in *The Republic*, as opponents of the democracy (of which Plato was the most notable example) could no longer rely on tradition and were obliged to construct their defence of social hierarchy on a wholly new foundation.

The Culture of Democracy

To get a sense of how much the issues of political theory permeated the whole of Athenian culture, it is worth considering how moral and political questions arose not only in formal philosophy but also in other, more popular cultural forms, notably in drama. The plays of Aeschylus, Sophocles and Euripides tell us a great deal about the atmosphere in which political philosophy emerged. We have already seen how political debate intruded into Euripides's *Suppliant Women*. In Aeschylus, the first of the major tragedians, the questions of political theory are introduced with greater subtlety but are also more integral to the dramatic action. Aeschylus was particularly well placed to judge the importance of the changes that Athens had undergone. He grew up in an age of tyranny and war. Having fought at Marathon, he saw the democracy come into its own. With experience of the past and steeped in its traditions, he was nevertheless very much a part of the new climate, in which citizens were forced to confront new questions about the moral and political responsibility of ordinary humans who no longer looked upon themselves as simply playthings of the gods or obedient subjects of lords and kings.

His classic trilogy, *The Oresteia*, appeared in 458 not long after the murder of the democratic leader Ephialtes, who had deprived the

Areopagus of its traditional functions, apart from its role as a homicide court. It is likely that Aeschylus was, among other things, conveying the message that this old aristocratic institution, while it still had a role to play in the democracy, had been rightly displaced by more democratic institutions. The trilogy has as its central theme a confrontation between two conflicting conceptions of justice, in the form of a contest between the endless cycle of traditional blood vengeance and new principles of judgment by judicial procedure. The first represents Destiny, the fury of uncontrollable fate; the other, human responsibility – an opposition that may also represent the antithesis of old aristocratic principles of kinship and blood rivalry as against the judicial procedures of a democratic civic order.

The murder of Agamemnon, king of Argos, by his wife, Clytemnestra, sets in train what could be an endless cycle of blood, as Orestes obeys an apparently natural law and avenges his father's death by killing Clytemnestra and her lover, Aegisthus. The inexorable laws of revenge mean that Orestes, pursued by the Furies, must also become the victim of blood vengeance, and so the cycle will go on and on. There is also, in a confrontation between the Furies and the god Apollo, a clash between old principles of kinship – represented by the Furies – and Apollo's commitment to patriarchal-aristocratic right, according to which the murder of a king is a crime in a way that matricide is not. The resolution comes in the last of the three plays with the establishment, on the instructions of Athena, of a court to hear the case of Orestes and end the matter once and for all. The jury will be manned not by gods or lords but by citizen jurors. Aeschylus still gives the gods a role, and fear will still play a part in enforcing the law – as the Furies become the more benign Eumenides. Nor does the tragedian repudiate the customs and traditions of the old Athens. But he is unambiguous about the importance of replacing the force and violence of the old order with new principles of reason, the rule of law and 'Holy Persuasion', the kind of order established by the polis and its civic principles – in particular, the democratic polis ruled by its citizens and not by kings or lords.

The attribution to Aeschylus of another play, *Prometheus Bound*, has been put in question, although his authorship was generally accepted in antiquity. Yet, whether or not it can be read as expressing his views, it tells us much about the culture of Athenian democracy, if we compare its telling of the Promethean myth to other versions of the story. The myth in what is probably its more conventional form appears in Hesiod. Prometheus steals fire from Zeus as a gift to humanity. In his anger, Zeus threatens to make humanity pay for this gift.

There follows the story of Pandora's 'box', a storage jar containing the threatened 'gift' from Zeus. Contrary to the advice of her brother-in-law Prometheus, she opens the jar and releases every evil, ending a golden age when the fruits of the earth were enjoyed without effort, and humanity was free of labour, sorrow and disease, although hope remains trapped inside. Hesiod combines this with another story about stages in the decline of humanity, which was once equal to the gods but is now a race that works and grieves unceasingly. For Hesiod, this is, in the main, a story about the pains of daily life and work. In Aeschylus's recounting of the Prometheus story, as in other variations on the same themes in Sophocles, and in the Sophist Protagoras, it becomes a hymn in praise of human arts and those who practise them.

In this first and only surviving play of a trilogy, (pseudo?) Aeschylus's Prometheus, being ruthlessly punished by Zeus for his pride, is presented as a benefactor to humanity. He has given them the various mental and manual skills that have made life possible and good, ending the condition of misery and confusion in which they had first been created. He also represents the love of freedom and justice, expressing contempt for Zeus's autocracy and the servile humility of the god's messenger, Hermes. As in *The Oresteia*, the tragedian is not here repudiating the gods or tradition, and there may be some right on both sides. But there is no mistaking the importance of the way he tells the Promethean story. Human arts, skills and crafts in his version betoken not the fall of humanity but, on the contrary, its greatest gift. The full political significance of this becomes evident not only when we contrast this view of the arts to the practices of Sparta, where the only 'craft' permitted to citizens was war, but also, as we shall see, if we compare it to Plato's retelling of the myth, where labour is again presented as a symbol of decline, in the context of an argument designed to exclude practitioners of these ordinary human arts, the labouring classes, from the specialized 'craft' of politics.

In Sophocles's *Antigone*, as in Aeschylus's plays, there are also two opposing moral principles in tragic confrontation, and again there is right on both sides. Eteocles and Polyneices, sons of the late ruler, Oedipus, and brothers of Antigone, have killed each other in battle. The new king of Thebes, Creon, has decreed that Eteocles, who fought on the side of his city, will be buried with full military honours, while Polyneices, who fought against the Thebans, will be left unburied. Antigone insists that she will bury her traitorous brother, in defiance of the ruler's decree and in obedience to immortal unwritten laws.

The play is sometimes represented as a clash between the individual conscience and the state, but it is more accurately described as an opposition between two conceptions of *nomos*, Antigone representing eternal unwritten laws, in the form of traditional, customary and religious obligations of kinship, and Creon speaking for the laws of a new political order. This is also a confrontation between two conflicting loyalties or forms of *philia*, a word inadequately conveyed by our notion of 'friendship' – a confrontation between, on the one hand, the ties of blood and personal friendship and, on the other, the public demands of the civic community, the polis, whose laws are supposed to be directed to the common good.

It cannot be said that Sophocles comes down decisively on one side or the other. It is true that we have great sympathy for Antigone, and increasingly less for the stubborn Creon; yet both the antagonists, Antigone and Creon, display excessive and uncompromising pride, for which they both will suffer. The tragedian here too clearly respects 'unwritten laws', but he also stresses the importance of human law and the civic order. Yet, for all of Sophocles's even-handedness, it becomes clear that Creon's chief offence is not that he insists on the supremacy of civic law but rather that he violates the very principles of civic order by treating his own autocratic decrees as if they were law.

In a dialogue with his son Haemon, Creon, having decreed Antigone's punishment, maintains that her act of disobedience was wrong in itself. Haemon believes it would be wrong only if the act itself were also dishonourable, and, he says, the Theban people do not regard it so. 'Since when,' Creon objects, 'do I take my orders from the people of Thebes?. . . I am king and responsible only to myself' – in a manner reminiscent of Xerxes in Aeschylus's *Persians*. 'A one-man state?' asks Haemon. 'What kind of state is that?' 'Why, does not every state belong to its ruler?' says the king, to which his son replies, 'You'd be an excellent king – on a desert island.'

In an ode that interrupts the action, the Chorus sings the praises of the human arts, and the rule of law which is the indispensable condition for their successful practice. We can deduce from this interlude that Sophocles regards the civic order and its laws as a great benefit to humankind, the source of its progress and strength. Yet he is also very alive to the dangers of allowing the polis to be the ultimate, absolute standard, discarding all tradition. Among the chief benefits of the civic order is the possibility of governing human interactions by moderation and persuasion. Perhaps the polis is, ideally, the place where different ethics can be reconciled. But one thing is clear: the possibility of resolution by discussion and persuasion, rather than by coercion, is greatest in a democracy, where one man's judgment cannot prevail simply by means of superior power.

There is also, in the ode, another indication of Sophocles's commit-ment to Athenian democracy. Of all the wonders of the world, he writes, none is more wonderful than humankind. What distinguishes humanity are the various human arts, from agriculture and navigation to speech and statecraft. In this poetic interlude, as in Aeschylus's *Prometheus*, human society is founded on the practical arts; and Sophocles here sums up the central values of the democracy: not only the centrality of human action and responsibility, but also the importance of a lawful civic order and the value of the arts, from the most elevated literary inventions to the most arduous manual labour. In the interweaving of these themes – the centrality of human action, the importance of the civic principle and the value of the arts – we can find the essence of Greek political theory, the terrain of struggle between democrats and those who seek to challenge them by over-turning democratic principles.

Democracy and Philosophy: The Sophists

The plays of Aeschylus and Sophocles bespeak the rise of the civic community, citizenship and the rule of law, as against traditional principles of social organization. They reflect the evolution of the democracy with its new conceptions of law, equality and justice, a new confidence in human powers and creativity, and a celebration of practical arts, techniques and crafts, including the political art. But their tragedies also manifest the tensions of the democratic polis, the questions it inevitably raises about the nature and origin of political norms, moral values, and conceptions of good and evil.

The dramatists speak for a society which has certainly not rejected the notion of unwritten and eternal laws, universal principles of behav-iour, or obligations to family, friends and gods. But it is also a society in which the very idea of universal and eternal values is open to question and nothing can be taken for granted. The experience of the democracy makes certain questions inescapable: what is the relation between eternal laws and man-made laws, between natural and positive law? It is all very well to connect the two by invoking some divinely inspired lawgiver (as the Spartans did, while the Athenians did not); but how do we account for the differences among various communities, which all have their own specific laws? And what happens when demo-cratic politics encourages the view that one person's opinion is as good as another's? What happens then to universal and eternal laws or conceptions of justice? Are these just man-made conventions, based simply on expediency, human convenience, agreement among ordinary mortals and the arts of persuasion? If so, why can we not change them at will, or, for that matter, disobey them?

From the middle of the fifth century BC, these questions were increasingly raised in more systematic form, first by the so-called sophists and then by the self-styled philosophers. There already existed a tradition of natural philosophy, systematic reflection on nature and the material world; and among the natural philosophers, some had begun to extend their reflections to humankind and society – such as the great atomist Democritus, who devoted his life to both science and moral reflection. But the sophists can claim credit for making human nature, society and political arrangements primary subjects of philosophical enquiry.

The sophists were paid teachers and writers who travelled from polis to polis to teach the youth of prosperous families. They flourished in Athens thanks to a keen and growing interest in education, especially in the skills required in the courts and assemblies of the democracy, the arts of rhetoric and oratory. Athens, with its cultural and political vitality, attracted distinguished teachers from other parts of Greece: Prodicus of Ceos, a student of language; Hippias of Elis, whose interests were encyclopedic; the brilliant rhetorician, Gorgias of Leontini, who came to Athens not as a professional teacher but a diplomat; and above all, the earliest and greatest of the sophists, Protagoras of Abdera, friend and adviser to Pericles, about whom more in a moment. Among the other sophists were Thrasymachus, whom we shall encounter in our consideration of Plato's *Republic*; and the second-generation sophists, such as Lycophron, who is credited with formulating an idea of the social contract; Critias, the uncle of Plato, who also appears in his nephew's dialogues; the possibly fictional Callicles, whom Plato uses to represent the radical sophists' idea that justice is the right of the strongest; the so-called 'Anonymous Iamblichi', who countered the radical sophists by arguing that the source of power is in community consensus; Antiphon, perhaps the first thinker to argue for the natural equality of all men, whether Greek or 'barbarian'; and, much later, Alcidamas, who insisted on the natural freedom of humanity.

We should not be misled by the unflattering portraits of these intellectuals painted in particular by Aristophanes and Plato, for whom they represented the decline and corruption of Athens. It is impossible to judge the portrayal of the sophists by these critics without knowing something about the historical moment in which they were writing. During this phase of the democracy, even democratic aristocrats like Pericles were being displaced by new men such as the wealthy but 'common' Cleon. In Plato's aristocratic circles, there was, not surprisingly, an atmosphere of disaffection and nostalgia for the good old days. Unfortunately, the aristocratic grumbles of a small minority have tended to colour views of Athenian democracy ever since, creating a myth of Athens in decline which has been very hard to shift. Aristocratic disaffection did have more serious consequences, which left a deep mark on the democracy. There were two oligarchic revolutions: a brief episode in 411 but more particularly the coup in 404 which, with the help of Sparta, established the bloody rule of the Thirty (the Thirty Tyrants). With the support of a 700–man Spartan garrison on the Acropolis, the Thirty murdered and expelled large numbers of Athenians. Thousands fled the city, and only 3,000 Athenians – perhaps 10 per cent of the citizenry – retained full rights of citizenship. Yet, when the democracy was restored in the following year, it displayed remarkable restraint in dealing with the oligarchic opposition, instituting, at Sparta's behest, an amnesty which ruled out the political persecution of the oligarchs and their supporters; and despite the catastrophes that brought the golden age to a close, the fourth century was to be the most stable period of the democracy, which enjoyed widespread support among the poor and even the rich. This was also a period in which the culture of Athens flourished and when it truly became what Pericles had earlier called 'an education to Greece'. There was no further serious internal threat to the democratic regime, and it came to an end only when Athens effectively lost its independence altogether to the Macedonians in the last quarter of the century.

The notion that the late democracy was a period of moral decay is largely a product of class prejudice. To be sure, there were serious problems, especially economic ones; and the Athenians had paid a heavy price in the Peloponnesian War, to say nothing of the plague. But the myth of democratic decadence has more to do with the social changes that marked the decline of the old aristocracy, which were accompanied by political changes in both leadership and style, a new kind of popular politics that brought to maturity the strategy adopted by Cleisthenes at the beginning of the democracy, when he made the people his *hetairoi*. Critics described these changes as the triumph of vulgarity, materialism, amoral egoism, and 'demagogic' trickery designed to lead the ignorant demos astray. What is most striking about the attacks on a leader like Cleon – by figures as diverse as Thucydides, Aristophanes and Aristotle – is that they invariably suggest objections of style more than substance. Aristotle, for instance, can think of nothing worse to complain about than Cleon's vulgar manner, the way he shouted in the Assembly and spoke with his cloak not girt about him, when others conducted themselves with proper decorum.

For critics like Aristophanes and Plato, the sophists became the intellectual expression of this alleged moral decadence and were made to stand for the decline of traditional values. They were portrayed as representing a polis where even young aristocrats had given up the high moral standards of their ancestors, a polis in which all standards of right and wrong had been abandoned, and even those who knew the difference were likely to prefer wrong to right. The rhetorical strategies perfected by the sophists, and the lawyer's adversarial principle that there are two sides to every question, were interpreted by critics as simply a way of 'making the worse cause seem the better'. But, while some sophists may indeed have been unprincipled opportunists, among them were thinkers who made substantial and innovative contributions to Greek culture and the traditions emanating from it. Even while their ideas have come down to us only in fragments or in second-hand accounts, especially in the dialogues of a generally hostile Plato, enough remains to justify the claim that the sophists, and Protagoras in particular, effectively invented political theory and set the agenda of Western philosophy in general.

The sophists varied in their philosophical ideas no less than in their politics. What they generally had in common was a preoccupation with the distinction between *physis* (nature) and *nomos* (law, custom or convention). In a climate in which laws, customs, ethical principles, and social and political arrangements were no longer taken for granted as part of some unchangeable natural order, and the relation between written and unwritten law was a very live practical issue, the antithesis between *nomos* and *physis* became the central intellectual problem. The very immediate political force of this issue is dramatically illustrated by the fact that, with the restoration of the democracy, magistrates were prohibited from invoking 'unwritten law', an idea that now had powerfully antidemocratic associations.

The sophists in general agreed that there is an essential difference between things that exist by nature and things that exist by custom, convention or law. But there were disagreements among them about which is better, the way of nature or the way of *nomos*, and, indeed, about what the way of nature is. In either case, their arguments could be mobilized in defence of democracy or against it. Some, in support of oligarchy, might argue that there is a natural division between rulers and ruled and that natural hierarchy should be reflected in political arrangements. Others, in defence of democracy, might argue that no such clear division exists by nature, that men are naturally equal, and that it is wrong to create an artificial hierarchy, a hierarchy by *nomos* as against *physis*. But other permutations were possible too: a democrat could argue that a political equality created by *nomos* has the advantage of moderating natural inequalities and permitting men to live in harmony. Or it could be argued that, however similar men may be by nature, life in society requires differentiation, a division of labour, and hence some kind of inequality by *nomos*.

If sophists could be either oligarchs or democrats, it was democracy itself that had brought such issues into sharp relief. In the context of civic equality, the seemingly self-evident observation that, as Thucydides put it in the Melian Dialogue, 'the strong do what they can and the weak suffer what they must' could no longer simply be taken for granted and was up for discussion in unprecedented ways. There were now indeed two sides (at least) to the question. The juxtaposition in practice of civic equality and 'natural' inequality, the inequality of strength and weakness, produced particularly fruitful tensions in theory, which found expression both in Thucydides's history and in philosophy.

It is not as easy as Plato would have us believe to distinguish between the intellectual activities of the sophists and true 'philosophy', or love of wisdom, as practised by Plato himself and the man more commonly credited with its invention, Socrates. To be sure, Socrates was not a paid teacher, though he could always rely on the largesse of his almost uniformly wealthy and well-born friends and acolytes – such as his greatest pupil, the aristocratic Plato. But both Socrates and Plato conducted their philosophic enterprise on the same terrain as the sophists. Not only were the 'philosphers' also concerned primarily with human nature, society, knowledge and morality, but they also proceeded in their own ways from the distinction between *nomos* and *physis,* between things that exist by law or convention and those that exist by nature. They certainly transformed this distinction, in a way that no sophist did, into a philosophical exploration of true knowledge. Unlike the sophists, who tended towards moral relativism or pluralism and never strayed far outside the sphere of empirical reality, Socrates and Plato were concerned with a different kind of 'nature', a deeper or higher reality which was the object of true knowledge. The empirical world was for them, and more particularly for Plato, a world of mere appearances, the object of imperfect conventional wisdom, at best (more or less) right *opinion* but not real knowledge. The philosophers drew a distinction between learning and persuasion, suggesting that the sophists, like lawyers, were not really interested in learning the truth but only in making a case and persuading others of it. Yet even if, for instance, Plato's conception of the division between rulers and ruled is grounded in this hierarchy of knowledge and not on a simple test of brute strength or noble birth, we can still see the connections between the philosopher and those sophists who opposed the democracy on the grounds that it created an artificial equality in defiance of natural hierarchy. More particularly, we can see that the sophists, especially the democratic ones and Protagoras in particular, set the questions the philosophers felt obliged to answer.

Socrates and Protagoras

Socrates, probably the ancient Athenian most revered in later centuries, is also in many ways the most mysterious. He left none of his ideas in writing, and we have to rely on his pupils, especially Plato but also Xenophon, for accounts of his views. Although the differences between Plato's and Xenophon's Socrates have often been vastly exaggerated, it is certainly true that each of these two very different witnesses, the philosopher and the rather more down-to-earth and unphilosophical general, brings something of his own disposition to the portrait of his teacher. There has been heated debate about the 'real', 'historical' Socrates; about the degree to which Plato's philosophy represents an extension of Socratic teachings or a clear departure of his own; and, not least, about Socrates's attitude to the democracy.

The trial and death of Socrates have presented enormous problems of their own. While commentators seem, on the whole, to agree that the death sentence was a grave injustice, they differ on what it tells us about the democracy. On the one hand, there are those who see only an injustice perpetrated by a repressive democracy against a man of conscience, the model of the courageous intellectual who follows his reason wherever it takes him in defiance of all opposition and threats. On the other hand, some commentators see not only an injustice but also a beleaguered democracy, which had just come through a period of oligarchic terror and mass murder after a coup against the democratic regime; and they see in Socrates not only a philosopher of courage and principle but also a man whose friends, associates and pupils were among the leading oligarchs – a man who, as democrats fled the city, remained safely in Athens among his oligarchic friends, with every indication that they were confident of his support.

This is not the place to rehearse all these debates.[12] We can confine ourselves to a few less controversial facts about Socrates, his life and

---

12 For detailed discussion of these disagreements, see Ellen Meiksins Wood and Neal Wood, *Class Ideology and Ancient Political Theory: Socrates, Plato, and Aristotle in Social Context* (Los Angeles and Berkeley: University of California Press, 1978), Ch. 3; and Wood and Wood, 'Socrates and Democracy: A Reply to Gregory Vlastos', *Political Theory*, Vol. 14, No. 1, February 1986, pp. 55–82.

work, and then proceed to an analysis of those ideas that had the
greatest consequences for the development of political theory. All we
can confidently say about his life is that he was an Athenian citizen
of the deme of Alopeke, born around 470 BC, son of Sophroniscus
and Phaenarete; that he participated in some military campaigns,
most likely as a hoplite (which required enough wealth to arm oneself
and support a retainer) during the Peloponnesian War; that he took
part as a member of the Council in the trial of the generals of 406
BC; and that he was tried and condemned to death in 399. There is
little evidence to support the tradition that his father was a sculptor
or stonemason (he may have owned slaves employed as craftsmen,
as did the fathers of Isocrates and Cleon) and his mother a midwife,
and even less that Socrates followed in his father's footsteps. There
is some evidence that he was a man of comfortable means, though
certainly not among the very wealthiest. His friends and associates,
however, were almost uniformly wealthy and well born; and the
picture of Socrates regularly holding philosophical discussions with
artisans around the streets and markets of Athens should be taken
with a grain of salt.

During the oligarchic coup and the regime of the Thirty, Socrates
stayed safely in Athens, as one of the privileged 3,000 citizens. Some
time after the democracy was restored, a charge was brought against
him for not duly recognizing the gods of Athens, introducing new
gods and corrupting the youth. It seems likely that these accusations
were, at least in part, a substitute for more overtly political charges
ruled out by the amnesty; but, in any case, there can be no doubt that
Athenians looked upon the philosopher with suspicion because of his
association with the enemies of the democracy. This does not detract
from his dignity and courage; and the main reason given for his refusal
to escape with the help of his friends – that he must honour the laws
of his polis – testifies to his principled commitment to the rule of law.
In this respect, he was quite different from many of his oligarchic
friends. But nor do his courage, dignity and loyalty to principle make
him a supporter of the democracy.

The question then is whether the suspicions aroused by his associations are supported by what we know of his ideas. Here, again, we
have little to go on. What we know with some degree of certainty is
that he adopted a particular method of inquiry: engaging in dialogue
with one or more interlocutors, he begins with a very general question
about the nature of knowledge or the meaning of a concept such as
virtue or justice, proceeding by a painstaking series of questions and
answers to enumerate the manifold particular instances of 'virtuous'

or 'just' actions; and, with his characteristic irony, he searches out the inconsistencies and contradictions in his interlocutor's definitions. Although he typically professes ignorance and an inability to teach, it becomes clear that, by seeking the common qualities of all the specific instances of 'virtuous' or 'just' actions, he attempts to find a 'real' definition of virtue or justice – not a rule-of-thumb characterization of specific acts in the empirical world but a definition that expresses an underlying, universal and absolute principle of virtue or justice. The object of the philosophic exercise is to elevate the soul, or *psyche*, the immortal and divine element in human nature to which the flesh should be subordinate. Applied to politics, the object of philosophy is to fulfill the higher moral purpose of the polis.

In itself, neither the Socratic method nor even the conception of absolute knowledge associated with it has any necessary political implications. But Socrates's most famous paradox, that virtue is knowledge, is altogether more problematic. On the face of it, this principle simply implies that people act immorally out of ignorance and never voluntarily; and, whatever we may think of this as a description of reality, it seems at least benevolent in its intent, displaying a tolerance and humanity towards those who do wrong which appears to rule out retribution. Nor is there anything political in the admirable first principle of Socrates's moral teaching: that it is better to suffer wrong than to inflict it. But there is more to the identification of virtue with knowledge, which has far-reaching consequences, not least political and antidemocratic implications. The combined effect of this identification and the moral purpose he attributes to the state is, for all practical purposes, to rule out democracy and even to make 'democratic knowledge' an oxymoron.

The implications of Socrates's formulation become most visible in the confrontation with the sophist Protagoras, depicted in Plato's dialogue, *Protagoras*. If we can rely on Plato's reconstruction of the sophist's argument, he seems to have laid out a systematic case for democracy; and it is based on conceptions of knowledge, virtue and the purpose of the polis opposed to those of Socrates. What we know from Plato's portrayal and from the very few genuine surviving fragments of the sophist's writings is that Protagoras was an agnostic, who argued that we cannot really know whether the gods exist; that we can rely only on human judgment; and that, since there is no certain arbiter of truth beyond human judgment, we cannot assume the existence of any absolute standards of truth and falsehood or of right and wrong. Human beings, indeed every individual, must be the final judges – an idea famously summed up in his best-known aphorism,

'Man is the measure of all things, of things that are that they are and of things that are not that they are not.'

Such ideas were significant enough. But in Plato's *Protagoras*, there is a discussion between Socrates and Protagoras which effectively sets the agenda for the whole of Plato's mature philosophical work and the intellectual tradition that follows from it. Although this dialogue is no longer commonly regarded as among the earliest of Plato's works, it has been described as the last of his 'Socratic' dialogues, after which he strikes out on his own, developing his ideas more elaborately and independently of his teacher. *Protagoras* opens up the questions to which the philosopher will devote the rest of his working life and which will, through him, shape the whole of Western philosophy.

What is most immediately striking about the dialogue is that the pivotal question is a political one. Socrates presents Protagoras with a conundrum: like others of his kind, the sophist purports to teach the art of politics, promising to make men good citizens. This surely implies, argues Socrates, that virtue, the qualities of a good citizen, can be taught. Yet political practice in Athens suggests otherwise. When Athenians meet in the Assembly to decide on matters such as construction or shipbuilding projects, they call for architects or naval designers, experts in specialized crafts, and dismiss the views of non-specialists, however wealthy or well born. This is how people normally behave in matters regarded as technical, involving the kind of craft or skill that can and must be taught by an expert. But when the Assembly is discussing something to do with the government of the polis, Athenians behave very differently:

> . . . the man who gets up to advise them may be a builder or equally well a blacksmith or a shoemaker, merchant or shipowner, rich or poor, of good family or none. No one brings it up against any of these, as against those I have just mentioned, that he is a man who without any technical qualifications, unable to point to anybody as his teacher, is yet trying to give advice. The reason must be that they do not think this is a subject that can be taught.[13]

Protagoras gives a subtle and fascinating answer, introduced by yet another story about Prometheus. He sets out to show that Athenians 'act reasonably in accepting the advice of smith and shoemaker on

---

13 *Protagoras* 319c–d, transl. W.K.C. Guthrie.

political matters'.[14] There is no inconsistency, he says, between the claim that virtue can be taught and the assumption that civic virtue, or the capacity to make political judgments, is a universal quality, belonging to all adult citizens regardless of status or wealth. His argument turns out to be less a case for his claims as a teacher of the political art than a defence of Athenian democratic practice, insisting on the capacity of ordinary, labouring citizens to make political judgments. Although there is a brief defence of democracy in Herodotus (III.80), Protagoras's speech is the only substantive and systematic argument for the democracy to survive from ancient Greece. It is true that we have to rely on Plato to convey the sophist's views, and we have no way of knowing how much of it Protagoras actually said. But, in contrast to Plato's attacks on other sophists, Protagoras emerges as a fairly sympathetic and deeply intelligent figure, and Socrates somewhat less so than is usual in Plato's dialogues. In any case, whether or not these are the authentic ideas of Protagoras, they certainly express a coherent democratic view; and Plato spends the rest of his career trying to counter it. Much of his philosophy thereafter, including his epistemology, seeks to demonstrate that virtue is a rare and lofty quality and the political art a specialized craft that can be practised only by a very select few, because it requires a special and elevated kind of philosophic knowledge.

It is not always clear that Plato regards natural inequalities among human beings as great enough in themselves to justify the division between rulers and ruled. But there is no ambiguity in his belief that there is an absolute and universal hierarchy of knowledge, which must be reflected in the organization of the polis. Whatever the innate qualities of human beings and their natural capacities to acquire knowledge, it is impossible, in the real world, for the majority to achieve the kind of philosophic knowledge required to make sound political judgments. In particular, the practioners of ordinary and necessary crafts – Protagoras's shoemakers and smiths – are politically incapacitated not only by their lack of time and leisure to acquire philosophic knowledge, but even more by their bondage to labour and material need, their life 'among the multiplicity of things'. True knowledge requires liberation from the world of appearance and necessity.

Protagoras's argument proceeds, first, by way of an allegory. Human beings, he recounts, at first had no means of providing for themselves as other animals did. Prometheus found them 'naked,

---

14 *Ibid*. 324d.

unshod, unbedded, and unarmed.'[15] So he gave them the gifts of fire and skill in the arts. But, while they now had the resources to keep themselves alive, they were unable to benefit from the arts they had acquired, because they lacked political wisdom. They had speech and the means to make houses, clothes, shoes, and bedding, and to get food from the earth; but, unable to live together and cooperate for their mutual benefit, they scattered and were devoured by wild beasts. Zeus instructed his messenger, Hermes, to give humanity the qualities of respect for others (*aidos*) and a sense of justice (*dikē*), to create a bond of friendship and union among them, so they could live together in civilized communities. Hermes asked Zeus whether these qualities should be distributed just to a few, on the grounds that only one trained specialist is enough for many laymen – as one doctor is enough to care for many untrained people – or should they be given to all alike. Zeus replied that all should have their share, because there could never be cities or civilized life if only a few had these virtues.

Protagoras's allegory from the outset entails a conception of the state's purpose quite different from that of Socrates. The polis exists not to achieve some higher moral purpose but to serve ordinary human interests by providing conditions in which human beings can live reasonably peaceful and comfortable lives. The allegory is intended to demonstrate that political society, without which humanity cannot benefit from the arts and skills that are its only distinctive gift, cannot survive unless the civic virtue that qualifies people for citizenship is a universal (male?) quality. He then goes on to show how virtue can be a universal quality that nonetheless must and can be taught – and here the argument moves from allegory to what might be called anthropology.

The necessary qualities are not, he argues, the kinds of characteristics that are given by nature or chance. They require instruction and learning. Yet the required instruction is available to all. Everyone who lives in a civilized community, especially a polis, is from birth exposed to the learning process that imparts civic virtue, in the home, in school, through admonition and punishment, and above all through the city's customs and laws, its *nomoi*. In a remarkable passage, Protagoras illustrates his point by insisting that no rational man would inflict punishment for a crime simply to avenge the offence, which in any case cannot be undone. Because we believe that civic virtue can be taught, punishment looks not to the past but to the future, either to prevent the same person from repeating the offence or to teach by example to others.

---

15 *Ibid.* 321d.

No man, argues Protagoras, can be a layman in civic virtue if the state is to exist at all, and any civilized community has the means to ensure that all its members can obtain the necessary virtue. Life in a civilized and humane community, which has courts of justice and the rule of law, as well as education, is the school of civic virtue; and the community's customs and laws are the most effective teachers. Civic virtue is both learned and universal in much the same way as one's mother tongue, which is taught and learned in the normal transactions of everyday life. The sophist who, like Protagoras himself, claims to teach virtue can only perfect this continuous and universal process, and a man can possess the qualities of good citizenship without the benefit of the sophist's expert instruction. Again, the object here is not to defend the claims of expert teachers but, above all, to give credit for virtue and civilized life to the *nomoi* generated especially by a democratic community.

Protagoras's emphasis on the universality of virtue is, of course, critical to his defence of democracy. But equally important is his conception of the process by which moral and political knowledge is transmitted. Virtue is certainly taught, but the model of learning is not so much scholarship as apprenticeship. Apprenticeship, in so-called 'traditional' societies, is more than a means of learning technical skills. It is also the means by which the values of the community are passed from one generation to another. There is no better way of characterizing the learning process described by Protagoras, the mechanism by which the community of citizens passes on its collective wisdom, its customary practices, values and expectations.

It is not quite so easy to interpret the argument of Socrates. He begins the discussion apparently suggesting that virtue cannot be taught and mischievously concludes at the end of the dialogue that he and Protagoras seem to have changed sides on the question. But he is being somewhat disingenuous. It is, after all, not Socrates himself who begins with the view that virtue is not teachable and that it is effectively a universal quality. He is, with a fair degree of irony, suggesting that the Athenians themselves behave as if this were so. The essence of his argument is not that virtue is unteachable, or requires no teaching, but rather that it is inconsistent to argue both that virtue is teachable and that it is a universal quality.

The point, of course, is that Socrates and Protagoras, from the beginning, have different conceptions of knowledge. Although Socrates does not here lay out a systematic argument, he is certainly moving in the direction of identifying virtue – the condition for enjoying political rights – with philosophic wisdom, the knowledge of a universal and absolute good. Protagoras, as we saw, is talking about a different and more mundane kind of knowledge, as the condition of a more mundane kind of political virtue and to serve the mundane purposes of the polis. His position on virtue and how it is acquired never changes throughout the discussion. What Socrates mischievously presents as a contradiction in Protagoras's argument is simply his refusal to accept the identification of virtue with philosophic wisdom. Socrates, too, remains consistent; and, while he never quite answers the question about political virtue himself, he already hints at an answer, to be developed by Plato, which effectively repudiates Athenian democratic practice: virtue can and must be taught (though Plato makes it clear that the final perception of the Good, after painstaking guidance by the teacher, is not something that is directly taught but occurs as an almost mystical illumination); but if virtue is taught and learned, it is as a rare and highly specialized knowledge, a knowledge that only a few can acquire. The dialogue ends with a tantalizing suggestion that the discussion of virtue will be left for another occasion. In fact, Plato will devote much of his life to it.

The principle invoked by Socrates against Protagoras – at this stage, still rather tentatively and unsystematically – is the principle that virtue is knowledge; that is, philosophic knowledge, the knowledge of one single good that underlies the appearances of many particular goods. This is the kind of knowledge that allows its practitioner not only to display this or that specific ordinary virtue but to grasp the fundamental and all-encompassing principle of virtue as a single entity, which underlies all the qualities we associate with various multiple virtues. The principle that virtue is knowledge was to become the basis of Plato's attack on democracy, especially in *The Statesman* and *The Republic*. In Plato's hands, it represents the replacement of Protagoras's moral and political apprenticeship in the community's values and norms with a more exalted conception of virtue as philosophic knowledge – not the conventional assimilation of the community's customs and values but a privileged access to higher universal and absolute truths, which are unavailable to the majority who remain tied to the world of appearance and material necessity.

So the political question posed by Socrates opens up much larger questions about the nature of knowledge and morality. Epistemological and moral relativism, as Protagoras formulates it, has, and is intended to have, democratic implications. Plato responds to this political challenge by opposing Protagoras's relativism with a new kind of universalism. In the democracy, in the atmosphere of public deliberation and debate, there could be no ruling ideas, no individual or social group whose unchallenged dominance allowed it to claim universality for its own values and impose them on others. The only effective way of challenging the conventional wisdom of shoemakers and blacksmiths, and their ability to participate in public speech and deliberation, was to trump conventional wisdom altogether with some higher form of knowledge, a knowledge not of mundane empirical realities but of absolute and universal truths.

Platonic universalism is of a very special kind, and it is perhaps only in relation to this philosophical universalism that Protagoras's ideas can be called morally relativist at all. He certainly did reject the notion that there are higher moral truths accessible only to philosophic knowledge, but he put in its place what might be called a practical universalism, rooted in a conception of human nature and the conditions of human well-being. His argument presupposes a conviction not only that men are in general capable of making political judgments, and that their well-being depends on participation in a civic order, but also that they are *entitled* to the benefits of civic life. It is true that, in his view, the specific requirements of well-being will vary in the infinite diversity of the human condition in different places and times, and social values will vary accordingly. But the underlying human substratum remains the same, and the well-being of humanity does provide a kind of universal moral standard by which to judge social and political arrangements or to assess the relative value of opposing opinions, not on the grounds that some are *truer* than others but that they are *better*, as Protagoras is made to formulate it in Plato's dialogue, *Theaetetus*.

In these respects, Protagoras and Plato are poles apart both politically and philosophically, and the differences between them are traceable to their very different attitudes towards democracy. Nevertheless, there is one respect in which they proceed from a common starting point, and both of them are equally rooted in the democracy. Plato too draws on the common experience of democratic Athens, appealing to the familiar experience and values of the labouring citizen by invoking the ethic of craftsmanship, *technē*, and seeking to meet the democratic argument on its own terrain by constructing his definition of political virtue and justice on the analogy of the practical arts. Only this time, the emphasis is not on universality or the organic transmission of conventional knowledge from one generation to another, but on specialization, expertise and exclusiveness. Just as the best shoes are made by the trained and expert shoemaker, so the art of politics should be practised only by those who specialize in it. No more shoemakers and smiths in the Assembly. The essence of justice in the state is the principle that the cobbler should stick to his last.

Only the few who are not obliged to work for a living, whether in farming, craftsmanship or trade, can have the qualities required to rule.

Both Protagoras and Plato, then, place the cultural values of *technē*, the practical arts of the labouring citizen, at the heart of their political arguments, though to antithetical purposes. Much of what follows in the whole tradition of Western philosophy proceeds from this starting point. It is not only Western *political* philosophy that owes its origins to this conflict over the political role of shoemakers and smiths. For Plato the division between those who rule and those who labour, between those who work with their minds and those who work with their bodies, between those who rule and are fed and those who produce food and are ruled, is not simply the basic principle of politics. The division of labour between rulers and producers, which is the essence of justice in the *Republic*, is also the essence of Plato's theory of knowledge. The radical and hierarchical opposition between the sensible and the intelligible worlds, and between their corresponding forms of cognition, is grounded by Plato in an analogy with the social division of labour which excludes the producer from politics.[16]

Plato: The *Republic*

After the *Protagoras*, Plato would never again directly confront a democratic argument. He certainly continued his debate with the sophists; and every attack on them was in a sense an attack on democracy, since, even when they were antidemocratic, he often treated them as products or expressions of democracy (which, of course, in a sense they were) on the grounds that they reflected and encouraged the moral and intellectual decadence of a polis in which one man's opinion was as good as another's. In the *Gorgias*, for instance, we are given to understand

---

16 It has been suggested that this opposition is the most distinctive characteristic of Greek thought, which has set the agenda for Western philosophy ever since. See, for instance, Jacques Gernet in 'Social History and the Evolution of Ideas in China and Greece from the Sixth to the Second Century BC', in Jean-Pierre Vernant, *Myth and Society in Ancient Greece*, transl. Janet Lloyd (Sussex: Harvester Press, 1980). The suggestion that the opposition between sensible and intelligible worlds is uniquely Western may be misleading; but there is a uniquely antagonistic conception of the relation between them in the Western philosophical tradition since Plato; and this owes much to the antidemocratic convictions on which his argument is based. The connection drawn by Plato between this epistemological division and the division between rulers and ruled is critical here; and a philosopher who could take for granted the division between rulers and producers (as Mencius did, for instance) might not have felt the same compulsion to emphasize the antithesis between these two worlds, with their corresponding forms of cognition.

that the amoral, unprincipled Callicles, with his contention that justice is the right of the strongest, is the logical outcome of the democratic attitude, even when the idea that might makes right is invoked in support of oligarchy. Yet, while Plato conducted his case against democracy without ever directly engaging a serious argument in its favour, Protagoras remained his primary, if nameless, adversary.

Protagoras, as we have seen, presented the practical arts as the foundation of society. The 'argument from the arts', which lies at the heart of Plato's political theory, is intended to turn Protagoras's principle against itself. It uses the ethic of craftsmanship, which was so much a part of Athens's democratic culture, to argue against the democracy. We can understand the full significance of this argument for Plato only if we consider its relation to the culture of the Athenian aristocracy and its disposition at that historical moment.

Plato, born in 427, belonged on both his parents' sides to the most distinguished of Athenian families, perhaps not among the very wealthiest – though his wealth was not inconsiderable – but certainly among the most noble in pedigree. There can be little doubt about the generally antidemocratic feeling among his associates, and his close relatives were leaders of the oligarchic coup that established the reign of the Thirty Tyrants. Plato himself, if we are to believe the *Seventh Epistle*, had political ambitions in his youth and had great hopes for the regeneration of Athens by the oligarchic revolution.[17] But he was, to his credit, unable to accept the excesses of the regime established by his friends and relations, refusing to join them as he was expected to do. When the Thirty were overthrown, his political ambitions were briefly renewed, only to subside again with the restoration of the democracy. Plato praised the moderation of the returning democrats, who generally treated their enemies with great restraint, especially in contrast to the bloody excesses of the oligarchs; and this remained his judgment despite the trial and death of Socrates. Yet the restored democracy seemed to him to signal the moral corruption of Athens, which 'was no longer ruled by the manners and institutions of our forefathers', and where 'the whole fabric of law and custom was going from bad to worse at an alarming rate'.[18]

After the death of Socrates, Plato embarked on an extended journey, not only to expand his own education but offering his wisdom to the

17 The authenticity of the *Epistles* is controversial, although the *Seventh Epistle* is more generally accepted as Plato's own work.
18 *Seventh Epistle*, 325d–e.

royal court of Syracuse in Sicily. He visited Syracuse both under Dionysius I and his successor, Dionysius II, with whom the philosopher fell out. In about 385 BC Plato founded the Academy, about a mile outside the city walls, to teach subjects such as mathematics, astronomy, harmonics, and philosophy, both natural and political. His own political ambitions were never again revived and, given his associations, were in any case unlikely ever to succeed. But the political purposes of the Academy are unmistakable. Its students – the sons of wealthy Athenians and foreign families – were educated in Platonic politics and sent forth as consultants to rulers and cities throughout the Mediterranean world.

At home in Athens, disaffected aristocrats were withdrawing from politics, and Plato's philosophical enterprise developed in this climate of disaffection and withdrawal. There would still be aristocratic leaders even in the late third century, notably Lycurgus; but politics was no longer the favoured career it had once been. The historical moment of popular politics and aristocratic estrangement, when well-born and educated men turned their backs on the polis, posed itself for Plato as a philosophical problem: the separation of thought and action. He set himself the task of reuniting them. Wisdom as he conceives it is in its very essence related to practice and especially to politics. We cannot hope to understand how he envisaged his philosophical task if we abstract it from the political problem as he perceived it. His philosophical project was never divorced from Athenian political realities, and his search for absolute and universal truths was never dissociated from the mission to regenerate Athens. Plato cannot be dismissed as simply an ideologue of the aristocratic-oligarchic faction in Athenian politics, nor is his conception of philosophic virtue reducible to the values of aristocratic culture. But his political philosophy leaves little doubt that his hopes of moral and political regeneration required the reconciliation of aristocracy and politics. Nor is this a simple matter of replacing one political form with another. The separation of thought and action has very specific social conditions, and to reunite them will require a social transformation.

The democracy, as we saw, had evolved in tandem with the civic principle; and the estrangement of the aristocracy from politics was the culmination of that historical process. The establishment of the Athenian polis as the dominant principle of association, the civic community with its laws and the new identity of citizenship, had at the same time been a consolidation of popular power, in opposition to aristocratic dominance. Civic identity, the jurisdiction of the polis and the rule of *nomos* in Athens all tended towards a kind of equality, set against aristocratic principles of rule and hierarchy. Plato's task was to reclaim the polis for the aristocracy. This required breaking the bond between politics and democracy and making hierarchy, not equality, the essence of the polis. The polis, in other words, had to replace the hierarchical *oikos*, the lordly household of the Homeric epics, as the natural terrain of aristocracy. So Plato had to devise a conception of the polis in which the essential political relation would no longer be interaction among citizens but, again, the division between rulers and subjects, even rulers and producers. He also needed to elaborate a conception of justice that would reverse the increasingly close association, in the democracy, between the concept of *dikē* and the notion of *isonomia*. In his great classic, the *Republic*, Plato constructed a conception of *dikaiosune* which identified it with inequality and the social division of labour between rulers and producers.

The dialogue begins with an exchange between Socrates and his interlocutors concerning three conventional conceptions of justice: first, the simple morality of the honest businessman whose basic rules of right conduct are that one should always tell the truth, never cheat anyone, and pay one's debts; second, the traditional maxim of helping one's friends and harming one's enemies; and finally, the observation that justice is defined by the interest of the strongest. Plato, in the person of Socrates, quickly dismisses the first, on the grounds that specific actions, such as returning something borrowed, may be good and just in some circumstances but not in others. Polemarchus tries to deal with this by proposing, first, that justice is giving every man his due. But that, of course, raises questions about what is due to whom, and here Plato already introduces the analogy of the arts which will be the core of his whole argument: to judge what is due to someone is akin to the expert judgment made by the practitioner of a specialized art, *technē*, about what good practice is in any particular circumstances; and this requires knowledge about the purpose of the art involved, the ends it is meant to achieve. Just as doctors, builders or shoemakers must have specific knowledge about the ends and means appropriate to their arts, so a man can live a good and just life only if he knows the true purpose of life and how to achieve it. Polemarchus then specifies that justice means doing good to friends and harm to enemies. This, too, is found wanting, since it cannot be just, for instance, to do harm to enemies who are themselves good. Polemarchus is forced to concede that what he means is that we should do good to friends who are good and harm to enemies who are bad. But this simply opens him to the objection that it surely cannot be just to harm others, especially since the only real harm we can do them is to make them worse than they are. How can it be just to make someone less good? So we must still seek out the underlying principle of justice that stands apart from any specific example and allows us to judge any particular action by a universal standard that applies to all cases.

The argument with Thrasymachus and his definition of justice as the interest of the stronger is the most revealing and significant. He begins with a descriptive observation that, in any given situation, the interest of the stronger or ruling elements will be defined as just. This is not, at first, intended as a moral judgment. At this stage, Thrasymachus is expressing the kind of anthropological insight we might expect from a serious sophist, with which even Protagoras could agree. It is a simple proposition about the conventional foundations of morality, with the added observation that the ideas of ruling groups, for better or worse, have tended to be the ruling ideas of their societies. But Plato creates a trap for the sophist, which allows the philosopher not only to mobilize and elaborate the arts analogy but also to transform a reasonable sophistic insight into an objectionable amorality.

Socrates responds to Thrasymachus's original observation with the objection that rulers can be wrong about their interests and leads the sophist to the conclusion that a ruler is only a ruler insofar as he makes no mistakes – a conclusion that leads easily to the proposition that ruling is a specialized art. Thrasymachus shifts his position, moving away from his purely empirical observation and boldly asserting the moral principle that 'might makes right'. As is typical of Plato's dialogues, Socrates's interlocutor has conveniently been pushed to a conclusion that need not follow from his first premise. There is no logical reason why Thrasymachus's anthropological insight is more consistent with the moral judgment that might makes right than with Protagoras's principle that justice is something like the greatest good of the greatest number. But Plato's strategy, as a prelude to his own exploration of justice, is not to grapple with the useful insights of the sophists so much as to undermine even the reasoned arguments of Protagoras through a kind of guilt by association, while also establishing the principle that government is a specialized art. He goes on to suggest that justice is the specific virtue of the soul which allows the soul to perform its special function most effectively. That function is to live well, and Plato here also establishes a principle that will prove crucial to his argument: that among the basic functions of the soul essential to the truly good life, functions that only the soul can perform, are actions such as 'deliberating or taking charge and exercising control'. We begin to understand that justice has something to do with a proper balance among various functions, with reason in control.

It is striking that, in seeking a definition of justice, Plato never engages a conception that expresses the principles of the democracy. He never, for instance, directly confronts an argument that justice has something to do with equality, that *dikaiosune* has something to do with *isonomia*. If anything, apart from the first definition canvassed in the *Republic*, which he lightly dismisses, he conducts a debate with conventional principles that were fundamental to the old aristocratic ethic. Here, the division between friends and enemies, as well as between rulers and subjects, had a special meaning, deriving from a society in which aristocratic power was rooted in a network of friendship groups, the *hetaireiai*, and the values of a ruling class were meant to be a universal standard. Plato challenges these principles not on behalf of democratic values but rather in the conviction that conventional aristocratic principles are far too vulnerable in the democracy. In democratic Athens, the main political arena is not *hetaireia* but polis; and the demos, not the aristocracy, can be regarded as the strongest or the ruling element. What is needed is a new aristocratic ethic, which is less dependent on convention and tradition, far more universalist and absolute, and yet rooted in the polis.

Plato then sets out to replace the conventional wisdom of the oligarchic faction with a *philosophical* defence of inequality. One distinguished classicist has even suggested that Plato's doctrine of Ideas is 'directly descended' from the old aristocratic ethic of hero-models, as in Homer. But now the *paradeigma* or example for imitation, which was so central to the old aristocratic code, is translated into, as Plato himself defines the Ideas, 'patterns established in the realm of Being'.[19] His argument depends on situating justice within the realm of absolute Ideas, the ultimate reality to which only philosophical reason has access, beyond the sphere of everyday life, the world of appearances and 'the multiplicity of things'.

The stated objective of the dialogue is to find a conception of justice that is not merely conventional, nor merely concerned with appearances, rewards and punishments. The task is to discover an absolute and universal idea of justice as something that is good in itself. Socrates suggests that, although he hopes to identify the qualities of the just man, it is easier first to seek out justice in the larger model of the state. Some commentators have taken this to mean that the *Republic* is not essentially a political work and that Plato's fictional state appears in it simply as a means of defining justice in the soul by analogy. But

---

19 Werner Jaeger, *Paideia: The Ideals of Greek Culture* (New York: Oxford University Press, 2nd edn, 1945), Vol. I, p. 34. The definition of Ideas appears in *Theatetus*, 176–e.

as the argument proceeds, it becomes increasingly clear that the philosopher is laying out some essential principles of politics, which are never secondary to, and are always served by, the analogy of the soul.

Socrates proposes to follow a state in imagination as it comes into being and develops from a simple form to a more prosperous society of luxury, so that we can observe the point at which justice enters the picture. The very first essential principle laid down in this imaginary reconstruction is that the state is based on a division of labour. This means that the state is not simply a conventional creation but is based on the natural principle of human interdependence, the inability of any single human being to perform all the functions necessary for survival, and the variety of innate abilities which fit different people for different occupations. As Socrates builds his imaginary state, it begins to emerge that justice will have something to do with this division of labour, the proper balance among the constituent elements.

We should here take note of the fact that there is nothing in the social division of labour as such that makes it intrinsically hierarchical. Yet Plato requires a hierarchical division of labour in which some elements control or rule over others, and establishing this hierarchical principle may be the most important step in his argument. It is at this point that we can appreciate the function of the analogy between individual soul and the state.

We might expect the typical Athenian citizen to dispute the notion that there is a natural division between those who rule and those who must be ruled. He would, at any rate, object to the application of this notion to himself and other Athenians. But he might more readily accept the principle that a healthy soul, the one more conducive to a morally good life, is one in which reason commands the 'lower' appetites. We need not assume that the notion of a two-part soul was conventional wisdom in Athens; but at least such a principle would not violate the fundamental values of the democratic culture, and the citizen would probably have little difficulty in appreciating the distinction between reason and the appetites. Now, analogy can be a persuasive tool of argumentation only if there is some basic agreement about one of its terms, which can then be extended – by analogy – to support a more contentious proposition. To an Athenian audience, the political principle in Plato's argument is undoubtedly the controversial one, and it would be pointless to invoke it in support of some other allegedly analogous proposition. Despite what the philosopher tells us about his primary intention to elucidate the nature of the soul and the just individual, his strategy makes far more sense if we understand that the object of his argument is to defend a deeply controversial political principle, by drawing on a less contentious notion of the soul. In any case, in spite of what Socrates tells us about the order of argumentation, he has already introduced the notion of a balance between the controlling, rational element of the soul and the lower appetites before he embarks on his reconstruction of the state, and he freely draws on the analogy as he proceeds.

It is worth noting, too, that to make the critical move in his argument, establishing the natural division between ruler and ruled, Plato invokes only two parts of the soul, 'better' and 'worse', or reason and the appetites, although he will go on to propose a tripartite soul. The tripartite soul, which appears only sporadically in Plato's work, has its own, more specific political purpose in devising a kind of tripartite state – or rather, a bipartite state with a ruling class exercising two distinct functions. But the more fundamental division between rulers and ruled is supported by a two-part soul. In his other major political work, the *Laws*, he again requires only a division between reason, the 'natural sovereign', and the passions, appetites or lower functions of the soul; and even in the *Republic* the essential division is between the sovereign reason and the baser elements, just as the primary division in the state is between rulers and producers. The tripartite soul, in which a 'spirited' element ideally assists deliberative reason, simply allows him to delineate the two distinct functions of a ruling class, deliberative and military, as against the 'lower' functions of the farming classes and the practitioners of other practical arts. At every stage of his argument, in every aspect of the analogy between the soul and the state, it is difficult to mistake the direction of argumentation: the doctrine of the soul serves the theory of the state.

As Plato spells out the qualities of the good soul, he is also elaborating the qualities appropriate to a ruling class and those characteristics that must consign men to political subjection. What is particularly striking about his delineation of the 'philosophic nature', the qualities of the soul appropriate to rule, is the extent to which the philosophic virtues correspond to more conventional aristocratic traits. It is impossible to detach moral qualities from social status in Plato's doctrine, in much the same way that the English concept of 'nobility' implies both a moral attribute and a social position; and like other aristocratic critics of democracy, the philosopher attaches great importance to style and deportment as reflections of some deeper moral virtue. More particularly, the realization of the philosophic nature depends on the life conditions of a leisured aristocracy, able to appropriate the labour of others and free from the need to engage in productive work.

Plato's argument here is significant for several reasons. It means

that social conditions are more decisive than innate differences in
determining the qualities of soul that divide human beings into rulers
and ruled. To be sure, people are born with varying abilities – which
is, again, why the division of labour is a natural principle. Yet the
differences among them are not enough to account for the vast and
permanent division between rulers and ruled. Even the differences
between 'gold' or 'silver' souls, on the one hand, and 'iron' or 'brass',
on the other, turn out, in the main, to be socially determined. The
unbridgeable gulf between the few who are by nature qualified to rule
and those who must be ruled is grounded in more profound differences
in the conditions of life which divide the privileged classes from the
labourers, craftsmen, merchants and farmers tied to the world of material necessity. Each condition of life has its own specific virtue, the
qualities best fitted to fulfil its proper role. But the majority engaged
in base and menial occupations can never rise above the relative virtues
of their station, and it soon emerges that the highest virtue of these
classes is voluntary submission to their betters. True virtue requires
liberation from the 'multiplicity of things'. The conditions for the
realization of true virtue, however, are not simply the social circumstances of the individual. A polis governed by the lower appetites –
that is, a polis in which 'banausic' classes dominate – will inevitably
corrupt the most admirable soul. The life of the virtuous soul can be
achieved only in a polis that allows the necessary social conditions to
flourish and is governed by rulers who personify the soul's higher
elements. At the very least, it requires a philosopher king who embodies
the necessary virtues and rules the polis absolutely according to his
philosophic wisdom, unfettered by law.

When Plato goes on to trace the stages in the decline of the polis,
he confirms the dependence of virtue on social conditions. The watershed in the decline is the fall of the second-best form, timocracy, a
warrior state like Sparta, which is motivated by the love of honour,
and its replacement by oligarchy, which is driven by the love of money.
Oligarchy is rule not just by the wealthy but specifically by those in
possession of alienable property, not a landed aristocracy but moneyed
men; and the transition from timocracy to oligarchy marks the beginning of rule by the lower parts of the soul, as the 'spirited' element
gives way to baser appetites. Nothing could be clearer than the close
association in Plato's moral doctrine between qualities of soul and
social conditions. Even the prevailing form of property is decisive in
shaping the moral disposition of the polis. A change from aristocratic
and hereditary property to moneyed wealth crosses the critical dividing
line between, on the one hand, a society in which the ruling class –

in timocracy, the fighting class – 'will abstain from any form of business, farming, or handicrafts', and on the other hand, a society in which the leading elements are men who have scraped together a fortune by earning their living.

The fact that the ruling class in the ideal polis of the *Republic* has no property at all, while subordinate classes apparently do, should not mislead us about the aristocratic values that permeate the dialogue. References to Plato's 'communism' – in relation to the communal property, and the community of wives and children associated with it – are particularly misguided. What is important for Plato in his conception of property is that the rulers belong to a group that can live on the labour of others and are free of material necessity, the most fundamental distraction from pure intellection. In the real world, the closest approximation to his ideal – a ruling class that can 'abstain from any form of business, farming, or handicrafts' – is a hereditary landed class, secure in its possession of largely immobile and inalienable property, commanding the labour of others and never reduced to sordid commercial dealings. In the *Laws,* Plato will make explicit this connection between the ideal and the 'second-best' polis.

It is significant, too, that when Plato blames 'bad upbringing' for the corruption of promising individuals, what he has in mind is not the ill-effect of the wrong kind of family life or a poor education but rather, above all, the corrupting influence of the mob. Here, Plato again turns Protagoras against himself. He adopts the sophist's view that the community, and not any individual instructor, is the most effective teacher, best able to transmit its values and promote the character traits it most prizes. But while Protagoras regarded the democratic polis, with its customs and laws, as the surest source of virtue, for Plato it is the breeding ground of vice. The demos is capable only of a relative virtue specific to its lowly station, but its corruption is more absolute. The vice of the banausic multitude is not only its specific class attribute but the source of the corruption infecting other classes too – as it infected, Plato tells us in the *Gorgias*, even its greatest leader, Pericles.

The possession of true virtue and the 'philosophic nature', then, depends both on the individual's social position and on the quality of the polis as a whole, in particular the social character of the people who dominate it. The importance Plato assigns to the social conditions of virtue must inevitably affect how we understand his theory of knowledge and the practice of philosophy. It is clear that for Plato true knowledge, which Socrates has identified with virtue, requires not only epistemological liberation from the material world of appearances but also social liberation from material necessity in everyday life. We already know that freedom from material necessity is a requirement for those who practise the 'Royal Art' of politics or statesmanship; and, as Plato explains the process of acquiring true knowledge, he makes it clear that the essential qualification for the Royal Art is knowledge of the 'Human Good', the true purpose or *telos* of humanity, which is not mere pleasure, power, or material wealth but the fulfilment of the human essence as a rational being. The social condition Plato requires of his ruling class, in other words, is also the minimal condition of true knowledge.

As Plato lays out the programme of the philosophic education, freedom from material necessity begins to appear not simply as a precondition but an integral step in the process of acquiring knowledge of the Good. The object of Plato's education is to lead the student to a knowledge of goodness in itself, the ultimate Idea or Form of the Good as a single, unchanging essence beyond all specific instances of goodness. This, in his view, requires understanding of a greater cosmic order, the expression of a higher Reason. Plato never offers us a definition of the Good, because its apprehension is a kind of revelation, even a mystical experience. But the process that leads the student to the point of revelation is spelled out in great detail, as Plato enumerates the various forms of cognition, together with their proper objects, in ascending order. The essential dividing line is between the world of appearances and the intelligible world, and each of these is subdivided into lower and higher forms: the form of cognition most tied to appearances is imagining, the object of which is images, and above that is belief or opinion, which concerns visible things. We cross the line to the intelligible world in the process of *thinking* about mathematical objects, and from there we rise to intelligence or knowledge of the Forms. This takes us finally to the threshold of the Good.

The process of education is a gradual progression in detaching the soul from 'the multiplicity of things' and mere appearances; and the freedom of body and soul from material necessity is no less a part of that progression than is the hierarchy of cognition. The practical liberation from everyday material necessity is the first and essential moment of the soul's epistemological liberation from the world of appearances.

The *Statesman* and the *Laws*

We shall return to Plato's theory of knowledge as laid out in the *Republic* to consider how, or even whether, our judgment of his whole philosophical system – not only his political philosophy but also his epistemology – should be affected by its material presuppositions and ideological implications. For the moment, a brief consideration of his two other important political works, the *Statesman* and the *Laws*, will help to clarify the political assumptions that permeate his philosophic project.

It can be misleading to look upon the progression from *Republic* to *Statesman* to *Laws* as simply a two-stage descent from the ideal. It is certainly true that the *Laws* is explicitly presented as a 'second-best' polis, and it is also true that the *Statesman* provides a conceptual transition to the later work. But it is important to acknowledge that all three dialogues express the same fundamental principles, which Plato elaborates from different vantage points. The *Republic* undoubtedly displays a greater allegiance to philosophic principles than to aristocratic politics, and it certainly reflects his disillusionment with the attempt to establish an Athenian oligarchy. In the *Laws*, Plato will spell out in great detail a constitution that does not depend so much on rule by philosophic wisdom as on carefully crafted institutions and laws designed to imitate as much as possible the effects of philosophic rule. Although this polis is at best an imitation of the ideal, adapted to the harsh realities of material and social life, there is a sense in which it is even more revolutionary than the *Republic*. If the *Republic* represents a kind of thought experiment, not intended as a model for the ideal polis but rather as statement, in poetic or metaphorical style, of certain fundamental principles – the *Laws*, however utopian it may be, converts those principles into an institutional blueprint. It proposes a complete transformation of political and social relations as they are in the Athens of Plato's day, a radical departure from everything essential in Athenian political practice and its social underpinnings, down to the most basic conditions of property and labour. The polis of the *Laws* makes Plato's political commitments even clearer than the ideal state in the *Republic*. The *Statesman*, while it presents no blueprint for an ideal or even second-best constitution, elaborates political principles introduced in the *Republic* and develops them to lay a foundation for the revolution of the *Laws*.

The *Statesman* is above all an elaboration of the argument from the arts, which already played a major role in the *Republic*; and it redefines the rule of law, which will be given concrete form in the *Laws*. In effect, it creates a bridge between the rule of philosophy and a philosophic rule of law. The first premise, again, is that politics is a specialized art, requiring refined expertise – though here, more than in the *Republic*, Plato stresses the differences between statesmanship and more conventional arts, in order to emphasize the incompatibility between the art of politics and ordinary occupations. The emphasis, as ever, is on expertise and the exclusiveness of specialized arts, and perhaps the most critical point is that the true expert must have free rein in the practice of his art. This principle, which absolves the statesman from obedience to law, will set the stage for redefining the rule of law.

But first, Plato seeks the best analogy for the art of statesmanship. He begins by suggesting that the art of politics is essentially one with the arts of household management. We should hardly need reminding how significant it would have been in Plato's Athens to treat the polis as an *oikos* writ large, with everything this implies about its hierarchical structure; and Plato is especially provocative in identifying the statesman with the household lord, even the slave-master, the *despotes*. Yet this is not enough to characterize the political art, so Plato ventures further afield. Here, he introduces the myth of the cosmic cycle, which we encountered in our discussion of the Promethean story. Human beings in the philosopher's own time are living in the Age of Zeus, the bottom of the cosmic cycle, with all its pains and labours and bereft of divine guidance or assistance, in sharp contrast to the Age of Kronos, when the herd of humanity was governed and physically nurtured by the divine shepherd. This suggests the possibility of an analogy between statesman and shepherd; but, although Plato acknowledges certain affinities, he cannot unequivocally accept this analogy. To be sure, it has the advantage of emphasizing that the art of politics is about rule and not citizenship; but, for reasons that will soon become apparent, he is unwilling to accept that the political art, like the art of tending sheep, entails the physical nurture of its subjects.

The art that most resembles statesmanship, Plato finds, is weaving. The art of weaving selects appropriate materials, rejects others, and joins a multiplicity of different strands into a variegated but unified fabric. The art of politics is similar to weaving because its object is to create a social fabric out of various human types. The statesman supervises the selection and rejection of materials and creates the web of state out of the warp and woof of humanity. He must weave together the strands that truly belong to the web of state, while 'enfolding' in it other elements, not integral parts of the state but necessary for its maintenance. Plato distinguishes between the art of weaving itself and other, ancillary arts: those that are 'subordinate' to weaving but part of the process, such as carding and spinning, and those that are merely 'contributory', in the sense that they do not belong to the process of weaving but simply produce the necessary tools, such as shuttles. Analogously, there are subordinate and contributory arts in the realm of politics. In particular, those who practise the contributory arts can have no share in the royal art of politics – and these politically excluded arts turn out to embrace everything that produces the community's physical requirements: its food, tools, clothing, shelter, conveyances, and other materials used to maintain existence and health, provide amusement, or give protection. Aristotle, who joined the Academy in 367 when Plato's *Statesman* was taking shape, would later make a distinction with similar political effect, between the 'parts' and the 'conditions' of the polis: those that have a share in politics and those who simply create the conditions that make it possible.

Having established the nature and purpose of the royal art, Plato is able to redefine the rule of law accordingly. His first premise is that law, at least as it is commonly understood in democratic Athens, is incompatible with art. *Nomos* and *technē* are antithetical, because the rule of law restricts the free play of the craftsman's art and because non-experts are effectively dictating to experts. Doctors, for instance, cannot be told what to do by those who are ignorant of medical arts. They must be free to respond creatively to each situation as their knowledge and skill best instruct them. The rule of law as understood by the Athenians violates that principle of art and ties the hands of those who govern them. *Nomos* acts as a check on leaders no less than on those who are led; and (as we saw earlier in considering the contrast between *nomos* and *thesmos* as two very different conceptions of law) it is an expression of the people's role – the role of non-experts – in determining their common life.

Yet Plato finds a way of reappropriating the law by redefining its function. The rule of law, in his new definition, should imitate, not thwart, the political art. Its object should be to create and maintain a certain kind of social fabric, not to introduce an element of civil equality into the polis but, on the contrary, to embody inequality, in particular to fix in place the hierarchical relation between those who practise the political art and those who simply 'contribute' by serving the needs of the polis.

Plato goes on to classify the types of constitution, adopting the traditional distinctions among rule by one man, rule by the few and rule by the many, but dividing each into law-abiding and lawless forms. Just as one-man rule can be a lawful monarchy or a lawless tyranny, rule by the few can take the form of aristocracy or oligarchy, which are distinguished not on the grounds that one is rule by the 'best' and the other simply rule by the rich but rather on the basis that one form of rule by the rich abides by the law and the other does not. Here, Plato makes a grudging concession to democracy, suggesting that, among the evil constitutions, the lawless form of democracy is easiest to bear – not because it is more virtuous than others but simply because it is weaker and can do less harm. Yet the most revealing point is his suggestion that among the law-abiding constitutions, democracy is the worst, the most distant from the art of politics and its objectives.

Plato puts these principles into practice in the *Laws*, which delineates in great detail a polis governed by a system of laws designed to imitate the art of politics. As the *Statesman* has led us to expect, the rule of law is here conceived as a way of rigidly structuring social behaviour by means of a legally fixed separation of human types. Its principal objective is to divide the inhabitants of the polis permanently into predetermined social positions or classes, even castes, to prohibit any confusion among them, and especially to separate those who are suited to citizenship from those engaged in occupations that corrupt the soul and disqualify their practitioners from political participation. This will be accomplished by establishing a sharp and legally defined distinction between landowners, who are free of necessary labour, and non-landowning labourers, who will perform all necessary labour. Land will be carefully allotted to prospective citizens and made entirely inalienable. The landed class produced by this means will have access to the labour of others and will hence be qualified for citizenship. Although the citizen class contains people of modest means (in movable property), as well as those of more substantial wealth, Plato has effectively restored the rule of a hereditary agrarian aristocracy, except that now the polis, not the *oikos*, is its principal platform. The remaining landless inhabitants, ranging from slaves and farm labourers to craftsmen and merchants, will have no political rights. Indeed, anyone performing necessary labour will be scarcely distinguishable from slaves in dependence and servility.

It soon becomes clear that Plato has very consciously set out to subvert the Athenian constitution, deliberately replacing its democratic principles with antithetical aristocratic standards. He even signals his intention by ostensibly adopting certain Athenian institutions – like the Solonian division into classes of wealth and Cleisthenes's division of the population into tribes – and adapting them to his antidemocratic purposes. The classes of Solon, for instance, become not a means of conferring a political identity even on the poorest classes but rather a reinforcement of their exclusion. The new classification simply subdivides the ruling class itself into four sections based on the amount of their movable wealth, and the rest of the population are defined by their complete omission.

This legally fixed class structure is designed to make the polis less dependent on the judgment of wise rulers. In separating good from bad, as little as possible will be left to chance, to guard against the danger that virtue will be contaminated by a confusion of noble and banausic. Yet if much of philosophy's work will be done in advance by a rigid system of law, philosophy will still play a major role in the daily life of the polis. Nowhere, in fact, are the political intentions of Plato's philosophy more evident than in his account of the Nocturnal Council, which will oversee the laws. With a striking resemblance to Plato's Academy, engaging in philosophical studies with an emphasis on mathematics, astronomy and theology, the Council is nonetheless an overtly political institution, with a central role in governance, like the unreformed Areopagus in Athens. It will act as a supreme court to interpret the laws, a continuous constitutional convention to revise them when necessary, a school for public officials and a moral censor; and as guardian of the law, its principal function will be to protect the rigid class system which for Plato is the essence of lawfulness. In the *Laws*, it is even harder than in the *Republic* to avoid the political implications of his philosophic system.

Philosophy and Ideology

Let us, then, return to the *Republic* and the question of how we should judge the philosophy of Plato if we accept that knowledge and virtue as he conceives them have a clear and forceful ideological meaning. Considering this question in relation to Plato, at this founding moment in the development of Western philosophy, may also shed light on our whole historical enterprise and the implications of a 'social history' for our appreciation of political theory.

Even if we interpret the *Republic* as above all a discussion of the individual soul, a dialogue on the attainment of knowledge rather than an essentially political work, there is no escaping the social conditions of true knowledge as Plato conceives it. Even if the polis appears only for the purpose of analogy, it remains significant that he defines knowledge in these terms. Plato's philosophical idealism turns out to be remarkably materialist: true knowledge, the knowledge of Ideas or Forms, has very concrete material conditions. Again, the material freedom of the person is an irreducible condition of true knowledge not only in the sense that the long and arduous process of education leading to knowledge of the ultimate Good requires leisure time but, more particularly, because a life of necessary labour damages the soul and makes it unfit for philosophy. Philosophy is inevitably dishonoured when it is illegitimately pursued by those 'whose souls a life of drudgery has warped and maimed no less surely than their sedentary crafts have disfigured their bodies.'[20]

What does all this mean for our appreciation of Plato's philosophical project? If we acknowledge its social and political meaning, even its ideological motivations, are we obliged to disparage his philosophy? Is it still possible, for instance, to derive profound epistemological or moral insights from the *Republic* even while we recognize its anti-democratic purpose? These are the kinds of questions we inevitably confront with every great thinker who is also politically engaged – as all the political theorists of the Western canon were, in one way or another.

The simple answer is that no amount of disagreement with their ideological propensities obliges or permits us to dismiss the theoretical merits of their ideas or to suspend our intellectual judgment. The historicity of an idea or even its partisanship does not preclude significance and fruitfulness beyond its time and place or outside the politics of its originator. The object of a contextual reading, in the sense intended here, is not to discredit or to validate ideas by their ideological origins or purposes but rather to understand them better by identifying the salient issues that confronted the theorist and the terms in which those issues were being contested. This kind of reading has the added advantage of enabling a critical distance from our own unexamined assumptions. Our assessment of ideas cannot end with recognition of their historicity, but that is certainly a useful place to start. To appreciate the philosophers' answers, we need to understand the questions they are addressing, and those questions are historically constituted, however much the theorist may be looking for a universal answer.

The notion of universality itself has a history of changing meanings rooted in specific social conditions and steeped in ideology. Plato's idea of universal truths, for example, is something very different from the universalism of the Enlightenment; and the differences in philosophical substance are grounded not only in different historical conditions but also in divergent social and political motivations. The characteristically Greek identification of universal truth and philosophic reason grew out of a distinctive social and political experience. While Plato was addressing questions already raised by thinkers before him about the existence of universals and whether, or how, it is possible to know them, these questions posed themselves to him not only as philosophical but also as practical, political problems. We need not insist that Plato's

---

20 495d–e.

motivation was solely political in order to acknowledge the ways in which his conception of reason and universal truth grew out of an engagement with the politics of the democracy. He was nothing if not clear about the practical intentions of his philosophy and about the central role of politics in achieving the good life, which was the object of the philosophic quest. So the problem of reason and truth was for him immediately and essentially political.

The nature of truth and human access to it had a particular meaning in the democratic culture, which ascribed to human reason an unprecedented role in determining the fate of humanity and in judging, indeed creating, authority. Plato's philosophical mission was driven not only by his engagement with thinkers like Pythagoras or Parmenides but by a confrontation with the politics of the democracy, its conception of authority and its apparently indiscriminate attention to all kinds of opinion, whatever their source. His solution, while directed against the democratic conception of reason and truth, was still characteristically Greek. He did not deny the power of reason. If anything, reason, as the guide to higher universal truths, became still more powerful. But he redefined its appropriate object, and in so doing placed true rationality for all practical purposes outside the reach of ordinary people. Yet, for all his antidemocratic motivations, who can deny that his struggle with the culture of democracy was exceptionally fruitful, or that debate on the nature of knowledge was immeasurably advanced by his attempt to find a truth beyond the transience and mutability of empirical reality?

We cannot go far wrong if we begin by acknowledging that passionate engagement, while it can often overwhelm the critical faculties, can also be the surest source of human creativity. It is, indeed, difficult to think of any lasting contribution to the culture of humanity, from the arts to science and philosophy, that has not been driven by some kind of passion. In the case of political theory, it seems reasonable to suppose that the relevant engagement is political; perhaps a passion for social justice, however defined, or even something less exalted, like a fear of losing power or a drive to guard the interests of one's class. We shall hardly do justice to the philosophers if we simply point out the political commitments secreted even in their most ostensibly abstract, disinterested and universalistic ideas. But neither will we give them their due if we evade the issue altogether by assuming that any idea that claims to be disinterested or universalistic cannot also serve partisan interests.

At the same time, we should also acknowledge the complexities of the relation between ideas and contexts. Even if we were inclined to

judge Plato's philosophy on primarily political criteria, we would have
to recognize its inextricable connection with Athenian democracy.
Although – or, more precisely, because – his elaboration of Greek
rationalism and his particular brand of universalism were in deliberate
opposition to the prevailing democratic culture, his philosophical
approach was determined as much by the democracy as by his own
aristocratic inclinations.

Aristotle

It has been said – most notably by Samuel Taylor Coleridge – that
'one is born either a Platonist or an Aristotelian'. This observation
may have more to do with temperament than philosophy, but there
are also differences in philosophic style. In some respects, indeed, the
two philosophers do seem to represent polar opposites: Plato's abstract
idealism against Aristotle's materialism, or at least his abiding interest
in the material world; Plato's Socratic 'dialogical' method against
Aristotle's 'technical' approach; Plato's eyes fixed on the heavens and
pure, disembodied Forms, seeking the kind of knowledge captured by
astronomy and mathematics, against Aristotle's grounding in the
physical world of animate and inanimate bodies, the world of physics
and biology; Plato's insistence on the primacy of absolute, eternal and
universal truths, against Aristotle's preoccupation with motion and
change, his sympathy for conventional opinion and his pragmatism;
Plato's insistence that virtue is knowledge, against Aristotle's less
demanding acceptance of ordinary, unphilosophical virtues, gentlemanly behaviour and the golden mean. Seen from a slightly different
angle, the more down-to-earth Aristotle seems the more disinterested
scholar, a cool logician and a man of scientific temperament, as against
Plato, whose literary style suggests an artist's disposition, while his
political passions are present at every level of philosophy, beginning
with epistemology.

However we look at them, these two philosophers present a host
of striking contrasts. We shall consider some of these at least briefly
in what follows, but it may be necessary to acknowledge at the outset
the challenge they may seem to pose to the social history of political
theory advocated in this book. It will be argued here that whatever
else may divide these two philosophical giants, their social values and
political commitments are, for all intents and purposes, the same. They
are both opposed to the Athenian democracy, from the standpoint of
aristocratic values. Might it not be possible, then, to object that, if
the connection between politics and philosophy is as close as we say

it is for these great political thinkers, the same political commitments and social ideologies should produce essentially the same philosophies? Or, at the very least, are we not entitled to question the usefulness of this social-historical approach if the connections between politics or social attitudes and philosophy is so variable, so lacking in what might be called predictive value?

Nothing argued here so far would justify a simplistic reading of what is entailed or promised by a contextual analysis of political theory, even one that attaches great importance to the political and social dispositions of the theorist. But it may be worth emphasizing a few points. While it should be fairly obvious that any ideology can be sustained by a wide variety of theoretical strategies, even this is not the crucial issue. The point is rather that, for the truly great and creative theorists, historical contexts and political commitments present themselves not as ready-made answers but as complex questions. A historical and political reading of the classics can never predict the thinker's theoretical solutions. It can only illuminate them after the fact – and this is surely no small benefit – by shedding light on the questions to which the theorist was seeking an answer, questions that were posed and contested in historically specific forms.

At the same time, it should also be obvious that no two contexts are ever the same, however close in time and space they are, to say nothing of differences in temperament and personal experience, family background, and education. Plato was an Athenian citizen, Aristotle a metic in Athens, a resident alien from Stagira in Macedonia. For that matter, Plato's philosophy already belonged to the historical context in which Aristotle conceived his ideas. There is also a critical difference between the political moment in which Plato was writing, after the golden age of Periclean democracy but at a moment of declining aristocracy, and, by contrast, the period of Macedonian hegemony, which was Aristotle's context and very present in his mind as he thought about the polis. The Macedonian conquest of Greece effectively marked the end of the polis as an independent political form, but Aristotle saw new possibilities for it within the imperial embrace. While Plato's aristocratic authoritarianism was fairly hopeless and nostalgic, at a time when a rampant democracy seemed to have triumphed, only a few years later Aristotle could imagine a political dispensation more congenial than Athenian democracy, watched over and enforced by a Macedonian garrison.

Aristotle was born in 384 BC, the son of a distinguished family. His father was physician to Amyntas III, King of Macedonia, and the philosopher was probably brought up in the royal household, beginning his lifelong friendship with the king's son, two years his junior, who would become Philip II, conqueror of Greece. The political environment in which Aristotle grew up – both the oligarchy of Stagira and the tribal kingdom of Macedonia – was very different from democratic Athens; and Aristotle's first exposure to Athenian democracy came through the antidemocratic medium of Plato's Academy, where he came to study in 367, escaping the bloody dynastic struggle following the death of Amyntas. He remained as a teacher apparently until 348, the year before Plato's death, perhaps compelled to flee by the growing anti-Macedonian sentiment in Athens. Although evidence is scanty, according to tradition he served from 343 or 342 to 340 as tutor to Philip's son, the future Alexander the Great. It is likely that he also undertook other missions for Philip, such as negotiations with various *poleis* before the final conquest of Greece in 338.

The philosopher returned to Athens in 335, after Philip's assassination and Alexander's suppression of various revolts, including one in Athens. This time, Aristotle came as a member of the Macedonian establishment, with the support of local aristocratic-oligarchic factions; and he lived under the protection of his close friend and patron, Antipater, Alexander's autocratic viceroy in Greece. The philosopher would live and teach in Athens for another dozen years; and, although the famous Lyceum was technically founded by his friend and student, Theophrastus, it was essentially Aristotle's intellectual creation, as the Academy was Plato's. On Alexander's death, Aristotle was forced yet again to leave Athens. When, the following year, he died in Chalcis, a wealthy man with an estate far larger than Plato's, the executor of his last will and testament was Antipater. A few years later, the new ruler of Athens, Demetrios of Phaleron – an Athenian of the pro-Macedonian aristocratic-oligarchic faction, student of Theophrastus and possibly of Aristotle, and something like a philosopher king who apparently lectured at the Lyceum himself – introduced political reforms in the spirit of Aristotle and his philosophic predecessors.

Aristotle, then, was probably more directly engaged in the politics of his day than Plato had been. Although he never directly took part in everyday politics, he was certainly closer to power. But his engagement expressed itself in his philosophy in rather different ways. We have seen how Plato attacked the very foundations of the democratic culture; how, with his epistemology and the principle that virtue is knowledge, he set out to uproot the conceptions of knowledge and virtue that justified democracy. His higher reality of absolute and universal Forms, accessible only to philosophic wisdom, was intended to displace the world of change and flux that was the object of conventional opinion, a world in which there was no higher good than the ordinary virtues of the common citizen. Aristotle challenged Plato's conception of truth and the process of knowing, rejecting the notion of Forms as a separate reality, while placing high value on conventional morality and practical wisdom, accessible without some special philosophic vision. In this, he seems closer to Protagoras. To be sure, he concurred with Plato in rejecting epistemological and moral relativism, of the kind proposed by sophists; but he was very critical of Plato's failure to confront the realities of change and motion, regarding the Platonic theory of Forms as particularly unhelpful. Although the natural state of things was rest, according to Aristotle, and everything tended towards a motionless state, the world was constantly in motion. There was, in his view, a critical need for a form of knowledge capable of dealing with the problem of motion and change; and Plato's theory of immutable Forms, which seem to have an independent existence separate from the changing world of particulars and sensible experience, could contribute little to that kind of knowledge.

For Aristotle, every substance is a complex of matter and form, which are conceptually distinguishable but always exist, and must be studied, together. He agrees with Plato that form, which persists through change, is the proper object of knowledge, and that we can distinguish universal forms from concrete particulars; but for Aristotle this means that the primary objective of knowledge is not to abandon the natural world for a higher, immutable reality but rather to discover the *order* of nature, that which is permanent and unchanging in a world of change. Instead of escaping the world of particulars to contemplate the Universal Forms, we acquire knowledge by proceeding from particular to general, investigating generality by studying particulars, the mutable world we inhabit, which is best known to us. This conception of knowledge attaches importance not only to observed facts but also to commonly held opinions, and in that respect could hardly be more different from Plato's counterposition of empirical fact and opinion, on the one hand, to knowledge and truth, on the other. Since that counterposition lies at the very heart of Plato's moral and political philosophy, in particular his challenge to democracy, we might expect to see a commensurate difference in ethics and political theory.

Aristotle, like Plato, denies that standards of right and wrong are mere conventions; but, he argues, we have no way of discovering rigorous absolute rules. There is no single Form of the Good, no single definition that applies to all cases; and even if there were, the kind of knowledge that could apprehend it would be of little use in understanding particular goods as they apply to us in our everyday lives.

That kind of knowledge could not make someone a better craftsman or doctor; nor could it ensure a morally good life. Morality is more a matter of habituation than of philosophic learning. Aristotle certainly distinguishes between intellectual and ethical virtues or virtues of character; and, having also distinguished between two intellectual virtues, theoretical and practical wisdom, he identifies contemplation or *theoria* as the highest virtue. But ethics, like medicine, is a practical, not a theoretical discipline, whose aim is action, not just understanding. In determining the good, we can only proceed from what is given in experience, with all its confusions and uncertainties, and try to reach some kind of reasoned universal judgment. This means that we must consider conventional opinion and adopt as much as possible of popular morality. To be sure, the practical intelligence that guides us to the good life is an intellectual as well as a practical quality; and the best and most complete life, the fulfilment of humanity's true nature, includes not only bodily goods but goods of the soul, the contemplative life, the life of reason. But moral virtue is not knowledge, in the Platonic sense. It is something closer to what Plato might call right opinion.

The most general and universal feature that defines Aristotle's virtues is adherence to the mean in every quality. Every practice, every temperament, has its excess as well as its inadequacy; and the morally good person is the one who consistently displays a disposition to that golden mean – as (there is here a certain circularity in Aristotle's argument) the man of practical intelligence would define it. His moral principles are more like universal rules of thumb than abstract absolutes. Yet he tells us enough about the qualities of the virtuous man to make it clear how closely tied the virtues are to aristocracy. The four most important ethical virtues – generosity; magnificence; the nameless mean between ambition and its absence; and, 'the crown of the virtues', great-souledness or high-mindedness (*megalopsychia*) – are qualities available only to the wellborn and wealthy. The great-souled man in particular is by definition an aristocrat, whose qualities include a (justified) feeling of superiority, pride, self-confidence and even haughtiness. He can concern himself with 'great and lofty matters' because he (like Plato's philosophic nature) is free of the petty and vulgar preoccupations that come with having to work for a living. 'A high-minded person', the philosopher writes in a passage that could have come from a handbook of aristocratic manners,

> is justified in looking down upon others for he has the right opinion of them, but the common run of people do so without rhyme or reason. . . . He will show his stature with men of eminence and

fortune, but will be unassuming toward those of moderate means. For to be superior to the former is difficult and dignified, but superiority over the latter is easy. Furthermore, there is nothing ignoble in asserting one's dignity among the great, but to do so among the lower classes is just as crude as to assert one's strength against an invalid. He will not go in for pursuits that the common people value. . . . He cannot adjust his life to another, except a friend, for to do so is slavish. That is why . . . all flatterers are servile and people from the lower classes are flatterers. . . . He is a person who will rather possess beautiful and priceless objects than objects which are profitable and useful, for they mark him more as self-sufficient.[21]

The philosopher then goes on to list the elements of style – the slow gait, low voice and deliberate manner of speaking, the absence of hurry and excitement that mark the great-souled man. Readers may remember that Aristotle (if he was indeed the author), in *The Constitution of Athens*, singles out the lack of just such gentlemanly style as the principal defect of the democratic leader, Cleon. Vulgarity, it seems, is a serious breach of morality.

Aristotle's *Politics*

The moral conventions that Aristotle respects clearly have more to do with aristocratic codes than with popular morality. And yet, the fact remains that, far more than Plato, he is prepared to give consideration to conventional opinion, not only in the aristocracy but even among the 'middling' sort. This is reflected in his politics not in the sense that his attitude to democracy and his preference for aristocratic oligarchy are any less pronounced than Plato's, but rather in the sense that he raises questions which Plato never bothers to confront – at least in part, perhaps, because the younger philosopher has more hope of seeing his principles put into practice. Just as in his approach to the sciences and metaphysics Aristotle grapples with the material world of change and motion, instead of turning his gaze immediately to a world beyond mundane reality, in his political theory he looks not only for the ideal state but for the sources of motion and unrest in the polis as it is, with a view to correcting them.

Aristotle enumerates several different forms of polis, based on the

---

21 *Nichomachean Ethics*, transl. Martin Ostwald, 1124b5–1125a16.

numbers who rule – monarchy, aristocracy, polity, and their perversions, tyranny, oligarchy and democracy. This classification is accompanied by another, which plays a smaller part in his own political theory but which would, as we shall see in subsequent chapters, figure more prominently in medieval philosophy: the distinction among different forms of authority – despotic, economic, regal and political. But in his attempts to identify the principal causes of civil strife, he is mainly concerned with the two principal types of the Greek state, democracy and oligarchy, not only to judge them against some abstract ideal but to investigate what kinds of safeguards are needed to preserve each actually existing form by reducing the strains that engender conflict and civic disorder, or *stasis*.

To understand the vantage point from which Aristotle constructs his theory of politics, we can consider it in light of what has been said here, earlier in this chapter and in Chapter One, about the distinctive development of the polis, especially in Athens, and the very particular problems it posed for the maintenance of social order in general and the position of propertied classes in particular. Here is a particularly striking illustration of how historically specific questions, posed by specific social conditions, have set the agenda for philosophy and shaped the template on which a system of ideas has been constructed.

Two essential and related features of the polis stand out: the absence of a clear demarcation between rulers and producers, in a civic community combining landlords and peasants, together with other producing classes; and the lack of a powerful state apparatus to act on behalf of propertied classes in maintaining order and their dominance over producers. In other precapitalist societies, appropriators have been directly organized in the state, as in the ancient bureaucratic kingdoms, or have been able to rely on state power to maintain their positions of dominance and to suppress unrest among subordinate producers. There have been some cases, notably in the feudal West, in which dominant classes have, for a time, managed without a strong central state; but even a strongly militarized dominant class could not stave off the threat of disorder forever. Feudal lords were under great pressure to create a unified power to defend them, to counter the centrifugal forces generated by their intraclass conflicts; and the 'parcellized sovereignty' of feudalism gave way to a process of state centralization. While the modern European state was certainly marked by tensions between monarchs and propertied classes, it was the best available protection of property and class domination and was accepted as such, with varying degrees of reluctance, by Europe's ruling classes.

In ancient Greece, as we have seen, a loosely organized propertied class never had such a state at its disposal. The polis presents a rare, even unique, case in precapitalist history in which a propertied class for various historic reasons had neither the military nor the political predominance required to sustain its property and powers of appropriation. Instead, post-Homeric landlords were compelled to rely on various political accommodations to maintain social order and protect their property. The reforms of Solon and Cleisthenes illustrate how the distinctive class relations of ancient Attica were managed in the absence of a clear class dominance, in a civic order where appropriators and producers confronted one another directly as individuals and as classes, as landlords and peasants, not primarily as rulers and subjects. Without assuming that these reformers were driven by democratic sympathies, we can recognize how the configuration of social power in the ancient polis obliged them to reach accommodations with the demos if civic order was to be maintained and, indeed, if the rich and well born were to protect their own positions.

Aristotle's political theory can be situated in this long political tradition. Just as early modern European political theory would be shaped by the three-way relationship among landlords, peasants and monarchical states, so Aristotle's theory responded to the specific questions thrown up by the polis and its own very particular disposition of social power. He made it very clear that his preference, like Plato's, would have been for a clear division between rulers and producers. But in the actually existing social order, with its distinctive class configuration, he felt obliged, like Athens's legendary reformers, to consider what kind of civic accommodation could save the polis from the social conflicts that threatened to destroy it. We can better understand him if we keep in mind that his conception of political order, as it is possible in the real world, is always informed by his conviction that ruling and production are best kept apart. In the states he clearly favours, such as Egypt or, in Greece, Crete, something like this division exists, for instance in the separation of military and farming classes; and in his outline of the ideal polis (to which we shall return), he proposes just such a division.[22] But in dealing with realities in which the ideal is impossible, he compromises this principle, while always keeping it in view.

Aristotle, then, argues that the general cause of *stasis* in both the two principal forms of polis, especially in recent times, is inequality,

---

22 *Politics*, 1328a–b.

specifically the conflict between the rich and well born on one side and the common people on the other. These social conflicts are expressed politically in different conceptions of justice, a democratic conception which demands equality and an oligarchic one which insists on inequality, or, to put it another way, two opposing conceptions of equality: 'numerical' and 'proportionate', or arithmetic and geometric. It is true, the philosopher argues, that there should be political equality among men who are equal, and also that unequal men should have unequal political rights. But both democratic and oligarchic conceptions are incomplete, because they ignore the proper criteria of equality and inequality, the qualities that properly dictate what is, in true justice, due to each man. The democrat assumes, in effect, that all free-born men are equal, while the oligarch treats wealth as the measure of inequality. But true justice requires that political rights and offices should vary according to the contribution men make to the fulfilment of the state's essential purpose. That purpose is not mere life, material prosperity or even safety and security. Although the state does serve all these ends, its essential purpose is the truly good life; so honours and offices should, in true justice, be distributed according to a principle of civic excellence apart from wealth or free birth. Nevertheless, if both oligarchic and democratic notions are imperfect, the oligarchic commitment to proportionate equality is the best of the incomplete conceptions of justice, the one that more closely approximates the perfect form, while the democratic idea of justice as numerical equality is certainly the worst.

Yet, since the rich and the poor will always exist, there will always be conflicting conceptions of justice in both democracy and oligarchy; and means must be found to contain the conflicts generated by this inescapable reality. In oligarchies there are also the problems posed by conflicts within the ruling oligarchic class itself. At the same time, the rich and well born are, as we know, uniquely equipped to pursue the good life in ways denied to those whose bodies and minds are bound to the necessities of work. This means that preserving, or even advancing, the well born and wealthy minority, with its natural superiority and its critical role in any kind of state, is for Aristotle an essential objective in both cases. The measures intended to eliminate *stasis* must never go beyond the minimum necessary to avoid instability. His general prescription is a judicious combination of oligarchic and democratic principles, in various forms depending on the circumstances; but while the avoidance of *stasis* may require concessions to democracy, the presumption is clearly in favour of oligarchy, because it is among the oligarchic aristocrats that at least a handful of virtuous men will be found.

The 'best practicable' polis, the 'polity' (an Anglicization of *politeia*, which Aristotle is using here in a narrower sense than the general term often translated as 'constitution'), would be just such a combination, in which, despite some democratic elements, the effective primacy of oligarchic principles is clearly visible. Property would be a qualification for active citizenship, even for membership in the Assembly; and, while independent farmers of moderate means would be included and might belong, as hoplites, to the fighting element that is the backbone of the polity, ordinary shopkeepers, artisans and wage-labourers would not qualify. When Aristotle describes the best forms of democracy and oligarchy, they turn out to be very like the polity; and even in democracy, the role of the solid citizen of moderate means, the middling independent farmer, would be limited, because such men, as Aristotle points out, 'not having any great amount of property, are busily occupied; and . . . have thus no time for attending the assembly'[23] – which is all to the good, as government will, for all practical purposes, be concentrated in the hands of the rich and well born.

The philosopher's political values are most clearly visible in the incomplete outline of the ideal polis in what are conventionally numbered Books VII and VIII of the *Politics*. There are significant similarities between this ideal polis and the polity, and indeed the best forms of oligarchy or democracy. But the fundamental principles are more explicitly stated. In particular, the proposal is based on one fundamental premise:

> In the state, as in other natural compounds, [there is a distinction to be drawn between 'conditions' and 'parts']: the conditions which are necessary for the existence of the whole are not organic parts of the whole system which they serve. The conclusion which clearly follows is that we cannot regard the elements which are necessary for the existence of the state, or of any other association forming a single whole, as being 'parts' of the state or of any such association.[24]

We encountered a similar principle in Plato's *Statesman*, in his distinction between the art of statesmanship and other, ancillary – 'subordinate' and 'contributory' – arts, which excluded from citizenship all those who worked to serve the daily needs of the polis. Aristotle's

---

23 *Pol.*, 1218b.
24 1328a.

ideal polis, too, relegates such people to the sphere of necessary 'conditions' and not integral 'parts' of the polis. 'The state', he declares, 'is an association of equals, and only of equals' – though now he makes it plain that the relevant criterion of equality is after all a social one, even in the ideal state: we must, he seems to suggest, always assume that those who do the necessary work cannot make a contribution to the essential, higher purpose of the polis. The presumption must always be in favour of those whose material conditions and social position suit them for the good life, whether or not they actually achieve or contribute to it; and they are the integral parts of the polis:

> Upon these principles it clearly follows that a state with an ideal constitution – a state which has for its members men who are absolutely just, and not men who are just in relation to some particular standard – cannot have its citizens living the life of mechanics or shopkeepers, which is ignoble and inimical to goodness. Nor can it have them engaged in farming: leisure is a necessity, both for growth in goodness and for the pursuit of political activities.[25]

There are, of course, necessary functions not subject to this political exclusion: the functions of governance themselves, military and deliberative. These functions are in some respects separate, if only because young men do the fighting and deliberation is best left to older, more experienced citizens. But together they constitute the practice of rule, and they must be performed by men of property, never by those engaged in other necessary arts. Nor should farmers, craftsmen and day-labourers be allowed to serve as priests. The state should be divided into classes, and, in particular, there should be a division between farming and fighting classes. Indeed, all cultivation should be done by slaves or serfs, preferably non-Greeks.

Although Aristotle criticizes Plato's political theory in various ways, the similarities between his own ideal state and Plato's 'second best' polis should already be clear. Nor is this likeness accidental. The affinities between them are indicated even in specific proposals, such as Aristotle's suggestion that every citizen should have two plots of land, one near the central city and one on the frontier, which, like other measures, he borrows directly from Plato's *Laws*. That this polis is for Aristotle a perhaps unrealizable ideal and for Plato only 'second best' tells us very little about any differences between them in their

---

25 1328b–1329a.

opposition to democracy or their commitment to aristocratic principles. It tells us more about the differences in the tasks each man set himself and the very specific historical moment in which he thought about the polis. Even Aristotle's criticisms of his predecessor are often motivated by the values they share, on the grounds that some of Plato's proposals, such as his views on property or the community of wives and children in the *Republic*, would endanger, not advance, the goals both philosophers would like to achieve. Such proposals are not only impracticable but tend to dilute the differentiation of men and the self-sufficiency which both agree is essential to the polis.

Politics and Nature

We must also consider how Aristotle's antidemocratic sentiments, while moderated for the real world, penetrated his most fundamental ideas and even his most analytic or descriptive 'science'. At the beginning of the *Politics*, he lays out his basic definitions and applies his 'analytic-genetic' method to politics as he does elsewhere to other natural phenomena. His political preferences are already visible here; and when we move from the *Politics* to the non-political works in which his philosophical and scientific methods are developed, it is hard to escape the political assumptions that imbue them.

Aristotle begins the *Politics* by defining the basic forms of human association, of which the polis is the highest. Each one has its own specific purpose or *telos*, corresponding to various aspects of human nature. The most basic form is the *oikos*, the household, which deals with biological necessity, the daily recurrent needs of life. Then comes the village, an association of households, which contributes to the satisfaction of material necessities but also deals with something more than daily recurrent needs and is, in a sense, a bridge to the highest form, the polis. The polis, though it also incorporates and adds to the functions of the other two, has as its distinctive purpose the realization of humanity's essential nature. It is natural in the sense that it develops from other natural associations; but, more particularly, it is natural in the sense that it is the perfect completion of human development. 'Man is by nature a polis-animal', a creature intended to live in a polis, because it is only in the polis that he can fulfil his own *telos* as a rational and moral being.

The nature of the polis is defined in relation, as well as in contrast, to the *oikos*. The household is characterized by three principal sets of relationships: master and slave, husband and wife, parents and children. It is in its very essence a hierarchical and patriarchal institution marked by fundamental inequalities. At the very outset, the philosopher lays out his theory of natural inequality, on the premise that there is a principle of rule and subordination operating throughout all nature, and that the soul rules the body. In this respect, he is in agreement with the fundamental dualism in Plato's theory of knowledge and the cosmos. Aristotle goes on to say that, while slaves, women and children do possess the different parts of the soul, they do so in different ways. Women possess the faculty of deliberation, but in an incomplete form; and in children it is immature. They are therefore naturally subordinate to the man of the house. But there are some men whose powers are basically those of the body, while their understanding is capable of no more than following the orders of someone else's reason. It follows that some men are naturally suited to rule and others to be ruled, some are by nature free and others are natural slaves. Since the master is the rational being, the subordinate condition of the slave is both just and beneficial to all concerned.

Aristotle goes beyond most Greeks, and indeed Romans, in justifying slavery on the grounds of natural inequality. While the ancients were prepared to justify slavery on other, often simply pragmatic, grounds, the idea of natural slavery, based on innate differences among individuals or races, seems never to have been widely accepted. The distinctiveness of the philosopher's justification is certainly significant, but it is also important to note that the natural division between rulers and ruled operates for him also in the absence of such innate inequalities. The principle of hierarchy remains natural, even if it corresponds to no naturally inborn inequalities among human beings. Indeed, his political theory requires a principle of natural hierarchy between rulers and ruled that applies not only to the relation between masters and slaves – or even between men and women, adults and children – but also to aristocracy and common people, the leisured few and the labouring many. To widen the scope of this hierarchical principle Aristotle, like Plato, relies not only on fundamental innate differences among men to justify rigid divisions between those who are suited to rule and those who should be ruled. Even without substantial innate inequalities, those whose lives of labour bind them to necessity – and such men must always exist – cannot possess the qualities of soul required to rule.

It is true that Aristotle explicitly distinguishes between the slave and the free artisan, on the grounds that their degrees of servitude are different, the artisan less bound to a master; nor is the artisan naturally what he is in the way that the slave is by nature a slave. Yet the conclusion the philosopher draws from this is simply that the master has an obligation to produce in the slave the limited moral goodness of which he is capable, while there is no such obligation to the free man. The differences between free artisan and slave turn out to be less important in establishing Aristotle's political principles than are the similarities in their respective conditions, in particular their function in supplying the basic necessities of life. The division between 'banausic' types and those whose life conditions fit them to rule is, in its way, no less grounded in nature than that between natural masters and natural slaves.

Those who labour for a livelihood, whether in farming, commerce or the crafts, lack the leisure and freedom of spirit to fulfil the essential nature of humanity. Their bondage to necessity places them on the wrong side of the divide between those who contribute to the fulfilment of the state's essential purpose, its natural *telos*, and those who merely serve its basic needs – even if Aristotle acknowledges that, in practice, political concessions must sometimes be made to 'banausic' men of free birth. The polis, in contrast to the *oikos*, is an association of equals and only of equals; yet the principle of hierarchy established in the *oikos* is critical to the definition of relations in the polis too. The criterion of equality and inequality that Aristotle regards as appropriate in the distribution of political rights derives from the distinction between the principles of necessity and freedom established in the household.

There is also another way in which the *oikos* sets the terms of political right. It is in his discussion of the *oikos* that Aristotle lays out his views on property and the art of acquiring it, and these are essential in defining the character of the proper ruling class. The art of household management (*oikonomia*) strictly speaking is concerned with the use, not the acquisition, of things necessary for life and comfort; but the art of household management must involve itself with acquisition, or, more precisely, with supervising the process of acquisition. We must, then, distinguish between 'natural' forms of acquisition, having to do with obtaining and securing things required by the household, and the unnatural mode of acquisition whose object is the making of money, retail trade for profit. There are certainly legitimate forms of exchange in which households acquire from others things they do not produce for themselves, and some gain may even be involved. But because monetary gain is not the object, these are in a sense extensions of *oikonomia*, or, in any case, they represent a more natural form of *chrematistic*, the art of acquisition. Unnatural *chrematistic*, exchange for the primary purpose of monetary gain, is concerned not with well-being or 'true wealth' but the acquisition of money, and this kind of exchange has become increasingly prevalent.

Aristotle here makes a distinction that was to become theoretically fruitful many centuries later and serves as a fine illustration of how an idea shaped by its specific historical context and even by particular social values can reach far beyond its time, place and ideology. 'All articles of property', he argues, 'have two possible uses . . . The one use is proper and peculiar to the article concerned; the other is not.'[26] A shoe, for example, can be worn or it can be used as an object of exchange for profit. More particularly, there is a distinction between production for use and production for profitable exchange. A shoe produced for one's own use, or even simply to exchange it for necessary money or food, is one thing, while a shoe produced for making profit is something else; and these forms of production are quite different in their consequences. One is associated with acquisition which is limited in its objectives, while the other is in principle unlimited. Karl Marx would develop the distinction to quite different ends, but for Aristotle it plays an essential role in establishing the aristocratic principles that inform his conception of the polis.

As the argument proceeds, it becomes increasingly clear that the philosopher's political preferences are embodied even in his most basic and ostensibly neutral definitions. Even as he develops his definitions of the various associations and applies his analytic-genetic method to them, we form a picture of the 'equals' who properly constitute the polis. They are, to begin with, heads of patriarchal households, engaged in supervision but not in labour, while slaves do the necessary work. Since the truly natural form of acquisition is from land and animals, the political class is properly a class of landowners; and, if the *telos* of the polis is truly to be realized, their property is substantial enough to free them from the need to work. Nor should their property be acquired by sordid commercial means. The hereditary property of the well born is certainly the cleanest kind of property. Those practising 'unnatural' *chrematistic*, retail trade or any other form of money-making such as usury, as well as those engaged in necessary labour, do not properly belong in the political realm, however important they may be to its maintenance. The fact that Aristotle is prepared to compromise on these principles in varying degrees in various circumstances does not make them any less significant in identifying his social values and political preferences, which play their part even in his most pragmatic proposals.

It is even difficult to detach his non-political theory from his politics.

---

26 1257a.

The argument of the *Politics*, as we have seen, deliberately proceeds from certain basic principles derived from his general theory of nature. Aristotle's objective in studying nature is to explain the anomaly of constant motion in a natural world where everything tends toward rest. He seeks to discover the principles of order that remain constant throughout the processes of change. Two themes are essential to his explanation: the first is the notion of purpose or the *telos* towards which every process tends, and the second is the intrinsic hierarchy of the natural order.

When we speak of the *telos* or 'final cause' of objects created by humans, we mean the conscious, deliberate purpose of the craftsman who creates them; but we can still speak of such 'final causes' even where, as in the natural world, there is no deliberate purpose, no divine mind controlling natural change from without (here Aristotle tends yet again to differ from Plato, who sometimes seems to be suggesting a divine intelligence). In nature, the *telos* is immanent in the object itself, the final state 'for the sake of which' the natural processes of growth and development take place – as the oak is the *telos* of the acorn; and every immature object or being, including the human child, is *potentially* what it will (or ought to) be when it matures. Moreover, these processes, while not consciously willed, are not random but orderly and regular. Different outcomes are possible, if things go wrong, but there is only one true *telos* for every thing and every being in nature. How Aristotle puts this principle to use in his political theory is clear enough, as he develops his conception of the human *telos* and the political conditions necessary for its realization. Even clearer is the political application of his second principle: that there is, everywhere in nature, a ruling element and a ruled. Aristotle insists that the natural order is universally hierarchical and that the condition of rest towards which all nature tends forms a Great Chain of Being, in which every natural being is situated, from the highest to the lowest. The polis must in its way reflect that natural hierarchy.

It may be difficult to determine what comes first, the natural 'science' or the politics, or, more precisely, which has the overriding force. No doubt this doctor's son was exposed very early to his lifelong scientific interests, particularly in biology, and no doubt these continued to shape his thinking in every domain. But it is also possible that Aristotle's conception of nature was affected by his predisposition to social and political hierarchies. The issue here, however, is not whether we can unravel the complex order of causality in Aristotle's thinking, or, indeed, in that of any other complicated human being. If, in his philosophy, aristocratic principles govern both the natural and political order, it is enough for us to recognize that the questions he was seeking to answer in both his scientific and political speculations were put to him by his social no less than his natural context.

FROM POLIS TO EMPIRE

From Aristotle to Alexander

Plutarch, in one of his accounts of Alexander the Great and his achievements, writes that Aristotle advised his pupil to distinguish between Greeks and barbarians and to deal with the former as a leader or *hegemon*, while behaving towards the latter as a master, a *despotes*. Alexander, says Plutarch, did just the opposite. Refusing to divide men between Greek friends and barbarian foes, he chose rather to distinguish simply between good men and bad, whatever their origin. Alexander, it has been said, was in effect inventing the notion of a *cosmopolis*, which received its theoretical expression in Stoic philosophy, replacing the polis with a universal human community and stressing the equality and fraternity of humankind as against the particularisms of the polis.

Whether or not the story of Aristotle's advice to Alexander is authentic, it does correspond to a distinction between different kinds of rule that the philosopher draws in the *Politics*:

> There is rule of the sort which is exercised by a master [over slaves] . . . But [besides rule of the sort exercised by their ruler over persons in a servile position] there is also rule of the sort which is exercised over persons who are similar in birth to the ruler, and are similarly free. Rule of this sort is what we call political rule; and this is the sort of rule which [unlike rule of the first sort] the ruler must begin to learn by being ruled and by obeying – just as one learns to be a commander of cavalry by serving under another commander . . . [1]

Aristotle later elaborates on this distinction by contrasting two modes of government: 'One way is to govern in the interest of the governors: the other, to govern in the interest of the governed. The former way is what we call "despotic" [i.e. a government over slaves]; the latter is

---

1 *Pol.*, 1277b.

what we call "the government of freemen."[2] The rule of a master over slaves, 'though there is really a common interest which unites the natural master and the natural slave, is primarily exercised with a view to the master's interest, and only incidentally with a view to that of the slave, who must be preserved in existence if the rule itself is to remain.'[3] Here, he introduces another category, household management (*oikonomia*), rule over wife, children and the household in general, which 'is either exercised in the interest of the ruled or for the attainment of some advantage common to both ruler and ruled.'[4]

The philosopher's distinctions did not preclude a despotic relation between rulers and ruled in a polis; or a polis governed by a community of citizens rather than a single ruler, in which the relation between citizens and non-citizens might be comparable to that between a despotic ruler and his subjects. Aristotle wanted to preserve the civic ideal of the polis, its principles of freedom and equality, while giving new life to old principles of rule, grounded in a natural division between ruler and ruled. The political relation among citizens was a relationship among equals, but there remained a fundamental inequality between the civic community and those outside it. The notion of rule applied to the life of citizens only in the sense that citizenship involved an alternation between governing and being governed, and, ideally, a capacity in every citizen for both. But a far more rigid and permanent division was preserved for relations between the 'parts' and the 'conditions' of the polis, between true citizens and all those subordinate human beings whose purpose was to serve their rulers' interests, just as the purpose of slaves is to serve the *despotes*.

If Alexander really did refuse his teacher's advice, he surely cannot have done so because he rejected the principles of rule, a deep and abiding division between ruler and ruled or the duty of subjects to serve their imperial master. Readers hardly need reminding that he was a ruthless conqueror, an absolute ruler who built a vast empire on the foundations laid by his father, Philip, and declared his own divinity. His imperial ambitions and policies hardly bespeak a doctrine of human equality and brotherhood. If the accounts of Alexander's ostensibly humanitarian views are correct, it would be absurd to take them at face value without considering their ideological or rhetorical function in his imperial project. Perhaps he had in mind something like what Aristotle himself hints at in the *Politics*:[5] that if only the Greeks could achieve a single *politeia*, they would rule the world.

---

2 *Pol.*, 1333a.
3 1278b.
4 1278b.
5 1327.

To be as explicit as Aristotle was about the nature of despotic rule and its purpose of serving the interests of the ruler would not, to be sure, have been the most effective way of justifying it to its victims. But stressing the equality and brotherhood of all human beings is not, in general, the most obvious way to justify the subjection of some of them to others, whether in the form of monarchy or imperial hegemony. If Alexander did adopt this paradoxical strategy, he did so because in the Greek world it had a special propaganda value. It would have evoked the deeply rooted principles of Greek political life, their professions of freedom and equality. It is true that Alexander, and even more his successors in their struggles for power, invoked old principles of *eleutheria*, *autonomia* and even democracy in seeking the support of prospective subjects by promising them the right to live under their own laws and ancestral gods, free of tribute and imperial garrisons. But if this represented an appeal to the older particularistic values of the autonomous polis, Alexander's (putative) idea of the cosmopolis could have been intended to transfer those old political principles and loyalties from the polis to the all-embracing imperial state, while depriving citizenship of its political arena and replacing active citizenship with passive membership in a cosmic community. If Alexander really did think in cosmopolitan terms, his usage would have been largely ideological in its purpose, to describe and to justify empire and even its attempted, if not entirely successful, suppression of politics.

Whatever its ideological purpose, however, the cosmopolitan idea did express a historical reality. Not only was polis replaced by empire – if not, 'world order', certainly a unit much wider in geographic scope – but the empire established by Alexander was also composed of very diverse populations which were united under Macedonian rule. While Greek culture was already widespread in the Mediterranean world before the conquests of Alexander, he consciously utilized the strategy of Hellenizing subject peoples as an instrument of hegemony. The cosmopolitan principle found expression sometimes in the coercive suppression of difference but also in the encouragement of mixing and intermarriage among the various ethnicities, in the emergence of religious cults without frontiers instead of particularistic tribal and civic cults, and above all in the unifying dominance of Greek language and culture. Increasing commercial relations among the imperial cities were also a major factor in promoting the cosmopolitan idea. Transport and communication were enhanced by new roads, a more widely recognized currency was established, and Greek became the main commercial language from Massalia (modern Marseilles) to the borders of India.

In general, however, Hellenistic cosmopolitanism meant the Hellenization of local elites. Macedonian and Greek populations, together with Greek-speaking local elites, tended to remain apart from the subjects whose labour supported them; and lower classes, if they spoke Greek at all (or, at least, the simplified demotic form that would become the language of the New Testament), would have had little access to the glories of Greek culture. A similar mechanism would operate in the Roman Empire, which already by 30 BC included half of what had been the 'Hellenistic' world. Roman imperial rule too would rely on the cultural transformation and allegiance of Romanized local aristocracies. And just as Alexander had defined his imperial rule as cosmopolitan, the idea of the cosmopolis would be translated into the 'universal' Roman Empire and, above all, into Christianity, the 'universal (literally *catholic*) Church'.

This mode of imperial rule through the medium of local aristocracies allowed Alexander, like the Romans after him, to govern a far-flung empire without a massive imperial state. In this respect, both Hellenistic and Roman empires contrasted sharply with other great imperial civilizations like the Chinese, whose imperial states were more directly in command of their subjects, by means of much larger imperial bureaucracies. This also meant that the 'cosmopolitan' empire did in a sense preserve, or revive, at least the form of the Greek polis. Reliable cities could be permitted a degree of local self-government; and Alexander founded cities (often called Alexandria, like the most famous centre in Egypt) in his various domains, which were allowed a certain autonomy and laws of their own, although they were clearly subject to his imperial rule.

After his death, as his empire fragmented into the Macedonian or Antigonid, Seleucid and Egyptian kingdoms, the idea of a king governing through the medium of local municipal entities played a particularly important role in the power struggle over the successor kingdoms.[6] At least, the old liberties of the polis, their *eleutheria* and *autonomia*, served a useful propaganda purpose – though there were cases in which, with the help of one or another imperial rival, oligarchies established, for instance, by Antipater, actually were overthrown in favour of 'democracy'. Reality may not have measured up to rhetoric; but the old Greek culture of the polis, and even of democracy, was so deeply ingrained that no imperial ideology was likely to succeed without

---

6 See Eric S. Gruen, *The Hellenistic World and the Coming of Rome* (Berkeley and Los Angeles: University of California Press, 1984), Vol. 1, esp. Ch. 4.

invoking it. Thereafter, this strategy would survive, even if only in rhetorical form, as a means of maintaining friendly relations among monarchs and cities, as an excuse for war, or as a form of diplomatic language to describe the relations of domination by stronger over weaker powers.[7]

For all its 'cosmopolitanism', however, the 'Hellenistic' period, generally dated from Alexander's life to the late second century BC, was a period of political and social crisis. Alexander's conquests and the power struggles that followed his death aggravated existing social and political instabilities in the Greek world. The worsening conditions of the poor and the growing numbers of the landless led to demands for redistribution of land and the abolition of debts, giving rise to social conflicts, even a social revolution, which has been described as 'one of the great historic processes of Hellenistic Greece'.[8] Inevitably expressed in political upheavals, in conflicts between democrats and oligarchs, this social unrest intensified as the successor kingdoms vied for influence in Alexander's domains by mobilizing those ever-present social and political antagonisms and seeking to install or promote friendly governments. Sparta, paradoxically, which had remained a vigorous and independent polis, was also the site of a particularly notable revolution in the third century BC under kings Agis IV and Cleomenes III, instituting land reforms, cancellation of debts and an extension of citizenship based on fairly extreme conceptions of equality. The effect was to alarm the propertied classes throughout the Greek cities. Fearing social unrest and reform at home more than they did Macedonian dominance, they allied themselves with the Macedonians; and Sparta was finally defeated. The pervasive unrest, and the fear it inspired in propertied classes, form the background against which Hellenistic thinkers embarked on their philosophical projects.

Hellenistic Philosophy: Epicureans and Stoics

Hellenistic philosophy remained deeply indebted to its Hellenic past, but its ground had shifted in fundamental ways. Not only was Athens displaced as the cultural centre by Alexandria and Pergamum, with their great libraries, but philosophy was obliged to adapt itself to a

---

7 *Ibid.*, p. 156.

8 A. Fuks, 'Social Revolution in Greece in the Hellenistic Age', *La Parola del Passato* 111 (1966), p. 441, quoted in Andrew Erskine, *The Hellenistic Stoa: Political Thought and Action* (Ithaca: Cornell University Press, 1990), p. 36.

new imperial reality. If it is possible to speak of political theory in this period, its principal subject was no longer the polis of Plato and Aristotle.

The Hellenistic *cosmopolis*, to be sure, presupposed the *polis*. This is true not only in a purely etymological sense but also in the sense that the cosmopolitan idea absorbed and adapted the principal themes that had emerged from the life of the polis: themes such as *nomos*, *eleutheria*, *autonomia*, the principles of citizenship and the civic community, and even the democratic concept of *isonomia*. It is even possible to say that if Alexander, his successors or those who lived under their rule had any systematic notion of 'empire' at all, the idea of an imperial *state* played little part in it. The primary idea of the state that Hellenistic rulers had to work with was the old conception of the polis as a community of citizens. Imperial rhetoric, and even, up to a point, imperial reality, oscillated between, on the one hand, a conception of empire as a collection of poleis, each allowed at least nominal autonomy and governed by its own particular laws, and, on the other, the idea of the cosmopolis as one universal polis, with its *nomoi* writ large.

The Hellenistic period did produce theories of kingship, especially to legitimize the three kingdoms that succeeded Alexander; and the idea of monarchy was inevitably called upon to play a larger role than it had in the age of the free polis, if only to support the dynastic claims of particular rulers. The importance of monarchy in post-classical Greek political theory – such as it was – reflected the decline of the polis and the civic community. This gave rise to a literature on ideal kingship, which has no parallel in classical Greek culture and which draws on Persian, Egyptian and Mesopotamian ideas as well as Greek traditions going back as far as Homer, together with a tendency to deify kings.

Yet Hellenistic conceptions of kingship never completely detached themselves from the polis, at least in the sense that they were obliged to confront the cultural and ideological legacies of the polis and its civic principles. So, for instance, one of the most important ideas emanating from the Hellenistic theory of kingship is the notion of the king as 'living law' (*nomos empsychos*, in Latin *lex animata*), which would be transmitted to the medieval West via the Roman Empire in the Code of Justinian. The idea of the king as 'living law' has much in common with – and is related to the polis in much the same way as – Plato's redefinition of *nomos* in the *Statesman*. As we saw, he argues that *nomos* in its conventional Athenian sense is opposed to the art, the *technē*, of statesmanship; and he elaborates a new conception of the rule of law which would imitate, not thwart, the political art. Plato reappropriates *nomos* by detaching the rule of law from the community of citizens and personifying it in the monarchical statesman, who must be free to exercise his art on behalf of the community, unchecked by a self-governing community of non-expert citizens. Absolute rule replaces the civic traditions of the democratic polis by turning them against themselves.

There were other, more philosophically fruitful responses to the shift from polis to empire. As civic identity and agency gave way to different ways of being in the social world, philosophers such as the Epicureans and Stoics concerned themselves less with political order than with the individual's place in the cosmos. It is, indeed, sometimes said that a kind of individualism represents the greatest departure of Hellenistic philosophy from its Hellenic predecessors. While this judgment tends to neglect the role of human association in Hellenistic doctrines, it is certainly true that these philosophers were inward-looking in a way that their predecessors were not.

At the same time, even this inward-turning individual has roots in the polis. Stoic and Epicurean philosophy both, in their different ways, are responding to questions raised with particular force by the life of the polis. In the previous chapter, it was suggested that the conflict and debate that characterized the polis, the direct experience of shaping the conditions of everyday life and social arrangements, the constant challenge to prevailing political relations and values – meant a confrontation, in unprecedented ways and to unprecedented degrees, with the problems of human agency and responsibility. The civic consciousness was both confident in the possibilities of human agency and, at the same time, uneasy about the uncertainties, dangers and responsibilities associated with it. Stoic and Epicurean philosophies seem to derive their special character from a confrontation with the joys and fears of autonomy and self-determination, the consciousness of the citizen, but now in the absence of the polis. It may be too much to say that the individual of Hellenistic philosophy is, in one form or another, an introversion of the active citizen; but the dynamism of this introspective soul surely bears the mark of civic activism.

It remains true, nonetheless, that the period is marked by a conception of human agency and the possibilities of human action that no longer has the polis as its principal terrain. It is possible to read both Stoicism and Epicureanism as more or less apolitical responses to the decline of the polis or to the general uncertainty and turbulence of the times. It is certainly true that, as polis gave way to empire, the main arena of philosophical reflection shifted. The sphere of civic action and deliberation receded, bringing into focus the private individual at one extreme – most notably in Epicureanism – and the universal order of the cosmopolis at the other, especially as conceived by the Stoics. While there was certainly a place in Stoicism, especially in its later Roman form, for civic duty and political activism, both these major Hellenistic schools located human happiness not in the polis but in the individual's inner resources. In the case of Epicureanism, the shift away from politics is explicit and unambiguous. The case of the Stoics is rather more difficult, and we shall shortly explore its complexities (always keeping in mind that very little remains of their work, or, indeed, the work of any Hellenistic philosophers).

Epicurus was born in Samos in 341 BC, the son of Athenian parents. He would experience very directly the effects of the Macedonian conquests when, after the death of Alexander, the Athenian settlers were driven out of Samos by Perdiccas, the imperial regent. Epicurus eventually settled in Athens in 306, where he founded a school, from which derived a philosophical tradition that would retain its popularity and influence for something like six centuries. His work has survived only in fragmentary form or in the words of his followers. The most important extant Epicurean classic would be the epic poem by Lucretius (about whose life little is known), *De Rerum Natura* (*On the Nature of Things*), written much later, in the first century BC, in republican Rome.

For Epicurus and his followers, the highest good, even the purpose of life, is pleasure (though not in the amorally hedonistic sense commonly attributed to 'epicureans') and the avoidance of pain. Above all, happiness requires the peace that comes with the absence of fear, and this means in particular fear of death and the afterlife. If there is one single overriding purpose in Epicurean philosophy and its conception of nature, it is to banish such fears, which requires liberation from religion. This involves an explanation of natural processes without the intrusion of divine or supernatural forces, relying on a conception of material bodies composed of atoms, and an account of the human psyche in terms of materially generated sensations, which are, on the whole, accurate sources of knowledge. The consequence of this materialism is that death need not be feared, because it means complete annihilation. Nowhere, at any time in history, has this theme been more eloquently played out than in Lucretius's *De Rerum Natura*. But the materialist bent of Epicureanism and its unambiguous concentration on the goods (intellectual as well as, and more than, material) of this life were not expressed in a conception of human self-determination through the medium of the self-governing polis. Its central theme was not the life of the citizen but the experience and ethics of the individual person; and the highest relation among individuals was not the civic bond but personal friendship.

At the same time, while the shift from polis to empire created a powerful impetus to apolitical withdrawal, we need to remember that Hellenistic philosophers were writing against a background of war and social turmoil, particularly as, in various city-states, conflicts between classes or between democrats and oligarchs were drawn into imperial power struggles. Social upheaval and political instability certainly encouraged a search for comfort in the cultivation of one's own garden; but they also gave a new urgency to questions of order, hierarchy, domination and subordination. Stoic philosophers in particular responded in ways quite different from, and often consciously opposed to, their great predecessors, Plato and Aristotle.

The foundation of Stoicism is credited to Zeno of Citium (333–264 BC); but it would undergo various significant changes after its foundation and is generally divided into three periods, the Old, Middle and Later or Roman Stoa. Nothing but fragments remain from the earlier periods; and the only complete works belong to the later, Roman imperial phase, the works of Seneca (4 BC–AD 65), Epictetus (c.55–135) and the Emperor Marcus Aurelius (121–80), which are largely devoted to ethics. It is only from fragments or from reconstruction by later thinkers that we can piece together anything like a coherent picture of the epistemological and cosmological ideas of the earlier Stoics. What can be said with some degree of confidence is that significant shifts took place in Stoic philosophy as the Hellenistic age passed into imperial Rome and philosophers began to respond to the needs of Roman elites. An important shift undoubtedly took place some time between Zeno and the Middle Stoics, Panaetius (185/180–110/108) and Posidonius (135–51), who, though Greek in origin, spent time in Rome, were well connected with Rome's elite and supported Roman imperial rule.

Like Epicureanism, Stoicism is concerned above all with ethics and the well-being of the individual. The self-control, even self-abnegation, that we associate with 'stoicism', the aspiration to eliminate the passions that cause human misery and the emphasis on the internal goods of the soul, may seem to argue for a withdrawal from political life altogether. Although civic life did play an important part in the ethical philosophy of Stoicism, at least in some of its forms, Stoic cosmopolitanism, with its emphasis on the universal bonds of humanity against all social and political particularities, may seem to have an apolitical charge. There is, nonetheless, much to be said in favour of a more political reading of what the Stoics were about – although their doctrines are compatible with a fairly wide range of political attitudes.

The most important known political work of early Stoicism is Zeno's *Republic*, which can only be reconstructed on the basis of comments left by his critics and successors. Zeno was born in Citium in Cyprus, the son of a merchant, and seems to have been a merchant himself until, after studying with the Cynic philosopher, Crates, he founded his own school, the Stoa, named after the Stoa Poikile, the Painted Porch in Athens where he taught. His *Republic* portrayed an ideal polis lacking the familiar institutions of the real city-state, such as courts of justice, schools, temples, property and money, and relying for its cohesion entirely on harmonious relations among virtuous individuals. On the one hand, it has been described as a youthful aberration, depicting a completely imaginary, perhaps even playful, ideal which can hardly be taken seriously. On the other hand, it has been interpreted as a mature, radical critique of contemporary social and political realities, which eliminates from the ideal republic all the injustices and sources of conflict that plague existing states – not only confining its inhabitants to wise and virtuous men but removing all existing sources of inequality, domination and subordination, in direct opposition to Plato's *Republic*.

Whatever Zeno may have intended in this political dialogue, there are more fundamental questions to be asked about Stoic epistemology, psychology and cosmology; and, while their political implications are not self-evident, we can attempt to tease them out. At the heart of Stoic doctrine is the notion of *logos*, the universal reason of a divine cosmic order, the dynamic principle in material nature. The universe is completely unitary. In sharp contrast to the Platonic dualism of sensible and intelligible worlds, the rational and the non-rational, body and intellect, there is in Stoic philosophy – at least in its original form – no division between mind and matter. Mind permeates all material things, as the universe is united by the dynamic principle of cosmic reason, *logos*, which both activates the universe and holds it together. Human reason partakes of this universal *logos*. It is effectively one with the cosmic or divine *logos*. Epistemologically this means that human sensation and perception, which have direct access to reality, are reliable foundations of knowledge – not the imperfect sources, at best, of mere opinion, to be distinguished from the true knowledge that is accessible only to reason. It also means that, since there is no mind–body split in Stoic psychology, Stoic philosophy departs radically from the principles underlying the fundamental Platonic division between ruling element and ruled.

The ethical implications of this Stoic monism are even more significant, though not entirely unambiguous. Although all living beings and
inanimate objects belong to the rational cosmic order, only human
beings possess the rational capacity to understand it. At the same time,
and for the same reason, Stoicism suggests that human beings are
capable of acting in opposition to the *logos*, that is, in a less than
rational manner. In that sense, they have the freedom to choose or
repudiate virtue. If humans simply acted unconsciously or non-
rationally in accordance with the laws of nature, as animals do, it
would be impossible to speak of human virtue. But, by definition, the
truly rational – hence virtuous – person is the one who can live only
in accordance with the universal principle of nature, aligning the
individual soul with the divine cosmic order.

The suggestion of a natural law which applies to all human beings,
and the notion of a universal human community, can be understood
in different ways and with different moral or political effects. The
idea of a universal community, subject to a universal law, can be
understood as a counsel of universal compassion; but it can also
support a harsh moral rigidity. It can underwrite deeply egalitarian
principles; but, as we have seen, it can also be used to justify empire.
The idea of a transcendent natural equality, which attributes to all
human beings a common *logos*, can be used to underwrite social and
political equality, even the equality of women, and the repudiation
of slavery. But it can also serve as a pretext for accepting inequality
in the material world, while relegating equality to some higher realm
which leaves existing social and political hierarchies intact. This, as
we shall see, was certainly the effect of Stoic influences in Rome and,
for instance, in the political theory of Cicero. It would also find its
way into Christianity.

We can perhaps gain a deeper insight into the political implications
of Stoic doctrine by considering the provenance of their philosophy,
as they themselves perceived it. This will require us to go back further
in the history of Greek philosophy, even beyond the classical age of
Plato and Aristotle. In rejecting the dualism of Plato and Aristotle,
the Stoics purport to be returning to the Presocratics, and to Heraclitus
(535–475 BC) in particular. Heraclitus is the first thinker known to
have given a metaphysical meaning to the word *logos*, a wide-ranging
word commonly used to denote everything from the spoken or written
word to thought or opinion, measure, proportion, the truth of the
matter, an account of something, right reason, and so on. He has also
been credited with the first known philosophical use of the word
cosmos to denote the world order. The remaining fragments of his

thought are still controversial, and commentators cannot agree on whether the universal *logos* that gave order to the cosmos had epistemological implications for him as it later would for the Stoics. It is presumably significant that he used the term commonly applied to human word, thought or reason to denote the universal principle of cosmic order; and it seems reasonable to suppose that, if the *logos* represented both the cosmic order and human intelligence, this had implications for the possibilities of human knowledge. Nevertheless, it is possible that the Stoics drew out these epistemological implications for their own purposes. Heraclitus, who more than once expressed his contempt for the ignorant many, would have been unlikely to accept the egalitarian consequences of Stoic psychology. His *logos* was certainly that which is common; but the trouble with most human beings, according to him, is that they live in ignorance of what is truly common, as if according to a private wisdom of their own. It is possible that, in their opposition to Platonic doctrines, the Stoics invoked the authority of Heraclitus not because they wished to reproduce his views faithfully but precisely because of Plato's objections to the great Presocratic philosopher.

What, then, can we learn from Plato's objections? In the first instance, they concern two related ideas that are central to Heraclitus's philosophy: that everything is in continuous motion, so that, while the cosmos is lawful, its operative principle is a law of change; and that the cosmic order is constituted by opposites in tension, a harmony of opposites, so that strife and war are the universal principle of nature. For Plato, Heraclitus's conception of the cosmos leaves no room for the dichotomy between the constant change of becoming and the permanence of being, or for the essential distinction between knowledge and opinion and the two distinct levels of reality that correspond to them. Nor would Plato have approved of Heraclitus's strictures against Pythagoras. For Heraclitus, Pythagoras represented precisely the idea of cosmic peace and harmony he was opposing; while for Plato, Pythagoras epitomized the orderly, motionless world of true being. Aristotle (who cannot abide what he takes to be Heraclitus's violation of the principle of non-contradiction: the unity of opposites suggested by Heraclitus's view that things, in the process of flux, are the same and not the same at once) even suggests that Plato devised his conception of absolute Forms in reaction to Heraclitus and the unknowable world which, as Plato saw it, followed from the Presocratic philosopher's ideas.

In short, Heraclitus failed to acknowledge the dualisms that would unite Plato's epistemology with his political theory. It does not, however, follow that Heraclitus himself drew the political conclusions from his own cosmology that Plato ascribed to philosophical monism. If anything, though little is known of Heraclitus's political preferences, the evidence suggests that he had aristocratic leanings. But it is likely that the differences between Heraclitus and Plato had less to do with the logic of philosophical argumentation than with the historical changes that had intervened between them.

Heraclitus, whose birthplace Ephesus was near the Ionian city of Miletus, where Greek philosophy was born, was writing probably in the late sixth century BC, before the golden age of Greek democracy. Plato, of course, lived through the democratic golden age in Athens, into what he regarded as its decadent phase, and was obsessed with its consequences for all he held dear. When Heraclitus conceived his ideas on cosmic strife, Ionia, and Miletus in particular, had just passed through 'some of the most extreme civil conflicts of the archaic period'.[9] There had been a struggle for control between the Wealthy (*Ploutis*) – possibly those who derived their wealth from trade, since they were also called Perpetual Sailors (*Aeinautai*) – and the Manual Workers (*Cheiromachai*); and, 'after a number of atrocities on both sides over two generations', the conflict was settled by arbitrators from another city who placed control in the hands of the landowners – or, as Herodotus puts it:

> they called the people together . . . and made proclamation that they gave the government into the hands of those persons whose lands they had found well farmed; for they thought it likely (they said) that the same persons who had managed their own affairs well would likewise conduct aright the business of the state. The other Milesians who in times past had been at variance they placed under the rule of these men.[10]

Is it fanciful to suppose that Heraclitus's conception of the cosmic order was shaped by these events? There is a striking correspondence, at any rate, between the recent social experience of Miletus and the philosopher's notion of strife as the operative cosmic principle, resolved not by complete suppression of one or the other of the warring parties but by a balance in tension between them – albeit with advantage to the propertied class. Just as the archer's bow is constituted by the

9 Oswyn Murray, *Early Greece* (Glasgow: Fontana, 2nd edn, 1993), p. 233.
10 Herodotus, *The Persian Wars*, transl. George Rawlinson, V.29.

tension between bow and string, which gives the deceptive appearance of motionlessness, so stability in society is not a state of rest but a constant tension of opposites held in precarious balance.

But even if Heraclitus himself did not associate social and cosmic orders in quite this way, there can be little doubt that Plato thought in such terms. Writing in democratic Athens, however, he could not have envisaged a Milesian resolution to the social conflicts of his day. Athens had already long ago passed through the kind of balance in tension which Solon, for instance, had sought to establish. The balance had long ago shifted too far towards the demos, and Plato could no longer imagine a stabilization of tension in the interests of the wealthy or the aristocracy. The demos now had to be unambiguously subordinate. His idea of social and political stability was uncompromisingly an order of motionless hierarchy, with lower elements in complete submission to the higher.

When the Stoics revived the *logos* of Heraclitus, they did so in conscious opposition to Plato's principle of order, at a time when the danger to property seemed very real, and dominant classes were certainly in fear of social revolution. Although it cannot be said that the early Stoics recommended an explicitly democratic order, they did reject the Platonic conception of *homonoia*, a concord based on rigid hierarchy. 'For Zeno', writes one commentator, '*homonoia* was not a relationship between classes that would not work, but a relationship among individual wise men; it was based not on suppression of recalcitrant elements, a potential source of conflict, but on their absence.'[11] If this utopian ideal fell short of democratic advocacy, how it identified the sources of conflict is significant enough. In any case, in the civil strife of Hellenistic Greece, Zeno's alternative idea of *homonoia* would certainly have been more attractive to supporters of democracy and far less welcome to their opponents than was Plato's uncompromising hierarchy.

It is not, therefore, unreasonable to emphasize the radical possibilities of the cosmological, psychological and epistemological monism of Stoic philosophy, at least in its original form. While it could be interpreted as an other-worldly doctrine with no practical implications for everyday social life, the doctrine of the all-pervasive *logos* certainly can have egalitarian consequences. The principle that, in this unitary cosmos, virtue is a unity and human beings who all share in the divine *logos* are free and equal, certainly was used to support the contention that slavery is contrary to nature, as is the inequality between men

---

11 Erskine, *op. cit.*, p. 31.

and women. It is, of course, possible to justify domination and subordination, inequalities of class and status or the relation between rulers and ruled, even in the face of natural equality. Even Plato defends the principles of rule and subordination less consistently on the basis of natural inequalities than on the grounds that there is a universal principle dividing ruling elements and ruled, reason and non-reason, and that a necessary division of labour in society will always mean that some people are rational and others are not. But it seems reasonable to draw certain radical political conclusions from Stoic philosophy, if only because the Platonic and Aristotelian dualism, which Stoics like Zeno deliberately rejected, applied the same principles to their political theories as they did to their theories of knowledge and nature.

It is significant, too, that later Stoics, especially those associated with Rome, who were more favourably disposed to empire and even slavery (if only on pragmatic grounds), felt compelled to modify the psychological monism of their predecessors. The Middle Stoics, Panaetius and Posidonius, for instance, harked back to Platonic and Aristotelian psychology. As for the truly Roman Stoics, they hardly bothered with such fundamental philosophical questions and were far more interested in ethics on its own terms, without any grounding in systematic theories of the cosmos or psychology.

To sum up, then, the social and political implications of Stoic cosmology, psychology and epistemology are in general not easy to read; and, in any case, their doctrines varied in different historical circumstances. When the early Stoics rejected the dualism that pervaded the cosmology, psychology and epistemology of their great predecessors, Plato and Aristotle, they also seem to have made corresponding judgments about slavery, freedom and empire. When the later Stoics retreated from the more radical positions of their predecessors, they were accommodating themselves to new social and political realities, most notably the rise of Rome and the conservatism of its ruling classes.

The dangers of Stoic egalitarianism became especially apparent in the context of the Spartan revolution. Military victories by the reforming king, Cleomenes, and especially the destruction of Megalopolis in 223 BC, were particularly alarming to propertied elites. To what extent the revolution was inspired by Stoic doctrine is a matter of conjecture; but the Stoic philosopher, Sphairos of Borysthenes, who wrote a tract on the Spartan constitution, was the tutor of Cleomenes and is said to have helped him institute his reforms.[12] At any rate, in the climate

---

12 See *Ibid.*, esp. Chs 6 and 7.

of the times, it is hardly likely that propertied classes would have welcomed any principle of natural equality or social justice that recognized no differences of class or status, any challenge to existing hierarchies, or any doctrine that might represent a threat to property (which for the Stoics is, in any case, a conventional, not a natural, institution, in a cosmos where all things are common), even if only by identifying property as the source of strife and instability. In the wake of the revolution and with the rise of Rome, its dominant aristocracy and growing empire, there emerged a Stoic current more congenial to the ruling elements.

The threats to property seemed that much more immediate when Rome's own resident radicals, the brothers Gracchi, came on the scene, with their ideas on agrarian reform and, perhaps, some kind of popular sovereignty. They certainly knew Greek and Greek philosophy, as did their opponents, who now mobilized Stoic arguments in defence of property, empire and even slavery. We shall return to these arguments, to the ideas of later Stoics such as Panaetius and the Romans who were influenced by them, notably Cicero. But something must be said first about the Roman context, as the new imperial power eclipsed its Hellenistic predecessors while absorbing the Greek world and its culture.

The Rise and Fall of Rome

Rome, like Athens, developed as a small city-state; and like the Athenian polis, the Roman Republic was governed by a small and simple state apparatus. By 265 BC, the republic was already governing most of Italy south of the Po, and its subjects outside Rome were 'citizens' only in very loose terms. Yet even then the ruling aristocracy, more powerful than its Athenian counterpart, was keen to maintain the state in its rudimentary form and long resisted the emergence of a professional state apparatus, preferring to govern themselves as amateurs. The aristocracy governed collectively, with individuals holding office for limited periods and every senator subject to principles of collegiality. But if this arrangement suited their purposes, it created problems of its own, requiring, again as in Athens, careful management of often tense relations between aristocracy and people and among rival aristocrats themselves.

In Rome, with its dominant aristocracy, the political form of the accommodation was not a democracy in the Athenian manner but a republic dominated by the aristocratic senate. Yet, while aristocratic dominance is a constant theme of Roman politics throughout both republic and empire, there was from the beginning a tension at the heart of the republic. It was a state built on private wealth, an instrument of individual ambition and acquisition for a ruling class of private proprietors who competed with one another for wealth and power but whose class position, in the absence of a superior state power, was sustained only by their own fragile collegiality. This form of state also implied an ambiguous relationship between the aristocracy and subordinate classes. Like Athens, Rome departed from the pattern of other ancient 'high' civilizations where a clear division existed between rulers and producers, monarchical states and subject peasant communities. In Rome, as in Athens, peasants and urban plebeians belonged to the community of citizens. While the balance of class forces between landlords and peasants in Rome, unlike Athens, had produced an aristocratic state, its dominant class was obliged to enlist the political and military support of its subordinate fellow-citizens, so that here, as in Athens, some of the characteristic legal and political arrangements of the republic are traceable to aristocratic conflicts and accommodations with popular forces – such as the office of tribune, in which a member of the elite was elected by the people to represent their interests (though tribunes were never regarded as 'magistrates', which meant that their office did not entitle them to sit in the senate).

In the early years of the republic, the Roman peasantry was relatively strong, but the history of the republic is a story of peasant decline and an increasing concentration of land and power in aristocratic hands. While the expansion of Rome into a huge territorial empire depended on the peasantry which manned what was to become the largest military force the world had ever known, their mobilization and deployment away from Rome made them more vulnerable to expropriation at home. As the army was effectively professionalized, peasants were turned into soldiers and the aristocracy benefitted on the home front too, while the agricultural labour force in the imperial homeland was increasingly given over to slaves, available in unprecedented numbers through conquest and trade.

As new lands were captured in Rome's imperial expansion, the issue of their distribution loomed very large on the political agenda, particularly the issue of land set aside as *ager publicus*, state lands available for colonization by citizens or for leaseholds at nominal rents. Some members of the aristocracy who served as tribunes of the people did seek to utilize the *ager publicus* to redress the balance between the rising aristocracy and increasingly impoverished peasants; but they were bitterly opposed by the ruling class in general, and the reforming agrarian laws seem to have had no lasting effect. The most famous attempt to effect a more equitable land redistribution, the reforms of the Gracchi, ended with the murder of the tribune Tiberius Gracchus at the hands of the aristocratic opposition, and later the violent death of Tiberius's brother Gaius, who had sought to continue and extend his brother's reforms and seems, unlike Tiberius, to have had a radical anti-senatorial political agenda.

With slaves and peasants (whether as tenants or as soldiers) creating wealth for the landlords, and urban masses in the huge metropolis of Rome living in appalling slums, overcrowded, unsanitary and dangerous, the differences of income between rich and poor at their peak have been estimated at 20,000 to 1, in contrast to the ratio of a few hundred to 1 in Athens after the Peloponnesian War. 'No administration in history', as one distinguished historian of Rome has remarked, 'has ever devoted itself so whole-heartedly to fleecing its subjects for the private benefit of its ruling class as Rome of the last age of the republic.'[13]

By the time the republican era drew to a close, replaced by an imperial state (conventionally dated from the foundation of the principate under Augustus Caesar in 27 BC), the Roman ruling class had amassed private fortunes of staggering proportions, by means of exploitation and corruption at home – from their landed estates, urban slum tenements, usury, trading in property, government contracts, and so on – and even more spectacularly by systematic plunder of their expanding empire. The administration of the empire provided the Roman aristocracy with unprecedented opportunities for looting and extortion. Proconsular office in imperial domains was a sure means of lining the pocket and for the most prominent Roman oligarchs to consolidate their personal power by acquiring what increasingly amounted to private armies. The empire also had the advantage of shifting the burden of taxation – at least for a time – away from citizens, including peasants, and onto imperial subjects. This undoubtedly lowered the risk of popular unrest in Rome, but the price paid by peasants was the increasing concentration of land in the hands of the aristocracy.

Yet the very success of the republic as an instrument of aristocratic gain proved its undoing. The irony is that it was the triumph of the aristocracy which eventually led to the fall of the republic, as the weakness of the threat from below deprived the ruling class of any unity it might have had in the face of a common enemy. The growth of the empire aggravated the inherent weaknesses of the republican

13 Ernst Badian, *Roman Imperialism in the Late Republic*, 2nd edn (Oxford: Blackwell, 1968), p. 87.

state by enlarging the scope of oligarchic competition and raising the stakes. With an increasingly unruly oligarchy, the vast military apparatus of imperial expansion was bound to be deployed in the service of personal ambition and intra-oligarchic rivalry. The empire also placed intolerable strains on the administrative capacities of the republic and its principle of government by amateurs. With no strong state to keep the warring aristocracy in check the republic descended into chaos. It is not surprising that the fabric of republican government gave way under the strain.[14]

The most famous period of Roman history, the moment of Julius Caesar and Marcus Tullius Cicero, was the end of the republic: a time of unceasing intra-oligarchic conflict and violence, corruption, and breakdown of order, which spilled over into the vast expanses of the empire as ambitious aristocrats brought their proconsular armies into play. The time of troubles was brought to an end, and the cohesion and class power of the oligarchy preserved, only by the establishment of an imperial state in place of the city-state form of the republic. If the class interests of the oligarchy had created and sustained the republic, the acquisitive and expansionary logic of that same oligarchy had now driven it beyond the narrow bounds of the republican form.

What is most striking about the history of Rome, and what is most important for our understanding of its political and cultural life, is the Roman preoccupation with private property. The monumental scale of its land-grabbing project, both in the concentration of oligarchic property at home and in imperial expansion, was unprecedented and unequalled in the ancient world. It reflected a distinctive system of social relations and class reproduction, quite different from other ancient civilizations where centralized states ruled subject peasant communities and access to the surplus labour of others was typically achieved by direct possession of the state. State-appropriation in these other civilizations did not, as we have seen, necessarily preclude private possession of land, either for those who acquired it as a perquisite of office or for peasant-smallholders; but access to substantial wealth – that is, to the surplus labour of others on a large scale – tended not to be a function of property as such but rather of state power. In Rome, by contrast, landed property was the only secure and steady source of wealth.

---

14 The classic discussion of this period is Ronald Syme's *The Roman Revolution* (London and Oxford: Oxford University Press, 1960).

As in other pre-capitalist societies, juridical status and political power remained critical factors in the relations of exploitation. But in the absence of a centralized appropriating state superimposed on subject communities of producers, and without a clear monopoly of juridical privilege and political power for the ruling class, private property became an end in itself in unprecedented ways. Land-ownership became the major condition of surplus extraction, and there developed a compelling pressure to acquire land, even to dispos-sess smallholders. Since the citizenship of peasants precluded their juridical dependence, their exploitation – as tenants or casual labourers – depended on their economic vulnerability. If expropriated, they could be replaced by slaves as a labour force on large estates; and in the last century of the republic, in Roman Italy (agricultural slavery was less important in other parts of the empire such as North Africa or the east) one third of the population consisted of slaves. As the empire grew, the juridical and political status of the peasantry declined, while the burden of taxation increased.

The collective power of the aristocracy was sufficient (unlike that of ancient Athens) to achieve an unprecedented concentration of land in the hands of the oligarchy; and the principal career for the Roman ruling class was the acquisition and management of property. Even imperial service in the provinces was a way of looting subject popu-lations to obtain the means of investing in property. Public office was in general just a moment in that career; and, while imperial office was certainly a road to fame and fortune, aristocrats were not always keen to take it. The characteristic aspiration of the Roman aristocracy was *cum dignitate otium* (leisure with dignity), and their principal moti-vation for seeking release from public duties was quite simple: 'Their primary function and activity after all was the supervision and main-tenance of their wealth.'[15]

When the distinctive social property relations of Rome outgrew the republican state, they produced a new imperial system, an 'under-governed' empire. Although some parts of the empire were under more direct Roman rule than others, its administration of such far-flung territories could not have been achieved without a network of more or less self-governing cities (often newly founded and in largely rural areas), which amounted to a massive class federation of local aristoc-racies. This municipal system made possible what has been described

---

15 Chester Starr, *The Roman Empire, 27 B.C. to A.D. 476: A Study in Survival* (New York: Oxford University Press, 1982), p. 63.

as 'government without bureaucracy'. While the imperial state did, of course, have its share of centrally appointed officials, the empire 'remained undergoverned, certainly by comparison with the Chinese empire, which employed, proportionately, perhaps twenty times the number of functionaries.'[16]

This imperial system, with its diffuse administration, enhanced and extended the power of private property. The Roman Republic had established the rule of property as never before, and the empire pushed forward the frontiers of that regime. It constituted a historically unprecedented partnership between the state and property, in contrast to all other known civilizations in which a powerful state meant a relatively weak regime of private property. Even many centuries later, in late imperial China, for instance, with its long history of well-developed property in land, the imperial state consolidated its power by expanding the smallholder economy while discouraging large land-ownership, and centralized administrative power by co-opting large proprietors into the state. The result was a huge imperial bureaucracy, living off taxation of the peasants, while great wealth and power resided not in the land but in the imperial state, in an elite at the top of which stood the court and imperial officialdom. The Roman Empire was very different, with its distinctive mode of coexistence between state and private property.

But the strengths of the Roman regime were also its weaknesses.[17] The mode of administration, and the system of private property on which it was based, meant that the empire tended towards fragmentation from the start; and in the end, that tendency prevailed. The imperial bureaucracy grew, above all for the purpose of extracting more taxes – as always, largely to maintain the empire's military power. But the growth of the bureaucracy was a sign of weakness, not of strength. With no significant new and permanent conquests after the first century AD, the Roman army was overstretched in keeping control of the existing empire, while the bureaucracy and the tax-hungry state grew in order to sustain the army. The burden this imposed on Rome's imperial subjects simply hastened the decline. The so-called 'barbarian' invasions were less a cause than an effect of Rome's disintegration. In fact, it can be very misleading to speak of invasions at all, since Rome

---

16 Peter Garnsey and Richard Saller, *The Roman Empire: Economy, Society and Culture* (London: Duckworth, 1987), p. 26.

17 The rest of this paragraph and the following one are taken from my book, *Empire of Capital* (London: Verso, 2005), pp. 36–7.

had long had more or less friendly interactions with the 'barbarian' neighbours within its orbit, using them both as a source of military manpower and in commercial relations. By the time incursions across the imperial frontiers became a fatal threat and not just an annoyance, a crumbling state had long since become an intolerable burden to peasants and a dispensable nuisance to landlords.

It is a striking fact that the so-called 'fall' of the empire took place in the west and not in the imperial east, where the pattern of rule was more like that of other ancient empires: a bureaucratic state in which land remained largely subordinate to office. It was in the western empire, where state rule was diluted and fragmented by aristocracies based on huge landed estates, that the weaknesses of the empire proved fatal. As the imperial state imploded, it left behind a network of personal dependence binding peasants to landlord and land – a development encouraged by the state itself when, in a time of crisis, it tied many peasants to the land, no doubt for fiscal purposes. The simple opposition between freedom and slavery would be gradually replaced by a spectrum of dependence.

In the centuries following the 'decline and fall', there would be various attempts to recentralize this fragmented system under one or another dynastic monarchy, with successive cycles of centralization and repeated fragmentation, as one or the other element in the uneasy Roman fusion of political sovereignty and landed property prevailed. But the regime of private property had left its mark; and the fragmentation of the Roman Empire is still recognizable in European feudalism, a system of 'parcellized sovereignty' based on property, with political and economic power united in a feudal lordship dominating and exploiting a dependent peasantry without the support of a strong central state.

The Culture of Property: The Roman Law

The Roman property regime, and the particular form of Rome's class accommodations, shaped not only the political life of both republic and empire but also their cultural formation. Although the Romans would thoroughly appropriate Greek culture as their empire absorbed the Hellenistic world, they would never overtake their teachers in the characteristically Greek domains of philosophy and political theory. They certainly left their mark on their adopted cultural traditions – particularly, for instance, in Stoic philosophy; but their most distinctive contributions to the theorization of social and political worlds are to be found elsewhere: in the law and in Christianity, or at least the form of Roman Christianity that ultimately triumphed to become the 'universal' Church.

We can begin to appreciate the specificity of Roman political culture by considering more closely how the Roman resolution of its early social conflicts differed from the Athenian. The Athenians, as we saw, managed the conflicts between peasants and landlords, 'mass' and 'elite', largely on the political plane. The effect of their democratic reforms was gradually to dilute legal or status distinctions among free Athenians in the common identity of citizenship. The Romans to some extent also pursued the political course, and the citizen body also included both rich and poor; but, while property increasingly trumped heritage, even status distinctions among citizens, notably between patricians and plebeians, continued to play a role, with patricians enjoying privileged status and disproportionate representation in assemblies. The Romans did, to be sure, devise political institutions and procedures to regulate relations between different types of citizen – such as the particularly distinctive office of the tribune. But, while influenced at first by Greek law, the Romans constructed a much more elaborate legal apparatus, relying more than the Greeks on the law to manage transactions between mass and elite, between propertied classes and less prosperous citizens. Social relations between these groups were in large part played out not in the public domain of political life but in the sphere of private law – a distinctively Roman category; and the regulation of property would constitute by far the largest part of Rome's civil law.

The founding moment of the Roman law, the enactment of the Twelve Tables in the middle of the fifth century BC, was understood by Romans looking back at their legal history as a response to plebeian grievances about the old system of customary law, which had been interpreted and applied by patrician judges. But the Twelve Tables probably did not fundamentally transform the substance of traditional law or its aristocratic bias, and certainly did not dilute the distinction between patricians and plebeians. Instead, plebeians had to make do with the commitment of the law to a written code, which explicitly outlined their rights. While many adjustments and additions would later be required, especially as the republic grew into a massive empire, the system of private law which emerged from this early written code would remain the basis of the Roman law.

Both in its origins and in its substance, the Roman law was rooted in the old relations between patrician landlords and plebeian farmers, many of whom may, in the early years, have been in a dependent condition, occupying and working surplus land allowed them by landlords in exchange for political and military support. This traditional relation of *patronus* and *cliens* would soon change its form, and the division between patricians and plebeians would no longer entail the same relation between landlords and dependent peasants; but patronage would continue to denote a relationship between men of unequal status, in which a member of the Roman elite would offer help and protection to social inferiors (or sometimes, in a public capacity, to groups and even cities), who became his clients, in exchange for their loyalty, deference, political support and various kinds of service. The distinctively Roman conception of patronage and the relation between patron and client, which had no Athenian analogue, would continue to shape Roman conceptions of social and political dependence.

Even in the absence of the personal relation between patron and client, social relations between classes continued to play themselves out in the private sphere, where the law regulated property and all the various rights and obligations associated with it. This bespeaks a concept of the public realm very different from the Greek. The Greeks made various distinctions between state and non-state spheres. In the previous chapter, we encountered such a distinction, for instance, in Sophocles's play, *Antigone*. But a reminder of what was at issue in that play may also help to clarify the ways in which these Greek distinctions differed from the Roman antithesis of public and private. Although *Antigone* is often read as a clash between the individual conscience and the state, it has more to do, as we saw, with the opposition between two conceptions of *nomos*, Antigone representing eternal unwritten laws, in the form of traditional, customary and religious obligations of kinship, and Creon the laws of a new political order. The play also deals with two conflicting loyalties or forms of *philia*: on the one hand, the ties of blood and personal friendship and, on the other, the public demands of the civic community, the polis whose laws are supposed to be directed to the common good. In neither of these cases is the non-state realm adequately described as *private*, since both polis and non-polis principles concern communal obligations.

The Greeks come closest to a public–private dichotomy in the distinction between *oikos* and polis. As Thucydides makes clear in his account of Pericles's Funeral Oration, Athenians certainly distinguished between a citizen's domestic concerns, or an individual's own business, and the common affairs of the polis. But in Greek political theory, the distinction between *oikos* and polis, as elaborated most clearly by Aristotle, has to do with two forms of association and the different principles that govern them – in particular, the inequality of household relations and the civic equality of the polis, or the *oikos* as the realm of necessity and the polis as the sphere of freedom. A man denied access to the political sphere because of his bondage to necessary labour was, for Aristotle, not so much a private individual, as against a citizen, but rather a 'condition' of the polis, as against a 'part' of it. Democrats would have disagreed with Aristotle about the political consequences of social inequality, or whether a life of necessary labour disqualified people from politics; but they would have shared his view that the distinctive characteristic of the political sphere was civic equality – which is, of course, why democrats and antidemocrats disagreed so fiercely about access to that privileged sphere for the poor and labouring classes.

The Romans, by contrast, elaborated some fairly clear distinctions between public and private, yet these had little to do with the criteria which, for the Greeks, distinguished *oikos* from polis. For the Romans, for instance, inequality was formally present in the political sphere and was not therefore the criterion that marked off public from private. It was certainly not a question of distinguishing between a domestic sphere in which superior ruled inferior and a civic sphere in which social unequals met as political equals. In Rome, relations between social unequals in the private sphere of property were reflected in the public sphere of hierarchical citizenship. The Romans created a new and probably unprecedented kind of private sphere; and their distinction between public and private represented a new form of dichotomy, which is clearly visible in the distinction between public and private law that lay at the heart of the Roman legal system.

The only extant elaboration of the distinction defines it like this: 'Public law is concerned with the Roman state (*status rei Romanae*), while private law is concerned with the interests of individuals, for some matters are of public and others of private interest. Public law comprises religion, priesthoods, and magistracies.'[18] Private law was by far the greater concern of the Roman legal system, and the apparatus of law to deal with matters of public administration was fairly rudimentary by comparison. The primacy of private law is in itself significant, as is the mere fact that the Romans felt the need to draw such a clear line between public and private. The determining factor cannot have been simply the growth of the state. The republic had a

---

18 This formulation is by the Roman jurist, Ulpian (d. 228 AD). The compilation of the Roman law under the emperor, Justinian I (*c.* 482–565) – the *Digest* of Justinian – is said to owe something like one third of its content to Ulpian and begins with this distinction between public and private law.

minimal, virtually amateur state, while even the empire was 'under-governed'; and other ancient civilizations had far more elaborate states. What set the Romans apart from all other high civilizations was their property regime, with its distinctive legal conception of property; and with it came a more sharply delineated private sphere in which the individual enjoyed his own exclusive dominion.

The contrast with Greece is here particularly striking. It has often been remarked that the Greeks had no clear conception of ownership, indeed no abstract word for it at all. An Athenian might claim a better right than someone else to some piece of property but certainly nothing like the exclusive claim entailed by the Roman concept of *dominium*. In disputes over property, the difference in practice may not have been as great as it seems in theory, but its significance should not be under-estimated. It tells us a great deal about how the Romans conceptualized the social world. The word *dominium* 'and the actual law relating to ownership', writes one commentator on Greek law, emphasizing the contrast with Rome, 'serve to underline the strongly individualistic character of Roman ownership, which comes out forcibly in the plain-tiff's words in a *vindicatio* [the ancient legal action in which a Roman citizen asserted a more or less exclusive right of ownership over some-thing]'[19]: 'I claim that this thing is mine by the *ius Quiritum*', that is, by the legal right of private exclusive individual ownership which only Roman citizens could enjoy. In this way, 'The Roman citizen asserts a claim against all the world, based on an act of his own will.'[20] The concept of *dominium*, then, marks out the private sphere with an unprecedented clarity, and the private is inseparable from property.

The idea of an exclusive private and individual sphere of mastery contained in the concept of *dominium* would develop in tandem with the concept of a distinctly public form of rule. The *imperium*, which designated military command and also the right of command attached to certain civil magistrates, would evolve to encompass the rule of the emperor, eventually approaching something like a notion of sovereignty,

---

19 A.R.W. Harrison, *The Law of Athens: The Family and Property* (Oxford: The Clarendon Press, 1968), p. 201. It may be misleading to call Roman property 'absolute', but perhaps no more misleading than is the concept of 'absolute' property itself. If 'absolute' means completely inviolable, without restrictions on its use, or without any obligations (such as taxation) attached to it, there has never been a truly absolute form of property. But it would be a mistake not to acknowledge the distinctively *exclusive* quality of Roman property, the degree to which it belonged to the individual to the exclusion of others, even if certain obligations might be associated with it.

20 *Ibid.*

which distinguished the Roman idea of the state from the Greek conception of the polis as simply a community of citizens. The partnership of *dominium* and *imperium*, then, sums up both the distinction between public and private and the alliance of property and state that was so distinctively Roman.

To say that the Romans devised a conception of property more individualistic and exclusive than ever before, or that they differentiated private and public in historically unprecedented ways, is not to say that they anticipated modern liberal individualism. Their concern was not, for example, the protection of individual rights from incursions by the state. Indeed, they scarcely had a conception of the state, or of individual rights, of the kind that would be required to think in these terms; nor were their social relations and institutions of a kind to generate such ideas.

Rome was not a capitalist society, nor a 'liberal democracy'. It is certainly true that, unlike any other ancient civilization, the Romans created a regime with two distinct poles of power, in which a well-developed central state coexisted with strong private property; and it is no doubt also true that, as the imperial state grew, there were tensions between propertied classes and an increasingly burdensome state. But there never existed in Rome a system of appropriation, like capitalism, which depended on intensive growth, rooted in profitably competitive production, rather than on the extensive growth of property in a massive grab for land. Territorial expansion in the empire was an extension of land concentration at home; and the public power of the state, its coercive force, played a more immediate role in the acquisition of private wealth.

Roman ideas of property and its relation to the public sphere expressed this distinctive partnership of property and state. The emblem of the Roman state, SPQR, *Senatus Populusque Romanus*, the Senate and the Roman People, does not convey a formal, abstract concept of the state so much as a snapshot of the relations between dominant and subordinate classes, as well as alliances and rivalries within the ruling class itself. It is significant that *Senatus* is distinguished from, and placed ahead of, *Populus*, in a formula that denotes the dominance of the propertied classes in the senate and their limited accommodation with the people, a 'mixed constitution' containing popular elements but governed by an aristocracy. The absence of any abstract notion of the state is particularly clear in the republic, with its amateur government by members of the propertied elite taking time out from the management of their private wealth. In that context, the distinction between private and public represented not an antithesis between two poles of power but rather the dominant class in its two different aspects.

The clear delineation of public and private spheres, then, was not, in the main, intended to protect the private from public intrusion. It was more a matter of managing the private sphere itself. In the first instance, especially in the form of private law, it contributed to the regulation of relations between classes by recognizing the sanctity of property while spelling out the rights and obligations associated with it. Later, the ruling class's descent into self-destructive conflict would add a new dimension to the management of the private sphere, as we shall see in the work of Cicero; and as republic gave way to empire, the relation between public and private would inevitably change. Yet even when the polarities increased with the growth of the imperial bureaucracy, the state remained a distinctive collaboration between property and state, as private appropriation continued to depend on imperial power, while the imperial system relied on a network of alliances among landed elites.

The Roman law also mapped the social world in other significant ways. The distinction between the *ius civile*, the law specific to Roman citizens, and the *ius gentium*, which applied to other peoples, contains a wealth of information about the Roman world. This distinction between the Roman civil law and the law of nations in the first instance set Roman citizens apart from others, while at the same time acknowledging the need to provide some means of regulating the transactions between Romans and non-Romans, in a growing system of international trade and an expanding empire. The idea of the *ius gentium* both acknowledged that other peoples operated according to their own laws and customs and also sought to find principles common to all which could form the basis of transactions among them and be applied in Roman courts. This applied not only to principles having to do with relations among nations, such as the inviolability of treaties, but also to a wide range of private law matters concerning the performance of contracts, conditions of buying and selling, and so on.

The exclusiveness of the civil law became increasingly irrelevant as the Roman citizenship expanded, but the *ius gentium* continued to serve other purposes. The identification of certain universal principles accepted by all peoples had opened the way to a concept of *natural* law, a *ius naturale*, deriving from natural reason. At the same time, the idea of the *ius gentium* as simply the observable commonalities among social practices in various nations also allowed for the kind of Roman pragmatism that could, for example, regard slavery as an essentially unnatural institution while treating it as legitimate just on the grounds that it was (allegedly) a universal practice accepted by many particular systems of custom and law.

The 'undergoverned' Roman Empire, composed of diverse and loosely connected fragments and relying on an alliance of propertied elites spread over a huge territory, depended for its cohesion not only on a vast military force but on cultural ties and universalistic ideologies that could help to bind the imperial fragments together. The part played by the Roman law in maintaining the cohesion of the empire had at least as much to do with its cultural and ideological effects as with its role in governance. Even at the height of imperial dominion, Roman law never completely overshadowed the particularities of local law and custom; but the spread of the empire was accompanied by an increasing assertion of universalism against legal, political and cultural particularisms of various kinds, a universalism expressed in the natural law or the *ius gentium* no less than in Stoic cosmopolitanism and, finally, in Christian doctrine and the 'universal Church'.

The Culture of Property: Stoic Philosophy in Rome

The topography of a social world shaped by a distinctive property regime is visible also in Roman philosophy, particularly in its variants of Stoicism. Let us remind ourselves of the changes that Stoic doctrine underwent as Roman hegemony spread. In general, the most obvious transformation as Stoic philosophy came within the Roman orbit was a decreasing interest in cosmological, psychological or epistemological questions and a growing preoccupation with ethics alone. But before Stoicism became a truly Roman phenomenon, there were already moves away from the doctrines of the early Stoics and even from their cosmological and psychological foundations. Posidonius of Apameia (135–51 BC), with whom Cicero studied, not only modified Stoic ethical doctrine but also challenged the psychological and cosmological monism that underlay the ethics and politics of Stoicism; and the evidence suggests that this was already true of Posidonius's teacher, Panaetius of Rhodes (c. 185–109 BC), who first brought Stoicism to Rome and who greatly influenced Cicero. In their hands, Stoicism became a philosophy more congenial to the interests of the Roman ruling class. While early Stoic doctrine could be read as a challenge to slavery, empire and even, perhaps, to property itself, this 'Middle' phase of Stoicism provided the philosophical means to defend them. But even short of that, the modifications in ethics made Stoicism more adaptable to the values of Roman elites.

Panaetius came to Rome during the late republic after studying with Stoic philosophers in Greece, where he had met the Roman general, Scipio Africanus the Younger, also a student of Stoicism. He would later return to Greece to head the Stoa in Athens. But while in Rome, he remained close to Scipio and introduced Stoic ethics to the so-called Scipionic circle of intellectually inclined conservative aristocrats, who played a major role in disseminating Panaetius's ideas.[21]

What made his teachings especially attractive to men of this kind was that he adapted the ethical doctrine of Stoicism to the particular virtues most highly prized by them in their aspirations to honour and glory, placing an emphasis 'on such active virtues as greatness of soul or magnanimity, on generosity or liberality, on decorum and propriety, and on energy and industriousness, as against the traditional Stoic stress on fortitude and justice'.[22] More fundamentally, Panaetius eased the rigidity of Stoic ethics, making the doctrine more adaptable to ethical ambiguities and compromises of the kind that would be regularly encountered by Rome's aristocracy, in a world made up not of sages but of ordinary people; and he attached greater value to lesser goods, which fell short of the highest Stoic ideals. Stoicism had always allowed for a distinction between moral goods and goods that were morally indifferent but which could be rated in respect to preferability on other grounds. Material wealth was a typical example of the morally indifferent but preferable good. Now, such secondary goods were given higher status than the Early Stoics had granted them.

Justice, in this view, had more to do with positive legality than with higher moral laws – as one might expect in a society so imbued with legalism. This meant that strict moral principles might have to give way to existing Roman practices, to the requirements of contracts and the exigencies of everyday life in business and politics, as long as they remained within the law. But once this legalistic notion had replaced the old Stoic conception of an absolute and universal justice above man-made law, it was possible to temper legal justice by supplementing it with less exalted moral principles of equity. This would have significant implications for some of republican Rome's most important political controversies.

---

21 Some scholars regard the Scipionic circle as a fiction – which appears, for instance, in Cicero's *De Amicitia* (*On Friendship*). But whether or not there existed any such more or less formally organized 'circle', there can be no doubt that there was a significant conservative sector of the Roman aristocracy, of which Scipio was a prime example, which was influenced by the ideas of the Middle Stoa.

22 Neal Wood, *Cicero's Social and Political Thought* (Berkeley and Los Angeles: University of California Press, 1988), p. 48.

The role of the Scipios in Rome nicely illustrates the political significance of these changes in Stoic philosophy. In 134, Tiberius Sempronius Gracchus, cousin of Scipio Africanus the Younger and himself a successful general, was elected to serve the following year as tribune of the people. With the help of his brother, Gaius, he proposed a radical agrarian law to redistribute public lands in the interest of impoverished farmers. The opposition to the Gracchan reforms was led by their cousin, Scipio Africanus; and, in the hostility aroused by Tiberius's tribunate among the Roman aristocracy, he was murdered in a riot by senators and their supporters, led by P. Scipio Nasica.

In the debates surrounding Tiberius's agrarian law, Stoic principles may have been invoked on both sides. The earlier Spartan revolution, with its radical programme of land redistribution and debt cancellation, had been informed by the egalitarian ideas of Early Stoicism, together with its principle that, in a cosmos regulated by a single common *logos*, all things were fundamentally common; and these ideas may also have inspired Tiberius. But in the wake of the Spartan revolution the modification of Stoic principles, especially by Panaetius, had weakened the threat they posed to property. If the case for the Gracchan reforms could be supported by Stoic ideas on equality, social justice and the principle of commonality, the opposition could, and did, appeal to the modified Stoicism that identified justice with existing law but also tempered law with notions of fairness or equity. On the basis of those later Stoic principles, no higher standard of universal justice had any decisive bearing on the question of agrarian reform; and, while its legality was certainly an issue, because nothing could be just that was illegal (just as nothing that was lawful could be called unjust), beyond legality there were also requirements of equity.

It is striking that principles of equity were invoked by Rome's leading thinkers not in support of, but in opposition to, land redistribution. In *De Officiis (On Duties)*, a work that on the author's own testimony is profoundly influenced by Panaetius, Cicero comments on the damage done by both the Spartans and the Gracchi, as examples of the consequences that flow from violating equity in the redistribution of property. Having said that 'it is the peculiar function of the state and the city to guarantee to every man the free and undisturbed control of his own particular property', Cicero goes on to castigate the 'ruinous' measures adopted by land reformers who 'do away with equity'. '[H]ow is it fair', he asks, 'that a man who never had any property should take possession of lands that had been occupied for many years or even generations, and that he

who had them before should lose possession of them?'[23] Cicero seems
to share the view of his teacher, the Stoic Posidonius, student of
Panaetius, who maintained that, while there was nothing illegal about
what Tiberius did, he deserved the punishment he got.

It would, of course, be possible to argue that the practical ethics
of the Middle Stoa serve no particular social or political interests but
provide for ethical standards that can be met by ordinary people and
not just sages, or at least by Roman grandees faced with the imperfect
realities of everyday political and economic life. The moral rigidities
of Early Stoicism, it might be said, are not particularly congenial or
even humane; and surely principles of equity are good for everyone.
If Stoic arguments were used in defence of ruling class interests, can
the philosophers themselves be held responsible; and what is the point
of spelling out the immediate political sources and consequences of
these ideas? The least that can be said in response to such objections
is that, even if we leave aside the known associations of a philosopher
like Panaetius and his close connection to Roman leaders with a clear
political agenda, there is something to be learned from identifying the
particular historical conditions that placed certain urgent questions
on the political agenda and shaped the ways in which those questions
were answered. At the same time, it is not simply a matter of exploring
historical contexts to help understand ancient texts. To historicize, as
we said in Chapter One, is to humanize; and there is something deeply
troubling about analyses of political theory that are insensitive to the
pressing social issues to which it is addressed.

If we acknowledge the historical circumstances in which the ethical
doctrine of the Middle Stoa was rooted, and even the specific social
interests that it served, we can nonetheless accept that its social and
political implications are not necessarily one-sided and that its softening
of Stoic rigidities has a wider appeal. But Panaetius did not confine
himself to easing the requirements of Stoic ethics. The surviving evidence
suggests, for example, that he accepted slavery in a way his predecessors
had not. This might be expected of an ethical doctrine that allowed for
adaptations to normal if less than ideal Roman practices; but there is
also evidence of a more fundamental shift in psychology and cosmology
designed to provide a philosophical foundation for the defence of social
hierarchy and even slavery. Apparently dividing the soul between a
controlling reason and subordinate appetites, he revived the old dualism
which had underpinned the hierarchal philosophies of Plato and

---

23 Cicero, *Off*. II, 78–80, Loeb Library translation.

Aristotle. In relation to slavery, it was now again possible to argue, as Plato had done, that subordination of some men to others was good for both, if it accorded with the principle of rational control over baser elements. It was even possible to maintain, as Aristotle had done, that slavery was good for both parties in the relationship, as those fit only to obey can only benefit from subjection to a superior master.

Similar doctrines were applied in defence of Roman imperialism. Whether Panaetius himself made such an argument is unclear, but Cicero in his *Republic* deploys it in justification of both slavery and empire. In this dialogue, which purports to take place in the garden of Scipio Africanus the Younger, Cicero gives a speech to Laelius, one of the most important members of the Scipionic circle and clearly of Stoic persuasion, about the dominion that Rome has achieved 'over the whole world'. 'Do we not observe', says Laelius, 'that dominion has been granted by Nature to everything that is best, to the great advantage of what is weak? For why else does God rule over man, the mind over the body, and reason over lust and anger and other evil elements of the mind?' There is, to be sure, a difference, he says, between the kind of rule exercised by a king over his subjects, or a father over his children, and the rule of master over slave. The first – and this also applies to various other kinds of political arrangements – governs in the way that the mind governs the body, while the second is like the rule of reason over lust and 'other disquieting emotions', in that its object is to restrain and overpower slaves, just as reason, 'the best part of the mind', restrains 'the evil parts of the mind . . . with a stricter curb. . . . ' Since the empire is the product of just wars in defence of Rome's allies, we are given to understand that, while imperial domination may have elements of the first kind of rule, it also belongs, justly, to the second, in which lesser beings or nations are forcefully subjected to their superiors for their own benefit.[24]

---

24 *Rep*. III, 36–7, Loeb Library translation. The translator remarks that these fragments 'are part of the argument for the justice of slavery and imperialism, in which it is maintained that certain nations and individuals are naturally fitted for and benefited by subjection to others.' He points out that St Augustine later explained the meaning of these passages in *The City of God*, XIX, 21. The relevant passage in St Augustine reads ' . . . the rule over provincials [according to Cicero's *Republic*] is just, precisely because servitude is the interest of such men, and is established for their welfare when rightly established; that is, when licence to do wrong is taken away from wicked men; and that those subdued will be better off, because when not subdued they were worse off. In support of the reasoning a striking example is introduced, as if drawn from nature, and stated as follows: Why, then, is it that God commands man, the soul commands the body, the reason commands lust and the other vicious parts of the soul?' (Loeb Library translation).

That Cicero was putting into Laelius's mouth ideas derived from Panaetius is suggested near the beginning of the dialogue, when Laelius refers to conversations those present used to have 'with Panaetius . . . in company with Polybius – two Greeks who were perhaps the best versed of them all in politics'.[25] Doubts may remain about Panaetius's rejection of Early Stoic monism, or about his application of a psychological dualism to social and political relations; but the evidence for a restoration of Platonic dualism, between a ruling rational element and the irrational subjected to it, is clearer in the work of his pupil, Posidonius, described by his contemporaries as a great admirer of Plato and Aristotle. Posidonius also refers to historical cases of domination that seem to be examples of inferiors being subjected to superiors, for the good of the subject. In any case, the theory of empire which emerges from the various scraps of evidence concerning Panaetius's view, and/or the views of those strongly influenced by him, is, at the very least, that imperial domination is justified if it works to the benefit of its subjects. This may not go as far as Aristotle's notion that some men are natural slaves and so can only benefit from enslavement to superior masters; but the conception of what is beneficial to the subject is itself clearly coloured from the start by the Platonic and Aristotelian idea – inconsistent with the Early Stoic notion of a universal *logos* in a unitary cosmos – that there is a natural division between ruler and ruled and that some men are better off ruled.

Cicero

No one gave voice to the Roman culture of property better than the statesman, orator and thinker, Marcus Tullius Cicero. His political ideas may not have been deeply original; but his synthesis of the prevailing currents, including Stoicism, was brilliantly adapted to the conditions and interests of the Roman senatorial class, at that particularly turbulent moment in the late republic. By this time, when the republican form

---

25 *Rep.* I, 34. The historian Polybius (*c.* 203–122 BC), though a Greek, had become close to the Scipios and a supporter of Roman imperial rule. His grand history, which seeks to explain how Rome achieved its conquests, gives much of the credit for Roman success to its mixed constitution, the equilibrium and interdependence of classes created by the collaboration of consuls, Senate and multitude. Outlining the various forms of constitution, their origins and, in the manner of Plato, their process of degeneration, he seems to be making a case for Roman imperial rule addressed to a Greek audience. (See Peter Green, *Alexander to Actium: The Historical Evolution of the Hellenistic Age* [Berkeley and Los Angeles: University of California Press, 1993].)

was no longer able to maintain the delicate balance within and between social classes, the chief social problem confronting the dominant elites was no longer the threat from below but, above all, their own self-destruction. In his political theory, as we have already seen, Cicero certainly guarded his flank against popular threats, including the redistribution of property; but his principal concern was to restore the unity and stability on which the property regime depended. The challenge he took on was to defend the primacy of property and the dominance of propertied classes while counselling the ruling class to self-restraint.

Cicero was born in 106 BC, the son of a fairly prosperous and prominent, though not senatorial, landed family. As a member of the equestrian rank and a 'new man', he was no doubt subjected to snobbery; but his family was well connected, and he enjoyed all the benefits of a gentlemanly life, including the best education. As a young student of law, he came into contact with the type of Roman statesmen who would be his political models throughout his career, upholders in his eyes of the ancestral constitution and austere exemplars of the republican virtue which was waning in his own turbulent time. His education also encompassed philosophy, and he spent some time in Athens, studying oratory and rhetoric. He came away from his philosophical education with a great admiration for Plato, yet also with a mild philosophical scepticism, based on the teachings of Philo of Larissa, and an element of Stoicism – its ethics rather than its epistemology or metaphysics – none of which he regarded as antithetical to Plato.

Returning to Rome to practise law, he entered so actively and successfully into politics that he went through the sequence of offices with remarkable speed, becoming *quaestor* at the age of thirty, performing financial and imperial duties assisting the provincial governor of Western Sicily. This also entitled him to enter the senate, and he was eventually elected – at the earliest possible age of forty-two – to the consulship, the highest office the republic could offer him. By now, he was well established as a defender of conservative republicanism, an opponent of agrarian and democratic reforms and regarded by conservative senators as an effective counter to popular leaders like Caesar and Catiline, aristocrats who – as their critics perceived them – pandered to the multitude. One of Cicero's main accomplishments was to defeat the agrarian reforms of the tribune Publius Servius Rullus; but by far his most famous political act was his defeat of Catiline, who was allegedly plotting to seize power with the support of the urban masses and dispossessed or indebted peasants.

This notable success may also, however, have contributed to Cicero's undoing. He dealt with the conspirators with a ruthlessness and disregard for the law which antagonized even conservatives. In any case, the political winds in Rome were shifting towards his enemies. He was driven into exile and the comforts of philosophy. He returned to Rome in 58 BC and in 51 was sent to Cilicia to fulfil the duties of proconsul, which were required of every former consul. In charge of the civil and military administration of this imperial province, he did a creditable job, extracting less profit from his post than was usual among Roman proconsuls. Although we should have no illusions about Cicero's attitude to wealth, including his own personal property (he was, among other things, an enthusiastic slum landlord[26]), by Roman standards he undoubtedly performed his duties with admirable rectitude, and even had one modest military success in his province. On his return to Rome, he found his beloved republic in a state of civil war, the opposing sides led by Caesar and Pompey with their respective private armies. Cicero sided with Pompey, regarding Caesar's victory and dictatorship as the end of the republic, and indeed the Roman state. But he never suffered at the hands of the triumphant Caesar, who, on Cicero's own testimony, treated him with the utmost courtesy. On the assassination of Caesar, Cicero allied himself with the assassins and became for a short while effectively ruler of Rome. When his allies were, in turn, defeated by Caesar's lieutenant, Marc Antony – whom Cicero had ferociously attacked – the new triumvirate proscribed their predecessors, including Cicero, and he was finally murdered by their soldiers in 43 BC.

Cicero is certainly not a systematic thinker, and even less a methodical philosopher in the manner of Plato or Aristotle. But certain principles emerge fairly unambiguously not only from major works such as the Pro Sestio (In Defence of Sestius), De Re Publica (The Republic), De Legibus (The Laws), and De Officiis (On Duties), but also from other speeches and letters. In what follows, we shall not try to follow a detailed line of argument in any single work, as we did in the case of Plato and Aristotle; but an effort will be made to assemble

---

26 Cicero's letters to his friend, Atticus, reveal an avid interest in his own properties and a keen eye for profit. It is hard not to be amused, for instance, at the following passage from one of his letters: 'Two of my shops have collapsed and the others are showing cracks, so that even the mice have moved elsewhere, to say nothing of the tenants. Other people call this a disaster, I don't call it even a nuisance. Ah Socrates, Socratics, I can never repay you! Heavens above, how utterly trivial such things appear to me! However, there is a building scheme under way, Vestorius advising and instigating, which will turn this loss into a source of profit' (Att. XVI.9, 1).

a more or less coherent political theory, tracing the connections among the essential principles laid out in his various works and considering their sources, significance and implications.

Although Cicero's political thought is commonly neglected now, it has been remarkably influential in the Western tradition, if only because of its enormous popularity in the seminal early modern period. European and American thinkers, especially from the sixteenth to the eighteenth century, found in his work, especially *On Duties*, a whole range of congenial ideas, some of which have led commentators to credit Cicero with an implausible modernity, despite his firm roots in antiquity. These ideas have been summed up as follows:

> ... the principles of natural law and justice and of universal moral equality; a patriotic and dedicated republicanism; a vigorous advocacy of liberty, impassioned rejection of tyranny, and persuasive justification of tyrannicide; a firm belief in constitutionalism, the rule of law, and the mixed constitution; a strong faith in the sanctity of private property, in the importance of its accumulation, and the opinion that the primary purpose of state and law was the preservation of property and property differentials; a conception of proportionate social and political equality, entailing a hierarchy of differential rights and duties; a vague ideal of rule by a 'natural aristocracy'; and a moderate and enlightened religious and epistemological skepticism.[27]

Cicero was not, of course, alone among ancient Greek and Roman thinkers to believe in some kind of moral equality, or to advocate liberty, the rule of law or the mixed constitution; and he was certainly not alone in his conception of social and political hierarchy or a species of 'proportionate' equality and rule by a natural aristocracy. What is more distinctive is his conception of natural law, which allows him to combine advocacy of aristocratic rule and political hierarchy with a principle of universal moral equality. This apparent contradiction would become a staple of Western political thought, especially in the early modern period, when ideas of natural human equality and the equal moral worth of all individuals were (as in the case of John Locke) accompanied by political hierarchy, and sometimes even used paradoxically (most notably by Thomas Hobbes) to justify not only hierarchy but absolute rule. Cicero, while certainly influenced by

---

27 N. Wood, *op. cit.*, p. 4.

Stoicism, developed the concept of natural law as the Stoics never did and is perhaps the first major thinker to elaborate this paradox. There are significant contrasts on this score between the Roman thinker and his classical Greek predecessors, Plato and Aristotle.

We have seen how Plato, writing in the context of Athenian democracy, challenged the democratic polis by positing a natural principle of inequality. This may not have meant that, in his view, natural inequalities among men were enough to account for the division between ruler and ruled; but that division itself was for him a natural and necessary principle, based on the partition of the soul between 'better' elements and 'worse', which is reproduced in the inevitable division of labour between those who work for a livelihood and those who govern them. Aristotle too insists that there is a universal and natural division between ruling elements and ruled, and in his ideal polis that division is reflected in the distinction between the 'conditions' and 'parts' of the polis.

Cicero has a different approach to the question of inequality. He certainly shares the views of Plato and Aristotle on the necessity of political inequality. He even has a notion of the bipartite soul, which, as we saw in Laelius's speech in the *Republic*, he explicitly translates into a principle of political and imperial hierarchy. As he makes particularly clear in *On Duties* and elsewhere, he certainly believes in a social division of labour which subordinates men in base and vulgar occupations to those who live a gentlemanly life. At the same time, he follows the Stoics in their conception of a cosmos permeated by a universal principle of reason, which not only governs the universe but resides in every human soul. This divine rational principle takes the form of absolute, universal, immutable and eternal laws, which regulate the cosmic order and establish the ethical norms of human behaviour. All human beings are, in principle, innately capable of knowing these natural laws, since they all partake of the same cosmic reason; and this innate and universal reason constitutes a universal community, a cosmopolis, to which all human beings, in all times and places, belong.

We have, of course, already encountered the kind of cosmopolitan principle that is able to coexist, perhaps even to reinforce, the distinction between rulers and ruled. But, especially when combined, as it is for Cicero, with both the bipartite soul ruled out by early Stoic theories of the cosmic order, and an unambiguous commitment to an inegalitarian political order, the Roman Republic dominated by an aristocracy, this principle appears paradoxical enough to require explanation. It could simply be dismissed as an irreducible inconsistency; but, since Cicero, more statesman than philosopher, is at pains to elaborate the concept of natural law in a way the Stoic philosophers themselves never did, it is at least worth exploring what purposes it served in the pursuit of his political aims.

Moral Equality, Political Inequality

Let us first place the question in a longer historical perspective. Western political theory did not invent the notion of human equality. Ancient Chinese philosophy, for example, has its own forms of natural egalitarianism. But Western political theory, at least at certain seminal moments in its history, confronted the very specific problem of finding ways to explain and justify domination *on the basis* of natural equality. Or, to put it another way, given the assumption of equality, it had to find ways of explaining and justifying domination as such. The notion of natural equality became a troublesome issue when and because it was coupled with a challenge to the very idea of rule and domination. As long as the principle of domination was more or less unchallenged on its own terms – whether as the mandate of heaven or even simply on the basis of tradition – it was perfectly compatible with fundamental human equality. But once the principle of domination itself was thrown into serious question, it was a very different matter. The burden of justification fell much more heavily on human inequality, as a natural basis for social inequality and domination; and in those circumstances, a notion of natural equality could represent a serious threat to dominant elites. When people questioned authority by invoking natural equality, theoretical and ideological strategies had to be devised to overcome that threat and to turn democratic ideas against themselves.

The history of this strategy begins in ancient Greece. The principle of domination was, as we saw, challenged there, in theory and practice, in particular ways that distinguished it from other high civilizations. In the community of citizens that constituted the ancient Greek polis, the principal political relation was not between rulers and subjects but among citizens. This did not mean that citizens were socially or economically equal; but landlords and peasants belonged to the same body of citizens, sharing a civic equality. This produced a new political sphere, in which deep social divisions, and class conflicts in particular, played themselves out in political terms, not just in overt struggles for power but in the daily deliberations and debates of assemblies and juries. This also meant that, probably for the first time in history, there could be a significant tension between economic inequality and political equality.

This is the context in which notions of equality presented new problems for those wanting to justify domination; and much of ancient Greek philosophy, as we have seen, was motivated by the need to deal with those problems. In challenging democracy and trying to defend a principle of social hierarchy, Plato, for instance, opted for the strategy of finding a new, supra- if not supernatural principle of hierarchy which transcended any natural equality. This seemed the safest strategy in a context where democracy was a real challenge to dominant elites. Yet the separation of civic equality and class inequality had opened up new possibilities. Until then, it had always been clear that the state represented domination, even, or especially, where men were assumed to be naturally equal. But now, the state itself – in fact, the state above all – represented equality. In spite of all existing social inequalities, all citizens were equal in their new political identity. This meant that relations of domination could be disguised in wholly new ways, if only they could be clothed in the mantle of citizenship and civic equality. This was not, of course, a simple matter; but, as we saw, something like this strategy was adopted by Alexander the Great and his successors, as they claimed the values of the polis, and even of democracy, in defence of the new imperial cosmopolis.

Propertied elites in republican Rome confronted some of the same problems as their Greek counterparts. Here too they were obliged to reach political accommodations with the lower classes to preserve social order and safeguard their own property, and here too landlords and peasants shared a political identity as citizens. But there were also significant differences between the Roman Republic and Athenian democracy, which allowed, or required, different ideological strategies. The republic was clearly dominated by the senatorial aristocracy, its dominance acknowledged even in the civic sphere; the Romans never developed a notion of one citizen, one vote but counted only group votes; the identity of citizenship did not dissolve or overshadow the division between patricians and plebeians, patrons and clients, the Senate and the Roman People; private property not only had a clearer legal definition but also a more decisive political priority; and Rome's vast territorial empire was very different from the loose network of Athenian alliances and dependencies.

As the republic disintegrated in the time of Cicero, the most urgent issue facing the senatorial aristocracy was not a threat from below but its own self-destruction. Cicero's political theory was clearly a response to this crisis of the Roman aristocracy. His perception of the crisis and its causes undoubtedly shaped his theoretical responses and may, among other things, give us some insight into his conception of natural law.

Cicero traces the republican decline to the moment of the Gracchi, as he explains in *In Defence of Sestius*. A staunch opponent of redistributive agrarian reforms and members of the ruling class who advocate them, he regards this as the moment when the golden age of the republic ended. From then on, the senatorial elite was fatally divided between those who wanted to preserve senatorial authority and ancient traditions, the *mos maiorum* or customs of their ancestors, and those who pandered to the multitude by supporting the tribunate, agrarian reforms and the rights of popular assemblies in opposition to the senate. This division between *optimates* and *populares*, which reached a peak in the Catilinarian conspiracy, remains, in Cicero's eyes, a mortal danger to civic peace and stability; and the responsibility lies squarely with the *populares*.

Cicero sets his major work on the fundamental principles of the state, the *Republic*, in the time of the Gracchi, though it is clearly a comment on his own day. The work is perhaps also, as some commentators have suggested, a response to Lucretius's *De Rerum Natura*, which was being widely read in elite circles, because Cicero seems to regard its Epicurean principles as a threat to civic life and the *mos maiorum*. In the dialogue, Cicero unambiguously aligns himself with the distinguished participants who are well-known enemies of the Gracchi. These are men whom Cicero venerates as personifications of the old traditions and the *mos maiorum*; and he holds them up as models in his own time of strife, in which the senatorial elite is driven instead by insatiable greed for power and wealth, without the constraints of tradition, noble purpose or civic duty. Cicero hopes to restore a republic marked by *cum dignitate otium*, peace or leisure with dignity – a slogan that suggests both his wish for a dignified civic harmony in which every man receives what he deserves according to his worth, and also the aristocratic aspiration to a life of leisure with dignity.

Under the circumstances as Cicero perceives them, how might the Roman ruling class be persuaded to return to the ways of its ancestors? How might they be persuaded to adopt the *mos maiorum* as their guiding principle and to restore a republic marked by civic peace and dignity, a harmonious state in which rights and rewards are properly distributed among men according to their worth, on the principle of proportionate equality, and where both the state and its ruling citizens enjoy *cum dignitate otium*?

Certain principles are obviously necessary to his purpose. What Cicero has to say about the state and property is strategically indispensable. We saw in our discussion of the Stoics that, in his view, 'it is the peculiar function of the state and the city to guarantee to every man the free and undisturbed control of his own particular property'; and we also saw how redistributive land reforms – in which 'a man who never had any property should take possession of lands that had been occupied for many years or even generations, and that he who had them before should lose possession of them' – violate the principles of equity. These passages are significant not only because they display his commitment to the sanctity of property, his dedication to the interests of the landed classes, and his strong opposition to reforms and reformers; but also because of what they suggest about Cicero's conception of the state. What is striking is not only that he attaches such importance to the protection of property as an, if not the, essential purpose of the state, but the very fact that he offers a formal definition of the state in a way that no Western philosopher had done before.

As we have seen, Rome's well defined conception of exclusive property was accompanied by a particular distinction between public and private. This invited a definition of the public sphere, specifically the state, in a way that Greek experience did not. Just as the Greeks never elaborated a clear idea of property, they never went beyond the notion of the public sphere, the polis, as synonymous with the community of citizens. The Roman Republic, and the Roman law, encouraged a perception of a clearly defined public sphere and a conception of the state as a formal entity apart from the citizens who comprised it, even distinct from the particular persons who governed them at any given moment. Cicero takes on the challenge of defining the state in a manner befitting the Roman conception of property and the relation between property and state. He does this for fairly obvious reasons. His ideal ruling class is one that combines the enjoyment and enlargement of their estates with the demands of civic virtue, and so he sets himself the task of conceptualizing the relation between public sphere and private in such a way as to maintain the sanctity of private property while stressing public duty.

At the heart of his definition is his characterization of the state as 'a union of a large number of men in agreement in respect to what is right and just and associated in the common interest'.[28] Justice and the common interest are inextricably linked in Cicero's formulation, which requires that, in all matters private and public, we should give each person his due, his *dignitas,* while preserving the common interest. To give each person his due means that everyone should refrain from injuring another without due cause, keep promises and contracts, and

---

28 *Rep.* I, 39.

respect all property, private and public. But what is due to any person depends on his worth; and Cicero leaves us in no doubt that, whatever else may determine the value of a man, wealth and birth are critical, and the life of a gentleman is worth more than that of a labourer. These principles of justice are dictated by natural law, contrary to philosophers, notably Epicureans and Sceptics, who have suggested that justice is merely conventional. There is such a thing as natural justice, argues Cicero; and it must also be reflected in customary and statutory law. If man-made laws do not conform to the dictates of natural law, they are not true law; and a state governed by such laws is not a true state.

The hierarchy of law, descending from the law of nature, is at the centre of Cicero's political theory. Law, he writes,

> is not a product of human thought, nor is it any enactment of peoples, but something eternal which rules the whole universe by its wisdom in command and prohibition. Thus they have been accustomed to say that Law is the primal and ultimate mind of God, whose reason directs all things either by compulsion or restraint. Wherefore that Law which the gods have given to the human race has been justly praised; for it is the reason and mind of a wise lawgiver applied to command and prohibition.[29]

In the *Republic*, having insisted on the universality and immutability of true law, he goes on to warn that 'We cannot be freed from its obligations by senate or people'.

By placing natural justice at the heart of his conception of the state, Cicero has certainly ascribed some kind of moral purpose to the state. Yet that purpose is impossible to dissociate from his notion of the common interest, which has less to do with any higher moral goal than with the mundane interests of property, peace, security and material well-being. In that respect, his view of the state and its purpose appears to have more in common with Protagoras than with Plato, being less concerned with the fulfilment of some higher human nature than with the normal comforts of everyday life. In the *Laws*, his praise of human rationality includes an appreciation of the practical arts not so very different from that of Protagoras; and there is even a certain similarity between Cicero's conception of justice as an innate and universal human sense, which enables people to live together in comfort

---

29 *Laws* II, 8.

and harmony, enjoying the benefits of reason and the arts, and Protagoras's conception of the innate and universal sense of justice and respect for others which make possible the civilized, comfortable life of the polis.

But Cicero's political conclusions are different from those of Protagoras. He comes down on the side of Plato and his antidemocratic judgments on the political capacities of shoemakers and smiths. In his speech, 'In Defence of Flaccus', this great admirer of Greek culture reveals his strong dislike of Athenian democracy, attacking 'those cobblers and belt-makers', those 'craftsmen, shopkeepers and all the dregs' in the Assembly, who were the ruin of democratic Athens and represent a salutary lesson to the Roman Republic's own brand of demagogues. In the *Laws*, as well as other works and speeches, he makes very clear his disdain for those engaged in menial occupations and his utter contempt for the poor, as if they were criminals, while heaping praise on occupations appropriate to gentlemen, such as war, politics or philosophy, and farming or commerce on a large scale. The ideal gentleman and political leader is the substantial landed proprietor, and even the profits of commerce should ideally be invested in land.

It is not surprising, then, that when, in the *Republic*, Cicero surveys the various types of constitution, he concludes that, of the simple types – kingship, aristocracy and democracy – democracy is clearly the worst. Democratic equality, even when the demos governs wisely, violates the principles of justice and equity by denying men their just – unequal – deserts: 'For when equal honour is given to the highest and the lowest – for men of both types must exist in every nation – then this very "fairness" is most unfair; but this cannot happen in states ruled by their best citizens.'[30] The best type of state is a mixed constitution, striking a balance in the class conflict between rich and poor, which, while granting some degree of *libertas* to every man, distributes it unequally according to the unequal *dignitas* among its citizens. As in the Roman Republic, there is a hierarchy of social orders, and with it a hierarchical order of political rights.

Cicero thus manages to combine what appear to be democratic principles of arithmetic equality with an aristocratic notion of 'proportionate' equality, attributing to all men a sense of justice in the manner of Protagoras, while identifying justice with social and political hierarchy in the manner of Plato. Cicero sees no contradictions between his own political principles and Plato's and presents himself

30 *Rep.* I, 53.

as following in the Athenian philosopher's footsteps, even down to the titles of his two major works in political theory. But he distinguishes himself from his great predecessor on the grounds that Plato's philosophy was too abstractly utopian, while his own intentions are very explicitly political and practical. It is also possible that the egalitarian dangers of the cosmopolitan idea seemed less immediate to a defender of the propertied elites in republican Rome, where their supremacy was effectively unchallenged, than a principle of equality seemed to propertied classes in democratic Athens.

It may be useful here to recall the role played by 'unwritten law' in Athenian democracy. While democrats – philosophers, dramatists or ordinary citizens – might remain wedded to the idea of universal laws, such as obligations of kinship or reverence for the gods, the relation between such laws and the *nomoi* of the polis had become an urgent practical issue in ways that put unwritten laws in question altogether, whether they were man-made or decreed by nature. We witnessed the tensions between unwritten, timeless laws and civic law in Sophocles's *Antigone*; but they were particularly visible when, after the oligarchic coup of the Thirty Tyrants, the conflicts between democrats and oligarchs prompted the restored democracy to prohibit the invocation of unwritten law because of its deeply oligarchic associations. For supporters of democracy, it was not simply a question of committing laws to writing in order to make them known to all citizens and protect them from aristocratic judges. More fundamentally, the notion of unwritten law had come to be identified with oligarchic principles of natural inequality, the idea that men were unequal by *physis*, which, in the eyes of democrats, had been rightfully challenged by civic equality. Plato, of course, was the principal philosophical exponent of this oligarchic view, especially in his identification of justice with inequality, on the basis of a higher principle of cosmic order. For his democratic opponents, unwritten law represented injustice, not justice, and men had to turn to the laws of the polis to get their just deserts. The polis and its *nomoi*, as we saw in Greek drama, had also replaced the endless chaos of blood vengeance and irrational violence. In that sense it was civic law, not unwritten laws of nature, that represented the triumph of reason and 'Holy Persuasion'.

In Cicero's conception of natural law we see something quite different. It is certainly true that his natural law included norms of behaviour that would have been congenial to democrats no less than oligarchs, as would his conception of a universal moral equality among all men. But inscribed in his universal law of nature and the transcendent laws of reason is a fundamental human inequality, which means that the principles of oligarchy are divinely ordained and superior to civic law. It is not for nothing that he regarded himself as a follower of Plato. His notion of natural law can, at least in this respect, indeed be understood as a translation of Plato's ethereal philosophy into the idiom of mundane Roman politics.

The combination of natural law and proportionate equality, as Cicero presents it, seems to come down to this: equality of obligation, inequality of rights. With his specific political project in mind, it is not surprising that the burden of natural law is 'restraint', 'prohibition' and 'compulsion' – which applies to all classes, calling upon elites to act with restraint and the people to stay in their place. In the immediate historical and political circumstances confronted by the Roman statesman, the advantages of his formula are clear. It underwrites precisely the kind of 'mixed constitution' he favours, granting all citizens a certain moral and even political status, while vesting rule in an aristocratic elite. It also has the virtue of calling an unruly aristocracy to order, reining in its excesses while respecting its property and its political dominance. Finally, although Cicero has remarkably little to say about the empire he served and from which he benefitted personally, his political formula has its uses in defending Roman imperialism, giving philosophical support to the Roman idea of a benevolent empire, in which the superior rule the inferior in the interests of both, according to the law of nature.

In this defence of empire, as in its Hellenistic predecessors, the idea of the cosmopolis is combined with, or rather derived from, the civic ideology descended from the polis. On the one hand, the Roman Empire depended in large part on the so-called municipal system, an alliance of ostensibly self-governing units dominated by local aristocracies. And, on the other hand, just as Alexander had defined his imperial rule as cosmopolitan, the idea of the cosmopolis could be translated into the 'universal' Roman Empire, which would extend Roman citizenship far beyond the borders of metropolitan Rome. Citizenship, of course, no longer meant what it had done in the democratic polis, but it was an effective ideological instrument of imperial hegemony. Eventually, that ideology would transmute the Roman imperial cosmopolis, together with the natural law that governed it, into the 'universal Church' of Christianity.

Roman Christianity: From Paul to Augustine

At least to the secular imagination, the roots of Christianity in the specific conditions of the Roman Empire seem all but self-evident. The peculiar blend that is Christian theology could hardly have been born anywhere else, amalgamating Judaic monotheism, Greco-Roman paganism, the Greek philosophical tradition, the legacy of Hellenistic kingship (and Alexander's self-deification) in the Roman imperial idea, together with Rome's universalistic aspirations and the Roman law.

The emergence of the specifically Roman Christianity that would from then on shape the tradition of Western political theory can be best understood by tracing the transformation of the Christian faith from an essentially tribal sect into a universal(ist) religion, and from a rebellious Jewish faction into an ideological bedrock of empire. The story of that transformation begins with Paul of Tarsus and culminates in Augustine of Hippo. Its essence is the creation of a distinctive universalism which allows the supreme omnipotent authority of one God to coexist with the more or less absolute temporal powers of emperors and kings, and the equality of all humanity before God with the most extreme social inequalities and rigid earthly hierarchies – not unlike the delicate balance we have already encountered in the modified cosmopolitanism of Roman Stoicism and Cicero's concept of natural law.

The doctrinal balance effected by Roman Christianity had very particular social, political and cultural conditions. It certainly presupposed the distinctive imperial blend perfectly embodied in Saul of Tarsus/St Paul, Hellenized Jew and (perhaps) Roman citizen.[31] But, while the capital of empire would move from west to east, from Rome to Constantinople, with the establishment of Christianity as the imperial religion by the Emperor Constantine in the fourth century AD, the triumph and elaboration of Pauline Christianity depended on the increasing divergence of Eastern and Western empires, which saw the emergence of a distinctively Latin theology rooted in the western provinces and reaching fruition in Romanized North Africa.

Christianity developed in tandem with the imperial state. The development of Christian doctrine, its conception of divinity and the relation of humanity to God, is inextricably bound up with the Roman imperial idea, which underwent significant changes in the first few centuries of the Christian era. As imperial state displaced the old republic and developed according to a logic of its own, the early imperial myth of the *princeps* governing in tandem with the senate

---

31 There has been considerable debate about the Roman citizenship attributed to Paul in *Acts*. But even those who question it are prepared to accept that, at the very least, he would most likely have belonged to a kind of *politeuma*, a community granted certain autonomous rights by the Roman Empire, which, if not actually amounting to Roman citizenship, enjoyed some analogous freedoms and privileges.

inevitably gave way to the emperor conceived as absolute *dominus*. At the same time, the republican notion of empire as the product of legitimate conquests by the city-state of Rome would be replaced by a more cosmopolitan idea of a 'supra-national world empire', in which all peoples were equally ruled by one absolute ruler no longer centred just in Rome.[32] It is surely not fanciful to see the Christianization of the empire as the cultural completion of this transformation.

The Empire went through a crisis in the mid-third century, its unity threatened by fatal fragmentation and its frontiers collapsing. When it re-emerged for a time with new vigour, it was thanks to a military and bureaucratic revolution, which would be completed by the Christian emperor, Constantine, and buttressed ideologically by his conversion of the empire to Christianity. But the consolidation of the state bureaucracy did not mean a weakening of the imperial aristocracy. On the contrary, it produced a new and larger ruling class, an 'aristocracy of service', whose military and official functions gave its members unparalleled access to wealth.[33] At the same time, the western provinces, where the gulf between rich and poor was growing ever wider, were increasingly dominated by the landed aristocracy, which had amassed wealth estimated on average at five times that of the first-century senatorial class. This also meant a significant change in the urban culture of the empire, as the public life of ancient civic communities gave way to inward-looking domesticity, and aristocratic civil benefaction gave way to lavish displays of private wealth.

Both the consolidation of the imperial state and the ascendant aristocracy, especially in the west, shaped the evolution of Christian theology. While changes in the imperial idea can persuasively be represented as the triumph of the Hellenistic East over the Roman West, and eastern notions of kingship over Roman republicanism, there is another thread in the process which belongs specifically to Western Christianity. Byzantine 'Caesaropapism' emerged in the east, a unity of religion and state in which Christianity acknowledged its subordination to political authority, leaving a spiritual residue of mysticism outside the state. By contrast, the West would eventually produce its distinctive notion of two equal powers, temporal and spiritual, each

---

32 Wolfgang Kunkel, *An Introduction to Roman Legal and Constitutional History*, 2nd edn. (transl. J.M. Kelley) (Oxford: Clarendon Press, 1973), pp. 50–1, 62–3.

33 Peter Brown, *The World of Late Antiquity: From Marcus Aurelius to Muhammad* (London: Thames and Hudson, 1971), pp. 24–7.

with its own earthly institutions and hierarchies. The idea of two equal powers may always have been as much myth as reality, but it points to certain underlying features of the Western empire which decisively shaped its theological formation.

The sources of Western Christian dualism may be found in social and cultural conditions we have already encountered in our discussion of the Roman property regime and the distinctive public/private dichotomy that it engendered. The Romans, in their very specific social conditions, elaborated a conceptual apparatus which lent itself particularly well to apprehending distinct but coexisting structures of authority – as in their conceptions of property and state, or *dominium* and *imperium*. The same distinctions could be used to modify the principles of universality and commonality, such as those established by the Stoics, allowing the particular and private to intrude upon the universal and common.

So, for instance, Seneca (*c*.3 BC–AD 65) explicates Stoic doctrine by demonstrating how all things can be considered common, at least to wise men, while still remaining individual and private property. He draws a significant analogy with the rights of the emperor: 'all things are [Caesar's] by right of his authority [*imperio*]'; yet at the same time the sense in which everything is his by right of 'imperium' must be distinguished from the way things belong to him as his own personal property by right of inheritance, 'by actual right and ownership', or *dominium*. Seneca then goes on to apply the analogy to the gods, allowing us to trace the conceptual logic that joins the idea of divine authority to Roman conceptions of property: 'while it is true that all things belong to the gods, all things are not consecrated to the gods, and . . . only in the case of the things that religion has assigned to a divinity is it possible to discover sacrilege.'[34]

Here, then, was a way of thinking about property and spheres of authority that made it possible to insist on one universal cosmic *logos,* a universal and common natural law, the equality of all human beings, and even the exclusive supremacy of one omnipotent God; while still declaring the sanctity of private property, the legitimacy of social inequality and the absolute authority of earthly governments, including those that by any reasonable standard could be judged as defying the ethical principles of divine or natural law. It was a way of thinking that reflected the historical realities of a cosmopolitan empire, which appealed to universalistic principles to sustain its legitimacy, while

---

34 *On Benefits*, VII, vi–vii.

coexisting with, and supporting, a regime of private property of an unprecedented kind: a distinctive union of a powerful state and strong private property quite different, as we have seen, from other ancient high civilizations. Much of Roman Stoic philosophy, to say nothing of the Roman law, was dedicated to maintaining this distinctive balance, defending the claims of the state's *imperium* while consolidating the sanctity of private *dominium*. It required only minor conceptual adjustments to translate this dualistic logic, with its distinctive division between two spheres of authority, into the particularly Western Christian division of secular and spiritual realms.

The Bible attributes to Jesus himself the principle that we should 'Render unto Caesar the things which are Caesar's, and unto God the things that are God's.' Stated in this simple form, the principle is nicely consistent with Seneca's modified Stoicism. While certainly not questioning the supremacy of God, the universality of His divine law or His 'ownership' of everything in this world and beyond, it nonetheless finds room for Caesar's realm of absolute authority. God's cosmic *imperium* coexists with Caesar's earthly *dominium*, just as Caesar's temporal *imperium* coexists with the private *dominium* of the Empire's propertied citizens.

It was Paul, the founder of Christianity as we know it, who, in his defence of absolute obedience to earthly powers, began the process of translating into systematic Christian theology the doctrine of universal divinity and the spiritual equality of all human beings before God, combined with the earthly inequalities of property, social hierarchy and absolute political authority. He establishes his universalistic principles by dissociating Christianity from Jewish law, replacing the particularism of an essentially tribal religion with a transcendent moral doctrine that applies equally to all human beings, Greeks or Romans no less than Jews, and slaves no less than masters. The 'righteousness of God', he writes, manifests itself apart from any law. In this, he belongs to Hellenistic and Stoic traditions of cosmopolitanism, which he may have learned not only from Stoic philosophy but from the *Septuagint,* the Hellenistic Greek translation of the Old Testament, where the Hebrew Bible's Jewish exclusiveness is modified by a certain cosmopolitan opening to gentiles.[35] Yet Paul's universalism is a two-edged sword. On the one hand, it asserts the equal moral value of all human beings. On the other hand, it leaves completely unchallenged,

---

35 For a discussion of Paul and the *Septuagint*, see Calvin Roetzel, *Paul: The Man and the Myth* (Edinburgh: T. & T. Clark, 1999), esp. pp. 16–17.

indeed supports, the social inequalities of the temporal sphere, enjoining their acceptance, and emphatically asserts the absolute authority of the secular state:

> Let every soul be in subjection to the higher authorities, for there is no authority except from God, and those who exist are ordained by God. Therefore he who resists the authority, withstands the ordinance of God; and those who withstand will receive to themselves judgment. For rulers are not a terror to the good work, but to the evil. Do you desire to have no fear of the authority? Do that which is good, and you will have praise from the same, for he is a servant of God to you for good. But if you do that which is evil, be afraid, for he doesn't bear the sword in vain; for he is a servant of God, an avenger for wrath to him who does evil. Therefore you need to be in subjection, not only because of the wrath, but also for conscience's sake. For this reason you also pay taxes, for they are servants of God's service, attending continually on this very thing. Give therefore to everyone what you owe: taxes to whom taxes are due; customs to whom customs; respect to whom respect; honor to whom honor.[36]

This declaration of the emperor's divinely ordained authority can be interpreted in more than one way. The ideology supporting the first Christian emperor, Constantine, as spelled out by the Bishop Eusebius in his famous oration in praise of Constantine (which is hard to match in its obsequious grandiosity), would identify the emperor as God's representative, even his partner, the earthly embodiment of the divine *logos*. But as far-reaching in its consequences as this doctrine certainly was, there is in Pauline theology another theme, which would be fully elaborated only in the Christian West, in specifically western conditions: the emperor not as God's representative on earth or personification of the divine *logos* but as the (to be sure, divinely ordained) secular ruler of a fallen humanity.

It may be useful to consider the context in which Paul wrote his Epistle to the Romans and the significance his contemporaries would have attached to his assertion of universalistic, cosmopolitan principles against the particularism of the Jewish law. Apart from any other implications of Pauline doctrine, and whether a conflict between universalist 'Hellenists' and particularist 'Hebrews' ever actually took place

---

36 Romans 13.

among the early Christians, Paul's universalism had some very obvious
advantages for the pagan Roman authorities and imperial elites. Christianity may have begun as a movement of the urban poor; but Paul's
message to the prosperous classes was decidedly more reassuring than
were, for instance, the convictions of other early Jewish Christians
who, following Jesus, preached an egalitarianism not confined to the
moral or spiritual sphere, repudiating materialistic values and calling
upon Christians to give up their wealth to their community. Even Paul's
emphasis on salvation by faith rather than works had clear advantages
to those who stood to lose from strict adherence to the social Gospel.

Slavery itself was compatible with Paul's doctrine of universal
equality. He calls upon servants to 'be obedient to them that are your
masters according to the flesh, with fear and trembling, in singleness
of your heart, as unto Christ . . . knowing that whatsoever good thing
any man doeth, the same shall he receive of the Lord, whether he be
bond or free.'[37] Pauline principles oblige the master to recognize his
servant's moral equality by treating him well, but they represent no
challenge to the institution of slavery.

Paul's most basic theological principles would also have been far
more congenial to Roman state authorities than were Judaism or Jewish
Christianity. At a time when rebellious Jews were resisting Roman
hegemony and refusing to acknowledge the divinity of the emperor,
while Jewish Christians pointedly denied the divinity of Caesar by
asserting the lordship of Christ, Paul's universalistic attack on Jewish
particularism, and his replacement of Jewish monotheism with a
cosmopolitanism which at the same time renders unto Caesar the things
that are Caesar's, nicely undercut any such challenge to imperial authority. It gave support to the secular universalism of the Roman Empire,
replacing, among other things, the temporal pretensions of the Jewish
law with a universalistic monotheism that, unlike the Jewish version,
left Caesar's authority intact.

Pauline Christianity, in other words, effected an adaptation of universalism analogous to the changes in Stoic doctrine, which blunted its
egalitarian implications and its potential challenge to existing authorities, making the doctrine more congenial to Roman elites. It might
be said that, like the Roman Stoics, Paul – who was familiar with and
influenced by Stoic philosophy – achieved this effect by reintroducing
a kind of dualism that allowed a separation between, on the one hand,

---

37 Ephesians 6: 5–9. See also Paul's Epistle to Philemon, in which he asks a wealthy
Christian to receive humanely the escaped slave whom Paul is sending back to him.

the moral or spiritual sphere, in which the cosmic *logos* dictated a universal equality, and, on the other hand, the material world in which social inequalities and even slavery prevailed and political authority was entitled to impose an absolute and universal obedience, just as masters could compel their slaves.

But Christianity required its own distinctive means of dividing the spheres of authority. For the Stoics, it was enough to acknowledge that, in the real world, not all human beings are wise, so that the ordinary earthly life of ordinary earthly men and women must be governed by some kind of practical ethics and a legalism tempered by equity. The Stoic case for Roman property, political hierarchy and empire was obviously strengthened by attempts to replace the Early Stoic monism with something like Platonic principles of rule and subordination. But for the most part, Roman Stoics, as we saw, contented themselves with concentrating on the field of ethics unencumbered by deeper speculations on psychology, cosmology or metaphysics. Christianity required something more.

There would, of course, emerge a Neoplatonist strand in Christianity, which adapted Plato's conception of a transcendent realm beyond empirical reality and posited the One, the ultimate unitary and unknowable divine reality from which all other levels of reality emanated. Platonic philosophy could, to be sure, supply a cosmic principle of rule and subordination, which could be used – as some Stoics did use it – to justify earthly hierarchies; and perhaps the idea of the One from which descending orders of reality all emanated could be invoked in support of the emperor's absolute power, for instance in the manner of Eusebius and his invocation of the divine *logos* personified in Constantine. The old Platonic opposition of sensible and intelligible worlds could also lend support to a Pauline Christian dualism. But Christian Neoplatonism was not particularly well suited to give positive support to existing social and political arrangements. It tended rather to devalue earthly existence and the material realm, and encouraged Christians to seek mystical release from it, always striving to attain the spiritual realm and assimilate the human soul to God as much as possible. This could no doubt encourage a passive acceptance of worldly injustice and in this way support existing authorities at least by default; but it did little to bolster the claims of property and state. For Christians a defence of the Roman social, political and imperial order posed a very particular challenge, in the face of a theological universalism, governed by one omnipotent God; and Western Christianity met that challenge in very particular ways.

In the final analysis, the whole Pauline structure of dual authority depended on the concept of sin. It is a striking fact that the emphasis on sin was a distinctly Western phenomenon; and while it would be foolish to explain this solely in relation to the ideological requirements of Roman hegemony, it would be no less foolish to ignore the role of sin in buttressing the principle of 'render unto Caesar'. Earthly governments and total obedience to them are necessary, according to this version of Christianity, because and only because human beings are sinful by nature. It is true that, for Paul, Christ represented salvation from the universal taint of sin, but in this life, if not the next, there was no escaping human sinfulness; and that made Caesar's authority an unavoidable necessity. The principle that human sinfulness legitimates earthly authorities, already present in Paul, would reach its full development in Augustine; and here begins a long tradition in Western political theory, which attributes the necessity and legitimacy of private property as well as earthly government to the fallen condition of humanity.

At the same time, among the earthly institutions that organize this fallen world, there is the Church – and here too the distinctiveness of Western Christianity is manifest. The focus on the role and structures of the Church belongs to the West no less than does the emphasis on sin and personal salvation. In the development of Christianity from the Eastern Roman Empire through Byzantium, the state effectively became the Church. The empire was the Church on earth, as the emperor was its head. The Western approach was different. Here, the Church was responsible for organizing the personal salvation of Christians, who could have no hope of seeing true harmony and justice in this world and who were obliged to rely on Caesar – not as sacred representative of God on earth but as profane political authority – to regulate their fallen lives.

The Church, in fact, became a parallel structure, a mirror image of the Roman state, in which religious functions were conceived as offices. Even the outlines of the Western Roman social hierarchy were mirrored in the Church, with bishops playing the part of the landed senatorial aristocracy. Indeed, the ecclesiastical aristocracy tended to be drawn from the same social source; and the episcopacy would become one of the landed aristocracy's principal institutions, a relocation of aristocratic power at a time when secular authority was crumbling.[38] Western bishops were, in fact and in conception, the product of Rome's distinctive social order, the unique autonomy of landed property and the predominance of aristocracy. They would

---

38 Patrick Geary, *Before France and Germany: The Creation and Transformation of the Merovingian World* (New York and Oxford: Oxford University Press, 1988), pp. 32ff.

continue to represent as much a secular as an ecclesiastical power; and the particular development of Western Christianity would, as we shall see in the next chapter, continue to mirror the destiny of landed aristocracies, sometimes reflecting their dominance and at other times manipulated by kings engaged in centralizing projects against aristocratic autonomy.

It is one of history's many ironies that, while the empire collapsed in the west, as the imperial state gave way to a fragmented order dominated by the landed aristocracy, it was the west that preserved Roman imperial structures and institutions, in the hierarchy of the Church. While the seeds of these developments are already present in Paul's *Epistles*, a truly Roman, Latin theology emerged only at the end of the second century. For a long time, the culture of educated Christian elites was practically indistinguishable from that of their pagan fellow citizens, with an emphasis on literature and rhetoric, in contrast to the philosophical concerns of the east.[39] It should by now be no surprise that the first major figure in the development of a distinctively Western theology, the son of a Roman centurion based in Carthage, was trained in Roman law and that, in the absence of any Latin theological tradition, he drew on the concepts and language of the Roman law. Tertullian's legalistic temperament and training may also help to explain his particular emphasis on sin; and his doctrine of original sin (he has even been credited with inventing the term), as inherited by every human individual from Adam, made each member of humankind the bearer of guilt – a doctrine perhaps particularly well suited to a theology that conceived of the cosmic relationship between God and humanity in general in legalistic terms, on the analogy of secular crime, judgment, and punishment or pardon. At any rate, Western Christianity would thereafter continue to develop under this legalistic influence. Tertullian's legalism can hardly be just the accidental consequence of his personal experience. He was surely a creature of the Western Roman Empire; and against the background of Pauline doctrine and its place in imperial history, there is nothing surprising about the reflection of Roman institutions and the Roman law in the organization and teachings of the Church.

The imperial model of church organization was also most fully spelled out in Carthage, when, in the third century, Cyprian, bishop of Carthage and a Roman citizen of noble birth, elaborated the most authoritative Latin doctrine on the hierarchy of the Church in his *De*

---

39 *Ibid.*, p. 31.

Catholicae Ecclesiae Unitate (*On the Unity of the Catholic Church*).
But by far the most important product of the western empire – yet
again based in North Africa – was Augustine, bishop of Hippo.

Augustine of Hippo

Augustine's masterpiece, the *City of God*, is conventionally taught in
English-speaking universities as a classic of medieval political thought;
but, while it profoundly influenced medieval Christianity, it is very
much a product of the late Roman Empire. It is precisely his engagement
with imperial realities that compelled him to break new ground, not
only in theology but in political theory. In his interrogation of the
relation between Christianity and empire, which took to new extremes
the dualism of St Paul and his doctrine of obedience to even the most
sinful of temporal powers, Augustine departed from the classical
conception of the state and its moral purpose and in so doing opened
new questions about political obedience and obligation.

Augustine was born in North Africa in 354, to a Christian mother
and a pagan father of the curial class – the prosperous, if not aristocratic, class from which local magistrates were drawn and who were
responsible for funding various public functions. After studying and
teaching, first in Rome and then in Milan, and having flirted with
Manichaeism and Scepticism, he finally underwent his own conversion
to Christianity, which was powerfully influenced by Neoplatonism. He
was particularly affected by its idea of God as spirit and the conception
of evil as withdrawal from God rather than an independent malign
force, but also by the belief in the possibility of attaining virtue in
this life through philosophical contemplation – a belief he would later
abandon. Throughout his life, he enjoyed the friendship and patronage
of the Romanized aristocracy; and, after spending much of his youth
in the fleshpots of Rome, he became bishop of Hippo in his native
North Africa in 395.

This was the granary of the empire, a land of huge estates, worked
not by slaves but by peasants, many of them dependent. Augustine's
life in the late empire was a time of acute economic and social strife
in the region, plagued by agricultural decline, rural unrest, popular
revolts against Roman colonial rule, a polarization of the population
and depopulation as peasants fled the land. Estates in Augustine's part
of North Africa were increasingly dependent on itinerant labour, the
social type that would, many centuries later, be described as 'masterless
men' by social critics fearful of the disorder engendered by footloose
labourers.

The social unrest that accompanied economic decline was aggravated by the Christianity of the African peasantry and schisms like the Donatist Church, which included some members of the educated classes and their clients but whose base of support was among the lower orders. An extremist fringe of Donatism, the Circumcellions, probably drawn from Libyan-speaking landless peasants, some renegade slaves and migratory labourers, represented not only a theological or political danger but also a social one.[40] While there has been much debate about whether the motivations of this movement were primarily social or religious, there seems little doubt that Romanized landed elites perceived it as a threat to their very way of life.

While the Donatist schism and the Circumcellion threat were part of the larger context for Augustine's hardening views on heresy and the necessity of state suppression, the immediate occasion of his *City of God* was that of barbarian raids and the sack of Rome by Alaric, king of the Visigoths, in 410. North Africa was spared Alaric's attack by a storm that turned back the invaders, and Carthage became a haven for aristocratic refugees from Rome. Among them were wealthy educated pagans who blamed the disaster on the abandonment of ancient ways, above all the repudiation of paganism in favour of Christianity. Augustine set out to demonstrate to such imperial elites that Christianity was not their enemy, that it was not inconsistent with earthly government, social order or duty to the state – or, indeed, to property and social inequality. In the process of making his case for the exoneration of Christianity, he succeeded in arguing a brief for absolute obedience to even the most unchristian of worldly rulers.

The essence of Augustine's doctrine is, again, the fallen condition of humanity and the stain of original sin. He underpins this doctrine with a particularly harsh conception of predestination. Not only are some predestined to enjoy God's grace and salvation, whatever their own acts on earth, but the separation of others from God's grace and their eternal punishment is also predestined, not a function of their own uniquely sinful acts – an extreme version of predestination that would later be adopted by Calvin but by very few others. Augustine denies that it rules out free will; and it is certainly true that the doctrine of predestination, precisely because it makes grace and punishment independent of specific human actions, has no necessary implications

---

40 See Neal Wood, 'African Peasant Terrorism and Augustine's Political Thought', in *History from Below: Studies in Popular Protest and Popular Ideology in Honour of George Rude*, ed. Frederick Krantz (Montreal: Concordia University, 1985), pp. 279–99.

for individual free will. But the fundamental purpose of the doctrine is not to resolve the conflict between the principles of individual freedom and determinism but rather to construct a foundation for his conception of two 'cities', the City of God and the earthly city.

In his earlier years, Augustine essentially shared the view of other Christians concerning the role of the Roman Empire as God's providential instrument for the Christianization of the world, in the manner proposed by Eusebius in praise of Constantine. But the disasters experienced by the western provinces, both from external threats and internal disorder, posed a challenge to such Christian optimism and put in question the position of Rome as God's chosen earthly medium of salvation. Had Augustine written the *City of God* in different historical circumstances, at a time when Constantinian triumphalism may have seemed more convincing, it might be plausible to suggest, as some commentators have done, that Augustine's most important accomplishment in that work was to 'relativize' the empire by challenging its universalistic claims. But history had already made a mockery of Rome's presumption, whether pagan or Christian; and in that context, Augustine's argument was less a challenge to Rome's imperial pretensions than, on the contrary, a new way of buttressing imperial authority without appealing to an implausible divine election.

Western Christianity, in contrast to the Byzantine East, faced very specific difficulties because of its relation to the Roman Empire. The empire in the West preceded Christianity, and after its conversion – in many eyes, because of it – seemed on the verge of destruction. The East faced no such complications. Imperial Christianity and the eastern empire were born together under Constantine, and the east did not face the same barbarian threat. There are no doubt many reasons for the theological divergences between Western and Eastern Christianity, but we should not underestimate the doctrinal consequences of their divergent relations with secular empire. While the East was able to assume the unity of empire and Christianity, Church and state, and even the subordination of the Church to the secular state, Western Christianity was obliged to deal not only with the rupture between imperial paganism and Christianity but also with the near-collapse of empire after its conversion. That precluded any easy assumptions about relations between Church and state. This affected not only teachings with immediate consequences for the understanding of divine and secular authority but even the most arcane of Christian doctrines, such as interpretation of the Trinity. Much of Augustinian theology was an attempt to come to terms with a secular authority whose Christian foundations were ambiguous and a Christianity which seemed to endanger secular order.

An essential element in Augustine's defence of Christianity against the charge that it was responsible for the calamities facing the empire was a consideration of Cicero's definition of the state, in the speech attributed to Scipio in the *Republic*, which we have already encountered: the state, says Scipio, is 'a union of a large number of men in agreement in respect to what is right and just and associated in the common interest'. Augustine rejects this definition, on the grounds that it does not conform to historical experience. Neither the Roman Republic, nor the Roman Empire (despite its many contributions to the welfare of humanity), nor indeed any other pagan state could ever fit this definition, since justice cannot exist except under the rule of God. But Augustine's objective is not to delegitimate the pagan state. On the contrary, the effect of his argument is to make it clear that the pagan state is no less a state and no less entitled to obedience than any other state on earth. It is striking that, while his discussion concentrates on pagan states and the City of God, no special status is granted to the Christian state – which, when all is said and done, is prey to all the evils of humanity's fallen condition. His purpose is not to maintain that Christian states are more entitled to obedience than pagan rulers but simply to insist that Christians cannot be blamed for the corruption of the Roman commonwealth. On the one hand, Rome was never a commonwealth in Cicero's sense because it never enjoyed true justice, so Christianity cannot be blamed for destroying the Roman commonwealth; and, on the other hand, in the transformation from paganism to Christianity, it retained the qualities of a genuine state despite the absence of true justice in both cases. There is nothing, then, in Christian doctrine which can be used to advocate disobedience to the imperial state or to promote civil disorder.

To explain the evils facing Rome, while at the same time justifying obedience to its earthly authority, required something very different from a conception of the Roman Empire as the fulfilment of God's purpose on earth. Augustine repudiated altogether the notion of Rome's Christian mission. By now, he had also given up some of his earlier Platonism, in particular his youthful optimism about the attainment of virtue by means of Platonic contemplation. Just as he lost faith in the empire's divine purpose, his hopes for human virtue were replaced by a preoccupation with humanity's innate sinfulness. Augustine also now rejected his earlier Platonist belief in the rational order of the cosmos descending from the heavens to earth, and any conception of natural law in which human law is an earthly reflection of a divine cosmic order. In place of such ideas, he proposed his doctrine of two cities.

The Augustinian idea of two cities is not easy to grasp. Although it undoubtedly owes much to the tradition of Roman dualism and its Christian adaptations, it is nothing so simple as a distinction between earthly and heavenly realms, or secular and spiritual authority. Augustine invokes various dichotomies to characterize the antithesis of divine and earthly cities: the one represents the saintly, holy, elect, pious and just; the other designates the impure, impious, unjust and damned. But, while the two are antithetical, they exist inextricably together; and both run inseparably through every human society. Augustine even rejects the distinction between the sacred and profane as two discrete spheres – so that the Church itself, while holy, is for him an earthly institution plagued like all others by the conflict between holiness and sin.

Even those who belong to the City of God must pass through the earthly city and share its tribulations; and the conflict between the two forces will go on until the end of history, when the City of God will finally triumph. In the meantime, the earthly City remains dominant, and history will remain a tragic spectacle, in which true harmony and justice can never prevail. The best that can be hoped for until the end of historical time is the maintenance of earthly peace and social order, which are no less necessary to the City of God as it passes on its earthly pilgrimage than they are to the damned while they live on this earth. Every person and all institutions, the holy no less than the transparently unholy, must therefore subject themselves to the earthly powers whose purpose is to maintain peace and order in this world – not a just or rightful order but a measure of security and physical comfort, to ameliorate the disorder that inevitably follows from the essential nature of the earthly world and the flawed human beings who populate it.

At the root of this pessimism is, of course, the notion of humanity's fallen condition and the power of sin. In this, Augustine was a true and explicit follower of Paul; and like Paul, he concluded from this that Caesar's earthly power, while not fulfilling any truly divine mission, was nevertheless providentially ordained by God. But Augustine takes the doctrine much further, systematically elaborating the reasons for obedience to a pagan emperor like Julian the Apostate, no less than to Constantine the Christian, even after the Christianization of the empire, which Paul, in the early days of Roman Christianity, could hardly have foreseen. If anything, the burden of Augustine's argument is virtually all on the side of obedience to imperial authority; and this explains even his hardening attitude, as bishop, to heresy, which has led some commentators to accuse him of fathering the Inquisition.

It may, at first glance, seem inconsistent to adopt such a repressive line towards heresy while taking as limited and pessimistic a view of what the Church can do in this world and identifying the Church itself as an inevitably flawed secular institution. The very notion of 'heresy', in fact, is, on Augustinian assumptions, theoretically problematic. But there is no mystery about it if we consider that Augustine's principal aim is to sustain the power of existing authorities and the imperial state. The effect of his doctrines was not only to uphold the authority of an imperfect Church, whose right to obedience did not depend on the personal virtues of its clergy, but also to underwrite obedience to the secular state. His notorious campaign against the Donatists, for instance, was directed against their challenge both to the Church and to the imperial power. Their doctrine of a 'pure' Church represented a threat both to a corrupt and sinful clergy and to the ecclesiastical authority of the emperor. Augustine was keen both to preserve the inviolability of the Church hierarchy and to circumvent the problem of relations between secular and ecclesiastical authority, effectively declaring the supremacy of imperial power in the absence of any possible justice on earth. By identifying the Church as a secular institution, not a distinct sphere that must be rendered unto God, he ensured that the principle of 'render unto Caesar' could not be understood as *limiting* the emperor's authority.

To understand the role of predestination in this argument, let us consider the task faced by Augustine. Here is a Christian bishop who is seeking to assert the supremacy of secular authority, as well as to preserve the social arrangements based on the rights of property conferred by the authority of kings and emperors. These secular authorities, which Christians are enjoined to obey, may include non-Christians and even the unholiest of tyrants; yet their authority applies equally to saints and to sinners. Now, it is much easier to justify the subjection of all humanity, regardless of virtue or vice, to the same worldly tribulations, or to insist on the absolute obligation to obey ungodly authority, instead of resisting it on holy principle, if grace and punishment are set apart from any human choice or action. No human being can be compelled to disobey authority or to challenge unjust institutions on the grounds of higher moral principles if such moral resistance is as futile on earth as it is inconsequential in heaven.

This was the crux of the dispute between Augustine and Pelagius, another victim of his anti-heretical zeal, who not only insisted on human free will but utterly rejected the idea of original sin and the necessity of divine grace. Adam, according to Pelagius, was certainly a bad example, but he was not the bearer of a universal guilt imposed on all humanity, just as Christ was a good example but not a necessary source of redemption from original sin. Human beings, obliged to live a virtuous life, were intrinsically capable of living without sin. The issue between these two theologians had less to do with free will itself – a problem which, as we have seen, Augustine sought to finesse – than with the underlying concept of original sin and its implications for human conduct in this world. The Pelagian heresy may seem very harsh in the demands it makes on free human beings, imposing on the individual the responsibility of a holy and ascetic life; but it challenges the realities of Roman society and the values of the imperial aristocracy in a way Augustine's theology does not. While Augustine gave comfort to a wealthy and predatory ruling class, making demands on their thoughts but not on their deeds, Pelagius exposed the immorality of wealth and was a uniquely harsh critic of Roman society. Augustine's campaigns against Donatists and Pelagians, argues his biographer, Peter Brown, together represent 'a significant landmark in that process by which the Catholic Church had come to embrace, and so to tolerate, the whole lay society of the Roman world, with its glaring inequalities and the depressing resilience of its pagan habits.'[41]

The doctrine of original sin, especially with the burden Augustine places on it, makes great demands on every aspect of Christian theology. It can, for instance, be argued that it allows no ambiguity about the full divinity of Christ. The tradition of 'heresies', such as Arianism, which denied that full divinity, might well be understood as a challenge to any strict notion of original sin, if only because they make it harder to understand how an excessively human Christ could be exempted from the universal taint. Augustine, in particular, clearly felt the need to respond to these heresies by elaborating an interpretation of the Trinity according to which the Holy Spirit 'proceeds' from both God and the Son, instead of from God alone, who conferred it on the Son. He strongly opposed the version of the Trinity more common among early Greek Christians, which seemed to suggest not only that Christ received the Holy Spirit from God but that ordinary mortals partici-pated in the Holy Spirit in much the same way as did the Son, 'begotten' of God. The Augustinian version of the Trinity drove a wedge between ordinary mortals and a direct experience of the Holy Spirit and made

---

41 Peter Brown, *Augustine of Hippo* (London: Faber and Faber, 1967), p. 350.

them more dependent on intercession by the Church.[42] At the same time, it buttressed the doctrine of original sin which had as its corollary the obligation to obey the temporal powers of both Church and state.

It is surely significant that the schism between Eastern and Western Christianity would later come to a head over the so-called 'filioque' controversy, concerning the addition of the clause 'and the Son' to the Nicene Creed, so that the Holy Spirit was seen to proceed not only from God but from the Son. Eastern Christianity never faced the same political dilemmas as confronted the West and perhaps for that reason was not so compelled to resort to doctrines of original sin or all the theology supporting them. When Charlemagne, as we shall see in the next chapter, provoked the separation between Rome and Byzantium by insisting on the 'filioque' clause, following Augustine, he certainly had immediately opportunistic reasons for asserting the theological superiority of Rome over Byzantium; but we should not overlook the deeper political significance of such arcane doctrines in sustaining temporal powers in the West.

Augustine provides a powerful, and Christian, justification for both ungodly rule by non-Christian rulers and ungodly or unchristian behaviour by Christian emperors and kings. He not only finds a way of reconciling Christian morality with amoral earthly rule but even establishes Christianity as a way of *justifying* immoral earthly rule.

---

42 Elaine Pagels, in her book, *Adam, Eve, and the Serpent* (New York: Random House, 1988), has argued that the transformation of Christianity into an imperial religion by the conversion of Constantine was accompanied by 'a cataclysmic trans-formation in Christian thought' effected by Augustine, who replaced the early Christian doctrine of moral freedom with an ineluctable bondage to original sin, providing a justification for Christian submission not only to ecclesiastical authority but to imperial power. Christian attitudes on sexuality were part of this transformation. But these transformations were surely already present long before the conversion of Constantine, in the doctrines of St Paul, whose attitudes on sin and sexuality, no less than submission to imperial authority, prefigured Augustine's. Paul may not have transformed Christianity into an imperial religion – a change that awaited the Constantinian conversion – but he certainly made Christianity compatible with submission to imperial power, on the grounds of humanity's inevitable sinfulness. Augustine's version of the Trinity, however, was truly distinctive and took Christianity even further in the direction of submission to both ecclesiastical and secular power. Eugene Webb has argued that, by interpreting the symbols of Father, Son, and Holy Spirit in a way that made impossible the Christian's experience of participation in the filiality of Christ, Augustine took a final step in transforming Christianity into a doctrine of command and coercion. ('Augustine's New Trinity: The Anxious Circle of Metaphor', *Religious Innovation: Essays in the Interpretation of Religious Change*, ed. Michael A. Williams, Collett Cox and Martin S. Jaffe (Berlin: Mouton de Gruyter, 1992), pp. 191–214).

What makes the paradox even more paradoxical is that Augustine has put a Christian theory of political immorality in place of the old Greco-Roman pagan theories of civic virtue.

Augustine departs from the ancient traditions of Greek and Roman political theory not only in his answers but also in his questions. Greek political theory, as we saw, emerged in response to the dissolution of traditional relations between rulers and ruled and the emergence of a new form of political organization, a civic community. Its central category was citizenship, not rule and obedience, and it conceived of politics not as a relation between rulers and ruled, or masters and servants, but as a transaction among equal citizens. Antidemocratic philosophers like Plato and Aristotle, who sought to restore a relation between rulers and ruled, still felt obliged to operate within these civic categories. Plato did much to re-establish the principle of rule as the central category of political thought; and the idea of a universal cosmic hierarchy was certainly used by him and his successors (including Aristotle) to justify a permanent division between rulers and ruled. But that division was presented less as a political relation between those who ruled and those who were obliged to obey them than as a relation between a political sphere and those outside it. Plato, for instance, in the *Statesman* distinguishes between the royal art of politics and other, subordinate arts which serve the political without partaking of it. For Aristotle, the relations that characterized the polis, as distinct from other forms of association like the *oikos*, were relations among equals, while relations among unequals – between, for instance, 'parts' and 'conditions' of the polis – were not political.

The civic categories of Greek political theory persisted in Rome, even when empire replaced republic; and political theory was slow to take up the challenge posed by the renewed relations between rulers and ruled. The fact that these questions re-emerged in a context where traditional principles of domination and obedience had long been undermined by the civic relations of polis and republic, where there could be no easy assumptions about an inevitable division between rulers and ruled or about a correspondence between class inequality and political hierarchy, meant that the Roman Empire had distinctive ideological requirements in constructing a case for obedience to rule. It is true that Western political theory would not produce systematic theories of political obligation until the early modern period, when arguments had to be found to impose the obligation to obey authority on men who were naturally free and equal. But the Roman Empire broke new ground in justifying inequality and domination. We have seen how thinkers like Cicero sought to meet the requirements of justifying inequality; but no one before Augustine was so systematically preoccupied with questions of rule and obedience – and it was Christianity that provided the necessary conceptual tools.

The development of Western Christianity was, as we have already seen, shaped in very particular ways by the specificities of Greco-Roman political life. We have also seen how the special conditions of the Roman Empire encouraged a theology of sin. Augustine was preoccupied with the immediate question of Rome's decline and how, in those conditions, to explain the need for obedience to a secular authority which could no longer be plausibly regarded as the privileged agent of God's mission on earth. But obedience and obligation posed more general problems in a political culture imbued with Greco-Roman civic principles.

Imperial rule, which required obedience to one supreme ruler, meant that it was no longer enough simply to divide the social world between a political community of citizens and those outside it, as Plato and Aristotle had done. In any case, the equality of human beings before God was an essential principle of Christianity, so political rule could not be justified in Christian terms by dividing humanity between those who belonged to a civic community and those outside and subordinate to it. Within those constraints, the most effective way to justify a secular imperial authority was to abolish the civic sphere altogether. Even the passive variety of Roman imperial citizenship is emptied by Augustine of any residual substance. If the old Greek principles of political community presupposed some kind of human capacity for self-government – whether innate in all men, as assumed by Protagoras, or confined to a few, as in Plato's political theory – those civic principles could best be challenged by denying any such capacity for civic virtue or self-rule. Nothing was more aptly suited to that purpose than the Augustinian doctrine of sin.

4

THE MIDDLE AGES

From Imperial Rome to 'Feudalism'

'[T]here seems little doubt,' writes the eminent medieval historian, Rodney Hilton,

> that peasantries were the basis of the ancient civilizations out of which most European feudal societies grew . . . In fact, viewed from the standpoint of this most numerous class of rural society, the difference between late Roman and early medieval civilization may not have been all that easy to discern.[1]

Yet, despite this fundamental continuity, some conventions of Western culture have produced a sense of profound rupture between classical antiquity and 'feudal' society, as the western empire descended into the 'Dark Ages' after the 'decline and fall'. Enlightenment conceptions of progress and classical political economy, for instance, tended to view the Middle Ages as an interruption in the progressive development of Western civilization from its roots in classical antiquity, a hiatus that delayed the inevitable triumph of rationalism and/or 'commercial society' after their promising beginnings in the ancient Mediterranean. The natural course of history, it seems, resumed only with the Renaissance.

Feudalism, in these conventions, often appears to come out of nowhere, or at best from outside, imported into the imperial territories by barbarian invaders. When the feudal order has been presented as a synthesis of Roman and barbarian elements, the Roman past still seems to be a hollow memory rather than a living social legacy. More

---

1 Rodney Hilton, *Bond Men Made Free: Medieval Peasant Movements and the English Rising of 1381* (London: Temple Smith, 1973), p. 10.

recent scholarship has done much to correct this disconnected view of history. But the legacy of old conventions has been hard to uproot, not least because the continuities are more visible from the vantage point of peasants, and history has seldom been recorded from the standpoint of the peasantry. Even historians who are more sceptical of the 'decline and fall' as rupture, or question 'Germanic' influences, or reject the idea of a medieval hiatus by finding the roots of modernity in the Middle Ages, have sometimes tended to emphasize the void left by a dying Roman Empire, which was to be filled by a thoroughly new feudal order, whether transmitted by barbarian invasions or born out of the wreckage of empire, the chaos of social disorder and war.

The history of political thought may seem immune to these ideas of historical rupture, because the legacies of ancient thinkers, the Roman law and Christianity are so obvious in medieval culture. But the continuous history of philosophy and 'canonical' political theory, which is particularly circumscribed by the experience of dominant classes and cultural elites, is perhaps even more inclined to obscure the underlying social continuities in relations between landlords and peasants.

To emphasize the continuities is not at all to deny the social transformations that took place in the dying years of the empire and thereafter. On the contrary, the point is to observe the development of feudal society precisely as a transformation and not an alien intrusion. What is at issue here is not immobility but change as a continuous historical process. To be sure, the intruding 'barbarians' brought with them practices and institutions that would shape the feudal order; but their institutions merged with already existing social relations. Medieval social and political forms are inexplicable without reference to the specificities of Roman society or its distinctive forms of property. Nor does stressing the continuities require us to excavate a history of Western political thought derived from the utterances of peasants, a history that is simply not there to discover, even in the records of peasant rebellion. It is enough to acknowledge that landlords are what they are because of their relations to the property and peasants over whom they exercise their lordship, and medieval agrarian relations were firmly rooted in their Roman antecedents.

The concept of feudalism is often said to be of questionable value, and there has certainly been much variation in its usage. Yet there can be little doubt that developments in the western empire produced distinctive social forms without which the later history of Europe is inexplicable, and some kind of shorthand designation seems all but indispensable. For the sake of convenience, unless and until a generally accepted designation is found to replace it, we can apply the term 'feudalism', or perhaps feudal society, to these social forms, while acknowledging that there was no single feudal order unvarying throughout the West.[2]

Between the sixth and tenth centuries, the period commonly identified as the era of feudalization, the Roman Empire was replaced by what has been called the 'parcellization of sovereignty'.[3] Persuasive arguments have recently been made that the process was much more sudden than medieval historians have conventionally suggested and that there was a 'feudal revolution' only at the end of this period;[4] but whether the process was gradual or revolutionary, the imperial state gave way to a patchwork of jurisdictions in which state functions were vertically and horizontally fragmented. Domination by an overarching imperial state was replaced by geographic fragmentation and organization by means of local or regional administration, perhaps in the form of contractual arrangements within the ruling class, between kings and lords or lords and vassals – though these arrangements could take many different forms, and the very existence of vassalage has been put in question.[5] This administrative, legal and military patchwork

---

2 For an important discussion of feudalism and specifically differences between England and France, see George Comninel, 'English Feudalism and the Origins of Capitalism', in *The Journal of Peasant Studies*, July 2000, pp. 1–53.

3 Perry Anderson, *Passages from Antiquity to Feudalism* (London: Verso, 1974), pp. 148ff.

4 There have long been fluctuations between histories of feudalism that insist on continuities and those that emphasize more revolutionary transformations. A case for a 'feudal revolution' was made by T.N. Bisson in *Past and Present* in 1994 ('The "Feudal Revolution"', *Past and Present* 142, February 1994, pp. 6–42), which generated a debate among several historians in subsequent issues (152, August 1996, and 155, May 1997). Among the participants was Chris Wickham, who, with some reservations about Bisson's argument, judiciously and persuasively defended the idea of a 'feudal revolution'.

5 Susan Reynolds, in particular, has argued that the concept of vassalage is virtually meaningless, while even the concept of 'fiefs' is too vague and variable to be very useful (*Fiefs and Vassals: The Medieval Evidence Reinterpreted*, New York and Oxford: Oxford University Press, 1994). The argument here, as will be explained in what follows, in no way depends on the existence of vassalage or, indeed, on the notion of fiefs. Reynolds has also taken issue with arguments that, in her view, attribute too much importance to intellectual constructs, including the revival of ancient Greek philosophy, in constituting social and political relations in the Middle Ages. She emphasizes 'traditional bonds of community' and communal practices established long before, and independently of, such ideas. It should already be clear that this criticism cannot apply to the concept of feudalism employed in this chapter.

was generally accompanied by a system of conditional property, in which property rights entailed jurisdictional and military service.

This is not the place to consider whether, or to what extent, feudalism was a product of Germanic influences – even if it were possible to identify any single 'Germanic' entity or culture. It is, however, misleading to imagine invasions of the Roman Empire by more or less pristinely 'Germanic' tribes, emerging more or less untouched from the forests of the north. The interactions between the Romans and the 'Germans' go much further back than the late mass migrations commonly regarded as 'barbarian invasions'. These included long-standing relations of exchange, which served to aggravate social differentiation within the German tribes and to destabilize relations among Germanic communities themselves, provoking constant warfare and increasing militarization. By the time their incursions into Roman territory became a decisive factor in determining the fate of the empire, the Germans were already deeply marked by their long interactions with Rome.

There has been considerable debate about whether relations between landlords and peasants should be included in the definition of feudalism. At one extreme is the argument that relations between seigneurs or manorial lords and their dependent labourers cannot be called feudal, because feudalism has to do not with domination and dependence but with contractual relations among juridical equals – at least among people of lordly status, even if some owed service to others. At the other extreme is a definition of feudalism entirely based on relations among landlords and peasants, which is sometimes applied not only to the specifically Western medieval forms of peasant dependence but to any type of agrarian exploitation by means of rent-extraction. Both these extremes seem unhelpful.

On the one hand, it should go without saying that feudal lords, however we define them, depended for their very existence on their relations with peasants. Wherever there were lords, there were peasants whose dependent labour sustained them. On the other hand, a diluted definition of 'feudalism', which embraces any kind of relationship between landlord and peasant, obscures the specificities of agrarian relations in the medieval West. What is distinctive about the Western case is the exploitation of peasants by lords in the context of parcellized sovereignty – with or without the relations of vassalage. The concept of 'feudalism' is useful because, and to the extent that, it draws attention to this distinctive formation.

In the very particular unity of economic and extra-economic power that emerged in medieval 'Europe', economic relations of appropriation were inextricably bound up with political relations, as they had been in ancient bureaucratic states. But, in sharp contrast to those ancient civilizations where subject peasants were ruled by monarchical states, the feudal state was fragmented by parcellized sovereignty; taxation by the state gave way to levies collected by lords and appropriation in the form of rent; and lordship combined the power of individual appropriation with possession of a fragment of state power. Lordship, which constituted a personal relation to property and command of the peasants who worked it, took over many of the functions performed in other times and places by the state. The effect was to combine the private exploitation of labour with the public role of administration, jurisdiction and enforcement. This was, in other words, a form of 'politically constituted property', a unity of economic and extra-economic power, which presupposed the uniquely autonomous development of private property in ancient Rome.

In the preceding chapters, there was some discussion of property relations in ancient Greece and Rome, emphasizing their distinctiveness when compared to other 'high' civilizations. Property in land was more thoroughly separated from the state than in the 'bureaucratic' kingdoms where it tended to be closely bound up with state service. In such king-doms, peasant producers were subject to surplus extraction less in the form of exploitation by individual private proprietors than in the form of collective subjugation to an appropriating, redistributive state and its ruling aristocracy, typically in the form of taxation and compulsory services. In Rome, private property developed as a distinct locus of power in unprecedented ways; and peasant producers were more directly subject to individual private appropriators, who extracted surplus labour in the form of rent. These developments, as we have seen, were reflected in the Roman law, which formally recognized the exclusiveness of private property and elaborated a distinction between two forms of domination, the ownership of property and the power of state rule, the powers of *dominium* and *imperium*. The conceptual elaboration of these two distinct foci of power would have enormous implications for the development of political theory.

When a massive imperial state did emerge, with its own bureaucracy and system of taxation, it was already fundamentally different from the other imperial or monarchical states of antiquity. Even at the height of the empire, the primary form of appropriation by dominant classes was not through state office by means of taxation but the acquisition of land and direct exploitation of the labour that worked it, whether peasants or slaves. Landlords and peasants confronted each other more directly as individuals and classes, as distinct from rulers and subjects, while imperial governance itself depended on a network of local landed aristocracies, especially in the western empire. This mode of imperial rule had the effect of strengthening property, in contrast to other ancient states which impeded the full and autonomous development of private property or propertied classes independent of the imperial bureaucracy. When the empire adopted the expedient of paying for military services by grants of land, this property in land preserved the attributes of Roman ownership.[6]

The existence of two poles of power, the state and private property, meant that there was a tendency to fragmentation at the very heart of the imperial state. When the empire disintegrated – precisely in the west, where state rule existed in tension with aristocracies based on huge landed estates – aristocratic autonomy would continue to grow, even when some form of public power continued to exist. The devolution of public functions to local lords occurred even where monarchical powers succeeded, at least for a time, in their attempts to recentralize the state. Monarchies typically depended, to varying degrees but always unavoidably, on territorial aristocracies which exercised functions – judicial, administrative and military – formerly belonging to the state.

---

6 An interesting but, in my view, flawed argument has been proposed by an eminent historian of late Rome and the Middle Ages, Chris Wickham, who has more recently modified his view but without completely replacing what seem to me its most problematic aspects. In his original formulation, he invoked the notion of the 'tributary system', in which surplus extraction takes place by means of taxation, and contrasted it to feudalism, in which surplus extraction takes the form of rent instead of tax. ('The Other Transition: From the Ancient World to Feudalism' and 'The Uniqueness of the East', originally published in 1984–5 and both republished in *Land and Power: Studies in Italian and European Social History, 400–1200* (London: The British School at Rome, 1994). The tributary system includes the bureaucratic redistributive kingdom as I have described it here; but in Wickham's view, it also includes the 'ancient' form exemplified by Greece and Rome, in which the city rather than a central monarchical state is the tax-extracting entity. The Greco-Roman case was distinctive, he argues, also because the tributary form coexisted with 'feudalism'. The transition occurred, he suggests, when the tensions between these two coexisting modes of production led to the decline of the tributary element (in particular, the imperial state) and the growing predominance of the feudal form. I find this account problematic for several reasons: each category, the 'tributary' and the 'feudal', is far too undifferentiated and explains very little – especially because any relations of rent-extraction between landlords and peasants are called 'feudal', which tends to obscure the particularities of Western landlord/peasant relations, while any form of taxation appears to partake of the 'tributary' form. The approach is more taxonomic than historical, positing two modes of production with no historical beginning and no internal dynamic that might help to explain the transition – the 'feudal' form is simply there and, in its tension with the 'tributary form', there is no apparent reason for its eventual predominance; and above all, this approach fails to capture the specificity of the 'ancient' form. It is not enough

Even when, in the eighth century and thereafter, the Franks, especially under Charlemagne, restored some kind of unity and order to the chaotic remnants of the Western empire, creating their own large imperial dominion, the Frankish realm was administered by regional counts, while newly conquered territories were controlled by local military strongmen. This fragmented administration continued even after Charlemagne's coronation in 800 as *Imperator* in the Roman manner, which appeared to revive the universal empire. The so-called Holy Roman Empire which ensued would, in the centuries that followed, even aggravate the conflicts of fragmented jurisdiction, adding yet another claim to temporal authority, in an already combustible mix of lordly, royal and papal authority.

Kingship in the medieval West was always characterized, in varying degrees, by a tension between monarchical power and lordship, between centralized and local authority. This tension would produce uniquely Western conceptions of rule, in which a resolution between competing

---

to say that the tributary form here was different because the city was the tax-extracting entity or even to say that it coexisted with 'feudalism'. The point, at the very least, is that the city and even the empire, with their systems of taxation, were themselves already shaped by the uniquely autonomous development of private property. The city-state of the Roman Republic was constituted by specifically Roman relations between landlords and peasants, and the empire that grew out of it presupposed the development of a historically unique landed class.

More recently, Wickham has replaced his distinction between tributary and feudal *modes of production* with a distinction between two types of *polity* or state: one based on taxation and the other on land. This distinction has certain advantages over the other, but it is still far from characterizing the specificities of the Roman tax-based state and the differences between it and, say, a tax-based state like imperial China, where the relation between state and landed property was significantly different. For that matter, it is difficult to do justice to the divergences between the Western and Eastern Roman empires without acknowledging such differences in their state/property relations. In the east, the imperial state was typically superimposed on already existing and highly developed state structures. In the west, where no such structures had existed, the development of aristocratic landed property – and its centrifugal effects – went much further, and it was here that the empire disintegrated. In any case, except in some ahistorical taxonomy, there probably has never existed a simple land-based state, in opposition to a tax-based state. Wickham's model for the land-based form seems to be the fragmentation of the state or 'parcellization of sovereignty' based on a hierarchy of landed property which emerged in feudal Europe (he cites the great historian of feudalism, Marc Bloch, as the scholar who has best analyzed it); but that feudal form surely presupposes the distinctive development of Roman property and Rome's landed aristocracy, as well as the Roman imperial state, with its system of taxation. Wickham's own magisterial and persuasive analysis of the early Middle Ages confirms this, yet his conceptual framework tends to obscure it.

claims to authority was sought not by asserting the simple and unambiguous predominance of central over local power but rather by invoking some kind of mutuality, an agreement between two legitimate forces conceived in contractual or, eventually, constitutional terms.[7] It is hard to imagine how such a dispensation could have emerged without the distinctively Western development of property as an autonomous force in tension yet in tandem with the state.

After the end of the ninth century, there was, in effect, no sovereign state, if the hallmark of state sovereignty is legislative power (as distinct from the application of existing law). Some public institutions, particularly certain kinds of courts, continued to exist; but there was effectively no legislation at all for two centuries, except for changes in customary law. The disintegration of Western Frankish rule in the tenth century left local castle lords in command, while the east, particularly Germany, was controlled by powerful duchies. By the early eleventh century, even the functions of public courts fell into the hands of local lords, with regional counts appropriating jurisdictions not as public offices but as private property. If any legal and political order existed in these regions, it has been said, the only sector of the population that remained subject to any social discipline was the peasantry, under the control of individual lords. [8] Aristocratic autonomy now truly became the parcellization of sovereignty.

To put it another way, the public or civic sphere completely disappeared. This was so not only in the sense that the state apparatus effectively disintegrated but also in the sense that public assemblies in which free men could participate, of a kind that survived throughout the Carolingian realm, no longer existed.[9] Clear distinctions between free men and slaves gave way to a complex continuum of dependent conditions. The category of 'free' man effectively disappeared in the former Frankish empire, where even owners of free land might be subject to seigneurial jurisdiction and feudal obligations, while the

---

7 See Janet Coleman, *A History of Political Thought: From the Middle Ages to the Renaissance* (Oxford: Blackwell, 2000), p. 18, for a discussion of the peculiarly Western resolution of tensions between local and central authorities.

8 It is argued, in *The Cambridge History of Medieval Political Thought: c.350–c.1450* (Cambridge: Cambridge University Press, 1988) that the coincidence of lordship and ownership, which made peasants both tenants and subjects at once, applied throughout the West, including England (p. 195). As we shall see, however, the English case was exceptional, because the coincidence of lordship and ownership did not take the form of parcellized sovereignty in the way that it did on the Continent.

9 I owe this point to George Comninel.

concept of slavery was overtaken by a spectrum of dependence, in relations between lords and 'their' men.

By the thirteenth century, more firmly established feudal monarchies restored effective systems of administration. This was also a period when the Holy Roman Empire, now led by German kings, achieved its greatest power as a central European state, while the papacy was asserting its own authority in the temporal domain. Yet even then, although the feudal subjection of peasants to lords was eased to some extent, the autonomous powers of lords, with their administrative and jurisdictional challenges to royal authority, would remain defining features of the medieval order. When a public realm and spheres of civic participation re-emerged, it typically took the form of corporate entities, internally self-governing yet bound by charters defining their corporate relation to superior authorities. Far from resolving the old jurisdictional conflicts, the new configuration of power in the later Middle Ages created even more virulent contests, with seigneurial and corporate claims to autonomous jurisdiction vying with, and intensified by, the powers of emperors and popes.

There were, to be sure, patterns of social order in Europe other than the characteristically 'feudal' relations between landlords, peasants and kings, even at the height of feudalism. Where urban concentrations had survived the collapse of the Roman Empire, and where landholding patterns produced a larger proportion of free peasants as distinct from serfs, the seigneurial system was comparatively weak. This was true in northern Italy, where towns had remained relatively strong, and the legacy of the Roman municipal system was more persistent. Just as towns had been the social and political domain of Romanized local elites, who effectively governed the surrounding countryside, the city continued to be the administrative centre of the secular and ecclesiastical authorities that carried on the legacy of Rome. A typical pattern was administration by bishops who preserved something of the Roman Empire and its municipal government, though this relatively unified civic administration increasingly gave way to a more fractured system of governance by various corporate entities and guilds. While the imperial elites had been overwhelmingly landed classes, in medieval Italy – especially from the beginning of the eleventh century – there emerged a powerful urban patriciate. Some of the urban communes became prosperous commercial centres, with dominant classes enriched by commerce and financial services for kings, emperors and popes. Collectively, they dominated the surrounding countryside, the *contado*, extracting wealth from it in one way or another, not least to sustain the public offices that, directly or indirectly, enriched many members of the urban elite.

Much confusion has been generated by historical accounts of feudalism that identify commerce with capitalism, treating money and trade as inimical to feudal relations. Yet money rents were a prominent feature of relations between landlords and peasants, while commercial transactions – typically, in luxury goods – were very much a part of the feudal order.[10] The thriving commercial centres of northern Italy may have stood somewhat apart from the seigneurial system, but they served a vital function in the larger European feudal network, acting as trading links among the segments of that fragmented order and as a means of access to the world outside Europe.

Nor did these cities escape the parcellization of sovereignty. While other parts of Europe were experiencing feudalization, municipal administration was undergoing its own fragmentation. The communes became and remained, in varying degrees, loose associations of patrician families, parties, communities and corporate entities with their own semi-autonomous powers, organizational structures and jurisdictions, both secular and ecclesiastical, often in fierce contention with each other and in battle among warring civic factions. A lethal ingredient in this mix was the intrusion of papal and imperial powers. Even while civic communes were to a greater or lesser extent autonomous from larger temporal authorities, they were often fierce battlegrounds in those wider power struggles, which played themselves out as vicious factional rivalries within the civic community – what would come to be known as the conflict between Guelf (papal) and Ghibelline (imperial) factions; typically, but not necessarily, corresponding to divisions between merchant classes and landed *signori*.

Interpretations of medieval 'republicanism', especially conceived as a foretaste of political modernity, can be misleading not only because cities with effective civic self-government were essentially oligarchies, but also because they never constituted a truly united civic order, with a clearly defined public sphere detached from private powers of various kinds. In moments of more effective republican government, greater efforts were made to unite the civic community; but no medieval Italian commune ever succeeded in transcending its inherent fragmentation or the fusion of public power with private appropriation. The triumph

---

10 The view that capitalism emerged when and because the expansion of trade destroyed feudalism was decisively challenged in the so-called 'Transition Debate', sparked in the early 1950s by a debate between Maurice Dobb and Paul Sweezy, followed by a discussion among several other Marxist historians. (*The Transition from Feudalism to Capitalism*, introduction by Rodney Hilton [London: New Left Books, 1976]).

of more despotic oligarchies did not represent a major rupture with
republican forms but belonged to the same dynamic of what we
might call urban feudalism. Nor did their attempts to extend and
consolidate their own rule truly overcome the feudal fragmentation
of governance. Even the most centralized of 'Renaissance' states in
post-medieval Italy would continue to be divided by party, privilege
and confused jurisdictions.

The most notable exception to the feudal breakdown of state order
in the West was England, with significant implications for later European development and for the history of political theory. Although
the collapse of the Roman Empire in Britain seems to have produced
a breakdown of material and political structures more catastrophic
than anywhere else in the West and a more drastic discontinuity with
Roman forms, in Anglo-Saxon times a process of state-formation was
already well advanced, with kings, landlords and church hierarchy
working in tandem to produce an unusually centralized authority.
While France was disintegrating, the English forged a unified kingdom,
with a national system of justice and the most effective administration
in the Western world. There also began to emerge a new kind of
national identity – 'the Anglo-Saxons', and later 'the English'.

Anglo-Saxon kingdoms were certainly administered with the help
of local aristocracies who had considerable powers; yet local lords
governed – in principle and even in practice – not as autonomous
regional counts but as partners in the royal state from which their
administrative authority derived. In England there would emerge a
distinctive relation between central government and the lesser nobility.
Local elites, with considerable local authority, would govern not as
feudal lords but in effect as delegates of the royal state, and not in
tension with the central state but in tandem with the rise of a national
Parliament as an assembly of the propertied classes ruling in partnership with the Crown.

In the eleventh century the Normans would bring with them
elements of Continental feudalism, but the feudal parcellization of
sovereignty never took hold in England as it did elsewhere. The Norman
ruling class arrived, and imposed itself on English society, as an already
well organized and unified military force and consolidated the power
of its newly established monarchical state by adapting Norman traditions of aristocratic freedom to Anglo-Saxon traditions of rule.

It is certainly true that lords of the manor in England had substantial
rights and jurisdictional powers over their tenants; but the centralized
power of the monarchy remained strong, and a national system of law
and jurisdiction emerged very early, in the shape of the common law,

the king's law. The development of the English monarchy was, and continued to be, at bottom a cooperative project between monarchs and landlords.[11] Even when open conflict and, indeed, civil war erupted between king and aristocracy, the stakes had less to do with a contest between centralized government and parcellized sovereignty than attempts to correct imbalances in the partnership between monarchs and lords. The baronial challenge to monarchy in the documents that make up Magna Carta, for example, can certainly be construed as an appeal to reinstate some kind of feudal right; but, while barons may have been demanding that they should have the right to be tried by their peers in their own courts, they were not asserting their own jurisdiction over other free men. Unlike their counterparts in France, where seigneurial and royal jurisdiction would long continue to be regarded as in conflict with each other, English barons were claiming their rights at common law, that is, as rights deriving from the central state. The barons took that state for granted hardly less than did the king himself; and this would continue to be true in every episode of conflict between the monarchy and propertied classes, up to and including the Civil War and the Glorious Revolution of the seventeenth century.

The relative strength of the centralized state in England, however, did not mean the weakness of the landed aristocracy. In significant ways, the contrary is true. There emerged a cooperative division of labour between the central monarchical state and the landed class, whose power rested not on fragmented sovereignty but on its command of property. It is true that the Roman system of property, like the Roman state, suffered a more complete disruption in England than elsewhere in the former empire; but, just as effective central administration was re-established in England more quickly than elsewhere, a strong and exclusive form of property would emerge in England as it did nowhere else.

English property law would, on the face of it, become the most 'feudal' in Europe. This was so in the sense that here, as nowhere else in feudal Europe, there were no exceptions to the principle of 'no land without its lord', and there was no allodial land. Yet the paradox of English 'feudalism' is that the condition for the complete feudalization

---

11 For a discussion of relations between aristocracy and monarchy in the process of feudal centralization in England, in contrast especially to France, see Robert Brenner, 'The Agrarian Roots of European Capitalism' in ed. T.H Aston and C.H.E. Philpin, *The Brenner Debate: Agrarian Class Structure and Economic Development in Pre-Industrial Europe* (Cambridge: Cambridge University Press, 1985), esp. pp. 253–64.

of property was the centralized monarchy, together with its law and courts – not parcellized sovereignty but, on the contrary, its absence. If all land had its lord, it was only in the formal sense that the monarch was conceived as the supreme landlord. Yet, in practice, tenements held directly, in common law, under the jurisdiction of the king – including certain types of humble property held by tillers and free-holders who owed no military service and were free of lordly jurisdiction – constituted private property more exclusive and less subject to obligations to an overlord than anything that existed on the Continent, despite (or in some ways because of) the growing dominance of the common law in preference to the Roman law.[12] Monarchical rule and exclusive private property, in other words, were developing together.

For all the feudal trappings of English property, and the departures of the common law from the legal traditions of Rome, private and exclusive property would develop more completely in England than in any of the Continental states where Roman law survived and where the parcellization of sovereignty prevailed. In England, the total breakdown of the Roman imperial order may have had the paradoxical effect that, when the Roman legacy was reintroduced from the Continent – not only by the Norman Conquest, but even before, by Anglo-Saxon kings availing themselves of Continental legal expertise – the regime of exclusive private property was more forcibly implanted and rigorously imposed.

---

12 It should be emphasized here that the development of the common law in England and its relation to the establishment of exclusive rights of property was not, as is often suggested, the simple transition from feudal relations of mutuality under feudal law to individual and exclusive property rights in common law, defensible in a common, national court. (See, for instance, Coleman, *op. cit.* p. 616). The common law had its roots in Anglo-Saxon England and thus preceded 'feudalism', so that when the Normans brought feudal law from the Continent, it was implanted in the context of an already established common law. It is also important to recognize that the possibility of defending property rights before a national court, as existed elsewhere in Europe too, did not in itself represent a negation of feudal property. In France, for example, when peasants had the right to defend their property in royal courts, property was still held on feudal principles, with attendant obligations, and each seigneurie continued to have its own system of law and its own autonomous jurisdiction. Nor did the fact that the land might be alienable change the feudal obligations associated with it or the right of the seigneur to interpose himself in the transaction. It is misleading to suggest that, by the late Middle Ages, property both in England and on the Continent was well on the way from feudal to capitalist, simply because property rights were increasingly defensible at law, before a national court. Quite apart from the misleading conflation of absolute property with capitalism, the fact remains that property in England developed in ways quite distinct from other European cases, and even with its feudal trappings was more 'absolute' and exclusive than anywhere else.

Nonetheless, despite this significant exception, parcellized sovereignty continued to be a dominant theme in medieval European history. It is true that, by the end of the twelfth century, more or less stable political administrations began to re-establish themselves in various parts of Europe, either in the form of monarchical states or as autonomous urban communes. The classics of medieval political philosophy belong largely to this later period, and are preoccupied not so much with tensions between feudal lords and monarchical states as with conflicts among kings, popes and Holy Roman emperors. Nevertheless, even as kings contended with ecclesiastical and imperial hierarchies, monarchs would continue to rely on, and compete with, the lordly jurisdictions of landed aristocracies; and corporate entities of one kind or another continued to assert their autonomy against various claims, secular and ecclesiastical, to a higher unified sovereignty.

In all these cases, the question of legal and political sovereignty was always inseparable from tensions between the authority to govern and the power of property; and political conflicts were often conducted through the medium of controversies on property rights. In the feudal unity of property and jurisdiction, institutions claiming legal or administrative powers of any kind were inevitably obliged to confront competing rights of property; and questions about the relation between *imperium* and *dominium* were bound to pose themselves with special urgency.

Church, State and Property

Christianity added its own distinctive features to the complexities of feudal governance. The division of labour between Church and state which had emerged in the Roman Empire would be shaped by the disintegration of the imperial state and the medieval tensions between seigneurial and royal power. The effects of parcellized sovereignty are strikingly apparent in the development of Christian doctrine.

The classic statement of the division between secular and spiritual power was written in the late fifth century by Pope Gelasius. Although it was intended to deal with a very specific problem at a particular moment of schism between East and West, it would continue throughout the Middle Ages to be the *locus classicus* of Western Christian doctrine on the relation between the two spheres. In a letter to Emperor Anastasius in Constantinople, conventionally entitled *Duo Sunt*, Gelasius defended the Roman Church against the imperial claims of Byzantium by insisting on the superiority of the spiritual over temporal power:

There are two powers, august Emperor, by which this world is chiefly
ruled, namely, the sacred authority of the priests and the royal
power. Of these that of the priests is the more weighty, since they
have to render an account for even the kings of men in the divine
judgment. You are also aware, dear son, that while you are permitted
honorably to rule over human kind, yet in things divine you bow
your head humbly before the leaders of the clergy and await from
their hands the means of your salvation. In the reception and proper
disposition of the heavenly mysteries you recognize that you should
be subordinate rather than superior to the religious order, and that
in these matters you depend on their judgment rather than wish to
force them to follow your will.[13]

This manifesto nicely reveals the paradoxes at the heart of Western
Christianity in its relation to secular power. Its assertion of spiritual
superiority could be, and certainly was, invoked to support the temporal
authority of popes. Yet it not only presupposes the duality of power
but, like Pauline doctrine, it can also – and perhaps even more readily
– be understood as leaving the secular power essentially in command
of this world, while relegating the Church to an elevated sphere beyond
the daily practices of governance. The message seems to be that the
'two swords' which govern the world should be wielded by two different
hands, and the sword of temporal power should be rendered unto
Caesar. But, as the empire disintegrated, Christianity was obliged to
adapt to new conditions. The relation between secular and ecclesiastical
authority became more complicated, especially when the institutions
and doctrines of the Church were elaborated by the Franks as a supplement to state administration.

   An essential element of the Carolingian strategy for dealing with
an extensive empire in the absence of a central state power adequate
to the purpose, and dependent on regional lords to administer order,
was to mobilize Christian religion as a unifying force and a discipline.
Charles Martel's principal strategy in consolidating his rule was to
use the Church hierarchy and episcopacy, with all its property and
perquisites, as a means of countering the challenge of aristocratic
autonomy by creating a friendly aristocracy of his own. He also
established an alliance with the papacy, largely in order to detach
Christianity from local loyalties (including reverence to local saints)
which had helped to sustain regional lords opposed to his centralizing

---

13 J.H. Robinson, *Readings in European History* (Boston: Ginn, 1905), p. 72.

project. This alliance between papacy and monarchy or empire would later, of course, become deeply problematic and the conflict between them a central theme of Western political thought; but at this stage it was congenial to both these temporal powers.[14]

Charlemagne would continue to mobilize the ecclesiastical apparatus to sustain his own rule. This meant, above all, that Christian conversion was imposed and enforced by the sword, and that he sought to make religion uniform throughout his realm. His religious strategy required, among other things, a literate clergy; and this requirement was not the least important motivation in the cultural renaissance conventionally attributed to his reign. It also meant that Christian dogma and ritual were made to encompass all aspects of life with increasingly complex liturgical forms, placing an increasing emphasis on sin and on the correctional, disciplinary role of religion.

Charlemagne's reign was responsible for entrenching certain fundamentally Augustinian doctrines in Western Christianity, and in so doing, bringing about the final schism between East and West. This is not the place to canvass the debate on the arcane question of the 'filioque' clause (discussed in the previous chapter); nor can we judge to what extent the Frankish insistence on including this clause in the Nicene Creed was, as is often suggested, simply an opportunistic move in the struggle between the Franks and the Byzantine East, branding as effectively heretical the Eastern Greek interpretation of the Trinity, in support of a strategy to establish the Frankish empire as the true Rome. But it is at least worth considering that, for Charlemagne as for Augustine before him, the filioque clause might have had the added advantage of reinforcing the doctrine of original sin and the necessity of obedience to prevailing authority.

The state administration was supplemented by the Church bureaucracy, from bishops, the Church aristocracy, down to lowly priests who were conceived as a means of transmitting the royal will to peasants.[15] The clergy was just as much a part of the state's administrative hierarchy as were regional counts. It is not surprising, then, that Carolingian rule is often described as theocratic, not only because its claims to legitimacy relied on its association with the Church and

---

14 For a discussion of this strategy, see Patrick Geary, *France Before Germany: The Creation and Transformation of the Merovingian World* (Oxford and New York: Oxford University Press, 1988), esp. pp. 212–20.

15 On the distinctive role of the Church in the Carolingian state, see the *Cambridge History*, *op. cit.*, esp. pp. 220–1.

mutual obligations in the community of faith but also because the state apparatus was so dependent on the clergy. Yet it seems fruitless to ask whether Carolingian kingship was more 'theocratic' than 'seigneurial' or 'feudal' and more useful simply to acknowledge the complexities of the medieval order in the West, the inevitably tense collaborations between monarchs and lords, and the role of the Church in the contests between them.

However much relations between Church and state would fluctuate throughout the Middle Ages and beyond, the doctrinal effects of Christianity's administrative and correctional function would remain deeply ingrained in Christian theology. At the same time, the fragmentation of secular authority and jurisdiction would be aggravated by the parallel structures of ecclesiastical power and property. Although Carolingian rule represented a partnership between Church and secular state, it was bound eventually to increase tensions between them, precisely because it confirmed the Church itself as a temporal power. These tensions would be felt throughout our period. When, in the later Middle Ages, monarchical states consolidated their rule, they were increasingly challenged by ecclesiastical authority, especially by the growth of papal government and papal claims to a 'plenitude of power'. The division of labour between secular and spiritual spheres, which may have seemed a relatively simple matter in relations between the Roman Church and Caesar, was implicated, in ever more intricate ways, in the complex contestations between kings, emperors, popes, and various other autonomous powers.

As conflicts between royal or imperial and ecclesiastical authority became more intense, the doctrine of Gelasius was developed accordingly, with wide-ranging implications not only for ideas on Church and state but also for other aspects of political theory. Successive popes went beyond the Gelasian division of labour between secular and spiritual authority to assert the temporal superiority of ecclesiastical power far more unambiguously than Gelasius himself had done. At a particularly critical moment in the eleventh century, Pope Gregory VII set out to deprive kingship of any remaining sacral or theocratic elements, bolstering papal claims to a plenitude of power by asserting that kings were simply secular, and above all removable, officials. He skilfully turned Germanic notions of elective monarchy against the German emperors themselves, insisting that the suitability of candidates for royal office was a matter for papal approval, with the ultimate sanction of excommunication.

Later popes would go even further in consolidating the Church as a governmental power, with jurisdiction not only in spiritual matters but in the public domain. It is significant that this issue played itself out in theories of private property, elaborated by civil and canon lawyers as well as philosophers. The spiritual role of the Church had to do with the inner being, the soul, of every Christian, while ecclesiastical authority in the public sphere, its jurisdiction over mundane and material matters, was identified with its control of wealth and property. The vast wealth of the Church could become the basis of a claim to temporal authority on the grounds that it was held on behalf of the whole Christian community. It was a short step from this assertion of temporal power over the material well-being of the Christian community to the claim that ecclesiastical authority trumped that of the secular state. Defenders of papal authority would, for instance, argue that *dominium* or ownership of the Church's temporal goods resided in the Christian community as a whole and that therefore the ecclesiastical establishment which administered the vast wealth of the Christian community – that is to say, exercised jurisdiction over it – was in effect a governmental power, wielding coercive force on behalf of the faithful in pursuit of the common good, just as secular governments purported to do on behalf of their own subject communities. Ecclesiastical jurisdiction thus challenged the jurisdiction of secular powers on their own terrain. Claiming to be acting in the common good of the whole Christian community, for both its spiritual and temporal benefit, the papacy could claim superior authority.

The final conceptual step was taken by Pope Boniface VIII, at the beginning of the fourteenth century, in conflict with Philip IV of France over the very temporal matter of taxation. Declaring the pope's plenitude of power in the most uncompromising way, his papal bull, *Unam sanctam*, proclaimed the unambiguous superiority of papal authority over every temporal power, the spiritual sword over the secular. Pope Boniface clearly overstepped the mark and lost his battle with the French king. Others might have been more circumspect in asserting papal authority; but, once relations between secular and ecclesiastical powers had been cast in the terms of competing jurisdictions, it would have been only a matter of time before one pope or another made something like this conceptual move.

We should not take it for granted that the battle between ecclesiastical and secular powers was bound to take this jurisdictional form, nor should we assume that conflicts between competing authorities inevitably implicate conceptions of property. That such conflicts expressed themselves in these terms in medieval Europe speaks to the very particular relation between state and property in Western

development and conceptions of power defined by the duality of
state and property. The preoccupation with, perhaps even the
conception of, jurisdiction presupposes the kind of boundary disputes
generated by parcellized sovereignty and the overlapping claims
associated with it. Parcellized sovereignty, in turn, presupposes the
autonomous development of property in classical antiquity and the
emergence of aristocratic power grounded in landed property, as
against the public power of the state. The various overlapping and
contending jurisdictions of feudalism were all shaped by that original
duality of power. A bureaucratic state in which authority is delegated
from the centre and the boundaries of office are well defined –
imperial China comes to mind – may generate its own conflicts
between emperors and local officials. But these disputes are of a
different kind and need not produce a legal apparatus designed to
negotiate contesting and overlapping jurisdictions or, indeed, the
discourse of jurisdictional disputes. This kind of legal and discursive
apparatus is distinctively Western.

The feudal parcellization of sovereignty, then, produced a very
particular need to negotiate jurisdictional disputes in theory and
practice; but the idea of jurisdiction in the West would not have taken
the form that it did without the legacy of Roman property, and the
history of Western political theory would continue to be shaped by
the relations between property and state inherited from Rome. In the
empire, as we saw, the distinction between *imperium* and *dominium*
was relatively clear, representing two distinct forms of power, public
and private, in varying degrees of tension depending on the claims
asserted by the imperial state against the rights of private property.
The legacy of Roman property survived the parcellization of
sovereignty; but as the imperial state gave way to fragmented
jurisdictions, there were corresponding changes in the concept of
dominium and its relation to governmental power, changes already
underway in the complex relations between the imperial state and
'barbarian' kingdoms. While feudal lordship certainly presupposed
the autonomous development of property and landed aristocracies in
ancient Rome, the complete and exclusive ownership suggested by
dominium could not accommodate the conditional property of feudalism. Nor could the distinction between *imperium* and *dominium*
adequately capture the unity of appropriation and governance in the
'politically constituted property' of feudal lordship. Changes were
needed on both sides of the duality.

On the one hand, the line between *dominium* and possession could
no longer be so clearly drawn. The Roman law in classical times had

provided for rights in property short of absolute ownership, so that possession or usufruct could be separated from legal ownership. Medieval adaptations of the Roman law were obliged to go further in blurring the line between ownership and possession to allow for conditional and overlapping rights in property. On the other hand, the feudal unity of private property and public power meant that the sphere of public governance could no longer be easily defined in the terms of the Roman *imperium* or the distinction between public sovereignty and private property, or for that matter, in terms of the dichotomy of public and private at all. In conditions of parcellized sovereignty and politically constituted property, the powers of government did not belong only to public officers of a central state. Jurisdiction could be exercised by authorities without *imperium*, or authorities apart from, and indeed opposed to, the secular state; or it could even be vested in the property rights of lordship in which private rights and public powers were united. Jurisdiction could belong to landlords or popes no less than to emperors or kings. The distinction between *dominium* and *jurisdictio* did not require a clear separation of private property and public power; yet, while it allowed for the unity of property and government, it did not rule out a distinction between *dominium* and administration or control – so that, for instance, the ecclesiastical establishment could exercise jurisdiction over Church property, which in principle belonged to the *dominium* of the whole Christian community.

The question of property opened a series of disputes across the whole range of political theory and practice. The confusions of possession, use and ownership involved in feudal property inevitably raised questions about the relations among them, in particular whether people with acknowledged rights of use could claim, simply by virtue of use, the kind of mastery implied by *dominium*. If effective ownership could be derived from use, did this mean that property was a kind of natural right, independent of law and convention? Or was property a right conferred by civil government, entailing only such rights acknowledged by law, and their attendant obligations?

Property rights were an issue for secular rulers seeking ways to assert their public authority over claimants to autonomous powers without denying them their rights of private property. For the Church, matters were even more complicated; and it was here that debates about the nature of property were most systematically pursued. The Church's own vast properties, as well as the private possessions of the faithful, had to be defended. Ecclesiastical authority also had to be asserted against secular power; and, as we saw, the concept of property could be mobilized to that end. Yet the Church was also confronted with internal opposition to its own great wealth, which stood out in provocative contrast to the poverty of Christian multitudes.

This was particularly true with the rise, in the twelfth and thirteenth centuries, of 'heretical' sects who denounced the ostentatious wealth and corruption of the Church. This, in turn, gave rise to the new mendicant orders whose self-imposed poverty was meant, among other things, to defend Catholic orthodoxy against such heresies. The poverty of the mendicant orders then required explanation: did it represent a challenge to property itself, or was there a way of reconciling 'apostolic' poverty with rights of property? Since mendicants made use of material goods to sustain themselves, were they effectively asserting rights to property; or was use, in this case as in others, distinct from ownership? Beyond that lay questions about the moral order ordained by God: must Christians assume that the existing disposition of property and power on this earth, whatever its apparent evil, is divinely ordained and, in that sense, 'natural'; or can there be a conflict between temporal realities and a divinely ordained moral order?

In ancient Rome, there had been varying views on the right of property, but in general Roman jurists regarded property as a convention established by states and enforced by civil law. In the late empire, the Church fathers, notably St Augustine, had proposed a resolution that would continue to be influential throughout the Middle Ages and beyond. Both government and property, according to this doctrine, were necessary evils after the Fall. This meant that, while property was a human convention created and enforced by the state, its function in maintaining peace and social order, like the function of government itself, was sanctioned by divine authority. It followed that apparently inequitable dispositions of property and power could command the acquiescence of Christians, just as Caesar could command their obedience.

In the later Middle Ages, the Franciscan order required something more to sustain its commitment to apostolic poverty. St Francis, the son of a merchant family, appeared to take a fairly extreme view, making no allowance for individual property among the brethren and repudiating commercial transactions. Such an extreme separation from the commercial economy that surrounded them at least in medieval Italy, and on which their survival depended, could hardly be sustained; and Franciscan thinkers found ways of demonstrating that use could be separated from ownership. The theologian and philosopher Duns Scotus (1266–1308) in particular argued that, in the state of innocence, all things had been used in common. This meant that common use was ordained by natural law. But common use did not entail common ownership, since everyone was only entitled to use what was necessary without excluding use by others. It followed that use and ownership were separate; and no form of ownership, let alone private property, could be regarded as natural – even if the complex relations of civil society required the institution of property in order to maintain the peace and civil order.

The Franciscan doctrine of poverty generated debate both about the question of property and, more generally, about relations between ownership and jurisdiction. This, as we have seen, had wider implications for relations between Church and state, papal authority and secular power. The Franciscans adopted the view that, since God gave the world to humanity for its common use, no one, neither individual nor corporate entity, could claim rights of ownership grounded in nature. Both ecclesiastical and secular powers could never do more than administer property as stewards. In the first instance, this principle could be construed as giving an advantage to ecclesiastical authority, if only because, since both ownership and jurisdiction derived from God rather than from any temporal power, the pope, who represented Christ on earth, could effectively claim to act on behalf of the true owner and to exercise superior jurisdiction, while other authorities, both secular and ecclesiastical, enjoyed only jurisdiction delegated by the pope. For all, or most, practical purposes, then, the jurisdiction of the papacy amounted to *dominium*.

The Dominican order would take issue with the Franciscan argument. On the one hand, Dominicans (most notably Thomas Aquinas) argued that use could not be separated from ownership, and that a transfer of use amounted to a transfer of ownership. On the other hand, they insisted on the separation of ownership and jurisdiction and denied that there was any sense in which either secular or ecclesiastical authorities could claim effective ownership or *dominium* over the property that they administered. We shall look at the Dominican argument more closely in our discussion of Thomas Aquinas, and at the Franciscan case as elaborated by William of Ockham. For the moment, it suffices to say that, while the Franciscan position seemed at first more congenial to papal authority, by the early fourteenth century it would be treated as a threat and even a heresy. The commitment to apostolic poverty, and all the arguments constructed to sustain it, came to be seen as a challenge to the Church establishment, with all its vast wealth. Dominican counter-arguments would then find papal favour, and Thomas Aquinas would eventually be canonized.

The strongest argument against the Franciscan position was laid out in Pope John XXII's papal bull, *Quia vir reprobus*. The pope maintained that God's *dominium* over creation was analogous to human *dominium* over earthly possessions, that this was true before the Fall as well as after, and hence that property was indeed natural. Furthermore, use and ownership could not be separated. Only ownership could justify the consumption of goods – that is, in effect, their destruction – because only owners had the right to destroy their own possessions; and even the use of non-consumable goods required a *right* to use.

Medieval debates about the right of property would continue to shape the development of Western political theory. In the fourteenth century and thereafter, the issue would be complicated by the various crises of feudalism, from the plague to peasant rebellions, which would bring about 'transitions' from feudalism to other economic and political forms. Yet we must resist the temptation of thinking that efforts to clarify the conception of property in the late Middle Ages represent a transitional moment from feudal property relations to capitalism. If anything, it was the realities of feudalism itself that demanded a systematic clarification of property. The need was more urgent precisely when and where the complexities of feudal jurisdiction were most powerfully at work: where there was a consistent blurring of lines between property and public power, or between ownership and posses- sion, to say nothing of the needs of the Church in administering its massive wealth.

It is even arguable that precisely where feudal relations of parcellized sovereignty were weakest – that is to say, in England – the feudal idea of property could be preserved, at least in formal law. English property law may have been, in formal principle, the most 'feudal' in Europe, but it comfortably adapted itself to forms of private property that were unusually exclusive and free of feudal obligations. In much the same way, a systematic theory of sovereignty in later centuries would emerge first in France, where a centralizing monarchy was doing battle with parcellized sovereignty, not in England, where the reality of central sovereignty was already well established and there seemed no pressing need to devise a formal doctrine.[16]

---

16 When Jean Bodin in the sixteenth century elaborated his conception of absolute sovereignty in *Six Books of the Commonwealth*, he was not expressing the reality of a clearly sovereign monarchy in France but confronting the challenge posed to monar- chical centralization by the autonomous powers of the nobility and corporate bodies. These were very evident in the Wars of Religion when provincial nobles mobilized Huguenot doctrines in support of their powers against the king.

Religion, Philosophy and Law

Ecclesiastical institutions inherited from imperial Rome belonged to the essential fabric of the medieval legal and administrative order, and the disciplinary doctrines of the Church were an indispensable tool in maintaining social order where the institutions and coercive force of public authority were not enough. But if the legacy of antiquity remained alive in medieval Christianity, Christian doctrine posed its own specific problems in the reception of ancient philosophy. The Greco-Roman legacy was transmitted not only by Roman Christianity and the traditions of the Roman law but, in the wake of Muslim conquests, by the Islamic revival of ancient Greek philosophy. Inevitably, the transactions between philosophy and theology took different forms in the various religious traditions; and this meant that the reception of the classical legacy was determined by the distinct and sometimes mutually exclusive doctrinal requirements of the three monotheistic faiths, Jewish as well as Christian and Islamic.

For all three of them, the central issue in negotiating relations between religion and philosophy was the status of law. Their most striking commonality was, as one commentator has put it, 'a divinely-revealed religion, the appearance of Greek political philosophy within a community that is constituted – either wholly or in its highest aims – by divinely-revealed Law, and the disagreement or conflict between the demands of the divine Law and the political teaching of the philosophers.'[17] All three religions would also accept the classic distinction, most notably outlined by Aristotle, between practical and theoretical sciences, and, in general, the superiority of the theoretical. But their conclusions about the connections between divine and secular law, and hence between theology and philosophy, inevitably differed. To be sure, there were many variations on this score among Christian thinkers themselves, as there were among Muslims and Jews. Yet in one crucial respect, Western Christianity as a whole differed in its very essence from the other two. This difference, which grew out of the very particular experience of Christianity as a product of the Roman Empire, would be elaborated in medieval theory and practice, adapted to the multi-layered fragmentation of authority in feudalism.

Both Islam and Judaism were distinguished from Christianity by their belief in a single divinely revealed system of law, encompassing

17 Eds Ralph Lerner and Muhsin Mahdi, *Medieval Political Philosophy* (Ithaca: Cornell University Press, 1972), p. 1.

the whole range of human practice, secular as well as religious. Christianity, by contrast, had been transformed from an essentially Jewish cult into a 'universal' Church and an imperial religion precisely by distancing itself not only from the old Law of Judaism but from the very idea of a single all-embracing religious law applied without distinction to both matters of faith and the mundane practices of everyday life. The 'universal Church', in other words, was born out of the distinction between Caesar and God and a conviction that each had his own proper sphere. The effect, perhaps indeed the purpose, of this distinction was to legitimate Caesar's claims – that is, the claims of the secular state – as the dominant temporal authority and as a source of law. At the same time, it gave theology its own exalted status, as, at least in principle, the highest form of knowledge, uniquely grounded in divine revelation.

Christian doctrine was capable of underwriting the obligation to obey even the most irreligious and sinful secular power, while still imposing rigid demands in the domain of faith. This did not necessarily. preclude the invocation of religious principles to *oppose* this or that secular power; but, however much the boundaries between the spheres would be disputed in medieval Europe, the defining principle of Western Christianity remained the rendering unto Caesar and God their respective domains of law and obedience. Indeed, in the absence of that principle, which recognized both the support that each sphere derived from the other and the ever-present tensions between them, there would have been no such boundary disputes. The battles, theoretical and practical, among multifarious claims to temporal power in the medieval West cannot be understood without it.

Christianity's distinctive dualism had significant theoretical consequences. It meant, among other things, that theology as a distinct form of knowledge, sustained and enforced by its own institutional base in the Church, encountered very specific dilemmas when confronting classical political philosophy. It is certainly true that the early doctrines of the Church were already shaped by the classical legacy, from Platonic cosmology and Aristotelian epistemology to Ciceronian ethics; but classical political philosophy, and especially its Aristotelian revival in the thirteenth century, posed its own particular challenges. The Church was obliged to consider not only whether there were doctrinal incompatibilities between theology and philosophy but whether philosophy was intruding into its own theological domain, whether boundaries of authority were being dangerously crossed, and whether – or when – the principles of faith obliged them to draw an inviolable line. Various answers were, to be sure, compatible with Christian doctrine. It was possible, for instance, to construct a philosophy, as Thomas Aquinas notably did, that combined theological reflections with theories about human political organization and law, even raising questions about the connections between divine and civic law, or where the boundaries between them lay. Yet, however capacious Christian doctrine may have been, it remains significant that the question of connections and boundaries was there to be asked.

Islam, which had no institutional power comparable to the Christian ecclesiastical establishment and no such autonomous power specifically devoted to policing theology, seems to have found it easier to accommodate philosophy without drawing lines between its proper sphere and the realm of theology. To be sure, the unity of the law could lead to the complete delegitimation of philosophy and all the secular sciences. Yet it was also possible, while remaining true to Islam, to acknowledge that reason and faith could reach the same truths by different means, without provoking boundary disputes. Since there was only one law and only one source of legal authority, there was no reason to regard philosophy as a dangerous temporal rival. It could be treated as another route to the same eternal truths revealed by religion, the latter accessible to anyone, the former only to an intellectual elite. Philosophy and the secular sciences could be pursued on their own merits.

At any rate, because there was no possibility of conflict between two legal authorities, the relative virtues of philosophy and religion did not take the form of a jurisdictional dispute; and the question of incompatibility between philosophical teachings and Islamic law was a matter for jurists, not for theologians protecting their own authoritative turf. There were certainly Islamic thinkers who insisted on the dangers of philosophy; but philosophy could be defended on equally Islamic grounds, even to the point of giving it priority – as was famously done by the great Arab philosopher, Ibn Rushd (Averroes) whose commentaries on Aristotle were a, if not the, major resource for Christian thinkers like Aquinas.

A distinguished and high-ranking legal scholar and jurist, as well as a physician and philosopher, Ibn Rushd (1126–98) was born in Cordova. Apart from a period of disfavour and banishment (later revoked), he served the Almohad dynasty in North Africa and Moorish Iberia. In his *Decisive Treatise* he lays out the relation between the religious law and philosophy, arguing his case as if before a court of law, and using the Islamic law as his standard of judgment. He not only concludes that the two are compatible, and that the attacks on philosophy current in his day have no basis in Islamic law, but even hints that philosophy is inherently superior as a means to the truths at which religion aims. But since the rational and demonstrative methods of philosophy can only be understood by the few, religious methods of persuasion are the best means of approximating the truth for the benefit of the multitude. Religion and philosophy, then, can and must coexist in fruitful alliance.

It is significant that Ibn Rushd, while he was certainly taking issue with a strong Islamic current, was not speaking as an anti-Islamic outsider but as a defender of the Almohad rulers' patronage of philosophy. Although this argument is sometimes dismissed as a tactical ploy on the part of a fundamentally anti-religious rationalist and defender of philosophy, it seems more useful to acknowledge its fundamental compatibility with Islam. A not dissimilar argument had been made earlier by al-Farabi (870–950), often called by Muslims the founder of philosophy in the Islamic world, who distinguished between those who arrive at truth through their own intellect by means of demonstration (as in philosophy) and those, the 'vulgar' multitude, who are given access to the truth by means of persuasion and imaginative representation, the methods of religion. Ibn Rushd's argument can perhaps be understood as giving the last word to philosophy when religious principles are found to be incompatible with demonstrable truth, and this might be taken as an attack on religion. But, whether or not we accept at face value his insistence on accommodation between the two approaches to truth, the important point here is that for Islam, theology did not have the same exalted claims to superiority, even infallibility, conferred on Christian dogma by a powerful ecclesiastical establishment; so there was no reason embedded in Islamic doctrine to regard theologians as better interpreters of truth, even of religious truth, than philosophers.

Ibn Rushd has been credited with an almost modern secularism and rationalism; but we cannot capture the flavour of medieval Islam and the contrasts with Christianity without acknowledging the ways in which the Muslim religion itself encouraged the reception of classical philosophy, as it promoted science. To treat Ibn Rushd's approach as simply secular, opposed to Islamic religiosity, may be to impose on Islam a distinctively rigid Christian dichotomy: it is as if, when philosophy crosses jurisdictional boundaries, it can only be justified by rejecting religion altogether. In fact, even the concept of Averroism as applied to those, including Christians, who believed in a 'double truth' and the separation of philosophic and religious worlds, is based on a dichotomy that certainly does not appear in Averroes himself and is arguably alien to Islam. No such dichotomy was required by Islamic doctrine.

However much today's Islamic fundamentalism appears to rule out the kind of open-mindedness available to medieval Muslims, it is a striking fact that Islamic religious doctrine could in some important ways afford a greater intellectual flexibility than did Christianity. The other side of the same coin may be that Christianity, precisely because it so jealously guarded the sphere of theological authority in the division of labour between state and Church, produced its own negation in a kind of anti-clericalism that was alien to Islam. But as attractive as the anti-clerical mentality may be to committed secularists (including the author of this book), we have to be aware of the contrasts between Christian theological rigidities and the freedom of Islamic thought in the Middle Ages.

It may be that philosophy appeared less threatening to Islamic authority at least partly because the Arabs had only limited access to classical *political* thought, while other aspects of philosophy did not challenge the law so directly. It is also possible that the Platonic political philosophy available to them was better suited to Islamic purposes. Although Ibn Rushd was a great admirer and interpreter of Aristotelian ideas on science and philosophy, his exposure to Greek political theory, like that of Arab scholars in general, was mainly through Plato; and he wrote a commentary on the *Republic*, which he felt able to recommend to his fellow Muslims without much reservation. Perhaps he would have taken a different view of Aristotle's *Politics*, which was not available to him. In that classical text, the civic culture of the polis figured more prominently than it seemed to do in Plato's deeply anti-democratic work; and that might have made the *Politics* less congenial than Platonic texts, where the division of rulers and producers was so sharply defined.

It is even possible (though there is no evidence to support such a presumption) that, quite apart from the contingencies of availability, the more obvious dangers of Aristotle's civic philosophy help to explain the absence of the *Politics* from the Islamic canon. Perhaps the Platonic conception of rule conformed better to the aspirations of the caliphate, while the feudal parcellization of sovereignty made it easier for Western Christianity to absorb, or at least to finesse, the civic principle inherited from classical philosophy. Perhaps the clear Platonic division between ruler and ruled was less important in the medieval West, where the ostensibly settled relation between ruling elements and their subordinates took second place in political thought to conflicts among the various claimants to rule; or maybe the Aristotelian notion of 'political' rule was more easily adapted to an idea of secular kingship subject to secular law than to a notion of rulers descended from a divinely inspired prophet.

At any rate, the approach to the relation between religion and philosophy in medieval Latin Christianity was deeply rooted in the institutional dualism of feudal society. The same dualism is reflected in the distinction between civil and canon law, which has no analogue in Islam or Judaism; and it is characteristic of medieval political thought that much of it was conducted within and between these two legal discourses, by their respective experts. The Latin Christian duality, as we shall see in our discussion of Thomas Aquinas, was also at work in the concept of natural law, which plays a central role in Western political theory but is completely absent from Islamic political philosophy.

Redefining the Political Sphere

Up to this point, we have dealt with medieval ideas about government, property and jurisdiction without systematic discussion of any major political thinkers. The complexities of medieval governance, as we have seen, meant that such ideas were discussed in a variety of discourses, especially legal and theological, other than political philosophy as the ancient Greeks and Romans had understood it. This was especially true at the height of feudal fragmentation of the state. The reconsolidation of government in the later Middle Ages was certainly a spur to political philosophy; but even then, while there was a wealth of innovative legal and theological reflection on matters of power, authority and jurisdiction – reflections in some ways more immediately engaged with the concrete practicalities of governance than Greek and Roman political theory had been – it is significant that there were very few, if any, original contributions to specifically *political* theory on the order of the ancient or early modern classics. Medieval thinkers, especially with the translation into Latin of Aristotle's *Politics* in the thirteenth century, certainly adopted the classical tradition of political philosophy with great enthusiasm and inventiveness; but what was most inventive was their adaptation of that tradition, with its well defined political subject, to a very different setting, not easily captured by the political discourse of classical antiquity.

It was not simply a matter of extending ancient political theory to encompass a wider variety of political forms, city-states, kingdoms and empires distinct from the ancient Greek polis. The point is rather that medieval social arrangements were so different from ancient forms that they were not readily comprehended in the theoretical language of Aristotle's political philosophy. It can, indeed, be argued that one of feudal society's defining characteristics was the virtual disappearance of a clearly distinct political sphere of the kind conceptualized by Aristotle. Even in the later period, when centralized states were establishing firm roots, the complexities of legal and administrative order, the confusions of parcellized sovereignty and complex spheres of jurisdiction, the elaborate network of consensual or contractual relations, meant that the boundaries of the 'political' were ill-defined and fluid. The laborious reasoning of canon and civil lawyers was better suited to accommodate these complexities than was classical political philosophy.

To say this may seem to run counter to some widely accepted views about the strength of the civic principle in medieval Europe. It certainly raises questions, as has already been suggested, about the tendency to treat the political theory of the medieval commune as the precursor of modern republicanism – an interpretation we shall submit to closer scrutiny when we consider Marsilius of Padua, whose *Defensor Pacis* is often read as a pioneering republican tract. For the moment, let us consider a more general suggestion put forward by a distinguished historian of political thought, who argues that medieval political theory and practice, at least when compared to ancient Rome, were more, rather than less, attuned to active citizenship and the civic community:

> Medieval political theorists and practitioners were to take literally and then transform the maxim of late Roman law that 'what touches all should be approved by all' (*quod omnes tangit ab omnibus tractari et approbari debet*), wrenching it out of the context in Justinian's *Codex* where they found it, and thereby emphasizing a deliberative participation by the 'people' in consenting to the laws. Furthermore, the people would be declared capable of electing removable public officials as the executive government . . . This was something of which the ancient Romans . . . would never have approved because 'the people' for them were never considered to be a deliberative body.[18]

'[M]edieval jurists', the argument continues, 'gave preference to the substance of citizenship rather than simply to the abstract principles of Roman legal rules'; and this preference derived from 'the peculiar contractual genesis of medieval city communes, where the citizen was an active rather than a passive member of the city.'[19]

The contrast suggested here between medieval conceptions of active citizenship and the passive variety devised in ancient Rome does point

---

18 Coleman, *op. cit.*, p. 6.
19 *Ibid.*, p. 8.

to certain significant differences between them. The Romans certainly invented a new conception of passive citizenship when they conferred a civic identity on their imperial subjects, and even the Roman people themselves never exercised the deliberative functions of the Athenian demos. Whatever doubts we may have about the medieval civic community (which will be explored in what follows), it is certainly important to acknowledge distinctively Western conceptions of rule by consent and how they are rooted in the medieval experience, with its unique dependence on contractual arrangements of various kinds. It is also true that these conceptions implied distinctive notions of participation in sovereignty which suggest a kind of active citizenship absent in ancient Rome. Yet it is no less important to recognize how such notions of consent, or ideas about participation in the feudal distribution of sovereignty, differed from ancient Greek notions of active citizenship and the civic community. A comparison between medieval and ancient conceptions should not disguise the ways in which medieval forms of parcellized sovereignty shifted political discourse away from what the Greeks in particular regarded as 'political', and away from citizenship as its principal subject. This was true, as we shall see, even in the urban republics of northern Italy, where the city commune was particularly strong.

In previous chapters, we explored the conditions in which political theory emerged in ancient Greece. We saw that the civic sphere of the polis, where the citizen was the essential political agent and political relations were relations among citizens, not between rulers and subjects, presupposed specific social conditions distinct from others in the ancient world. The democratic polis represented a case perhaps unique in pre-capitalist history in which a propertied class for various historic reasons had neither the military nor the political predominance required to sustain its property and powers of appropriation. Unable to impose an unambiguous dominance, it depended on political accommodations with subordinate classes. The reforms of Solon and Cleisthenes, as we saw, were designed to manage class relations in the absence of a clear class dominance, creating a civic order where appropriators and producers confronted one another directly as individuals and as classes, as landlords and peasants, not primarily as rulers and subjects. This also created an unprecedented juxtaposition of, and new tensions between, economic inequality and civic equality.

In the new civic sphere, deep social divisions played themselves out in political terms, not simply in overt struggles for power but in the deliberations and debates of assemblies and juries. This was the setting in which the theory and practice of active citizenship emerged, as a means of comprehending and negotiating a very specific configuration of social power and the very specific conflicts it engendered. While the classics of ancient Greek political theory were written by philosophers who had no great love for the civic unity of rich and poor, their ideas were inevitably shaped by it. Even an antidemocratic thinker like Aristotle, in his philosophical reflections, followed in the tradition of Solon and Cleisthenes by considering what kind of civic accommodation between classes could save the polis from the social conflicts that threatened to destroy it.

The constitutive social relations of feudalism precluded the kind of civic accommodation that underlay the ancient polis and political theory. Relations between landlord and peasant depended on precisely the kind of juridical inequality ruled out by ancient Greek citizenship – or, indeed, Roman republicanism, for all its oligarchic limitations on the civic role of lesser citizens. The economic power of feudal landed aristocracies, their access to the labour of peasants, was inseparable from their extra-economic status and privilege, their political, military and jurisdictional powers. Lordship was economic and political at once. This meant that a civic identity uniting the appropriating and producing classes in one political community in the way landlords and peasants, as well as craftsmen, were united in the ancient polis – or even in republican Rome – would, by definition, have been the end of feudalism.

Theories of government in the medieval West, then, did not concern themselves with a civic relation between landlords and peasants; but nor was their principal theme a relation between rulers and producers. The constitution of relations between feudal lords and peasants as essentially a nexus of rulers and producers was taken as given, and the relation between classes ceased to be the central subject of political discourse. The questions addressed by political theory revolved around the nature and location of rule itself, together with relations among the various competing and overlapping claims to rule. Even when the ultimate power was said to derive from 'the people', this principle was invoked to support the claims of one ruling power – kingly, imperial or papal – against another. Conceptions of consent or popular participation in sovereignty could be mobilized as instruments of rule by those who claimed their own authority on the grounds of popular consent; but they could also be employed even more ingeniously – not to say cynically – to challenge the legitimacy of a competing power by questioning its consensual authority, as we saw in the case of Pope Gregory's challenge to European kings and Holy Roman emperors.

Even to the extent that feudal relations were relations among equals, they were not political transactions among citizens but the contractual agreements among, so to speak, fragments of the state, the bonds of mutual obligation that organized parcellized sovereignty. It is certainly true that various corporate entities, from guilds to civic communes, might practise self-government within their particular spheres; but it cannot be said that the internal transactions of corporate bodies, even the deliberative practices of the civic commune, were the principal subject of political philosophy. We may accept that questioning the right to rule and making it dependent on some form of consent represented, in principle, an advance in the development of accountable government; but the fact remains that the emphasis here was not on active citizenship but on the right to rule.

Ideas of active citizenship as conceived in classical antiquity would, later in the development of Western political theory, be replaced by conceptions of passive, indeed tacit, consent. In their more benign forms, these notions of consent simply extended the principles of medieval corporations, grounded in Roman law, according to which the corporate whole could be bound by the decisions of the few who represented it. But the early modern idea of consent, whether corporate or individual, could be compatible even with absolute monarchy (most notably in the work of Thomas Hobbes), and with notions of sovereignty deriving from 'the people' in which the people, however narrowly conceived, played no effective part at all. Such notions of consent and sovereignty owed more to medieval (and, indeed, imperial Roman) conceptions of rule than to ancient ideas of active citizenship. People whose political role was as passive as this might just have been accepted as 'citizens' by, say Augustine; but, by Aristotle's standards, they would have been 'conditions', not 'parts', of the polis.

How far removed medieval political discourse was from the classical vocabulary of political theory is nicely illustrated by a mistranslation of Aristotle in the first complete translation of the *Politics*. William of Moerbeke (*c.*1215–86), apparently at the instigation of Thomas Aquinas, translated the whole of Aristotle's works into Latin, including, in about 1260, the *Politics*. His mistranslation of one important passage would be taken up with significant consequences by St Thomas himself, among others. It is significant not simply because it exemplifies the contingent effects of one man's ambiguous translation but rather because it expresses the medieval understanding of politics itself.

We have alluded in previous chapters to Aristotle's distinction among different forms of rule. There is, for instance, the kind of rule exercised over men in servile conditions; but there is also a 'political' kind of rule among free men, in which political equals govern and are governed in turn. What makes this form of rule 'political' is that it occurs in, and only in, a civic community, a community of citizens of intrinsically equal status, all of them entitled to participate in rule. There is a certain ambiguity in Aristotle's conception of 'political' rule and whether it can apply to all forms of polity, from democracy to monarchy – whether, in particular, a monarchy can be 'political'; but what is clear is that rule can be political only among men who are free and equal, in principle capable of ruling as well as being ruled. In Aristotle's ideal polis, where the civic community is limited to the rich and well born and where that community rules over subordinate producing classes excluded from citizenship – that is, a polis that distinguishes between the 'parts' of a civic community and the 'conditions' necessary to, yet always governed by, the citizen body – the relation between conditions and parts, rulers and ruled, is not 'political'.

Aristotle, like Plato before him, was undoubtedly keen to reinforce the division between ruler and ruled; but he confronted the issue in the terms imposed by the experience and discourse of Athenian democracy. Because the civic community was so central to Athenian political practice and theory, in outlining his ideal polis he defined the relation between ruler and ruled as a relation between the civic community and those outside it. The civic community consists of citizens, the 'parts' of the polis, who are qualified to rule and who are therefore in a position to rule and to be ruled in turn. This is not to say that ruling and being ruled occur, for Aristotle, simultaneously; but it is the essence of a truly *political* community that its citizens are, in principle, fit for political praxis.

In Moerbeke's translation, 'in turn' becomes 'in part', and Aristotle's reference to ruling and being ruled 'in turn' no longer applies to a civic community whose members are all entitled to rule but rather to a ruler who is 'in part' both ruler and ruled. Whatever Moerbeke's intention may have been, for Thomas Aquinas, as we shall see, rule is 'political' to the extent that the ruler himself, like his subjects, is bound by laws. The 'political' sphere as a relation among civic equals altogether disappears. It is, indeed, far from clear that the category of citizenship as Aristotle understood it was meaningful at all in medieval terms. People might enjoy rights by virtue of lordship, or as members of a guild or corporation with a charter of freedom; but the complex hierarchical structure of feudal lordship and corporate entities that constituted the medieval order was something very different from the ancient Greek community of citizens.

This is not to deny that medieval philosophers reflected on the whole range of political forms from imperial or monarchical rule to popular government; and some, including Thomas Aquinas, even acknowledged the benefits of rule by popular consent. But the medieval distinction between 'regal' or 'kingly' rule and 'political' rule reflects not only a political order very different from the ancient Greek polis but also a preoccupation with causes of disorder and conflict very different from those that dominated Aristotle's political thought. The conflicts between rich and poor, which for Aristotle were the ultimate source of *stasis* in the polis, the conflicts that most required political solution, played no such central role in medieval philosophy. Such conflicts, needless to say, certainly existed; but they were replaced at the core of political thinking by disorders produced by overlapping and competing powers of rule. The political relations at issue were neither relations among citizens nor between a community of citizens and those outside it, and the questions addressed by political theory did not implicate the civic community or citizenship in the way that they did in ancient Greece.

The forms in which these questions posed themselves varied according to the diverse configurations of power in different parts of medieval Europe, the specific forms and relative strength of competing claims to temporal authority and the intensity of the contestations among them. In jurisdictional contests among landlords, kings, popes and emperors, lordly power was stronger and monarchy weaker in some kingdoms than in others, just as emperors or popes were greater threats to some kings than to others. France and England, for instance, differed from each other in all these respects, not least because in France corporate entities were stronger than in England, where the relative weakness of corporate powers in relation to the monarchy gave greater prominence both to a unified central state and to the private individual, or to relations between private rights and public sovereignty. These differences, as we shall see, expressed themselves in theory no less than in practice. Nevertheless, in neither case was the political domain defined by a civic community.

Italy was different again. In the north, where landlordly power was relatively weak and, instead, an autonomous civic commune exercised a kind of corporate, collective lordship over the *contado*, we might expect to see the civic community reinstated at the core of political discourse. Yet here too competing autonomous powers and conflicting jurisdictions were the dominant preoccupations of political philosophy. While lawyers and rhetoricians no doubt had much to say about civic life and citizenship, the relations that figured most prominently in major philosophical reflections on government were neither the relations among citizens as equals in a civic community nor the conflicts

– which were often intense – between the dominant urban oligarchies and forces beneath them.

The geographic proximity of papal power and the immediacy of its temporal pretensions represented a very particular challenge to the governing classes of Italy, as did imperial claims in those parts of Italy more vulnerable to intrusions from German kings in their capacity as Holy Roman emperors. In the relatively small civic republics of the north, where the material interests of urban elites were heavily invested in the commune – not only in its power over the *contado* but more particularly in its commercial strength and the profits of civic office – support by one or another of the greater powers, papal or imperial, could be critical to the dominance of this or that civic faction and its access to wealth. Although conflict between urban elites and those beneath them was always a central fact of civic life, it is not surprising that politics in the republics typically took the form of factional struggles within the urban patriciate, often with external support, for control over the lucrative resources of the commune. Even, indeed especially, Marsilius's *Defensor Pacis*, for many commentators the quintessence of medieval republicanism, has less to do, as we shall see, with active citizenship in a civic community than with the struggle between pope and emperor.

It is worth keeping in mind that, if these Italian cities represented any direct continuity with Greco-Roman antiquity, it was with the municipal system of Roman imperial rule, not the civic community of the polis or even the Roman Republic. Even when the civic community takes centre stage in medieval political philosophy, it is typically as a player in the conflicts among contesting powers. The civic commune might assert itself against signorial rule, or against intrusions from papal or imperial power; or, on the contrary, it might (as we shall see in our discussion of Marsilius of Padua) be invoked to support one or another of these antagonistic powers. But the principal subject of political philosophy was not the civic life of citizens in a self-governing community.[20] The fact that, in practice, there was a vibrant civic life in these medieval urban communes, and that there is a rich body of documentation

---

20 The continuities in political thought from medieval Italy to the Renaissance can be misleading. We might, for example, be inclined to include Machiavelli in a discussion of medieval Italian political theory, on the grounds that he represents the culmination of a tradition rooted in the medieval urban communes. But there is a significant difference between the role of the civic community in medieval political philosophy and the reflections on republican autonomy and civic life which emerge in Renaissance Italy, when the main threats to civic autonomy come not from popes and Holy Roman emperors but post-feudal monarchical states.

testifying to its deliberative activities, only serves to emphasize the distinctive preoccupations of medieval political philosophy.

Medieval political theory involved a particularly complex relation to the legacy of classical antiquity. It was complicated not only by relations between secular and ecclesiastical authority but also by the ever-changing scope of secular state power and ever-present tensions between the processes of state centralization and the forces of parcellization. The legacy of empire, together with its classical inheritance, continued to structure the parcellized sovereignty of feudalism, both in practice and in theory. It survived both in the theological doctrines of Christian universalism and in the institutional hierarchy of the Church; but these were always in tension with the particularities of plural kingdoms, lordly jurisdiction and autonomous corporations of various kinds. At the same time, political philosophy had to adapt to the absence of a neatly defined political terrain, not a civic community such as the polis but a particularly convoluted network of secular and ecclesiastical institutions, together with the unity of property and jurisdiction.

Medieval Political Thought?

Much of this chapter has been devoted to medieval reflections on authority and jurisdiction in the absence of a clearly defined *political* sphere. It has been suggested that political theory as a specific mode of thought was not ideally suited to the distinctive conditions of medieval governance. *The Cambridge History of Medieval Political Thought* even begins with the proposition that 'The character of "medieval political thought" is problematic', suggesting among other things that, in the medieval context, modes of 'political' thinking appropriate to the experience of the classical polis or of 'the state' in the post-medieval Western world have little application.[21] Since 'few writers in that period can be meaningfully described as "political thinkers" at all; and very few indeed can be regarded as having made a major individual contribution to the subject', a history that proceeds by studying the work of outstanding figures 'can hardly fail to yield an imperfect and distorted picture of political ideas in the medieval centuries.'[22]

On these grounds, the *Cambridge History* chooses to adopt a thematic or conceptual approach instead of systematically discussing the ideas of each major thinker in turn. Given the peculiarities of

---

21 *Cambridge* History, *op. cit.*, p. 1.
22 *Ibid.*, p. 4.

medieval governance and the forms of theoretical reflection it produced, there is much to be said for this choice; but it may be useful nonetheless to look at a sample of outstanding figures to illustrate how the tradition of political theory inherited from antiquity was adapted to medieval conditions, and how adaptations varied in specific medieval contexts.

If any thinkers have a claim to 'political theory' in the medieval West, they belong to the later Middle Ages, at a time when more or less stable governments, in the form of monarchies and city-states, were on the rise, and while conflict between secular and ecclesiastical powers, or among kings, popes and emperors, was especially intense. This is also the time when the influence of classical political philosophy gathered momentum, especially with the translation into Latin of Aristotle's *Politics*. We can gain some insight into the particularities of political thinking in that period by looking at a few major figures who, while subject to similar intellectual influences and in varying degrees adopting the language of classical political thought and of Aristotle in particular, put them to work in different local contexts and in pursuit of different ends.

Thomas Aquinas (*c*.1225–74), Marsilius of Padua (1290–1342) and William of Ockham (*c*.1288–*c*.1348) were all in one way or another caught up in the characteristic conflicts of their time and responded to them philosophically, at varying degrees of conceptual distance from political events and power struggles. The most immediately engaged of the three was Marsilius, who was very intensely involved in the bitter struggle between Pope John XXII and the imperial aspirant, Ludwig of Bavaria, arguing the case, in his classic philosophical work, *Defensor Pacis*, for the emperor against the pope. The work of the other two was more substantially theological, although both of them were mobilized to fight the battle of the mendicant orders, Thomas on the side of the Dominicans and William of Ockham later on the side of the Franciscans – with all the implications this had not only for theology but for the temporal interests of the Church and the papacy. Both also had some more direct involvement in public life and the conflicts among various temporal powers. Aquinas not only dealt with the practical affairs of the Church, even as adviser to the pope on public matters, but also for a time advised Louis VIII of France (technically, King of the Franks and Count of Artois), to whom he was related. His ideas would be taken up and adapted by others more directly engaged in power struggles – for instance, by John of Paris (d. 1306), who, as we shall see, elaborated Thomistic doctrines to support King Philip IV of France in his conflict with Pope Boniface VIII. William of Ockham, like Marsilius, found himself caught up in the struggle between Pope John XXII and Ludwig of Bavaria when his own interventions on behalf of the Franciscans angered the pope. The philosopher sought refuge at Ludwig's court – an experience which, needless to say, was very much at the heart of his writings on the relation between secular and ecclesiastical power.

Whatever else may distinguish these thinkers from each other, it is worth considering the differences among the immediate contexts in which they confronted similar theoretical questions. While the contrasts among them are certainly not reducible to divergences in their respective contexts, there are some notable conformities between their ideas and the particular circumstances in which their philosophies were formulated. The differences between William of Ockham and the other two are particularly striking, in ways that reflect the specific conditions of medieval England. Before we explore the ideas of these three thinkers, then, let us briefly remind ourselves of the variations among the networks of power and politically constituted property in France, and more specifically Paris (where Aquinas was engaged not only in theological disputes but in both ecclesiastical and secular politics), northern Italy (Marsilius's political terrain) and William of Ockham's England.

The feudal parcellization of sovereignty was still a major fact of life in thirteenth century France, where seigneurial rights and jurisdictions were very much in evidence – as they would continue to be until the rise of a strong central state in the form of an 'absolutist' monarchy in the sixteenth and seventeenth centuries, never to be completely eradicated until the revolution of the eighteenth century. At the same time, the monarchy had made important advances in its territorial ambitions, and by the late twelfth and thirteenth centuries was already working to establish Paris as a national centre, not only a seat of government but the fount of education and culture. The royal project was, however, in tension not only with seigneurial autonomy in the surrounding countryside but also with the claims of autonomous urban corporations. Even the government of Paris, by now a thriving commercial centre, was a complex network of royal and corporate institutions, much of its public life governed by powerful merchants and guilds. Beyond the kingdom's still unstable boundaries, there were challenges from the German princes of the Holy Roman Empire, whose authority the French refused to recognize, and bitter conflicts between the royal power and the papacy, culminating in the struggle between King Philip IV and Pope Boniface VIII.

Earlier in this chapter, we considered the ways in which the city-states of northern Italy and the kingdoms of England both before and after the Norman Conquest diverged from the feudal pattern of parcellized sovereignty exemplified by France. For our purposes here, it suffices to recall the complex organization of the Italian urban communes: their autonomy and relative independence from centralizing powers of one kind or another, and, at the same time, their internal fragmentation, the semi-autonomous powers and corporations within them, the pressures exerted on them by emperors and popes, together with internal factions associated with one or the other superior power. The corporate principles on which the city-states were organized – both the civic corporation itself and the corporate entities within it – would be particularly significant in the development of political theory emanating from the civic communes, as we shall see in the case of Marsilius.

The English differed from both these cases in ways that would have particularly important implications for political theory. Instead of parcellized sovereignty, in contrast to France, the English developed a precociously centralized state in tandem with uniquely exclusive individual property. In place of seigneurial jurisdiction, the English established a unitary state, while the common law increasingly recognized an individual 'interest' in property independent of any extra-economic claims, privileges or obligations. This was distinct from the right, also enjoyed by the French in the later Middle Ages, to defend individual property rights before the law. The latter, even before royal courts, could (as in France) exist where property was still held on feudal principles, with the attendant obligations, and where each seigneurie continued to have its own system of law and its own autonomous jurisdiction. In England, the individual right of property itself was far more independent of feudal obligations and seigneurial jurisdiction.

In contrast to both France and Italy, where corporate principles were stronger and where the constituent units of political order were corporate entities, the English state was increasingly constituted as a collection of free individuals, subject to no lord except the king (notwithstanding the private powers of manorial lords). These differences would be reflected in the English system of representation, giving rise very early to a unitary parliament, conceived as representing not corporate bodies (as the French estates represented corporate entities) but the whole national community, composed of individual free men and propertyholders. Parliament would also exercise legislative powers far earlier than French representative bodies, the powers of propertied classes not as possessors of feudal jurisdiction but as participants in the centralized state.

Thomas Aquinas, John of Paris, Marsilius of Padua and William of Ockham all in their various ways made use of classical political theory and of Aristotle in particular. No doubt each thinker possessed his own distinctive genius. No doubt, too, they differed in purpose and political commitment. Yet their adaptations of, and departures from, their classical antecedents vary in significant ways that are unmistakably related to their contextual differences.

Thomas Aquinas

Thomas Aquinas was born, probably but not certainly in 1225, into an aristocratic family – his father was Count Landulf, while his mother was related to the Hohenstaufen dynasty of Holy Roman emperors – in Seccarocca, between Naples and Rome. Belonging to a prominent landed family in the Kingdom of Sicily, at a time of bitter conflict between its king, Frederick II, and Pope Gregory IX, Aquinas learned very early and at close hand about the struggles between ecclesiastical and secular power. His formal education began in the Benedictine monastery where his uncle was abbot, and continued at the University of Naples, where, against the strong wishes of his family, he fell under the influence of the new Dominican Order. This was a time of intellectual and religious ferment, with new universities playing an increasingly prominent role, not least to satisfy a growing need for an educated clergy, and purveying the 'new learning' profoundly influenced by classical sources. As a doctor of philosophy, Aquinas went on to teach in various Italian cities; but it was in Paris that he engaged most intensely in theological disputes and debates on the mendicant orders. It is reasonable to assume that it was in Paris, too, in his management of church affairs and as adviser to the king, that he found himself most personally engaged at the intersection of ecclesiastical and secular power.

The implications of political events and conflicts for Thomas's work are not immediately apparent. His case for the Dominican conception of property certainly had, as we have seen, practical implications for the temporal affairs of the Church; but unlike Marsilius or even William of Ockham, he is not, in his philosophy, taking obvious sides in the power struggles of his day – unless it is to support, in general principle, monarchical power such as that of his relative Louis VIII. We should perhaps concentrate our attention on another, broader sense in which Aquinas's political philosophy, and his adaptation of Aristotle, reflect the conditions and preoccupations of his time.

It was suggested earlier in this chapter that Aristotle's political theory was ill-suited to the realities of medieval governance. A system of thought grounded in the civic life of the ancient polis could be made to fit medieval conditions only by means of significant conceptual leaps. Yet there was one essential function that Aristotelian political philosophy was well designed to perform. With certain adjustments, which Aquinas accomplished, it provided a conceptual framework for situating secular government in a larger cosmic order in a way that neatly met the temporal needs of medieval Christians.

This may seem an odd proposition. On the face of it, the political theory of a pagan philosopher like Aristotle may seem far more adaptable to the study of medieval government in its mundane operations than to theological reflections on humanity's place in a Christian universe. Yet it is precisely in the elaboration of such theological reflections that Aristotle played a crucial role. Medieval Christian philosophers like Aquinas continued to be deeply influenced by early Christian Neoplatonism, particularly in its Augustinian form; but their needs were different from those of earlier Christians. The other-worldliness of Neoplatonism, with its devaluation of earthly existence in favour of spirituality and mystical release from the material realm, served Christians reasonably well in the later Roman Empire. Where the civic community had given way decisively to imperial rule, there was no need for Christian subjects to concern themselves with the intricacies of secular governance. It was enough for theologians like Augustine to underwrite the division of labour between Caesar and God; and good Christians, while rendering obedience to Caesar, could get on with minding their own spiritual business. But something different was required to explain the preoccupation of medieval Christians with the complexities of feudal (and post-feudal) governance, not least their obsession with the conflicts among various claims to temporal power. Aristotle's theory of politics, and the place he accords it in his philosophical system, provided a conceptual framework for Christian thinkers to acknowledge the supremacy of the spiritual realm while treating temporal and even secular government as the highest of Christian concerns in this world.

Let us consider, first, the essential Aristotelian principles adopted by Aquinas, in very simple outline. We can then go on to explore his departures from Aristotle, as he responded both to the requirements of Christian theology and to the realities of medieval governance. The argument of Aristotle's *Politics*, as we have seen, proceeds from his general theory of nature. In his effort to explain the principles of order that remain invariable in a natural world of constant motion, he emphasizes two principles: the purpose or *telos* towards which every process tends, and the intrinsic hierarchy of the natural order. Aristotle applies these principles to the polis by arguing that this form of human association is the highest form, and that it perfects human development;

that 'man is by nature a polis-animal', a creature intended to live in a polis, because it is only in the polis that he can fulfil his own *telos* as a rational and moral being. It is the polis, with its customs and laws, that habituates people to living in accordance with the principles of virtue and the good required for the happiness appropriate to human beings. As for what kind of polis is best, Aristotle proposes an ideal form, in which the basic hierarchical principle of nature, the division between ruling elements and ruled, is clearly reproduced in the division between 'conditions' and 'parts' of the polis; but he suggests that the 'best practicable polis' is one that combines elements of oligarchic and democratic forms, to reduce the disorder generated especially by the conflicts between rich and poor and their divergent conceptions of justice.

Aquinas's Aristotelianism, spelled out above all in his *Summa Theologica*, begins with the treatment of humanity as part of the natural order, in which each part is directed toward its own proper natural *telos*. Human beings are uniquely endowed with reason, and, as rational creatures, have a unique cognitive access to reality, which includes a natural capacity to understand the fundamental moral principles required to achieve the happiness specific to humanity. The human *telos* is to realize those rational capacities, in pursuit of the good, which is accessible to natural reason.

The cognitive capacity to understand the nature of things is, for Aquinas as for Aristotle, extended by practical reason, enabling human beings to make rational judgments not only about how things really are but also about right actions. While the principles of goodness are accessible to reason, human goodness in practice is a function of feelings directed by reason. It is a matter of training and habituation, which produce a disposition not only to pursue the good but to love it; and, like Aristotle, Aquinas argues that life in a 'political' community trains people to moral principles and habituates them to loving the good for humanity. For this reason, human beings are by nature 'political' animals, in the sense that the natural *telos* of humanity is best achieved in 'political' communities governed by law. The highest virtue is justice: affording to people that which is due to them; and this can probably best be achieved in some kind of 'mixed constitution'.

The 'naturalization' of man, virtue, justice and the 'political' community in the manner of Aquinas is a major departure from earlier Christian doctrines, and in this respect he differs substantially from Augustine. Aquinas's account of life in this world is very different from his great predecessor's treatment of human history in this sinful earthly existence. For Aquinas history is not just a tragic spectacle, in which no harmony, no just or rightful order, can prevail: in such a world the best that can be hoped for is a certain degree of security and material comfort, as long as subjects, including Christians, obey Caesar, while seeking release in the spiritual realm. This is not to say that the Fall and sin have no bearing on Aquinas's theology, but political association for him is not just a necessary evil to deal with a fallen humanity. Since political order is natural, it must have existed before the Fall, even if the tendency of human beings to sin has required coercion to maintain peace and order in a way that it did not in the prelapsarian condition. The Fall has not meant the loss of natural reason; and, while human beings are capable of choosing not to follow the principles of reason, their distinctive rational capacities allow them to understand and follow natural law. They can achieve happiness or fulfilment (*beatitudo*) in this world by living in accordance with the principles of reason and morality. The temporal political order, directed towards a common good, is the means to accomplish that end. It is worth adding here that such a conception of temporal power would have been all but indispensable to a Christian defence of monarchical secular power.

Commentators may differ about the degree to which, or even whether, complete and ultimate fulfilment for Aquinas can be achieved only after death, in a world beyond this one (as commentators differ about Aristotle's views on the relative value of *praxis* as against the contemplative life); but, just as even the most extreme reading of Aristotle's commitment to a life of contemplation cannot deny the importance he attaches to the polis, there can be no mistaking the value for Aquinas of the *beatitudo* available in the here and now to human beings living in 'political' communities. It is also clear, although he never systematically elaborates his views on the relation between spiritual and temporal powers, that he grants a substantial degree of independence to the secular political community, the *civitas*. There certainly remains a vital function for the spiritual community and the Church that represents it, in preparation for eternal life; but this does not detract from, or even subordinate, the function of secular associations, whether families or states, in their pursuit of earthly happiness. Nevertheless, Aquinas is, after all, a devout Christian; and to accommodate the doctrines of Christianity required some adjustments in Aristotle's cosmos.

Aristotle's conception of the *telos*, as we saw in a previous chapter, includes 'final causes', the ultimate condition 'for the sake of which' natural processes of growth and development take place. These are immanent in objects themselves (as the potentiality of the oak is immanent in the acorn), requiring no deliberate purpose, no control from without, and no divine mind. His idea of the 'unmoved mover', the first cause of motion which is not itself set in motion by any prior cause, does not suggest divine intelligence or purpose. It is simply a way of stating the principle that, in a cosmos where motion is constant and eternal, there must exist some moving principle that sets things in motion without itself being moved, or else we must suppose an infinite regress of movers, which for him is an impossibility. For Aristotle, in other words, the unmoved mover is a principle of physics, not theology. For Aquinas, needless to say, there must be something more than an unmoved mover in this sense. There must be a *creator*, and the cosmic order presupposes the purpose and intelligence of God.

For political theory, the most important implication of this view lies in the concept of law. Aquinas constructs a bridge between theology and the principles of earthly government by distinguishing among various kinds of law: divine, eternal, natural and human or positive. Divine law, directed to eternal life and humanity's relationship with God, is the subject of divine revelation in scripture. This is conceptually distinct from eternal law, which represents the principles of a cosmic order governed by God. To the extent that human reason has access to this cosmic order, we can speak of natural law. Natural law is that aspect of divine regulation accessible to human reason, establishing the basic principles of the good in human practice and legitimate government. This, in turn, should be embodied in the positive laws enacted by governments on earth.

Aquinas's concept of natural law represents a significant departure from Aristotle. There have been disputes among scholars about whether Aristotle himself has a theory of natural law. Yet, while he certainly believes standards of virtue exist not merely by convention but by nature, he never formulates these principles in terms of law (as the Stoics and Cicero would do later). However much he may have contributed to later conceptions of natural law with his naturalization of virtue and justice, there is certainly no sense of legislation and, even less, of an ultimate lawgiver, never mind some kind of punishment for breaches of the law. His 'natural' principles of virtue are not even absolute, rigorous rules discovered by reason but often appear to be little more than rules of thumb as embodied (almost tautologically, as we have seen) in the man of practical wisdom. Natural law for Aquinas, by contrast, is very clearly and indispensably understood as *law*, implying legislation and an ultimate lawgiver.

The transformation of Aristotle's unmoved mover into a divine creator and legislator has an obvious role in Aquinas's theology and his Christianization of Aristotle. But there is more to be said about the function of natural law in medieval political theory, which has as much to do with the realities of medieval governance as with the requirements of Christian theology. We have already observed that the concept was absent, for example, from Islamic philosophy; but it is not enough to say that the concept plays a unique role in Western political thought simply because the Roman legacy, including Cicero's theory of natural law, was more readily available to Latin Christians than it was to Arabs. We also have to take account of the theoretical needs that were met by the concept of natural law: needs that existed in Christianity, in the context of Western feudalism, as they did not in the Islamic world.

We have already commented on the difference between Christianity and both of the other monotheistic faiths on the subject of law, the uniquely Christian separation between a divinely revealed religious law and the civil law of everyday life. Yet it did not suffice for medieval Christians simply to imagine a divine lawgiver, who legislated from on high and punished those who strayed from his law. It is precisely because medieval Christianity was constantly obliged to negotiate the division between divine and civil law, just as it was always faced by the tensions between ecclesiastical and secular powers, that Christian philosophy needed a conceptual bridge between them. It needed a sphere of law that in a sense had one foot in each camp, without violating the integrity of either or challenging its authority. There had to be a law ultimately sanctioned by the divine lawgiver but accessible to ordinary mortals in ways that did not require divine revelation, even if divine revelation served to confirm the discoveries of natural reason. A Christian Aristotelian like Thomas Aquinas could not settle for a truly Averroist solution, which presupposed a single system of law; so, unless he was prepared to accept a 'double truth' relating to two completely separate worlds, natural law was an exceedingly useful idea.

Not the least of its functions is that it can both situate secular associations in a divinely ordered cosmos and at the same time grant the secular *civitas* its independence from spiritual authority by empha- sizing that human reason, even without divine revelation, has substan- tial access to the good. Human convention can, indeed, supplement natural law, or perhaps even modify its secondary principles. For exam- ple, although all men are equal by nature, slavery, which exists by the *ius gentium*, can be justified in relation to natural law: while there is no principle of nature that dictates that one man should be a slave and another man not, the enslavement of one man by another may be natural in another sense – on the grounds of utility, which dictates that it may be useful, as Aristotle said, for the slave to be ruled by a wiser man.

The serviceability of natural law as conceived by Aquinas is nowhere better illustrated than in his conception of property. We have already seen how the Dominican argument on property responded to the critics of the Church and served to make its vast wealth consistent with the principles of the mendicant orders; but Aquinas, here as elsewhere, also strikes a neat balance between principles of Christian theology and the mundane requirements of secular life. God, he argues, has *dominium* over the nature of material things, but man has effective *dominium* over their use. There is no principle in nature that determines whether possession is, or should be, private or communal; but private property does exist by the *ius gentium*. While the material world was originally intended for the use of all humanity, the utility of private property has made it consistent with natural law. It even serves a higher purpose, contributing not only to the sustenance of families but also to relief of the poor and promotion of the common good.

There are in Aquinas's work severe moral strictures against such economic practices as usury or fraud, and commerce for him is not a particularly noble activity; but, although the idea of 'just price' is central to his ethical philosophy, he certainly accepts the benefits of trade – as one might expect of a philosopher so deeply rooted in a major medieval commercial centre like thirteenth-century Paris. If he perceives moral dangers in wealth and commerce, which require regulation of property and commercial activity by civil law and even princely rule, he clearly favours private property and wealth when used in accordance with reason.

The Displacement of Civic by Legal Relations

The duality of Western Christianity is, however, still not enough to explain the critical role played by natural law. We must also take into account the overwhelming importance of law in general to the medieval order. While Aristotle was certainly concerned with the role of *nomoi* in the polis, there is nothing like the same preoccupation with law as the constitutive principle of social order that characterizes the philosophy of Aquinas. This divergence reflects the difference between the civic community of the ancient polis and the complex network of legal and contractual relations, within and among various corporate entities, that constituted the medieval order. If Aristotle's political theory had to do with the civic accommodation between classes in a single civic community, medieval thinkers were more concerned with mapping out the spheres of authority among overlapping and competing jurisdictions and negotiating interactions among multiple communities. It was not for nothing that the theorization of medieval governance was dominated by lawyers, civil and canonical. The concept of natural law, already imbued with ancient Roman legalism, neatly extended the legalistic conception of order to the cosmos as a whole.

The displacement of civic by legal relations runs very deep in medieval political philosophy. It is, for instance, visible in Moerbeke's mistranslation of Aristotle, in which the definition of the 'political', as we have seen, has less to do with relations among citizens than with the lawfulness, or otherwise, of rule. In Aquinas's commentary on the *Politics*, it is revealing that, although he follows Aristotle's discussion of citizenship, he renders the distinction between 'kingly' or 'regal' and 'political' regimes in the manner of Moerbeke. Just as the household is characterized by a twofold rule, domestic and despotic, the one over members of his family, the other over slaves, the city too 'is governed by a twofold rule, namely the political and the kingly. There is kingly rule when he who is set over the city has full power, whereas there is political rule when he who is set over the city exercises a power restricted by certain laws of the city.'[23] The immediately striking point about this passage is that it takes monarchical government for granted, distinguishing not between monarchy and other forms of polity but between lawful and unlawful forms of princely rule. There may even be grounds for doubting that Thomas unambiguously prefers 'political' monarchy – though he is so unclear about this that he has been called everything from an absolute monarchist to a forerunner of modern constitutionalism. The fundamental question here, however, concerns the criterion on which this distinction is made and how Aquinas redefines the 'political' in contrast to Aristotle.

It is certainly true that Aristotle distinguishes between lawful and unlawful rulers, or rulers who act in the common interest and rulers who act for themselves. But the defining characteristic of 'political' rule, by whomever it is exercised, is not simply that it is lawful but that it occurs within a community of citizens – not, it should be emphasized, just free men but citizens, who in principle are qualified for political participation. For St Thomas, by contrast, as for other medieval thinkers, the centre of political discourse shifts away from the community of citizens, as he adapts the 'political' to the conditions of the feudal order, its hierarchy of juridical status and corporate entities.

23 *Politics* I,1,13.

There are, to be sure, suggestions in Thomas's work that, even if he takes princely government for granted, rule in accordance with the common good entails some kind of consent on the part of those who are ruled that the relation between them and the ruler has something like the character of a covenant and that tyrannical rule – that is, rule in the interests of the ruler and not the common good – is a breach of the covenant which may perhaps produce an entitlement to depose or even kill the tyrant. [24] This is, however, not a private but a public right, nor is it a civic right belonging to individual citizens; and, while Aquinas is never precise on this question, it is likely that the public authority in which it resides is, for Aquinas as for his contemporaries in general, a function of feudal or corporate status.

The rational capacities of humanity, which enable individuals to judge the rectitude of law, seems to suggest that all of them are entitled to some share in sovereignty, residing in the whole community or in some representative entity; and this may mean that laws which do not conform to the principles of reason carry no absolute obligation to obedience. Disobedience may even be required when individuals are ordered to commit a sinful act. Yet even if we take these suggestions of consent and representation to the limits of interpretation, it is important to acknowledge the differences between these ideas and the ancient Greek conception of citizenship. We should acknowledge that, although we have become so accustomed in the modern world to thinking of civic participation in the terms of consent and representation, ideas such as those of Aquinas are very much rooted in the medieval order. Such notions of a share in sovereignty, as was suggested earlier in this chapter, have less to do with active citizenship in a civic community, or even the kind of civic participation still existing in the early Middle Ages in assemblies of free men, than with the distribution of sovereignty and jurisdiction in a complex organizational network, with a multiplicity of corporate communities, and the coexistence of various hierarchies, secular and ecclesiastical. The central 'political' agent in this medieval order is not the individual citizen of the classical polis, or the free man of the Carolingian era, but the possessor of some feudal jurisdiction or a corporate entity endowed with its own legal rights, a degree of autonomy, and probably a charter defining its relation to other corporations and superior powers.

It is perhaps in this light, too, that we can best understand Thomas's conception of, and apparent inclination towards, a 'mixed constitution',

24 See for example, *In Rom.* 13.1 V.6.

which combines monarchy with elements from other forms of polity. This idea may seem inconsistent with his unambiguous preference for princely rule, until we consider the realities of feudal monarchy, always balanced to some degree by autonomous lordly and corporate powers. Thomas may, if anything, lean further towards unchecked 'regal' monarchy than many of his contemporaries, and there may even be some justification for calling him an absolute monarchist *avant la lettre*; but in his time and place, an 'absolute' monarchy completely free of parcellized sovereignty was all but inconceivable.

Even Aquinas's conception of justice is shaped by these distinctive medieval realities, defined by its legalism and corporate organization. Justice, again, entails giving others their due. As a general principle of morality, it expresses the Christian rule of 'doing unto others as you would be done by'. Since it presupposes a concern with the good of others, its proper sphere is the community, the *civitas*, whose object is the common good where people learn to love the good of others as their own. Yet there is, as one commentator has nicely put it, 'a whiff of the feudal' in Aquinas's conception, together with a Ciceronian deference to rank and differential entitlements:[25] 'A thing is due', St Thomas writes, 'to an equal in one way, to a superior in another, and to an inferior in yet another; likewise there are differences between what is due from a contract, a promise, or a favour conferred.'[26] This is a reasonably clear departure from Aristotle. To characterize this departure, we could just point to the difference between Aquinas's conviction that 'what is due depends on the status of the recipient', and Aristotle's view 'that status is ideally a consequence of moral merit'.[27] Yet there is another way of looking at this difference, which perhaps tells us more about the divergences between the medieval order of Aquinas and Aristotle's polis.

It is certainly true that even Aristotle's notion of proportionate equality is not predicated on the principle that just deserts are determined by some clearly defined social status. It is, for example, compatible with a polis in which different classes share a civic status. Yet it surely cannot be said that social differences play no part in his conception of justice and what is due to any individual. In his discussion of the conflict between democratic and oligarchic conceptions of justice, the one committed to 'numerical' equality, the other to 'proportionate', Aristotle makes it very clear that both are incomplete, since they ignore the proper criteria

25 Coleman, *op. cit.*, p. 97.
26 Quoted in *ibid.*, pp. 97–8.
27 *Ibid.*, p. 97.

of equality and inequality, the qualities that properly dictate what, in true justice, is due to each man. It is wrong to assume, as the democrat does, that all free-born men are equal, and it is also wrong to treat wealth as the relevant criterion, in the oligarchic manner. The proper measure is the contribution men make to the fulfilment of the state's essential purpose, the truly good life. At the same time, the oligarchic commitment to proportionate equality, for Aristotle, most closely approximates the perfect form, while the democratic idea of justice as numerical equality is undoubtedly the worst. It is also clear that, for Aristotle, men of wealth and good birth are more likely to achieve the necessary virtues required for honours and offices. This means that, while some accommodation must be reached to avoid social conflict, the balance should never be tilted towards the democratic view of justice, or towards the participation of the demos in the civic life of the polis, more than is absolutely necessary to avoid *stasis*.

It would, then, be misleading to say that Aristotle's conception of justice is intrinsically more democratic than Aquinas's, or less concerned with social difference. In the polis, where classes share the same civic and legal status, proportionate equality and differential justice cannot be determined by legal status differences; but, if anything, Aristotle is more, rather than less, preoccupied with social difference, with class relations between rich and poor. His conception of moral virtue itself, as we have seen, is deeply influenced by social difference and even matters of style. It often appears that his principal moral standard is the aristocratic gentleman. In Aquinas's universe, by contrast, where class differences are inextricably bound up with 'extra-economic' powers and 'politically constituted property', the criteria of difference have less to do with simple distinctions of wealth and more to do with legal relations, juridically defined status differences, contractual networks and corporate hierarchies. Aristotle's conception of justice, in other words, reflects, yet again, his preoccupation with the civic accommodation between classes, while Aquinas is more concerned with the intricacies of medieval governance and jurisdiction, in a society where economic power is still closely tied to legal status, corporate identities and jurisdictional rights.

John of Paris

Although Aquinas may not have been so directly engaged in the power struggles of his day, his ideas would immediately be mobilized by other thinkers in more open defence of one temporal power against another. So, for instance, John of Paris, who probably studied with Aquinas and certainly used Thomistic arguments, in *On Royal and Papal Power* (*c*.1302) intervened in the debates generated by the conflict between King Philip IV of France and Pope Boniface VIII. Responding directly to the pope's *Unam sanctam*, John elaborated the Dominican conception of property, and the relation between *dominium* and *jurisdictio*, to make an argument not only about the relation of Church and state to property but also about the relation between ecclesiastical and secular power, as well as conflicts between kings and Holy Roman emperors.

In keeping with distinctively French preoccupations (to which Aquinas, in his Parisian involvements, was surely not indifferent), John had to strike a delicate balance: while the French king was in conflict with the pope, the kingdom did not accept the legitimacy of the empire and its German princes. This meant that an argument in favour of secular monarchy against papal supremacy could not be cast in terms that would strengthen imperial claims. John of Paris asserts the spiritual authority of the pope while denying his absolute *dominium* and hence his temporal supremacy. At the same time, he argues that the universality of the spiritual realm cannot apply to secular kingdoms, with their diverse conditions, which means there can be no universal empire.

John draws on Aquinas's theory of kingship and builds on his theory of property. The argument proceeds from a defence of private property, as against communal ownership, on the grounds that, if everything were held in common, it would be difficult to keep the peace. The common good can best be achieved by permitting individuals to put their property to fruitful use under supervision by some kind of secular power whose object is the common good. John, however, adds an important refinement to the Dominican distinction between ownership and administration. Defining *dominium* in narrow terms as *dominium in rebus* – that is, in material things – and not as lordship in a wider sense, he argues that individuals have inalienable rights in property deriving from their own labour and industry, which precede both secular and ecclesiastical institutions.

The secular state, then, has jurisdictional power to regulate the property of individuals and to arbitrate disputes among them, but it has no *dominium*. The fact that propertied individuals retain their rights and autonomy in relation to the powers of the state implies that the state is, in some sense, a fiduciary power whose authority is conditional on its pursuit of the common good. As for the Church, while the ecclesiastical corporation owns property collectively in material things, this property does not belong to the Church and its priests as vicars of Christ or apostolic successors but derives from concessions granted to them by pious rulers or laymen. This means that neither the state nor the papacy has absolute *dominium*; but it also emphasizes the temporal independence, even the priority, of secular kings in relation to the pope.

John of Paris's arguments on property, kingship and temporal authority clearly reflect the preoccupations of his time and place, not least the particularly complex French relations between the monarchy, the papacy, the empire and various lesser claims to the autonomy of property, whether from seigneurs or urban corporations. His emphasis on individuality and individual rights need not be understood as an anticipation of modern individualism or even modern constitutionalism. On the contrary, his argument on private property is inseparable from feudal principles and corporatism.

The right-bearing individuals of John's political thought are individual *propertyholders*, and much depends on how property itself is conceived. Even feudal property, however conditional it may be and whatever obligations it may entail, is vested in individuals; but these individuals are themselves defined by their juridical or corporate identity. They hold their property not simply as free men but as lords, or as landholders subject to feudal obligations and lordly jurisdiction. Perhaps even more fundamentally, John's view of private ownership coexists with a conception of the political community as constituted by corporate entities. If the state is in some sense accountable to individual propertyholders, this does not mean that it is constituted by a multitude of individuals. In medieval terms, it is much more likely to mean that the state is constituted by, and accountable to, the 'people' as a corporate entity, or even a collection of corporate bodies, whose representatives speak for them. Even the idea that the attribution of inalienable rights to individuals makes government in some sense a fiduciary power is not so much an anticipation of modern constitutionalism, as a residue of feudal parcellized sovereignty and claims to seigneurial or corporate autonomy against a centralizing state.

The idea that government derives its authority from the 'people' was widely accepted by medieval thinkers, and it was generally agreed that kings had a duty to protect the rights of their subjects. Yet these principles were compatible with a broad range of political commitments, including the conviction that monarchical power should be virtually unlimited. If anything, the 'people' – as a corporate entity – was more often invoked in support of monarchical authority than as a limitation on its power, let alone in favour of more democratic forms of government. Even when the 'people' were granted a right to depose kings who failed in their duty, that right was typically vested in a corporate entity or its representatives, not least in feudal magnates of one kind or another. For John of Paris, for instance, the rights of individuals do seem to constitute significant limits on government, even entailing a right to depose kings. Yet he invokes this right on behalf of feudal magnates and he does so primarily in order to deny that right to the pope, while the prince remains the arbiter of the common good.[28]

This is not to deny that feudal conceptions of the fiduciary relationship between kings and the people, however narrowly the 'people' was defined, could place severe restrictions on monarchical power. Nor is it to deny the profound influence that such medieval ideas would have on the development of modern constitutionalism, however misleading it may be to speak of them as anticipations of modernity. Precisely because they were predicated on the autonomous powers of magnates or corporate bodies, they could, indeed, be more restrictive than some later conceptions of individual consent, which (as in the case of Hobbes) could even underwrite absolute monarchy. The radical resistance theories of the sixteenth century in France, for example, would continue to be based on the autonomy of magnates and urban corporations.[29] There were also corporatist theories that challenged autocratic rule by invoking not only the autonomous powers of particular corporate entities but the superiority of a large, inclusive general corporation, on the principle that the ruler or pope might be superior to any lesser individual, but that he was inferior to the corporate entity constituted by the whole community. This doctrine – applied by John of Paris himself among others – was used against the pope, arguing that the general body of the Christian faithful, in the shape of a general council, was the ultimate ecclesiastical authority, which could even depose popes.

This idea would be developed in so-called conciliar theory, which flourished in the fourteenth and fifteenth centuries. By the mid-fourteenth century the papacy at Avignon had increasingly come under the influence of the French monarchy, and competing claimants to the papacy in Avignon and Rome were inevitably embroiled in inter-state rivalries between France and its European neighbours. In response to the growing conflicts within the Church, which eventually gave rise to

28 According to the *Cambridge History*, 'In France, the people's right to depose kings was normally discussed only in the context of rebutting papal claims to be able to do so.' (p. 517)

29 Huguenot resistance tracts like the *Vindiciae contra Tyrannos* asserted the 'people's' right to resist by invoking the independent powers of nobles and magistrates against the king.

the so-called Western Schism, conciliarists would elaborate the idea
that it was not the pope but the corporate body of Christians in the
form of a general Church council that held ultimate authority in
spiritual matters. Although a resolution would emerge from a series
of Councils, conciliarism would give way to a revived papal dominance,
while surviving as a model for secular theories of consitutional
government.

It is, nevertheless, important to keep in mind that conceptions of
the social contract as a deliberate transaction between consenting
individuals and a government whose only purpose is to protect their
lives, liberties and property are grounded in conditions quite different
from those assumed by John of Paris or Thomas Aquinas. Whether
such conceptions are invoked in defence of absolute monarchy or to
support some kind of limited, constitutional government, they presuppose, on the one hand, a centralized state not fragmented by parcellized
sovereignty and, on the other, a political community of individuals
detached from corporate identities. It is not insignificant that such an
idea would first emerge clearly in England, where corporate principles
were weaker and Parliament was conceived as both a representative
body – representing a national community of free individuals – and
a partner in the legislative functions of the central state, without whose
consent the king could not govern.

Marsilius of Padua

Corporate principles, as we have seen, played an essential role in both
France and Italy in ways that they did not in England; and this difference
represented divergences not only in processes of state-formation but
also in the nature of property. Corporate autonomy, like other forms
of feudal power, belonged to the structure of parcellized sovereignty
in opposition to a centralized state. Corporate liberties, privileges and
powers, not unlike feudal lordship, were forms of politically constituted
property, a fusion of public power and private appropriation, in contrast
to appropriation independent of extra-economic status or jurisdictional
powers.

The contrasts between Marsilius of Padua and William of Ockham
nicely illustrate the effects of these contextual differences. Both philosophers argued the case against papal power, and both as a consequence
sought refuge at the court of Ludwig of Bavaria, whose imperial claims
had brought him into conflict with the pope. Yet their strategies of
argumentation were quite different, and their differences cannot
simply be put down to political or temperamental disagreements: the

extremism of Marsilius's anti-papal arguments as against William's effort to strike a somewhat less one-sided balance between papacy and empire. The two thinkers proceed from divergent assumptions, and these divergences are strikingly congruent with the differences between Italian civic communes and the medieval English state.

Marsilius was born in Padua c.1275 into a family very much involved in the communal government, as civil lawyers, notaries and judges. Instead of following his family into the legal profession, he studied medicine, first in Padua and then in Paris, where he taught natural philosophy and, in 1313, became rector of the university. Although he was promised ecclesiastical preferment by Pope John XXII, his hopes were disappointed. Whether or not this disappointment had anything to do with his anti-papal venom, he went on to serve two of the great lordly families of northern Italy, the della Scala of Verona and the Visconti of Milan, both of whom, as was typical among the landed nobility, had strongly imperial (Ghibelline) loyalties, at a time when Padua was under papal (Guelf) lordship.

In his famous anti-papal treatise, the *Defensor pacis*, completed in 1324, Marsilius would single out for special praise Matteo Visconti, who ruled Milan as *podestà* or 'imperial vicar' and effectively destroyed communal government. It will be important to keep this in mind when we consider conflicting interpretations of the *Defensor pacis* as either a republican tract or a strong defence of imperial power. In any case, once its authorship was attributed to Marsilius, who had at first circulated it anonymously, he was forced to seek refuge with Ludwig of Bavaria; and he went on to give Ludwig his unambiguous support against the pope, even accompanying the king in his invasion of Italy. Marsilius's imperial connections may be more clearly reflected in his last work, the *Defensor minor*, than in his major work; but it remains for us to consider whether there are, in the *Defensor pacis*, indeed contradictions between the republican and an imperialist Marsilius of Padua.

Let us first examine his anti-papal argument. Marsilius regards the papacy as the main threat to peace in Europe, and he attacks the very foundations of the pope's claims to a plenitude of power, indeed the very notion that the pope and the clergy in general have a claim to temporal authority at all. His argument is not that there are separate spheres of jurisdiction, ecclesiastical and secular, but rather that the very idea of jurisdiction does not belong in the spiritual realm. He pursues his argument on two fronts, first by examining the origin, nature and purpose of the civic community, more or less in the manner of Aristotelian naturalism, and then by constructing a theological case and a historical argument which recounts the history of the Church after the Fall and traces papal claims to power back to their Roman imperial roots in the conversion of Constantine, the first Christian emperor.

The purpose of the civil community, as Marsilius already suggests in the first paragraph of the *Defensor pacis*, is to create the conditions of peace and tranquillity required to achieve 'the greatest of all human goods . . . the sufficiency of life.' Tranquillity in the city or realm means that each of its parts can perform its proper function according to reason and prevailing custom, in an organic harmony. This requires the imposition of law, and Marsilius's conception of law is significant for two principal reasons.

First, he emphasizes its coercive function, as a means of achieving peace and not, in the Aristotelian or Thomistic manner, as a means of habituating citizens to virtue. This emphasis, as he elaborates his argument, places jurisdiction firmly in the hands of secular authority and rules out ecclesiastical jurisdiction in the temporal sphere. Civil peace and tranquillity are the responsibility of secular powers, while the Church has no coercive function. The rewards and punishments promised by Christianity await the afterlife, since the benevolence of Christ allows repentance till the end. The priestly function is certainly an integral part of the civil order, as are military and judicial functions; but Marsilius makes it clear that the Church remains subordinate to secular power in the temporal domain. This does not mean, however, that his view of the state prefigures a modern secular state. His argument remains, in this respect as in others, firmly rooted in the medieval order, not only because of the importance he attaches to the priestly function but because, as we shall see in a moment, his challenge to the temporal authority of the Church is mounted on behalf of other unmistakeably medieval claims to temporal power.

Second, the law emanates from a human legislator, whom Marsilius identifies with the whole civic corporation, 'the universal body of citizens' (*universitas civium*). The ultimate authority of civil government derives from the whole corporation of citizens and requires its ongoing consent. This is where we confront the question of the philosopher's republicanism, and certain immediate problems arise. We have already remarked that there was nothing unusual in medieval political thought about the conviction that civil authority derived from the 'people'; and we have also observed that this proposition was perfectly compatible, and indeed commonly associated, with the defence of powers that were far from democratic, up to and including unlimited monarchy. Marsilius himself makes it clear that the corporation of citizens is represented and governed by a ruling part (*pars principans*), which may consist of many, few or even one. More significantly, he always qualifies his references to the universal body of citizens with 'or its prevailing part' (*valentior pars*, sometimes translated as the 'weightier part'), which apparently can be very limited in numbers. Not only the power to elect (or depose) the ruling or executive part but even the legislative function and the ultimate power of consent could, then, reside in a very small number.

Nevertheless, Marsilius does go substantially further than other medieval thinkers in his ascription of sovereignty to the corporation of citizens. His theory, writes one historian of medieval political thought, 'is medieval corporation theory with a vengeance', placing great confidence in the capacity of the corporate body (as distinct from any individual wise man or men) – both as the *unversitas civium* and as a community of faith, the *congretatio fidelis* or *universitas fidelium* – to judge and enact the laws most conducive to the sufficient life.[30] His theory is also distinctive in its insistence on the unity of jurisdiction, placing the legislative power entirely in the hands of the civic corporation. He denies the force, indeed the existence, of canon law, and this is certainly decisive in the attack on papal power. Yet there remains the question – to which we shall return – of how, or whether, these principles can be squared with a defence of imperial power or, for that matter, support for the kind of signorial power enjoyed by the Visconti.

The argument about the origin and purpose of the civil order is buttressed in the second discourse of *Defensor pacis* with theological arguments, interpretations of scripture and of various canonical sources on ecclesiastical authority, together with a complex historical argument about the origin of papal power. Marsilius uses scripture and the example of Christ, his poverty and his benevolence, to demonstrate that the Church has no role in temporal affairs or in coercive governance. The historical argument is intended to demonstrate that the history of the Church is, to quote one commentator, 'a history of gradual, papally inspired perversion', driven by 'greed for temporal possessions and ambition for secular *dominium*', as a consequence of which modern priests are antithetical to the example of Christ and his apostles.[31]

This process of corruption, according to Marsilius, began paradoxically with the conversion of Constantine. Before the conversion there

---

30 Coleman, *op. cit.*, p. 137.

31 George Garnett, *Marsilius of Padua and 'The Truth of History'* (Oxford: Oxford University Press, 2006), p. 146.

was a clear distinction between the Church and the human legislator, who was an infidel. This meant that the church and the bishop of Rome were obliged to assume a kind of institutional pre-eminence, acting on behalf of the Christian community, which could not freely assemble to deliberate on matters of faith. Once Constantine's conversion made it possible for Christians to gather and regulate questions of ritual and faith, it was no longer necessary for the Church or the pope to act on their behalf. Yet it was precisely then that the bishops of Rome asserted their pre-eminence over other bishops and priests. They did so on the basis of the so-called donation of Constantine, an edict that was supposed to have granted jurisdictional superiority to the Roman pontiff, St Sylvester. Although the authenticity of the donation was always in question, Marsilius chooses to accept it as historical fact, and argues that, while Constantine was simply and with good intentions following the practice of the early Church under infidel emperors, the circumstances had radically changed and the consequences would prove to be disastrous. Now that the human legislator was a believer, a new kind of division opened up between the Christian human legislator and the institutions of the Church. As the *universitas fidelium* and the *universitas civium* were united and the human legislator was perfected by Christianity, the institutions of the Church and the priesthood were gradually corrupted by temporal ambitions, the benefits of ecclesiastical office and property.

How the Holy Roman Empire figures in this argument is not immediately obvious. Although Marsilius suggests that human law can best achieve its purpose in creating the conditions of peace, tranquillity and the sufficient life when Church and civic community are one, he also allows for a diverse multitude of self-governing civic communities, such as Italian city-states. He does not, on the face of it, advocate a universal empire uniting the spiritual community of Christians with a coextensive temporal *imperium*. It has, however, been persuasively argued that, in this respect, Marsilius has much more in common than is commonly supposed with the poet Dante, who did, in his *De Monarchia*, make an unambiguous case for a single universal ruler (who turns out to be the Roman emperor).[32] While Dante accepts the need for different laws for different conditions, he insists that, in matters common to the whole of

---

32 The argument that follows here and in the next paragraph is outlined by Garnett, *op. cit.*, especially pp. 160–4. For a different view of Marsilius, see Cary Nederman, *Community and Consent: The Secular Political Theory of Marsiglio of Padua's Defensor Pacis* (Lanham: Rowman & Littlefield, 1995).

humanity, there should be one supreme prince. Marsilius does not go so far, indeed appears to deny any such a necessity. Yet his argument is not that a universal ruler is unnecessary to keep the peace among the faithful. It is rather that the need for one universal coercive judge has not yet been demonstrated 'as necessary to eternal salvation'; and he goes on to say that 'there seems to be a greater necessity among the faithful for this than for one universal bishop, in that a universal prince is more able to preserve the faithful in unity than a universal bishop.'[33]

If a universal prince would serve a useful purpose in maintaining peace among the faithful, and if unity among the faithful for the sake of salvation cannot be achieved without unity for the sake of peace, a case can certainly be made for some such universal ruler or coercive judge. Marsilius suggests several times in the *Defensor pacis* that, while various provinces or cities have their own legislators, they must be subordinate to the supreme human legislator of the Roman Empire, to avoid precisely the state of war that now exists within the Holy Roman Empire, where the pope has usurped the universal human legislator's role. This conception of a universal prince may not have quite the geographic reach of Dante's world empire, but it does suggest that the emperor has an essential role in reversing the papal usurpation which has destroyed the peace within the existing boundaries of the Holy Roman Empire. Marsilius's later work and his service to Ludwig of Bavaria are perfectly in keeping with this argument.

Can this reading of Marsilius be squared with the republicanism that is commonly attributed to him? If he was indeed a republican, do we have to accept that his republican leanings in the *Defensor pacis* were modified by his experience in Ludwig's court, making the *Defensor minor* more clearly imperialist? To put it another way, must we choose between imperialist and republican readings of Marsilius? Some commentators have pointed out, quite reasonably, that, given the realities of the Italian city-states, we need make no such choice, since even self-governing communes with an active civic corporation could exist under the lordship of the Holy Roman Empire (even if imperial power typically supported signorial rather than communal government). Yet something more needs to be said. What is striking about Marsilius's argument is that his call for unitary jurisdiction, which is so distinctive among medieval thinkers, applies only to the division between the Church and secular government. He makes no such argument against the feudal powers of *signori* and seems completely unconcerned by the

---

33 *DP* II.28.15. ed. and transl. Annabel Brett.

threat they pose to civil peace – a threat that certainly did not escape his contemporaries – in stark contrast to his apocalyptic vision of the danger posed by the papacy. Having established a single, apparently unified civic corporation, he leaves intact – indeed, in practice actively supports – one of the principal challenges to civic unity and unitary jurisdiction.

There is, perhaps, an explanation that can accommodate all the complexities in Marsilius's political theory. It would be perfectly reasonable to argue simply that, in his genuine horror at the threats posed to European peace by papal pretensions, he felt obliged, despite his deeply felt republicanism, to defend signorial supporters of imperial power. Let us, however, suppose for a moment that the reverse may be true: that he truly believed in the likes of Matteo Visconti and that his anti-papal argument was at least to some extent inspired by such signorial allegiance. Might there be a way in which his apparently republican ideas could serve that cause?

In the specific conditions of Italian city-states and especially his native Padua, which had experienced dramatic shifts between Guelf and Ghibelline dominance, his argument could readily be mobilized in support of a civic commune dominated by a seigneurial Ghibelline faction under imperial protection. Indeed, it is hard to imagine a more effective way of making the Ghibelline case in the context of Italian civic corporations, the case for something like the Visconti of Milan against the Guelfs of Padua. It is certainly possible, even likely, that Marsilius's support for the Visconti was tempered by sentiments in favour of more communal government than was practised by his signorial masters, even if the civic body in question might be a restricted oligarchy – though even signorial rule could maintain the forms of communal self-government. The least that can be said is that even the most republican reading of the *Defensor pacis* does not rule out oligarchy, while Marsilius's support for the lordship of the Holy Roman Empire tends toward the oligarchic dominance of feudal nobles like the Visconti.

It is significant that when Marsilius characterizes the 'parts' of the city or civic corporation, he does so in a way that accords a privileged status to precisely the military function conventionally associated with the feudal aristocracy. Of the various offices or parts of the city – following Aristotle, he says, these include 'agriculture, manufacture, the military, the financial, the priesthood and the judicial or councillor' – only the priesthood, the military and the judicial 'are parts of the city in an unqualified sense, and in civil communities they are usually called the notables [*honorabilitas*].'[34]

---

34 *DP* I.5.1.

The 'plebeian' multitude belong to the parts of the city only 'in a broad sense', because they service its needs. Those engaged in production or trade – and this presumably includes the commercial patriciate – belong, it appears, to something like Aristotle's category of 'conditions', while *signori* would be truly 'parts'. Even Marsilius's emphasis on the coercive function of the law seems to reinforce this point: '[G]iven that the sentences of judges on internal miscreants and rebels must be carried out by means of coercive force,' he writes, 'it was necessary to institute within the city a military or defensive part, to which many of the mechanical arts also minister.'[35]

The very argument that lies at the heart of Marsilius's 'republicanism', his elevation of the civic corporation, can be understood as playing a critical role in support of signorial interests. How persuasive would it be, after all, to argue the Ghibelline case against Guelf dominance and papal lordship by blatantly attacking communal self-government in favour of a ruthless *signoria* in the hands of an aristocratic family? Typically, the powers of mercantile anti-signorial factions resided in semi-autonomous, self-governing guilds and corporations. It would therefore surely be much more effective to begin by trumping the autonomous authority of lesser corporations, invoking the more general and inclusive corporation of the civic commune – corporatism indeed with a vengeance. An analogous strategy would later be adopted by absolutist monarchs, who claimed to represent the general will of an inclusive corporate entity, something like the nation, against the particular interests of feudal aristocrats, autonomous municipal authorities and other lesser corporations. Marsilius's conception of the civic corporation could then be buttressed by challenging the papal authority that supported anti-signorial corporate interests, and then defending the imperial powers that sustained aristocratic 'imperial vicars' like the della Scala and Visconti dynasties.

William of Ockham

Even a moment's reflection should make it clear how inconceivable such arguments would be in a different social context, such as the England of William of Ockham. Whatever other reasons an English thinker, reflecting on English conditions, might have for defending imperial against papal authority, the uniquely Italian civic conflicts between factions supporting, and supported by, one or another of these greater powers would not be among them. More fundamentally, even if we reject such a partisan reading of Marsilius and give his republicanism the benefit of every doubt, his reliance on corporatist arguments would have nothing like the same force in England that it did in northern Italy.

To accommodate English conditions, it would, at the very least, be necessary to redefine the corporation. This is precisely what William of Ockham does. The starting point of his arguments – epistemological, theological and political – is emphatically the individual; and even his conception of the corporation denies the very first premise of medieval corporatism as conceived, most notably, by Marsilius: the idea that a corporate body can assume a personality, with a corporate will, separate from, and entitled to represent, the individuals who compose it. While it would be foolish to ascribe Ockham's philosophical individualism to purely contextual determinations, it would be no less foolish to disregard the fact that his formative experience and education took place in England, where a particular relation between state, property and individual assigned a very different, and weaker, role to corporations than was the case elsewhere in Europe.

William of Ockham was born in the 1280s in Surrey and was educated at Oxford in theology and philosophy, continuing his studies and going on to teach as a member of the Franciscan order. There is some dispute about when and how he first came into conflict with the papacy, but the most common view is that he was summoned to Avignon to defend his theological and philosophical work before a papal commission for some suspected heresy and then found himself drawn into the dispute on apostolic poverty. John XXII's papal bull, *Quia vir reprobus*, was, as we saw, the most powerful challenge to the Franciscan position; and in his response, Ockham came to believe that the pope himself was guilty of heresy.

Although Ockham was never formally excommunicated, he fled to the court of Ludwig in the year that the king became Holy Roman Emperor. Like Marsilius, he supported Ludwig in his conflict with the pope, continuing to defend the doctrine of apostolic poverty and attacking papal claims to a plenitude of power, which compelled him to elaborate his view on the relation between secular and spiritual jurisdictions. He never produced a systematic political theory, and what he did say is subject to conflicting interpretations; but a theory of politics can be reconstructed from various works.[36] Whatever else can be said about his

---

36 See, for example, *Contra Benedictum*, *Tractatus* against John XXII, parts of the *Dialogus*, the *Breviloquium de potestate tyrannica* (*A short discourse on the tyrannical government over things divine and human*), and *De imperatorum et pontificum potestate* (*On Imperial and Pontifical Power*).

political ideas, there is no question about the originality and significance of his reflections on corporations and individual rights.

There is an unmistakeable congruence between Ockham's redefinition of the corporation and his individualist approach to philosophical questions in general, especially his theory of cognition. It might, therefore, be tempting simply to say that the former followed neatly from the latter without the intervention of contextual factors. Yet, while it would clearly be too strong to claim that his philosophy is entirely a by-product of English conditions, his theory of rights and corporations is so strikingly congruent with the realities of English law, property and governance that a failure to take note of the connections and correspondences would surely be a careless oversight.

Ockham starts from the premise that there is nothing in this world but individuals, and that no universals or essences exist except as abstractions constructed by the mind from reflection on particulars. Knowledge derives from individual cognition, which is by definition particular and contingent, and universal concepts do not reflect an external reality but rather the operations of the human mind. Universal concepts are names or signs human beings ascribe to particular things in the effort to find commonalities among them; and it is these linguistic creations, not the substance of things, that constitute the objects of knowledge.

Ockham's views on society and government start from analogous premises. The body politic, too, is a world constituted by individuals and nothing else. Collective opinion can never be more than a product of individual opinions, and no collectivity is ever more than the sum of its parts. This means that there can be no collective body with a corporate personality or will of its own, distinct from the sum of individual personalities and wills that compose it. Individuals do not, of course, exist in isolation from each other. They congregate for social, political and religious reasons; but they do so as free and autonomous beings, and the body politic does not exist as a sphere separate from the multitude of individuals that constitute it. There is no legally created imaginary persona which can claim to represent them. The collectivity or corporation is never anything other than a collection of autonomous rational individuals. Individual wills cannot be represented by a corporate entity, nor can individuals alienate their autonomy, their rights or their responsibilities.

It is, however, true, according to Ockham, that the Fall made secular authority necessary, since individuals could no longer rule themselves by their reason alone. Ockham not only allows for secular authorities that can impose their coercive powers on free individuals but even accepts the possibility of governments that stand above the law. Governments are established by the universal consent of individuals who will be governed by them; but thereafter circumstances will dictate whether the ruler will, or should, act in accordance with positive law. There is no need for repeated acts of consent by the governed. They have consented from the outset to government that will act and legislate in accordance with right reason, equity and the common good as demanded by particular circumstances. This may imply a right of resistance if and when that fundamental condition is not met, but there is no provision for continuous consent nor for any institutions to restrain the ruler. In the absence of any requirement for regular participation by the people or for institutional limits on government, William of Ockham's political stance has been described as 'absolutist'. At the same time, his is an absolutism firmly based on the principle that individuals cannot alienate their freedom and autonomy; and since no individual can claim absolute power over another, no such power exists for them to confer on anyone else. This insistence on the inalienability of human rights and freedoms has made it possible to invoke his doctrines to support the right of resistance and constitutional government.

What, then, of individual rights and especially the right of property? In the debate on apostolic poverty, Ockham explored the concept of *dominium*, distinguishing between conditions before and after the Fall. In the prelapsarian condition, humanity enjoyed a capacity to make use of all creation but not the ownership of property. Once Adam's sin transformed the human condition God provided the means of improving human life by giving humanity a capacity to appropriate temporal goods, in the form of individual property, and to protect their rights of property by instituting government. Ockham's immediate objective in the debate with the pope was to demonstrate that, since both property and government result from Adam's sin, they clearly belong in the temporal sphere, under the direction of secular authority, which means that the pope can claim no plenitude of power. His argument, however, has wider implications. Although property is a human creation, dependent on civil authority, the capacity to exercise *dominium* in its postlapsarian form was a gift from God. The utility of private property, recognized not only in civil law but in the *ius gentium*, suggests that it conforms to natural law, even if it does so in a different sense than did common possession before the Fall; and once acknowledged, it constitutes an inalienable right.

As a Franciscan defending apostolic poverty, Ockham opposed

Dominican doctrines on the unity of use and ownership, together with the separation of ownership and jurisdiction. But the principle that property was a civic institution had already been accepted by Dominicans like Thomas Aquinas and other medieval theologians. For Ockham's purposes, this doctrine had the advantage of under-cutting the pope's authority by placing property squarely in the realm of secular authority. He also had in common with Aquinas a distinction between different forms of natural law and the suggestion that private property is, in its own way, consistent with natural law. But if Ockham's theory of property, despite his insistence on its civic institution, nevertheless brings us closer than do other medieval theories to the notion of private property as an irreducible natural right, inherent in the human individual independent of civic authority, it is because of the priority he gives the individual as the most fundamental constitutive unit of the social order, in contrast to the corporatism of other medieval theorists.

There are certainly ambiguities in Ockham's political doctrine. The practical implications of his views on individuals and corporations are probably clearer in relation to spiritual authority than to secular power, and, indeed, his innovative treatment of corporate principles was most immediately intended to deal with the question of spiritual power. Confronting the relation between spiritual and secular jurisdictions, he does not choose Marsilius's solution of simply subordinating one to the other. Yet again, he seeks his answer in the all-important individual. Individuals, he argues, are both spiritual and secular beings, so any resolution between the two jurisdictions must acknowledge that duality. As spiritual beings, individuals are governed by divine laws, while as secular beings they are subject to positive law. Since individuals are irreducibly free and autonomous, they are entitled to establish their own secular governments with their own systems of law.

Ockham may not go as far as Marsilius's outright subordination of Church to state, but his separation of the two jurisdictions represents a significant challenge to the temporal power of the Church and the papacy. At the same time, just as he denies the primacy of corporations in the secular sphere, he gives little credence to general councils of the Church. Some individual Christian, even a child or a woman, might come closer to the truth than a general Church council. Just as there is no secular corporation that is more than the sum of its individual parts, with a right to represent them, no spiritual collectivity has any superior standing. Unlike Marsilius and John of Paris, whose cor-poratism extended to general councils of the Church, granting them an infallibility that endowed them with a right to depose popes, Ockham had no such corporatist weapon available to him and was forced to rely on individual members of the Church to resist papal heresies and misdeeds.

William of Ockham's redefinition of the corporation was, then, a two-edged sword. There is no question that his doctrine of individual autonomy and rights could be adopted in support of constitutional limits on government. Once the representative can no longer be identified by definition with the collectivity it represents, the way is open to raise questions about the conformity of the representative's will to the desires of the individuals he claims to represent and therefore about the accountability of representatives to their constituents. No such questions arise, by contrast, in Marsilius's theory of the corporation. The will expressed by the corporate body, in the person of its representatives, necessarily defines the common good, whatever any individuals may think or wish.

Yet medieval corporatism could and did provide a foundation for limiting state power, by asserting autonomous powers and rights independent of the central state. Ockham's rejection of corporatism as understood by his contemporaries denies him some of the most powerful weapons available to medieval thinkers for checking the powers of monarchs and popes. Although some of his ideas would be adopted by conciliarists, his views on general councils of the Church would seem to undercut conciliar doctrine fatally; and it is hard to see how any notion of corporate resistance to tyrannical authority, secular or ecclesiastical, could survive his redefinition of the corporation.

At the same time, there are, as we have seen in the case of Marsilius, ambiguities in corporatism too, especially when the corporation in question is coextensive with the whole civic community. A universal corporation – whether a general council of the Church or a secular body of citizens – could certainly be mobilized against a monarch or a pope, but autocratic rulers could also assert their superiority over lesser autonomous powers by claiming to represent a more general corporate interest.

Both corporatism and individualism were, then, compatible with a wide range of political options, from more or less absolute government to constitutionalism and a defence of civic liberties. In the following centuries there would be varying traditions of both absolutism and constitutionalism, not only in theory but also in practice; and these differences, which have their roots in medieval Europe, reflect significant divergences – notably between England and France – in the nature of the body politic and its constituent units.

Long after William of Ockham, another Englishmen, Sir Thomas Smith, then Queen Elizabeth's ambassador to France, in a treatise on the English body politic, would define a 'commonwealth' or 'societie civill' as 'a societie or common doing of a multitude of free men collected together and united by common accord and covenauntes among themselves, for the conservation of themselves aswell [sic] in peace as in warre.'[37] His contemporary, Jean Bodin, reflecting on French conditions, had a different conception of a commonwealth, as composed not of free individuals but of 'families, colleges or corporate bodies'.[38] The differences expressed in these two definitions were already well established in the thirteenth century, visibly present in systems of property, law and representation.

In England, as we have seen, the corollary of an unusually centralized state and a uniquely unified system of law was a distinctive type of 'free' man, subject only to the king and to no lesser lord. Landlords certainly enjoyed great local powers; but outside the manor, and in relation to free men, they acted as delegates of the Crown. While there remained a sharp distinction between freehold property and unfree tenures, subject to manorial lordship and with no access to the royal courts, the free Englishman was a unique formation, with an individual 'interest' in property, recognized in common law and independent of any extra-economic claims, privileges or obligations. In France, by contrast, free status was more ambiguous. Charters of freedom did not dissolve seigneurial obligation, and even peasants who owned land and had access to royal protection could still be subject to seigneurial jurisdiction and its attendant obligations, in a society governed, even at the height of absolutism, by hundreds of local law codes, customs, and fragmented jurisdictions.

The status of the free man in England entailed a distinctive political identity, without all the feudal and corporate mediations that stood between the state and individuals elsewhere in Europe. This relationship was reflected in a new conception of representation. When knights of the shire were elected to represent their counties in the Parliament of 1254, they were representing counties not as feudal entities but as administrative units under the Crown; and they were elected by county courts, which were assemblies of free men, the same kind of free

---

37 Sir Thomas Smith, *De Republica Anglorum*, ed. Mary Dewar (Cambridge: Cambridge University Press, 1982), p. 57.

38 Jean Bodin, *Six Books of the Commonwealth*, ed. M.J. Tooley (Oxford: Basil Blackwell, 1967), p. 7.

individuals who constituted the English jury. Englishmen, to be sure, were no less inclined than other Europeans to speak of the commonwealth as if it were a corporation. Yet, when, for example, the Chief Justice of England declared in 1365 that 'Parliament represents the body of all the realm', that 'body' was no longer the kind of corporate entity imagined by Marsilius; nor was it a collection of corporate entities, such as Bodin's 'colleges and corporations' or the French estates. It was more a collection of individual free men like that conceived by William of Ockham.

It is important to acknowledge that these differences are not just theoretical. European thinkers certainly shared a rich philosophical and cultural tradition, as well as certain important commonalities in the development of property and state; but the legacies they drew upon in common only emphasize the significance of the divergences among them and the degree to which they reflect significant variations in social and political conditions, which produced different social conflicts and offered different practical options for their resolution. In the following centuries, there would be several divergent patterns of European state-formation and economic development, which would be expressed in diverse traditions of political thought.

CONCLUSION

Why, then, end this volume here, in the middle of the fourteenth century? Its subject is a social history of political theory from classical antiquity to the Middle Ages; but the 'medieval period, perhaps more than most, is subject to debate about its boundaries, and especially about when it properly ends. Histories of medieval political theory will often end a century later (or more) than this one does. The *Cambridge History*, for instance, spans roughly the years 350 to 1450, on the grounds that 'somewhere around the middle of the fifteenth century we can detect enough of a decisive shift in the patterns of intellectual life to justify the claim that the principal movements of "medieval political thought" . . . were drawing to a significant close.'[37] This is, of course, a difficult judgment to make, since there was, as there always is in historical processes, a continuity in change. Yet, the argument goes, while many medieval themes and 'traditions' of thought persist 'with considerable vitality into the later fifteenth century and beyond . . . they survive increasingly in a situation of co-existence with other, newer (and no doubt at the same time older) ways of thinking.' Renaissance 'humanism' coexisted, but came into conflict, with the 'scholasticism' of medieval philosophy, 'and just as the great institutions of medieval society – the papacy, the empire, the "feudal monarchies", the canon and civil lawyers – survived only in changed forms, so medieval political ideas survived to play a part in changed circumstances and were themselves changed in the process.'

This may not tell us much about epochal shifts, and readers may find it hard to imagine any moment in history that could not be described in similar terms, as a unity of change and continuity. It may,

---

37 *The Cambridge History of Medieval Political Thought: c.350–c.450* (Cambridge: Cambridge University Press, 1988), p. 652.

indeed, be impossible to formulate our temporal parameters much more decisively than this. Yet there is something more to be said. If we take seriously the concept of feudalism as laid out in the previous chapter, the boundaries may be just a bit less difficult to draw. If we focus our attention on feudalism, it is possible to situate some significant epochal moments in the mid-fourteenth century and beyond: a time of plague, demographic collapse, peasant revolts and the Hundred Years War. Taken together, these developments spell the crisis of parcellized sovereignty, and we can begin to speak of 'transitions' from feudalism.

From the middle of the fourteenth to the late fifteenth century, there is a period of canonical scarcity, which ends decisively with Machiavelli.[38] When the story of the Western canon resumes, we are in a European world shaped by different relations between property and state. In the rising absolutist state, particularly in France, the monarchy is seeking to co-opt the nobility by replacing its feudal autonomy with privileges and perquisites of office. In England, where an already well-established central state had developed in tandem with a powerful landed aristocracy, we can begin to see the rise of agrarian capitalism. The city-states of northern Italy, for all the continuities in their communal forms, are now no longer battle grounds for conflicts between popes and Holy Roman emperors but for wars between French and Spanish monarchical states.

It was with one eye on these neighbouring states, which posed a wholly new challenge to civic autonomy in Italy, that Machiavelli reflected on the history and politics of Florence. In France, Jean Bodin, in support of monarchical centralization, would engage in philosophical disputes with constitutionalist thinkers defending the declining autonomous powers of provincial nobles and corporate entities; while in England, Thomas More (who served and eventually fell victim to a

---

38 Nicolas of Cusa (1401–64), who falls within this period of canonical scarcity, is certainly an important figure, though his inconsistencies and changes of position make him hard to situate in the history of the canon. Identified by some commentators as a major theorist of conciliarism, he has also been accused of helping to destroy it, when he ended by siding with the pope against the council of the Church. It is, in any case, arguable that his story, like that of conciliar theory in general, belongs to the crisis of parcellized sovereignty and the process of state-centralization, which will be left for another volume. Conciliarism flourished in a period when divisions in the Church, leading to a major schism, were aggravated and even generated by rising secular states, and especially the French monarchy, which bolstered their own power by aligning themselves with this or that pope.

powerful monarch) observed – and participated in – the dispossession of small producers by enclosure as, in his own words, 'sheep devoured men'.

These various 'transitions' from feudalism, and the diverse traditions of political theory that accompanied them, are the subject of another book. But if we can speak of a crisis – or crises – of feudalism, the mid-fourteenth century seems a natural place to end the medieval period. At the same time, we should keep in mind that the transitions which followed bore the marks of what preceded them. This is so not only in the sense that later developments in Western political thought inherited a powerful legacy but, more fundamentally, in the sense that the whole canonical tradition, in all its national variations, would continue to be shaped by the autonomy of property and distinctive tensions between property and state, which would play themselves out in all the various transitions.

The canon of Western political theory, while it includes some notably radical thinkers, is largely the work of members or clients of dominant classes. Popular voices are seldom heard in the canonical tradition. Yet it has been shaped by a complex three-way interaction between the state, appropriating classes and producers. Propertied classes have depended on the state to protect their property and dominance against the challenge from below, yet they have also been in conflict with the state and its intrusions from above. They have, in other words, always been compelled to fight on two fronts. This has also meant that challenge to political authority has come not only from resistance by subordinate classes to oppression by their overlords, but also from the overlords themselves in opposition to the state.

These complex interactions between the state and propertied classes have certainly sustained the traditions of Western political theory, raising fundamental questions about authority, legitimacy and obedience even when popular voices have been muted in their opposition to oppression. But this has generated certain ambiguities and paradoxes, which remain deeply ingrained in Western political theory and practice. It is, for example, significant that constitutional and even democratic doctrines in the West owe as much to the defence of aristocratic power and property as they do to popular struggles. The constitutive principles of Western liberal democracy, its ideas of limited and accountable government, have more to do with medieval lordship and its claims to autonomous power than with rule by the demos as conceived in ancient Athens.

It is not just that tensions have always existed between the idea of civic equality and the realities of class inequality. What is most ambiguous and paradoxical in the Western tradition of political theory, which was born in the civic community of ancient Greece, is that its foundational ideas of citizenship and civic equality have almost since the beginning been adapted to serve the cause of inequality and domination. We have seen, for example, how the idea of citizenship was used by the Romans as a hegemonic instrument of oligarchy and imperialism. Not only did the imperial idea of Roman citizenship replace civic agency with passive obedience, but even a republican thinker like Cicero found ways to finesse egalitarian ideas, turning democratic principles against themselves, by relegating equality to an abstract moral sphere beyond the inequalities of daily life and oligarchic rule.

Christian doctrine, too, would assert the equality of all human beings before God, while condoning profound inequality, oppression and even slavery in the mundane reality of life in this world. Early modern political theorists would declare that human beings (or at least men) were free and equal in the state of nature, and go on to construct arguments in favour of absolute monarchy (Hobbes) or rule by the propertied classes (Locke), not in opposition to but on the basis of natural equality, by applying the very elastic idea of consent. An emerging capitalist 'economy', with its purely 'economic' modes of class domination, would perfect the paradox, making it possible to relegate democracy to a formally separate 'political' sphere, while leaving intact the vast disparities of power between capital and labour in the market and the workplace and putting much of human life beyond the reach of democratic accountability, to be governed by market imperatives.

What is at issue here is not the familiar human inclination to profess one thing and do another. It is rather that such paradoxes lie at the very heart of Western political theory and practice. Ideas of limited and even democratic government have enjoyed a long and vigorous life in the Western tradition, not least because a particular formation of property, class and state power has made it possible for them to be adopted as ruling ideas, and not only expressions of popular power or resistance to dominant classes. But whatever this may have done for the longevity and vigour of such ideas, it has also restricted our conceptions of democracy. A more generous vision of human emancipation requires us to go beyond ruling ideas to a richer tradition of emancipatory struggle, in action and thought; but we can best reveal the limits of prevailing orthodoxies if we understand the canonical tradition and the historical experience in which it is rooted.

PART II.

LIBERTY AND PROPERTY:
RENAISSANCE TO ENLIGHTENMENT

ACKNOWLEDGEMENTS

I am finding it more difficult than usual to thank all the many people who have, in one way or another, helped me with this book. The 'early modern' period covered in this volume has been a special preoccupation of mine since I first started reading, then writing and teaching, the history of political thought nearly half a century ago; and everything I have written about contemporary capitalism, imperialism and democracy has been informed by my reflections on that earlier historical moment and by years of conversation with colleagues, friends and students who may never have seen a single page of this book. My greatest debt remains to Neal Wood, who died some years before I started working on it.

My particular thanks must go, of course, to those who read the whole manuscript: Perry Anderson and George Comninel, whose comments have, as on other occasions, been no less generous than trenchant, and Ed Broadbent, to whom this book is dedicated, who again superbly played the role of 'intelligent general reader' with his customary insight and unflagging support.

I also owe thanks to Frances Abele, Robert Brenner and David McNally, who have read parts of the manuscript or allowed me to try out bits of it on them. And then there are those who advised me on (and who were acknowledged in) previous related works, including editors who commented on and/or permitted me to use some of my earlier publications, parts of which have inspired or been absorbed into this book: 'The State and Popular Sovereignty in French Political Thought: A Genealogy of Rousseau's "General Will" ', *History of Political Thought* IV.2, Summer 1983, pp. 281–315; 'Locke Against Democracy: Representation, Consent and Suffrage in the *Two Treatises*', *History of Political Thought* XIII.4, Winter 1992, pp. 657–89; 'Radicalism, Capitalism and Historical Contexts: Not Only a Reply to Richard Ashcraft on John Locke', *History of Political Thought*, XV.3, Autumn 1994, pp. 323–72; *A Trumpet of Sedition: Political Theory and the Rise of Capitalism, 1509–1688* (London: Pluto Press, and New York: New York University Press, 1997 – this book was coauthored with Neal Wood, although the sections on the seventeenth century used in the present volume were written by me); 'Capitalism or Enlightenment?', *History of Political Thought* XXI.3, Autumn 2000, pp. 405–26; 'Why It Matters', *London Review of Books*, vol. 30, no. 18, 25 September 2008.

Finally, a note on sources: I have tried to keep the number of footnotes under control and make it easier for readers to locate citations from the political thinkers discussed in this book. Instead of footnoting page numbers from one particular edition or translation I have, wherever possible, cited the original chapter, section and paragraph numbers that can be found in any standard editions of the works quoted. Where such citations may not be specific enough, I have included footnotes with page numbers (as in the case of works by Bodin and Rousseau in Chapter 6); and, for readers who would like to identify specific translations, here is a list of the translated works that, in subsequent chapters, will be cited without footnotes in the body of the text:

John Calvin, *Institutes*, transl. H. Beveridge (Edinburgh: Calvin Translation Society, 1845).

Niccolò Machiavelli, *The Prince*, transl. W.K. Marriott (London and New York: Everyman's Library, 1992); *The Discourses*, transl. L. Walker (Harmondsworth: Penguin Books, 1983); *History of Florence and the Affairs of Italy* (New York: Harper Torchbook, 1966).

Charles-Louis de Secondat, Baron de Montesquieu, *The Spirit of the Laws*, transl. T Nugent (New York: Hafner, 1962).

Benedict Spinoza, *The Political Works*, transl. A.G. Wernham (Oxford: Oxford University Press, 1958).

Francisco Vitoria, *Political Writings*, eds. A. Pagden and J. Lawrance (Cambridge: Cambridge University Press, 1991).

1

TRANSITIONS

The decline of feudalism and the rise of capitalism, from its agrarian origins to the early phases of industrialization; the religious ruptures of the Reformation; the evolution of the nation state; the growth of modern colonialism; cultural landmarks from the Renaissance to the Age of Enlightenment; modern philosophy and a scientific revolution, rooted in the empiricism of Francis Bacon or the rationalism of Renée Descartes – all these momentous historical developments, punctuated not only by wars among states but by popular uprisings, rebellions and revolts of various kinds, up to and including civil war, have been ascribed to the so-called early modern period.

It may not be surprising, then, that the canon of Western political thought is disproportionately populated by 'early modern' thinkers. While historians may differ about the inclusion of this or that name, the period has more than its share of towering figures – from Machiavelli or Hobbes to Locke and Rousseau – whose canonical status is as unassailable as that of Plato or Aristotle. Yet all the historical landmarks that mark out the era and even their conventional names – Renaissance, Reformation, Enlightenment, to say nothing of 'feudalism' or the 'rise of capitalism' – regularly provoke controversy among historians. So, for that matter, does the designation 'early modern' itself. It seems, on the face of it, a fairly innocent, if imprecise, descriptive label indicating rough chronological boundaries, somewhere between the middle ages and full-blown modernity. We shall use the label here in that more or less neutral sense, just for the sake of simplicity and for lack of anything better. But there is more at issue than chronology. Whatever dates we settle on – let us say approximately 1500 (or 1492?) to 1800, or maybe 1789 or even 1776 – the early modern presupposes an idea of the modern, as distinct from the ancient, the medieval or at least the 'premodern', an idea of modernity that raises questions of its own.

Much intellectual effort has been expended on clarifying the idea of 'modernity', and we shall, in what follows, have occasion to confront some of the questions it poses. For the moment, it is enough to say that, although there has been disagreement about what exactly constitutes the 'modern' and whether it is good, bad or morally neutral, there is, in 'Western' culture, a deeply rooted and tenacious conception that cuts across divergent schools of thought which may agree on very little else. Even when sharp distinctions are made among various national histories, there remains a single, overarching narrative of European history and the advent of modernity, a narrative defined by discontinuities and at the same time transitional processes, passages from one age to another marked by fundamental transformations.

In that narrative, the modern era, whatever else it may be, is a composite of economic, political and cultural characteristics, uniting capitalism (what classical political economists liked to call 'commercial society'), legal-rational political authority (perhaps, but not necessarily, with a preference for its liberal democratic form), and technological progress – or 'rationalization' in its various aspects as manifest in markets, states, secularism and scientific knowledge. Emphases or causal primacies may vary, and different balances may be struck among the factors of modernity, economic, cultural or social. There may be fierce dispute about the processes of transformation that produced the modern age. The critical transition may be defined as a passage from feudalism to capitalism, the rise of the bourgeoisie, the forward march of liberty, a destructive rupture from tradition, and much else besides. But it is difficult to find a notion of the modern in which the culture of 'rational' inquiry, advances in technology, the market economy and a 'rational' state are not, in one way or another, for better or worse, inextricably connected.[1]

In recent years the lines between the early modern and the modern have been more sharply drawn in some historical accounts, as the early modern has tended to merge with the 'late medieval'. Among historians of political thought in particular, there are those who question the idea of an early modern period, on the grounds that there was no significant rupture between medieval thinkers and those described as early modern. Political ideas, in this account, remained strikingly consistent throughout the historic transformations that brought the 'middle ages' to an end. But even here, the concept of modernity, and the conventional narrative associated with it, have been remarkably persistent.

There are, to be sure, those who reject the very idea of modernity. It makes some people uneasy because of its association with conceptions of progress, which smack of teleology or, after the horrors of the twentieth century, appear in questionable taste. Others are opposed to 'grand

---

1 The issue here may be confused by debates about the late nineteenth- and early twentieth-century cultural phenomena described as 'modernism'. But whatever may be meant by 'modernism' (or, indeed, 'postmodernism'), whether it is treated as an intensification or, on the contrary, a repudiation of the 'modern' and its cultural forms, this much-disputed concept leaves the conventional idea of modernity essentially intact.

narratives' of any kind and prefer to discard the *longue durée* in favour of a focus on the local, the particular and the contingent. Since 'modernity' implies a very long historical sweep from ancient to modern, with at least implicit explanations of how one led to the other, this refusal of a longer view makes it hard to sustain an idea of the modern.

Yet, these controversies notwithstanding, the notion of modernity is rarely challenged from a vantage point that, while systematically questioning the conventional paradigm, still takes a longer view of history. The most influential 'grand narratives' – from Enlightenment conceptions of progress, to Marxist or Whig interpretations of history or Weberian historical sociology, and all their varied legacies – have tended to leave the conventional composite portrait of the modern era fundamentally intact, however divergent their judgments of modernity have been. The challenge to the standard story of modernity has more often come from various kinds of disconnected or fragmented history, 'postmodernist' or 'revisionist' accounts with no long view and little explanation of historical causality or, indeed, historical process – though even then the stubborn concept of the modern has tended to return through the back door.

Early Modern Europe?

What, then, does it mean to speak of early modern political thought? The growth of the 'modern' state, with its entrenchment of national boundaries, political, economic and cultural, is certainly a central feature of the early modern period; and, in one way or another, it affected all forms of political organization that came within its field of force. But the canon of Western political thought, which is the subject of this book, was in that period also shaped by political forms as diverse as the city-states of Italy, the bewildering variety of German jurisdictions, and the commercial republics of the Netherlands – to say nothing of the Holy Roman Empire, simultaneously a self-conscious throwback to imperial antiquity and an aspiring if ultimately unsuccessful nation state, in constant tension with all other claimants to sovereignty, secular and ecclesiastical. The concept of the early modern encompasses not just the early manifestations of the modern state or the modern economy but cultural and intellectual developments rooted in very different, and not conspicuously modern, social and political forms, such as the Italian city-states in which the Renaissance came to fruition or the Electorate of Saxony where Martin Luther, at least according to historical convention, launched the Reformation.

These cases differed not only in their political form but in the particular interactions among public power, private property, and the producing classes; and these differences would give rise to distinctive traditions of political discourse. This was true even among the city-states and principalities joined at one time or another under the rule, however tenuous, of the Holy Roman Empire: the Germans and the Spanish, the Italians and the Dutch. To be sure, Italians and Germans, Spanish and Dutch, or, for that matter, English and French, all shared a common cultural legacy; and our period begins at a moment of particular cultural unity, manifested in the Latin that united Western European scholars, the whole apparatus of Christian theology, the revived Greek classics of political philosophy, the 'republic of letters' constituted by European humanism. Yet this common intellectual vocabulary simply makes the variety of national traditions that much more striking. The inherited languages of Western political theory have been remarkably flexible in their adaptation to varying contextual circumstances; and, as each specific historical form has posed its own distinctive problems, the same traditions of discourse have been mobilized not only to give different answers but in response to different questions.[2]

Is there, nonetheless and despite all these divergences, a sense in which it is meaningful to speak of 'early modern Europe', or, more particularly, does it make sense to think of Western Europe as an entity distinct from other regions, which is, in the period covered by this book, experiencing a pattern of historical development that distinguishes it from others? In what follows, there will be much emphasis on the specificities of national development, but let us for the moment consider the common foundations.

In the first volume of this social history of political thought, it was argued that Western political theory, in all its variations, has been shaped by a distinctive tension between two sources of power, the state and private property. All 'high' civilizations have, of course, had states, and some have had elaborate systems of private property; but developments in what would be Western Europe, with roots in Greco-Roman antiquity and especially the Western Roman Empire, gave property, as a distinct locus of power, an unusual degree of autonomy from the state.

Consider, for instance, the contrasts between the Roman Empire and the early Chinese imperial state. A strong state in China established its power by defeating great aristocratic families and preventing their appropriation of

---

2 *The Cambridge History of Political Thought: 1450–1700* (Cambridge: Cambridge University Press, 1991), without, to be sure, dismissing national differences and certainly acknowledging the variety of national discourses, adopts what it calls 'a more illuminating approach to the subject as a whole', choosing, for the most part, a thematic rather than a national mode of organizing the material. It does so mainly on the grounds that not only the survival of the *res publica christiana* but the humanist 'republic of letters' produced an intellectual community that transcended national boundaries (p. 5). Whatever its virtues, this approach fails to do justice to significant differences in the application and elaboration of precisely this common European discourse in response to different questions posed by divergent patterns of political and economic development among the European states.

newly conquered territories, which were to be administered by officials of the central state.[3] At the same time, peasants came under the direct control of the state, which preserved peasant property as a source of revenue and military service, while ensuring the fragmentation of landholdings. Rome, by contrast, achieved imperial expansion without a strong state, governed instead by amateurs, an oligarchy of landed aristocrats, in a small city-state with a minimal government. While peasants were part of the civic community, they remained subordinate to the propertied classes; and as the empire expanded, with the help of conscript peasant soldiers on military service far from home, many peasants were dispossessed. Land was increasingly concentrated in the hands of the aristocracy, much of it – at least in Roman Italy – worked by slaves. When the republic was replaced by an imperial state with its own structure of office, the landed aristocracy continued to amass huge properties; and, while in China great riches were typically derived from office in the central state, in the Roman Empire land remained the only steady and secure source of wealth. Even at its height, the imperial state was, by comparison with China, 'undergoverned', administered through a vast network of local aristocracies.

The Roman Empire represents the first known example of a strong imperial state combined with strong private property. This powerful, if sometimes uneasy, partnership is expressed in the Roman concepts of *imperium* and *dominium*. The Roman concept of *dominium*, when applied to private property, articulates with exceptional clarity the idea of private, exclusive and individual ownership, with all the powers this entails, while the *imperium* defines a right of command attached to certain civil magistrates and eventually the emperor himself. While, in the history of Western legal and political thought, the distinction between private property and public jurisdiction would not always be so clear, the Romans certainly did break new ground in distinguishing between the public power of the state and the private power of property, in both theory and practice. In contrast to China, where there was a direct relationship between the state and the peasants whose labour it appropriated, in Rome the primary relation between appropriators and producers was not between rulers and subjects but between landlords and subject labour of one kind or another, whether slaves or peasants exploited as tenants and share-croppers. When the empire disintegrated, what remained was this primary relationship, which would survive as the foundation of the social order for centuries to come.

The existence of two poles of power, the state and strong private property, together with a mode of imperial rule dependent on propertied classes with a substantial degree of local self-government, had created a tendency

---

3 See Jacques Gernet, *A History of Chinese Civilization* (Cambridge: Cambridge University Press, 2nd edn, 2005), Chs 3–5.

to fragmentation of sovereign power even in the Roman Empire. In the end, the tendencies towards fragmentation prevailed, leaving behind a network of personal dependence binding peasants to landlords. When the empire disintegrated, and after several attempts at recentralization by the Merovingian monarchy, the Carolingian empire and the successor states, the autonomy of landed aristocracies asserted itself in what might be called the privatization of public authority, the feudal 'parcellization of sovereignty',[4] with the devolution of public functions to local lords and various other independent powers. This devolved public power was at the same time a power of appropriation, the power to command the labour of producing classes, appropriating its fruits in rent or in kind, in particular from peasants who remained in possession of land but worked in political and legal subjection to lords. We can, for lack of a better term, apply the much-disputed concept of feudalism, or 'feudal society', to this specifically Western parcellization of sovereignty, which invested private property with public power in historically distinctive ways. The 'medieval' period for our purposes is roughly marked out by the dominance of that distinctive configuration and its decline.[5]

This feudal parcellization existed in various forms and to varying degrees. Feudal monarchies were stronger in some places than in others; and parts of Europe were in varying degrees under the sway of higher authorities, the Holy Roman Empire or the papacy. But political parcellization affected even European political entities that did not conform to the model feudal system. Italy, for instance, has been called the 'weak link' of European feudalism because, especially in the north, urban patriciates were dominant, in contrast to seigneurial landed classes elsewhere. Yet, not only did the city-states of northern Italy have their own fragmented governance – what might be called a kind of urban feudalism – but the great commercial centres like Florence and Venice were what they were in large part because they served a vital function as trading links in the fragmented feudal order.

Wherever we choose to place the dividing line between the 'medieval' and the 'early modern', we can, by the late fifteenth century, identify a new configuration of political power, with new relations between property and state different from feudal parcellized sovereignty. Lords and autonomous corporate bodies did, to be sure, continue to play a prominent role; but centralizing monarchies – especially in England, France and the Iberian peninsula – were now taking centre stage, imposing a new political dynamic

---

4   The phrase 'parcellization of sovereignty' appears in Perry Anderson, *Passages from Antiquity to Feudalism* (London: Verso, 1974), p. 148.

5   For a discussion of the much-debated concept of feudalism, see Ellen Meiksins Wood, *Citizens to Lords: A Social History of Western Political Thought from Antiquity to the Middle Ages* ((London: Verso, 2008), Ch. 4.

even on different political forms, such as the Italian city-states or German principalities. While northern Italy, for instance, had been a battleground for rivalries between the Holy Roman Empire and the papacy, the challenge to the autonomy of city-states was increasingly coming from the territorial ambitions of monarchical states such as France and Spain.

Many explanations have been offered for the decline of feudalism. Some historians have argued that, just as the emergence of feudalism was marked, or even caused, by a contraction of trade, commercial expansion and the growth of the money economy inevitably brought feudalism to an end; while others have persuasively argued that trade and money were very much part of, and not intrinsically inimical to, the feudal order. Much is often made of the demographic collapse that occurred in the time of the Black Death, the pandemic that affected Western Europe in the 1340s; and it has been argued that the relationship between lords and peasants was fundamentally transformed as the drastic decline in population gave peasants an advantage in bargaining with lords in need of labour. Peasants, according to some historians, may have had yet another bargaining advantage, an escape route provided by the growth of urban centres as commerce expanded. Popular rebellions of various kinds were then provoked by the efforts of lords to reimpose and intensify peasant dependence; and, though rebellions in the West were successfully suppressed, the feudal order was effectively dead.

The development of the modern nation state may be attributed to the needs of landed aristocracies for a stronger central power to maintain order against the threat of rebellion, or – and perhaps at the same time – feudal monarchies may have been under greater pressure to consolidate their positions, as revenues derived from peasants became more precarious and the competition with landlords for access to peasant labour became more intense. The pressures became that much greater when aristocratic rivalries spilled over into wars between aspiring territorial states, as happened most dramatically in the Hundred Years' War, which began as a dynastic struggle over the monarchy in France and continued as a battle over the territorial boundaries of the French and English states. The incentive to consolidate centrally governed territorial states was further intensified by the commercial and geopolitical challenge of the growing Ottoman Empire, which made deep incursions into Europe and commanded east–west trade routes.

Yet, however important any or all of these factors may be, this cannot be the whole story. Commercial expansion, plague and demographic changes, peasant revolts and dynastic conflicts occurred in various parts of Europe; and we may even accept, as a very general principle, that all of them played a part in the decline of feudalism. But, quite apart from the variety of 'feudalisms', there was a wide variety of outcomes; and the feudal order gave way to more than one 'transition'. Serfdom, for instance, ended in

Western Europe, while Eastern Europe saw what has been called the 'second serfdom'. Even in Western Europe, which is our main concern here, relations between landlords and peasants turned out to be very different in, say, England than in France; and these differences were associated with divergent paths of state-formation. In England, where the monarchy had developed in cooperation with an unusually united aristocracy, lords had gained control of the best land, including properties left vacant by the demographic collapse. In France, the monarchical state, which consolidated the dominance of one aristocratic family against its rivals, helped to ensure that peasants remained in possession of by far the most land, as a vital source of tax revenues for the centralizing state.

In these different contexts, commercial expansion, too, had divergent effects. All the major Western European states, to say nothing of the highly developed economies of Asia and the Arab Muslim empire, were very much engaged in trade, both domestic and international; but a distinctively *capitalist* 'commercial society' arose 'spontaneously' only in England and produced a historical dynamic unlike any other, even in the most commercialized societies.[6] Capitalism, as it emerged in England, was not simply more of the same, more trade and more expansive commercial networks. The 'rise of capitalism' cannot be explained as just a quantitative process, 'commercialization' approaching some kind of critical mass. England, indeed, was very far from being the dominant commercial power in Europe when its economic development began to take a distinctive turn, giving rise to something different from traditional modes of commerce, the old forms of profit on alienation or 'buying cheap and selling dear'. English capitalism, which was born in the countryside, produced a new kind of society, with an economy uniquely driven by compulsions of competitive production, increasing labour productivity, profit-maximization and constant capital accumulation. When other European economies later developed in a capitalist direction, they were in large part responding to military and commercial pressures imposed by English capitalism.

Which 'Modern' State?

In the following chapters, we shall look at various distinctive patterns of development in Western Europe as they affected national 'traditions of discourse'; but for the moment, and to illustrate the contextual history proposed in this book, we can concentrate on the one overarching

---

6   See Robert Brenner's two contributions to *The Brenner Debate: Agrarian Class Structure and Economic Development in Pre-Industrial Europe*, eds T.H Aston and C.H.E. Philpin (Cambridge: Cambridge University Press, 1985). See also Ellen Meiksins Wood, *The Origin of Capitalism: A Longer View* (London: Verso, 2002).

development that had effects on all of them: the evolution of the 'modern' state, especially in England and in France.

Quentin Skinner, in his *Foundations of Modern Political Thought*, tells us that in the period from the late thirteenth century to the end of the sixteenth, 'the main elements of a recognizably modern concept of the state were gradually acquired.' He goes on to elaborate his definition of the modern state in terms derived, as he acknowledges, from Max Weber:

> The decisive shift was made from the idea of the ruler 'maintaining his state' – where this simply meant upholding his own position – to the idea that there is a separate legal and constitutional order, that of the State, which the ruler has a duty to maintain. One effect of this transformation was that the power of the State, not that of the ruler, came to be envisaged as the basis of government. And this in turn enabled the State to be conceptualized in distinctively modern terms – as the sole source of law and legitimate force within its own territory, and as the sole appropriate object of its citizens' allegiances.[7]

The elements of this modern state, Skinner explains, were by the sixteenth century visible at least in England and in France. The transition to a modern discourse of the state, he suggests, 'first appears to have been accomplished in France'. This was so not only because the intellectual preconditions were present – inherited from Italian humanism – but because 'the material preconditions' were more fully developed in France: 'a relatively united central authority, an increasing apparatus of bureaucratic control, and a clearly defined set of national boundaries'.[8] 'The next country in which the same fundamental conceptual shift took place', Skinner continues, 'appears to have been England', where, by the 1530s, 'a similar set of material as well as intellectual preconditions for this development had been achieved: an increasingly bureaucratic style of central government, together with a growing interest amongst English humanists in the problems of "politics" and public law.'[9]

This formulation obscures a wealth of differences between the two cases, both in the nature of their states and the forms of 'discourse' they engendered. Those differences also cast doubt on some other standard conventions about 'modernity' and especially about the connections between the capitalist economy – or 'commercial society' – and the 'rational' state. In subsequent chapters, we shall look more closely at the varying traditions of political discourse that emerged out of divergent patterns of historical development;

---

7 Quentin Skinner, *The Foundations of Modern Political Thought, Volume 1: The Renaissance* (Cambridge: Cambridge University Press, 1978), pp. ix–x.

8 Skinner, *Foundations, Vol. 2: The Age of Reformation*, p. 354.

9 *Ibid.*, p. 356.

but a broad preliminary sketch of the differences between England and France will serve to illustrate the 'social history' on offer here.

The story begins at least as early as the Middle Ages, at a time when the Frankish empire was disintegrating while the Anglo-Saxon state was the most effective centralized administration in the Western world.[10] Medieval Europe was generally characterized by what we have called a 'parcellization of sovereignty', the fragmentation of state power, as feudal lordship and other autonomous powers took over many of the functions performed in other times and places by the state, combining the private exploitation of labour – typically the labour of peasants – with the public role of administration, jurisdiction and enforcement. Yet England, for all the power of the barons – and, in some ways, precisely because of it – never really succumbed to parcellized sovereignty, while France never completely overcame it, even under the absolutist monarchy; and the centralizing project of the state remained on the agenda to be completed by the Revolution and Napoleon.

This meant, too, that there were major differences between England and France in the relations between state and dominant classes. In England, even at a time when English law was at its most ostensibly feudal and the manorial system was at its height, the process of state centralization continued. The Norman Conquest, when it brought feudal institutions with it from the Continent, also, and above all, brought a military organization, which vested power in a central authority and built upon the foundations of a centralized state that already existed in England. The Normans established themselves in England as a more or less unified ruling class, a conquering army that imposed itself as both a dominant class of great landholders and a governing power; and the central state was always its instrument. Thereafter, the centralization of the post-feudal state would remain a cooperative project between monarchy and landed aristocracy. This certainly did not rule out fierce dynastic rivalries; and, though some historians have questioned the very existence of, for example, the 'Wars of the Roses', there certainly were powerful incentives for battles over control of an already well-established central state. When, in the sixteenth century, the Tudor monarchy embarked on a programme of state-centralization, which has (controversially) been described as the 'Tudor revolution', it was not inventing but building on a long-standing unified state apparatus, which, when the Reformation came to England under Henry VIII, would have the added strength of a state Church.

This centralizing project was cooperative not only in the sense that the central state would develop as a unity of monarchy and the landed class in

---

10   These points are discussed at greater length in *Citizens to Lords*, as are the differences between feudal societies in England and France, among others. For an important discussion of those differences, see George Comninel, 'English Feudalism and the Origins of Capitalism', in *The Journal of Peasant Studies*, July 2000, pp. 1–53.

Parliament, nicely summed up in the old formula 'the Crown in Parliament'. The cooperative project also took the form of a division of labour between the central state and private property. As legislation and jurisdiction were increasingly centralized, the aristocracy would increasingly depend for its wealth on modes of purely *economic* exploitation. Recent scholarship has shown that smallholders may not have disappeared from the English countryside as completely as historians have sometimes suggested; but the fact remains that lords in England, while lacking some of the jurisdictional powers enjoyed by their counterparts elsewhere in Europe, had control of the best land, which was concentrated in the hands of large landholders to a greater degree than in France, where peasant property prevailed. When feudalism experienced its crisis throughout Europe, and serfdom declined in the West, English landlords were in a uniquely favourable position to exploit the purely economic powers that they still enjoyed, even as the state became increasingly centralized.

The English landed class was, in this respect, markedly different from those Continental aristocracies whose wealth derived from 'extra-economic' power, or what has been called 'politically constituted property', of one kind or another, various forms of privilege, seigneurial rights and the fruits of jurisdiction.[11] The concentration of landed property in England meant that land was worked to an unusual extent by tenants – increasingly on economic rents subject to market conditions – while landlords without access to politically constituted property came to depend on the productive and competitive success of their tenants. The result of this distinctive development was agrarian capitalism, which was 'capitalist' in the sense that appropriators and producers were dependent on the market for their own survival and the maintenance of their positions, hence subject to the imperatives of competition, profit-maximization and the need constantly to improve labour productivity.

Because of uniquely English relations between large landowners and tenants whom we might call capitalist farmers, English agriculture began to respond to new requirements of market competition with no historical precedent. The particular relations between landlords and tenants, in the context of a distinctive kind of domestic market, meant that already in the seventeenth century both parties were compelled to enhance the land's productivity for profit – to promote what they called *improvement*. Improvement and profitable production became the preferred strategy for the ruling landed class. What this meant was not – at least in the first instance – mainly technological innovation. It had more to do with methods and techniques of land use; but it also meant, and more fundamentally, new forms and conceptions of property. Agricultural

---

11   The phrase 'politically constituted property' has been used by Robert Brenner in various historical works.

improvement and the enhancement of profit for capitalist agriculture ideally called for a concentration of property; but above all, they required the elimination of various customary rights and practices that interfered with capital accumulation. Improving landlords and capitalist tenants needed to be free of obstructions to the productive and profitable use of property.

Between the sixteenth and eighteenth centuries, there was growing pressure to extinguish customary rights – for instance, disputing communal rights to common land by claiming exclusive private ownership; challenging customary tenures which granted smallholders rights of possession without outright legal title; eliminating various use rights on private land; and so on. This meant the establishment of property that was literally *exclusive* – excluding other individuals and the community, eliminating various kinds of restrictions on land use imposed by custom or communal regulation.

The detachment of economic from 'extra-economic' powers meant that the processes of state-centralization and capitalist development, although sometimes in tension, were closely intertwined. There were obviously conflicts between the landed class and the monarchy, which would come to a head in the Civil War. But those conflicts had a particular character and intensity precisely because of the underlying partnership between dominant class and monarchical state. The interests of the English ruling classes were, from very early on, deeply invested in a unitary Parliament, with legislative powers, which was very much a part of the centralized state. The aristocracy was also committed to a national system of law, and jurisdictional conflicts between king and the nobility ended quite early. Even in the early thirteenth century, at a time of violent tension between monarchy and barons, when Magna Carta claimed the rights of the barons to be tried by their peers, it did not assert their rights of jurisdiction over other free men. The common law – which was, in the first instance, the king's law – became the favoured legal system for the aristocracy as well as for free peasants who could seek protection from the Crown, while the rule of law was understood to mean that the monarchy itself was subject to the law.

This uniquely unified system of law, in an unusually centralized state, produced a distinctive type of 'free' man, subject only to the king and to no other, lesser lord. Landlords enjoyed great local powers, but outside the manor they acted as delegates of the Crown in relation to free men. There remained land subject to manorial lordship; but the 'free' Englishman, with an individual 'interest' in freehold property recognized in common law and free of lordly claims or obligations, was a unique formation. In France, for example, even charters of freedom did not dissolve seigneurial obligation; and even free peasants with access to royal protection could still be subject to seigneurial jurisdiction.[12]

---

12   See Comninel, 'English Feudalism'.

The English common law did eventually come to represent parliamentary power *against* the Crown, with Parliament asserting its supremacy as the interpreter of common law. In the Civil War in the seventeenth century, the conflict between monarch and Parliament, common lawyers tended to side with Parliament, against the prerogative courts allied with the king. But this was not a case of parcellized jurisdictions asserting themselves against the central state. On the contrary, it was an assertion of the aristocracy's essential role in the partnership that constituted the central state, at a time when that partnership was being challenged by the monarchy. At the same time, while the ruling class was claiming its share in the public sphere of the central state, it was also asserting its power in the private sphere of property, as landowners rather than as officers of state. From this point of view, the issue was less an assertion of public jurisdiction than of private rights, intended to protect the ruling class against the Crown's violation of its partnership and the division of labour between property and state.

The English Revolution – the whole period from the Civil War in the 1640s to the so-called Glorious Revolution of 1688–9 – saw major upheavals, and, as we shall see in a subsequent chapter, it produced uniquely radical ideas. But it did not fundamentally transform social property relations in England, which were hardly less capitalist before the Revolution than after. Nor, for that matter, did it fundamentally transform – bar the 'interregnum' – the relation between Parliament and monarchy. Even if we attach great importance to the settlement of 1688 in establishing parliamentary supremacy, it did little more than consolidate what was already on the table before the Revolution, before the Stuart monarchy attempted, unsuccessfully, to establish a Continental-style absolutism in a society where there was little political support and even less social foundation for any such project. If the old cooperative enterprise between monarchy and Parliament was increasingly giving way to parliamentary supremacy (and we should not exaggerate the extent to which this was true even in the eighteenth century), what remained was the characteristic division of labour between state and property, the separation of economic and extra-economic powers, which had marked out Britain from its neighbours.

The long history of partnership between aristocracy and central state, and the role of Parliament as the public face of private property, has meant that the ruling class in Britain has, on the whole, been consistently committed to parliamentarism. But the other side of the coin is that the dominant historical narrative and mainstream political culture have marginalized the truly revolutionary and democratic traditions that emerged during the English Revolution, the tradition of the Levellers, Diggers and other radical movements. Democratic popular forces were defeated by the parliamentary oligarchy; and, though their legacy has never completely disappeared from the British labour movement, the dominant parliamentary tradition owes more to the victorious propertied classes.

The process of state-formation in France was quite different. If in England there was a transition from feudalism to capitalism, in France it was rather a transition from feudalism to absolutism – absolutism not simply as a political form but the absolutist state as a form of politically constituted property, a means of enriching office-holders by exploiting the peasantry. The monarchy emerged out of feudal rivalry, as one aristocratic dynasty established itself over others in a context of parcellized sovereignty. The monarchical state continued to confront the challenge of feudal parcellization, not only opposition from dynastic rivals but claims to independent powers and privileges by the aristocracy and various corporate entities, guilds, estates, provinces and towns.

The monarchy certainly did pursue a centralizing strategy with some success; and royal courts did emerge, which, among other things, could be used to protect peasants from lords (not least, in order to preserve the peasantry as a source of state taxes). But the dominant class continued to depend to a great extent on politically constituted property – that is, on means of appropriation deriving from political, military and judicial powers, or 'extra-economic' status and privilege, in contrast to the English landed classes and their dependence on competitive production. In France, in contrast to England, even in the eighteenth century peasants still dominated agricultural production, and relations between landlords and tenants had very different effects. There was, for instance, nothing like the culture of 'improvement' nor the improvement literature that had been so important in seventeenth-century England. Village regulation of production and restrictions on land use continued to be important in agriculture even beyond the Revolution. For French landlords, extra-economic strategies – political and legal – for enhancing their power to squeeze more surplus out of peasants were still more important than agricultural improvement. This meant, among other things, that peasants were more plagued by taxes than by attacks on their property rights.

The state developed as a competing form of politically constituted property, a primary resource, a mode of direct appropriation for state office-holders by means of taxation, which some historians have called a kind of centralized rent. If the absolutist state was able to undermine the independent powers of the aristocracy, it did so in large part by replacing those powers with the lucrative resource of state office for a segment of the aristocracy. An elaborate bureaucracy developed not just for political and administrative purposes but as an economic resource for office-holders, proliferating state offices as a form of private property.

Nor was there anything in France like England's long parliamentary tradition. No such tradition existed before the Revolution. There was, to begin with, a stark historical contrast between the unitary national Parliament in England, with its early legislative role, and the fragmented estates in France. The estates had no legislative function and were divided by locality – even on the rare occasions when they met on the national plane of the Estates General. They were also divided by corporate hierarchy, above all the division between, on the one hand, the two privileged estates, the nobility and the Church, and, on the other hand, the Third Estate, which encompassed both bourgeoisie – the more prosperous non-privileged classes, often urban notables – and peasantry. The emergence of a representative legislative body in France had to await the Revolution; and one of the most striking differences between England and France is that, in France, even when estates were replaced by a national assembly, important sectors of the dominant classes remained opposed to the Republic. The revolutionary transformation created both a new parliamentary tradition, even a radical republicanism, and at the same time a dangerously anti-parliamentary, anti-republican formation, which persisted well into the twentieth century and explains much that would happen in France in the Second World War.

The French legal system also developed in ways sharply different from the English. Not only was there a long-standing division between the Roman law which survived in the south and the Germanic customary law of the north, but in addition, on the eve of the Revolution there were still approximately 360 different law codes in France, with various seigneurial, local and corporate powers contesting jurisdiction with the monarchy, and customary law challenging the supremacy of state legislation. Although the absolutist state succeeded to a considerable degree in limiting seigneurial and local jurisdiction, jurisdictional conflicts remained a constant feature of the ancien régime and a major preoccupation of French courts. The aristocracy and corporate bodies clung to their autonomy and independence from the national state, while the monarchy continued its efforts to co-opt and integrate them.

When monarchical absolutism gave way to Revolution, the centralizing project of the state continued. The French *état légal* evolved not as a defence of private rights against public incursions but as a means of asserting the power of the central state against fragmented jurisdictions and independent local powers. This limited the independence of the judiciary, effectively absorbing it into the civil service. It remained for Napoleon to complete the project begun by the Revolution. While the judiciary would regain some of its autonomy in the Fifth Republic of 1958, the historic function of the law in asserting state sovereignty against autonomous jurisdictions remains a powerful legacy.

Relations between central state and landed aristocracy, then, were quite different from the English case. In contrast to the close English partnership between the aristocracy and monarchy, in France the tensions between aristocratic privilege and monarchical power, between different modes of extra-economic exploitation, persisted until the Revolution. At the same time, the aristocracy itself was divided between those with power in the central state and the many who remained dependent on their privileges and local powers; and this division continued to be fluid. The centralizing project of the state can be understood as in large part an attempt to overcome that division by replacing autonomous aristocratic powers with perquisites and privileges deriving from the state – for instance, by granting privileged exemption from royal taxation in place of seigneurial jurisdiction.

As for the bourgeoisie, throughout the ancien régime and beyond, state office would be a favoured career. Notwithstanding the conventional conflation of 'bourgeois' with 'capitalist', the French bourgeoisie was not in essence capitalist. While France was certainly a major trading nation, the majority of 'bourgeois' were urban notables or functionaries of various kinds, office-holders, professionals, intellectuals; and even those engaged in commerce (who might also be inclined to use their wealth to buy ennobling office) were operating on familiar principles of non-capitalist commercial profit-taking.[13] When the Revolution came, the revolutionary bourgeoisie – typically consisting precisely of those office-holders, professionals and intellectuals – was less concerned with breaking the shackles impeding the development of capitalism, as is often suggested by the notion of the 'bourgeois revolution', than with preserving and enhancing their access to the highest state office, 'careers open to talent'. It was, indeed, a threat to the access they already enjoyed under the absolutist monarchy that probably more than anything else provoked the bourgeoisie into revolution and a confrontation between bourgeoisie and aristocracy.

Although private property in office was abolished by the Revolution, state office remained a lucrative career, in which office-holders appropriated the surplus labour of peasants through taxation. Even after the Revolution, even after Napoleon, the state continued to serve this economic function for the bourgeoisie. The peasantry, which remained in possession of most land in France, continued to be exploited by extra-economic means, through the medium of state taxation. The Revolution did not radically transform the social property relations between the state and small agricultural producers which had prevailed in absolutist France.

While the Revolution may have been 'bourgeois', then, there was little that was 'capitalist' about it. If, in its political principles and in its legacies it went far beyond the 'bourgeois' impulses that first set it in motion, there remained strong continuities between the ancien régime and the post-revolutionary state. What is so striking about the post-revolutionary period,

---

13   For a discussion of this point, see George Comninel, *Rethinking the French Revolution: Marxism and the Revisionist Challenge* (London: Verso, 1987), esp. pp. 180ff.

throughout much of the nineteenth century in France, is the persistence of the tax/office structure, in which appropriation took the form of direct exploitation of peasant producers by the state through taxation. Not only did the economy continue to be based on small-scale agricultural production, but the state continued to relate to that production as a primary exploiter of direct producers through the medium of taxation, for the benefit of office-holders.

One has only to read Marx's account of nineteenth-century France in the *18th Brumaire* to see how persistent this formation was. He speaks of the 'immense bureaucratic and military organization', a 'frightful parasitic body', in which the *'material interest* of the French bourgeoisie is most intimately imbricated. It is that machine which provides the surplus population with jobs, and makes up through state salaries for what it cannot pocket in the form of profits, interest, rents and fees.' This bourgeois tradition would continue well into the twentieth century, if not until today, in a culture where state office would remain the highest career, with a tradition of mandarinism, dominated by a hereditary elite of office-holders and their exclusive academies.

Economic development in a capitalist direction was, in France, largely driven from without, in particular by military pressures. After the Revolution, the defeat of Napoleon not only made clear the military advantage that a victorious Britain had gained from the economic growth and wealth created by capitalism but also opened the former Napoleonic empire to the purely economic pressures of British capitalism in unprecedented ways. The state responded to those external imperatives by bringing about a state-led development of the economy. In a sense, the development of capitalism preceded social transformation; and, in contrast to England, capitalist class relations were more a result than a cause of industrialization.

Modern Political Thought?

It is certainly true that the emergence of national states with clear territorial boundaries and a more or less unified sovereign power created conditions for new developments in Western political thought – but perhaps not quite in the ways that Skinner has suggested. It does make sense to identify the rise of territorial states in Europe as a major historical development, a departure from the parcellized sovereignty of previous centuries; but it helps very little to describe these states as 'modern' if that label disguises important historical differences, such as those we have already observed between England and France. Is absolutist France more modern because of its elaborate bureaucracy, the sign of a 'rational' state? Or should we give the prize to England, because its centralized state, however 'irrational' in Weberian terms, has more completely asserted its sovereignty against autonomous powers of various kinds and has largely ceased to be a form of property?

It also makes sense to single out the rise of the 'market economy' as a critical development, but what precisely makes a market 'modern' as distinct from 'ancient'? There were vast commercial networks in various parts of the world long before the advent of 'modernity', and it is not at all clear that the trade we see in 'early modern' Europe is operating on significantly different principles, the age-old practices of buying cheap and selling dear. It cannot be simply a matter of scale, or else why should Europe in the sixteenth century be more modern than India or China even centuries before? If there is a fundamental rupture in the age-old pattern of commercial exchange, it occurs in England (a point to which we shall return in later chapters), with the rise of agrarian capitalism; but England is at first a fairly minor player in the global trading network compared to, say, Venice or Portugal; so which of them is more modern? If we try to identify a uniquely modern complex of a rational state, a 'rational' economy, and a culture of 'reason', where, if anywhere, did it exist?

If the notion of the modern state conceals as much as it reveals, what does it mean to speak of modern political thought? There seems to be an irresistible temptation among historians of political thought to identify the first modern political thinker in the Western canon. Pride of place is commonly awarded to Hobbes or Machiavelli. The reasons for selecting Hobbes may have to do with his theory of government, grounded in a systematically secular, materialistic account of epistemology, human psychology and morality. Or the reason may be that, however ambiguously, he bases his theory of politics on a conception of individual freedom and rights. Or it may simply be that, by elaborating a definitive conception of sovereignty, he best represents the triumph of territorial monarchies, or even 'nation states', over medieval forms of governance. Hobbes has even been called a 'bourgeois' thinker, an exponent of a 'possessive individualism' associated with a modern market society.

If Machiavelli is chosen, with or without denouncing his 'Machiavellian' amorality, it is likely to be on the grounds that he, before Hobbes, gave an account of politics divorced from moral or religious principles, or even that he is the first political *scientist,* on the side of the 'empirical' instead of the 'normative' study of politics, 'facts' rather than 'values'. Or it may be on the grounds that his republicanism, albeit more visible in the *Discourses* than in his most famous work, *The Prince,* mobilizes ancient ideas of civic autonomy against feudal hierarchies and in support of more modern conceptions of liberty and citizenship, a pivotal moment – as in John Pocock's 'Machiavellian moment' – in the development of modern republican ideas. Or at least, it might be said, if he has one foot in the ancient world, he is a 'transitional' figure; and, even if the city-state of Florence that produced him fails to fit the model of a modern nation state, it was, after all, a centre of commerce, which is supposed to be a prelude to a modern capitalist economy.

The Cambridge School, which dominates the field of early modern political theory in the Anglo-American academy, may have muddied the waters – making it harder to award the modernity prize to any one thinker – by eschewing the very idea of a 'canon' and replacing it with discursive contexts that include a host of not-so-canonical writers who have in their various ways contributed to language 'situations'. This approach certainly has its advantages, but it may – as we have seen in the case of Quentin Skinner – simply shift the question to which political language or discourse represents a modern break from ancient or medieval precedents. The conventional language of ancient and modern persists even when traditions of discourse span centuries of historical change, indeed even when ancient and modern languages of politics are allowed to coexist in historical time, in conflict or in paradoxical unity – as in the notion of 'civic humanism' or, for that matter, 'republicanism'.

But whether applied to a single major thinker or to a collective 'discourse', the concept of modernity, in all its conflicting forms, is loaded with assumptions that shed little light on historical processes. Might it not be better to look for historic transformations, even ruptures, without being obliged to define them as breakthroughs to modernity? And what kinds of transformations might we find if we set aside the elusive search for modernity? In particular, what significant changes would we find in the discourse of politics in the era we are exploring here?

During the medieval period, at the height of 'parcellized sovereignty', there scarcely existed a distinct political sphere.[14] The elaborate feudal network of competing jurisdictions, bound together – when not in open conflict – by a complex apparatus of legal and contractual relations, meant that the boundaries of the 'political' were ill-defined and fluid. The main 'political' agent was not the individual citizen but the possessor of some kind of secular or ecclesiastical jurisdiction, or a corporate entity with its own legal rights, a degree of autonomy and often a charter defining its relation to other corporations and superior powers. Legal and political thinking was preoccupied not, as ancient political philosophy had been, with portraying the political transactions among citizens within a civic community, but with mapping out the spheres of authority among overlapping and competing jurisdictions or negotiating interactions among them. The emergence of territorial states in the early modern period would change these conditions (though, as we shall see, we should not exaggerate the speed or degree of these transformations), creating a new political domain, new political identities, and new political ideas to suit them.

Among the most significant developments were new conceptions of individual rights in relation to political authority. Although there has been

---

14 There is a detailed discussion of these themes in my *Citizens to Lords*, Ch. 4.

much debate about when and how the concept of 'subjective' rights originated, the idea of rights inherent in the person, prior to and independent of civic authority or positive law, certainly had roots in the Middle Ages, in the writings of canon lawyers and philosophers. The very idea of a Christian conscience, for instance, presupposed a human capacity for understanding principles of right (in the 'objective' sense, as 'what is right') and a responsibility to follow them.[15] That responsibility implied both a moral obligation and a certain individual autonomy, the capacity to disregard the principles of right no less than to respect them. From that individual autonomy it was possible to deduce a notion of individual freedom from which followed certain entitlements – which might include a 'right' to be free of enslavement, or a 'right' of self-preservation and self-defence; and it also entailed respect for the same entitlements in others, if only on the basis of the Golden Rule.

These principles of right did have some implications for political thought. An insistence on individual autonomy or natural freedom seemed, for instance, to require an acknowledgement that civil authority is constituted by consenting individuals – which was consistent with the prominent role of contractual relations in the feudal order. But none of this had any necessary implications for the rights of individuals in relation to the state, once established. As long as the central category of political thought remained not citizenship but jurisdiction, and as long as the principal political agent was not the individual citizen but the bearer of some jurisdictional authority – a feudal lord, perhaps, or some corporate entity endowed with legal rights and liberties – there was no obvious connection between individual rights and limitations on the state, nor, indeed, any need to demonstrate by systematic argument that individual rights do not preclude almost unlimited civil power.

A monarch might, for instance, invoke a doctrine of consent, based on rights, to buttress his own authority against the claims of popes or emperors. What may look to us like a paradox seemed to medieval thinkers not so paradoxical. The creation of the body politic was quite distinct from the conditions of rule. The idea that civil authority is constituted by the 'people' (typically conceived as a corporate body) was perfectly consistent with the

---

15   The history of 'rights' is difficult to trace not least because the Latin *ius* has such variable meanings, denoting both 'objective' principles of right or justice, established by positive or natural law, and 'subjective' rights in the sense of entitlements inherent in the individual person. Some of the same complexities exist in modern European languages, as in the German *Recht* or the French *droit*. Since the principles of 'objective' right derive their moral force from their availability to the same rational, responsible and autonomous individual who is the subject of 'subjective' rights, it is that much harder to draw a neat line between 'objective' and 'subjective' right in the development of Western political thought.

view that such authority was almost unconditional – not least because the right of resistance to illegitimate authority, if it existed at all, was typically vested not in individual citizens but in jurisdictional authorities. Even in the 'early modern' period, there would continue to be doctrines of resistance in which the right to resist civil authority was not a right of private individuals or citizens but an attribute of office, the authority of one jurisdiction pitted against another.

A right of private property might be emphatically acknowledged; but even that right was conceived in the context of competing jurisdictions, typically to assert lordly autonomy or to mark out a domain of private power, the power of the head of the household over his family and possessions, or perhaps the remnant of jurisdictional authority construed as a right of *dominium*, against some higher *imperium*.

If the universal possession of natural rights and natural liberty did not guarantee universal entitlements to full political rights, much the same can be said about notions of natural equality. It is, as we shall see in subsequent chapters, a striking characteristic of Western political thought throughout much of its history that ideas of natural equality among men did not rule out the unequal distribution of political rights; and elaborate arguments have been constructed to legitimate relationships of rule and domination among naturally equal men. Men might all be equal under God or natural law, but some might be entitled to rule others nonetheless. The determinants of property and class could trump all natural equalities.

It has even been possible for political thinkers to go some distance in conceding the equality of women, while taking for granted their complete exclusion from the political domain – for example, on the grounds of their child-bearing functions or men's monopoly of coercive force. Few thinkers exceed Thomas Hobbes in acknowledging the natural equality of men and women, just as few go beyond him in insisting on natural equality among all men; yet none of these concessions to equality pose any obstacles to his convictions on the legitimacy of absolutist rule. Nor is John Locke inhibited in his views on the unequal distribution of political rights among men by his belief in their natural equality, or the total exclusion of women from politics by his denial that God decreed the subjection of Eve to Adam or women to men.

The compatibility of natural equality with political inequality would remain a persistent theme in Western political thought. But the emergence of a sovereign state in which the contest among jurisdictions ceased to play a central role undoubtedly created, as we shall see, conditions for new conceptions of 'natural right'; and, in that respect, the rise of sovereign territorial states clearly had a bearing on the development of Western political theory. Yet the differences among the European states were no less decisive in shaping 'traditions of discourse'. If we look beyond the most formal characteristics of a centralized state, the 'material' conditions in the two cases identified by Skinner as the sources of 'modern' ideas of the state look very different. It is not unreasonable to identify those cases as, in one way or another, emblematic of the 'modern' state, in theory and in practice; and, largely for that reason, the chapters devoted here to England and France will be longer than the others. But, even if we ignore the fact that it was England more than France that first experienced a centralization of the state unencumbered by 'parcellized sovereignty', while French absolutism even at its height remained in constant tension with various competing jurisdictions, their patterns of political and economic development are strikingly divergent.

This is not to deny that France and England shared a common intellectual legacy and, indeed, important material roots traceable at least to imperial Rome, its mode of imperial rule and its system of property. Nor is it to deny that their national histories were always inextricably intertwined, by virtue of proximity, shifting territorial boundaries, war, trade, commercial rivalries, and even recurrent alliances. But the historical moment we are exploring here – the moment of rising territorial states and national economies – is precisely the period of diverging national histories, with their distinctive patterns of development.

As we shall see in what follows, the national differences we have already observed had fundamental implications for the development of political thought. When, for instance, French political theory, especially in the person of Jean Bodin, clearly and systematically articulated a 'modern' conception of state sovereignty, it was not because the French had already established one clear and undisputed centre of political authority but, on the contrary, because the centralizing power was still contending with competing jurisdictions. Bodin's political theory, in other words, reflected not the reality of undivided sovereignty in France but its absence. He was proposing his idea of a single, indivisible and absolute power in order to support the king's claims to authority over the nobility and other autonomous powers, at a time, during the Wars of Religion in the sixteenth century, when the monarchy was being challenged by rebellion and radical ideas about the right of resistance.

Those ideas of resistance were themselves deeply rooted in the persistent tension between the central state and the remnants of parcellized sovereignty. When the French *monarchomachs* insisted on the people's rights of resistance to the monarchy, the people they had in mind were not private citizens. They were corporate bodies, provincial aristocrats and local magistrates, who claimed a right of resistance in their capacity as office-holders. The main resistance tracts – which will be discussed in a subsequent chapter – were expressing the interests of local aristocracies and various corporate entities. When they invoked some kind of popular sovereignty, they did so as officers asserting their jurisdictional rights against the central state; and, when the absolutist monarchy invoked the concept of state sovereignty against them, it was professing to represent a more general interest, as opposed to the particularities of these fragmented jurisdictions. It claimed to be acting on behalf of a more universal corporation than the particularistic corporate bodies that were challenging its sovereignty. Even as late as the eighteenth century, when revolutionaries challenged the existing hierarchy of corporate power and privilege, they purported to act on behalf of the corporate 'nation'. The concept of equality that has figured so prominently in French political discourse and the revolutionary tradition owes much to the Third Estate's struggles over corporate privilege and its battle for access to office, 'careers open to talent'.

In England, where there was no such fundamental conflict of jurisdiction between the monarchy and ruling classes, there was no strategic need to assert the power of one against the other with a clear idea of indivisible sovereignty. In fact, the English tended to avoid the issue of sovereignty altogether (a thinker like Thomas Hobbes was one striking exception, and even he formulated an idea of sovereignty significantly different from the French). The idea of a 'mixed constitution' – anathema to Jean Bodin – conformed very nicely to English conditions and the interests of the ruling class. The partnership between Crown and Parliament had created a delicate balance which neither side was anxious to upset by claiming ultimate authority. Even when the conflicts between them came to a head, as the king threatened the partnership with Parliament, parliamentarians were very slow to invoke their own sovereignty as representatives of the people. To assert the sovereignty of Parliament against the king and on behalf of the people threatened to unleash more dangerous claims to popular sovereignty from the truly radical forces mobilized by the Revolution, without the protection of intermediate powers between Parliament and people. A degree of vagueness seemed prudent even among republican elements in Parliament.

The particular formation of the state, the distinctive relation between aristocracy and monarchy, the unity of Parliament and Crown, the evolution of a unified system of law on which the ruling class depended to sustain its property and power, meant that political conflict did not in general take the form of jurisdictional disputes among fragments of sovereignty. It also meant that corporate principles were weak. From early on, the relation between state and individual was not mediated by corporate entities, and political rights were vested in the individual rather than in corporate bodies.

In England, where the primary political relation was not among competing jurisdictions but between individual and state, the idea of individual rights was bound to have different implications than it did elsewhere in Europe. It is significant, as we shall see, that the first systematic discussion of the relation between individual rights, the rights of private individuals, and sovereign power was produced by an English theorist, Hobbes, though not in defence of individual rights against the state but in favour of absolute sovereignty. At the same time, any theory of resistance or popular sovereignty would, in that context, represent a greater challenge to the power of propertied classes than did the French resistance tracts. When such theories did emerge in England, they effected a revolution in political thought – as, for instance, when the Levellers in the English Civil War insisted that consent to government, on which freedom depends, must be given not only once in a single transfer of power but continuously, and by a multitude of individuals, the people outside Parliament, not by some corporate entity which claims to represent them.

The differences between England and France are visible, too, in conceptions of the relation between state and economy. We are accustomed to associating 'political economy', in the tradition of Adam Smith, with the development of 'commercial society' in its Anglo-Scottish mode. Yet the very first writer to use the term 'political economy' in the title of his work was a Frenchman, Antoine de Montchrétien. Already in the early seventeenth century, as we shall see in Chapter 6, he elaborated an idea of commerce as a means of harnessing private interests and passions to the public benefit, so that civic virtue was no longer necessary. In his *Traité de l'économie politique,* published in 1615, he insists that selfish passions and the appetite for gain, far from threatening the common good, can be its very foundation, without any reliance on virtue or benevolence. But his argument was critically different from what followed in Britain, and French arguments would continue to be different for a long time thereafter. French thinkers who, like Montchrétien, extolled the benefits of *le doux commerce* took for granted that the necessary condition for the positive effects of trade was a forceful monarchy to integrate and harmonize particular interests and transform private vices into public benefits. This assumption is rooted in the realities of absolutist France, a society in which there is still no integrated market or competitive capitalism, and where the polity is still fragmented by a welter of corporate entities and privileges. French thinkers were bound to look, as the English were not, for ways of dealing with this structural divisiveness when they reflected on the replacement of virtue by commerce.[16]

In the eighteenth century, the same assumptions are present in

---

16 The fact that monarchy is regarded as the necessary unifying principle should be enough to distinguish these views from modern conceptions of the state as simply a means of 'articulating' and 'aggregating' interests. It is true that the idea of private passions and 'vices' producing public benefits would emerge in a different form in the Netherlands, as we shall see in a later chapter, with roots in the philosophy of Spinoza and culminating in Bernard Mandeville's *Fable of the Bees.* While a Dutch thinker like Spinoza might still feel the need for political harmonization of private vices, in the context of the Dutch commercial republic, a republican form of government might seem more practicable than an absolutist monarchy. Yet this is not because Dutch republicans had in mind the 'invisible hand' of the market but largely, as will be suggested in the discussion of Spinoza in Chapter 5, because a republic can bind private greed to public office.

Montesquieu's views on monarchy. Unlike republican government, he tells us, monarchy has the advantage of making it possible to promote the common good with minimal virtue or self-sacrifice. Private interests can be the source of public benefits. But, while Montesquieu is less convinced than some of his contemporaries that commerce among nations need be a zero-sum game, this is not because he imagines that the common good will emerge naturally out of the interplay of private interests through an autonomous market mechanism. On the contrary, the monarchy must play that harmonizing role. Even the physiocrats, who most admired English agrarian capitalism and held it up as a model for France, shared classic French assumptions about the primary role of the state in harmonizing particular and corporate interests; and heavy traces of that view are still visible even in post-revolutionary France, in Napoleonic conceptions of the state.

The English – or, more precisely, the Anglo-Scottish – argument proceeds on the basis of different social and economic conditions. In the Anglo-Scottish version of *le doux commerce* in the eighteenth century, the burden of harmonizing private interests falls much more heavily on the market, on the discipline of competition in organizing production. The state, to be sure, plays a critical role in producing and maintaining the conditions for commercial development; but the purpose of the state is not to impose harmony on competing private interests. On the contrary, its role is to facilitate the operations of the market, which has that integration as its primary object.

What is critical, then, is not that commerce is presented as a substitute for civic virtue (more on this in a later chapter) but rather that commerce itself is conceived in new ways, in practice no less than in theory. We are now dealing with a competitive national market far more integrated than any other in Europe, and this market has a dynamic completely different from old forms of trade. The old forms of profit on alienation in transactions between separate markets really do look like a zero-sum game which inevitably leads to conflict. But the new dynamic of England's economy allows Adam Smith, for instance, to regard competition as itself an integrative force. It is precisely the discipline required to keep self-interested commercial classes in check.

The state undoubtedly plays a vital part in Smith's economy, above all to ensure that the market mechanism operates as it should – which seems to include, among other things, protection against employers combining to drive down wages. He also believes firmly in the importance of education for the lower classes. He does, to be sure, make debatable assumptions about the role of market mechanisms not only in advancing general prosperity but also in enhancing a more equitable distribution of wealth, which is, for him, a major reason for advocating free markets (in sharp contrast to our contemporary 'neoliberals', who may acknowledge that markets are more likely to increase inequality but regard that as a fruitful outcome). The freedom of the market that Smith has in mind requires intervention by the state to sustain it; and he does indeed believe that merchants lack the moral fibre or traditions of the landed classes, though concentrations of landed property represent a danger too. But the solution is not to find some kind of counter-weight to commerce. On the contrary, the solution must be sought in commerce itself. The market imperatives that come with a mature commer-cial society impose their own discipline on all the participants, and it is not the function of the state to counteract them. Intervention by the state is necessary to sustain the mechanisms of the market; but its purpose is not to suppress or to lessen but to intensify the imperatives of competition – against, for example, the monopolistic inclinations of merchants.

Smith's analysis of market mechanisms certainly owed much to the French and particularly to the physiocrat Quesnay (more in Chapter 6). But this debt makes even more striking the differences between the French and the Anglo-Scottish views on what is required to ensure the proper function-ing of the 'invisible hand'. Both regard a stable social order as a necessary precondition of a prosperous economy, and for both this requires interven-tions by the state. But Smith not only takes for granted a new form of commerce, such as already exists in England, but a unitary state with a unitary representative, while Quesnay assumes the need for a politically constituted integrating force, a kind of 'legal despotism', to deal with the fragmented system of estates and corporate bodies; and this kind of state, according to physiocratic doctrine, is needed not only to sustain but to create a new form of economy, which exists in English agrarian capitalism but not in France.[17]

The different patterns of 'political economy' in English capitalism and French absolutism would continue to have implications in the realm of ideas, in what many historical narratives depict as the age of 'Enlightenment'. But, even while it has become fashionable to acknowledge national differ-ences by speaking of 'Enlightenments' in an ever-proliferating plural, the very idea of 'Enlightenment(s)' has tended to obscure some critical diver-gences – which will be explored in the concluding chapter of this book.

A Social History of Political Thought

The purpose of this book is not to enlarge the canon or to argue for a more inclusive canonical literature that does justice to popular or democratic forces. It will confine itself largely to political thinkers who are most typi-cally regarded as 'canonical', or who have had substantial influence on

---

17   For an important discussion of these points, see David McNally, *Political Econo-my and the Rise of Capitalism: A Reinterpretation* (Berkeley and Los Angeles: University of California Press, 1990), esp. pp. 121–9.

thinkers more generally included in the canon, particularly for their ideas on legitimate rule and domination. Like any other survey of this kind, this one will, if only for reasons of space, leave out or briefly summarize the ideas of thinkers who may, in their various ways, be no less important than are the major figures treated here at greater length. Even major philosophers like David Hume, whose work belongs to the philosophical canon but for whom political theory was a more marginal concern, will get short shrift. We shall not, in general, deal with theorists best known for their theories of relations among states, with the notable exception of Grotius, whose views on private property and public jurisdiction are especially germane to our main themes. The primary aim of this study is to illustrate our social–contextual approach, and how it differs from others, by applying it to major thinkers whose status in the canon of political thought has been accepted by convention.

It should already be clear that the 'social history' of political thought on offer in this book departs from other accounts of Western political theory in the 'early modern' period, not least because it is based on a historical narrative that questions the conventional story of modernity. It aims, among other things, to disentangle the disparate threads of the 'modern'. For example, it distinguishes 'bourgeois' from 'capitalist'; it seeks to detach the culture of 'reason', or what postmodernists call the 'Enlightenment project', from the development of capitalism; it suggests that there was not just one overarching historical trajectory but several 'transitions' in the Western European passage to 'modernity', which have shaped divergent traditions of political thought; and it puts in question some fairly conventional wisdom, but also recent scholarship, on what it means to speak of 'modern' states and 'modern' ways of thinking about politics.

To those interested in the arcana of the discipline, it will also be clear that this social history departs from other contextual approaches not only in substance but in form and method. Like other modes of 'contextualism', it requires us not only to decipher texts but also to situate them in their specific historical contexts. Yet it entails an idea of 'context' that differs from others, in particular the school of contextualism that, in the Anglo-American academy, has dominated the history of political thought and especially the study of the early modern period, the so-called Cambridge School.

Both the Cambridge approach and our social history start from the premise that, to understand the ideas of political thinkers, we must know something about the questions they are seeking to answer. Both approaches treat those questions as constituted by specific historical conditions. Yet, while both accept that thinkers are likely to respond not only with a cool intelligence but with a sense of urgency and often passion, neither form of contextualism assumes that ideas can be simply 'read off' from a thinker's situation within a given context. Great thinkers, indeed, are likely to be those who shed light on their historical setting by thinking at an unpredictable angle from it, often as uncongenial to their friends as to their enemies – such as Hobbes, an absolutist whose works were burnt by the monarchy. The Cambridge School would on the whole agree with our social history that even when thinkers offer idiosyncratic answers or seek to transcend the specificities of time and place, the questions confronting them are posed in specific historical forms. Where the two contextual approaches differ is in their conceptions of what form these questions take and how they are configured by the specificities of history.

For the Cambridge School, contexts are 'discourses', utterances or 'language situations'. Social relations and processes are visible only as either literary and theoretical conversations, or the discursive transactions of high politics. A Cambridge School historian like Skinner is, to be sure, concerned with what theorists were 'doing' and why, given the range of political vocabularies available to them, they chose specific languages and strategies of argumentation, in the specific political circumstances of their own time and place and often for very specific political purposes. But the social conditions in which words were deployed are deliberately excluded. The period covered by Skinner's history of political thought was marked by major social and economic developments that loomed very large in political theory and practice, yet he tells us virtually nothing about them. We learn little, if anything, about – for instance – relations between aristocracy and peasantry, about agriculture, land distribution and tenure or disputes over property rights, about urbanization, trade, commerce and the burgher class, or about social protest and conflict. John Pocock is generally more interested than is Skinner in the languages of civil society and political economy, not simply in the discourses of formal political theory; but his subject remains discourse and language. Social relations, if they are visible at all, appear in the form of conversations among literate elites.

The social history of political thought raises questions about how the political sphere itself is constituted by social processes, relations, conflicts and struggles outside the political space – producing, for instance, different patterns of state-formation in England and France and different traditions of political discourse, even while sharing common languages of politics. It raises questions about how social conflicts set the terms of political controversy – as, for example, in England, conflicts over property rights and even the very definition of property were playing themselves out between landlords and commoners before they reached debates in Parliament, philosophy or classical political economy.

It is not here simply a matter of attending to popular voices as distinct from, or in addition to, elite conversations. No one can deny that subordinate classes have tended to be voiceless in the historical record. To be sure, even when there remains no record of their discourse, if we are attentive we can detect their interactions with dominant classes in the great theoretical efforts devoted by their masters to justifying social and political hierarchies, and, of course, in theories of property. But the principal question is where we should look to discover the meanings and motivations of discourses, whether popular or dominant.

For the social history of political thought, it is not enough to track relations among thinkers, their utterances and texts; but nor is it enough to situate them in the historical context of very specific political episodes, such as the Engagement Controversy in which Hobbes may have sought to intervene (see below, p. 242) or the Exclusion Crisis, in which Locke was almost certainly engaged (see below, p. 256). There is no doubt that such historical moments may have far-reaching consequences in shaping political languages – as the revolutionary crisis of the Exclusion controversy shaped Locke's political ideas. But for the social history of political theory, the questions confronting political thinkers are framed not only at the level of philosophy, political economy or high politics but also by the social interactions outside the political arena and beyond the world of texts.

To identify these questions is likely to require greater attention to long-term historical processes of a kind the Cambridge approach eschews altogether. We might, for example, situate Locke not only in the context of the Exclusion Crisis but also in the context of a long-term process like 'the rise of capitalism'. This is not to enlist him as an advocate of the system we now know as capitalism, nor to attribute to him a kind of supernatural prescience about the eventual development of a mature industrial capitalism, nor even to credit him with anything like an idea of a 'capitalist' economy. The point is rather that a process of transformation in the property regime (the development of 'agrarian capitalism' discussed here in this chapter and in Chapter 7) was being contested in Locke's own time and place, and was generating conflicts over the definition of property. We are much more likely to discern the issues at stake if we observe them, as it were, in the process of becoming, as existing social forms are being challenged or displaced.

Whether we choose to call the new property regime 'agrarian capitalism' or something else altogether, we may wish to point out that it had some bearing on what came after, not least on the emergence of 'commercial society', which figures very prominently in Cambridge School accounts of eighteenth-century England. But even if we choose to abstract Locke's brief historical moment from any longer processes of social transformation, the least that can be said is that these social transformations generated conflicts over property in Locke's own time and place; and the issues at stake were very much the stuff of his ideas.

There are certainly moments when history intrudes with special urgency into the dialogue among texts or traditions of discourse, when long-term developments in social relations, property forms and state-formation episodically erupt into specific political–ideological controversies that meet the requirements of the Cambridge School; and it is certainly true that political theory tends to flourish at times like this. But it is not enough to identify those moments; and we cannot get the measure of a thinker like John Locke if we fail to acknowledge the questions that were posed to him not just by this or that political episode but by larger social transformations and structural tensions, which made themselves felt beneath the surface of high politics.

Without in any way dismissing the importance of specific political moments in shaping ideas (which are often admirably covered by exponents of the Cambridge School), this book, and the social history of political theory it offers, will place more emphasis on the kinds of social contexts and historical processes commonly overlooked, if not explicitly discounted, by other modes of 'contextualization'. Consideration of what might be called deep structural contexts and long-term social transformations does not in the least imply a neglect of historical specificities, including national differences. On the contrary, we shall in the following chapters be keenly attentive to such differences; and the chapters will be organized along these lines, exploring certain historical landmarks in the development of Western political thought in their varied political and social contexts. If anything, the social history of political theory is more attuned to historical specificities than is a mode of contextualization devoted to 'language situations' in which common vocabularies may disguise important historical differences. Despite the Cambridge School's insistence on the specificity of every historical moment, its conception of linguistic contexts and their detachment from social conditions occludes all kinds of historical specificities, the differences of meaning that even common languages may have in different social contexts, not only giving different answers but posing different questions.

As we track the various Western traditions of discourse in the early modern period, it is nonetheless important to keep in mind that, for all the variations, the tension between two sources of power – the state and private property – and the complex three-way relations between state, property and the producing classes, had clear implications for the development of political thought throughout Western Europe and its colonial dependencies. If there is in this book a single overarching theme, it has to do with certain distinctive transformations in the relation between private property and public power that took place in our period. Earlier in this chapter, and at greater length in *Citizens to Lords*, the first volume of this social history, we traced the development of the relation between property and state from classical antiquity to 'feudal' society and took note of the very particular effects of Roman property, the privatization of public authority with the devolution of public functions to local lords and other autonomous powers. This volume deals with a period when fragmented sovereignty was giving way to more centralized states, and new tensions emerged between property and state. It is also a period in which, with the advent of capitalism, property and political power, *dominium* and *imperium*, became structurally disentangled in historically unprecedented ways.

In what follows we shall be especially attentive to the distinctive tensions between private property and public power in Western Europe. We shall also emphasize their national divergences. But for now, and as a general rule, we can say that appropriating classes, even when they were competing with the state for access to surpluses produced in the main by peasants, also relied on the state to maintain order, conditions for appropriation and control over the producing classes whose labour sustained and enriched them; yet they also found the state a burdensome nuisance, as a threat to their property or as a competitor for the wealth derived from subject labour. Propertied classes, in other words, were always fighting on two fronts; and the Western canon of political thought has always reflected this three-way relation.

Challenges to authority have come from two directions. Subordinate classes have resisted oppression by their overlords. But overlords themselves, while always looking over their shoulders for threats from their subordinates, have sought to protect their autonomy, their 'liberties', privileges, jurisdictions and properties, against intrusions from the state. This has meant that, even while the canon has generally been the work of ruling classes or their clients, and even when social and political hierarchies have been at their most rigid, there has been a continuous and vigorous tradition of interrogating the most basic principles of authority, legitimacy and the obligation to obey.

The canon of Western political thought has owed much of its vigour to the fact that the discourse of liberty has belonged to ruling classes asserting their mastery, no less than to those resisting oppression by their masters. One objective of examining the canon in its social context is to suggest that even – or especially – now that capitalism has decisively transformed relations between property and power, our conceptions of freedom, equality, rights and legitimate government are constrained by their roots in the defence of ruling-class power and privilege; and even ideas of democracy have been distorted by this complicated legacy.

2

THE RENAISSANCE CITY-STATE

It has been said that 'one of the most essential factors separating Renaissance from later philosophy [is] its fully international character, based on the use of Latin as an almost universal language of scholarship', not divided by modern linguistic or national boundaries.[1] Yet this period is precisely the age in which territorial states, defined by national boundaries, were becoming the dominant political force in Western Europe. It is certainly true that these states were not the homeland of the cultural phenomenon called by convention the Renaissance (a convention often questioned by historians these days); but this international culture was born in an even more particularistic setting, the Italian city-states most fiercely attached to their local autonomy.

The poet and scholar Petrarch, who, for his recovery of ancient classics and his Latin writings, is often called the 'father of humanism', or even of the Renaissance itself, is also, by virtue of his Italian poetry, considered one of the principal founders of a national language and literature. His revival of antiquity appealed not only to philosophers but to princes, emperors and popes who were keen to invoke Italy's glorious past for their own political purposes. 'Humanism' would become the discourse of thinkers who have come to be called 'civic humanists', in defence of civic liberty and of their city-states' autonomy. Yet the Renaissance would flourish as the city-states were in decline, and civic humanism would reach its pinnacle when the political independence and economic prosperity of the major city-states were most severely threatened by a new world order of 'national' states.

Whether we call this period the 'Renaissance' or something else, the dichotomy of 'ancient' and 'modern' cannot help us very much to understand these paradoxes. It is far more trouble than it is worth to determine whether civic humanism – if it exists at all as a distinct and coherent body

---

1 *Cambridge History of Renaissance Philosophy,* eds C.B. Schmidt et al. (Cambridge: Cambridge University Press, 1988), p. 2. This insight, or at least full justice to it, is credited to the German philosopher and intellectual historian Ernst Cassirer.

of thought (about which more in a moment) – partakes of the ancient because it resists the trend towards large territorial or national states and because it adopts an ancient Greco-Roman discourse, or whether it is more modern than ancient because it supports the principles of civic liberty against monarchical or feudal rule. Nor, for that matter, is it particularly useful to describe this cultural form as transitional, or even as a synthesis of contradictions. We can, and clearly should, take note of the discourses available to thinkers; but we can better understand the particular ways in which political theorists chose to exploit them not by locating them along some abstract continuum from ancient to modern but by situating them in very specific historical processes.

Renaissance City States

The medieval city-states of northern Italy (which were discussed in the first volume of this history) represented an exception to the Western feudal model of seigneurial domination. Landed aristocracies certainly existed and in some city-states continued to play a prominent role; but urban concentrations which had survived the collapse of the Roman Empire, together with landholding patterns that preserved a free peasantry in contrast to the serfdom that had emerged elsewhere, produced a distinctive configuration: more or less autonomous city-states, governed by urban elites, often – as in the case of Florence – exercising what has been described as a collective lordship over the surrounding countryside, the *contado*. Some developed into prosperous commercial centres, serving a fragmented feudal Europe as trading links, providing goods to landed aristocracies and offering financial services to kings and popes.

But, if these city-states departed from seigneurial patterns of lordship, they had their own forms of parcellized sovereignty. The civic communes were always fairly loose associations of patrician families, factions, parties and corporate entities with their own liberties, organizations, jurisdictions and powers. In the Middle Ages, they were also battlegrounds for larger temporal authorities. In particular, they were caught up in struggles between the papacy and the Holy Roman Empire, which conducted their rivalries through the medium of factions within the civic commune – most notably, the infamous battles between Guelf (papal) and Ghibelline (imperial) factions, which typically, though not always, coincided with divisions between merchant classes and landed *signori*. These self-governing cities were, on the whole, oligarchies; and even when more effective republican governments came to power, they never succeeded in overcoming their internal fragmentation. Still later, even the most centralized Renaissance kingdoms continued to be divided by party, privilege and competing jurisdictions. For all the talk of civic humanism, the civic order never marked out a clearly defined public sphere detached from private corporate powers of various kinds.

Nor did the commercial activities of the civic communes mark a significant departure from feudal economic patterns. Their commercial success depended not, in the capitalist manner, on cost-effective production and enhanced labour productivity, in a market driven by price competition, but rather on 'extra-economic' factors, that is to say, factors external to the 'economic' transactions of production and exchange: not just the quality of goods but political power, monopoly privileges, sophisticated financial techniques, and military force. In external trade, which was the most lucrative economic activity for a major commercial centre like Venice, success clearly depended on military power and a symbiotic connection between commerce and war. Venice's command of east–west trade required control of eastern Mediterranean sea routes, no less than rivers and mountain passes on the Italian mainland. To maintain that control, the Venetians developed a powerful military force, which itself became a marketable commodity, as Venice offered military aid to other powers – notably the Byzantine Empire – in exchange for commercial privileges and rights to trading posts.[2]

In general, economic rivalries took the form of power struggles among merchants, cities or states over direct control of markets; and city-states were constantly at war with one another. The major centres such as Florence and Venice consolidated their commercial dominance by forcibly incorporating their less powerful neighbours into larger city-states. It is certainly true that Venice, and even more Florence, traded in commodities produced in their own cities, such as Florentine textiles; and great merchant dynasties did invest in production. But substantial wealth and power depended on command of trading networks, which in turn depended not simply on the quality or price of goods produced at home but on superiority in controlling and negotiating markets, to say nothing of dynastic connections, patronage, personal networks among patrician families, and leading positions in ruling oligarchies.

Even where, as in Florence, wealth was heavily invested in production, it was no less dependent on 'extra-economic' factors, not least on office in the city-state's administration. The career of the Medici speaks volumes: they began in the wool trade, then moved on to achieve their greatest wealth, with the help of family connections and personal networks among the Florentine patriciate, not as producers but as bankers to European princes and popes. Three Medici themselves became popes. The dynasty finally reached the summit of its ambition as effectively rulers of the Florentine republic, leaving the wool trade far behind.

---

2 For more on these points, see Ellen Meiksins Wood, *Empire of Capital* (London: Verso, 2005), pp. 54–61.

In Renaissance Florence, in other words, political and economic power were inextricably connected in the feudal manner; and this was true not only for city elites. The guilds that organized the wool trade and other occupations were principal players not only in the economic sphere, protecting the interests of their members and sheltering them from competition, but also in the political domain. The guilds themselves had autonomous corporate powers, governed by charters and systems of rules that had the force of law. It may even be misleading to speak of *citizenship* in the republic, since active membership in the civic community did not reside in individuals but in these corporate entities.

Internal conflicts in the city-states were shaped by this unity of political and economic power. Economic rivalries among merchant families could never simply take the form of competition in the marketplace but were always political rivalries at the same time. The pursuit of high office and the dominance of any family depended on its standing in a complex network of patrons and clients, inevitably embroiled in factional struggles, often with support from foreign powers. It has even been suggested that this helps to explain the remarkable cultural richness of these city-states and their patronage of the arts, creating not only great wealth but a climate of competitive achievement and conspicuous consumption – especially in times and places where, as in the Florentine republic, artisanal guilds played a major political role.

In Venice, which remained an oligarchy even when ostensibly ruled by one man, the Doge, it was largely a matter of rivalry among noble families. In Florence, other strains and conflicts were also at work. Patrician family connections or membership in major guilds afforded the only consistent access to the political sphere; and political battles throughout the history of Florence often revolved around the political standing of lesser guilds. There were constant struggles over access to the political domain among *signori*, rich merchants and guildsmen, as well as between major and lesser guilds. Outside the guilds, the *popolo minuto*, the 'little people' or labouring classes, including large numbers of skilled and unskilled workers in the wool trade, were completely excluded from the political sphere, except for one brief democratic moment, the Revolt of the Ciompi in 1378, one of the most famous incidents in Florentine history. The *ciompi* rebels briefly seized control of the government and then, with support from some members of the minor guilds, obtained guild privileges, which meant access to the political domain – only to lose it soon thereafter when the *popolo grasso*, their wealthy 'fat' compatriots, now with the help of the minor guilds, deprived them of guild and political privileges.

This episode would long remain, for better or worse, a vivid memory in the consciousness of the republic, not least for Machiavelli; and it illustrates most dramatically the distinctiveness of the civic domain in the Italian city-states. When, just three years later, the English peasant revolt erupted, its leader, Wat Tyler, is reported to have said, 'No lord should have lordship save civilly', and all men should be equal but the king. He was advocating not the peasant's access to the civic domain but rather certain rights of property against the claims of lords and, perhaps, access to common-law courts to protect those property rights. The contrasts between this English case and the Revolt of the Ciompi are striking. For English peasants the issue is lordship, not citizenship; but, while the Italian case may seem in this respect less 'feudal', it is distinctive not because it presages some modern principle of individual autonomy and citizenship. The issue for the *ciompi*, no less than for the English peasantry, is the exclusive extra-economic powers and privileges, or 'politically constituted property', of their superiors. We might even be tempted to say that the English assertion of property rights against the claims of lordship have more in common with modern conceptions of citizenship than do the demands of Florentine labouring classes for a share in corporate privileges.

What singles out the Italian case, and what helps to explain the particularities of Renaissance Italian political thought, is that 'politically constituted property' is indeed political – that is to say, the extra-economic rights and privileges upon which economic power rests derive from the civic community, depending not on individual powers of lordship but on membership in the civic corporation. Social conflicts play themselves out on the civic terrain, not only in open struggle or organized rebellion but in the daily transactions of civic life, in an urban setting where all contenders, as individuals and as collective entities, are always face to face as citizens or aspirants to civic status. The inextricable connection between economic power and 'extra-economic' force means that economic rivalries, or social conflicts over property and inequalities of wealth, are inseparably struggles over civic power, always on the brink of open war.

'Civic Humanism' and Machiavelli

This very particular configuration of the civic domain produced distinctive traditions of political ideas. The designation 'civic humanism' to describe the main currents has become conventional among many historians of political thought. For the German historian Hans Baron, who coined the phrase, 'civic humanism' was a specifically Florentine conjunction of cultural humanism, with its educational ambitions, and the city republic's defence of civic liberty against imperial domination. This, in his view, marked a decisive break from medieval religion and feudal hierarchy, towards modern ideals of political liberty, economic progress, secularism and intellectual creativity. Although he would, over several decades, develop and modify his views on civic humanism – and would later be more inclined than he was at

first to include Machiavelli in that tradition – his original intention in identifying this historic rupture was not only historiographical but also political.
He was seeking to promote a conception of modernity as the advance of
human autonomy, at a time when, in Weimar Germany, such ideas were
under threat from anti-democratic strains of German nationalism.

Baron's idea would later find its way into the anglophone academy,
adapted to various Anglo-American 'republican' traditions (the most notable example being John Pocock's 'Machiavellian moment'). Recent
scholarship has, nonetheless, tended to correct Baron's exaggeration of the
rupture between medieval and Renaissance political thought. More attention has been given to the continuities between scholasticism and humanism,
indeed their coexistence and revival in the later Renaissance. Yet these
corrections have failed to dispel the notion that 'republican' political theory,
especially in its humanist mode, somehow points us towards the modern
world. We shall in subsequent chapters raise questions about the very idea
of 'republicanism', especially in its application to seventeenth-century
English thinkers; but, for the moment, it is enough to say that, even if we
acknowledge the existence of something like a 'civic humanist' tradition, it
is profoundly misleading to characterize the political ideas of the Italian
Renaissance – and of Machiavelli in particular – as a breakthrough to
modernity. The very characteristics that give a 'modern' appearance to ideas
like Machiavelli's are rooted in a dying political form that would soon give
way to 'modern' states. These states would generate their own political
predicaments, together with modes of discourse designed to confront them
in ways that 'civic humanist' or 'republican' ideas were unable to do.

There are, to be sure, significant differences between Machiavelli and, say,
Marsilius of Padua two centuries before.[3] These differences can even be
characterized, without too much exaggeration, as having something to do
with the contrasts between scholasticism and humanism. But much depends
on whether we define those differences as products of transformations in
language and discourse or place our emphasis on social relations and historical processes. It may be true that civic humanism had introduced a new
language of politics, quite different from that of medieval scholasticism. It
may even be true that Machiavelli belongs to the humanist tradition in a way
that Marsilius did not. Yet both political thinkers were deeply rooted in the
Italian city-state; and the differences between them have as much to do with
changes in the circumstances of the city-states as they do with transformations in discourse.

The differences between Marsilius and Machiavelli also have to do with
their differing relations to the social conflicts of their day. Marsilius was
preoccupied not with the survival or autonomy of city-states but the

---

3 Marsilius of Padua is discussed at greater length in *Citizens to Lords*, pp. 218–25.

factional struggles between papal and imperial parties. It can even be argued (as was done in the first volume of this study) that his defence of imperial power was driven less by fear of the papacy and its threats to civil peace than by his support for great aristocratic families like the Visconti of Milan and the della Scalas of Verona, who had strong imperial (Ghibelline) loyalties (as was typical among the landed nobility) and in whose service Marsilius worked. This allegiance to signorial power is masked by inter-pretations of Marsilius's doctrine that treat him as a forerunner of modern republicanism, which also obscure the immediate issues confronting this late medieval thinker.

For Marsilius the problem, in the medieval manner, was a complex network of competing jurisdictions. When he outlined his idea of a single unitary jurisdiction, the civic corporation, he was certainly depart-ing from the medieval norm of parcellized sovereignty; but he was by that means quite consciously supporting one claim to temporal author-ity against another, not so much the civic commune against all other jurisdictions but the Empire against the papacy, and Ghibelline *signori* against their civic rivals. He showed no concern for the threat to civic unity and jurisdiction posed by the feudal powers of the landed nobility, while his notion of a single unitary civic corporation represented a clear challenge to autonomous guilds and their anti-signorial powers. His notion of one undivided civic corporation simply trumped the claims of lesser corporate bodies.

Machiavelli's Florence presented different problems, and his responses to them were shaped by different allegiances, perhaps more truly republican and certainly less inclined to the interests of the *signori*. The very survival of the city-state as anything like an autonomous entity was indeed at stake; and the immediate challenge was coming not from various fragmented juris-dictions, or from struggles between papal and imperial authorities, or between the civic factions they sustained, but from increasingly centralized and expanding states. The most powerful external forces were now rising territorial monarchies like France and Spain; and internal disorders in Florence were shaped by this new political reality.

The Italian city-states had already suffered from the general European crises, famine and plague of the fourteenth century. But even in good times their prosperity and success had depended on the fragmented governance of European feudalism and could not long survive the rise of strong territorial states. In constant rivalry and often open war with one another, the Italians were especially vulnerable to the territorial ambitions of the European monarchies. The role of commercial centres such as Venice and Florence as indispensable trading links in feudal Europe declined as feudal fragmenta-tion gave way to centralized state powers, sustained by military superiority and the commercial advantages of imperial expansion.

By the fifteenth century, Venice and Florence stood almost alone as inde-pendent city-states. The Ottoman Empire deprived Venice of its dominance in east–west trade, capturing Constantinople in 1453, while European monarchies challenged both the political independence and the economic prosperity of the remaining city-states. Portugal extended its commercial reach to India, Spain gained access to the wealth of the New World, and France invaded Italy in 1494. Economic stagnation, social unrest and politi-cal upheaval in the city republics were immensely aggravated by years of war following the French invasion, as France, Spain, and the Holy Roman Empire battled for control of Italian territory – even while culture flourished in the city-states at the very moment of decline, when wealthy patrons of the arts, now more rentiers than entrepreneurs, engaged in ever more passionate conspicuous consumption.

It was the military disasters facing Italy, in 1494, and the political insta-bility associated with them, that more than anything else concentrated the minds of Italian political thinkers, particularly in Florence. They were forced to reflect not only on the conditions of civic success and decline but also on the fundamental human traits that encouraged or impeded them. Niccolò Machiavelli's generation was formed in this context, and its shadow looms over everything he wrote. He was born in 1469, the son of a distin-guished lawyer, at a time when republican government had given way to Medici rule. Although of moderate means, his family seems to have belonged to a long line of Florentine notables. Machiavelli, who received a classic humanist education, began his career of public service as a clerk in 1494, the very year of the French invasion and the expulsion of the Medici from Florence, and would go on to serve the restored Florentine republic in vari-ous civil, diplomatic and military functions from 1498 to 1512.

When the Medici returned, Machiavelli was thrown out of office. In 1513, accused of conspiracy against the Medici, he was imprisoned and tortured. On his release, expelled from the centre of power, he retreated to the coun-tryside outside Florence, where, as he would famously write in a wistful letter to his friend Vettori, he whiled away the time in idle rural pursuits all day and

When evening comes I return home and go into my study, and at the door I take off my daytime dress covered in mud and dirt, and put on royal and curial robes; and then decently attired I enter the courts of the ancients, where affectionately greeted by them, I partake of that food which is mine alone and for which I was born; where I am not ashamed to talk with them and inquire the reasons of their actions; and they out of their human kindness answer me, and for four hours at a stretch I feel no worry of any kind; I forget all my troubles, I am not afraid of poverty or of death. I give myself up entirely to them. And because Dante says that understanding does not constitute knowledge unless it is retained in the memory, I have written down what I have learned from their conversation and composed a short work *de Principatibus*[4]

And so he produced his most famous work, *The Prince,* though it was published only later, in 1532. His advice to princes has been variously described – for instance, as an effort to ingratiate himself with the Medici, in an attempt to revive his career; or even as a coded message to opponents of the Medici, and others like them, exposing their methods of obtaining and retaining power. Whatever his intentions, Machiavelli remained confined to his rural retreat, where he also wrote the *Discourses,* which more clearly expressed his republican convictions. The Medici would eventually call again on his services, but his later career was less notable for his official duties than for his work in other fields, such as his great *History of Florence* and his play *La Mandragola.* He died in 1527.

The rising monarchical states, and the French monarchy in particular, would figure prominently in the formation of Machiavelli's political thought. He was sent several times on diplomatic missions to the court of Louis XII to enlist the aid of France in various battles on Italian territory, not least the rivalry between Florence and Pisa, or to ensure that Florence would not be implicated in territorial wars among the European monarchies. His early missions inspired a growing conviction that Florence should free itself of dependence on foreign powers by mobilizing its own citizen army, in sharp contrast to the Italian tradition of mercenary soldiers. Machiavelli supervised the formation of the Florentine army in the restored republic, which won a famous victory against Pisa in 1509; and a strong commitment to citizen militias would lie at the heart of his political thought. When Spain supported the Medici in their efforts to recover their power in Florence, the republic turned for help again to France, to no avail – with dramatic consequences for Machiavelli's career. Whatever else he may have intended when he wrote *The Prince,* one bitter inspiration may have been Louis XII's betrayal of the Florentine republic. Machiavelli would invoke the example of the French king as a primary lesson to princes not for his successes so much as for his failures, which, in Machiavelli's eyes, had brought such tragedy to Italy.

European territorial monarchies, then, would always be in Machiavelli's line of sight as he elaborated his political ideas. In the conclusion to *The Prince,* with its passionate call for the liberation of Italy from the 'barbarians', his main target is patently obvious. Yet it would be a mistake to interpret this call for a strong and united Italian defence against expanding

---

4 Quoted in Roberto Ridolfi, *The Life of Niccolò Machiavelli* (London: Routledge & Kegan Paul, 1963), p. 152.

territorial states as a demand for the unification of Italy – or even its north-central regions – into a 'modern' nation state like France. These developing territorial states were already becoming the dominant force in Europe, but for Machiavelli they represented not so much models to be emulated as external threats to be resisted. He does, to be sure, cite France as the best monarchy, for its lawfulness and apparently for its suppression of the nobility. But it cannot be said that he sheds much light on the nature of the rising monarchies. He can speak of the French king in terms hardly different from those he uses to describe the infamous Cesare Borgia. Machiavelli remained rooted in the city-state of Florence. Although he certainly shared his city's expansionist ambitions and would have welcomed an extension of Florentine rule over its neighbours, of the kind the republic had enjoyed in its more prosperous days, he retained a firm commitment to the city-republic. Visible even in *The Prince*, this is the very essence of the *Discourses*.

Machiavelli was deeply rooted in the civic corporation; and the very particular force of his 'modern' approach to political 'science' derives from his attachment to the independent city-state at a very specific historical moment. Conditions were very different from what they had been in Italian city-states when his great predecessor, Marsilius of Padua, devised his theory of the civic corporation. It is the threat to the very survival of the city-state that gives Machiavelli's political thought its particular edge. Renaissance conceptions of human autonomy and civic liberty may seem to presage modernity even while reviving ancient ideas; but the 'modern' sensibility attributed to Machiavelli derives from a particularly archaic feature of the Italian city-state, the characteristic blend of civic and military values that sustained it.

In Machiavelli's political works, as distinct from his history of Florence, there is no evidence that the context in which he was writing was one of the great commercial centres of Europe. Commercial values are nowhere visible, and commercial activity barely figures at all. Yet the spirit of his work is very much the spirit of the Italian commercial city, the city-republic in which a commercial economy existed under a highly militarized urban rule, armed to withstand external threats, to dominate the *contado*, to defeat commercial rivals and extend the city-state's commercial supremacy, in what might be called an urban and commercial feudalism.

Political and economic power, as we have already observed, were inextricably conjoined in the commercial republics, which in this respect had more in common with medieval social forms than with modern capitalism. Governed by collectives of urban elites, whose political and economic rivalries were never far from violent struggle, these cities relied on armed force not only to dominate their neighbouring territories but to defeat commercial rivals and expand their own supremacy in trade. Even conflicts between rich and poor, or between the *popolo minuto* and *popolo grasso*, had the character of power struggles always on the verge of violence. In the late fifteenth century, the immediate threats from foreign powers, which also exacerbated internal conflicts, added a particular urgency to military questions. In these circumstances, Machiavelli was not alone to see the civic domain in military terms.

It was not unusual to ascribe the success of commercial republics to the warrior mentality of urban elites, nor to blame commercial decline on a loss of martial spirit. Republicans who decried the corruptions of Medici rule were likely to share the view of Machiavelli's friend and critic Francesco Guicciardini, that 'the Medici family, like all narrow regimes, always tried to prevent arms being possessed by the citizens and to extinguish all their virility. For this reason we have become very effeminate, and we also lack the courageousness of our forefathers.'[5] This assessment might be shared by all kinds of republicans, whether they subscribed to a less restrictive republican citizenry, a *governo largo*, as Machiavelli did, or, like Guicciardini, to a *governo stretto*, a republic in which the aristocracy played a more important role. It may even be possible to say that a certain martial spirit, as much as any other quality, sets civic humanism apart from scholastic philosophy.

The humanists are noted above all else for reviving the literature of classical antiquity, both Greek and Latin; but in civic humanism there is no mistaking an inclination towards Rome. The novelties of humanistic discourse, in contrast to the scholastic tradition, are akin to the Roman departures from Greek philosophy, the characteristically Roman interest in the active life, in rhetoric and ethics for its own sake, less systematically grounded in theories of the cosmos, metaphysics or psychology. If Aristotle was the prophet of scholasticism, in civic humanist discourse he was displaced, or at least supplemented, by Cicero, whom Petrarch called 'the great genius' of antiquity. Aristotle may have been no less attached to the life of the polis than to the life of the mind; but Cicero, the consummate politician and orator, spoke more directly to the spirit of republican activism. It is Cicero who was likely to be invoked to counter Christian, and especially Augustinian, fatalism about the possibilities of human excellence and action in attaining a good life in this world; and it is Cicero who guided republican views on the education needed to achieve that excellence, especially the skills of rhetoric so vital to the active public life.

But the Roman example meant something else, too. When Aristotle spelled out his classic characterization of man as a political animal, and his theory of the polis as the terrain of human excellence, he was not concerned to defend the city-state from external threats to its very survival. The polis,

---

5 Francesco Guicciardini, *Dialogue on the Government of Florence*, ed. Alison Brown (Cambridge: Cambridge University Press, 1994), p. 34.

after the Macedonian conquest, was already effectively dead as an independent political form. But the philosopher embraced, and even served, the Macedonian hegemony; and he envisioned a new life for the polis under imperial rule, in keeping with Alexander's distinctive mode of imperial governance, through the medium of local aristocracies in ostensibly self-governing municipalities. Macedonian hegemony had the added advantage, for Aristotle, of supplanting radical Athenian democracy, enhancing the power of the aristocracy against unbridled rule by the demos. This delicate balance of class power required the suppression of social strife, especially the conflicts between rich and poor, the philosopher's main practical concern. The ideal Athenian citizen, then, governed by Macedonian agents under the watchful eye of imperial garrisons, was not a man of struggle or of military virtues.

The Roman case could hardly be more different. The republic was itself an imperial power, whose conquests had created a huge territorial empire with what would become the largest military force the world had ever known. While Roman thinkers such as Cicero were no less committed than Aristotle to a 'mixed' constitution in which the common people were subordinate to aristocracy, in Cicero's Rome the civic culture was at heart a military ethic. Against the background of the threat to Florentine autonomy, it was this above all that spoke to Machiavelli, who took the civic humanist idea of 'virility', or *virtù*, to the limits of its martial spirit.

The Prince

In his most famous, not to say notorious, work, *The Prince*, Machiavelli lays out his 'Machiavellian' challenge to any conception of political power that invokes moral principles to distinguish between legitimate and illegitimate uses of power. There is, evidently, no such thing as rightful authority, and power is to be maintained by any means necessary. How far Machiavelli meant to push this principle remains a matter of dispute. Whatever his motivations, whether he was seeking the approval of the Medici or was simply driven by a bitter sense of irony in his exile from politics, commentators who regard him as a 'realist' are no doubt closer to the truth than those who treat him as the emblematic advocate of political evil. There is, at any rate, no mistaking the differences between *The Prince* and the *Discourses on the Ten Books of Titus Livy*, which almost certainly expresses Machiavelli's own disposition more precisely, displaying a preference for republican government that requires him to make the kinds of judgments about good government that he refuses in *The Prince*.

Much has been written about Machiavelli's relation to, and divergences from, the civic humanist tradition; and, more specifically, about where to situate *The Prince* within a genre familiar to his contemporaries: humanist advice-books to princes. For Machiavelli, as for other writers in the genre, writes Quentin Skinner, 'the prince's basic aim, we learn in a phrase that echoes through *Il Principe,* must be *mantenere lo stato,* to maintain his power and existing frame of government. As well as keeping the peace, however, a true prince must at the same time seek "to establish such a form of government as will bring honour to himself and benefit the whole body of his subjects"'.[6]

Where Machiavelli significantly and famously departs from other humanists, as Skinner observes in his account of what it means to *mantenere lo stato,* is in his insistence that the willingness to use force is essential to good princely government, in contrast to the conventional humanist distinction between *virtus* or manliness, and *vis,* that is, brute force, and in his dissent from humanist accounts of princely virtues, which require both the highest standards of personal morality and a strict adherence to principles of justice.[7] But this departure may have less to do with differing views about how best to maintain what Skinner calls 'the existing frame of government' than with Machiavelli's concentration on external military threats, which puts war at the centre of his doctrine.

What Machiavelli means when he speaks – as he so often does – of *lo stato* remains a subject of scholarly debate. Yet again, the issue turns on whether he has in mind a 'modern' concept of the state as an impersonal legal and political order, or a pre-modern idea of political authority as a personal possession or *dominium,* or something in between and 'transitional'. There is still much of the pre-modern personal in Machiavelli's *stato,* with its emphasis on the personal power and honour of the prince. But if there is also an element of the impersonal, it may have less to do with a 'modern' conception of the state than with Machiavelli's military preoccupations and the threats that loom from without.

In *The Prince* Machiavelli tells us that

> A prince ought to have no other aim or thought, nor select anything else for his study, than war and its rules and discipline . . . there is nothing proportionate between the armed and the unarmed; and it is not reasonable that he who is armed should yield obedience willingly to him who is unarmed, or that the unarmed man should be secure among armed servants . . . He ought never, therefore, to have out of his thoughts this subject of war, and in peace he should addict himself more to its exercise than in war. (XIV)

---

6 Quentin Skinner, "Political Philosophy," in *Cambridge History of Renaissance Philosophy,* p. 431.

7 *Ibid.,* pp. 432–3.

Machiavelli's military model goes beyond the art of war. In *The Prince* he not only identifies war as the prince's main concern. His conceptions of leadership, political morality, and the conditions for sustaining a successful civic order are at bottom the conditions of a successful military power. Ideally, in his view, this is best achieved by a difficult balance between ruthless leadership and popular support, a capacity for cruelty and frequent departures from conventional morality, combined with an ability to mobilize the loyalties of the rank and file. The fact that Machiavelli has no use for a traditional military aristocracy and that his ideal military organization is a citizens' militia makes the conditions of success even more exacting – and, as becomes clearer in the *Discourses,* at this point his views on military success become inseparable from his republicanism.

Machiavelli's views on religion are also a subject of controversy, not least because, especially in the *Discourses,* he suggests that conventional Christianity has had the effect of weakening the manly vigour, the *virtù,* required for the active civic life. Yet his attitude has much in common with that of other humanists in his challenge not to Christian faith in general but to scholastic Christian fatalism, which requires submission to the blind power of fate and fortune and views the frivolous goods of this world – wealth, power, honour, fame and glory – as useless and unworthy of pursuit. Again like other humanists, he challenges these beliefs not by denying that much of human life is determined by circumstances beyond our control – the dictates of *fortuna* – but by emphasizing the scope of human action within the limits imposed on us by fate or fortune or God's will. Fortuna can be a friend to the man of *virtù,* instead of a pitiless enemy beyond the reach of human capacities and action. Every civic order will, to be sure, inevitably decline; and then a new order will have to be founded, which will make even greater demands on *virtù.* On this score, too, Machiavelli is not so distant from other humanists. Where he departs from humanist conventions is in his insistence that *virtù* may run counter to conventional morality; that political stability is possible despite – or even because of – humanity's most stubborn defects; and that men of *virtù* must often commit acts of violence, especially in the foundation of new states.

Machiavelli's views on the conditions for the creation and maintenance of a successful civic order depend, of course, on certain convictions about the possibilities available to human action; and his military principles are supported by more fundamental assumptions about history and human nature. He never precisely spells out his conception of human nature, though he certainly assumes the worst by emphasizing the insatiable desires of human beings, their short-sightedness and envy, even their general untrustworthiness. But the important point for him is that, because human nature remains essentially immutable, we can learn from historical experience, imitating successful actions while avoiding those that have failed. Human beings can adapt to varying circumstances. They can indeed, up to a point, shape those circumstances and, in so doing, shape themselves; and the very qualities that seem to militate against stability and social order can be channelled to positive ends.

Machiavelli's military model of political order, then, encompasses his most familiar 'Machiavellian' strictures on the necessity of force and violence in creating and sustaining the body politic; the importance of fear in the maintenance of leadership (it is best, of course, for a leader to be both loved and feared, but if he has to choose, fear must prevail); the need for ruthless treatment of one's adversaries, even if that means violating the most cherished principles of conventional morality; and so on.

The opposition of the armed and the unarmed lies at the very heart of Machiavelli's political theory. In *The Prince*, one of his principal criticisms is levelled against a man who was also one of the most famous leaders of the Florentine republic, Girolamo Savonarola. A Dominican friar, preacher and prophet, Savonarola led Florence when the Medici were expelled in 1494; but, says Machiavelli, he was an 'unarmed prophet', in sharp contrast to others who had founded a new order but who, unlike the prophet unarmed, were able to maintain their positions: 'armed prophets' such as Moses or leaders like Cyrus, Theseus and Romulus. The whole of Machiavelli's political theory is in many ways directed at the failings of the unarmed prophet.

Savonarola had predicted the French invasion, placing the blame on the corruption and decadence of Florence in the era of Medici rule. He began, in fact, by predicting the downfall of the city, doomed by the will of God as punishment for its own sins; but he would go on to extol the Florentine republic, which would, he declared, restore itself by banishing moral corruption. When the Medici fled and the French withdrew, the preacher's credibility was vastly enhanced, and his vision of an incorruptible Christian republic held sway for a few years, finding its most emblematic moment in a 'bonfire of the vanities'. Since his attacks on moral corruption included the clergy, he had powerful enemies in the Church. Having lost the support of the Florentine people who had tired of his moralistic rule, he was excommunicated by Pope Alexander VI and executed in 1498.

Savonarola's defence of the republic was essentially scholastic in its mode of argumentation. Humanistic speculations about human autonomy and excellence, while certainly not alien to Christianity, were less congenial to the preacher's uncompromising convictions about the primacy of divine will. While he extolled republican liberties, they were to be preserved not by struggle but by banishing corruption and suppressing conflict within the civic order. After his execution his followers, who remained a significant political force in Florence, would prefer the example of aristocratic Venice ruled by its Great Council, or of Florence in the era of *governo stretto*, the restricted civic order that governed the republic on the eve of Medici rule and was advocated by the Florentine aristocracy.

On these scores, Machiavelli disagreed with Savonarola and his supporters on every count. There has been much debate about Machiavelli's attitude towards Savonarola. Some commentators have suggested that he respected the preacher as much as he condemned him; and he certainly does praise him, for instance in the *Discourses*. But Machiavelli's doctrine of struggle, conflict and military prowess is in direct antithesis to the 'unarmed prophet', in opposition to Christian fatalism and the invocation of God's will as responses to disasters like the French invasion.

The *Discourses*

Machiavelli's conviction that every state will eventually decline suggests, on the face of it, that he shares the views so typical of his contemporaries and predecessors about the cyclical processes of history and the inevitable decline of even the most stable and powerful political order, however well endowed with *virtù* their leaders may be. In the *Discourses* he also – at least pro forma – draws on his ancient predecessors, especially Polybius, in outlining the different forms of government and the conditions of their rise and decline. But it soon becomes clear that he has something else in mind. He tells us that others who have written about such matters have said that there are three principal forms of government: principality or monarchy, aristocracy and democracy. Moreover, he continues, they have said that there are actually six, three good forms and three bad, each good form having a tendency to degenerate into a pernicious variant: principality can easily become tyranny, as aristocracy can readily become oligarchy, and democracy anarchy. Machiavelli then ascribes to the classics the view that all six forms are actually pernicious, the 'bad' because they are bad in themselves and the 'good' because they can so easily corrupt. To avoid the inevitable evils of these basic forms, he tells us, classical writers tend to opt for a mixed constitution.

Machiavelli goes through the motions of summing up the early history of Rome as a process of transition from monarchy to aristocracy to democracy. But it soon emerges that he differs fundamentally from his predecessors, because he is addressing a rather different problem. He is not primarily concerned with the forms of constitution as defined by the ancients. He is interested in the forms of state that immediately affect his own time and place: above all the city-republics of Italy, governed by civic bodies that range from the oligarchic to the more inclusive, though never democratic, as well as (up to a point) the rising monarchies, such as France or Spain, by which the city-states are threatened. He offers – without systematically spelling it out – a classification different from the ancient one, a simple opposition between principalities and republics, the latter either democratic or aristocratic; and his principal objective in exploring these two forms is even more specific: to consider the conditions for maintaining liberty. That, when all is said and done, is the main theme of the *Discourses*. In this respect, it already asks questions different from those that concerned Plato in his account of political rise and decline, or even Polybius, whose idea of the 'mixed constitution' Machiavelli appears to adopt. But, if his concerns with republican liberty have more in common with his contemporary civic humanists than with ancient ideas on political cycles, he makes an observation that sets him on a rather different path; and in retrospect, it also sheds light on *The Prince*.

Describing the cycle of rise and decline, he writes:

This, then, is the cycle through which all commonwealths pass, whether they govern themselves or are governed. But rarely do they return to the same form of government, for there can scarce be a state of such vitality that it can undergo often such changes and yet remain in being. What usually happens is that, while in a state of commotion in which it lacks both counsel and strength, a state becomes subject to a neighbouring and better organized state. Were it not so, a commonwealth might go on for ever passing through these governmental transitions. (I.2.13)

This observation is not simply a prelude to the remarks that follow it about the advantages of a constitution that can claim to combine – as did the Roman republic – the three major forms, monarchy, aristocracy and democracy, in a way that enhances stability. On this score, Machiavelli appears to have much in common with other advocates of a 'mixed' constitution. At the same time, he departs from convention by insisting that, in Rome, 'it was friction between the plebs and the senate that brought this perfection about'. He departs from the classic view of the mixed constitution as a mode of consolidating oligarchic rule. In the context of Florentine politics, he has little use for the nobility. While he is no democrat, he prefers *governo largo* to *governo stretto;* and, given a choice between democracy and oligarchy, his preference would seem to be democracy.

Yet his comments suggest that he is less concerned with classifying governments, or with the internal conditions that preserve or destroy particular forms of government, or with the mechanisms of transition from one form to another, than with the maintenance of the commonwealth itself and above all its capacity to resist threats from without. The cycles of governmental change could, for better or worse, go on forever, were they not cut short by conquest. The fundamental criterion of political stability is not the quality or duration of any specific political form but the capacity of the state, whatever its form, to withstand external military threats.

This is not to say that Machiavelli is interested only in military readiness and not in the general conditions of a stable civic order or the well-being of the people; but, even when he departs from the amorality of *The Prince*, his preoccupation with external threats colours everything he says about political success. In the *Discourses* he remains concerned with the survival of states in the face of foreign invasions, and he is as direct and uncompromising as ever in his advocacy, when necessary, of violence and deception. Here, too, domestic conflicts are conceived in terms not very different from wars between states. But now he extends his analysis beyond the most basic conditions of *mantenere lo stato* against external threats; and his demands are more exacting than in *The Prince*, because the issue is no longer mere survival, or even the preservation of the state's liberty from external domination, but also the preservation of civic liberty within the state. This requires more than the absence of tyranny. The fundamental condition is still the city-state's autonomy, its freedom from foreign conquests and, not least, from dependence on foreign powers; but there is more at stake. While he certainly discusses the conditions for maintaining principalities, his chief concern is the foundation and preservation of a free republic.

It is, nonetheless, striking how much of the *Discourses* is devoted to military matters, and how much his preference for republican governments itself is cast in military terms. Republican liberty may be good in itself, but popular government also generally gives rise to more reliable armies and to better soldiers – even if they must submit themselves to leadership. It could even be said that, for Machiavelli, what makes a republic on the whole a better bet than princely government is that it tends, as Roman history so clearly demonstrates, to produce a more effective fighting force.

It is here that Machiavelli's military preoccupations merge with his republicanism. His military ideal, the citizen's militia, certainly requires leadership, but it is leadership that can inspire loyalty and love among the rank and file. Ordinary soldiers cannot simply be obedient cannon fodder but must enjoy the respect of their leaders and must themselves partake of military virtues. While a mercenary army is typically led by a traditional military aristocracy, a citizen's militia requires the subordination of the aristocracy to the larger civic community. When Machiavelli extols the benefits of social conflict, untypically for his time and in sharp contrast, for instance, to Aristotelian principles, he has in mind not simply its effects in maintaining the militant spirit of the citizens but also the necessity of constant struggle to keep the aristocracy in check. On this score he departs even from Cicero, who shared Aristotle's predisposition to aristocratic dominance and the kind of social harmony required to sustain it.

Yet even if Machiavelli's preference for republican liberty is in large part shaped by a conviction that it produces better armies, the military cast of his arguments is not just a matter of defending against external threats. If he were simply writing about the art of war – as he does in his book of that name, which he regarded as his greatest achievement – his characteristic 'Machiavellian' principles would be less startling than they are when applied to the daily transactions of politics. What he has to say about violence and deception would hardly seem alien to a military strategist. Nor would his insistence on the need to adapt oneself to the times and to existing circumstances – which commentators have singled out as a particularly significant departure from the standard views of his contemporaries and predecessors, who measured politics against some universal moral standard. The advocacy of deception and the necessity of adapting to changing conditions were, after all, central to one of the earliest masterpieces of military literature: *The Art of War,* attributed to Sun Tzu in China in the sixth century BC. What is new in Machiavelli is the application of these military principles to politics; and this is rooted in the very specific conditions of Renaissance Florence.

The military model of politics belongs to the essence of the *Discourses* no less than to that of *The Prince*. Maintaining a republic, he insists, requires ruthless leadership, which is prepared to violate conventional morality – as his friend and mentor, Piero Soderini, failed to do when he led the Florentine republic, with, as Machiavelli tells us, disastrous results. But understanding Machiavelli's preoccupation here with domestic liberty and order demands something more, a closer look at the conditions of civic disorder and decline. In his *History of Florence*, he recounts at some length the story of the *ciompi* rebellion, presenting it as a turning-point in the history of his city, the culmination of its endless factional and social conflicts. In a speech attributed to a *ciompi* militant, he sums up in the most dramatic terms what is at stake. Just as the economic rivalries of the urban patriciate played themselves out in political factions, so, too, did the economic grievances of the urban poor over inadequate remuneration for their labours turn into conflict over guild privileges and then a struggle for political power. Power struggles of this kind all too readily took on the character of war:

> [O]ur opponents are disunited and rich; their disunion will give us the victory, and their riches, when they have become ours, will support us. Be not deceived about that antiquity of blood by which they exalt themselves above us; for all men having had one common origin, are all equally ancient, and nature has made us all after one fashion. Strip us naked, and we shall all be found alike. Dress us in their clothing, and they in ours, we shall appear noble, they ignoble – for poverty and riches

make all the difference . . . [A]ll who attain great power and riches, make
use of either force or fraud; and what they have acquired either by deceit
or violence, in order to conceal the disgraceful methods of attainment,
they endeavour to sanctify with the false title of honest gains. Those
who either from imprudence or want of sagacity avoid doing so, are
always overwhelmed with servitude and poverty . . . Therefore we must
use force when the opportunity offers; and fortune cannot present us
one more favourable than the present, when the citizens are still disunited, the Signory doubtful, and the magistrates terrified; for we may
easily conquer them before they can come to any settled arrangement.
By this means we shall either obtain the entire government of the city, or
so large a share of it, as to be forgiven past errors, and have sufficient
authority to threaten the city with a renewal of them at some future
time. (III.3)

This dramatically captures the realities of Florentine politics and, perhaps
more than any other passage in Machiavelli's writings, starkly sums up his
understanding of the problems his political theory is meant to confront. He
is not here advocating the violence proposed in the speech, but he sees how
and why things have come to this pass. He even suggests that it was inevitable and, in the circumstances, preferable to what the *signori* had done. Yet in
the *Discourses* a bloody outcome like this is precisely what he sets out to
avoid in his recommendations for a successful republican order – that it be,
at the same time, an effective military force.

The balance at which he aims is difficult. Civic liberty requires that
the aristocracy be kept in check and that the people have some role in
politics. Military success, which is far more likely to be achieved by a
citizens' militia than by untrustworthy nobles and their mercenary
armies, also depends on some kind of equilibrium among the social
classes; and this requires some degree of civil strife, a fruitful tension
between people and patriciate. The problem is that civil strife can always
descend into outright war. It was the Romans who, at least for a time in
the days of the republic's imperial expansion, struck the right balance.
They built their empire not by simple oligarchic rule and the suppression
of the common people – as in ancient Sparta or in Venice. They found a
middle way between oligarchy and democracy by giving the people a
voice through the tribunate, which institutionalized and channelled
social strife. Contrary to all conventional opinion, which condemns the
quarrels between the nobles and the plebs, says Machiavelli, it was those
very quarrels that preserved Roman liberty.

If Machiavelli seems to be a political 'scientist' or even a political 'realist'
avant la lettre, these qualities have more to do with his grounding in the
political realities of his city-state, with its military civic culture and the

immediate dangers it confronted, than with any modern conception of the state or some affinity to scientific methods.[8] His military model of politics conformed to the realities of domestic politics in Florence, where political rivals and factions were always on the verge of war, no less than to the threats that faced his city from without. More than other civic humanists, he proceeded unambiguously on the premise that the object of war, foreign or domestic, is to win, in conformity with moral principles if possible but with cruel violence, deceit and stratagem if not. Machiavelli's military model was, in the context of Florentine realities and the culture of civic humanism, a relatively small change of perspective; but it was enough to shift the focus away from the just political order or the virtuous prince to the means of seizing and maintaining power, pure and simple. Especially when cast in Machiavelli's vivid and uncompromising prose, that seemed a shocking innovation.

It is, then, precisely his commitment to a practically defunct political form that produced what many commentators have interpreted as Machiavelli's most 'modern' political ideas. His views on governance, on how to achieve and maintain power, on relations among citizens and even between princes and their subjects, are steeped in the conditions of the city-state. It is the city-state that for Machiavelli defines the political terrain. This affects his military model of politics, which gives his political theory the aura of 'realism' that to some commentators seems distinctly modern; but it also produces a conception of civic liberty that gives his ideas a flavour in some ways more familiar to modern audiences than political ideas

---

8 A different understanding of Machiavelli's lasting insights, if not his 'modernity', is offered by Louis Althusser in *Machiavelli and Us*, transl. Gregory Elliott (London: Verso, 1999). What is distinctive about Machiavelli, he argues, is not a 'scientific' approach that seeks to discover general laws but rather his concentration on political 'conjunctures'. There are indeed constants that recur in various cases, and they must be clearly understood; but they manifest themselves in different ways in different cases, which means that the general and the particular combine in different ways in each specific historical 'conjuncture'. Machiavelli's particular strength, according to this argument, is not that he proposes certain universal laws but that he grasps conjunctural particularities and the 'aleatory' nature of political practice. Whatever his own political preferences might be, his primary concern is the conjunctural conditions in which political action must take place, which will require different responses. This argument (though it may exaggerate the absence of 'conjunctural' considerations in the history of Western political thought) certainly captures something distinctive about Machiavelli's approach; but, as has already been suggested here, a 'conjunctural' approach as uncompromising as Machiavelli's might have seemed more familiar to military strategists and was expressed in terms not so fundamentally different in China many centuries before. Machiavelli's originality in this respect may, again, lie in his application of such military principles to politics, for reasons that are not particularly 'modern'.

emanating from the rising territorial monarchies that would shape the new world order of modern nation states.

In the classics of sixteenth-century French political thought, for example, the political domain is not a civic community, a community of citizens. It is a contested terrain among various competing jurisdictions: the monarchy, the nobility, local magistrates and various corporate bodies. When Jean Bodin outlined an argument in favour of an 'absolutist' monarchy and devised a theory of sovereignty that has been called a landmark in the evolution of the modern state, he was addressing the position of the monarchy in relation to various corporate powers with varying degrees of autonomy. Even the anti-absolutist arguments of, say, the Huguenot resistance tracts, had little to do with the rights and powers of citizens. Instead, when they asserted the rights of the 'people' against the centralizing monarchy, they were asserting not the rights of citizens but the autonomous powers of various office-holders, 'lesser' magistrates, the provincial nobility, urban corporations and other corporate powers.

In England, which had long before become the most effective centralized administration in Europe, corporate powers were weaker than in France; and even at moments of the greatest tension between monarch and nobility, from Magna Carta to the Civil War, the issue was not jurisdictional disputes of the kind that defined the political terrain in France. Yet the political sphere was typically conceived as a partnership of Crown and Parliament, and the English were slow to formulate the tensions between these two partners in terms of popular sovereignty. We shall return to the peculiarities of England in a later chapter and to the radical ideas that challenged the prevailing wisdom; but for now it suffices to say that, even when royalists and parliamentarians came to blows, the English were, for their own distinctive reasons, disinclined to conceptualize a political domain defined by the rights and powers of citizens as distinct from the rights and powers of Parliament. Even 'republicans', as we shall see, did not always make clear that citizenship meant something more than the right to be (actually or 'virtually') represented by Parliament – which did not necessarily entail the right to vote for it.

By contrast, the Renaissance city-republics extended corporate principles and corporate autonomy to the civic community as a whole; and this produced something more ostensibly akin to modern ideas of popular sovereignty, the sovereignty of citizens, in contrast to the discourse of territorial monarchies. We are, in today's liberal democracies, accustomed to thinking of citizens' rights as a hallmark of a truly modern politics. That, among other things, is what allows some commentators to identify 'civic humanism' or even Renaissance 'republicanism' as a window to the modern world. But it may be misleading to describe membership in the civic corporation in medieval and Renaissance Italy as 'citizenship', since it vests political rights in corporate bodies and not individual citizens, while the republican discourse has less to do with the advent of the 'modern' state (unless it is as a threat to the survival of city-republics) than with the distinctive unity of civic, commercial and military principles in a political form that would not survive modernity.

3

THE REFORMATION

Martin Luther is one of very few, even among canonical thinkers, for whom a persuasive case can be made that, had he never been born, history would not have unfolded as it did. He may, for this reason alone, seem to present a special challenge to a social-contextual history like this one. If the ideas of one man can seem to change the course of history in such dramatic ways, must we not reconsider the primacy of discourse? Yet to ask the question in this way would be to misunderstand what is entailed by the kind of contextualization proposed in this book. Whatever doubts we may have about the decisive role of this or that historic figure, the social history of political theory does not require us to denigrate the creativity or world-historic influence of individuals. It does not oblige us to think that a Protestant movement would have emerged more or less in the form that it did with or without Martin Luther, nor does it suggest that if Martin Luther had never existed he would have had to be invented, or, for that matter, that Protestantism had no significant effects on the truly 'basic' processes of history.

How, then, should we pose the question? We shall certainly want to ask how the particularities of Luther's time and place shaped the particular configuration of problems he sought to resolve; and we shall want to consider how it came about that the same ideas were mobilized so differently, to such divergent purposes, in different contexts. But in the case of Luther more than most other thinkers, we are compelled to ask how a conceptual shift in the realm of ideas could have had such massive historical consequences; and it may turn out that the greater the world-historic effects we claim for Luther's ideas, the more – not the less – we must appeal to a contextual explanation.

The Roots of Reformation

Some historians have questioned the very existence of a Reformation conceived as a radical discontinuity in Christian dogma and reactions to it. The ideas of Luther and other major Protestant thinkers, they point out, were deeply rooted in the medieval Church, which was already alive with debate and projects for internal reformation; and there had long been heresies to challenge the institutions, no less than the theological orthodoxies, of the Catholic Church. Conflicts in the Church had been vastly aggravated by geopolitical rivalries among rising territorial states, as the papacy at Avignon had increasingly come under the influence of the French monarchy, and competing papal claimants in Avignon and Rome became embroiled in inter-state rivalries between France and its European neighbours. In the late fourteenth century, these rivalries produced the so-called Western Schism, which would last for decades and helped to generate a climate of reform and outright heresy.

The conciliar movement, which flourished in the fourteenth and fifteenth centuries, elaborated the idea that it was not the pope but the corporate body of Christians in the form of a general Church council that held ultimate authority in spiritual matters. While the movement would give way to a revived papal dominance, its influence remained alive, even if more as a model for secular theories of constitutional government than as a programme for reform of the Church. More scathing attacks on the papacy, as well as on the abuses and corruptions of the Church, would come from the Englishman John Wycliffe (1330–84) and, most importantly, from the Bohemian Jan Hus (1369–1415), whose influence on Luther would run very deep. Both Wycliffe and Hus denied that the ecclesiastical hierarchy, from pope to cardinals to priests, constituted the Church; and both called on secular rulers to initiate reform of the Church. They even demanded that ecclesiastical possessions should be subject to secular rule, on the grounds that the Church did not enjoy ownership but only use rights conditional on good behaviour.

Renaissance humanism, too, played a critical part. Indeed, there may be something artificial about distinguishing the 'Reformation' from 'Christian humanism'. The humanist preoccupation with ancient texts would be extended to the Bible, encouraging theologians to mobilize scripture in challenging the current practices of ecclesiastical authorities. The spread of printing, needless to say, gave a new force to this kind of textual challenge. Christian humanism, especially in the person of Erasmus, may have remained committed to internal reform of the Church and deeply suspicious of the Lutheran 'reformation'; but it also encouraged, if not necessarily outright anti-clericalism, at least the subjection of Church rituals and orthodoxies to critical scrutiny and the moral judgment of the individual. All these challenges to clerical authority, both Christian humanist and 'Protestant', would at the same time, directly or by implication, affect attitudes towards the powers of secular rulers.

Ideas such as these – not only criticism of the Church and its abuses but also, and not least, the elevation of secular authority – would be central to the Reformation. Yet even if we acknowledge that the institutions of the

Church were in the end resistant to the necessary changes, and even if we treat Luther's ideas as a profoundly revolutionary transformation in theology, the magnitude of the Lutheran rupture seems incommensurate with the novelty of his theology. There is also a massive disparity – which, of course, there often is with major thinkers but which, in Luther's case, is particularly striking – between the meaning or intentions of his doctrine and the direction of the changes that emerged in its wake. It will be argued in what follows that the scale and consequences of the break had less to do with the originality and revolutionary import or intent of Luther's ideas than with the geopolitical and social conflicts into which they were drawn.

That Luther challenged some of the beliefs and practices of Roman Catholicism with drastic effect is beyond question, as is, needless to say, the separation of 'Protestants' – in all their various and often antithetical guises – from the Catholic Church. We shall look at the nature and implications of Luther's challenge to medieval Catholicism, but Luther's doctrine was something else too. Inextricably connected with his attacks on the Church, not only its corruptions but its very claims to jurisdiction, are his views on secular government. For all Luther's occasionally stinging attacks on German princes, there hardly exists in the Western canon a more uncompromising case for strict obedience to secular authority; and this, as we shall see, belongs to the essence of Lutheran doctrine no less than does the attack on the medieval Church's practice of indulgences or Luther's idea of justification by faith.

Yet, while this fundamental aspect of Protestant doctrine was certainly not lost on German princes or on European kings, it was also somehow transformed into its opposite, a doctrine of rebellion. The question, then, must be how such a rigid doctrine of obedience could have such revolutionary effects and, beyond that, how a doctrine that seems far better suited to defending than to challenging the supremacy of princely power could be transformed into a doctrine of resistance. The answer lies in specificities of context, which both impelled Luther to formulate his doctrine of obedience and also permitted it to be transformed into its opposite.

Martin Luther

If the sixteenth century was a period of rising territorial states in Western Europe, Germany, like Italy, represented an exception. While in other cases the crisis of feudalism had meant a growing challenge to parcellized sovereignty from centralizing monarchies, in Germany it gave new life to the fragmentation of governance. Feudal lordship may have given way to princely government, and the feudal powers of the lesser nobility may have been weakened; but German principalities and duchies vigorously resisted the kind of monarchical centralization that was taking place elsewhere in Western Europe and produced in its stead a new kind of parcellized sovereignty.

In the Holy Roman Empire, which was the nearest thing to a national state in German territories, the emperor's authority was severely and explicitly limited by the autonomous powers of local duchies, principalities and cities. In the thirteenth century, Frederick II – partly in a fruitless effort to maintain the presence of the Empire in northern Italy – had ceded even more powers to local German lords, including princes of the Church. Although German landed classes in the west were never able to consolidate their powers over peasants in a 'second serfdom' as their eastern counterparts would do, the Empire had effectively transformed them from feudal lords into local rulers, territorial princes with state-like powers of their own, not least the power to tax. This gave them access to increasing revenues from peasants, especially from more prosperous peasant farmers who, even while freed from feudal dependence, bore the greatest burden of taxation. This would become a major source of grievance in the peasant war of 1524–5.

Secular authority had been further fragmented, especially from the twelfth century, with the foundation of cities by both emperors and dukes, for administrative or commercial purposes. These cities would challenge the powers of both emperor and local princes. Like the Italian city-states, German cities often governed their surrounding villages, exacting taxes from the peasantry by means of a collective urban lordship; but they stood in a different relation to landed aristocracies and princes than did the Italians. In northern Italy, the major city-states could trace their urban lineage back to imperial Rome, and the landed aristocracy was, in general, weaker than it was elsewhere in feudal Europe. The German cities, by contrast, owed their late foundations to superior lords. Even as they built upon the independence granted by higher authorities, they were obliged to defend their autonomous powers, inseparably political and economic, against other claimants within the imperial hierarchy, from emperors to princes.

Here, as in Renaissance Italy, political struggles were difficult to disentangle from economic rivalries and conflicts. Just as German princes relied on their political and military dominance for access to the revenues derived from cities and especially from peasant labour, so too was the success of the commercial cities dependent on their 'extra-economic' powers and privileges. The commercial dominance of the Hanseatic League in Northern Europe, for instance, relied on the League's coercive powers, the capacity to enforce monopolies, embargoes and blockades, which might require military interventions up to and including outright war. The League's dominance was threatened not so much by the purely 'economic' superiority of its commercial rivals – the kind of competitive advantage enjoyed by cost-effective capitalist producers – as by their more effective geopolitical reach and military power.

In 1519, the Habsburg King Charles I of Spain became the Holy Roman Emperor Charles V. His reign would be marked by intense and varied conflicts with German princes and municipal authorities, to say nothing of the peasant revolt. Charles was constantly distracted by the Empire's rivalries with other rising states, as well as Spain's project of imperial expansion, revolt on Spanish soil and the ever-present Turkish threat. He never succeeded in subduing local powers in the German territories. His reign would play a decisive role in the life of Martin Luther and in the Reformation, which flourished in the context of the Holy Roman Empire, not only because the emperor's attacks on Luther helped to concentrate the theologian's mind but because Lutheran doctrine proved so useful to various protagonists in the rivalries among competing powers.

Born in 1483 into a reasonably comfortable family, Luther was intended for the law; but he soon gave up his legal education for the Church and became an Augustinian monk. The monastic life seems to have generated little but doubt and despair. The Christianity he had learned from preachers and a very pious mother was obsessed with sin, repentance and the wrath of God. It did, to be sure, suggest that repentant sinners can make some contribution to their own salvation; and theology appeared to teach that, even if salvation is a matter of God's grace and not just a simple reward for a virtuous life, believers can and must engage in a constant struggle to cooperate with God – always, of course, with the help of the Church. But, to Luther, this appeared to mean that, torn between virtue and sin, between God and the devil, we can in this life never know whether all our efforts are enough to please God. Not even the extreme asceticism he adopted in the monastery could offer any certainty or comfort. As he described his own experience, it only turned his soul upon itself. He began to break free from this tormented struggle when his superior, Johann Staupitz, convinced him that repentance is not a matter of seeking God's love, which is already evident in the sacrifice of Christ, but, on the contrary, begins with our own love of God.

Luther was also persuaded by Staupitz, who was dean of the new University of Wittenberg, to pursue an academic career in biblical theology; and it was not as any kind of activist but as professor of theology that Luther launched his attack on the corruptions of the Church. He would later attribute his theological innovations to a transformative moment, a rebirth, which came to him while grappling with the doctrine of St Paul. 'For therein is the righteousness of God revealed from faith to faith:' said Paul in Romans 1: 17, 'as it is written: the just shall live by faith.' Luther would later recount that, while lecturing on the Psalms, he finally came to understand this passage to mean that the righteousness of God was not revealed by punishment. Instead, in his grace, he declared the sinner righteous – or 'justified' him – by means of faith alone. Salvation was not, in other words, the uncertain outcome of a lifelong human effort but a free and loving gift of God.

Luther never resolved the question of predestination, and debate still rages about what he meant on this score. Lutherans would come to distinguish themselves from Calvinists on the grounds that, while both theologians believed in election by God, only Calvin insisted on a 'double' predestination, according to which God also chose those who are damned. Luther, they maintain, never taught that some were predestined to eternal damnation. Yet, if this is so, some would argue, Luther remained caught in an irreducible contradiction, which undermined belief in God's total sovereignty. It might be better simply to accept that Luther deliberately refused to confront the conundrum of predestination, because preoccupation with this issue was, in his eyes, a distraction from acknowledging our sinfulness and from unwavering faith in God's grace and salvation through Christ. This would also, as we shall see, have the effect of strengthening Luther's doctrine of obedience to secular authority.

Whether or not Luther's revelation was as sudden as he later made it out to be, the doctrine of 'justification by faith' represents a revolutionary moment in the history of Christianity. It is true that St Augustine had elaborated a doctrine of salvation that seemed to leave very little scope for repentance and good works as the road to salvation. For him, too, salvation was a free and unearned gift of God through grace; and he had a particularly uncompromising view of predestination. But Luther, as influenced as he was by St Augustine, was convinced that, once he had experienced his revelation on St Paul, he had put Augustine behind him.

For Augustine, justification by God's grace was not something that happened all at once. It was a process that occupied a lifetime in this world and could only be completed in the next, while, for Luther, it was God's immediate and unconditional gift in this life. Augustine may have been no less intent than was Luther on emphasizing that salvation was an unearned gift from God; but his formulation may have seemed open to the interpretation that human beings could in their lifetime, at least in some small way, cooperate in their own transformation by divine grace. In any case, whatever St Augustine had intended, the authority of the Catholic Church clearly depended on maintaining the sinner's role in achieving salvation, with, of course, the necessary help of sacramental interventions by the Church; and Augustinian theology would be interpreted by medieval popes, such as Gregory the Great (590–604), in just this way. Luther would have none of that – not on the grounds that Christian virtue and good works meant nothing to him, but on the grounds that, while they should be undertaken freely for the love of God, they had nothing to do with earning God's love and the free gift of justification. Sinners are saved not by their own righteousness but, all at once and in this life, by the righteousness of God, which means that, even while remaining sinners, they are 'justified' by faith alone. This doctrine had fatal implications for the sacramental functions of the Church, but its implications for obedience to secular authority may have been even greater.

Whenever Luther's doctrine of justification by faith reached maturity – and commentators disagree on when and how it happened – Luther's challenge to the authority of the Catholic Church did not at first depend on it. The most famous moment in his career, which is conventionally depicted as the Reformation's true beginning, was his attack on the corruptions of the Church, and especially the practice of indulgences, in his *Disputation on the Power and Efficacy of Indulgences,* commonly called the 95 *Theses,* which he issued in 1517, nailing them, as tradition (if not historical evidence) tells us, to the door of the Castle Church in Wittenberg. His target was the pope's claims to powers that were, for Luther, God's alone: the power to award salvation or to affect the scope and duration of penance in the after-life. This attack on the pope did not require, nor did Luther invoke, the doctrine of justification by faith as he would later formulate it.

Luther would soon be threatened by a papal ban, which would lead to his excommunication; and his personal fate became enmeshed in public conflicts between the Church and secular authorities over the distribution of tempo-ral power. His immediate response to papal threats was a series of treatises in 1520, the first of which was his *Address to the Christian Nobility of the German Nation.* Here, his theological preoccupations shifted, significantly, from the disposition of power between God and the pope to the conflicts between the Church – specifically the pope, together with the Holy Roman Emperor – and German secular authorities.

This would be followed in rapid succession by two other treatises, laying the groundwork for his mature theology: *On the Babylonian Captivity of the Church,* which, written in strongly vituperative terms, attacked the papacy and challenged the sacramental functions of the Church; and *On the Freedom of a Christian,* which, though framed in more conciliatory language and even dedicated to Pope Leo X, outlined the principles that would constitute the doctrine of justification by faith. Luther here elabo-rated on the dualism, or the paradox, at the root of his theology: the simultaneity of human sin and divine justification, the nature of humanity as irreducibly sinful yet saved.

Human beings, Luther argued, are at once sinners by nature and saints by faith. Redeemed by God, they may freely undertake service to others; but, while Luther can be interpreted to mean that justification by faith is simultaneously a free commitment to good works, he insists that ordinary human beings are free as any lord or king and subject to no overlord in matters affecting the soul. Yet, at the same time, as he would soon make clear, the irreducible sinfulness of humanity requires temporal authorities to whom all Christians owe obedience. It is true that, in these early works, Luther not only challenged the division of the world into temporal and spiritual jurisdictions but established the principle that all baptized Christians are equally priests; and the idea of a universal priesthood would be taken up by radical forces as a justification of rebellions far beyond anything envisaged by Luther himself, including the peasant revolt. But this radical appropriation of Lutheran doctrine should not disguise the fact that Luther's account of the simultaneous duality of sin and justification entailed both a denial of ecclesiastical jurisdiction and an insistence on strict obedience to secular authority.

In 1521, Luther was called before an assembly of the estates of the Holy Roman Empire at the Diet of Worms; and, refusing to recant the views expressed in the 95 *Theses* and other writings, he was outlawed by the emperor, Charles V. Under threat of arrest, he disappeared for a time. Despite imperial orders for his apprehension and punishment, declaring it a crime to shield him, he was offered protection at Wartburg Castle in Eisenach by a leading German prince, Frederic III, Elector of Saxony. It was then that he began his translation of the Bible into German, which would be printed in 1534 and can reasonably be regarded as his most far-reaching accomplishment, with influences well beyond the German language or Lutheran theology.

The Doctrine of Obedience to Secular Authority

In Luther's treatises of 1520, ideas essential to the Reformation, challenging the spiritual authority of the Church, its monopoly on the interpretation of scripture and its sole right to call a council of the Church, were formulated with direct reference to the relation between ecclesiastical and secular authority. Whatever effects these treatises may have had in undermining ecclesiastical authority, their implications for obedience to secular government were very different. To challenge the claims of the Church as privileged mediator between humanity and God, it might have been enough to reject, as Luther did in the 95 *Theses,* its efforts to usurp divine powers of punishment and absolution. Challenging the Church's claims to temporal power and its usurpation of secular authority required something more, and even that would not suffice to impose on Christians a strict obedience to secular government. The doctrine of justification by faith would achieve all these effects.

Commentaries on Luther's theology have tended to identify his greatest innovation as his challenge to the Church's sacramental, sacerdotal powers. By the late Middle Ages, they say, a clear distinction had been established between the sacramental powers of the Church and its jurisdictional authority in the temporal domain, its coercive powers in the public realm (*in foro exteriori et publice*), its 'plenitude of power'. Indeed, others before Luther, such as Marsilius of Padua, had challenged its temporal authority. But Luther took the extra step.

No one had yet gone quite so far in questioning not just the Church's temporal authority but even its powers over the souls of the faithful.

Yet, if we follow the logic of Luther's theological development, it is striking that it proceeds in the opposite direction. He begins by questioning the Church's power to punish sins, to excommunicate or to confer benefices and indulgences, and then advances from there not simply to attack the temporal authority of the Church but to support secular governments and their claims to almost unconditional obedience. It is at this point that the doctrine of justification by faith becomes truly essential. That doctrine may have contributed even more to the defence of secular authority, and the necessity of obedience to it, than to the attack on the sacramental powers of the Church.

The Lutheran creed of obedience looks back to St Augustine and St Paul, who had, at different moments in the history of the Roman Empire, enunciated doctrines of obedience to secular authority.[1] In the first volume of this history, it was argued that the defining principle of Western Christianity was the rendering unto Caesar and God their respective domains of law and obedience. The 'universal' Catholic Church was born when what had been a Jewish cult detached itself, in accordance with the doctrines of St Paul, from Judaism's all-embracing religious law, which applied to both matters of faith and the mundane practices of everyday life. The distinction between Caesar and God, each with his own proper sphere of obedience, would perhaps more than anything else set Christianity, especially in its Western form, apart from the other monotheistic religions.[2] It was this, above all,

---

1 St Paul and St Augustine are discussed in my *Citizens to Lords*, pp. 144–63.

2 There has been much confusion about Islam and the consequences of its belief in a single divinely revealed system of law, encompassing the whole range of human practice, secular as well as religious. We have become familiar with a strain of Islam for which this view of the law requires an 'Islamist' state, replacing secular governance with a fundamentalist theocracy. But this was certainly not characteristic of medieval Islam. The belief in a single divinely revealed law meant not the dominance of *mullahs* but, on the contrary, the absence of an institutional power comparable to the Christian ecclesiastical establishment, with its own distinct claims to authority and obedience. There was no autonomous Islamic power such as the Catholic Church for policing theology, let alone laying claim to authority over the whole temporal domain. There were no jurisdictional claims and disputes of the kind that characterized Christianity; and this permitted, among other things, an openness to the idea that truth could be arrived at in various ways – for example, by means of secular philosophy no less than by means of Islamic theology (see vol. 1 of this history for a discussion of the relation between Islamic theology and classical philosophy). By the same reasoning, a secular government could be perfectly consistent with Islamic theology – and perhaps without all the tensions engendered by jurisdictional conflicts of Western Christianity. Christian theology did not prevent secular governments from claiming their authority as divinely ordained; and, if anything, the jurisdictional dualism of Christianity could easily accommodate, indeed invite, a doctrine of strict obedience to secular authority imposed on sinful human beings, in the manner of Augustine and Luther.

that permitted Christianity to become an imperial religion, which relinquished to Caesar the right to rule this world.

Before the Constantinian conversion, St Paul had already invoked this principle to impose upon Christians a need to obey imperial authority. After Christianity had become the official religion of empire, St Augustine elaborated the principle of obedience to secular power into an even more uncompromising doctrine, which still included submission to pagan rulers. He accomplished this by transforming the old Christian dualism into a rather more complex dichotomy. Instead of a simple distinction between earthly and heavenly realms, or secular and spiritual authority, or even the sacred and the profane, Augustine proposed a dichotomy between the divine and earthly 'cities', which are antithetical but inextricably united in this world: the one representing the saintly, holy, elect, pious and just, the other representing the impure, impious, unjust and damned, which runs through every human society and every human institution, including holy institutions of the Church. Since all human beings and all human institutions are tainted by unholiness and sin, no truly just and rightful order is possible in this world; and they must all subject themselves, by divine ordination, to the earthly powers whose purpose is not to achieve some higher principle of holiness or justice on this earth but simply to maintain peace, order and a degree of physical comfort.

For early Christian theologians under imperial rule, a doctrine of obedience to Caesar may have been a relatively simple matter. The issue became infinitely more complicated when empire gave way to the medieval fragmentation of temporal power, in which ecclesiastical authorities were major players. Now theologians had to confront not only a division of labour between Caesar and God, with their respective claims to obedience, but also between Empire and Church, or princes and popes, among a bewildering variety of other autonomous powers, from feudal lords to civic corporations. It is not surprising that much of Christian theology soon took the form of legalistic arguments on jurisdiction.

No philosopher or theologian could ever have decisively resolved the boundary disputes between ecclesiastical jurisdiction and secular governments, especially between the papacy and rising feudal kingdoms, which increasingly plagued Western Christendom in the later Middle Ages; but medieval Christian theology was at least obliged to confront the question in a way that early Christianity was not. It may have been enough in the time of St Paul to elaborate the principle of rendering unto Caesar and God their respective domains; and it may have been enough in St Augustine's time to construct a theology of other-worldliness, like Christian Neoplatonism, which allowed obedience to Caesar to coexist with a devaluation of earthly existence and a philosophy of mystical release from the material world. But, in the age of Thomas Aquinas, theologians were compelled to contend with, and even to justify, the preoccupation of medieval Christians with the intricacies of worldly governance and conflicts among competing claims to temporal power.

This was a time when rising kingdoms like France were contending with other temporal powers, such as the German princes of the Holy Roman Empire and above all with the papacy. Christian theologians confronted not only the contests between spiritual and secular domains but ecclesiastical powers that laid claim to temporal authority on the grounds of their privileged access to the spiritual domain. Aquinas himself never systematically spelled out in practical terms his views on the relation between spiritual and temporal powers; but, drawing on the rediscovered Aristotle, he did find a way of situating the secular sphere in the cosmic order, retaining for the Church its own rightful domain while securing the position of secular governments. Although he placed the secular political sphere in a descending hierarchy from the divine to the mundane, he ascribed to it a positive function in the greater scheme of things, not simply in the role of necessary evil, as it had been for Augustine. The spiritual realm still reigned supreme in the cosmic hierarchy, and the Church still had its privileged position in that sphere; but secular government, which was granted substantial autonomy, could, on Thomistic principles, be treated as the highest of Christian concerns in this world.

Here, too, the cosmic order was defined in legalistic terms, as Thomas distinguished among various kinds of law, divine, eternal, natural and positive. Natural law was that aspect of divine regulation and the cosmic order accessible to human reason and hence available to secular governments no less than to ecclesiastical authorities. Political society was not directly instituted by God but by natural law as mediated through positive law. This doctrine went some distance in sustaining the authority of secular princes against ecclesiastical powers claiming temporal supremacy. While Aquinas himself remained aloof, his doctrines were soon deployed in favour, for instance, of Philip IV of France in his struggles with Pope Boniface VIII.[3]

Lutheran theology disrupted this neat Thomistic structure. The hierarchy of the cosmic order was replaced by a particularly rigid separation of spiritual and temporal domains, which denied any temporal jurisdiction to the Church. As we have seen, Luther took this further than ever before by denying the jurisdiction of the Church *in foro interno*, no less than *in foro externo,* not only depriving it of authority in matters temporal but restricting even its formal sacramental functions, divesting the Church's officers, the priesthood, of their role as humanity's only and official channel to God.

---

3   Thomas Aquinas is discussed in greater detail in *Citizens to Lords*, as is the preoccupation with jurisdiction in medieval theology.

The powers of coercion belonged solely to secular government, to which Christians owed their obedience.

In spiritual matters affecting the soul, Christians were, to be sure, obliged to follow their Christian conscience; and, if commanded to act in ungodly ways, they might be obliged to disobey. Yet this obligation did not constitute a right to resist or rebel. If Christians felt compelled in conscience to disobey, they were obliged simply to accept the punishment for disobedience. True Christian liberty belongs to the soul and is perfectly consistent with bodily imprisonment. The right of refusal was reserved to the individual Christian conscience and could not be translated into active, collective and organized resistance to secular authority. A radical reading of Luther might seem to suggest that civil authority could not reside in ungodly princes, and more radical resistance theories would interpret Lutheran doctrine in this way. But the master himself would make very clear, most emphatically during the peasants' revolt, that the ungodliness of rulers is no warrant for rebellion.

Luther would, in his later years, reluctantly accept – at the strong and repeated urging of German princes – a right of resistance that went beyond his earlier convictions; but the issue then was whether the princes had a right, even a duty, to form a league to resist the emperor, which Luther had earlier opposed. Some supporters even appealed to Roman civil law in support of the right to resist force with force and to disobey unjust judges. There were those who argued, invoking 'private law', that an unjust ruler might forfeit his public authority and effectively become a private person subject to resistance on the grounds of self-defence. Even Luther himself with great hesitation accepted the 'private law' doctrine; but, while some did indeed interpret the doctrine as implying a more radical right of individual resistance, for Luther the narrowly circumscribed issue was the right of lesser authorities like German princes actively to resist the higher authority of the emperor.[4] The argument developed by rebellious princes to justify resistance to the imperial power was intended, from beginning to

---

4   See Skinner, *Foundations, Vol. 2: Age of Reformation*, esp. pp. 199–202. While Skinner argues that Luther's change of mind was indeed a real one, he also takes pains to emphasize that the Lutherans were 'of course' 'anxious to avoid at all costs' any interpretation of the private-law doctrine as implying that private individuals had a right of violent resistance to public authority or any confusion between private individuals and public office (p. 200). See also Cynthia Grant Bowman, 'Luther and the Justifiability of Resistance to Legitimate Authority', *Cornell Law Faculty Publications*, Paper 151, 1979. 'It is important to note that in voicing this new position Luther based his stand solely upon the cautious, tightly circumscribed grounds of constitutional law', on the question of whether lesser authorities could resist higher ones. Private citizens could refuse to obey their emperor and to participate in the war on his side; but 'only those who had public authority to do so, and that seemed in the light of the jurists' arguments to include the princes, should actively oppose the Emperor' (pp. 11–12).

end, to be formulated in such a way as to ensure that resistance was not conceived as a general right residing in the people. It was meant, from the start, to be a constitutional argument about the rights of princes and other officials to resist the higher authority of the Empire, especially in matters of religion, and even to repel the emperor with military force. Even if the emperor had become a private person by governing unjustly, his punishment remained a public duty, performed by proper authorities, and not a private right.

Other Christian theologians had devised theories of obedience to secular authority, but Luther faced specific problems that no other theologian had effectively confronted. Unlike, for instance, Marsilius of Padua, who attacked the papacy on behalf of the Holy Roman Empire and its allies in Italian civic communes, in particular the Ghibelline nobility, Luther was asserting the authority of secular rulers, sometimes kings but in particular local princes, who were in conflict with both pope and emperor. To establish that Christians owed obedience to German princes, it was not enough to declare that the Church had no jurisdiction, public or private. This might suffice to shift the balance of authority in worldly affairs from Church to secular government, but princes whose authority was in no way derived from divine associations – such as even the Holy Roman Emperor enjoyed – would seem to have a tenuous claim on the strict obedience of Christian believers. Augustine had gone a long way in establishing the principle that secular and even pagan rulers could command the obedience of Christians; but there remained some loopholes, which were closed by Luther's doctrine of justification by faith.

Augustine had certainly argued that temporal government is providentially ordained by God to deal with a fallen humanity. Since the purpose of government was simply to maintain peace, order and a fair degree of comfort among sinful human beings who could expect no justice in this world, even pagans could fulfil this modest purpose and could command obedience on the same grounds as did a Christian ruler. The principle of obedience was underwritten by his doctrine of predestination, which seemed to leave little, if any, scope to human effort in achieving salvation. At the same time, as we have seen, Augustine's view of salvation appeared, in the eyes of some interpreters, to leave room for human effort in cooperating with the grace of God, while his attitude to heresy and his support for its brutal suppression by the state might be understood to imply that Christians did, after all, stand in a different relation to secular authority than did heretics or non-believers. Some might even be inclined to interpret the distinction between the sinful mass of humanity and the elect, rooted in the doctrine of predestination, to mean that secular government was necessary to control the many but that the few might somehow be exempt.

Luther decisively closed all the doors left ajar by Augustine. The

Reformation would, to be sure, produce sects, in particular the Anabaptists, who believed that true Christians were subject only to the Word of God and not to the temporal sword. But Luther's theology is emphatically on the side of obedience to secular government and the need for Christians to submit to it. Whatever he may have believed about predestination or the division between damned and elect, his doctrine of justification by faith effectively rendered them irrelevant to the question of obedience to secular authority, while at the same time giving secular government an unambiguous claim to divine ordination.

Luther accepted the Augustinian opposition between the realm of God and the earthly realm, or the devil's; but that antithesis was trumped by another distinction, between temporal and spiritual realms, with their corresponding modes of authority, both of which are divine. The antithesis of divine and diabolic 'kingdoms' remained important; but it figured in the argument on divinely ordained temporal and spiritual realms only in the sense that it reflected the dual nature of humanity, the simultaneous unity of sin and justification that characterizes Christians, whose human sinfulness requires the temporal sword.

The distinction between temporal and spiritual realms, or between the kinds of order to which they are respectively subject, does not, then, correspond to the antithesis of God's realm and the devil's, because, as we have seen, both orders are divine. Nor does Luther situate temporal and spiritual orders in some kind of Thomistic hierarchy. Each has its rightful and inviolable domain and its own mode of governance: the spiritual realm is the domain of the Word, with no business in the sphere of jurisdiction or coercion, which is the preserve of secular government. The line of demarcation between the two domains is clear, and any confusion between them is the work of the devil. This formulation puts paid to the temporal pretensions of the Church, while elevating secular authority to a status no less divine than the spiritual order.

Obedience Transformed into Resistance

Despite the doctrine of obedience, there was always a danger that attacks on abuses of clerical power might put in question any religious legitimation of secular authority; and Lutheran theology was – selectively – invoked by radical Protestants to justify rebellions of a kind Luther himself vehemently opposed. In his absence from Wittenberg after the Diet of Worms, some of his followers promoted more radical reforms of the Church than he had envisaged; and their rebellion did not stop with ecclesiastical authorities but extended to the government of civic magistrates. Luther responded, already in 1521, with *A Sincere Admonition to All Christians to Guard Against Insurrection and Rebellion*. He was, to be sure, critical of German princes; but even in his treatise *Temporal Authority: To What Extent It Should Be Obeyed* (1523), which most clearly expresses his reservations about how princes are actually using their divinely ordained power, he never abandons his call to obedience. Luther admonishes the princes – without much hope, it must be said – to behave like Christians; and he also appears to suggest that true Christians are obliged to sustain the powers of secular government only out of Christian love and service to others who are more in need of coercive correction. Yet his principal message is that, while the Christian soul is governed by the Word, Christians, whether because of their own sinfulness or in service to others, are in the temporal domain no less subject than anyone else to the sword of secular authority and the obligation to obey.

On his return to Wittenberg, Luther managed to subdue his most radical followers; but this did not prevent others – notably the Anabaptist Thomas Müntzer, who had broken with him – from supporting and leading the peasant rebellion. While Müntzer certainly had Luther in his sights when he excoriated a view of the world in which all things and creatures have been turned into property, support for the peasants' revolt did not require anything quite as radical as an attack on the very institution of private property. But even short of that, given Luther's unambiguous insistence on obedience to secular authority, it may not be immediately obvious how Lutheran doctrine could lend support to a popular uprising.

Luther's attack on the Church could be more readily mobilized against the ecclesiastical hierarchy, princes of the Church and the imposition of tithes, which were indeed a major grievance. But during the peasant revolt the challenge to authority went beyond ecclesiastical jurisdiction to include secular authorities, the ever-increasing burden of taxation and gross inequalities of property and power. To justify rebellions such as these in Lutheran terms required a considerable stretch. If Luther advocated the personal and passive disobedience of Christians when commanded to act in an ungodly way, his radical followers transformed that principle into militant collective rebellion against 'ungodly' rulers, in a way Luther never intended. His doctrine of a universal priesthood or the equality of all baptized Christians before God had to be translated, in distinctly un-Lutheran ways, into principles of social equality and challenges to any kind of earthly lordship.

If some peasant rebels were driven by Lutheran ideas and expected support from the master, they were soon disillusioned. In *Against the Robbing and Murdering Hordes of Peasants,* Luther left no ambiguity at all about the obligation to obey the secular authorities, however ungodly their behaviour. Whatever legitimate grievances the peasants may have had, they were in the very act of rebellion guilty of terrible sins against God and man; and for that they must be brutally suppressed. 'Therefore let everyone who can, smite, slay and stab, secretly or openly, remembering that nothing can be more poisonous, hurtful or devilish than a rebel. It is just as when one must kill a mad dog; if you do not strike him, he will strike you, and a whole land with you.'[5]

This invitation to princely brutality may seem a far cry from Luther's earlier admonitions to misbehaving princes, and there can be no doubt that the peasant revolt aroused his anger as never before; but his strictures against rebellion follow seamlessly from the insistence on obedience to secular authority that lies at the heart of his theology. When the rebellion was finally defeated by German princes and their troops, there remained a sharp rupture between radical sects that challenged the temporal sword, and Luther's Reformation, which supported secular powers and enjoyed their protection. In the end, he would even compromise his basic principles about the sharp dividing line between temporal and spiritual authority, allowing secular governments to invade the spiritual domain in order to defend true religion, even, when needed, by force.

The doctrine of obedience that lay at the heart of Protestantism was certainly a boon to German princes, and this advantage was certainly not lost on other European kings. Where territorial monarchs were already far advanced in their centralizing projects and (unlike, say, the Spanish monarch, who was also Holy Roman Emperor) not dependent on attachment to the Catholic Church, Protestant doctrine could easily be deployed in support of monarchical power. This was particularly true in England. Henry VIII in his earlier, orthodox years wrote an attack on Luther that earned him a papal endorsement as 'defender of the faith'. But, while his attitude towards Lutheranism remained at best ambivalent, Protestant doctrine was soon enlisted in the cause of royal supremacy, which granted the monarch command of state and Church at once. The same ideas would be no less serviceable to James I when he claimed the divine right of kings.

The irony is that, while (mis)interpretations of Lutheranism were used to justify the peasant revolt, the most systematic and influential Protestant doctrines of resistance emerged not from radical rebellion but from assertions of power by secular authorities. It should be no surprise that this transformation first took place in the Holy Roman Empire, with its intricate web of competing jurisdictions. Rivalries among various claimants to secular authority spawned new ideas of resistance to power quite different from those that drove radical sects or the peasant revolt. It was one thing for peasants to rebel against their superiors. It was quite another for princes to rebel against Holy Roman Emperors, or civic magistrates against both emperors and princes. When princes challenged the emperor, or civic magistrates

---

5 Luther, *Against the Robbing and Murdering Hordes of Peasants*, in *Martin Luther (Documents of Modern History)*, eds E.G. Rupp and Benjamin Drewery (London: E. Arnold, 1970), pp. 121–6.

resisted princes, they were certainly pursuing their own economic interests by defending or augmenting their hold on political power, just as burghers and guildsmen fought urban patriciates to gain the material advantages deriving from a greater share in civic governance, or peasants rebelled against princes to free themselves of tithes and taxes. The difference was that, in their resistance to higher authorities, princes or civic magistrates could claim to be acting not in their private interests but in defence of their own public powers.

Luther's theology proved well adapted to these conflicts; and its success must be at least in part explained by its capacity to serve the interests of secular powers in various ways, depending on the balance of forces in any given principality or city at any given time. The complex of ideas that combined separation from the Catholic Church with a doctrine of obedience to secular authority served princes and civic authorities particularly well. The adoption of Lutheranism, however genuine the spiritual motivations, had distinct political and economic advantages. It freed principalities and cities from papal jurisdiction and taxation, while also challenging imperial authority and the diversion of German resources to other imperial territories.

So, while Luther himself was quick to denounce the peasant revolt against princes and other secular powers, his doctrine of obedience did not prevent princes themselves from mobilizing Lutheran theology – nor did it prevent Luther from supporting them – against the Holy Roman Empire. Their resistance could remain consistent with the doctrine of obedience because they launched their opposition not as private citizens resisting authority but rather as one competing temporal jurisdiction against another. Much the same would be true of Protestant urban elites, who challenged higher authorities not to defend the liberties of citizens so much as to assert the rights and jurisdictions of 'lesser' authorities against emperors and princes. At the same time, princes and civic elites could invoke the doctrine of obedience to secular authority in countering threats of rebellion from below.

In 1531, when Emperor Charles V threatened to suppress Lutheranism by military means, a group of principalities and cities, led by two powerful German princes, the Landgrave of Hesse and the Elector of Saxony, formed the Schmalkaldic League to defend the Protestant faith. A theory of resistance was devised, which invested in 'lesser magistrates' – the lower levels of imperial government, such as local civic officials – a right to resist by military force. It was made very clear that no such right belonged to private citizens: never again should there be such a thing as a peasant revolt. Indeed, the right to resist was less a right than an official duty.

Luther himself – belatedly and reluctantly – had come around to this point of view, having been repeatedly called upon by the Elector of Saxony and others to write in support of the princes' political moves against the

Empire or the Catholic Church. At first, he supported the princes on narrowly constitutional grounds, saying that if the lawyers were right in their interpretation of the imperial constitution and the rights of lesser officials, then the princes were entitled to resist the emperor. Even then he narrowly defined the right of those public authorities and explained his change of mind on the grounds that imperial law itself, that is, law imposed by the emperor himself, called for resistance to a notorious injustice wrought by government. For German princes and their supporters, resistance remained a prerogative of office, and the right of other authorities to repel force with force rested on the emperor's having himself become a rebel – whose punishment was clearly a duty of office. Even when the argument expanded from purely constitutional principles to arguments from natural law, the issue was still the rights of princes, or at least the right to disobey the orders of the emperor to take up arms against Protestants.[6] For Luther, if the private citizen had any rights, they almost certainly did not go beyond the citizen's right to join his prince's army against the emperor.

Later, under the influence of Calvin, who was himself – as we shall see – a strong advocate of secular obedience, this defence of Protestant religion against imperial threats would be transformed into a doctrine of secular resistance against any overweening royal power; but even then it remained – as in the Huguenot resistance tracts in France – not a declaration of individual freedom but, above all, an assertion of autonomous powers belonging to provincial nobles and civic officials.

John Calvin

The city of Geneva, where John Calvin would find his spiritual home, had, like other cities in the Holy Roman Empire, long been a battleground for power struggles among bishops, counts and dukes. In the Middle Ages, the bishop of Geneva had been a prince of the Empire; but there were constant battles between the bishops and other princely claimants, eager to gain

---

6   Luther was not above invoking natural law, if only on rhetorical grounds, but his theology did not lend itself to – and he avoided – a systematic theory of natural law. Lutheran theology, from its very first premise, makes appeals to natural law – for instance, in judging the legitimacy of any government – very problematic, since no Christian doctrine can, in Luther's view, be constructed on the assumption that a fallen humanity is capable of following, or even comprehending, divine will or natural law. Christian theology must always proceed from the premise of humanity's innate sinfulness. That is why, in his doctrine of justification by faith, salvation relies on a free gift of God and not on adherence to principles of Christian virtue. His doctrine of obedience to secular authority was constructed on the same premise, making it difficult to argue that obedience to secular authority depended on the virtue of the ruler.

access to the fruits of the city's commercial success. When the House of Savoy sought to turn Geneva into a duchy, the city countered the threat by joining the Swiss federation in 1526; but this union would soon be disrupted by a division between Catholic and Protestant cities. When Geneva finally asserted its autonomy as a republic in 1536, it did so under the banner of Protestantism, for obvious practical and economic no less than spiritual reasons, and managed to maintain its independence as a city-state against prevailing trends.

Calvin would arrive in Geneva the year of its establishment as a Protestant republic, and – except for a period of exile from 1538 to 1541 – he would stay there until his death in 1564. Born in France in 1509 as Jean Cauvin, he began his career as clerk to a bishop; intended for the priesthood, he studied philosophy in Paris, but then gave up the Church for the study of law. At the University of Bourges, he came under humanist influences. The exposure to humanism clearly played a major part in his religious conversion; and like other humanist reformers, he would soon abandon the Catholic Church. On his return to Paris, caught up in conflicts between the reformers and the orthodox Catholics, he was compelled to flee and in 1535 settled for a time in the Protestant city of Basle.

It was during his stay in Basle that Calvin, in 1536, published the first edition of his major life's work, the *Institutes of the Christian Religion*, a catechism of his faith and the principles of reformation to which he subscribed. Written first in Latin, it would later appear in French editions, which would have an enormous influence not only on theology but also on the French language. He would continue to edit and amplify this work throughout his life. On his return to Paris from Basle, finding his reforming views unwelcome in his native France, he set out for the free imperial city of Strasbourg; but, forced by circumstances to take a detour, he arrived in Geneva, and there he would remain.

Calvin settled in Geneva at the urging of another Frenchman, who invited him to join in reforming the Church. Their proposals for ecclesiastical reform, undertaken at the behest of civic authorities, were immediately accepted by the city council. Although Calvin would find himself in conflict with the council in 1538 and yet again forced into exile, the civic authorities of Geneva invited him to return in 1541 to carry on his project of reform. In November of that year, the council amended and passed the Ecclesiastical Ordinances drafted by Calvin, which spelled out the organization and functions of the Church in what amounted to a blueprint for a division of labour between civic and ecclesiastical jurisdictions in governing the city. The Ordinances struck a difficult balance between separating the functions of Church and state, allocating each its proper domain, and at the same time establishing a partnership between them in governing the city according to the principles of the reformed religion. There would be other moments of conflict and danger for Calvin, especially when some Genevan notables challenged the Ordinances, in opposition to the strict discipline imposed on them by both civic and ecclesiastical jurisdictions. But in the end, the so-called *libertines* were defeated and their leaders banished or executed.

It is difficult to disentangle Calvin's theological development from the evolution of his political consciousness. His first book, a commentary on Seneca's *De Clementia*, which he began writing while still a law student, was not a work of theology but a humanist essay on a classical text. Seneca's work, addressed to the emperor Nero, has been called a forerunner of what would become the humanist genre of 'mirrors for princes'. While it would be too much to say that Calvin's commentary was intended as a comparable lesson to Francis I, some of the essential principles of his later views on civil government already make an appearance here. There is, for instance, a significant note citing St Paul's Romans 13 to demonstrate that Christianity requires obedience to princes; and there are several references to princes as the vicars or delegates of God, an idea that would play a central part in his mature political theology. By the time he wrote the first edition of the *Institutes* after his conversion, his theological principles were already bound up with his views on civil government; and, whichever came first, Calvin's political ideas are securely grounded in the most fundamental tenets of his theology. The inextricable connection would be firmly sealed by his career in Geneva.

The first edition of the *Institutes* was introduced by an epistle dedicatory to Francis I of France, which presents the catechism that follows as a defence of the reformed religion against threats faced by French Evangelicals. In his effort to demonstrate that the reformed faith poses no threat to the king's authority, Calvin proceeds on two fronts: he seeks to show that the Roman Church, in its usurpations of temporal power, represents a more sinister challenge to the monarch's authority, while at the same time the theologian opposes radical reformers, notably the Anabaptists, who deny the legitimacy of civil governance. The book ends with a long chapter on civil government, which may be read as a continuation of his letter to the king; but it also confronts a different set of questions, posed not by the threat of the Catholic Church but by the distinctive relations between civic authority and a reformed Church within the free Protestant city.

It has been said that Calvin's theology, like that of Zwingli and Bucer, is 'the result of the Reformation message filtered through the actuality of the free city'.[7] It is true that the very specific relationship between secular and spiritual spheres that characterized the Protestant cities, where civic and ecclesiastical authority were both separate and intertwined in such

---

7 Bernd Moeller, *Imperial Cities and the Reformation* (Philadelphia: Fortress Press, 1972), p. 89.

distinctive ways, posed different problems for theology than those that preoccupied Luther. When Calvin wrote the first edition of the *Institutes*, he was certainly concerned with the fate of French Evangelicals under threat from the Catholic Church; but he was also compelled to address a very different set of questions, which did not have to do with the rival claims to temporal authority in conflicts between kings or German princes and the Holy Roman Empire or the papacy. While maintaining a distinction between secular and spiritual realms, he could not rely, as Luther did, on denying any jurisdiction to the Church; but nor could he simply assert the authority of secular government over the Church. He was obliged to explain the division of labour between secular and ecclesiastical authorities, both of which had an essential role in sustaining the reformed faith and both of which played a central role in governing the earthly city.

Political life in a city like Basle or Geneva thus placed a special burden on Protestant theology. For Luther, in a different context, it was enough to confine the functions of the Church to preaching the Word and administering certain sacraments, while asserting the exclusive jurisdictional claims of secular government against ecclesiastical pretensions, yet asking little more of earthly government than that it rein in a sinful humanity. His theology achieves this effect by stressing the simultaneous duality of sin and justification: God's loving grace 'justifies' humanity as a free and unearned gift, even while the sinfulness of human beings, their implication in the devil's 'kingdom', requires submission to secular government, which is divinely ordained.

Calvin may have been more reluctant to give secular governments a dominant authority over the Church; but within its own domain he demanded more of secular power than did Luther, and his views on civil government therefore required a different theology. He certainly shares the principal tenet of Lutheranism, the doctrine of justification by faith; but his emphasis is less on God's loving grace than on his total sovereignty.[8] While justification remains an unearned gift, which is not a reward for virtue, good works, or freedom from sin, the godly life of the Christian community is not just a matter of service and good works freely undertaken by the Christian faithful in answer to God's loving grace. It follows from God's unconditional will that Christians must in this world live a life of godly discipline.

Calvin's theology underwrites a partnership between secular and spiritual authorities, in which both, equally under the sovereignty of God, exercise temporal jurisdiction. This not only restores to the Church its own temporal authority but also elevates the role of civil government. Its function is not simply to maintain civil peace and good order among sinful human beings but, in a joint project with the Church, to impose a godly discipline on the

---

8   Francis Oakley, 'Christian Obedience and Authority', in *Cambridge History*, p. 182.

Christian community in recognition of God's total sovereignty. Civil government, in other words, is not just a divinely ordained institution to cope with the 'kingdom' of the devil as it manifests itself in human sinfulness. Civic authorities act together with the Church in the fulfillment of God's sovereign will. This means that, even while the Church ministers to the soul as civil government takes care of more mundane concerns (which include defending the true faith), there can be no clear distinction between the godly standards upheld by the Church and some kind of lesser, more modest, less divine criteria applied to civic life.

Calvin's doctrine of predestination may seem to complicate the issue. After all, if human beings are damned or saved through no fault or virtue of their own, what can it mean to demand of them that they live according to the dictates of a godly discipline? Yet if we start not with predestination but with God's sovereign will, the logic of Calvin's argument may be easier to trace: the doctrine of predestination – the idea that our fate depends entirely, without condition, on God's determination – follows directly from the notion of God's total and unconditional sovereignty, as does the idea of godly discipline and the role of both jurisdictional spheres in maintaining it.

It is almost as if Calvin arrives at his doctrine of predestination less because it expresses his deepest convictions than because it seems an unavoidable consequence of God's total sovereignty, which is central to his views on the role of the Church and civil government. In the *Institutes,* the argument for predestination – the predestination of the damned no less than of the elect – comes down to this: we must believe in it, because to do otherwise is to detract from the glory of a totally sovereign God. But, in Calvin's view, there is little to be gained by dwelling on it. Precisely because it represents God's unconditional sovereign will, which cannot be understood or judged by any human standards, it must remain a mystery; and we should not attempt to penetrate God's judgment on our own fate in the afterlife. The best that Christians can do, in their humility and unconditional obedience to God, is to act in this world with confidence in the goodness and generosity of God's justification, proceeding in their earthly callings as if they and their fellows belonged to the elect, with faith that not only their souls but their works are justified by divine grace.

Christians, then, must serve their community in accordance with the principles of godly discipline. This certainly elevates earthly callings to a new respectability and even grants an element of godliness to the most humble human labours. But, while Calvin's idea of the calling, more than Luther's, invites the faithful to take an active part in shaping the social and political conditions of their lives on this earth, it also means that civil governments must be regarded as representatives of God; and this carries with it a strong obligation to obedience: 'When those who bear the office of magistrate are called gods, let no one suppose that there is little weight in that appellation. It is thereby intimated that they have a commission from God, that they are invested with divine authority and, in fact, represent the person of God, as whose substitutes they in a manner act' (IV.20.4). It follows that Christians owe obedience to civil government, and even tyrants must be treated as the delegates of God: 'even an individual of the worst character, one most unworthy of all honour, if invested with public authority, receives that illustrious divine power which the Lord has by his word devolved on the ministers of his justice and judgment, and that, accordingly, in so far as public obedience is concerned, he is to be held in the same honour and reverence as the best of kings' (IV.20.25). Christians should obey secular government not simply out of fear 'but because the obedience which they yield is rendered to God himself, inasmuch as their power is from God' (IV.20.22).

Nevertheless, if Calvin's doctrine of obedience to civil authority seems hardly less, or even more, stringent than Luther's, his roots in the free Protestant city do make a difference. When considering the various forms of government, he expresses a preference for collective governments instead of kings, if only on the grounds that human imperfections make it useful to have magistrates who can keep an eye on one another. The ideal might be a city like Geneva, governed by civic elites through the medium of magistrates and city councillors, who have an official duty to preserve the city's liberty. This means that, on the whole, aristocracy is best, or perhaps a mixed constitution in which aristocracy is leavened by an element of popular government. There is nonetheless, Calvin tells us, no point in discussing which government is best, since that depends on circumstances; and, in any case, we must assume that, whatever the prevailing type of government in any given circumstance, it was decreed by God. While the Lord may take vengeance against 'unbridled domination', 'let us not therefore suppose that that vengeance is committed to us, to whom no command has been given but to obey and suffer' (IV.20 31).

There seems to be no ambiguity in Calvin's views on strict obedience, but here he introduces a qualification that would have major consequences for political theory. 'I speak', he says, 'only of private men'; because there have existed public offices – presumably decreed by God – whose duty it has been 'to curb the tyranny of kings', such as the Ephori in Sparta, the tribunate in Rome, the Demarchs in Athens, and perhaps even the assembled three estates in a kingdom like France (IV.20.31). It has been the public duty of these 'lesser magistrates' to defend the people against the tyranny of rulers. Although Calvin himself would never go beyond the observation that there have existed public offices whose official duty is to represent the interests of the people as a check on princely power, the doctrine of the 'lesser magistrate' would become the basis of more wide-ranging and militant resistance theories.

That doctrines supporting the power of temporal authorities, and even the need for obedience to them, could be mobilized in support of resistance to power and even popular rebellion is a peculiarity of Western culture. Other societies have certainly created doctrines of rebellion, but they took a very special form in Western Europe. The fragmentation of political power in feudal Europe, and the constant jurisdictional battles that followed from it for centuries thereafter, produced quite distinctive effects. The assertion of one jurisdiction against another could be formulated as a right to resist illegitimate power or tyranny. While this meant that ideas of resistance could be adopted and disseminated by ruling classes, landlords and civic elites, it also meant that their interests would shape and constrain Western conceptions of democracy, in ways that persist to this day.

Protestantism and the Rise of Capitalism?

What, then, should we make of the proposition that Protestantism had something to do with the 'rise of capitalism'? It is certainly true that Lutheranism became a powerful force when it established itself in great commercial centres. It is also true that, in some commercial cities, where urban patriciates had become rentiers instead of active merchants and where they restricted access to the political domain, burghers and new merchants without political privileges might use Protestant doctrine to challenge patrician dominance. It may even be true that Protestantism, and Calvinism in particular, removed ecclesiastical constraints on commercial activities, or that Protestant doctrine, and especially Calvin's doctrine of the calling, called into question old verities about the unworthiness of commercial pursuits and the acquisition of wealth, or about work as a curse and simply a punishment for original sin. But, even if we accept that Protestantism promoted a 'work ethic' or that it had certain benefits for merchants, and even if we set aside its equal usefulness to nobles, princes and kings, its bearing on the 'spirit of capitalism' is another matter altogether.

Let us first be clear about what is meant by capitalism and the conditions of its 'rise'. Conventional wisdom – and, indeed, a great deal of scholarly work – treats the rise of capitalism as little more than the quantitative growth of commerce or exchange for profit. Capitalism, in other words, is 'commercial society' as understood by classical political economy, a society in which commercial practices that have existed since time immemorial have, with the expansion of cities, markets and trade, become the economic norm. Human beings have, time out of mind, engaged in profitable exchange, and capitalism is just more of the same. This means that, if the birth of capitalism requires any explanation, all that needs to be explained is the growth of market opportunities and the removal of obstacles to the expansion of commerce.

Yet this understanding of capitalism takes no account of the very specific economic principles that came into being in early modern Europe, principles very different from anything that had existed before even in the most commercialized societies: not simply the growth of market opportunities with the expansion of vast trading networks, but the emergence of wholly new *compulsions*, the inescapable imperatives of competition, profit-maximization, constant accumulation and the endless need to reduce the costs of labour by improving labour productivity. These imperatives did not operate in the age-old practices of commercial exchange even in its most elaborate forms. Traders made their fortunes not by means of cost-effective production in integrated competitive markets but rather by negotiating separate markets, the 'buying cheap and selling dear' that was the essence of pre-capitalist commerce. A revolutionary transformation of relations between producing and appropriating classes, as well as changes in the nature of property, would be required to set in train the imperatives of the capitalist market – as happened in English agrarian capitalism

Once we identify capitalism with market *imperatives*, the search for its origins must take a different form. The question then becomes not how commercial opportunities expanded and economies were freed to take advantage of them, or even how the cultural and moral climate changed to justify pursuit of profit, but rather how social arrangements and the production of basic human needs were so fundamentally transformed as to impose compulsions and necessities unlike any that had governed human social life before.

This is not a question addressed by the most influential advocates of the view that Protestantism in one way or another promoted the development of capitalism – Max Weber and R.H. Tawney – nor, indeed, by their later supporters and critics. Both traced the evolution of Protestantism, especially in its Calvinist form, into a particular variety of Puritanism, especially in England, that encouraged 'capitalist' values and practices; but neither of them actually argued that Protestantism *caused* the emergence of capitalism. It would be fair to say that in both arguments the development of Protestantism into a doctrine favouring capitalism (in the sense they understood it) *presupposes* the existence of certain forms of property and economic practices that, if not already fully 'capitalist' (in their terms), are 'capitalist' in embryo and mark a significant break from feudal forms and principles.

Weber was perhaps more inclined than Tawney to emphasize the growth of cities and the process of commercialization, while Tawney, despite a more or less conventional association of capitalism with the commercial classes, had a greater interest than did Weber in the transformations of landed property which took place in England as a precursor to commercial and industrial capitalism.[9] Tawney may go further than Weber in tracing the transformation of Calvinism into a capitalist-friendly Puritanism, and he certainly is clearer about the ways in which existing economic practices shaped the formation of religious ideas. But both suggest that, if there had not already existed property forms and classes disposed to operate on 'capitalist' principles, Protestant doctrine would not and could not have been – selectively – appropriated and adapted to the 'spirit of capitalism'. Without these pre-existing elements of 'capitalism' there could, by definition, have been no 'elective affinity' (as Weber himself described it) between Protestantism and capitalism.

The argument being offered here departs from both Weber and Tawney not because it gives 'material' factors priority over ideas. Neither the German sociologist nor the English historian treats religious ideas as autonomous and primary, as against material determinants; and both have complex understandings of causality. Nor does the present book deny complex interactions of causation or the efficacy of ideas. Where it differs most fundamentally from other views on the connection between Protestantism and the rise of capitalism is that it insists, in a way the others do not, on the specificity of capitalism, its radical rupture from preceding social forms, including earlier forms of commerce. However much Weber and Tawney emphasize the break from feudal practices and attitudes, they both take for granted that capitalism is an extension of commerce, which already existed in the interstices of feudalism (and, indeed, before). The rise of capitalism, in this view, took place when and because commercial classes and the practices of commerce were liberated and encouraged to grow by the removal of obstacles – institutional, cultural or attitudinal – and/or by the construction of ethical supports for commercial profit-taking that were lacking before.

---

9   More than a decade before the publication of *Religion and the Rise of Capitalism*, Tawney published his great work, *The Agrarian Problem in the Sixteenth Century*, which clearly outlines the new market principles that were already driving English agriculture before the advent of Puritanism. Just as Tawney's work on religion should be read against the background of that book, so too should Weber's *Protestant Ethic and the Spirit of Capitalism* be situated in his whole body of work on economic history and especially his writings on the city. Although Weber sees elements of 'capitalism' even in ancient Rome, the medieval city, in his view, prefigured modern industrial capitalism when and because it became a 'centre of production' and not just of consumption, as it was, he maintains, in classical antiquity. But this development seems to have been for him a natural consequence of the liberation and political elevation of burgher classes in the medieval West. There is a question-begging slippage at precisely the critical juncture in the argument, since the work ethic that, in Weber's account, encouraged modern industrial capitalism is, in his account, nothing more than an elaboration of the age-old principles of profitable exchange, for the first time given free rein and positive ethical support. For more on this point, see Ellen Meiksins Wood, *Democracy Against Capitalism: Renewing Historical Materialism* (Cambridge: Cambridge University Press, 1995), Ch. 5.

The argument in this book, by contrast, starts from the premise that capitalism represents a fundamental break from other forms of commerce no less than from what Weber and Tawney regard as 'feudal' – that is, in their terms, non-commercial – principles and practices.

Seen from this perspective, the historic role of Protestantism looks rather different. On the one hand, whatever we may say about the usefulness of certain Calvinist principles in sustaining a philosophy of life congenial to commercial profit, it tells us very little about the rise of capitalism. We may place our emphasis, as Weber does, on a 'work ethic' more or less directly derived from Calvin's ideas of predestination, 'limited atonement' and the 'calling'; or we may stress, as Tawney does, the revolutionary Puritan modification of Calvinism that discarded one essential aspect of Calvin's own doctrine, its commitment to a godly discipline and even a kind of collectivism, in favour of an economic individualism. Either one or both may tell us something (though even here a certain caution is required) about strategies of self-justification adopted by people seeking to avail themselves of market opportunities or about psychological adaptations to the uncertainties of commerce. But neither tells us anything about the systemic *imperatives* imposed on capitalists, which compel them to maximize profit, whatever their own motivations and values and however limited their greed.

At the same time, if we acknowledge the specificity of capitalist imperatives, we may be more inclined to consider the ways in which Protestantism had less to do with capitalism or even a commercial ethic than with the maintenance of power in distinctly non-capitalist forms. In the case of England, where capitalist social property relations did emerge, it might be possible to speak of an 'elective affinity' between Protestantism and capitalism, if only in the sense that *all* forms of English Protestantism, including High Church Anglicanism no less than Cromwell's Puritanism, were shaped by the specificities of property and state in England. But this specific case should not be allowed to obscure the distinctly non-capitalist origin and substance of the Reformation.

Luther's theology served the purposes of German princes, but it was also deployed by civic magistrates and became a major historical force when adopted by important commercial cities. Yet Lutheranism emerged at a time when Germany's commercial cities were in a process of decline. The Hanseatic League's domination of trade in Northern Europe was giving way to rising powers, such as the Swedish and the Dutch; and the independence of some cities was threatened by territorial princes with stronger military force at their disposal, not least the princes of the Church endowed with the powers and prerogatives of secular rulers. Maintaining civic autonomy became an ever more costly business, which aggravated social tensions between urban patriciates and other classes that were subject to burdensome exactions. Civic magistrates defended their city's autonomy by challenging the authority of emperors and princes and often pursued anti-clerical policies to avoid the burdens imposed by ecclesiastical jurisdiction. Burghers demanded a share in civic governance against dominant urban patriciates; and urban elites asserted their rule against threats from below. In all these battles Lutheran doctrine proved distinctively useful, for reasons that had nothing to do with the 'spirit of capitalism'.

Much the same can be said of Calvinism. Calvin's theology was eminently suited to the needs of civic magistrates, not because of anything to do with the doctrine of predestination, the calling or the 'work ethic', but rather because of his elaborate discussion of civil government, to which a large part of the *Institutes* is devoted, promoting the idea that magistrates are 'gods'. This doctrine had direct and obvious implications for the civic governance of Calvin's Geneva. Yet the very same principles that made Calvinist doctrine so useful to civic magistrates could as easily be, and were, applied to other secular authorities seeking to preserve their extra-economic powers, at a time when the economic interests of all classes were (in sharp contrast to capitalism) dependent on political status and privilege, or 'politically constituted property'. Just as Lutheranism could be mobilized in the interests of princes no less than of civic authorities, so too did Calvinism, for all Calvin's devotion to his adopted city and its civic institutions, serve the purposes of French provincial nobles or even English kings.

THE SPANISH EMPIRE

In the 1530s, in his lectures at the University of Salamanca, the Spanish Dominican theologian Francisco de Vitoria presented an interesting variation on Western Christianity's defining principle about the rightful domains of Caesar and God. 'In this way and by this title', he said,

> the Roman Empire was enlarged and extended – that is, by taking over by law of war the cities and provinces of enemies from whom they had received any injury; and yet the Roman Empire is defended as just and legitimate by Augustine, Jerome, Ambrose, St Thomas, and by other holy doctors. In fact, it may be seen as approved by our Lord and Redeemer Jesus Christ in that famous passage: 'Render therefore unto Caesar the things which are Caesar's. etc.', and by Paul, who appealed to Caesar (Acts 25: 10) and advised us (Romans 13) to be subject to the higher powers and to be subject to the princes and render them their tributes – all of which princes at that time had their authority from the Roman Empire. (*De Indis et de jure belli*, III.56)

The principle of 'render unto Caesar' was here being invoked not simply, in the customary Western Christian way, as a warrant for obedience to secular authorities but more particularly as, apparently, a defence of empire. Vitoria's stance on Spain's far-flung empire remained ambiguous. He has been variously cited both against the imperial regime and, at least ambivalently, in its favour; but his lectures at the University of Salamanca elaborated doctrines that would have considerable significance for European political thought and its conceptions of natural law, natural rights, the law of war, and international law.

In the decades following Vitoria's lectures, there would be a flowering of Spanish political thought; and, if there is one defining feature that distinguishes this tradition of discourse from others among Spain's European neighbours, it is that the central questions confronted by the so-called School of Salamanca arose not just from jurisdictional disputes between a centralizing state and various 'parcellized sovereignties' but from Spain's distinctive experience of imperial expansion. Reflecting on empire and the treatment of indigenous peoples had the effect, among other things, of putting on the agenda ideas of natural rights residing in the individual that went beyond what the tradition of Western political thought had yet been able to contemplate in its reflections on the state.

State or Empire?

Spain in the sixteenth century has been called Europe's, even the world's, most powerful nation. Yet this claim can hardly be ascribed to its preeminence in forging a 'modern' or unified national state, with more or less unambiguous sovereignty over its domestic territory, or at least a reasonably well delineated sphere of national jurisdiction. It is certainly true that Ferdinand and Isabella challenged the independent powers of the nobility and did much to establish a strong monarchy in Spain, while weakening the *cortes*, descended from what has been called the first Parliament in Western Europe. Not the least of their efforts in strengthening monarchical authority was their institution of the Spanish Inquisition, which, whatever else it may have done, was clearly intended to replace papal hegemony over religious orthodoxy in Spain with control by the Catholic monarchy. Their successors would continue the centralizing project; but even in the imperial golden age of the Habsburg rule of Charles I and thereafter, the Spanish state was still a tenuous national entity. Its constitutive elements were two very distinct and autonomous kingdoms, Castile and Aragon, with their own very distinct political institutions and traditions.

When the two ruling families united to form a single royal state, each kingdom brought to the union its internal jurisdictional conflicts among parcellized sovereignties, corporate, local and regional. The kingdom of Aragon was a federation consisting of several separate realms, not least Catalonia, with its own jurisdictional tensions, a well-developed feudal structure, and the so-called *pactisme,* in which the power of the central authority was constrained by more or less contractual agreements with the aristocracy. The kingdom of Castile, which led the imperial project, had no strong tradition of feudal lordship; but war with the Moors had produced not only a class of warlords with fairly autonomous powers over the kingdom's expanding territories in Spain but also an armed class of small proprietors. The medieval *reconquista*, recapturing Moorish lands in Europe, had been less the work of a powerful kingdom than a partnership not unlike the classic feudal exchange between monarch and military leaders, in which conditional rights of property and jurisdiction had been vested in the lord in exchange for military services. In the early modern period, a very large proportion of Spain remained outside royal jurisdiction: in 1600 two-thirds of its towns and half of its villages were under private control, while the king had no standing army and no bureaucracy or civil service, generally farmed out taxes, and governed his provinces with the cooperation of elites.[1] The royal state would produce bureaucracies both at home and in the colonies, but the weakness of state sovereignty in Spain remained a constant theme throughout our period.

The Spanish nonetheless created the largest overseas empire the world had ever seen. This would become the essence of the kingdom's wealth and power. Its prosperity depended above all else on gold and silver from the colonies; and this wealth, together with growing colonial demand, did for a time fuel the economy at home. Colonial wealth undoubtedly strengthened the position of Spain in its conflicts with other European kingdoms, such as the French. Yet even in its massive empire the weakness of Spain as a national entity, political or economic, was on display. The circulation of colonial wealth in external trade would come to be controlled less by Spanish traders than by merchants in Genoa and Antwerp, and the weaknesses of the royal state were reproduced in colonial governance.

Imperial expansion in the Americas was modelled on the reconquest of European lands from the Moors and its spread into Africa and the Canaries. While it is certainly true that Spanish monarchs always sought to protect their own royal powers and succeeded in preventing the emergence of a hereditary feudal aristocracy in the colonies, they presided over Spain's massive imperial expansion by farming out the tasks of empire to private conquerors in pursuit of private wealth. Just as the process of royal centralization would be constantly dogged by domestic conflicts over jurisdiction, so too would the empire be marked from beginning to end by the tensions between monarchs and private conquerors or their heirs in the colonial landed classes.

Imperial expansion was achieved with a remarkably small military force, and the Spanish military presence in the colonies was never very large. Nor was the conquest intended to exterminate indigenous peoples in order to occupy their lands. With Spain's dependence on gold and silver from mines in the Americas, the imperial rulers had more to gain from preserving the local population and exploiting its labour. The civilizations they encountered ranged from nomadic hunter-gatherers to densely populated, socially stratified and technologically complex empires; and, while the conquest destroyed these advanced civilizations, the conquerors stood to benefit from their technologies, their agricultural skills and their experience of large-scale public projects.[2] Nonetheless, whatever its intentions, the conquest

---

1 Henry Kamen, *Spain 1469–1714: A Society of Conflict* (Harlow: Pearson/Longman, 3rd edn, 2005), p. 160.

2 On the Latin American peoples encountered by the conquerors, see Mark A. Burkholder and Lyman L. Johnson, *Colonial Latin America* (Oxford: Oxford University Press, 4th edn, 2001).

would prove genocidal, spreading disease and imposing a brutally destructive system of exploitation.

The Spanish monarchy may have succeeded in its efforts to prevent the formation of a feudal aristocracy in the colonies and to avoid the emergence of representative institutions like the *cortes*, but there remained the problem of commanding the subject labour force. Here the Spanish state had to strike a difficult balance between controlling local landholders and allowing them the power to exploit the Indians. Having outlawed formal slavery in 1500, the colonial power produced the *encomienda* system, modelled on the settlement of recaptured Moorish lands in Europe.

In theory, the *encomienda* was not a grant of land to colonial settlers. The Indians were subjected to tributary labour, ostensibly in exchange for religious education and military protection by the settlers; but the indigenous people were in principle recognized as owners of the land, even while nearby plantations might belong to the *encomendero* and be worked by the same Indians. Nor did the *encomendero* have formally acknowledged political jurisdiction over the indigenous population. But, in practice, these formal limits on the *encomendero*'s ownership of land and on his jurisdiction had little effect in containing the settlers' control over their subjects or in moderating the harshness of the system. It became a murderously extreme form of exploitation, little short of slavery and responsible for killing huge numbers of Indians. In the Caribbean it destroyed itself within a generation, while its persistence elsewhere continued to arouse opposition both from the Church and, if inconsistently, even from the royal state, which had its own reasons for seeking to check the powers of *encomenderos*. But when laws were passed to modify or abolish the system, they had little effect. The *encomienda* long remained, in one form or another, a defining feature of Spanish imperial rule, leaving its mark on other colonial forms of landownership and labour.

The monarchy did implant local administrations to counteract the power of the settlers. In Peru, for instance, it created an elaborate state bureaucracy in large part for the purpose of regulating forced labour in the mines. But the Spanish state was never able to govern its colonial territories without permitting local landed classes to dominate the land and its people. Even the all-important gold and silver eluded the royal grasp. The Crown, finding it impossible to exploit this source of huge wealth on its own, was compelled to relinquish its hold on the mines, giving them up to local ownership or leasing them out in exchange for a share of the yield.

Spain's growing dependence on bullion imported from the colonies, instead of on domestic agriculture and industry, and even at the cost of colonial production, has often been blamed for the decline of the Spanish economy from the seventeenth century onward. But, however important such factors may be in explaining the dramatic decline of what for a time had been the greatest imperial power the world had yet seen, it is also true that there was from the start an inherent instability in this world empire. It depended for its dominance neither on a powerful political and military force, nor even on commercial strengths, but rather on vesting powers in colonial landed classes. The later rebellions of colonial ruling classes and the wars of independence that were to follow had less to do with the emergence of a revolutionary bourgeoisie in the colonies, as some historical accounts suggest, than with the legacy of the uneasy colonial balance between a distant imperial state, with a tenuous hold on its own domestic sovereignty, and local power based on landed property.

The School of Salamanca

Spain was a world empire long before it was a proper 'nation state'; and that distinctive reality is clearly reflected in Spanish political thought. The usual Western European jurisdictional disputes – between ecclesiastical and secular authorities, or among monarchs, popes, Holy Roman Emperors, aristocracies, and municipal elites – were certainly all present. The historical moment in which the Salamanca School began to flourish was the reign of Charles I, the grandson of Ferdinand and Isabella, who became the Holy Roman Emperor Charles V; and this period, as we have seen, was fraught with tensions between emperor and pope, as well as German princes, to say nothing of the rivalries among the rising European kingdoms and the always looming Turkish threat. But, in Spanish political thought, these conflicts were typically filtered through the preoccupations of empire. Other rulers, like the French or the English, might claim to be 'emperors' in their own kingdoms; and this would shape European conceptions of sovereignty. But, in the Spanish case, the imperial idea had less to do with the sovereignty of the royal state at home, where its powers were limited by various more or less explicitly contractual relations with competing jurisdictions, than with the colonial domination of far-flung territories and their indigenous peoples.

The contested sovereignty that plagued other monarchs, such as the French, certainly encouraged theoretical debates about what constitutes legitimate political authority, but in Spain the empire raised especially sharp questions. It was one thing for the king to claim *dominium* over his kingdom at home as if it were his private household. It was quite another matter to assert his domination over distant colonial territories and their indigenous populations, especially those with their own complex modes of organization and governance. The 'high' civilizations of the Americas made it more difficult to invoke traditional conceptions of domestic lordship or natural hierarchy. Defenders of the empire and the *encomienda* system did, to be sure, appeal to Aristotle's conception of natural slavery; but Indians with elaborate technologies and complex forms of government were not so easily dismissed as slaves by nature or as irrational creatures, subject to the authority of their natural superiors; and claims to empire on these grounds were contested almost from the beginning. Once even their lack of Christian belief had been challenged as a justification for subjecting indigenous peoples to imperial domination, it became that much more pressing to confront fundamental questions about how legitimate rule should be defined. The Spanish mode of imperial expansion had created its own ideological needs, and Spanish political thinkers had particular reasons to reflect on the natural rights of colonial subjects or the limits imposed on their imperial masters by natural law.

The Reformation, and especially the translation of Protestant doctrine into theories of resistance, would pose problems for the Spanish royal state engaged in a contested process of centralization, as it did for other European monarchies, notably the French. But the realities of imperial conquest presented a distinctive challenge. Debate on this subject preceded the Reformation and would help to shape the Spanish Counter-Reformation. The huge influx of silver and gold would have been enough to generate fierce debate among theologians long accustomed to disputes about the rightful attitude of Christians towards property and wealth;[3] and the Spanish would, among other things, produce innovative theories of money and exchange, which have even been credited as the origin of modern economics. But the fact that imperial wealth was acquired by brute force made its defence even more complicated. While the empire was won by relatively small military forces, there was no mistaking Spanish America as anything but an empire of conquest. It may have been less deliberately murderous than the English colonial project in North America, which was shamelessly intended to clear the land for settlers; yet – or perhaps for that very reason – the Spanish, dependent as they were on ruling and exploiting a large and visible mass of indigenous labour, found it harder to disguise the nature of their imperial enterprise.

Defenders of imperial domination were unambiguously explicit that what they were justifying was indeed conquest, in contrast to the peaceful virtues of commerce and agriculture that would be invoked to support (no less bloody) English, and to some extent French, imperial ventures.[4] At the same time, since Spanish imperial rule was being imposed, and by violent means, on high civilizations with their own complex modes of governance,

---

3 See my *Citizens to Lords*, esp. pp. 182–6 for a discussion of medieval debates on property, particularly between Franciscan and Dominican theologians.

4 For an illuminating discussion of Spanish imperialist ideology, in contrast to British and French, see Anthony Pagden, *Lords of All the World: Ideologies of Empire in Spain, Britain and France c. 1500–1800* (New Haven: Yale University Press, 1995).

the defence of conquest was more difficult, raising fundamental questions about the property and sovereignty, indeed the rationality and natural rights, of colonial victims.

The complexities were greatly aggravated by their implication in the usual jurisdictional disputes. Early justifications of the empire were based on donation from the pope, but the uneasy relations between the monarchy and the papacy, especially when Charles became the Holy Roman Emperor and found himself in conflict with the pope, made papal donation an awkward defence. Papal donation was also vigorously challenged by Spain's European rivals, contesting Spanish claims to imperial territories, which made it even more useful to find alternative justifications.

Under Holy Roman imperial rule, the Empire could be presented as something like a mission on behalf of a universal empire or the Christian world order, much as the ancient Roman Empire had claimed to be acting on behalf of a universal world order; but theological arguments against the claims of the papacy, which worked in favour of the monarchy, tended also to argue against the 'universal empire' and against the Spanish conquest. Theologians of the Salamanca School argued that the pope, though he was the spiritual leader of Christendom, had no temporal authority over the world, nor did the pope – or the Church he represented – have authority of any kind over non-Christians. This could be taken to mean that there was no such thing as a universal 'holy' temporal empire, but it also cast doubt on the defence of conquest on the grounds that it was bringing Christianity to infidels or punishing savages for violations of natural law.

The Spanish crown also had other reasons for encouraging such arguments against colonial oppression, with or without its conflicts with the papacy. In its attempts to control the feudal ambitions of colonial settlers and to prevent the emergence of a hereditary aristocracy in America, it had very practical reasons for welcoming attacks on the *encomendero*'s brutality and on the *encomienda* system itself. The restrictions imposed by the monarchy on the growth of slavery and its attempts to abolish the *encomienda* system may have been in part genuinely motivated by ethical and religious concerns, but there can be little doubt that the effort to curtail the independent power of the settlers was an overriding consideration.

Whether motivated by humanitarian revulsion at imperial atrocities or simply defending the monarchy, powerful arguments were launched by theologians and jurists challenging Spanish domination in the Americas; and this forced defenders of empire to change their strategies. It was a particularly delicate business for monarchist defenders of empire, who were obliged to attack the *encomenderos* without undermining the monarch's imperial claims. They might accept that the Church or the papacy had no universal temporal authority, but then turn – as is suggested by Vitoria in his observations about God and Caesar – to less grandiose claims and especially to the concept of 'just war'.

The 'just war' tradition had, from its roots in antiquity, been notoriously elastic, encompassing everything up to and including the most aggressive and predatory imperial adventures. Throughout its various permutations, the doctrine of just war enunciates a few basic requirements for going to war: there must be a just cause; war must be declared by a proper authority and with the right intention, and after other means have been exhausted; there must be a reasonable chance of achieving the desired end, and the means must be proportionate to that end. Yet these apparently stringent requirements would be made compatible with the most aggressive wars of imperial expansion and, later, commercial rivalry. The idea of just war had already done service in the *reconquista,* when the victors elaborated intricate codes for dealing with, and even enslaving, their victims.

Colonialism in the Americas, then, might not be justified on the grounds of papal decree or the Church's temporal authority; but, argued supporters of the conquest, there were various legitimate reasons for waging war. A 'just war' might be necessary to defend the 'innocent' or, much more broadly, to promote the values of 'civilized' life, in self-defence or on behalf of a universal 'human republic' threatened by behaviour that violated standards of peace and good order or impeded free commerce. Any conquest resulting from a just war could establish legitimate domination, which could be defined so broadly as even to justify slavery.

The debate began in the earliest days of the conquest. In 1493, Pope Alexander VI (the infamous father of the even more infamous Cesare Borgia) issued a papal pronouncement that was meant to settle disputes between Portuguese and Spanish claims to imperial lands. By 'papal donation', Spain was granted land in the Americas. From the beginning there were questions about papal jurisdiction; but even for those unwilling to challenge the pope's authority, or indeed the Spanish monarchy's right to rule colonial territories, ambiguities in the pope's proclamation generated passionate debate about whether he was sanctioning colonization by violent means – that is, by means of 'just war' – or simply the peaceful conversion of heathens. In either case, what is unambiguously clear is the pope's assumption that Spain did indeed have the right to establish its colonies and not only a right but an obligation to impose the Christian faith.

This controversy would figure decades later in the most famous debate – the Vallidolid debate of 1550–51 between Bartolomé de Las Casas and Juan Ginés de Sepúlveda – about the Spanish colonial regime. By this time, the debate was taking place against the background of growing controversy over the treatment of Indians. In 1511, a year after the Dominicans arrived in the colonies, a friar of the order, Antonio Montesino, had given a ground-breaking sermon addressed to the settlers and *encomenderos*. 'Tell me', he demanded,

> by what right and justice do you keep these Indians in such cruel and horrible servitude? On what authority have you waged a detestable war on these people who dwelt quietly and peacefully on their own land? . . . Are these not men? Have they not rational souls? Must not you love them as you love yourselves?

Las Casas had himself been an *encomendero;* and even when, partly under the influence of Montesino, he came to oppose the existing system of labour in the Americas, he would for a time support the enslavement of Africans. But, while he never opposed imperial expansion and remained convinced that Indians should be converted to Christianity, he became a forceful and consistent critic of the *encomienda* system and conversion by force of arms. His views certainly had their effects on Spanish opinion and influenced the Laws of Burgos, passed in 1512–13 to regulate the system, but these had little practical effect in improving the condition of the Indians and were still clearly based on the assumption that the conquest was legitimate. The brutal regime of *encomiendas* continued unchecked.

Las Casas would elaborate a powerful argument in support of the view that the Indians were rational beings with a complex civilization and capable of peaceful conversion. His views, although not yet spelled out as systematically as they would be in the Vallidolid debate, clearly influenced Pope Paul III. In 1537 the pope issued a papal bull proclaiming that 'the Indians are truly men and that they are not only capable of understanding the Catholic Faith but, according to our information, they desire exceedingly to receive it . . .' '[T]he said Indians', the pope went on,

> and all other people who may later be discovered by Christians, are by no means to be deprived of their liberty or the possession of their property, even though they be outside the faith of Jesus Christ; and that they may and should, freely and legitimately, enjoy their liberty and the possession of their property; nor should they be in any way enslaved; should the contrary happen, it shall be null and have no effect.

While this did not explicitly revoke Alexander's earlier edict, it could be so interpreted (though battles to persuade the Vatican to revoke it explicitly have continued to this day). At the same time, it could be, and was, understood by some to leave open the possibility of legitimate conquest – that is, a just war – to impose Christianity on those who proved themselves unable or unwilling to receive it peacefully.

Although Las Casas remained convinced that Christians had a duty to convert the Indians, in 1539 he presented to the royal court a shocking account of Spanish brutality. This would lead to the New Laws of 1542, intended to regulate the *encomienda* system more stringently; but these laws would be fiercely opposed by the *encomenderos* and would, in the end, do little to transform the system. If critics like Las Casas had limited effects in practice, they did set the terms of theoretical debate. In the same year that Las Casas reported so dramatically on the condition of the Indians, Francisco Vitoria delivered the lectures at the University of Salamanca that would be published as *On the Indians and the Law of War* (*De Indis et De Jure Belli*, extracts from his *Relectiones Theologicae XII*). Although Vitoria is commonly cited as an opponent of the empire, his argument can be seen as a response to critics of the *encomienda* system like Las Casas. While Las Casas's views on the Indians' rights of dominion went far enough to challenge any colonial claims to their lands, Vitoria may have been seeking to salvage the strongest case possible for imperial conquest, once the humanity and rationality of Indians had been conceded; or, to put it another way, he may have wanted to formulate an argument that would sustain the imperial legitimacy of the Spanish crown while undermining the *encomenderos*. This may help to explain some inconsistencies and ambiguities in Vitoria's arguments; but even if we read him as an apologist for empire rather than a critic, it was precisely this confrontation with the question of empire that pushed the theory of natural rights beyond its medieval limits. The Dominican friar would be credited with pioneering international law on the strength of the *Relectiones*; and the debates on empire impelled him, and others in the School of Salamanca, to elaborate on medieval conceptions of natural law and natural rights in ways that would have significant effects on the development of Western political thought.

It needs to be emphasized that something like an idea of individual natural rights, with medieval roots, was already well established by the sixteenth century. What was not so well established was its effect on questions of state power, or, more precisely, its implications for limiting state power. Medieval theologians and jurists had left a legacy in which it was not the function of individual rights to decide the contest among competing domestic jurisdictions. Nor was the doctrine meant to establish a right of resistance to overweening royal power. There were, to be sure, thinkers prepared, *in extremis,* to countenance tyrannicide committed by individuals; and radical sects would emerge that justified resistance to any princely power. But in the mainstream of European political thought, the normal right to resist or limit monarchical power would still in the sixteenth century typically be based not on individual rights but on the jurisdictional claims of corporate bodies, municipal authorities, or local aristocracies.

The appeal to certain transcendent principles beyond the civic sphere – the assertion of some kind of moral claim available to human beings that was not derived from positive law or civil authority – would later be elaborated in modern theories of resistance or limited government. But the doctrine of right in its medieval form was, if anything, more likely to be used in *defence* of royal power, especially against the papacy. The idea that government derives its authority from the 'people' was compatible with a broad range of political commitments, including the conviction that monarchical power should be virtually unlimited. The idea that the 'people' – as a corporate entity – was the ultimate source of authority was likely to be invoked less as a limitation on state power than in support of monarchical authority, in particular against the papacy. It was precisely on the grounds that the monarch derived his authority from the people that he had jurisdiction over the secular domain, which the pope could not claim.

The right of private ownership could also, in medieval thought, easily coexist with a conception of the political community as constituted by corporate entities. Even when the state was conceived as accountable to individual propertyholders, this could, in medieval terms, still mean that the state was constituted by, and accountable to, the 'people' as a corporate entity, or even a collection of corporate bodies, with official representatives to speak or act for them.[5]

It was possible, then, to go some distance in arguing a case for rights residing in the individual and yet still espouse the idea that political authority derived from the community as a corporate entity. The idea of natural rights inherent in the individual – notably the right to property – might require some explanation of the extent to which they could, or could not, be legitimately violated by the state; but even to say, for instance, that the monarchy must not interfere with the property of its subjects did not by itself have implications for the contest over jurisdiction and political authority. The conceptual problem (if such it was) posed by the doctrine of individual rights did not arise when political authority was invested in a corporate entity that transcended the individuals of which it was composed. It was not the idea of individual rights but the notion of the community as

---

5 In *Citizens to Lords*, I argued that 'Even feudal property, however conditional it may be and whatever obligations it may entail, is vested in individuals; but these individuals are themselves defined by their juridical or corporate identity. They hold their property not simply as free men but as lords, or as landholders subject to feudal obligations and lordly jurisdiction.' This also had implications for the principle that the royal state is accountable to the 'people': 'Even when the "people" were granted a right to depose kings who failed in their duty, that right was typically vested in a corporate entity or its representatives, not least in feudal magnates of one kind or another' (pp. 216–17). For instance, according to the *Cambridge History of Medieval Political Thought: c. 350–1450* (Cambridge: Cambridge University Press, 1988), 'In France, the people's right to depose kings was normally discussed only in the context of rebutting papal claims to be able to do so' (p. 517).

greater than any single individual, including the king, that was more likely to be invoked in support of limited, constitutional government.

There was, in other words, no obvious contradiction between asserting the inherent rights of (private?) individuals and supporting the monarch's absolute powers in his own political domain. It might be necessary for the monarchy to guarantee his subjects a sphere of private property, but this could be done without ceding royal jurisdiction to some other fragment of sovereignty. If anything, the notion of individual rights – which entailed no claims to jurisdiction or public authority – was, in the Spanish context as in the French, less threatening to royal power than was the idea of corporate rights, rights residing in corporate entities or their official representatives. It would be in England, where competing jurisdictions were not the central issue between the monarchy and those inclined to check its powers, that the idea of individual natural rights would be most unambiguously drawn into controversies on the absolutist state.

In the English case, as we shall see, the doctrine of natural rights residing in the individual would come to have a different meaning. For contextual reasons, having to do with the relatively minor role of corporate bodies and especially of competing jurisdictions in defining the political terrain, the problem of state power and its limitation was more likely to present itself as a question about the relation between the state and the individuals that constituted it. The doctrine of natural rights would then have more obvious and immediate implications for the limitation of state power. Even an ardent defender of the absolutist state like Thomas Hobbes would feel obliged not only to explain how the natural rights of individuals could be compatible with absolute monarchy but to argue that such a state was constituted by individuals, and only by individuals, with inherent natural rights and without corporate mediations.

In the Spanish context, where the contest over royal power was played out on the terrain of corporate jurisdictions, it was the empire, more than the tensions between monarchs and subjects, that shaped the conception of natural rights. Spanish thinkers did, like their medieval predecessors, raise questions about individual rights, in particular the right of property, in opposition to monarchical intrusions; but their elaborations of medieval Thomist ideas were shaped by the imperial experience. The right to liberty as seen through the prism of empire had less to do with the civil rights and liberties of Spanish subjects in relation to the state than with the rights of indigenous peoples to be free of outright enslavement to *encomenderos*; and the right of property was seen from the angle of the competing claims over colonial territory.

In contrast, then, to more familiar conceptions of natural rights that came after it, such as that of John Locke, the purpose of the theory that emerged from the School of Salamanca was not primarily to delineate the proper relationship between the individual and the community or between the state and its citizens or subjects. The Spanish doctrine of natural rights was specifically intended to confront questions concerning the legitimacy of the empire in general and its treatment of the Indians in particular; and it was articulated in ways designed to deal with Spain's imperial dilemmas, without immediate implications for the legitimacy of the monarchical state in relation to its subjects at home.

To establish the imperial rights of the Spanish crown in the Americas – not least its claims to property in the colonies and in particular the mines – required a battle on several fronts: against other European powers and, more particularly, as we have seen, against the papacy and *encomenderos*. One of the ironies in Spanish political thought is that the argument deemed by Spanish theologians to be most effective in sustaining the king's position against the challenges he faced from all directions was one that asserted the rights of indigenous peoples. It might, in their view, even be wise to argue that the Indians had rights of jurisdiction, so that imperial domination might have to be justified on the grounds that they had consented to rule by the Spanish crown;[6] but it was even more important to concede to Indians their rights of property. The idea of papal donation was dangerous not only because of the tensions between the Spanish monarch, especially in his capacity as Holy Roman Emperor, and the pope, but also because rival European claimants to colonial territories persistently challenged the pope's jurisdiction and his authority to 'donate' land in this way. This made it prudent for defenders of the Spanish monarchy to suggest that land in the Americas could belong only to the indigenous rulers, so that they had the same rights as did European princes, whose rights of property the pope could not infringe. It was for that reason useful to find other ways of justifying Spain's colonial dominance – such as the doctrine of 'just war'. Asserting the property rights of the Indians had the added advantage of denying the *encomendero* any autonomous claims to colonial land. At the same time, to grant the Indians their rights of *dominium* was not inconsistent with the claims of foreigners to things – such as gold in the ground – that had not been appropriated by anyone, which (as Vitoria would argue in *De Indis*) by the *ius gentium* will belong to the first taker.

A Spanish thinker like Vitoria, whose *On Civil Power*, an early *relectio*, was a defence of royal power against the threats posed by radical Protestantism, could, in his later reflections on war and indigenous peoples, readily move on to espousing an idea of natural rights residing in the

---

6   See Pagden, *Lords of All the World*, pp. 50–52 for a particularly useful account of why the School of Salamanca chose to argue that Charles could claim jurisdiction over the Indians only on the basis that they had consented to it, as German princes 'consented' to his supra-legislative authority.

individual, without feeling any need to justify the transition or attempting to demonstrate how natural rights and royal absolutism could coexist. There was no need for him to perceive individual natural rights as a challenge to monarchical authority. The challenge was coming from a different direction. Vitoria had composed *On Civil Power* in 1528, after the Revolt of the Comuneros, the rebellion of Castilians against Charles V, and after the peasant revolt in Germany. He was particularly keen to defend the authority of princes against the threats he perceived from radical theology. Although there are ambiguities in his account of secular authority, his principal strategy in that work is to insist that sovereign power derives not from a community of men but from natural and divine law. It is true that even in *On Civil Power* he sometimes suggests – and in his later lectures does so consistently – that kingly power does indeed originally come from the community, on whose behalf the sovereign reigns. But his emphasis in this *relectio* is on the origin of civil power in natural law. The coexistence of these divergent accounts may seem a careless oversight; but the two propositions may not have appeared so contradictory to Vitoria, since the idea that state power derives from the people had long been considered perfectly compatible with the absolute power of kings.

In another *relectio, On The Power of the Church,* Vitoria denounced the Lutheran view that all Christians are priests and that the power of the Church inheres in every believer, but his argument on the source of civil power was not so different from Luther's. Luther himself, as we saw, had argued for obedience and against resistance to secular authority, which he treated as providentially ordained by God. It would not, then, have been unreasonable for Vitoria to think that the real danger posed by Protestant doctrine to secular rulers resided less in Luther's views on the source of secular authority than in his conception of the priesthood and the Church, which certainly was elaborated by radicals to justify resistance to secular power despite the master's opposition.

Nonetheless, Vitoria was criticized by other Thomists for failing to recognize the threat posed by the Lutheran idea that political authority derives directly from God's grace. Luther had argued *against* the right of resistance, partly on the grounds that the legitimacy of secular authority cannot be judged by the standards of natural law or the principles of justice, since we cannot assume that a fallen humanity is capable of following, or even comprehending, divine will or natural law. For him, in other words, appeals to natural law could offer a dangerous pretext for rebellion. Yet natural law had quite a different meaning for the neo-Thomist theologians when they argued that political society was indeed grounded in natural law and that there was indeed an element of grace and justice in the human soul. Whatever their benevolent intentions, they had very immediately practical objectives, too. They were, of course, concerned to salvage a capacity in human beings to cooperate to some degree in their own salvation by God's grace, without which the Catholic Church had little meaning or authority. But they were no less concerned about the status of secular monarchies in their conflicts with each other and the papacy. They sought their solution in the concept of natural law inherited from Aquinas.

The Thomist distinction among various kinds of law – divine, eternal, natural, and human or positive – provided a means of asserting the autonomy of secular authority without denying its roots in God's will. Divine law, directed to eternal life and humanity's relationship with God, is the subject of divine revelation in scripture. This is conceptually distinct from eternal law, which represents the principles of a cosmic order governed by God. Natural law is that aspect of divine regulation accessible to human reason; but, while it establishes the basic principles of legitimate government, it exists in political society only as embodied in the positive laws enacted by governments on earth. The emphasis here is not so much (and less in some thinkers than in others) on natural law as a standard against which human legislation can be judged. The essential point is rather that, while political society is ultimately grounded in natural law, it exists only by human institution and through the medium of human legislation. Political society, in other words, does not derive directly from God's grace but is created by the human community to fulfil human ends.

Neo-Thomist theologians were far less worried about the subversive possibilities contained in a view of natural law as a standard against which secular power could be judged than they were about the threat to secular rulers presented by a conception of political authority as derived directly from God's grace. Protestant radicals had dangerously elaborated Luther's doctrine, in such a way as to imply that, if secular authority was founded by God's grace to deal with human sinfulness, his purpose could hardly be served by ungodly rulers. The Lutheran principle could be taken to imply that obedience to rulers is conditional on their godliness. This made it possible to argue that rulers could be not only passively disobeyed but actively resisted according to the dictates of the Christian conscience.

No less disturbing was the implication that 'ungodly' rulers could legitimately be deposed by conquest, an idea that was readily mobilized in conflicts among Europe's Christian monarchs. Such notions were particularly menacing at a time when Protestantism was being drawn into the tensions between monarchs or emperors and 'lesser' jurisdictions, such as the conflicts that would eventually issue in the French religious wars, or the rebellion against the Spanish empire in the Netherlands. It was, apparently, far safer to maintain that secular authority was grounded in natural law via human institution.

Thomist theologians therefore expended a great deal of energy on defeating the Protestant conception of political society and the doctrine of justification by faith that underlay it. At the same time, their arguments in defence of secular princes could put at risk the legitimacy of Spain's empire. The idea that political society is grounded in natural law but only via human institution also implied, for neo-Thomist theologians, that the only forms of dominance that follow directly from natural law are the positions of husbands and fathers. While the general principle of dominance derives from natural law, its political form exists only by human institution, simply to preserve a human community. This put in question the Spanish king's position as emperor in the Americas, even in his capacity as Holy Roman Emperor. He could not claim jurisdiction on the grounds of universal empire. He therefore had no better claim to jurisdiction over colonial territories than did other European princes; and indigenous rulers enjoyed the same legitimacy as any other political authority enacted by men to preserve their own community. If the requirements of European princes in asserting their authority at home took precedence over the monarch's imperial claims in neo-Thomist theology, some other justification would have to be found for Spain's imperial expansion.

Vitoria did later abandon the idea that secular authority derives directly from God and with it any notion that political society was implanted directly by nature. In the lectures on the Indians and on the law of war, he proceeded from the classic Thomist view that political authority derives its legitimacy not from direct divine institution but from natural law through the medium of human legislation. Although ultimately emanating from God, natural law is accessible to men through reason and implemented by them through positive law. Men, as individuals endowed with the right of dominion, voluntarily divided property and established civil authority. While man, according to Aristotelian and Thomistic notions, is by nature a 'political' or civil animal, political society is constructed not by nature but by law.

Vitoria goes on to adopt the fairly conventional view that the sovereign power is established by the transfer of powers originally inhering in the people. Yet, while this differs from his position in *On Civil Power*, the transformation may not indicate a significant change of view on the limits of state power. The idea that political society exists by human institution did not, as we have seen, have any necessary implications for limits on secular government. On the contrary, Thomist theologians were more likely to invoke this doctrine in support of secular authority, against the right of resistance or the powers of the papacy; and the idea of civil authority as originally constituted by the people was capacious enough to allow even absolute monarchy.[7]

---

7 Distinctions might be made between the *transfer* of power from the people to their rulers as against the unconditional *alienation* of power; but that distinction is not always so clear, since even in the case of a conditional 'transfer', the conditions that might permit rebellion could be so stringent as to leave the ruler's power all but absolute.

If the idea that individuals were endowed by nature with a right of dominion did not necessarily entail the limitation of civil authority, it did imply that Indians should not be enslaved by their colonial masters. Reflecting on the conquest of Peru and the destruction of Inca and Aztec civilizations, Vitoria ruled out any justification that appealed to the natural inferiority of the Indians or to Aristotle's theory of natural slavery. The Indians were, like other human beings, endowed with the right of dominion, with liberty and rights of ownership. This precluded conquest even to achieve their forcible conversion to Christianity. Nor could imperial domination be justified on the principles of 'universal empire'. Since civil authority is grounded in natural law only through the medium of human law, there can be no such thing as a temporal world empire that derives its authority directly from divine or natural law. The laws and institutions of the Indians have the same legitimacy as any Christian polity. If there are any universal expressions of natural law, it can only be in laws and customs that are common to various peoples throughout the world – the law of nature as embodied in *ius gentium* (variously translated as the 'law of peoples' or the 'law of nations').

The effect of Vitoria's argument was to narrow the scope of imperial justification. The only ground remaining was the theory of 'just war'. He was, nevertheless, at best ambivalent (and even inconsistent, from one work to another) about what could be legitimated by 'just war'. On the one hand, he seems to rule out the forcible conversion of unbelievers and conquest on behalf of a universal empire. On the other hand, he does, as we have seen, invoke the Roman Empire as an example of a legitimate form of forcible imperial expansion, approved not only by Church fathers but, in principle, by Jesus Christ himself. Although Vitoria's remarks on Rome are not explicitly related to the empire in the New World, they had clear implications for the Spanish empire in the Americas. More significantly, even his conception of the *ius gentium* provides a foundation for the justification of conquest. It represents a kind of natural human community, entailing certain universal principles such as the right of movement and free trade, which includes the right to 'trade' the Christian faith. A just war can be fought in defence of these principles against anyone who interferes with them. Vitoria has, then, conceded to Montesino and Las Casas their defence of Indians as rational human beings entitled to their liberty and property, and has also rejected the idea of a universal empire, while justifying conquest nonetheless. We might conclude that he has made an imperialist case against *encomenderos* but for the king of Spain.

Domingo de Soto, who would join Vitoria at the University of Salamanca, had preceded him in declaring the Roman Empire to be based on nothing more than the force of arms. Like Vitoria, he defended secular authority against what he took to be the Lutheran threat; but he would go on to make stronger arguments against the imperial regime, in 1553 undercutting even the 'just war' defence. Where Vitoria had invoked the authority of the Church fathers, and Augustine in particular, de Soto rejected this justification. Vitoria had gone some distance in narrowing the grounds of legitimacy on which the Roman Empire could stand, but de Soto went further by claiming that Augustine, far from approving Rome's imperial expansion by means of armed force, regarded it as an unjust pursuit of worldly glory, which for him was not a virtue but a vice. In any case, whatever legitimacy Rome may have gained in the eyes of later Europeans did not support the principle of a world empire. Yet even de Soto did not question the need for Christians to convert the Indians.

In 1545, the Council of Trent was convened. It would lay out the doctrinal terms of the official Counter-Reformation, elaborating arguments against Protestant heresies and setting in motion internal reforms in the Catholic Church. Charles V, as Holy Roman Emperor, appointed de Soto to be his theologian at the Council. Among the principal and most fiercely contested subjects was the doctrine of justification by faith alone.

In 1550, King Charles V summoned a *junta* of theologians and jurists to Valladolid to debate the legitimacy of the conquest and the conversion of the Indians by force, with de Soto presiding. Arguing in favour of conversion by just war was the humanist scholar and translator of Aristotle, Sepúlveda, who represented the interests of colonial settlers. In 1545, he had published his *Democrates alter sive de justis belli causis apud Indios* (Concerning the just causes of the war against the Indians). Although also a Dominican friar, he had made his arguments on largely secular grounds, rooted in Aristotle's theory of natural slavery. He was, to be sure, arguing in favour of the Indians' conversion; but he made his argument on the grounds that Spain was a superior civilization, which had the right to conquer these 'barbarous' people in order to prepare them for conversion. He would elaborate these arguments in the debate at Vallidolid, where his opponent was Las Casas, who was establishing himself as the Indians' principal defender.

In the debate Sepúlveda, invoking the doctrine of natural slavery, constructed his argument again on the basis that the Indians were a barbarian people governed not by reason but by passion. They were, he maintained, also guilty of violating natural law, committing 'crimes that offend nature', such as cannibalism, idolatry and sodomy, contrary to Spanish law and custom; and this, too, entitled the Spaniards to wage a just war against them. Moreover, since the Indians were in the habit of oppressing and killing the innocent among themselves, who were regularly offered as human sacrifices, their victims could be saved only by outside intervention – and here, Sepúlveda could draw on something like Vitoria's doctrine of *ius gentium* as a justification for war. Finally, the Christian mission of conversion could only be effected if the ground was prepared by conquest – just as the Christian emperor Constantine had in the fourth century brought pagans under Roman rule in order to convert them. Sepúlveda even appealed to scripture to sustain his case for conversion by force.

Las Casas responded to each of these arguments. He dismissed Sepúlveda's invocation of Aristotle not by arguing against the doctrine of natural slavery but by demonstrating that the Indians did not fit the Aristotelian category. Non-Christians they certainly were, but they were clearly rational, possessing elaborate languages and complex civilizations governed by law. Some, though few, communities did commit idolatry and sacrifice; but this had been true of many advanced civilizations throughout history and could not be cited as evidence of their rule by passion rather than reason. As advanced and rational people, the Indians could and should be converted not by force but by persuasion. Nor did Christians have any right to punish them for their wrongs, because neither the king nor the pope had jurisdiction over the Indians, who were not heretics subject to correction by the Church but pagans available to peaceful conversion. Even if idolatry and sacrifice were contrary to the *ius gentium* – and everyone is obliged to prevent such violations – to say that crimes against nature should be punished by force went against the teachings of Church fathers like Augustine. In any case, it was better wherever possible to avoid the greater of two evils, which was war.

Francisco Suárez

The debate had little effect in practice, but it certainly had theoretical implications. However powerful the arguments that challenged the legitimacy of the empire, they still left some room for a justification of conquest based on 'just war' in cases where war could be judged the lesser evil. Having emphatically ruled out the case for universal empire or natural slavery, it had the effect of placing the burden of justification on the doctrine of 'just war', together with the concept of *ius gentium,* the violation of which remained the most convincing case for waging war – and generally a fairly flexible one. These concepts would enter the mainstream of Western political thought not so much, as is commonly suggested, to place limits on the conduct of war but rather to defend the use of arms in pursuit of imperial interests.

Francisco Suárez, a Jesuit theologian and philosopher, would be the most important conduit for this kind of argument. He also elaborated his predecessors' ideas on natural law and natural right, in ways that have earned him credit for founding the early modern tradition of natural right; but here, too, he left an ambiguous legacy. He expressed views similar to those of Vitoria, de Soto and Las Casas on the Indians' right to dominion in their own lands; and his conceptions of natural law and natural right are sometimes interpreted as a more or less 'modern' defence of the individual's rights against the state. Yet if his predecessors had defended indigenous rights without having any wish to undermine the secular authority of European princes at home, Suárez made it even clearer that natural law and natural right were perfectly compatible with something close to absolute monarchy.

The neo-Thomist principle that political society is grounded in natural law through the medium of human legislation was used, as we have seen, in ways that may, to modern eyes, seem counter-intuitive: to buttress, not to limit, secular authority against resistance. The idea that political society exists by means of human institution in pursuit of human ends, while at the same time being subject in some way to standards of justice and natural law, and that certain rights inhere in individuals by nature, might on the face of it seem better suited to a doctrine of resistance than to a theory of political legitimacy not far short of royal absolutism. Yet for sixteenth-century European monarchies, in the specific context of the challenges they faced, a conception of secular authority such as that elaborated by the Spanish neo-Thomists was consistent with strict obedience to secular rulers or even royal absolutism, and the doctrine of natural right did not yet seem particularly threatening.

Suárez wrote as a theorist of law, and he perfected the legalistic neo-Thomist strategy of argumentation. Political society is, he argued, a human creation, constructed by men endowed with a natural inclination to live in communities, who establish polities to fulfil purely human and temporal purposes. Naturally free, individuals relinquish that freedom by common consent, agreeing to form a political body and set up government with legislative power. Political power thus resides not in individuals but in the community. At the same time, Suárez rules out the medieval principle that, even if the king is greater than any other individual, the community as a corporate body is greater than the king. The consent of individuals is not simply a delegation of power to their governors. It is an outright *alienation* of power; and its transfer to the ruler (whether in the person of a monarch or some other form of government) invests him with a full legal title to power, a kind of ownership, which is virtually unconditional. This means that, even while political power is different from the kind of natural dominion that resides in heads of household – the patriarchal authority of fathers and husbands – the ruler's possession of the legislative power, which is the hallmark of political society, cannot be rescinded or limited in the normal course of political events. The only right reserved by the people is the right to preserve the community from imminent destruction. Only in extreme cases, when a ruler threatens the very existence of the commonwealth, is resistance legitimate; but even then that right is a prerogative of public authority, not an individual right. The ruler can be called to account before a 'public' council; but if he is to be deposed, his deposition may, as we shall see in a moment, require papal authority.

In what sense, then, can it be said that natural law and natural right set the terms and conditions of political power? On this, Suárez remains at best ambiguous. In *De Legibus* he defines a right (*ius*) as 'a certain moral power that every man has, either over his property or with respect to that which is due to him' (I.2.5) . This suggests that rights exist by nature and independently of positive law. At the same time, Suárez tells us, this moral right is 'prescribed and measured by law'. The question, then, is whether positive law can be judged by any independent standard of right or justice. The legitimacy of positive law depends, he explains, on the good of the community, on what is rightful or just; and in that sense *ius* appears to be a standard against which human legislation can be judged. Yet in practice the legislative power residing in rulers can be resisted or constrained only in the most extreme circumstances; there is no normal legal instrument or process to limit it; and the ruler can override individual rights in the interests of the community as he defines them, with no recourse against that definition in the normal transactions of political life.

There is a further complication in Suárez's work. His strongest assertion of the right to resist secular authority occurs in his response to James I of England's *Apologie for the Oath of Allegiance,* which appeared anonymously in 1608 and in the king's name in 1609. It was James more than any political philosopher who, in various writings throughout his life, elaborated the doctrine of the divine right of kings, and this in its most extreme form, asserting the absolute authority of kings, its direct and hereditary derivation from God, and hence the immunity of kings to any resistance, secular or religious. The oath of allegiance explained in his *Apologie* was James's solution to the problem that had plagued English monarchs since the Reformation came to England: how to deal with English Catholics. This problem had acquired special urgency when the Counter-Reformation assumed a politically militant form, especially with the collaboration between the Catholic Church and Charles V's son, King Philip II of Spain, in his designs on the English crown. Throughout James I's reign, there remained a party of Jesuit-inspired English Catholics still wedded to that Spanish project; and the oath of allegiance – which had as its underlying premise the divine right of kings – was designed to deal with that threat.

At the behest of Pope Paul V, Suárez launched an attack on the king in *Defensio catholicae fidei contra anglicanae sectae errores.* It is here that he appears least absolutist, and it is here that he most emphatically asserts what appears to be the right of resistance. Yet the right to punish is, according to him, an act of jurisdiction, which is therefore always the act of a superior; and this is no less true in disciplining kings than in the punishment of any other wrongdoer. In this case the only legitimate superior is the pope, and much of Suárez's response to James I is devoted to asserting papal jurisdiction.

The issue for Suárez was not only the conflict between the pope and King James, or between Catholicism and English Protestantism, but also the political contest between the English Reformation and the Catholic monarchy of Spain. His predecessors in the School of Salamanca were still obliged to take account of the frequent tensions between the pope and King Charles I of Spain – especially as Charles V, the Holy Roman Emperor. The reign of Philip II and his son, Philip III, was a time of partnership with the pope. Suárez struck a complicated balance in his argument between sustaining the power of the Spanish king, as had his predecessors, and, at the same time, making an argument for the pope's superior jurisdiction against the king of England's claims. Against the divine right of kings invoked by King James, Suárez mobilizes the well-known neo-Thomist arguments about the source of political authority, arguing not only that political society exists by human institution but also that the authority of rulers derives from the people. Yet what he seems to give with one hand he takes away with the other, insisting not only that the people have alienated their power to their rulers but also that, on the very rare and abnormal occasions when they can act against him, that right is a prerogative of public authority, a jurisdictional matter, with the sanction of the ultimate superior, the pope.

Suárez is often credited with taking an important step in the formation of natural rights theory, which would increasingly situate rights in individual persons, emphasizing the natural freedom of the individual, detaching the moral force of natural rights from religious authority, and vesting it in the mundane requirements of human well-being, according to principles accessible to human reason. The critical step, it is argued, was to move away from Aquinas, for whom *ius* denoted 'the just thing', what was 'right' in an action or a situation, in a sense indistinguishable from what was just, in accordance with natural law. Suárez began to shift the concept of right from the justice of 'things' – actions or situations – to the entitlements of individual persons. Yet to say this may be to disguise some essential differences between his conception of rights and more familiar early modern 'subjective' theories of natural rights.

It must be emphasized first that the definition of right as a certain 'moral power' residing in a person, in relation to property or in respect to 'what is due' to that person, remains bound up with the condition or status of the person and leaves considerable scope for differential rights. Aquinas himself made it clear in his *Summa Theologica* that 'what is due' to an individual will vary according to status: 'A thing is due', he writes, 'to an equal in one way, to a superior in another, and to an inferior in yet another' – and this, in accordance with the principles of natural law, is justice. It would have been perfectly consistent with the master's doctrine of justice and right to say that the right of resistance is 'what is due' to someone not simply by virtue of his humanity but on the grounds of jurisdictional authority. Everyone has a right to his own property, as well as what is 'due' to him in his particular condition; and that means, for example (as Suárez makes clear), that the right of resistance to royal authority is not a universal right but a prerogative of office. It was even possible, given this conception of rights, to conceive of universal rights in such a way that they remained consistent with absolute royal power.

Since the available doctrines of individual rights and even popular sovereignty were still typically mobilized in support of royal power, not against it, when Suárez directs the idea of rights to sustaining monarchical power, rather than to placing limits on it, he is still following the medieval norm. If anything, he can feel secure in forcefully asserting the existence of rights precisely because the idea of rights vested in all men, and even the idea that secular authority derives from the people, belonged to the corpus of Western political thought as a support to royal power and not as a subversion of it. More dangerous to royal powers were claims to jurisdiction by other, 'lesser' public authorities against royal power. Suárez may direct his conception of rights against King James's notion of divine right, but the Spaniard makes sure that the right of resistance is very narrowly defined and ultimately dependent on the pope. If Suárez was restricting secular authority, then, it was by vesting rights in the pope, not in the 'people';[8] but even short of that, and even in the hands of political theorists who had their own reasons – whether in defence of kings or in support of Holy Roman Emperors – for insisting that the pope had no temporal authority, the idea that sovereignty derived from the people could be readily invoked to support monarchical power.

The doctrine of resistance as a right of jurisdiction would reach its height in sixteenth-century France. French constitutionalists took the idea of sovereignty derived from the people and the right of resistance vested in competing jurisdictions, or 'lesser magistrates', as far as it would go. It would be in England that this theoretical strategy became no longer viable. The English were faced with a conundrum that had not affected the French. When the English elaborated doctrines of resistance – most urgently in the seventeenth century – those who were defending the rights of Parliament against the Crown had to confront the possibility that invoking popular sovereignty might open much more hazardous floodgates, endangering not only the state but the whole social order. The right of resistance could not so easily be confined to the official acts of 'lesser magistrates'. The mediations

---

8   See Skinner, *Foundations, Vol. 2: Age of Reformation*, p. 179, for an argument that Counter-Reformation neo-Thomists like Suárez, while they did adopt some fairly radical and secularized notions of *imperium,* were no less keen to defend the temporal powers of the Church and the pope against theorists like Marsilius of Padua, who denied any coercive power to the Church, or William of Ockham, who denied the pope's right to intervene in temporal affairs.

between state and individuals endowed with rights, if not altogether non-existent, were weaker than they were elsewhere in Western Europe. In the English context corporate identities had become increasingly diluted, while economic power and property rights were increasingly detached from jurisdiction and corporate privilege. This placed an entirely new burden on the doctrine of individual rights. It is not surprising that England would produce more radically democratic ideas, including new ideas of rights such as those espoused by the Levellers. Less radical English political thinkers, whether defending royal absolutism or the primacy of Parliament, would find themselves obliged to construct their arguments in wholly new ways, on a foundation of unmediated free and equal individuals.

5

THE DUTCH REPUBLIC

In 1598 the Dutch child prodigy Huig de Groot, then barely fifteen years old, accompanied the Advocate of Holland, Johan van Oldenbarnevelt, on an extraordinary embassy from the States-General of the United Provinces to the French court. The purpose of the mission was to obtain whatever assistance it could from France against military threats to the Provinces' still precarious independence and stability as a free republic. Since William I (the Silent) of Orange had led a revolt of the Netherlands against Philip II of Spain in 1568, the Netherlands had been embroiled in more or less continuous conflict. Although the Dutch Republic was declared in 1588, the so-called Eighty Years' War with Spain would end only in 1648 with the Treaty of Westphalia; and throughout that period, which saw the Republic rise to extraordinary heights of economic and cultural success, its internal political life continued to be marked by intense civil strife.

Oldenbarnevelt would play a central role in the formation of the Republic's political institutions and, as architect of the United East India Company, in its immense economic success, becoming effectively the leader of the Republic. Hugo Grotius, later known as the pioneer of international law and, according to some commentators, a major theorist of natural rights and even a founder of modern theories of natural law, began his precocious career as protégé and then supporter of Oldenbarnevelt. While his close association with Oldenbarnevelt would, as we shall see, end badly when they fell victim to an especially ferocious factional dispute, his political ideas were rooted from beginning to end in the politics of the Dutch Republic, its civic conflicts and its vast commercial empire. The other canonical Dutch thinker to be considered in this chapter, Spinoza, may not have been as actively engaged in civic politics, but his political ideas are in their own distinctive way grounded in the conflicts of the Dutch Republic and its unique configuration of political and economic power.

The Dutch Republic

The man who bore the titles Charles I of Spain and Charles V of the Holy Roman Empire, who was born in the Low Countries in the Flemish city of Ghent, was always more at home in the language and culture of his birthplace than he ever would be in his Spanish kingdom. During his reign, the Habsburg provinces in the Netherlands looked set to be the European jewel in the imperial crown – or at least its principal cash cow. The commercial cities of the Netherlands had long been major trading links in the European economy. In the south, the city of Antwerp had become the hub of Europe's so-called rich trades, in spices, textiles, sugar and metals; while in the northern maritime provinces, Amsterdam, though its golden age would come after the Dutch Revolt from Spain, was already on the rise, soon to become what some have called the world's richest city as Europe's greatest transshipment point and a world financial centre. Neither Spain itself nor Habsburg Italy – over which the Empire's command had long been tenuous – could match the Netherlands' prosperity; and, as the contests among Europe's rising states intensified, the Habsburg monarchy was bound to increase its dependence on revenues from the provinces in building up its military capabilities. When France began to challenge Habsburg dominance in the Low Countries, Charles responded by bolstering his military strength, supported disproportionately by exactions from the Netherlands' commercial wealth. The more the king of Spain – and Holy Roman Emperor – depended on resources from the Low Countries, the more he was forced to rely on local elites to organize finances and collect taxes, which only served to aggravate the tensions.

For a time, local elites were prepared to play their part in the imperial project, and indeed to profit from it; but there had always been an inevitable conflict between the monarchy's centralizing mission and powerful forces in the Low Countries intent on preserving the provincial and civic autonomy of their city-states. Any effort to subject the provinces to Spain's monarchical administration was likely to encounter resistance from well-established civic institutions in an unusually urbanized society with powerful urban elites. Urban magnates resisted any challenge to their local powers or their networks of patronage; and, especially in Holland, the tensions between the monarch and the local patriciate were intensified by the Habsburg policy of elevating administrators from outside the leading local families, or sometimes officials from other, less dominant provinces. Charles's son Philip II, who broke the close personal ties his father had with the Low Countries, took the centralizing project even further. Aggravating tensions by ever more taxation, he presided over the final breach between Spain and its richest European dependency.

The conflict between local magnates and the Habsburg monarchy became entangled with religious controversies. Confessional divisions varied among the different provinces and cities; and there was no simple correlation between adherence to the Catholic Church and support for the Habsburg state, or between Protestantism and local resistance. But the northern provinces that broke free of Spanish rule were largely Protestant, while Catholicism prevailed in the south; and there is no question that Protestant religious doctrines were mobilized in the Low Countries, as elsewhere in Europe and notably in France, in support of local elites against the centralizing project of the monarchy. After the Revolt, Protestantism would itself become a fierce terrain of battle in the free Republic. Even divergent forms of Calvinism were pitted against one another in the struggles among civic factions. But in the conflicts leading up to the revolt against the Spanish crown, Protestants were united against the Catholic monarchy's attacks on their faith. Philip's fierce assault on Protestant believers was the final provocation.

The dominance of cities in the Netherlands explains a great deal about the Revolt and what followed in the politics, economy and culture of the Dutch Republic. In the absence of a strong central state, the Low Countries, divided among provinces with diverse political traditions and economic interests, had long been governed by relatively independent local rulers and increasingly by local urban elites, enriched by their city's commercial success. The province of Holland was becoming the most highly urbanized society in Europe, with a powerful urban patriciate presiding over the world's most commercialized economy. The urban centres had a vibrant civic life, with active corporate bodies of various kinds, such as guilds and militia companies. There were even 'chambers of rhetoric', which played a large part in literary and cultural life, especially in Holland, and in the 1520s and 1530s had served as a major conduit for humanism, with all its effects on religious and political debate. Well before the establishment of the Republic, city organizations and authorities had been increasingly involved in the maintenance of social order and civic welfare; and particularly in the northern provinces they would play a major role in the Revolt.

In the years following the Revolt, a new form of state would evolve, a confederation of provinces that maintained their autonomy and were governed largely by civic administrations in the cities. There was a supra-provincial governing body, the States-General of the Republic; but in the richest provinces, most notably Holland, powerful factions among the local ruling classes strongly resisted the formation of a centralized state, especially in the person of the stadtholder, an office inherited from pre-Revolt days. Once the sovereign's representative, this office had become the closest thing to a central state official in the free Republic. Particularly in Holland, whose wealth and power generally enabled it to impose its will on other provinces, there would be persistent conflict between the stadtholder – or, more specifically, supporters of the House of Orange, which claimed the office as its own – and civic leaders. Internal tensions were heightened as the urban patriciate, the regents, became increasingly exclusive and their government more oligarchic, driving less privileged classes to support the Orangists.

Civic conflict after the Revolt was exacerbated by its growing confessionalization. Although the Dutch maintained the separation of Church and state, officials were expected to be members of the Reformed Church. The Republic, with its headless and multi-polar government, relied heavily on the so-called 'public' Church to maintain not only communal welfare but civic order and discipline. Yet there were, from the start, divisions between strict Calvinists and more liberal preachers, which would erupt with particular venom in moments of political strife. In the battle between Oldenbarnevelt and his opponents in 1618, political conflicts – which proved fatal for him and disastrous for his supporter Grotius – were reinforced by a struggle between Arminians ('Remonstrants', after they issued their 'Remonstrance' against certain orthodox Calvinist doctrines) and 'Counter-Remonstrant' Calvinists (about which more later).

In the following decades, political factions, with their fiercely competing networks of patronage and clientage controlling access to civic office, sought to avoid such catastrophic confessional disputes. Civil strife continued to grow between Orangists, or followers of the stadtholder, and supporters of provincial and local power against the stadtholder's monarchical pretensions. The former were generally supported by strict Calvinists, the latter by more liberal believers; but both major factions nonetheless agreed on the importance of maintaining the unity of the public Church.[1] By the 1650s, in the years leading up to the next major crisis of the Dutch Republic, unity had broken down; and political divisions were deepened by confessional disputes.

At the heart of Dutch political development and conflicts, even at the height of the Republic's commercial success, was the importance of civic office not only as an instrument of government but as a guarantee of private wealth and power. The decentralized organization of the Republic created a particularly fertile field for public-service occupations, so the proportion of such occupations in the population of Dutch cities was very high. To be sure, while offices of various kinds often provided high incomes, it required substantial wealth from real property or finance to enter the urban patriciate, since to be part of the governing elite increasingly required abandoning private economic activities; but civic elites had good reason to maintain their hold on high office, which sustained their networks of power and patronage. Even in the Golden Age of the Republic's

---

1 Jonathan Israel, *The Dutch Republic: Its Rise, Greatness, and Fall 1477–1806* (New York: Oxford University Press, 1995), pp. 660–62.

commercial dominance, a wealthy landowner or financier would often choose to use his wealth for access to such offices. When, in the later seventeenth century, the European economy suffered a decline, access to office was even more highly prized, as a direct source of income no less than of power and patronage. By the eighteenth century, at a time when Britain was dominated by the wealth of capitalist landlords, among the highest incomes in the Republic were enjoyed by public servants. It is not surprising that political conflict over control of office, and the networks of patronage that sustained it, was particularly fierce.

We have already encountered societies, in medieval and Renaissance Italy, where urban patriciates extracted great wealth from commercial activities but relied for their success in large part on the privileges and powers associated with their status in the city. Here, too, political conflicts took on a particular ferocity and even violence, to say nothing of their regularity, because more was at stake than political interests and rights. Much the same logic applied to the commercial success of the city-state itself. Just as the wealth of civic elites in Italian centres of commerce depended on civic status, privilege and power, the commercial success of their city-states in rivalry with others depended less on competitive production than on 'extra-economic' advantage, up to and including military force.

The Dutch Republic certainly moved far beyond Italian city-states in its commercial reach and power. The Dutch commercial empire was much larger than the Venetian had been – eventually extending from the Baltic to North America, and from the East Indies to southern Africa – and commerce was the basic condition of Dutch life to a degree unprecedented in history. The Republic's domestic economy was dependent to its very foundations on trade and on the commercial empire that sustained it. But the Dutch no less than the Italians relied on 'extra-economic' advantages for their commercial dominance and always owed their prosperity disproportionately to their role as commercial mediators rather than producers. The Republic's great wealth would have been impossible without its pre-eminence in long-distance trade, circulating throughout Europe commodities produced far afield. It is, for example, indicative of where the Dutch Republic's economic interests lay that it gained more from its major role in the slave trade than it did from slave production. Like other commercial leaders in Europe before the commercial dominance of capitalist Britain, the Dutch typically relied not on competitive production in a single market but on superiority in negotiating separate markets: on dominance in shipping and command of trade routes, on monopolies and trading privileges, on the development of sophisticated financial practices and instruments; on an elaborate network of far-flung trading posts and settlements, and so on.

It is a measure of the Dutch economy's dependence on extra-economic power that its levels of taxation were higher than those of its European neighbours, its revenues devoted, above all, to sustaining military superiority. The complex and often disorderly political organization of the Republic did not prevent it from becoming a powerful military machine, a 'fiscal–military' state with an unusually effective mobilization of domestic resources for purposes of war, which made the Dutch Republic 'a model country that set the standard for European armed forces'.[2] Military aggression played a major part in achieving the Republic's commercial dominance, remaining an essential part of its economic strategy throughout the Golden Age and thereafter: in trade wars, in establishing monopolies and trading posts, in capturing strategic fortresses from commercial rivals. A particularly momentous military venture was the seizure by the Dutch East India Company in 1603 of a Portuguese ship containing an enormously valuable cargo of unprecedented proportions, large enough to affect the future course of Dutch economic development.

Nevertheless, during the Republic's 'Golden Age' there was a close linkage between commerce and production. Commerce itself generated needs that had to be met by industrial production and technological innovation, notably in ship-building, to say nothing of military technology; and the Dutch economy gained much from other sources, such as the textile industry and the herring fishery. The 'rich' trades generated significant industrial production for a thriving export trade in goods from tobacco and sugar to luxury textiles. Even agricultural production, in this highly urbanized society, developed in response to commercial opportunities. While an increasing proportion of the labour force had moved from countryside to city, agricultural productivity, enhanced by technological innovation, advanced beyond all European rivals; and the Republic was very close to being a net exporter of food. As the urban population swelled to service the Republic's growing dominance in shipping, trade and eventually finance, the expanding urban sector provided new markets for agricultural goods, as well as new sources of capital to exploit new opportunities for profit. Urban investors in agriculture became a major feature of the rural scene.

Dutch agriculture was constrained by ecological factors, which limited its capacity for the easy production of basic foods like grain. Yet the Republic's commercial dominance, and particularly the command of trade that gave it privileged access to Baltic grain, meant that Dutch farmers could concentrate on the production of semi-luxury commodities – from butter to flowers – sold in a large and prosperous market. A unique imbalance between urban consumers and rural producers created growing opportunities for commercial profit at home. While even agricultural producers became dependent on the market for access to grain and other basic necessities, the productive

---

2   Jan Glete, *War and the State in Early Modern Europe* (New York: Routledge, 2002), p. 141.

capacities of relatively small farmers were disproportionately enhanced by urban investment responding to growing commercial opportunities.

Its commercial successes have led some historians to describe the Dutch Republic as the first 'modern' economy, and there are even those who suggest that the Dutch Revolt was the first 'bourgeois revolution'.[3] Yet, for all its commercialization and impressive advances in production, it continued to operate on familiar non-capitalist principles, above all in its dependence on extra-economic powers. Public offices were, from beginning to end, no less important to Dutch elites than they would be, for instance, in the 'tax/office' structure of French absolutism; and Dutch commercial dominance depended, as we have seen, on various kinds of extra-economic superiority, particularly in shipping and military technology. Dutch producers were generally not, in the capitalist manner, acting in response to cost–price pressures in a competitive market where advantage depends on increasing labour productivity. Innovations in technology that enhanced productivity had less to do with improving competitiveness than with increasing volume to take advantage of a growing market.

As long as foreign and domestic markets were expanding, Dutch producers availed themselves of growing opportunities; and urban elites continued to invest in profitable production. But when, after 1660, the Dutch economy went into decline, as all Western European economies apart from England descended into crisis, wealthy elites disinvested in land and eventually in industrial production and turned even more to 'extra-economic' strategies. The traditional patriciate sought to tighten its grip on office and to restrict access to it (as the French aristocracy would later do, in a moment of crisis that led to revolution), and civic government became even more narrowly oligarchic. Merchants, who derived their profits from circulation rather than production, pursued pre-capitalist commercial strategies, seeking more lucrative means of trading in goods produced elsewhere by, for example, reviving monopoly privileges – such as the re-establishment of the Dutch West India Company or one company's monopoly on navigational charts. While industrial production for the 'rich' trades and export industry in general held on for a time, after 1720 the decline accelerated; and by the mid-eighteenth century non-productive rentiers, especially among the regents, would account for by far the greatest wealth. The disinvestment from land and even production during and after the European economic

---

3   See in particular Jan de Vries and Ad van der Woude, *The First Modern Economy: Success, Failure, and Perseverance of the Dutch Economy, 1500–1815* (Cambridge: Cambridge University Press, 1997). I have relied on this very important work for much of my discussion of the Dutch economy but have come to somewhat different conclusions, as I explain at length in Ellen Meiksins Wood, 'The Question of Market-Dependence', *Journal of Agrarian Change*, Vol. 2, No. 1, January 2002, pp. 50–87.

crisis represented a sharp contrast to England, where crisis and declining agricultural prices spurred an *increase* in productive investment, not least by landlords, to enhance labour productivity and cost-effectiveness, in the manner of capitalist producers responding to imperatives of competition in an integrated market.

The Dutch role in England's so-called Glorious Revolution of 1688 illustrates nicely the direction of Dutch economic development in the later seventeenth century. Here, the massive financial resources of the Republic were directed not at improving production, as they often had been during the Golden Age, but at achieving extra-economic commercial advantage by military means. The province of Holland in particular depended on the profits of commerce and was especially affected by the incursions of French mercantilism in the late seventeenth century, its interference with Dutch ships and its draconian tariffs. The preferred solution to this problem of commercial profitability was to defeat French mercantilism by means of an alliance with England, which seemed possible only with a friend on the English throne. The Dutch Republic committed its resources to supporting William of Orange's bid for the English monarchy. To the English, the Revolution may have seemed 'glorious' and largely bloodless. But from the Dutch point of view, it was nothing more nor less than an invasion, involving the occupation of London by Dutch troops, in full expectation of a war not only with the English but also with the French. Nor was this military venture just a classic case of geopolitical rivalry. It was an unmistakably commercial investment in pursuit of private profit, financed not simply by the public purse but by the Amsterdam stock exchange.

A Culture of Civil Strife

The cultural and intellectual life of the Netherlands was vibrant and creative long before the Dutch Revolt. In the rich commercial cities there was a large market – including, as ever, the Church – for the arts. A strategic location at the hub of international commerce and a highly concentrated urban population encouraged a lively, and not easily controlled, circulation of ideas; and the civic culture had produced an unusually literate public. The Low Countries, and the province of Holland in particular, were already on their way to becoming the relatively open and, within certain limits, tolerant intellectual and religious societies for which the Dutch Republic would be famous, making it a favoured destination for persecuted foreign intellectuals and religious refugees. By the seventeenth century it had become a major centre of innovative European thought. In 1630, for example, René Descartes moved from France to Holland; and his work would not only have profound effects on philosophy and science but would be taken up by thinkers engaged in very immediate political struggles. The other intellectual currents that shaped our period – the humanism of the late Renaissance and the Protestant Reformation – had established deep roots, especially in Holland. Humanism began to permeate the educational establishment; and Christian humanism was, in effect, a Dutch creation, in the person of the Rotterdam philosopher Desiderius Erasmus. Between 1490 and 1520, it spread more rapidly in the Low Countries than in any other part of Northern Europe.[4]

Despite Erasmus's distrust of Luther and a passionate dislike of public conflict, his teachings played a major part in advancing the Reformation in the Low Countries. In the Dutch-speaking Netherlands, Lutheran literature was more widely disseminated than in France, England or Scandinavia; and unlike elsewhere in Northern Europe, the Reformation in the Low Countries was not imposed by government but rose up from the bottom, in a population culturally primed to receive it.[5] This kind of popular Protestantism was a source of some unease not only to the Catholic Church but to local elites. Whatever attractions the Reformation may have had for them in their opposition to the Catholic monarchy, they clearly had reason to fear the kind of radical Lutheranism that had inspired German peasant rebels. Calvinism, though delayed in reaching the Low Countries, would prove much more to the taste of civic and provincial leaders. It laid a foundation for doctrines of resistance that could be mobilized against the Spanish crown, while preaching 'godly discipline' to keep the multitude in check.

Calvinist theories of resistance, in the form of Huguenot tracts, would have their most notable effects during the French Wars of Religion in the struggle against a rising absolutist monarchy (which will be discussed in the next chapter). In the Low Countries, too, Calvin's doctrine of the 'lesser magistrate' had an obvious appeal to civic elites. The doctrine was, after all, devised with the temporal authority of civic magistrates in mind. Resistance to encroaching monarchies was not, in the Huguenot resistance tracts, a right residing in the ordinary citizen or private individual; it was a right of officers, or 'lesser magistrates', deriving from some kind of jurisdiction vested in corporate bodies, aristocracies or municipal officials – more a public duty than a private right. In their struggles against the Spanish crown, Dutch Calvinists would certainly have been sympathetic to such notions of resistance; but the local elites of the Low Countries were very different from the provincial nobles in France who adopted the Protestant faith in their resistance to the French king's absolutist project. For Huguenot aristocrats, the principal issue was preserving what remained of feudal lordship, retaining or restoring their own autonomous powers and jurisdictions. That purpose was adequately served by some variety of constitutionalist doctrine. The urban elites of the Low Countries, especially in the northern maritime

---

4 Israel, *Dutch Republic*, p. 47.
5 *Ibid.*, pp. 80, 78.

provinces and most notably Holland, were not promoting feudal lordship but civic autonomy and collective – if oligarchic – urban government. This placed a greater premium on what might be called republican ideas of freedom, a concept of liberty identified with civic self-government.

The trope of freedom was invoked by William I of Orange himself in support of the Revolt against Spain. He cited the 'freedoms and privileges' of the provinces in the manner of medieval corporations asserting their autonomy; but he also defended the freedom of the people from enslavement by the Spanish monarchy. In the later conflict between stadtholders and civic elites, the opponents of the stadtholders turned the slogan against the House of Orange, asserting republican liberty against monarchical forces, with an ideology they called 'true freedom'.

This ideology of republican freedom would have a critical effect on Dutch political thought, but its message was at best ambiguous. There was, in the Republic, no simple opposition between an anti-democratic monarchy and a more democratic republicanism. Republican forces generally represented the wealthy civic elites, which had achieved their dominance at the expense of popular elements. While they argued passionately for the active role of citizens in governing themselves, they were likely to be just as passionate in their efforts to limit access to full political rights and especially to office. Civic magnates, as regents, had begun to constitute a self-perpetuating oligarchy in cities with a narrow political base. Craft guilds in the Dutch Republic, for instance, had less influence on urban government than did their counterparts in the Spanish southern Netherlands. This was not simply a matter of wealthy merchants opposing guild restrictions on their commercial activities but also – or mainly – a political conflict between urban elites and more popular forces over political power and access to office. The revolt of guilds, together with civic militias, especially in the city of Utrecht, would be a major source of unrest in the decade of social conflict that led in 1618 to Oldenbarnevelt's expulsion from office and his and Grotius's arrest.

Although this conflict was no less Byzantine in its causes and party allegiances than any other in the convoluted history of Dutch civil strife, it is worth noting that Grotius had by this time established himself as a theorist of a limited and oligarchic republicanism, while the chief engineer and beneficiary of the coup against Oldenbarnevelt, a coup supported by popular forces, was Maurits, the son of William I. As Prince of Orange and stadtholder, he would become the most powerful man in the United Provinces following the death of his father. Later, during the 'stadtholderless' period of 1650–72 – the high point of the free Republic, when the office of stadtholder was left unfilled – the political role of the people was, if anything, even more restricted. While the 'Orangists' were hardly democratic, when the stadtholderate was restored, it was, perhaps not surprisingly, popular forces that put another Prince of Orange back in office.

From one crisis to the next, the underlying reality was what might be called a politically constituted commercial society, a society in which economic interests were inseparable from extra-economic power, political status and privilege. The urban patriciate, with privileged access to office, jealously guarded its civic power and its command of a self-perpetuating governing elite, with its network of patronage and clientage, while the vast commercial empire in which their wealth was rooted depended more on powers of coercion than production. This accounts not only for war with rival states but also for fierce and frequent civic conflict. It also tells us much about Dutch political theory, in its own golden age from the Revolt and the establishment of the Republic to the crisis of the late seventeenth century.

Hugo Grotius

The Dutch Republic's distinctive configuration of political and economic power found its quintessential theorist in Hugo Grotius. Born in Delft in 1583 to a regent family replete with office-holders, he began his political career very early, as we have seen, and would devote himself throughout his life, in both theory and practice, to defending the interests of the Dutch commercial empire and its urban patriciate. At the age of sixteen, shortly after returning from the mission to the French court with Oldenbarnevelt, he was admitted as a lawyer to the provincial court of Holland and then to the supreme court of the provinces of Holland and Zeeland. In 1601, he became official historiographer for the states of Holland and was commissioned by Oldenbarnevelt to write a history of the Dutch struggle against Spain.

When ships of the Dutch East India Company famously seized the treasure-laden Portuguese ship *Santa Catarina* in 1603, the Company commissioned Grotius to write its defence against strong opposition to this legally questionable act. Although his treatise, *De Indis*, was never published fully in his lifetime, part of his deliberations, published in 1609 as *Mare Liberum*, was the work that would launch his reputation as a theorist of international and natural law. The issues he was compelled to address were not only legal – though the legality of the seizure by the Company and its retention of the prize without state authorization was questionable – but also moral, in response to objections raised even by Company shareholders, not least by Mennonites among them. Grotius's response to this range of legal, moral and religious objections was an argument based crucially on the doctrine of natural law.

Grotius went on to hold various public offices and in 1613 became Pensionary of Rotterdam, which placed him among the ranks of Holland's regents. In the meantime, Oldenbarnevelt had concluded a truce with Spain, widely supported in Europe and among regents in Holland but provoking fierce factional disputes and popular opposition. These political disputes became entangled with a major theological controversy between followers of Arminius, the head of the theological faculty at the University of Leiden, and strict Calvinists, who simultaneously opposed the Republic's policies of religious toleration under Oldenbarnevelt and the truce with Catholic Spain. Remonstrants came to represent the faction of the regents, particularly in Holland, with its view of the public Church as a partner with, if not a subordinate to, civil government. Counter-Remonstrantism became a rallying point for opposition to the regents' regime, uniting a mixed coalition of the regime's opponents, ranging from the old nobility and Orangists to small artisans and craft guildsmen.

Grotius had already established himself as a major spokesman for the Oldenbarnevelt regime and the idea of an oligarchic Republic. In several of his writings between 1602 and 1610, he spelled out a limited republican doctrine, arguing that the best way of preserving liberty, stability and virtue was a consultative government, but one restricted to a closed oligarchy, manned by people like Dutch regents, with the means to devote their time entirely to public business.[6] The stadtholder might have a limited role, in what could be called a type of 'mixed constitution'; but the urban oligarchy clearly reigned supreme. It was this kind of patrician Republic that Oldenbarnevelt was defending against stadtholder and Calvinist critics. The controversy between Arminians (Remonstrants) and Counter-Remonstrants posed an immediate danger when the latter called for English intervention to protect the Dutch Church from Arminian doctrines. Oldenbarnevelt called on Grotius to head a delegation to London both to negotiate the disputes over the East Indies between England and the Dutch Republic and to dissuade King James from supporting the Counter-Remonstrants.

Grotius's position in the theological controversy was carefully calibrated. On the one hand, he fully supported the Oldenbarnevelt regime and its policies of (limited) toleration, against the strict Calvinist position. In the battle between Arminians and Counter-Remonstrants, he and Oldenbarnevelt were certainly closer to the Arminian view that, while salvation is granted by grace, human beings have free will and can accept (or deny) the offer of salvation through faith in Jesus Christ – in contrast to strict Calvinist convictions about predestination. Since salvation in that sense depends on faith, it seemed to follow that religious toleration should extend to anyone of faith, irrespective of confessional differences. On the other hand, while supporting liberty of conscience, he was careful not to extend it too far. In the end, the public Church, as an ally of government, remained supreme as both an arbiter of faith and an instrument of social order. Freedom of conscience and expression might have to be limited in order to maintain stability, if necessary by coercion.

The Oldenbarnevelt regime remained precariously in power for the next

---

6 See *ibid.*, pp. 421–2.

few years, but by 1616 social unrest had reached a dangerous peak. Economic pressures affecting manufacturing cities were aggravating opposition to the oligarchic regime, especially from artisans and immigrant textile workers. High bread prices, as in so many other cases of revolt in medieval and early modern Europe, stirred some to protest (including, significantly, the wives of artisans); but, as always in the Dutch Republic, economic grievances could not be divorced from protests against restricted access to civic government. There emerged a militant popular movement of Counter-Remonstrance, which at the same time challenged the exclusive power of the regents.

Grotius yet again entered the fray, elaborating his brand of Christian oligarchic republicanism to mobilize humanist scholarship in support of the public Church as understood by the regents, against those who claimed their doctrines were inconsistent with the truths of Christianity. In the following months, the religious and political controversy came to a head in a final battle over state sovereignty, with the States-General of the Republic, represented by Maurits, commander of the Republic's army and soon to be the Prince of Orange, pitted against the provincial estates, or, more particularly, the province of Holland and its regents. Maurits won that battle. Oldenbarnevelt was arrested, later to be executed for treason, and Grotius was sentenced to life imprisonment and all his property confiscated.

Grotius would escape from prison, with the help of his wife, in a manner that has made him famous among Dutch schoolchildren even today. Carried out in a chest supposedly containing books, he fled to France, where he wrote the second major work on which his modern reputation rests, *De Jure Belli ac Pacis,* in the hope of returning to Holland and government service. In this work, written at a time when much of Europe was more or less constantly at war – in the series of conflicts called the Thirty Years' War – his defence of Dutch commercial imperialism took account of events in the intervening period, in which the Dutch East India Company was engaged in various military ventures to capture not just ships but rival trading posts and fortresses. Forced to leave France when he angered Richelieu by refusing to support the French against Holland, he did eventually manage to return to his homeland; but unable to resist involvement in current disputes, he was forced to flee yet again, this time to Sweden, where he became a Swedish citizen and even Swedish ambassador to France. He died in 1645 without ever resuming his career in Holland.

Grotius's major works elaborated an ideology well suited to 'extra-economic' strategies for establishing commercial supremacy; and they were transparently constructed to defend the very particular practices of the Dutch in their quest for commercial domination, not least by means of war. To build his case, he not only produced a theory of war and peace but elaborated conceptions of right and natural law, which, it has been claimed by some commentators, laid the foundation for modern theories of natural law.[7]

In *Mare Liberum*, Grotius was defending the East India Company's seizure of the Portuguese ship and its treasure. The Company, founded in 1602 , had been granted by charter a monopoly of trade in the East Indies, together with the right to establish trading posts and fortresses commanding trade routes and, significantly, among other state-like powers, the right to form its own military force, to be used, in principle, for defensive purposes. But the doctrine of 'just war', for all its flexibility and its history of imperial justification, was not so easily adapted to accommodate the pursuit of profit by a private enterprise, let alone a brazen act of piracy, which was hard to describe as a defensive action. Grotius would later, in *De Jure Belli ac Pacis,* elaborate the theory of war more systematically; but in *Mare Liberum,* he set out to demonstrate that this military aggression, committed by a private trading company and not a sovereign state, not simply in self-defence but for no other reason than commercial profit, was undertaken in accordance with natural law and the law of nations.

To justify the Company's act of war, he set out to demonstrate that all nations must have access to the East Indies, on the grounds that the law of nations requires the freedom to trade; that papal donation does not create a legitimate claim, because infidels have rights of ownership, public and private, of which they cannot be divested simply because they are infidels; that the sea and rights of navigation cannot become anyone's private domain, as the Portuguese were treating it; and nor can there be an exclusive right to trade with another nation. He starts from the premise that there is a universal human community, governed by certain universal principles of sociability required for survival, grounded in natural law accessible to human reason. God created the regions of the world with different and incomplete resources for survival; and, since the world is so constructed that no region has the means of self-sufficiency, it is a principle of reason that there must be free commerce among the regions and that obstruction of free commerce violates the law of nations.

In the course of his argument, Grotius begins to lay out a theory of property; but, although he raises such questions as those addressed by Vitoria concerning the right of *dominium* in the Americas, he is, in *Mare Liberum,* less concerned with rights of settlers than with the access of Dutch traders to the seas, to trade routes and to the fruits of commerce. This was in keeping with Dutch commercial strategies. Unlike their imperial rivals, the Dutch were not primarily interested in original colonization in newly discovered territories; and their strategies had less to do with establishment of settler colonies than with commercial supremacy. Even when they did establish

---

7 For a provocative, and persuasive, interpretation of Grotius, see Richard Tuck, *The Rights of War and Peace: Political Thought and the International Order from Grotius to Kant* (Oxford: Oxford University Press, 1999).

colonies, as they would later do, for example, in southern Africa, it was in the first instance for the purpose of provisioning commercial ships. In any case, Grotius's intention in *Mare Liberum* was not to justify colonization; and there was no need to elaborate a theory of property that could underwrite a claim to captured territory. All that was needed was a justification for the Company's act of armed aggression on the high seas.

Between 1603, the year of the *Mare Liberum,* and 1625, when Grotius wrote *De Jure*, the Dutch would embark on a series of military actions to seize trading posts, fortresses and colonial bases from other imperial powers like the Spanish and the Portuguese. It was then no longer simply a matter of maintaining the freedom of the seas but of contesting the power of rival states by capturing territory already claimed by them. Even while the seizure of territory was less for the purposes of wealth-producing settlement than for the promotion of commercial supremacy, it required a more positive theory of property rights, which Grotius would develop in his later work. But in *Mare Liberum,* where he is defending not the seizure and retention of colonial territory but the commercial movements of the Dutch East India Company against the trade monopolies of rivals, he is more concerned with what is *not* property than what is.

Like others before him, he begins with the world as common property, which is divided by human institution to deal with a growing division of labour, as well as the consequences of human sinfulness. Grotius certainly accepts that this institution, although created by human convention, conforms to the law of nature and the *ius gentium*, on the grounds that it is necessary to maintain the social order. It has even been argued by some commentators that he depicts property as an institution so ingrained in human nature and the needs of social life that it approaches a theory of property as a natural right.[8] Nevertheless, his objective in *Mare Liberum*

---

8   There has been much debate among commentators about whether Grotius is arguing that there is no right of property in the state of nature and that property depends entirely on agreement, or whether he does indeed posit something very close to a natural right, which requires agreement only to acknowledge, but not to create, the right of property, so that he makes a major advance in the direction of the idea of a natural property right as conceived by John Locke. But it can be argued that the difference between doctrines of property as a convention and as a natural right has been exaggerated. Many thinkers who start with the proposition the world is originally a common *dominium* and is divided into private property by human convention or law nevertheless treat property as a sacred right, instituted by divine providence, whether to deal with the consequences of human sinfulness or to provide the conditions of social cooperation and the division of labour necessary to human survival, according to the principles of reason accessible to human beings, with all the force of natural law. It will be argued in a subsequent chapter that Locke's break with tradition has less to do with asserting property as a natural right than with making the right of property dependent on something more than occupation, use, or even labour, grounding the right of property in the production of exchange value.

was to lay out certain limits on what can be claimed as property. Since his main concern was to argue for the freedom of the seas, to challenge the right of commercial rivals like the Portuguese to claim ownership of the seas and monopolize trade routes, his principal objective here was to deny the possibility of any proprietary interest in the sea. We can have a proprietary right, he maintained, only to things we can individually consume or transform. The sea cannot be property, because, like air, it cannot be occupied or used in this way and is therefore a common possession. Furthermore, what cannot become private property, he argued (contrary to traditional conceptions of political jurisdiction), cannot, by the same token, be the public property of the state either, since both private and public ownership come about in the same way. No state jurisdiction is possible where the kind of control implied by property is even in principle impossible.

It is not difficult to see how military intervention might be justified on these grounds against those whose only wrong had been to assert a hitherto accepted right of state jurisdiction over neighbouring waters or the right to regulate certain fishing grounds and trade routes. Nor, of course, did this principle preclude the de facto monopolization of trade that the Dutch themselves were aiming for in certain places, where they simply coerced local populations into trade, establishing monopolies by forcing treaties on them (in a practice of treaties among 'unequals' that Grotius would endorse in De Jure), while aggressively repelling their European rivals.

Grotius has been called the father of natural law, or at least its first 'modern' exponent, because he elaborates a conception of natural law that does not depend on a theological grounding. It is a precept of reason accessible to every rational person and binding on every human being without reference to faith. His work has been claimed by some commentators as a, if not the, major advance in the theory of natural right, elaborating a 'modern' conception of rights as 'subjective', in contrast to 'objective' rights as conceived, most notably, by Thomas Aquinas. For Aquinas, as we have seen, *ius* denoted 'the just thing', what was 'right' or just in an action or a situation in accordance with natural law, while Grotius was vesting rights in the person, a moral power or entitlement inherent in the individual. Other commentators have contested these claims to Grotius's originality, arguing, for instance, that Suárez had already made the innovative move – or, indeed, that the conception of 'subjective' rights can be traced to twelfth- and thirteenth-century theology and canon law. But, whether Grotius's ideas were truly original or largely derivative, his arguments proceed in novel ways, in answer to specific theoretical requirements, in unique historical conditions.

In *De Jure Belli ac Pacis*, Grotius begins by defining law and laying out his conception of natural law. Human beings are social creatures, not only possessing a strong inclination to society but also, by virtue of reason, capable of determining what is required to create and sustain a social order.

These principles of social order accessible to reason and hence to all rational beings are natural laws, both in the sense that they represent the basic requirements of the social order needed to sustain human life and well-being and also in the larger sense that they are inherent in human nature. In a proposition that shocked some of his contemporaries, he suggests that these natural principles would apply even if there were no God or if human affairs were of no concern to him. But, he hastens to add, we cannot and should not assume that no God exists. There is ample evidence of his all-powerful existence and the divine rewards of obeying natural law, so we can and should assume that natural law derives from God and that obedience to him requires adherence to natural law.

Human beings create a social order to meet their natural needs, and they do so by mutual consent, which gives rise to an obligation that derives from natural law and applies to civic laws, which human beings promulgate to sustain their social arrangements. These laws are specific to particular communities, devised for their own needs; but there are also laws that apply beyond the borders of any particular civic community and regulate relations among communities. These may exist by agreement; but there are also unwritten laws, principles of reason, that derive from nature. War itself is not immune to laws of this kind; and, while the laws of particular states do not apply to the conduct of war, those common laws – the law of nations – remain in force. Just as individuals undertake an obligation to laws designed to maintain social order, which they need to satisfy requirements they cannot meet on their own, even the most powerful states will sometimes need the help of others, either for purposes of trade or merely in self-defence. In this sense, they belong to an international community, also governed by law. The argument that follows is informed by the principle that the law of nature entails rights – moral qualities inherent in the person, the observance of which is dictated by right reason. There are also rights created by civil power rather than by nature, and this includes the right of property; but once established by civil law, the obligation to respect them is a principle of natural justice and carries the obligation of natural law.

Having defined law in the *Prolegomena* and the general sense in which the law applies to war, Grotius goes on to consider what is right or lawful in war, or what constitutes a 'just war'. He first proceeds to demonstrate that war is not inconsistent with natural law or the law of the Gospel and then, distinguishing between public and private war, goes on to show that private war, that is, war conducted by someone not lawfully authorized, can still be lawful, in keeping with the law of nature, which permits aggressive action to ward off injury. To be sure, even to insist that natural law applies to the conduct of war may by itself imply limitations on the conduct of war; and it is not unreasonable to invoke Grotius as a theorist of restrictions on war. Yet the concept of just war has always been notoriously flexible, easily adapted to justify the most aggressive imperialist wars. The limitations Grotius imposes do not in any way preclude, and in many ways support, the most aggressive actions taken by the Dutch, and the East India Company in particular, with no other object than pursuit of private gain.

War, argues Grotius, is above all a defence against violations of rights against the self or property; and he constructs a whole political theory on the principle that self-preservation is the first and most fundamental law of nature. This means that individuals and states are permitted, perhaps even obliged, to acquire for themselves 'those things which are useful for life'. Although they may not, in the process, injure others who have not injured them, their own self-preservation comes first; and they are entitled to commit aggressive acts to ward off injury. Grotius's notion of injury turns out to be very broadly permissive, at least for states and private agents like the Dutch East India Company, while the moral limits to which private agents and sovereign states at war are both subject are minimal.

The notion that there exists some kind of international society bound together by certain common rules is regarded as one of Grotius's major contributions to international law and a peaceful world order. But his argument had far less to do with what private agents or states owe one another than with the right they have to punish each other in pursuit of self-interest, not only in defending themselves against attack but 'proactively', as it were, in purely commercial rivalries. 'Grotius', concludes Richard Tuck, 'endorsed for a state the most far-reaching set of rights to make war which were available in the contemporary repertoire.'[9] On the one hand, Grotius argues that states, which can have no powers that individuals do not already have in nature, must, like individuals, be governed by the same moral principles. On the other hand, this conception, with all its wide-ranging implications for political theory in general, was elaborated by Grotius to defend the East India Company, on the grounds that individuals, like and even before states, have the right to punish those who wrong them.

This implied not only a very wide-ranging international right of punishment but also, finally, a right to appropriate territory. To buttress that right, Grotius was obliged to develop his theory of property. In *Mare Liberum,* it had been enough to demonstrate that the sea could not be claimed as property. But now something more was required to justify the capture of territory. Having argued that something could become property only if it could be occupied, and individually consumed or transformed, which might be true of land but not the sea, he now elaborated the other side of that argument: if usable things were left unused, there was no property in them, and hence people could appropriate land left unused by others. Grotius argued that no local authority could legitimately prevent free passage or the occupation of

9 *Ibid.,* p. 108.

unused land, and any attempt to do so could legitimately be challenged by military means.

Nevertheless, since land, unlike the sea, was in principle capable of transformation into property, it was also susceptible to political jurisdiction. Grotius never denied that indigenous authorities retained their general jurisdiction over the land – something that Dutch trading companies in principle accepted by seeking the approval of these local authorities and even paying them for taking land out of their jurisdiction. But the basic principle remained: land left waste or barren was not property and could be occupied by those able and willing to cultivate it. Grotius's argument had clear affinities with the principle, in Roman law, of *res nullius*, which decreed that any 'empty thing', such as unoccupied land, was common property until it was put to use – in the case of land, especially agricultural use. This would become a common justification of European colonization.[10]

It soon becomes clear that Grotius, in defining the ultimate right of self-preservation, was far less interested in the rights of individual persons than in the actions of a 'private' agent like the Dutch East India Company. It is significant that, at the very outset of his argument, immediately after laying out his basic propositions about what constitutes a lawful war and explaining his distinction between public and private war, Grotius devotes a chapter to the question of the right of subjects to resist their superiors. It is here, and not in discussion of wars among states or the military acts of private companies, that the moral limits imposed on aggressive action are most unambiguously stringent. Applied to the rights of an individual in relation to the state, the right of self-defence is very narrowly defined; and Grotius mounts a fairly conventional argument against the right of resistance, not only effectively denying any such right to private individuals but even questioning the rights of 'lesser magistrates'.

For all these strict limits on the rights of individuals, Grotius's painstaking elaboration of the conditions for and against the conduct of war makes it possible to justify the Dutch East India Company's seizure of Portuguese ships or Spanish fortresses and trading posts, on the grounds that these commercial rivals had breached the laws of nature by claiming command of the seas and trade monopolies. It is no less possible, on Grotius's terms, to justify exclusive Dutch trading rights – that is, monopolies – on the grounds that they have been established by treaty or agreements, which, as

---

10 Pagden, in *Lords of All the World*, has a useful discussion of this principle and its employment particularly by the English and, to a lesser degree, the French, and the reasons for its absence in Spanish imperial ideology. See pp. 77 *passim*. The principle was obviously more useful in cases where imperialism took the form of settler colonies which displaced local populations, but of little use to the Spanish, with their empire of explicit conquest.

he makes unambiguously clear, are no less legitimate for having been imposed by a stronger party upon a weaker one, not only by means of just war but simply by bald intimidation. The Portuguese unlawfully asserted their rights of property over the sea, when no such property is possible. This gave the Dutch East India Company the right to intervene with military force, in defence of free commerce, which, since commerce is a condition of survival, are ultimately grounded in natural law and the right of self-preservation. The Dutch, on the other hand, legitimately claimed command of trade routes, by occupying territory and asserting property in it, even when it remained under sovereign jurisdiction, which could not interfere with the Company's property rights; or the Company could gain monopoly privileges, and even use of already occupied territory, by agreement with weaker powers whose sovereign jurisdiction they formally recognized, even while imposing their own superior will by nothing more nor less than tacit threats of force.

There are some significant theoretical manoeuvres in Grotius's argument, which mark a break in the history of political thought, even if not precisely the kind of 'modern' innovations sometimes claimed for Grotius. Much of Western political thought since Roman times, which had delineated two distinct modalities of power, *dominium* and *imperium*, had been concerned with the relation between property and sovereign power or jurisdiction.[11] In his account of how property originates and how individuals acquire a right of property in any given thing, Grotius's views in *De Jure Belli* do not depart in any significant way from those of a long line of theologians and jurists who maintained that in the beginning all the world was held as a common *dominium*, and that private property exists not by nature but by agreement – though it is no less consistent with natural law. Even if we interpret his argument, as some distinguished commentators do (see footnote 7 above), as leaning further in the direction of property as a natural right, it would not represent a significant departure from what went before. Where his argument takes an interesting turn is in his view of the relation between property and jurisdiction. Ownership and jurisdiction are not only separate – as others before Grotius had, for various reasons, emphasized – they also seem to be on equal terms as claims to territory. This means that unoccupied territory, even when it is already under sovereign jurisdiction, can be claimed as property by an occupier from outside that jurisdiction.

The real novelty here is not in the concept of property. We shall see in a

---

11　See my *Citizens to Lords* for a discussion of the a discussion of medieval debates on this subject, the ways in which the struggles between ecclesiastical and secular authority were played out as debates about property and jurisdiction, and the complexities arising from the 'parcellization of sovereignty', which made the line between property and jurisdiction more difficult to draw.

subsequent chapter how the needs of a distinctive social form, capitalism, and a new form of imperialism would generate a truly new conception of property, which departs from the tradition that occupation or use constitute proprietary right. For the purposes of Dutch commercial imperialism, something like these traditional theories was enough – provided that it allowed the Dutch East India Company to claim as its property territory that fell within the jurisdiction of a sovereign state other than the Dutch Republic. For that purpose, a variation in ideas of jurisdiction was more important that an innovation in the idea of property. Grotius would go on to dislodge the rights of jurisdiction even more radically from the core of political thought, with significant, if unintended, consequences.

Grotius's ideas on natural law and 'subjective' rights arise not primarily in connection with competing jurisdictions, nor even in considering the relation between citizen and state. It is the very particular questions arising from the actions of a trading company on the international stage that determine the direction of his argument. He was confronting wholly new conceptual problems posed by the Dutch East India Company. The first multinational joint stock company, formed by investors in search of commercial monopolies and profit, it also performed functions that in other imperial powers, in particular the Republic's main rivals, Portugal and Spain, belonged to sovereign states. There was, to be sure, nothing unusual in pre-capitalist Europe about the unity of public power and private appropriation. That was, after all, the common pattern in societies where the wealth of dominant classes so often depended on coercive force and where revenues derived from jurisdictional powers at various levels, from feudal lordship to state office. But in no other society, not even the Italian city-states, was public authority so intricately bound up with commercial dominance. While private wealth was still heavily reliant on extra-economic powers and coercion, those powers, when they did not derive directly from office, were aimed at dominance in trade – such as monopolies maintained by military force. In the Dutch Republic, ruled by urban elites who identified the public interest with commercial profit, there was a hazy line between the sovereign state and a commercial enterprise – as would be baldly demonstrated some years later when Dutch military action to place William of Orange on the English throne for purely commercial reasons would be subsidized by the Amsterdam stock exchange.

It was not Grotius's intention to weaken the sovereignty of the Dutch state (although he might have been tempted to weaken the States-General in favour of the province of Holland). It was not, in other words, his intention to question the state's claims to sovereign jurisdiction; and nor did he ever question the sovereignty of the Spanish or the Portuguese state. What he did was simply to claim for a non-jurisdictional agent certain rights normally associated with jurisdiction and state sovereignty. He was confronting the challenge of justifying the quasi-state powers of the Company and particularly its right to undertake military actions in the pursuit of private gain. The issue in this case, then, was not competing jurisdictions, as it typically had been in the discourse on rights in relation to political authority. It was not a question of the Company demanding its autonomy and jurisdictional powers against intrusions from the state or other authorities, temporal or ecclesiastical. Nor was it the protection of the one commonly acknowledged private right, the right of property, against the claims of public jurisdiction. The problem here was the state-like powers of a commercial company in relation to rival states. In confronting this distinctive problem, Grotius detached rights from jurisdiction in unprecedented ways.

The Dutch East India Company did not lay claim to public jurisdiction, and nor did Grotius make such claims on its behalf. But he did have at his disposal certain conceptions of rights, which might include the right of self-defence, inherent in the private person – such as the idea, formulated by Suárez, of a right as 'a certain moral power that every man has, either over his property or with respect to that which is due to him'. Whatever Suárez's purpose may have been in formulating the concept of rights in this way (and we should, as we have seen, be careful not to make too much of the differences between his formulation and that of Aquinas), Grotius's intentions are fairly transparent. The right of the Company to engage in military ventures is assimilated to the rights of private individuals, who have no jurisdiction and no common status other than their humanity. He proceeds by ascribing to the individual certain rights that can by extension be applied to other private agents; and he accomplishes this by proclaiming the right of self-preservation as the ultimate right, the one right that individuals and states unquestionably have in common and that must apply to private agents no less than to public authorities.

Grotius's concern, then, was not the rights of private individuals but the state-like rights of trading companies against competing states. Yet, because he claimed those rights not as public jurisdictions in competition with the sovereign state but as the rights of private agents, the unintended consequence was to set the discourse of rights on what appears to be a 'modern' course, vesting 'subjective' rights in individuals in a more elaborate and systematic way than anyone had done before him. The conceptual consequence was to place rights residing in the private person, the sovereign individual, on a par with the sovereign rights of the state.

Benedict Spinoza

Just a few years after Grotius died, the office of stadtholder fell vacant with the death of William II. The province of Holland, to be followed by others, chose to leave the office unfilled; and from 1650 to 1672, the so-called first 'stadtholderless' era, the urban patriciate enjoyed a period of undiminished power, under the leadership of the Grand Pensionary, Jan de Witt. It was during this period that Benedict Spinoza reached maturity. While his interventions in philosophical and theological debates were radical and profoundly controversial, he was above all a philosopher and not a political figure in the manner of Grotius. He was, nonetheless, politically engaged; and his political allegiances seem to have been with the republican elite. While he was critical of his friends and allies, those allegiances are clearly reflected in his political philosophy. De Witt himself was a friend and protector of Spinoza; and among the strongest influences on the philosopher's political ideas were members of the commercial elite and de Witt's supporters – such as Lambert van Velthuysen and the de la Court brothers – who elaborated republican ideas, especially those who, as paradoxical as it may seem, drew upon Hobbes as their principal authority.

Spinoza was born in Amsterdam in 1632, the son of a Portuguese Jewish merchant whose family had taken refuge in the Netherlands. Benedict was well schooled in Judaism and may even have been educated for the rabbinate. Yet he was soon excommunicated from the Jewish community, as well as denounced by the Catholic Church, no doubt for ideas that foreshadowed his great work, the *Ethics*. He would establish connections with freethinking Protestants, who had come under the philosophical influence of Descartes and included precisely the kinds of Cartesian republicans who brought Hobbesian ideas to the Netherlands. Although he would manage to shock even those like Velthuysen, who had begun by supporting Spinoza's philosophical ventures, there is no mistaking his affinities, political no less than philosophical, with those Cartesian circles. In 1672, the Germans and French invaded the Netherlands, de Witt was assassinated, and the Orangist faction restored the office of stadtholder, establishing a regime – with the support of popular forces – under which Spinoza would continue to feel threatened until his death in 1677.

Spinoza began in 1663 with reflections on Descartes' philosophy but soon went on to elaborate his own distinctive views. In the *Tractatus Theologico-Politicus* of 1670, he laid out a provocative attack on the kind of reactionary Protestantism that supported the House of Orange, at a time when religious and republican liberties were under threat. Like others among his Cartesian republican associates, he promoted religious toleration; and like them, he called for the freedom of philosophy, as distinct from theology, even in interpretation of the Bible – which, in Dutch confessional disputes, had clear political implications. But he followed these principles to their limits in ways his friends were not always willing to do. Ultimately it would be Velthuysen, at first a friend and collaborator on the question of religion and philosophy, who would denounce Spinoza as an outright atheist.

The guiding principle of Spinoza's philosophy, which is elaborated in his

Ethics, was the unity of God and nature. To speak of a transcendent creator who by his own will and for his own purposes forged the universe seemed meaningless to the philosopher. There is one single reality, which we can call nature; and if God is its cause, he is an immanent cause, not standing outside nature but acting as the principle of nature unfolding its immanent necessities. Arcane debates have raged about whether this makes Spinoza a pantheist or even an atheist; but one thing remains certain: Spinoza had gone further than anyone else in the Western philosophical canon in denying any form of transcendence beyond or alien to nature or any dualism of matter and spirit. Humanity belongs to nature too; and, just as all of nature is a unique and single substance, there is no meaningful way to speak of a division in humanity between mind or spirit and matter. At the same time, our participation in this unique and single reality allows for real human knowledge. The material complexities of the human body are expressed in a complex and uniquely human capacity for apprehending the single reality of which the human being is an integral part. While as natural beings we are driven by our passions, having a unique capacity to know and understand the forces that drive us, we need not be slaves to our passions, or indeed to uncritical and unreflective adherence to religion, and can live a free life in accordance with reason. We shall see how these principles are reflected in Spinoza's views on the ideal polity.

That Spinoza was a groundbreaking philosopher, whose philosophical ideas had radical implications beyond the boundaries of scholarly debate, is surely not in question. But, although he has long held his place in the canon of philosophy, his political ideas have in recent years enjoyed a resurgence. It is striking that the dominant theme in this revival has been the philosopher's political radicalism, celebrated not only by a mainstream historian like Jonathan Israel, who situates him at the heart of a 'Radical Enlightenment', but also by Marxist thinkers from Antonio Negri to Etienne Balibar.[12] Israel goes beyond those historians of political thought who regard Spinoza, with his conception of rational freedom, as a, if not the, founder of 'liberalism'. The Radical Enlightenment, with its source in Spinoza, can, according to Israel, be credited with modern ideas of 'democracy, racial and sexual equality; individual liberty of lifestyle; full freedom of thought, expression, and the press; eradication of religious authority from the legislative process and education; and full separation of church and state.'[13] Indeed, whether or not we attribute directly to his influence the revolutionary movements that

---

12   Michael Hardt and Antonio Negri, *Empire* (Cambridge, MA: Harvard University Press, 2000), and Etienne Balibar, *Spinoza and Politics* (London: Verso, 1998).

13   Jonathan Israel, *A Revolution of the Mind: Radical Enlightenment and the Intellectual Origins of Modern Democracy* (Princeton: Princeton University Press, 2010), pp. vii–viii.

followed in the eighteenth century in North America and France, Spinoza, suggests Israel, virtually invented modern democracy. Marxist commentaries may seem still more extravagant in their claims for him, if we understand them as ascribing to him even more radically democratic and egalitarian doctrines than the kind of liberal democracy Israel has in mind.

There is no great mystery about why Spinoza's metaphysics, his 'monism', 'naturalism' and repudiation of transcendence have had a strong appeal to thinkers of the left, ever since Marx himself. Such ideas undoubtedly represented a powerful challenge to all forms of established authority, political, ecclesiastical or cultural. Some Marxist advocates of a radical Spinoza are also drawn to him because of what they understand as a materialism denuded of the teleologism that has dominated Marxist conceptions of history, deeply influenced by conventional Enlightenment conceptions of progress and by Hegelian philosophy. Yet Spinoza's political theory is a different matter. His conception of democracy remains far more ambiguous and paradoxical than recent interpretations suggest.

When all is said and done, the polity that was in practice closest to his theoretical democracy was the Dutch Republic, and especially the province of Holland, a civic order unambiguously dominated by wealthy commercial elites. He would certainly have preferred a republic with more popular support from the lesser classes who tended to side with Orangists and stadtholders against the urban elites. But, while this would have required something different from the self-perpetuating, self–co-opting oligarchy preferred by the regents, it is not at all clear that Spinoza's definition of democracy is inconsistent with an urban republic like the one in which he lived, where high office remained a prerogative of wealth. In his ideal 'democracy', the government would not be self-recruited, but he is careful to avoid identifying the inclusiveness of the citizen body or access to office as a criterion of democracy.

In the *Tractatus Theologico-Politicus*, Spinoza describes democracy as the most 'natural' form of state, the one most consistent with natural liberty, and the one least likely to commit acts of folly endangering self-preservation. (*TT-P* XVI) He also tells us that the most 'absolute' form of sovereignty 'if any such thing exists, is really the sovereignty held by a whole people'. But it is in his later, unfinished *Tractatus Politicus* that he provides his most elaborate definition of democracy. The difference between democracy and aristocracy, he stresses, is that, while in the latter, 'the right to govern is entirely dependent on co-optation', in a democracy 'it depends mainly on a kind of innate right, or a right acquired by fortune'. (*TP* VIII.1) A stable and successful aristocracy should have a large patriciate, but even if the whole population is admitted to the patriciate it remains an aristocracy as long as the right of entry is determined by express choice and not by some general law or inherited right. At the same time, a state can be 'democratic' even if that general or hereditary right is limited to a minority. He goes on to explain:

> [I]n aristocracy the appointment of a particular individual to the patriciate depends entirely on the will and free choice of the supreme council, so that the right to vote and undertake offices of state is in no case an hereditary possession, and no one can demand that right for himself by law; but in the state I am now discussing [democracy] the opposite is true. For here all who are of citizen parentage, or who have been born within the fatherland, or who have done good service to the commonwealth, or who qualify on other grounds recognized by law as entitling a man to civic rights, all these, I say, can legally claim the right to vote in the supreme council and to undertake offices of state; and it cannot be denied them unless they are criminals or persons of ill repute.
>
> Thus if it is laid down in the constitution of a state that only older men who have reached a certain age, or eldest sons as soon as they attain majority, or those who contribute a certain sum of money to the exchequer, shall have the right to vote in the supreme council and to handle public affairs, then, although such provisions would make it possible for its supreme council to be smaller than that of the aristocracy I have dealt with above, the state will still have to be called a democracy, since those of its citizens who are appointed to govern the commonwealth are not selected by the supreme council as the best, but are assigned this function by law. (*TP* XI.1–2)

On Spinoza's criteria, then, there is nothing to prevent an oligarchic republic ruled by commercial elites, with a small and exclusive governing council and even a limited citizen body, from being called 'democratic'.[14] Yet he never repudiates what appears to be the approbation for 'democracy' in his earlier work; and it is not self-evident why it seemed so important to him to claim the title of democracy for what, by any conventional definition, might still look like an aristocracy or even an oligarchy. 'Democratic' was far from being the word of high praise it has in recent times become. In early modern Europe, where the understanding of 'democracy' was still rooted in its ancient, original meaning as rule by the (common) people or even the poor,

---

14 It should perhaps be emphasized that Spinoza's conception of democracy cannot be explained as simply involving the kind of distinction elaborated (as we shall see in the next chapter) by Jean Bodin, between the nature of sovereignty and the form of government. Bodin can, for example, speak of a sovereign monarchy which can be 'democratic' if state office is accessible not only to the nobility or to men of wealth or virtue, as in an 'aristocratic' form of government; but, as should be clear from the passage quoted here, this is not what Spinoza has in mind.

it was more likely to be a word of condemnation, conjuring up the spectre of mob rule and, among propertied classes, a threat to their very existence. Even those who argued in favour of 'mixed' constitutions, in which the powers of kings and aristocracies were leavened by a 'democratic' element, were generally arguing in favour of oligarchic rule. There was, then, no immediately obvious reason for going quite as far as Spinoza did to attach the merits of democracy to an essentially oligarchic republicanism. Who, after all, was likely to be moved by such a designation? Was there any conceivable audience that might have been persuaded by it?

It may be tempting to think that Spinoza's insistence on using the word 'democracy' as if it were indeed high praise reveals his true democratic faith. Might this mean that he was, indeed, a democrat at least in his earlier days, and that, once having asserted his allegiance to democracy, he was in his later work – inspired by the shock of defeat – compelled simply, and somewhat unconvincingly, to redefine democracy just for the sake of consistency, so that his earlier praise might still apply to a form of state not obviously democratic? The bloody victory of the Orangist faction and the restoration of the stadtholder, supported by popular forces, may have required a certain rethinking; and it is almost as if Spinoza, once having insisted that democracy was the 'natural' form of sovereign power, was now seeking a definition of democracy that would allow the inclusion of far less democratic forms.

It seems more likely, however, that another kind of logic was at work. We have already seen how the idea that political authority derives from the 'people' and is grounded in consent could be used in favour of anything but democratic power, invoked to support even monarchies against not only popes but popular resistance. There is an element of that in Spinoza too. In the course of his discussion of democracy in *Tractatus Theologico-Politicus*, he makes a striking move, which seems to suggest that what he says about democracy even in his earlier work represents not so much approval of the democratic state as a means of legitimating other, rather less democratic forms. He tells us that he has two reasons for deliberately concentrating on the democratic state: the first is that it seems to be the most natural form – a proposition that appears to be not a normative judgment but an empirical observation that democracy is closest to humanity's natural conditions; and the second reason is that

> it best serves my purpose of dealing with the benefits of freedom in a commonwealth. I therefore pass over the bases of other governments; indeed, it is no longer necessary for us to know how they have arisen – and often arise still – in order to discover their right, which is abundantly obvious from what I have just shown. For whoever has sovereign power, whether it be one man, or a few, or all, has undoubtedly a perfect right to command everything he wishes. (XVI)

This means that aristocracies or kings have the same right to supreme power in their own forms of state as do the people in a democracy, since they are ultimately rooted in the same foundation (XVI). These other forms, in other words, may derive their legitimacy from their democratic origin.

Yet there remains something distinctive about Spinoza's characterization of 'democracy', which still needs to be explained. The logic of his argument may be easier to follow if we situate it in the context of Dutch political debate in that specific historical moment, at a time when the main objective of political thinkers, such as Velthuysen and the de la Court brothers, who supported de Witt, was to exclude the stadtholder altogether from any share in state authority. At the same time, the de la Courts in particular, who were newcomers to Holland from the southern Netherlands and did not belong to the governing regents, argued in favour of a more open republic with a less restrictive patriciate, elected by citizens in an assembly; and this was clearly a position favoured by Spinoza. Here the influence of Machiavelli and the Italian city-republics was very clear – though the model of Venice, or a *governo stretto*, figured more prominently than Machiavelli's Florence, in its *governo largo* mode, as the ideal for Dutch commercial interests. To be sure, the right to rule should, according to the de la Courts (as, indeed, for Jan de Witt), be confined to wealthy classes, and even the citizen body would ideally not include the plebs; but the ruling oligarchy, while restricted to the wealthy, should not be self–co-opting, as the regents' patriciate had increasingly become, especially as the European economic crisis took hold in the Republic. Only if the possibility of office were more open would it serve to harness private greed to public good.

The main theoretical requirement for these oligarchic republicans was to rule out, at almost all costs, any notion of a mixed constitution. That classic idea had, since ancient Rome, often done service in support of oligarchic republicanism; and even Grotius had invoked it. But now it was being used by Orangists to defend the position of the stadtholder, claiming, among other things, that this office protected the people from the oligarchs' excessive power. If the politics of the day precluded any concession by republican elites to theories of 'mixed' sovereignty, some other means had to be found to describe Dutch oligarchic rule, which factored out the monarchical element. For the de la Courts as indeed for Spinoza, there was the added requirement of replacing the self–co-opting regents with a more open oligarchy and finding other ways of attracting popular sentiment away from the Orangists. This posed a wholly new conundrum: how to introduce a 'democratic' element into the oligarchic Republic without conceding a divided sovereignty.

It was in this spirit that the Dutch republicans eagerly adopted Hobbes and his theory of indivisible sovereignty. They were clearly impressed by his argument sustaining a single, undivided sovereign power, even though they mobilized it not in favour of an absolute monarch, as did Hobbes himself, but for a civic Republic against the stadtholder's claim to a share in state power. On Hobbesian principles, the Dutch were able to argue that neither the House of Orange nor those clerics who opposed the civic government had any legitimate claim to state power in the Republic.

Hobbes was not the first political thinker to argue for indivisible sovereign power, but he did so on distinctive grounds, which seemed to have a special appeal to the Dutch. Unlike Jean Bodin in France, he was (for reasons that will be discussed at greater length in a later chapter) not principally concerned with the need to combat various corporate powers contesting jurisdiction with the monarchy. Instead, he took as his central theme conflicts among self-interested individuals whose overriding motivation was not to gain a share of public authority but simply to ensure self-preservation.

This seemed to suit Dutch purposes. The issue for them, as for the English, was not a conflict among corporate jurisdictions. During the Dutch Revolt, opponents of the Spanish monarch had, to be sure, typically asserted various claims to particular jurisdictions, privileges, liberties, and the powers of 'lesser magistrates' against incursions by the monarchy. But, in the course of the Revolt, the nature of the conflict changed, with opponents of the monarchy increasingly claiming a free and sovereign republican government. As the Republic was established, there emerged new doctrines of sovereignty belonging to the 'people' as a whole. That sovereignty was embodied in the nobles and urban patricians conceived not as 'lesser magistrates' but, in principle, as delegates of the sovereign people.[15] When, in Spinoza's day, republican elites challenged the powers of the stadtholder, they were no longer contesting his power as claimants to competing jurisdictions or the powers of lesser magistrates. They challenged the very existence of the stadtholder's office in favour of a single, undivided sovereignty.

Reflecting on human nature and the purpose of the state in recognizably Hobbesian terms, they argued that human beings are creatures driven by their passions, in pursuit of their own selfish interests and their principal aim, self-preservation. A stable state, they maintained, requires that these passions be held in balance, something that can be achieved only by an indivisible sovereign power. In the Dutch context this had a particular meaning: the aim was to achieve not only peace among self-interested individuals but, more specifically, a form of polity that would encourage the pursuit of wealth, sustaining commercial dominance without creating instability among rival civic interests, while preserving the position of commercial elites.

The specifically Dutch element in these arguments is what we have called

---

15 See introduction to *The Dutch Revolt,* ed. Martin van Gelderen (Cambridge: Cambridge University Press, 1993).

the politically constituted commercial society. This implies not only that the Dutch Hobbesians assume a society in which commercial interests are insep- arable from extra-economic power, political status and privilege, but also that, even in this profoundly commercialized society, the harmony of economic interests must, in their view, be achieved by political means. The critical instrument of harmony is not, as in the later Anglo-Scottish model of commercial society, the 'invisible hand' of the market. But neither is it, as in the French 'political economy', an absolutist monarchy. Political stability and harmony in this commercial society is best achieved by republican government, in which wealth is joined to public office.[16]

Although it would be a Dutchman, Bernard Mandeville, who, writing in early eighteenth-century England, would make famous the idea that 'public benefits' derive from 'private vices', something like that idea had already been proposed in France by Antoine de Montchrétien (as we have seen); even earlier, in sixteenth-century England, Sir Thomas Smith (about whom more in Chapter 7), had suggested that competing economic interests could be harmonized to forge a common good. For the Dutch, as for the French (and, indeed, for Thomas Smith), transformation of individual greed into commu- nal well-being required active guidance by the state. Even Mandeville would continue to emphasize the role of political guidance, in an interesting contrast to Adam Smith, who, although he certainly assigns the state an important role in ensuring the conditions of a truly competitive market, looks to the market itself to discipline competing interests. Smith's idea was rooted in a capitalist market of a kind that existed only in England and nowhere else, not even in a thoroughly commercialized society like the Dutch Republic. What was distinctively Dutch was a conception of commer- cial harmony produced by carefully balanced republican institutions, which would guide the pursuit of selfish interests to promotion of the common good by joining wealth to public office.

If Hobbes's views on human nature, passions and the sovereign powers of the civil magistrate provided the essential building blocks for Dutch republi- cans, an argument originally designed to underwrite the sovereign power of an absolutist monarchy required substantial modification to fit republican requirements. Hobbes had, to be sure, allowed for a plural sovereign; but his argument was constructed to make it clear that an indivisible, truly sover- eign, power resides most perfectly and absolutely in a single, undivided

---

16   Arguments like those of the 'Spinozan Marxists', who situate him – albeit ab- stractly – in the context of a 'market capitalism', tend to miss precisely what is distinctive about the Dutch commercial system. Spinoza's political philosophy seems more consis- tent and easier to comprehend in the context of what we are calling here a politically constituted commercial society, with all its assumptions about the unity of economic and 'extra-economic' power and about the political harmonization of interests.

mind or will, embodied in a monarchy. For the Dutch republicans, as for Hobbes, a 'mixed constitution' was not an option; but to make the strongest possible case for a sovereign power residing in a republican collective leadership, a republican power so indivisible that the stadtholder could have no place in it, required something more.

Whatever else Spinoza hoped to accomplish with his departures from Hobbes, he certainly sought to reverse the Hobbesian principle about the ideal location of indivisible power. A sovereign power must, it is true, express a common purpose; and Spinoza's theory faced the challenge of how such a common purpose could emerge from many minds and diverse passions. But there was no question of conceding to Hobbes that a monarchy was best, the surest way of translating a multiplicity of individual self-interests into a civil unity. An argument would have to be found that would give a plural sovereign the kind of primacy enjoyed in Hobbes's theory by a monarch.

Spinoza's argument, in simple terms, is that governments are generally stable to the degree that they enjoy the support of their subjects. Wide popular support, it would seem on the face of it, is more likely to exist if the people have a direct stake in government. The wider the scope of the sovereign power, the more 'absolute' it is, precisely because such a sovereignty is, by definition, more powerful, to the extent that it expresses the people's common purpose and is less inclined to stray from their common interests.

Yet the argument turns out to be more ambiguous than it seems at first sight. Does it, for example, mean that a democracy, as rule by an inclusive multitude, embracing a wider range of individuals and interests, must be more stable and secure than a less inclusive form, an aristocracy? Significantly, when Spinoza introduces the suggestion that sovereignty held by the whole people is more 'absolute', he does so not for the purpose of defending democracy but to demonstrate that an aristocracy with a council 'of sufficient size' is more 'absolute' than the rule of one man. A republic governed by a more open patriciate is, in other words, in this sense 'absolute'; and the passage even suggests that such an aristocracy is as close to 'absolute' as, in the real world, is conceivable. At the same time, even kings can garner popular support, if they govern for the common good (or even, possibly, if not?); and where they can maintain their power, the monarchy has no less right to rule than a democracy. Spinoza even suggests that monarchies have been historically more stable, while democracies have tended to degenerate into some other form like aristocracy.

Does this perhaps mean that democracy's claims to superiority have less to do with stability or security than with liberty? Even here, there are ambiguities. The philosopher does indeed claim that democracy is the form 'most consonant with individual liberty'; but he also tells us that freedom does not consist in acting simply in accordance with our own pleasures and passions, which may be contrary to our real advantage. True freedom means action in accordance with reason, which tends to be contrary to human inclinations. This means it requires strict obedience to a sovereign power, the sole legislative authority, acting in the common good, whether that sovereign power is a democracy or a monarchy. Indeed, a democracy that allows free rein to destructive or even simply useless passions is less free than a monarchy that governs for the people's benefit.

However radical Spinoza's philosophical system, his views on nature, reason or religion, may have been, it is virtually impossible to sustain an unambiguous case for his commitment to democracy in anything like its conventional meanings, ancient or modern, simply on the strength of what he explicitly says about the virtues and vices of specific political forms. Nor is it possible to brush aside the striking fact that his definition of democracy is carefully constructed to include an oligarchic republic, and that many of the observations seized upon by advocates of the philosopher's democratic radicalism are designed to underpin that kind of republican oligarchy. It is, nonetheless, fair to say that, whatever his intentions, his mode of argumentation opens certain democratic doors in strikingly unprecedented ways.

Here is how the case for Spinoza's democratic radicalism has been summed up by two of the principal advocates: while Hobbes, they say, 'plays a foundational role in the modern construction of a transcendent political apparatus', Spinoza is the philosopher of 'immanence', the philosopher who best expresses the idea that all power and authority are inherent in, and emanate from, the multitude. A similar, if rather more nuanced, argument has been made by Etienne Balibar. Spinoza, he suggests, asks a question never before raised by any political thinker, at least as an object of theoretical analysis: 'that of the basis of State power in the people, that is, in movements originating from within the "multitude" itself.'[17]

We can assess these claims by looking at how Spinoza's argument unfolds in relation to Hobbes's conception of the 'multitude'. Both philosophers start from the same premise: that, as Spinoza puts it in the *Tractatus Theologico-Politicus,* 'each has as much right as he has power' (II.8). Yet, if he identifies right with capacity or power in a manner similar to Hobbes, it is precisely here that, by his own account, he departs most significantly from the English philosopher: 'I always', he writes in Epistle 50 in response to a friend's enquiry about his differences with Hobbes, 'preserve the natural right in its entirety, and I hold that the sovereign power in a State has right over a subject only in proportion to the excess of its power over that of a subject'.

For Spinoza, in keeping with his philosophical 'naturalism', the emphasis here is on the 'natural', and the concept of right is defined in 'naturalist' terms, maintaining the identity of right and capacity or power, devoid of

---

17   Hardt and Negri, *Empire*, p. 83; Balibar, *Spinoza and Politics*, p. 56.

any normative significance. Hobbes, too, seemed to be arguing that anything individuals have the power or capacity to do in pursuit of self-preservation they have a natural right to do. Yet, because his conception of sovereignty allows for the unconditional transfer of rights to a sovereign power, which thereby acquires the right to decide for the subject what needs to be done to promote self-preservation, Hobbes has, in Spinoza's eyes, qualified the naturalist principle. If the sovereign power acquires an unconditional entitlement to rule by virtue of a voluntary transfer of rights from individuals, it would appear that right retains a normative element and is not entirely synonymous with power.[18]

On the face of it, Spinoza's unequivocal identification of right with power seems an even more unambiguous appeal to the prerogatives of power than Hobbes himself could contemplate. The English philosopher is reputed ruefully to have said to his friend John Aubrey that Spinoza had outdone him, having 'cut through him a barre's length, for he [Hobbes] durst not write so boldly.'[19] Yet Spinoza's daring formulation becomes not so much a statement of the principle that might makes right as a refusal of any idea that natural rights can be alienated and, arguably, an assertion of the multitude's political identity, in a way that contrasts sharply with Hobbes.

In his earlier work, Hobbes (who will be discussed at greater length in Chapter 7) had described democracy as the original form of sovereignty 'by institution' – that is, the first form of sovereignty created not by compulsion, nor by 'acquisition' or conquest, but as 'a creation out of nothing by human wit', by 'many men assembled together . . . which proceedeth from the assembly and consent of a multitude.' It is from this original form that the other forms – aristocracy and monarchy – derive (*Elements of Law* XX, XXI). In elaborating his idea of the contract in his later work, Hobbes abandoned this formulation. In *De Cive* and the *Leviathan*, he was not seeking to explain the historical origin of political authority but rather to emphasize that the voluntary transfer of rights to a sovereign power was absolute and unconditional, on the grounds that the multitude can never be more than a disparate collection of individuals, which can have no political identity.

Hobbes was confronting the problem of the 'multitude' in wholly new ways. The idea that sovereignty, of one kind or another, derives originally

---

18   In the *Leviathan*, a work Spinoza may not have known, Hobbes, as we shall see in the next chapter, seems to come closer to Spinoza by modifying his argument in a way that suggests the transfer of power is not as unconditional as it appears to be in *De Cive* and that the right to rule may indeed be conditional on the de facto power to maintain it – perhaps in order to justify Cromwell's accession to power and legitimate the Revolution that had overthrown a king.

19   'The Life of Thomas Hobbes of Malmesbury', in John Aubrey, *Brief Lives*, ed. John Buchanan-Brown (London: Penguin, 2000), p. 441.

from the people or a body of consenting individuals had, as we have seen, long been a convention in Western political thought; and it had no necessary implications for the people's political rights, within or against the state. It was typically invoked on behalf of one jurisdictional claim against another – for instance, by monarchies against the papacy, or by 'lesser magistrates' claiming to act as the people's corporate representatives in opposition to the king. But for Hobbes, as we shall see in Chapter 7, the 'multitude' presented a new kind of problem, which no political theorist had yet seriously confronted. Just as the language of individual rights took on a different meaning in the English context, where corporate powers were relatively weak and a new, less mediated political relation between private individual and state had displaced the old contest among jurisdictions, the question of the 'multitude' and its political identity took on a new significance.

In the English context Hobbes had felt compelled (as we shall see) to confront not only the conflict between Parliament and Crown but also the role of the people outside Parliament, the 'multitude', which had invaded the political arena in unprecedented ways. In his earlier work, it was enough to defend the crown against the claims of Parliament. By the time of *De Cive*, the work that established his reputation in the Dutch Republic, he was no longer simply defending the monarch against parliamentary forces or even against more radical claims to 'republican' liberty, but also seeking a way to deprive the multitude of any political identity.

In his earlier work, he had supported the Crown against Parliament by adopting an argument that, while certainly less grounded in corporatist assumptions, was not so different from that of his predecessors: that the people, as a collection of individuals, had created the sovereign by transferring their power. But in *De Cive*, he was confronting a different problem, the political role assumed by the people outside Parliament, who were taking to the streets in growing numbers and asserting a new kind of political identity. It was not here simply a question of tracing the sovereign power – whether of the monarch or of Parliament – to its original source in a multitude of consenting individuals. The problem Hobbes confronted was the multitude's assertion of its own direct political agency. His response was simply to say that the multitude had no political will or identity: 'When we say the People, or Multitude, wills, commands, or doth any thing', he insisted, it must be understood that it is the state itself 'which Commands, Wills and Acts by the will of one, or the concurring will of more, which cannot be done, but in an Assembly' (VI.1n). It is only once a multitude of individuals has given way to a united sovereign power that it is possible to speak of a political society.

Hobbes, then, was already grappling with the 'immanence' of the multitude's power in unprecedented ways. It could be said that, even if his objective was to demonstrate that the multitude's only political role was to relinquish and alienate its political agency, he went considerably further than Hardt and Negri or Balibar suggest in raising the question of the multitude as the direct and immediate, 'immanent' source of political power. He certainly went beyond anything proposed by medieval thinkers who had invoked the corporate 'people' or consent in the perennial contests over jurisdiction. *De Cive* may have set the terms of the debate for Dutch republicans; but any attempt to transform Hobbes's argument from a case for absolutist monarchy into a brief for an open republican oligarchy required a delicate balancing act, going one step further in establishing the 'immanent' power of the multitude, while retaining the dominance of the urban elite.

When Spinoza, in his earlier work, described democracy as the most 'natural' form of state, the one closest to the natural freedom of the individual, he was not so very far from Hobbes's early contention that democracy was the original form of state 'by institution'. Neither thinker was making a moral judgment so much as simply speculating on the most likely means by which a multitude of individuals might leave their natural state of freedom to institute political society. But both of them would later abandon this formulation, though for different reasons and in very different ways. Like Hobbes, Spinoza in his later work is no longer seeking the original, historical source of sovereignty. He no longer even mentions the idea of an original contract as the natural or primary source of sovereign power; but, unlike Hobbes, he seems to avoid any formulation, historical or normative, that may imply an original transfer of natural rights, however conditional, and takes for granted the political identity of the multitude. He allows for a kind of secondary contract, whereby the people, which already exists as a political entity, transfers powers to a king or aristocracy; and he even suggests that most aristocracies were originally democracies (*TP* VIII 12). This does imply that aristocracy and monarchy have a right to rule; and it may even suggest that democracies in reality have not typically been stable. Nevertheless, in Spinoza's formulation the political identity of the multitude remains at least in principle intact. Rights remain synonymous with powers – which means that sovereignty remains conditional on the maintenance of power and is likely to depend on a capacity to garner and to keep popular support.[20]

Yet, if this seems to lend some credence to those arguments that see a democratic essence in Spinoza's political theory, it remains entirely consistent with the view of the ideal polity espoused by prominent Dutch oligarchs: a commercial republic governed by an open urban aristocracy of wealth, in which republican institutions and the advantages derived from office help to channel private greed to the pursuit of common goods. Spinoza might prefer

---

20 Again, Hobbes would in the *Leviathan* come close to this, as we shall see in a subsequent chapter.

a more inclusive citizen electorate than did some of his compatriots, and the *TP* leaves tantalizingly open the possibility of a more unambiguously democratic argument. The work is suddenly cut off just at the point when Spinoza sets out to discuss the particular form of democracy in which, he says (for reasons that must remain unclear), he is most interested: an inclusive democracy whose citizen body consists of all independent men, all those subject to the laws of their government (as distinct from residents subject to other governments) and leading decent lives. Nevertheless, his definition of democracy itself, very painstakingly laid out, does not rule out exclusion of the plebs (to say nothing of women, whose relative natural weakness appears to justify their general exclusion from the citizenry[21]); and that definition has the virtue of embracing a de la Court–style oligarchy without conceding a divided sovereignty.

Nowhere, indeed, is there a clearer statement of the Dutch Hobbesian ideal than in Spinoza's observation that the state should be based

> on such laws as will cause the majority, not indeed to seek to live wisely – for that is impossible – but at any rate to be governed by those passions which are most useful to the commonwealth. Thus every attempt must be made to ensure that the rich, if they cannot be thrifty, are at any rate greedy for gain. For if this passion for gain, which is universal and constant, is reinforced by the desire for glory, most men will certainly make every effort to increase their wealth by honourable means so as to obtain office and avoid great disgrace. (*TP* X.6)

There is no mistaking the general principles Spinoza is outlining here: the greed for gain is a, perhaps even the, human passion most useful to the commonwealth; and it can be harnessed to the public good by making wealth a means to achieve the honour of office. Whatever we may think of the philosopher's observation that sovereignty is in principle most 'absolute' when it resides in the whole people, in the real world a republic governed by a commercial elite driven by greed seems best equipped to guide the passions of self-interested individuals towards the common good – and this apparently applies no less to the philosopher's 'democracy' than to an aristocracy. It is when greed is attached to republican office that governance by human passions can be most readily translated into the rule of reason.

We can gain some perspective on Spinoza's 'democracy' if we consider it

---

21 In his discussion of democracy, Spinoza considers at some length (*TP* XI.4) whether the exclusion of women from the political domain and their subjection to the authority of men exists by nature or merely by institution and concludes that the cause – and the justification – is their natural weakness. Their power, and therefore their right, is not equal to men's.

against the background of political developments elsewhere, which were accompanied by truly radical conceptions of the multitude and its claims to political agency. When the Dutch philosopher was still a boy, the political terrain was being redefined by the 'people' in England both in the streets and in the realm of ideas. We have already seen how Hobbes felt compelled to confront these popular intrusions into the political domain. But there were also far more radical expressions of the multitude's 'immanent' power. When, for example, Spinoza was fifteen years old, in the course of the English Civil War, a historically unique event took place in Cromwell's army, the so-called Putney Debates, in which fundamental questions concerning political rights and governance were discussed not by philosophers or theologians but by activists and soldiers who were truly speaking for the 'multitude', a 'rabble' of yeoman farmers, craftsmen, and the army rank and file. The extraordinary documentary record of those debates may not have achieved quite the canonical status of writings by a Hobbes or a Spinoza; and their theoretical influence, however significant, has been of a different kind. But the debates at Putney – to say nothing of even more radically democratic ideas that emerged out of the English Revolution – reveal a universe of democratic thinking that goes well beyond Spinoza's ideas on the 'multitude'.

6

FRENCH ABSOLUTISM

Between 1484 and 1560, successive French kings refused to summon the Estates General, the national assembly of regional estates, depriving France's representative bodies of their only significant function, the power of approving taxes. When they were finally recalled, it was a time of religious conflict during which exactions for the maintenance of soldiers added to the burden of taxation. The Estates General would meet again, without much effect, several times from 1560 to 1614, when they finally dissolved in disarray, not to be summoned again until 1789. France would have no national representative assembly, let alone a national legislative body, until the Revolution. The centralizing project of the monarchy had, at least in this respect, succeeded; and the 'absolutist' state prevailed.

Yet the failure of the Estates General was not a simple matter of monarchical success. If anything, the absence of a national assembly reflected the fragmentation of the French state no less than it expressed the power of the monarchy. The French monarchy, unlike the English, had emerged slowly, in a prolonged contest among rival feudal families; and, while in England the monarchy evolved as a cooperative project between feudal lords and kings, French absolutism never quite overcame the legacy of dynastic rivalry or the parcellization and particularisms of competing jurisdictions.

The royal state certainly succeeded in establishing its own apparatus of power, with a bureaucracy unmatched in Western Europe; but this was not simply a mark of its strength or of modern 'rationalization'. One of the monarchy's principal devices for gaining the support of its opponents was the distribution of patronage, especially in the form of state office; and the growth of the bureaucracy was in large part a consequence of buying off potential claimants to autonomous jurisdictions by offering the inducements of lucrative state office, to say nothing of the opportunities for plunder afforded by wars, foreign and domestic. The legacy of parcellized sovereignty would continue to shape French political theory and practice until the Revolution and even the Napoleonic state.

A System of Extortion and Embezzlement?

At the beginning of the sixteenth century, France was the most populous country in Europe. Of an estimated 18 million people, the vast majority, between 80 and 90 per cent, were peasants. Although in principle free and in secure possession of their land, they were still often subject to various seigneurial dues; and they also bore the brunt of growing state taxation. In the latter part of the sixteenth century the monarchy undertook a massive transformation of the state, expanding the bureaucracy and the tax burden with it, in a tax system that was evolving to finance not simply state projects but a 'massive spoils system', a 'semi-institutionalized system of extortion and embezzlement'.[1] Sections of the nobility, and a substantial part of the bourgeoisie, were co-opted by giving them access to the spoils of office as a means of private enrichment.

The distribution of offices no doubt increased support for royal power, but it also generated growing unrest among those who bore the burden; and even the beneficiaries of office proved unreliable. As the monarchy not only used the distribution of offices to consolidate its power base but also sold state offices to enhance its own fiscal solvency, this created a new dynastic class of venal officeholders, who would, in the seventeenth century, themselves become a source of opposition to monarchical power. Even when the 'absolutist' monarchy appeared to be firmly established, regional and corporate divisions persisted, as did the plethora of local legal systems.

Growing taxes and privileged exemptions from them were certainly enough to generate unrest, but the process of state centralization had produced increasingly complex social divisions. In a state where the monarchy had been the product of an inconclusive contest among rival noble families, dynastic rivalries continued to be fierce. At the same time, the centralizing monarchy was challenged not only by unprivileged classes that carried the burden of taxation but by nobles who had not been co-opted into the royal state and were defending their own jurisdictions. There were also conflicts not only between privileged and unprivileged estates but within the estates themselves. The Third Estate was divided in various ways, between rich and poor, bourgeois and peasant, urban and rural. Opposition to the monarchy was therefore never unambiguous. The bourgeoisie, while seeking to defend itself against excessive exactions, might also have reason to support the monarchy to strengthen its position against the aristocracy or to gain access to state office. Even peasants

---

1   Robin Briggs, *Early Modern France 1560–1715* (Oxford: Oxford University Press, 1977), p. 3; introduction to *Constitutionalism and Resistance in the Sixteenth Century: Three Treatises by Hotman, Beza, and Mornay,* ed. and transl. Julian Franklin (New York: Pegasus, 1969), p. 16. See also David Parker, *The Making of French Absolutism* (London: Edward Arnold, 1983), for an overview of the French state in the period.

might seek protection from the king against the aristocracy, while nobles co-opted into the state were pitted against those defending what remained of their seigneurial powers and local autonomy.

Nevertheless, as the royal state grew, so did opposition to it. Religious controversy sharpened the dividing lines, and there followed decades of conflict in which dynastic rivalries were compounded by confessional disputes and regional revolts of one kind or another. In France's fractured polity, religious dissent played a very particular role in unifying diverse oppositional forces and regions into a more or less united party of resistance. Ideas of resistance and popular sovereignty did cut across religious lines; but the Huguenots, though a minority movement, played a disproportionate role in generating what might be called the first organized resistance to royal power in Europe. While appealing to various classes for various reasons, Protestantism in France generated a forceful political movement when and because it was adopted by sections of the nobility, especially elements of the provincial aristocracy, for whom Catholicism, in the form of the Gallican Church, had become the creed of monarchy and the centralizing ambitions of the royal state. The most important political ideas bequeathed to the Western canon by the Wars of Religion in France were those that adapted Protestant doctrine to the interests of provincial nobles and municipal authorities asserting their local autonomy and particular jurisdictions.

The Reformation and religious division in France certainly crystallized political dissent, but the terms of religious conflict were politically defined from the start, shaped by the particular formation of the state. French Protestantism as an oppositional force, and the translation of its doctrines into theories of resistance and 'constitutionalism', belonged to a larger political struggle. In the series of bloody conflicts commonly described as the Wars of Religion, the battles between Catholics and Huguenots that erupted in 1562 and lasted for decades were inextricably bound up with rivalries among noble families for control of the monarchy, as well as conflicts between monarchy and aristocracy. At the same time, religious conflict aggravated already existing social unrest, not least by increasing the burden of taxation to finance the king's military forces. The development of the monarchical state as a means of private appropriation, always in tension with competing forms of 'extra-economic' power and 'politically constituted property'; its reliance on the proliferation and distribution of offices to sustain its power no less than its fiscal stability; the growth of the state not only as a means of maintaining order and protecting the private possessions of propertied classes but as itself a private resource – all this set the political agenda in specific ways and, with it, shaped religious controversy too.

There was, of course, nothing specifically French about the contest among competing jurisdictions; but the opposition between a centralizing monarchy and other claims to autonomous powers played a distinctive role. In the other major Western European monarchies the lines were drawn in different ways, and political discourse proceeded along different lines. In England, there was no fundamental challenge to a centralizing state, which served the interests of the aristocracy no less than of the monarchy; and, though the English Civil War would be ferocious, the contest between monarchy and Parliament – which jointly composed the centralized state – would not take the form of a battle between central state and other, partial jurisdictions. In Spain, the empire was, at least for systematic theorists of political theology, a more contentious issue than the royal state itself. In sixteenth-century France, the contest between monarchy and local jurisdictions played a central part in the formation of both 'absolutist' thought and theories of resistance.

The Reformation, the spread of Protestantism, the Wars of Religion, followed by the decline of the Huguenots and the rise of the Catholic League, brought to a head underlying social conflicts and provided ideological vehicles for conducting battles over taxation and tithes, privileges and exemptions, the powers of local patrician oligarchies, and royal absolutism itself. While the objects and intensity of struggle, as well as the nature and scope of social alliances, varied according to regional differences and variations in local privileges, parts of the country saw the outbreak of violent peasant protests and sometimes regional revolts in which peasants were allied with urban classes. Such outbreaks might begin as revolts against taxation and tithes and end as attacks on the whole system of power and privilege.

The period was rich in political ideas at every level of sophistication – the *cahiers de doléances*, which outlined the grievances of the three estates; the Huguenot resistance tracts; the political philosophy of Bodin – and all, in their various ways, reflected the distinctive configuration of the French state. The contrast between French and English political ideas is instructive. It was the English, not the French, who most readily adopted the idea of a 'mixed constitution', and they elaborated ideas of separated powers well before the French. This may seem paradoxical when we consider that it was the English, not the French, who possessed a more truly undivided sovereignty, and that even theorists of the 'mixed constitution' remained wedded to a centralized and indivisible sovereign power. But the 'mixed constitution' was, after all, perfectly consistent with a truly unitary state in which the sovereignty of the central state was shared by Parliament and Crown. In the English context the idea of a mixed constitution or divided power was not at all grounded in a fragmented sovereignty but, on the contrary, presupposed a unified sovereign state. The French were dealing with a different disposition of power and a more persistent contest among fragmented sovereignties, which called for different theoretical strategies.

English landed proprietors, who developed private and increasingly 'economic' means of appropriation, never came to rely so much on the state as a direct resource. Nor was the central state seriously challenged by corporate institutions, regional privileges, and politically autonomous urban communes. Royal taxation never played the same role for the English propertied classes that it did for the French; and the state never had the same reasons for either squeezing or protecting the peasantry as did the French state.

English property owners, when seeking to protect and augment their increasingly 'economic' means of appropriation, might struggle to defend their private rights of property against incursions by the Crown, to establish the supremacy of Parliament as an association of propertyholders, to thwart the consolidation of an absolutist monarchy by establishing 'limited government', while at the same time staving off threats from below. The propertied classes of France, who confronted the state both as a competitor for surplus labour and as a means of access to it, contended over taxation, the proliferation of offices and the means of distributing them, often struggling less to limit the state than to acquire property in it or prevent others from doing so. The English commoner, in defence against the landlord's efforts to augment his economic powers of appropriation, struggled against the enclosure of common and waste land. The French peasant, more oppressed by 'political' forms of exploitation, rebelled against royal taxation and seigneurial privilege. Englishmen asserted their individual rights; Frenchmen defended their corporate and regional privileges.

If the English were concerned with the relation between state and private property, the French were preoccupied with the state *as* private property. French anti-absolutism was not simply a matter of resistance to political tyranny but also an attack on the state as a means of private extortion. Popular resistance, too, often focused on exploitation by the state; and exploitation by means of direct seigneurial exactions might take second place to taxation (or the tax exemptions of others) as an object of grievance, just as the landlord might be less concerned about losing economic powers such as the right of enclosure than about relinquishing tax exemptions and political privileges.

French political discourse would long be preoccupied with the tax/office structure of the state and the fractured polity that underlay it. The principal issues typically had to do, as they so often did elsewhere in Europe, with contesting jurisdictions; but what distinguished French political debate was an emphasis on the role of the state as a proprietary interest, the monarchical state and its growing administrative and fiscal apparatus conceived as a means of private appropriation These questions were not, of course, specific to France; but they presented themselves to the French with particular force as the state became a major instrument of private appropriation for a growing class of office-holders, in ways and degrees unmatched elsewhere in Europe.

At the centre of French political thought in this period, then, stood a fragmented polity consisting of many particularisms whose unifying principle was yet another particularistic power, yet another proprietary interest. Advocates of monarchy were obliged to defend the monarch's right to rule, and especially his right to distribute office and impose taxation, by denying his particularity and claiming that he represented a public or general interest, transcending all the private and particular interests of his subjects or competing jurisdictions. His opponents might counter by insisting that the monarchy itself was nothing more than private and particular, just one proprietary interest against others, and that the various lesser jurisdictions truly represented 'public' interests.

Much of the debate surrounding the French monarchy concerned precisely this: the relation between public and private and who could claim to represent the public principle against the many private interests and jurisdictions that composed the polity of France. Arguments in favour of the centralizing monarchy, which claimed that the king embodied the public aspect of the state as against the private character of his subjects, suggested that a single superior will was required to bind together particular interests and produce a common good. A defender of the royal state like Bodin might claim that the will of the sovereign is law, on the grounds that the *res publica* or commonwealth – that which is common to all private individuals, families and corporate bodies – can only be constituted by a common subjection to the unifying will of the sovereign. Arguments against the centralizing mission of the monarchy voiced concern not only with the particularisms that divided the polity but also with the particularity of the state apparatus itself and the consequences of its use as private property – the proliferation and venalization of offices, the corruption of administration, the tax burden.

These conflicts did not necessarily pit monarchists against opponents of a monarchical state. Opposing sides were often embroiled in dynastic struggles in which one claim to royal power was contested by another. But even some adherents to an aspiring royal dynasty would often advocate the claims of lesser jurisdictions against a centralizing royal power. Even nobles or local magistrates who supported some kind of monarchy, or attached themselves to one dynasty against another, had reason to insist that royal power was rooted in, and created by, the nobility and other public officers, who therefore also had the right to depose kings. Against the monarch's claims to generality in contrast to their own particularity, these 'lesser magistrates', even while defending their particular jurisdictions, might claim to accept that the public interest or common good emanated from a unifying will or mind; but now, the unifying, generalizing will of the monarch, who was 'particular and single', was replaced by 'one mind compounded out of many', a collective will composed of nobles, 'lesser magistrates' or local authorities who acted as the people's public representatives.

From *Cahiers* to Constitutionalism

Jean de Bourg, arch-episcopal judge of Vienne, representative of the Third Estate to the provincial Estates and Estates General, from a province that experienced one of the country's bloodiest regional revolts in 1579–80, wrote the petition of grievances for the Dauphiné Third Estate to be presented at the Estates General at Blois in 1576.[2] He drew on philosophical principles and the classics of antiquity to support complaints and proposals for reform typical of his estate. The list of grievances he rehearsed focused on the privileges of the other two estates, especially their exemptions from taxation; the proliferation of useless offices with high salaries, secular and ecclesiastical; the tax burden imposed on the common people; and the inequitable political structure which gave the advantage of power to the privileged estates, so that they could manipulate the fiscal system for their own gain at the expense of the Third Estate. To these complaints – shared by bourgeois, craftsmen, and peasants – he added several of special concern to his own class, the bourgeoisie, and a few grievances of particular interest to the peasantry.

De Bourg's proposals for resolving these grievances included measures to strengthen the Third Estate, relieving its tax burden, augmenting its political powers in office and in the assemblies of Estates, and increasing the role of regional representative institutions. There were also suggestions in which the bourgeoisie's grievances against local oligarchies and seigneurial privilege converged with peasant complaints about rural administration. It is significant that these were met in part by proposals for restoring certain powers of local administration to the king in order to diminish the provincial powers of seigneurs, even though de Bourg pressed at the same time for reductions in the royal bureaucracy in order to reduce the burden of taxation.

De Bourg adduced philosophical arguments to support these proposals for reform. In particular, he developed the principle of corporate equality, drawing, for example, on Plato's concept of justice and Cicero's conception of a natural order based on a harmonious balance among the various social orders. It was this supposedly natural principle outlined by Cicero that, according to de Bourg, dictated the maintenance of social equality, not among individuals but among the three estates as corporate entities, and

---

2   I am relying for this account of de Bourg and the other lawyers on Le Roy Ladurie's *Carnival in Romans* (New York: George Braziller, 1980).

also (in particular, for purposes of tax assessment) among regions and cities. In this blend of philosophical speculation and political activism, de Bourg showed himself to be 'close to the great authors of Antiquity, and just as close to the aspirations of the common people of his own day, who had never read a word of Plato or Cicero'.[3]

De Bourg's main theme – the defence of a corporate balance among estates, especially with regard to taxation, based on the organic unity and harmony of the social order – remained the central focus of protest as voiced by his successors, the provincial lawyers who continued to do battle for the Third Estate in his region after the period of bloody revolt. Attacking the tax exemptions of the nobility, they invoked various organic metaphors – the mystical body of the state, or the musical metaphor of harmonious proportion so popular among the ancients from Pythagoras to Plato and Aristotle – in order to establish the fundamental unity of the state and the interdependence of its parts. By these means they sought to demonstrate the nobility's duty to the social whole and the essential function of the Third Estate in sustaining the body politic.

These protestors were not democrats. Men of substance, they represented essentially the interests of the urban bourgeoisie. The equality for which they strove was a corporate equality in which they would predominate over lesser members of their corporation, and a proportionate equality, an equality in difference, which acknowledged the hierarchical structure of the social whole. 'We . . . are not for government by the people, nor for equality, as the Nobles falsely claim', maintained Claude Delagrange in 1599. 'But our privileges are equal to [theirs].'[4] In other words, this was not so much an attack on the system of privilege, such as peasants or artisans might have wished, as it was a demand for access to it. 'The Third Estate needs the rules of harmonics, not arithmetic', wrote Antoine Rambaud. 'It does not want to make law of equality . . . It wants equal justice. But it does not want equal justice that follows arithmetic, with all things equal in weight and form. It wants the harmonic balance made up of different parts. Order and justice founded on proportional and harmonic equality, blending into one, are necessary to the survival of the State.'[5]

These conceptions of the state as a 'body', an organic unity, tended to be accompanied by a notion of a public or common good which was more than simply the sum of its parts, a principle of unity over and against the particularities comprising the body politic. Needless to say, the object of invoking this common good was to demonstrate that the nobility must subordinate its particular interests and privileges to the interests of the whole: 'The

---

3   *Ibid.*, p. 68.
4   *Ibid.*, p. 357.
5   *Ibid.*, p. 358.

Nobles use the privileges of the provinces as if they were theirs alone', complained Jean Vincent in 1598. 'The Nobles think they are born only for themselves. But according to Pericles as quoted by Thucydides, one should love the public good above all [and] consider oneself born not for the self but for the world.'[6]

For these bourgeois and far from radical protestors, the unity of the state, the 'One' to which the 'Multiple' must be subordinated, was embodied in the person of the king, the 'Father of the Common Welfare', as Vincent called him.[7] 'Aspiring to unity', explained Rambaud, 'does not mean making everything equal. Unity in music is nothing other than Monarchy in a State.'[8] It is not surprising that the lawyers should adopt this view, since the Third Estate might actually stand to gain from the appropriation of some (though not their own) corporate powers by the monarch. The corporate egalitarianism of these provincial lawyers was based on a view of society in which the unity of the state and the 'harmonious' balance of its constituent parts were expressed in and maintained by the sovereign power of the king. In this, they seem to have been true disciples of Bodin.

In contrast, Huguenot theorists advocated outright rebellion against the royal state. There is no reason to doubt that many Huguenots were motivated entirely by religious convictions (though similar ideas would later be adopted by the Catholic League); but it is equally certain that substantial numbers – especially among those social elements that transformed the movement into a powerful political force – were driven by other, less spiritual interests. The Huguenot resistance never had the support of more than 10 to 20 per cent of the French population, but it attracted disproportionate support among local notables, aristocrats and magistrates. For a time, Protestants controlled a great many towns, especially in the south of France; and in the 1560s, the Huguenot movement included close to half the nobility, at least in some regions of France, and especially the lesser, provincial nobility whose loss of feudal powers was not compensated by state office.

The Huguenots not only attacked the system of privilege and patronage, or fiscal and administrative corruption, but placed the blame squarely on the monarchy itself, with its bureaucratic apparatus in which royal office, including the office of king, was conceived as private property. This did not necessarily mean that they opposed the very idea of a monarchy. The most influential Huguenot resistance tract, the *Vindiciae Contra Tyrannos*, is attributed to a staunch supporter of Henry of Navarre, who would become Henry IV of France, the first Bourbon monarch – a king who would himself provoke opposition for his centralizing tendencies, which he would buy off (or threaten)

---

6   *Ibid.*, p. 353.
7   *Ibid.*
8   *Ibid.*, p. 359.

in the classic 'absolutist' manner. The fact that Henry was a Protestant (before converting again to Catholicism) is not, of course, insignificant; but to leave it at that, to explain Huguenot resisters' support for him simply on the grounds of their confessional allegiances, is perhaps to beg the question. It is surely worth considering the attractions that Protestantism, and especially Calvinism, held for various kinds of 'lesser magistrates', precisely because its doctrines offered support for their own power and autonomy when threatened by a centralizing monarchy.

The idea that no government is legitimate that is not in some sense based on the consent of the governed, that the king owes his authority to some kind of original compact with the 'people', was, as we have seen, not a new one. Nor was the idea that, while the king (as king, not as a person) was greater than any other individual, he was less than the community of the people taken together. It is certainly true that the French monarchomachs went further than some others in their elaboration of the principle that agreement to the king's rule is conditional, and that the king's legitimacy is contingent on fulfilling its terms. But for them, as for their medieval predecessors, the people remained a collective, corporate body, which is immortal, while individuals come and go.

The resistance tracts of the monarchomachs are often described as the beginnings of modern constitutionalism and modern ideas of 'popular sovereignty'. But, as we already know, much depends on what is meant by the 'people' – a flexible word that has had many meanings and served many different political purposes in Western political thought. The 'people' in this case was not simply a collection of private individuals. Individuals were not the basic constituents of the state, which was composed of corporate bodies, such as guilds, estates, provinces or towns; and the 'people' possessed political authority neither as individuals nor as a 'multitude' of individuals but as a collective, corporate body. The right, even the duty, to resist tyrannical power belonged not to individual citizens but to the body of the 'people' collectively, or, more precisely, to the officials who represented that collectivity. In fact, the authority – indeed, the duty – to resist tyrannical power was not strictly speaking an individual right at all but a function of office. Furthermore, the right that was being defended was not the right to give or withhold consent on a regular basis, as in periodic elections, but rather the right to resist in times of emergency, when the ruler failed to uphold his side of the bargain and was ruling tyrannically.

This undoubtedly helps to explain why in France, a largely Catholic country, the ideas of Protestants – at least for a time, when the centralizing monarchy was coming into conflict with the jurisdictions of local lords and magistrates – attracted large numbers of provincial nobles and municipal officials, in a war that was religious and political at once. Even if ideas like this were later appropriated by others and developed for more democratic purposes, and even if they established important principles of constitutional, limited and accountable government, there was nothing particularly democratic or 'modern' about them. These ideas were rooted in older, medieval principles, affirming the independent powers of lordship. The Huguenot doctrine of popular sovereignty had less to do with asserting the democratic rights of ordinary citizens than with defending older feudal powers, privileges and jurisdictions against encroachments by a centralizing state. The Huguenot solution to royal excesses was to augment the powers of other jurisdictions. While the case for the authority of magistrates or 'public councils' was formulated as a defence of the 'people's' inalienable right to resist, the insistence that this was not a private right of citizenship but a public function of officers or, in the Calvinist manner, of 'lesser magistrates', was intended both as an assertion of autonomous jurisdictions against the king, and, as in some other Protestant doctrines we have encountered, as a defence against popular rebellions and peasant revolts.

The Huguenot 'constitutionalists', then, were no more (and were in some respects less) democrats than were other sixteenth-century protestors who still looked to the monarchy for relief. It is not surprising that a substantial number of Huguenots and some of their leading spokesmen came from the ranks of the lesser, provincial nobility, precisely that section of the landed classes that had least to gain and most to lose from the growth of a strongly centralized appropriating monarchy. The most prominent Huguenot constitutionalists most commonly cited in histories of Western political thought, François Hotman, Theodore Beza and Philippe du Plessis-Mornay, all belonged to seigneurial families; and the social interests they represented are strikingly visible in the resistance tracts.

The first important text, Hotman's *Francogallia* (1573), formulated as a constitutional history of France rather than an overtly political tract, set out to demonstrate that, according to French tradition, the king was simply a magistrate, an office-holder; and even if he held his office in principle for life, he was subject to removal. The ultimate authority, which had been illegitimately seized in recent times by tyrannical kings, rightfully belongs to a 'public council' comprising the assembled estates, a council that has among its powers the power to create and depose kings. Beza, the spiritual leader of Protestants in France and Calvin's successor in Geneva, proceeded in his *Right of Magistrates* (1574) from a similar conception of French constitutional traditions but elaborated a more general doctrine of resistance, which unequivocally lodged the right to resist in 'lesser magistrates'.[9] While the

---

9   There were some attempts in Calvinist doctrine to defend a more inclusive right of resistance by extending the meaning of the 'lesser magistrate' to include private individuals, each acting as his own 'magistrate'; but this extension clearly – in fact, by definition – violates the meaning and intent of the original doctrine; and, in the case of the Huguenot

authority of magistrates derives from the people, resistance is, he insisted, a public function, not a private right, belonging not to private citizens but to public officers, 'among whom may be numbered dukes, marquesses, counts, viscount, barons, and chatelains', as well as 'the elected officers of towns'.[10]

The most influential Huguenot resistance tract, the *Vindiciae Contra Tyrannos* (published 1579, though perhaps written in 1574–5), attributed to du Plessis-Mornay, who was close to Henry of Navarre, developed Beza's doctrine into an outright call for revolt against the existing king. Starting from the premise that the king is no different from other men and that there is no natural division between ruler and ruled, this tract insists that kings are created by the people; but it becomes even clearer who the 'people' are and are not:

> When we speak of the people collectively, we mean those who receive authority from the people, that is, the magistrates below the king who have been elected by the people or established in some other way . . . And we also mean the assembly of the Estates, which are nothing less than the epitome of a kingdom to which all public matters are referred . . .
>
> In every properly constituted kingdom, this is the character of the officers of the crown, the peers, the lords, the patricians, the notables, and others chosen by the several estates who, in various combinations, make up the membership of the ordinary or the extra-ordinary council . . . For although these officers are severally below the king, they are collectively above him.[11]

Mornay does, very hesitantly and with exceedingly careful qualifications, suggest that there may be exceptional cases in which private individuals have been raised up by God to act as liberators; but, while his call to resistance may be more radical than that of other Huguenots, his argument in general is on the side of 'lesser magistrates', not in a metaphorical sense that includes private individuals, each acting as his own 'magistrate', but as public officials:

> [W]e are not speaking here of private individuals, who are not to be regarded as the basic parts of a community any more than planks, nails, and pegs are taken as the parts of a ship; or stones, beams, and mortar as the parts of a house. We are speaking rather of a province or a town, which is a part of the kingdom in the same way the prow, deck, and rudder

---

tracts, the intention is quite unambiguous.

10   Theodore Beza, *Right of Magistrates*, in ed. Franklin, *Constitutionalism and Resistance*, p. 110.

11   Philippe du Plessis-Mornay (?), *Vindiciae Contra Tyrannos*, in ed. Franklin, *Constitutionalism and Resistance*, p. 195. (The authorship of this tract remains in doubt.)

are the parts of a ship, or the roof, walls, and foundation are the parts of a house. And we are also speaking of the magistrate who is in charge of that province or town.

Huguenot ideas of resistance have been called a landmark in the development of modern constitutionalism largely on the grounds that they assume a sovereign community as the ultimate source of all political authority, which exercises its sovereignty by controlling the governing powers through institutions that represent the 'people'. Yet their conception of popular sovereignty was, if anything, more backward-looking than 'modern'. In defence of particular jurisdictions, the estates and 'lesser magistrates', they appropriated the principles that had long been used by monarchs to legitimate their own authority against, for example, emperors or popes, by claiming powers derived from the 'people' and even based on their notional consent. While such ideas could – and sometimes would – be adapted to more radical purpose, the contest between monarchy and 'lesser' authorities had more in common with medieval conflicts among jurisdictions than with modern democratic struggles for popular sovereignty or even just the limitation of state power.

Again, their arguments are based on a corporate and hierarchical conception of society. Since the right of resistance belongs to the 'people' not as private individuals but as properly constituted authorities, magistrates, and corporate bodies – the assemblies of estates, or towns and districts in the persons of their officials – rights are not individual but corporate. Indeed, in this argument – where the issue is not simply an appeal to the monarch to correct the imbalances among estates but a call to revolt against the monarch himself – the egalitarian aspect of the corporatist argument recedes; and its function as a limitation on popular rights comes to the fore at the very moment that the 'people's' rights are being so eloquently asserted.

To make the point that the right of resistance is based on the principle that it is the 'people' who constitute the king and not the reverse, the Huguenot resistance movement transforms the familiar idea of a unity in multiplicity, a common good emanating from a single unitary will, which others had used to justify the power of the king. Significantly, they do not abandon this idea of unity, nor do they propose a definition of the common good as a public interest whose substance consists merely of private interests and rights. Instead, they simply transfer the source of the unifying will from the monarch to the 'public councils' of the people. Much of their argument rests on contrasting the private, particular character of the king to the public, universal character of the 'people' embodied in their officers and councils, 'one mind compounded out of many'. The king as a person is 'particular and single';[12] the majesty of his office, its public character, derives

---

12   François Hotman, *Francogallia*, in *ibid.*, p. 78.

from the people – as represented by the notables who preside over them, the magistrates of towns, and (in keeping with the feudal interests of the nobility) the dukes, marquises, counts, and barons who 'constitute a part of the kingdom' and are established as 'guardians . . . for the several regions'.[13]

The Huguenot constitutionalists were in effect responding in kind to the advocates of royal power, adopting important aspects of their discourse; and they did so because this idiom was well-suited to deal with their grievances in a state conceived as private property. In particular, it provided useful language with which to assert the authority of the Estates to control the two major 'public' functions which lay at the heart of many grievances, the apportionment of taxes and the distribution of offices. While the 'particular and single' king, they argued, can dispose of his own private treasure at will and appoint his own personal counsellors, a careful distinction must be made between his private patrimony and that of the kingdom, the public treasury and public offices which are rightfully the province of the 'elders and experienced statesmen' who constitute the collective 'mind' of the kingdom.[14] While this theoretical strategy may be regarded as an important advance in 'modern' conceptions of public as against personal rule, it conceives the 'public' domain less as a modern impersonal state than as a composite of feudal jurisdictions.

The whole issue is summed up in the question: 'Is the King the Owner of the Kingdom?' More specifically, 'Does the king, then, have private property in the royal, or public, patrimony?'[15] The answer, of course, is no. And: 'Let me ask, furthermore, whether royal status is a possession or an office (*functio*). If it is a possession, then is it not at least a form of possession whereby the people, who conferred it, retain the proprietary right?'[16] As for the power of taxation, since taxes are intended for 'public purposes' – specifically the conduct of war – it cannot be the province of the king any more than the public domain is his private property. 'To guarantee that taxes will be used for public purposes', they must be authorized by the Estates, on the principle that the people 'taken collectively . . . are properly the owners of the kingdom' and their officers, as it were taken collectively, the only truly public being.

The Huguenot resistance movement may have failed in France; but monarchomach tracts were very soon taken up by resistance movements elsewhere, notably in the Netherlands and in England. Despite all the limitations of their resistance theories, the monarchomachs were articulating a relatively radical theory of consent. They certainly moved far beyond those

13 Mornay, in *ibid.*, p. 195.
14 Hotman, in *ibid.*, p. 79.
15 Mornay, p. 174.
16 *Ibid.*, pp. 175–7.

theories according to which the original agreement or contract that had founded political authority was an unconditional transfer of rights by the people to a ruler, and succeeding generations were bound by that original agreement. In medieval disputes between secular and ecclesiastical powers, for example, to defend royal power against the papacy, it had been argued that the emperor or king derived his power not from the pope but from God through the 'people'. This was something very different from the monarchomach idea that the authority of the king derived from the 'people', perhaps from a kind of compact between king and people, and that when the king exceeded his authority, violated the conditions of the compact and acted against the interests of the 'people', they had the right to rebel, even to the point of armed resistance. It may not, then, be unreasonable to claim for them a significant contribution to Western theories of popular sovereignty, the social contract, the supremacy of representative bodies, or at least 'constitutionalism'. But it is another testimony to the limits of the Western political tradition that ideas devised to reassert feudal rights against an encroaching monarchy, defending a hierarchical polity and the independence of corporate powers vested in nobles or municipal magistrates, as against a conception of active citizenship and popular power, can be treated as classics in the development of *democratic* ideas.

Jean Bodin

On a more abstractly philosophical plane, Jean Bodin addressed the same constellation of political problems. The theory of sovereignty, for which he is most famous, drew together several issues that were being contested in the struggles of the sixteenth century. The standpoint from which he sought to resolve these issues has much in common with that of the legal spokesmen for the Third Estate whom we have already encountered – and, indeed, Bodin was himself a lawyer and representative of the Third Estate for Vermandois at the Estates General of Blois in 1576. It is undoubtedly true that, when he wrote the *Six Books of the Commonwealth* in which his theory of sovereignty appeared, he was motivated in part by the desire to assert the sovereignty of the king against the dangers of rebellion and civil strife most dramatically embodied in the Huguenot resistance movement; but he also wanted to reform the structure of the state, the apparatus of office, the inequitable distribution of burdens created by the system of privilege and exemption.

Bodin was born in 1529 or 1530 in Angers, the son of a prosperous master tailor. Although his religious views in later life remain a subject of dispute, as a young man he joined the Carmelite order. He went on to study philosophy in Paris and law in Toulouse. His early work was humanist in inspiration, and he seems to have regarded humanism as a means of providing a unified education for all citizens, together with a single religion, to enhance political and religious harmony. The religious wars that ensued in France may, in his view, have been a necessity in the face of attacks against the 'true faith'; and religious unity was clearly for him a condition of civil peace. Yet, while religious diversity represented a threat to civil order, he would later make it clear that some kind of temporary accommodation with dissenters and a limited, and certainly not permanent, religious toleration would be a better means than violence to unify the commonwealth.

In 1560, Bodin became a member of the *parlement* of Paris. In the years that followed, he produced his most important political works: in 1566, the *Method for the Easy Comprehension of History* (the *Methodus*), spelling out the comprehensive historical and legal knowledge required to govern the state, and in 1576, the *Six Books of the Commonwealth* (*République*), on which his reputation as a theorist of sovereignty rests. The king began to consult him on matters of state; but, although as deputy for the Third Estate and then as president of the deputies, he took a very strong line against the privileged estates, he would also challenge the king on both financial and religious issues, opposing the monarch's rejection of accommodation with the Protestants and his efforts to appropriate the 'property of the people' as his own patrimony.

By the late 1580s, the country was in dynastic and religious crisis. With the assassination of the king and the ensuing rivalries, Bodin, by then a royalist magistrate in Laon, felt compelled – despite his own commitment to civil peace and at least a limited religious toleration – to join the Catholic League. It was, again, difficult to dissociate dynastic from confessional rivalries; and both were implicated in the classic jurisdictional battles: the major cities (and their magistrates) tended, for example, to side with the Duke of Guise and the League, while the nobility typically adhered to the Protestant King of Navarre. In that respect, the lines were drawn in ways that reflected the long-standing and complex relations among the estates and the monarchy; and Bodin came down on the side one might have predicted for a man of his estate and standing. When Henry of Navarre succeeded to the throne as Henry IV of France, the king remained under pressure from the powerful League; but, returning to the Catholic fold, he eventually brought about, in the Edict of Nantes of 1598, the kind of confessional accommodation Bodin might have wished for to maintain civil peace. By then, however, Bodin was dead, having succumbed to the plague in 1596.

There has been much debate about what to make of Bodin's theory of sovereignty and the changes it appears to undergo between his most important political works, the *Methodus* and the *République*. While the earlier work certainly outlines the idea of an indivisible sovereignty, it is not until the later work that this idea comes to be associated with the notion of 'absolute' power. To speak of Bodin as an advocate of 'absolutism' may be misleading if we take that to mean that he favoured monarchical power without limitation. There is no question that he was, from beginning to end, a believer in royal supremacy. Even in his earlier work, which contains no clear notion of 'absolute' power, the idea of indivisible sovereignty is already spelled out. Yet, while this certainly precludes a conception of the nobility or 'lesser magistrates' as joint or rival claimants to sovereignty, it does not rule out the limitations imposed on the ruler by natural or fundamental law nor the significant rights of office possessed by the estates or nobles according to the French juridical tradition. In his later work, Bodin combined the idea of indivisible sovereignty with a more unequivocal notion of 'absolute' power, that is, a comprehensive power including every legitimate state function; but even then, he never dismissed the political role of estates and corporations.

One eminent commentator on Bodin's political thought has suggested that the idea of sovereignty as 'absolute' represented an unfortunate resolution of a certain incoherence in Bodin's earlier work. To be sure, the idea of an indivisible sovereignty seemed to contradict the limitations on sovereign power implied by his concessions to the traditional authority of lesser magistrates and his conviction that certain actions of the king required the consent of the estates or *parlements*. But, this commentator argues, Bodin's resolution was a departure from conventional French discourse and not particularly well suited to French conditions. He might have done better 'to have defined the ruler's sovereignty as absolute (except with respect to the law of nature and fundamental law more narrowly defined), and conceded that its functions were divided among the king, the Parlements and the Estates'.[17] But having insisted on the notion of indivisibility, this argument goes, logic seemed to compel a kind of 'absolutism'; and what seemed to Bodin a logical compulsion became that much more powerful in the new historical circumstances, with the rise of the Huguenot movement and its doctrines of resistance.

Yet, whatever logical inconsistencies there may be in Bodin's notion of indivisible sovereignty, it does address the conditions of France, and, for all its innovations, in terms not at all foreign to his contemporaries. Although in response to armed resistance the *République* went further than the earlier work, both the *Methodus* and the *République* can be understood as seeking to limit the autonomous powers of the nobility and the 'parcellization of sovereignty' that continued to plague the monarchical state. At the same

---

17 Introduction to Jean Bodin, *On Sovereignty,* ed. Julian Franklin (Cambridge: Cambridge University Press, 1992), p. xxii. See also Franklin's *Jean Bodin and the Rise of Absolutist Theory* (Cambridge: Cambridge University Press, 1973); and his 'Sovereignty and the Mixed Constitution: Bodin and his critics', in the *Cambridge History of Political Thought 1450–1700* (Cambridge: Cambridge University Press, 1991), pp. 299–328.

time, both preserved important functions for lesser authorities and corporations. Even in his later masterpiece, despite his advocacy of an indivisible and absolute sovereign power vested in the king, Bodin clearly believed in enhancing the role of the Estates General, insisting, for example, that no tax could be levied without their consent. Indeed, his theory of sovereignty is not so distant from the views of those provincial lawyers who relied on the monarchy to maintain unity in a fragmented polity and to correct the social imbalance among its corporate constituents, in part by appropriating to itself the feudal prerogatives of the privileged estates.

Bodin's concern in constructing his theory of sovereignty was not simply to stave off rebellion of the Huguenot type but to deal with the underlying structural problems inherent in the French state and its political 'parcellization'. Whether he wanted to curtail the powers of the traditional nobility on behalf of the Third Estate or to strengthen the ruling class in spite of itself by bringing order to the anarchy of competing jurisdictions, he intended to transfer their particularistic, quasi-feudal powers to the monarchy, denying that noble prerogatives and offices belonged to their possessors by proprietary right (hereditary or otherwise) and rendering them dependent upon sovereign authority. The issue at stake was not simply the location of supreme and ultimate power but also the location of *unity*, the source of integration in a system of regional and corporate fragmentation: 'a commonwealth without a sovereign power to unite all its several members, whether families, colleges, or corporate bodies, is not a true commonwealth. It is neither the town nor its inhabitants that makes a city-state, but their union under a sovereign ruler.'[18]

Bodin's conception of sovereignty, then, represents in some respects an attack on feudal remnants, but it also presupposes a polity still organized on feudal, corporatist principles. It is in this light that his commitment to *indivisible* power must be understood. For representative institutions to share 'sovereignty' with the king would aggravate precisely the corporate fragmentation and political parcellization that Bodin's sovereign power was designed to overcome. But he did not envisage a society organized in a fundamentally different way, a society, like England, less divided into corporate fragments and integrated into a unitary state with a unitary representative body like the English Parliament. If anything, in some respects his argument was designed to strengthen certain corporate principles, and he regarded corporations as fundamental to the maintenance of social ties. It was the function of sovereign power to integrate and harmonize these necessary particularities.

Bodin nonetheless makes an important distinction between the form of state, based on the location of sovereignty, and the form of government, based

---

18   Jean Bodin, *Six Books of the Commonwealth*, ed. M.J. Tooley (Oxford: Basil Blackwell, 1967), p. 7.

on the principle by which lands, offices, and honours are distributed. A monarchy, for example, can be governed aristocratically or democratically, according to how the sovereign monarch chooses to grant honours and preferments. This distinction demonstrates that, however powers and offices may be distributed, these powers are ultimately vested in the sovereign and that it is in effect by the will of the sovereign that they are so distributed. The powers of office-holders or nobles are not held by proprietary right but by virtue of delegation from the sovereign – ideally, the sovereign in the person of a monarch. In this respect, the distinction between state and government, and the implied distinction between the sovereign legislative power and the subordinate power of execution, serves to reinforce Bodin's attack on feudal prerogatives and baronial anarchy, as well as on any other proprietary claims to political power apart from those of the sovereign. This feudal 'parcellization' of power, rather than 'divided sovereignty' in the English parliamentary sense, is, again, the main target of his insistence on the indivisibility of sovereignty. Whatever else he may have intended by distinguishing the form of government from the form of state, he clearly meant to sustain and enhance the authority of the monarchy against other particularistic claims to political power.

The notion of divided 'sovereignty' and limited government could, perhaps, more easily be elaborated in a polity that was not itself essentially divided and parcellized: a state which, like England, had achieved 'feudal centralization' with a relatively unified nobility, without territorial potentates like those of the Continent, with towns that lacked the political autonomy of Continental urban communes, and with unitary representative institutions for the ruling class, assemblies that were national in extent and represented a community of property holders not internally divided by region and estate. The unity of the English state, reflected in Parliament, made 'divided sovereignty' less threatening and more practicable; or perhaps the relative unity and strength of the ruling class made it inevitable. At any rate, Parliament quite early acquired legislative powers – at least the negative power to check the legislative activity of the king – in effect dividing between king and Parliament the very power which for Bodin constitutes sovereignty. In contrast, the French monarchy, whose power rested in part on the regional fragmentation of the state and the independent powers exercised by the nobility, remained largely free of limitation by representative bodies in this respect – if not in others, such as its fiscal powers. Bodin's concept of sovereignty, in short, speaks precisely to the historical conditions of France.

Political Economy

At the heart of Bodin's political theory, then, is a tension between a still feudal, corporatist, and fragmented social order and a centralized sovereign state, a tension characteristic of his time and place. The ruling class was still feudal to the extent that its mode of exploitation was a fusion of economic and political power, still rooted in the parcellization of the state. The tax/office structure of the monarchical state simply centralized this fusion of political and economic power, with a system of state taxation that has been described as a kind of 'centralized feudal rent'; and yet the state was at the same time anti-feudal in its attempts to unify the fragments of state power.

This tension is captured perfectly in the economic doctrines of the period, to which Bodin himself contributed. What is most characteristic of these economic theories is the unity of 'political' and 'economic' spheres, a view of the 'economy' as a politically constituted entity and an idea of the monarchy as the harmonizer of conflicting interests in a commercial order conceived as intrinsically divisive. Commerce certainly contributes to material prosperity and should be encouraged; but, in a commercial system based on 'buying cheap and selling dear' in transactions between separate markets, commercial activity is socially disruptive, and the function of the monarchical state is to integrate particular and conflicting economic interests, just as it unifies political particularisms. The economy was understood not as an integrated, self-sustaining mechanism but as subsumed under the political community. At the same time, the state itself, with its tax/office structure, was a form of politically constituted property, simultaneously a public, political institution and a private economic resource, quite different from the English economy, where purely economic modes of appropriation were far more developed.

The essential paradox that characterized both the French polity and its economy lies in the irreducible tension between their corporatist roots and an increasingly national economy, which required a more integrated market and the reduction of internal barriers to trade. Like the political theory of Bodin, contemporary economic doctrines depended both upon the maintenance of certain corporate powers, privileges and liberties, and on their transcendence by a powerful monarchy.

It is in this context that Bodin draws an analogy between the state and the household. The family, he suggests, is the origin of the state and its basic constituent unit; and household management is the model of good government. Taking issue with Aristotle and Xenophon for their separation of household management, *oikonomia,* and statecraft, he argues that the 'economic' art – knowledge of the acquisition of goods which Aristotle assigns to household management – is common also to 'colleges' and 'city-states'. Conversely, power, authority, and obedience, which apparently belong specifically to the political sphere, also belong to the family. In both cases the purpose of management is the acquisition of goods, the provision and prosperity of the household or state (as a condition, of course, for the good life in a higher sense). This object is best achieved under the supreme authority of a single head – the father in one case, the king in the other. The one fundamental difference between household and state is that the public character of the state exists in contrast to the private nature of the household, and this means that the former presupposes and must respect the private property of the latter.

The household/state analogy as formulated by Bodin represents a state dominated by an absolute ruler who, in promoting the acquisition of goods and increasing the prosperity of the state, guides and encourages the public 'economy', just as the father manages the household. Furthermore, since like the family the unity of the state should be grounded in concord and 'love', it is the task of state management to reconcile and bind together the constituent parts of the polity by creating a balance based on 'harmonic' justice. The presupposition of the analogy is an 'absolutist' monarchy which presides over a 'mercantilist' economy while it respects and protects the private property and (selectively?) the corporate liberties of its subjects.

Arguments in favour of the absolutist monarchy, then, were not confined to the political domain. The ideology of absolutism derived much of its force from the claims that were made for its role in promoting a prosperous economy; and it was not least on this basis that the notion of an 'enlightened despotism' would emerge. The idea that a successful commercial economy depended on an undivided sovereign power to harmonize conflicting interests, an idea which had already appeared in the work of Bodin, remained a recurring theme in French social thought. The state as an essential instrument of social integration would appear even in the work of the physiocrats, who, in the eighteenth century, articulated a groundbreaking theory of the economy as a systemic totality with its own internal operating principles, in the manner of modern 'economics'.

Even the term 'political economy' owes its origins to the kind of household/state analogy, together with its assumptions about the integrative role of the state in the economy, that underlay Bodin's theory of the monarchy. The analogy, together with language and logic strikingly reminiscent of Bodin, appeared in the work of Antoine de Montchrétien, as we have seen, who, if he did not actually invent the term, wrote what seems to have been the first book ever to contain the term 'political economy' in its title: *Traicté de l'oeconomie politique,* published in 1615. On the principle that the monarch should rule benevolently, like the father with an eye to the well-being, harmony, and prosperity of the household, he urged reforms that would encourage economic activity – especially measures to strengthen the Third Estate by protecting corporate liberties and equality, while integrating the polity into a national whole to encourage trade, presided over by a strong central state cleansed of its burdensome and corrupt system of office and taxation. Montchrétien eventually lost hope in the monarchy as the agent of reform and joined the opposition; but in the *Traicté,* he was writing in the tradition of those moderate reformers who looked to the king to protect them against the imbalance of power and privilege, and to integrate the body politic and the system of trade.

Montchrétien makes an interesting suggestion about the mechanism by which the desired effects of 'political economy' might be achieved. In a formulation that was to become very familiar in a different time and place, he suggests that selfish passions and the appetite for gain, far from threatening the common good, can be its foundation. In other words, Montchrétien proposes something very like the utility of selfish interests that was to be the basis of eighteenth-century, especially English (or, perhaps more accurately, Scottish). accounts of 'commercial society' and its capacity for promoting the common good without relying on the uncertainties of human virtue and benevolence.[19] But, in Montchrétien's argument, the social context for the operation of this principle was not English capitalism, with its integrated national market, driven by its own imperatives of competition. For Montchrétien, in French conditions, the mechanism for achieving the harmony of interest was not the 'invisible hand' sustained by a constitutional parliamentary state but rather the absolutist monarchy itself which was to serve as the agent of integration and harmonization. In this formulation, an active and forceful interventionist monarchy was the condition for transforming 'private vices' into 'public benefits'. This association of monarchy with the harmony of interests long persisted in French political thought.

The object of Montchrétien's proposal is especially to encourage economic activity and promote trade. His advocacy of selfish passions as the basis of public well-being is explicitly intended to defend the Third Estate, and in particular, the merchants who, he admits, are more commonly driven by selfishness and greed than by concern for the public good. These selfish passions ought not, he argues, be grounds for excluding such people (as, for example, Aristotle might do) from the citizen body as 'a kind of helot'.[20] It is these very appetites that motivate not only merchants but peasants, artisans, and lawyers to undertake and perform well the necessary and useful services on which the state depends.

The job of regulating these activities and establishing order among them belongs to the 'sovereign moderator of the State' and his officials, whose function is to protect the rights of the kingdom and 'particularly of each city'.[21] This regulation of the network of self-interest is to be achieved not only by ensuring just prices, stamping out corrupt commercial practices and frauds, and removing barriers to trade, but also by compensating for the

---

19 Antoine de Montchrétien, *Traicté de l'oeconomie politique*, ed. Th. Funck-Brentano (Paris: E. Plon-Nourrit & Cie, 1889), e.g., pp. 38–9, 140–4.

20 *Ibid.*, p. 141.

21 *Ibid.*

'inconsistency' of human 'inclinations' by introducing and managing (for example, through a system of royal manufactures) a division of labour and specialization now lacking in France – in contrast to the more commercially successful England and Germany.

The art of public management or 'political economy', then, consists, again, in maintaining a delicate balance between the preservation of corporate liberties and local privileges (in particular, the corporate liberties of the Third Estate and the urban communal privileges so vital to the bourgeoisie), and the unification of these particularisms into a 'harmonious' body politic and an integrated national economy. Again, the society presupposed by the notion of 'political economy' bears the traces of its feudal and corporatist lineage, while it takes for granted a strong monarchical state.

The Culture of Absolutism

By the end of the religious wars, France was effectively in social crisis and economic ruin. The 1590s were marked by famine, popular revolt and epidemics, as agriculture was fatally disrupted and many cultivators were forced off the land. The royal state began to seem the only viable solution to anarchy; and opposition to monarchical authority among its principal rivals receded, even while the monarchy introduced reforms that, among other things, redistributed the tax burden by excluding some privileged exemptions. Yet the seventeenth century would again be plagued by civil war. With the end of the Thirty Years' War and the Peace of Westphalia in 1648, the remnants of fragmented sovereignty reasserted themselves, aggravated not only by predatory bands of aristocratic soldiers returning from war but also by new dynasties of office-holders. In the time of the Fronde, the battles over jurisdiction, the burden of taxation, or access to state office and the profits of taxation, resurfaced in new forms. In a series of revolts from 1649 to 1652, there were successive waves of opposition to the king from the *parlement* of Paris defending its powers to limit the monarchy, from nobles asserting their autonomy, from popular forces resisting taxation, and finally from dynastic rivals.

The monarchy responded by consolidating central power. What followed is conventionally called the era of French 'absolutism': the revocation of the Edict of Nantes, which had granted significant rights to Protestants; reform of the fiscal and military apparatus to fortify the central state and weaken the aristocracy; a comprehensive programme by the state to promote commercial and industrial development; attempts to unify the legal system and to create a national French culture, from royal patronage of the arts to the standardization of the French language.

While the absolutist state survived the upheavals of the seventeenth century, the Fronde and peasant revolts, the grievances inseparable from the nature of that state – taxation, privileges and exemptions, administrative corruption, in a framework of regional and corporate fragmentation – continued to be the targets of social protest and proposals for reform. Absolutism would never overcome the fragmentation of the state; and the idea of a fragmented social order bound together by a single harmonizing will, a network of corporate entities integrated into an organic, hierarchical totality by a single sovereign power, would continue to shape French political thought. It also encouraged a conception of society in which the totality of social relations, including economic transactions, was subsumed in the *political* community. This constellation would continue to dominate French social thought up to the Revolution and beyond.

The 'parcellization' of political power in France, the survival of feudal prerogatives and privileges, their extension into new forms of patronage and proprietary offices, the persistence of regional and corporate particularisms, whether viewed from the perspective of the monarchy or the 'people', were often confronted theoretically by the notion of a single unifying mind or will which would bind them together. Defenders of the monarchy – whether motivated by the needs of a quarrelsome and self-defeating feudal nobility, the grievances of the Third Estate, or the proprietary interests of the monarchy itself – proposed that feudal prerogatives and proprietary rights in political office and power be appropriated by the monarchy, to constitute, as Bodin formulated it, a single, supreme and indivisible sovereign power. In moderate 'constitutionalist' doctrine, the royal will was to be rendered more truly public, cleansed of particularistic accretions in the form of a corrupt and venal administration, and tempered or informed by representative institutions, but not limited by sharing sovereignty with them.

Even in more radical attacks on royal absolutism, the public will of the state was not generally opposed, as in England, by asserting private interests or individual rights against it. Nor was the common good redefined as a public interest essentially constituted by private interests, in order to counter the public claims of a crown encroaching upon private rights. Instead, the public character of the absolutist state itself was questioned, and the location of the public will was shifted. The principle of generality in a system of particularisms was transferred in theory to representative institutions, the officers of the 'people', 'intermediate bodies'. Even where the common good was conceived as emerging from a harmony of private interests, the state – more specifically, the monarchy – tended to appear as the necessary agent of harmony, the unifying will that would integrate corporate particularities and partial interests. The threats posed by the state itself, its own particularistic and proprietary character, the growth of a burdensome administrative apparatus conceived as private property, were opposed not so much by attempts to defend the 'private' sphere from encroachment by the 'public', as by proposals for transforming the 'private' state into a truly public thing.

Under the Bourbon monarchy, the by now familiar argument that a unifying will in the person of the monarch was an inescapable necessity to maintain social order in an irreducibly fragmented state was taken to new extremes. In 1681 Bishop Bossuet, tutor to the son and heir of Louis XIV, had pushed the argument beyond all previous limits with the publications of his *Discourse on Universal History*. A staunch supporter of the king and the Gallican Church against both Protestants and papacy, he presented his pioneering work in 'philosophical' history as a lesson to the young dauphin. At the centre of the first volume, which covers a 'universal' history from the beginning of the world to the reign of Charlemagne, was the history of ancient Rome and the rise of Christianity. Bossuet's account of the later periods, up to 1661, would be reproduced from his notes after his death. The intention of this massive work was to demonstrate that the history of the world was providentially ordained in the interest of a unified Catholic Church; and one of its principal conclusions was that a single, indivisible sovereign monarch, as a repository of that single, unified Church, was required to fulfil God's purpose.

In the following century, the 'Age of Enlightenment', the culture of French absolutism would take a very different form; but the absolutist state remained at the core of the Enlightenment. However many national enlightenments there may have been, it was in France that the emblematic *philosophe* was born, a new kind of public intellectual whose mission to educate the modern reader was most vividly exemplified by the *Encyclopédie*, proposing to 'encompass not only the fields already covered by the academies, but each and every branch of human knowledge', and not only for the benefit of scholars but for the purpose of changing the 'common way of thinking'. This period is regarded as a distinctively cosmopolitan age in Europe and especially, perhaps, in France. Not unreasonably, the 'Enlightenment' is seen as a time when an 'Age of Discovery', three centuries of commercial and imperial expansion providing access to the material and cultural treasures of the world outside Europe, had driven European minds, and the 'republic of letters', beyond their narrow spatial boundaries. Encouraged by the intellectual legacy of humanism and a scientific revolution, this spatial expansion gave new life to universalistic visions of the world and human rights. Yet, for all their cosmopolitanism and inclusive ambitions, 'Enlightenment' reformers in France were still addressing specifically French questions about the proprietary state, patronage, taxation, and venal offices.

As the state long continued to be a major resource, even beyond the Revolution and Napoleon, complaints were often directed less at the inherent evils of the state as an instrument of appropriation than at the inequalities of opportunity blocking access to its fruits. If (as Jürgen Habermas has famously suggested) the Enlightenment created a new 'bourgeois public sphere', outside and independent of the state, allowing a new kind of critical distance, this had less to do with asserting 'bourgeois' interests against encroachments by the state, or marking out a new space outside the state for the development of capitalism, than with bourgeois demands for access to the state and to the fruits of office. It is not for nothing that, at a time when the traditional aristocracy was seeking to reassert its privileges, not least its privileged access to office, the slogan 'careers open to talent' had such resonance in the moments leading up to revolution.

The *philosophes* exposed the absolutist state and the Church to critical scrutiny, to say nothing of ridicule. They – though some more radically than others – espoused 'enlightened' principles of liberty and toleration with inimitable wit and eloquence. Their irreverence and their assaults on 'superstition' shocked many contemporaries and provoked established authorities, sometimes with dangerous consequences, including imprisonment. Even when their political views were far from democratic or displayed contempt for the common people, their educative mission was, by its very nature, liberating. For the most part the towering figures of the French Enlightenment – such as Voltaire, d'Alembert, Holbach, and Diderot – owe their intellectual force less to any systematic philosophical innovations than to that educative project.

Denis Diderot perhaps better than anyone else captures this specific quality and genius of the French Enlightenment. This is not to say that his views were typical of the *philosophes*. For all his flirtations with 'enlightened despotism' (he was invited to Russia to advise Catherine the Great), he was more democratic than, for example, Voltaire, and less inclined to display contempt for the 'common' people. He could be described as more progressive than was the norm on subjects like the rights of women or the wrongs of colonialism. But he has a special claim as representative of the French Enlightenment, because it was he, above all others, who sustained the *Encyclopédie*; and it was he who made most explicit the project of encompassing all knowledge in an inclusive, comprehensive educative mission, challenging both Church and state by changing 'the common way of thinking'. His own writings, which were wide-ranging and varied in style, would win the admiration of thinkers like Hegel and Marx. But the power of his vision, in a sense, depended on a conscious refusal of system. He can certainly be credited with a distinctive philosophical materialism, but its emphasis on change and uncertainty was perhaps best captured not by rigorous philosophy or political theory but by a characteristic work like *Rameau's Nephew*, a satirical dialogue ranging across a bewildering variety of subjects, full of confusions and contradictions, in which the standpoint of the author remains outside our grasp, yet which somehow succeeds in exposing enemies of enlightenment to ridicule.

Among the luminaries of the French Enlightenment, there were nonetheless at least two who could lay claim to systematic originality in social and political thought. Like the *philosophes* in general, Montesquieu and Rousseau, two of the most inventive and widely influential figures in the Western canon, belonged to a larger 'republic of letters', well schooled in cultural developments beyond the borders of France. Yet what is particularly striking about both these innovative thinkers is the degree to which their political ideas were deeply rooted in – and, in their very different ways, owed their distinctive character to – the specific discourse of French absolutism.

That the French Enlightenment's commitment to critical reason was, in one way or another, a response to royal absolutism is a commonplace. But to emphasize the cultural effects of absolutism is to say something more than simply that French arts and literature thrived under the extravagance of royal patronage and/or that the absolutist state provoked a culture of opposition, giving birth to an 'Age of Enlightenment' which celebrated reason, toleration, civil liberty and individual autonomy against oppression by an overbearing state supported by an intolerant Church and a culture of 'superstition'. Nor is it enough to acknowledge the continuity of grievances, from the sixteenth century to the Revolution. Throughout that period, the persistent tensions at the heart of the absolutist state remained at the core of French intellectual life in, so to speak, a more structural sense, presenting thinkers with specific questions and setting the terms of debate in particular ways. This is nowhere more visible than in Rousseau and Montesquieu.

Montesquieu

By the time Montesquieu published his *Considerations on the Causes of the Grandeur and Decadence of the Romans* in 1734, there was already a long tradition of debate on the origin and legitimacy of the French monarchy, as against competing jurisdictions. In the eighteenth century, old arguments like those of Hotman in the sixteenth century, which sought to challenge the monarchy's authority by invoking French historical traditions, were countered by alternative accounts of history – for instance, tracing the origins of monarchical authority to Roman imperial roots. Such arguments were challenged in turn by historical claims for the feudal powers of the nobility, which insisted that the absolute monarchy represented a historical corruption.

From this opposition would emerge the battle between the *thèse royale* and the *thèse nobiliaire*, the debate between those committed to an untrammelled, undivided sovereign monarchy and those who believed in a monarchical state limited by the autonomous powers of the nobility and corporate bodies. Whatever other ambiguities there are in Montesquieu's political philosophy, which have permitted commentators to describe him as everything from an apostle of reaction to a committed republican, his own contemporaries, including *philosophes*, had no difficulty situating him, for better or worse, on the side of the *thèse nobiliaire*.

In a letter to Montesquieu, for instance, Helvetius wrote:

> As to our aristocrats and our petty despots of all grades, if they understand you, they cannot praise you too much, and this is the fault I have ever found with the principles of your work . . . *L'esprit de corps* assails us on all sides; it is a power erected at the expense of the great mass of society. It is by these hereditary usurpations we are ruled.[22]

To be on the side of the *thèse nobiliaire* was not to oppose a monarchical state, as was clear to republican critics (not just in France but in America, for all the influence he is said to have had on the 'founding fathers') who denounced Montesquieu as a monarchist. Nor was there anything unusual or contradictory about asserting principles of liberty against the absolutist monarchy while remaining firmly wedded to the principles of aristocracy. But subscribing to the *thèse nobiliaire* did mean rejecting some of the most fundamental tenets of the absolutist state as embodied in the *thèse royale*; and the most efficient way of making sense of Montesquieu's apparent ambiguities is to place him in the context of that very French debate. At the same time, the conceptual innovations to which he owes his title as progenitor of modern sociology and/or the inventor of modern political science (or even political economy) are rooted in precisely his critical engagement with French absolutist ideology.

Montesquieu was born in 1689, the historical moment that in Britain produced the kind of 'balanced' government he would hold up as a model in his classic, *The Spirit of the Laws*. He came from an old and distinguished family of the *noblesse de robe*, an element in French society that would be at the very centre of his political ideas. Trained as a lawyer, he served in the *parlement* of Bordeaux and later became president; and this experience, as we shall see, would figure prominently in his theory of politics. A believer in venal office as a check on the central state, he sold his own office of president.

If the early movement of the *philosophes* began among courtly elites, it was Montesquieu who first moved significantly beyond the limits of salon conversation, with the publication of his *Persian Letters* in 1721. Like Voltaire's *Philosophical Letters*, published in 1734, Montesquieu's devastatingly witty epistolary novel, in which French society was viewed as through the alien eyes of a Persian visitor, advanced the Enlightenment,

---

22 Quoted by Franz Neumann in his introduction to Montesquieu, *The Spirit of the Laws* (New York: Hafner, 1962), p. xxvii.

as Robert Darnton puts it, 'from wit to wisdom', mixing 'libertine impieties with serious reflections on despotism and intolerance'.[23] But Montesquieu, unlike Voltaire, undertook a more ambitious intellectual project with his *Considerations on the Causes of the Grandeur and Decline of the Romans* in 1734, to be followed by *The Spirit of the Laws*; and it is here that the absolutist roots of French discourse in the 'Age of Enlightenment' are most visible.

Absolutist thought encouraged an idea of society as an interlocking whole, a systemic totality of social relations, constituted by political authority in the person of an 'absolute' monarch. The strategies adopted in defence of absolutism had the effect of encouraging totalizing visions of the social world and human history, which would have significant effects on the development of social theory. The 'philosophical history' of Montesquieu, as well as his theories of society and social change, belongs to that tradition. To say this may, on the face of it, run counter to interpretations of his work that treat him as a progenitor of modern sociology, whose discovery of 'society' as a self-subsistent entity, a network of relations with its own internal logic, had the effect of displacing the 'political' as the unifying force or organizing principle of human community. The 'laws' that Montesquieu has in mind are, according to such interpretations, not so much the products of human creativity and political agency as necessities arising from the nature of a given social system and its inherent systemic requirements. But, while it is certainly true that Montesquieu emphasizes the systemic interconnections among various factors – economic, ecological and cultural no less than political – his 'sociology' remains inescapably political and deeply rooted in the tradition of absolutist thought. Montesquieu's account of societies as systemic wholes, each with its own specific principle of coherence and change, represents an attempt to challenge absolutist arguments on their own ground, by offering a theory of social totalities – embracing everything from history and politics to economics – that did not inevitably point to absolutist monarchy. At the same time, if the absolutist monarchy is no longer the indispensable condition of social cohesion, political agency remains at the heart of his 'sociology'.

Bossuet's philosophical history, which sought to capture the totality of human history in a grand, all-embracing explanation, was the work that perhaps above all else inspired Montesquieu to embark on his own philosophical history of Rome, not simply a narrative of events and personalities but an account of a whole social order rising and declining according to its own intrinsic principles, as a counter to the bishop's 'absolutist' vision of the world. The *Considerations* introduced themes that would be developed

---

23   Robert Darnton, 'George Washington's False Teeth', *New York Review of Books*, 27 March 1997, p. 35.

in a different form in *The Spirit of the Laws*, on which his status in the canon of Western political thought mainly rests, published anonymously in 1748. In *Considerations*, Montesquieu's intent was not simply to present an alternative account of Roman history but to counteract justifications of royal absolutism by challenging the claims for Louis XIV as the divinely ordained agent of a universal history. He offers instead a 'natural' history of imperial Rome and the rise of Christianity, a 'philosophical' history but with only human agents, in sharp contrast to Bossuet's providential universal history.

Considerations is not an overtly theoretical work, but we can already detect the principles on which *The Spirit of the Laws* would proceed. In Montesquieu's history, there is no teleology or supra-human destiny of any kind. The history of Rome unfolds as a 'natural' process, and the rise of Christianity is nothing more than a part of that natural history. It has no more privileged historical status than any other Roman institution; and it is explicable in the same ways. But if history is a natural process, this is not to say that it proceeds in simple accordance with immutable natural laws. Human agency creates its own complexities. At the same time, history is not simply the product of great individuals. While the only historical agents are human, they act within specific contexts, specific institutions, common practices and the pervading culture, or the 'spirit' of the people, with their own intrinsic principles of change. It is in this sense that historical causes are general: the consequences of any particular cause – such as a military defeat – will be determined by a 'general' cause, the institutional framework of a specific society and the spirit of the people that pervades it. The early kings of Rome gave way to a republic not because of any great heroic acts by individuals but because the kings created an absolute monarchy, eliminating the intermediary powers of a nobility, and no such monarchy could be sustained for long. The republic achieved greatness, in power and size, not because of great individuals but because of the republican order and the particular public spirit that sustained it. Yet it was doomed to eventual decline because the nature and spirit of the republic encouraged, even required, constant conquests and expansion; and republics can survive only in a relatively small territory. Imperial expansion, while natural to the republic, was also the cause of its decline.

The Spirit of the Laws is a very different and more ambitious kind of work, but the amalgam of general and specific – the 'general' causes inherent in specific social forms – that appears in the *Considerations* is the guiding principle of Montesquieu's most influential classic. That sprawling work, with its huge temporal and geographical range, from France to China and beyond, while certainly acknowledged as a masterpiece, has also been accused of being contradictory, illogical and hard to follow, with ambitions that far exceed its accomplishments. But its weaknesses are at least to some extent the obverse of its strengths, the consequence of its author's innovative attempt to strike a theoretical balance between the general laws of social and political change and the distinctive operating principles or 'spirit' of specific political forms.

'I have,' he writes in his preface,

> first of all considered mankind, and the result of my thoughts has been, that amidst such an infinite diversity of laws and manners, they were not solely conducted by the caprice of fancy.
>
> I have laid down the first principles, and have found that the particular cases follow naturally from them; that the histories of all nations are only consequences of them; and that every particular law is connected with another law, or depends on some other of a more general extent. (SL)

One effect of treating all the many social forms and cultures on display in the world as equally 'natural' is to underwrite the toleration of diversity; and Montesquieu goes on to assure the reader that his purpose is not to censure the laws of any country whatsoever. His objective, he insists, is simply to illuminate the operating principles on which each type of government is based and the conditions conducive to its failures and successes, its rises and declines. 'Every nation will here find the reasons on which its maxims are founded.' The burden of proposing alterations 'belongs only to those who are so happy as to be born with a genius capable of penetrating the entire constitution of a state', and he himself would be happy simply to 'afford new reasons to every man to love his prince, his country, his laws' and 'to persuade those who command to increase their knowledge in what they ought to prescribe'. Yet, as Montesquieu proceeds, it becomes fairly clear that, however disinterested his scientific purpose, his exposure of the 'spirit' of all laws is, after all, also designed to promote the alteration of the existing French state. It is not too much to say that his grand scientific project is inevitably shaped by the particular requirements of a political programme.

Montesquieu starts from the premise that social and political change is intelligible, accessible to human reason; but to understand humanity's social and political practices requires something more than identifying certain fixed and invariable rules that are common to all nature. There are, to be sure, universal, immutable natural laws, which affect human beings as they do other natural bodies. 'Man, as a physical being, is like other bodies governed by invariable laws', but '[a]s an intelligent being, he incessantly transgresses the laws established by God, and changes those of his own instituting.' (I.1) These changes and transgressions are not unintelligible. The human 'laws' that are the subject of Montesquieu's study are no less susceptible to scientific knowledge than are the laws of nature as science understands them.[24] But the vast variety of social forms and customs, to say nothing of the vagaries of human passion, ignorance and error, means that it is not enough to discover the laws of nature in themselves – in the manner, for instance, of Hobbes, who tried to apply principles of physics and its laws of motion to human motivations. We must seek the internal coherence and logic of each specific social form.

We can certainly begin with certain common, fundamental human motivations, as does Hobbes when he describes the state of nature; and Montesquieu does briefly counter Hobbes's view: simple fear and the desire to dominate others can hardly explain how men live in society, and human motivations are far more complex. But the French philosopher is less interested in such primary motivations than in the complexities deriving from specific social forms. We can, he suggests, begin with the simple proposition that 'No society can subsist without a form of government'; and, in one way or another, all existing forms of government do conform to nature. But to say this is to tell us very little. 'Better is it to say', he goes on,

> that the government most conformable to nature is that which best agrees with the humor and disposition of the people in whose favor it is established . . . [and laws] should be adapted in such a manner to the people for whom they are framed that it should be a great chance if those of one nation suit another . . . They should be in relation to the climate of each country, to the quality of its soil, to its situation and extent, to the principal occupation of the natives, whether husbandmen, huntsmen or shepherds: they should have relation to the degree of liberty which the constitution will bear; to the religion of the inhabitants, to their inclinations, riches, numbers, commerce, manners, and customs. In fine, they have relations to each other, as also their origin, to the intent of the legislator, and to the order of things on which they

---

24 Louis Althusser, in *Politics and History: Montesquieu, Rousseau, Hegel and Marx* (London: New Left Books, 1972), makes an important argument about the 'revolution' of method accomplished by Montesquieu, in particular his redefinition of 'law'. While other thinkers had already secularized the concept of natural law, they had, argues Althusser, 'retained from the old version its teleological structure, its character as an ideal masked by the immediate appearances of *nature*. For them natural law was as much a *norm* (devoir) as a necessity. All their demands found refuge and support in a definition of law which was still foreign to the new one.' But Montesquieu 'proposes quite simply to expel the old version of the word law from the domains which it still held. And to consecrate the reign of the modern definition – law as a relation – over the whole extent of beings, from God to stones. "In this sense, all beings have their laws; the Deity his laws, the material world its laws, the intelligences superior to man their laws, the beasts their laws, man his laws" (I.1)' (p. 35).

are established; in all of which different lights they ought to be considered. (I.3)

Montesquieu proceeds to canvass a vast array of factors that set the terms of government and law, famously including long discussions of non-social determinants like climate and topography. But he still constructs his analysis on a familiar organizing principle, a formal typology of governments. He identifies three species of government: republican, monarchical, and despotic, each characterized by its own particular structure and the particular passions, or spirit, that ensure its survival. This classification is, of course, a departure from the ancient distinction among democracy, aristocracy, and monarchy (together with their corrupted forms); but, like much else in Montesquieu's work, it has roots in Machiavelli: instead of democracy and aristocracy, he proposes, as does Machiavelli, the republican form, in which the 'people' or some part of it possess supreme power and which therefore can be either democratic or aristocratic. But Montesquieu adds his own particular departure both from ancient classifications and from Machiavelli by proposing a distinction between monarchy and despotism: the distinctive characteristic of despotism is that 'a single person directs everything by his own will and caprice', in contrast to monarchy, 'in which a single person governs by fixed and established laws' (II.1).

The ancients did, to be sure, have a concept of 'despotic' rule. The word *despotes* in its original meaning simply described the head of a household or a master of slaves, a meaning that the Greeks by extension began to apply to their understanding of Asiatic forms of imperial rule, in contrast to Greek constitutions. In the sixteenth and seventeenth centuries, various thinkers – such as Bodin, Grotius, Hobbes and Locke – applied the term to denote regimes that effectively enslaved a subject people, or at least deprived them of rights, which these regimes could do legitimately on the grounds of just war. By the time Montesquieu elaborated his classification of political forms, which systematically included 'despotism' as one of the three major forms, the term had already become part of anti-absolutist discourse in France, to censure not an Asiatic 'despotism' or imperial rule over a subject population but a specifically European monarchy and its rule over its own people. In *The Spirit of the Laws*, Montesquieu makes the despotic form a central organizing principle of the whole work.

Montesquieu, then, proposes two types of formal criteria for distinguishing the principal forms of government: whether the state is governed by one person or more – which distinguishes republics from monarchies and despotisms; and whether the state is governed by 'fixed and established laws' – which distinguishes republics and monarchies from despotisms (although, as we shall see in a moment, this criterion is less straightforward than it may appear at first sight). It may be significant that whether the state is governed by a few or by many, a question so central to ancient classifications, does not have the same status as do those principal criteria: both aristocracies and democracies are republican forms. But this was true for Machiavelli, too, for whom the political universe was governed by a contest between principalities and city-republics, and the distinction between a *governo stretto* or a *governo largo*, his preference for the latter notwithstanding, was rather less important. For Montesquieu, the stakes, of course, are different. His classification of political forms seems designed to advance a particular agenda: the promotion of a monarchy, in which a government by 'fixed and established laws' is guaranteed by the autonomous powers of the nobility and other intermediate bodies.

How, then, is that purpose served by Montesquieu's distinctions among the forms of government, together with the very particular 'spirit of the laws' that sustains each one of them? Although he elaborates the differences between democratic and aristocratic republics, the most important message that emerges from his analysis of republican forms, whether democratic or aristocratic, is that they are very difficult – if not ultimately impossible – to sustain, requiring an onerous degree of probity or virtue not required by either despotic or monarchical states. The principle or 'spirit' that sustains the laws and institutions of democracy is a kind of civic virtue, a love of the laws and the country, that goes against the grain of other, simpler human passions. It can easily give way to 'the spirit of inequality', which drives people to put their own private interests and status above those of their fellow citizens, or, on the contrary, a spirit of excessive equality, which inclines people to disobey their governors in order to manage everything themselves. Aristocracies depend on a kind of 'moderation' that requires aristocrats to act in opposition to their inclinations and ambitions, which would naturally tend towards increasing the distance and the inequality between them and the common people, inevitably with corrupting and destabilizing effects. Republics, in other words, make unusually, even unnaturally, heavy demands on civic institutions, communal cohesion and devotion to the public good. To the extent that such demands can be met at all for any length of time, it is only in small and exceptionally homogeneous or integrated societies.

Montesquieu's discussion of republics, then, effectively rules out the republican form as a viable option for a country like France, or, indeed, for any other rising European power; but it does lay down certain ground rules of political survival, which can serve in analyzing other forms. We can, for example, analyze the monarchical form by discovering the principle that sustains it in a way analogous to civic virtue but without making the same demands on the people as republics do:

> In a monarchy policy effects great things with as little virtue as possible. Thus in the nicest machines, art has reduced the number of movements, springs, and wheels.

The state subsists independently of the love of our country, of the thirst of true glory, of self-denial, of the sacrifice of our dearest interests, and of all those heroic virtues which we admire in the ancients, and to us are known only in tradition. (III.5)

The basic principle of monarchy is honour, 'that is, the prejudice of every person and rank', which takes the place of political virtue and, when joined with the force of laws, can serve the purpose of government as well as virtue itself can do (III.6).

But there are very particular conditions that alone enable monarchy to sustain itself without demands on civic virtue, conditions without which rule by one man would simply be despotic. Governance by law means something very specific in the case of monarchy. Describing 'the relation of the laws to the nature of monarchical government', Montesquieu makes it clear that what finally distinguishes a lawful monarchy from a despotic form is the existence of 'intermediate, subordinate, and dependent powers' that stand between the people and the single ruler who governs by fundamental laws. Indeed, the very existence of 'fixed and established' fundamental laws presupposes such intermediate powers:

These fundamental laws necessarily suppose the intermediate channels through which the power flows, for if there be only the momentary and capricious will of a single person to govern the state, nothing can be fixed, and, of course, there is no fundamental law.' (II.4)

In the despotic form there are no such mediations, which means that, even if a despotism gives the appearance of governance by fixed and established law, it is really governed by the will and caprice of the ruler. Its operating principle is neither virtue nor honour but simply fear. Despotism is, in its way, certainly natural, driven by passions that come all too easily to human beings; but, while other forms of state are susceptible to corruption when their sustaining principles are compromised, despotic states are by nature corrupt from the start.

This brings us to another, more fundamental distinction among the types of state, the difference between 'moderate' and immoderate forms. The real danger of corruption comes not when 'the state passes from one moderate to another moderate government, as from a republic to a monarchy, or from a monarchy to a republic; but when it is precipitated from a moderate to a despotic government' (VIII.8). It is surely not insignificant that the principle specifically attached to aristocracy – the principle of 'moderation' – becomes the virtue of good government in general; and, indeed, Montesquieu goes on to make clear that a monarchy, as distinct from a despotism, is 'moderate' precisely because it is sustained by preserving autonomous aristocratic powers. What Montesquieu means by 'moderation' is revealed less by an explicit definition of this virtue than by the consequences he attributes to it and the means he prescribes to sustain it: a 'moderate government may, whenever it pleases, and without the least danger, relax its springs', unlike a despotism, in which the only guarantee of public order is blind obedience, driven by fear; and what ultimately makes this 'moderation' possible is a particular kind of balance among the powers of government:

> To form a moderate government, it is necessary to combine the several powers; to regulate, temper, and set them in motion; to give, as it were, ballast to one, in order to enable it to counterpoise the other. This is a masterpiece of legislation, rarely produced by hazard and seldom attained by prudence. (V.14)

This rare effect was achieved in republican Rome; and in Montesquieu's own time, he suggests, it exists particularly in England – although the English form as he describes it was, in reality, rather different from the monarchy he had in mind for France.

Here we come to one of the most disputed points in Montesquieu's work: whether what he was proposing was a 'separation of powers' in the sense that term is now conventionally understood. Debate surrounds his influence, or lack of it, on the American 'founding fathers' and the 'separation of powers' as encoded (though never specifically mentioned in those terms) in the US Constitution. It is certainly true that the 'founders' invoked Montesquieu and may even take credit for establishing his reputation as the inventor of the idea; but, however much the authority of Montesquieu was cited, the US doctrine of 'separate' powers, together with the 'checks and balances' it was meant to promote, produced something quite distinct from Montesquieu's intentions.

He tells us that '[i]n every government there are three sorts of power: the legislative; the executive in respect to things dependent on the law of nations; and the executive in regard to matters that depend on the civil law', the last of which can be called the judiciary power. (XI.6) But his account of 'moderate' government seems to suggest from the start that what he has in mind is not the separation of powers of a kind the US Constitution would produce. The most viable form of balanced and moderate government is monarchy; and he goes on to tell us that most kingdoms in Europe are 'moderate' because the prince, while possessing legislative and executive powers, leaves judiciary power to his subjects.[25] Yet it soon becomes clear that powers are

---

25 Althusser is right to suggest that the notion that Montesquieu proposed a 'separation of powers' is largely a historical illusion, a 'myth' (*Politics and History*, Ch. 5). But it should be added that, while there is debate about Montesquieu's meaning, there is

'separated' not in the sense that the three main governmental functions belong to different institutions. If anything, these functions are ideally combined but invested in more than one repository of power.

The ideal 'separation of powers' for Montesquieu clearly entails a monarchical state, in which the monarchy is checked and balanced by another source of power. In the English case, which he describes as the existing constitution most conducive to liberty, legislative power is embodied in the classic combination of 'the Crown in Parliament'. But there seems to be, for him, a different, perhaps even better, option, which has more to do with French conditions. Having told us that the 'intermediate, subordinate, and dependent powers constitute the nature of monarchical government', in which the 'fundamental laws necessarily suppose the intermediate channels through which the power flows', he goes on to explain that '[t]he most natural, intermediate, and subordinate power is that of the nobility. This in some measure seems to be essential to a monarchy, whose fundamental maxim is, no monarch, no nobility; no nobility, no monarch' (II.4, 15-16.).

This characterization of 'intermediate' powers suggests that there are two distinct issues at stake. It is one thing to distinguish among the various functions of the state and to insist that one or the other should not be placed entirely in the same hands. But to speak of the nobility in the way Montesquieu does is to raise a different set of questions.[26] The issue is not only the relation among legislative, executive and juridical powers but the survival of autonomous jurisdictions in relation to the central state.

Here, we can look back to the *Persian Letters* for some guidance about Montesquieu's preoccupations. The letters are set between 1711 and 1720. They span a period of crisis in the French state, with its climactic moment in 1715, the year of Louis XIV's death, followed by a regency which seemed at first to hold the promise of substantial change. 'The monarch who reigned for so long is no more', writes Usbek to Rhedi in 1715 (Letter XCIII). Usbek goes on to reflect on the possibilities that seem to have been opened, and it

---

nothing particularly novel or shocking about the contention that he never had in mind the 'separation of powers' in the now conventional sense. It is probably more common than otherwise among historians to point out that Montesquieu never meant what some Americans claimed for him.

26 The difference between these issues is perhaps more easily rendered in French. See Althusser, *Politics and History*, on the distinction between power as *puissance* and power as *pouvoir:* 'We then confront *two powers:* the executive and the legislature. Two *pouvoirs* but three *puissances*, to use Montesquieu's own words. These three *puissances* are the king, the upper chamber and the lower chamber, i.e. the king, the nobility and the "people" . . . The famous *separation of powers* is thus no more than the calculated division of *pouvoir* between determinate *puissances:* the king, the nobility and the "people"' (pp. 90–1). Yet even this formulation may not quite capture what Montesquieu has in mind.

is striking that his principal concern is with the *parlements*. These old institutions

> resemble those ruins which are trampled underfoot but are reminiscent always of some temple famed in the antique religion of the people. They now interest themselves only in judicial questions, and their authority will continue to weaken unless something unforeseen rejuvenates them. These great bodies have followed the destiny of all things human: they have yielded to time, which destroys all, to moral corruption, which enfeebles, and to supreme authority, which overthrows everything.

Yet there is hope:

> [T]he regent, who wishes to make himself agreeable to the people, has so far appeared to respect this shadow of public liberty. As if he intended to rebuild the temple and the idol, he has decreed that they may be regarded as the support of the monarch and the base of all legitimate authority.

In *The Spirit of the Laws,* Montesquieu appears to be reviving the hope that these 'great bodies', these embodiments of 'public liberty', might renew the monarchy of France. The *parlements* fit his account of 'intermediate bodies', the essence of 'moderate' government, more aptly than does any other institution; and this distinctive feature of the French political tradition makes sense of Montesquieu's obscure account of 'balance' among powers in a way the English 'Crown in Parliament' does not.

The *parlements* embodied all the characteristic tensions of the complex relation between the French monarchy and other jurisdictions. They had played a critical part in extending royal authority, acting as a conduit for royal administration in the provinces; yet, as venal offices, they had become the hereditary property of office-holders, the *noblesse de robe*, with autonomous claims against the king; and they came to represent opposition to the monarchy in the name of the people and French constitutional liberties. They had become above all courts of law, as distinct from representative legislative assemblies in the manner of the English Parliament; yet they combined judicial powers with other state functions, administrative or executive – at least, they did so, as Montesquieu suggests in *Persian Letters*, before they were weakened under Louis XIV. They enjoyed police powers across a wide spectrum, from religion and morality to trade and industry; but their most important political function was to register royal decrees, or to object to them by invoking the *droit de remonstrance*, the right to protest royal edicts, which was revoked by Louis and restored by the regency. This right may not have been particularly efficacious and could be circumvented by the king; but, in the eyes of the French public, the *parlements* succeeded to a remarkable degree in identifying the interests of a venal, quasi-feudal oligarchy with the protection of French liberties.

Montesquieu, whose own political experience was rooted in the *parlement* of Bordeaux, had no illusions about the benevolence and rectitude of this institution and had, indeed, subjected his colleagues to harsh criticism. But there is no doubt that, with a certain amount of idealization, the *parlement* represented for him the model 'intermediate power'. It is the quintessential institution of the *noblesse de robe*, a group that can perform its essential and distinctive function because of its location between the great nobility and the people (*SL* XX.22). Combining aspects of all three 'separate' powers, the *parlement* 'balances' the powers of the monarchy by acting as the channel through which royal authority flows, retaining a degree of aristocratic and regional autonomy, protected by the rights of venal office (which Montesquieu supports), without fatally compromising the political and legal unity ideally conferred by the monarchy on a fundamentally fragmented state. What emerges is a model of 'moderate' government in which a strong and stable centralized power is balanced and checked by preserving a degree of fragmentation and regional particularity, together with the autonomy of noble powers in *every* function of the state, executive, legislative and judiciary – a model that remains far closer to the realities of French absolutism than to the English pattern even in idealized form.

The political balance that Montesquieu attempts to strike is distinctively French. He clearly approves of a strong central power and would even advocate a kind of unified national system of law, which England then had but France, for all the absolutist pretensions of the king, had yet to achieve. Nevertheless, he still identifies liberty with the preservation of autonomous powers vested in the nobility and corporate bodies, in a manner very different from the English state.

Montesquieu's discussion of judiciary power is at once both ambiguous and revealing. He tells us that, of the three powers, 'the judiciary is in some measure next to nothing; they remain, therefore, only two' (XI.6). At the same time, the judiciary power is the one whose possession by the 'people' seems the most critical in defining moderate government; and since moderate government is the minimal condition of liberty, it is reasonable to assume that a properly constituted judiciary power is the ultimate guarantee of liberty. It is, perhaps, possible to reconcile these two apparently conflicting propositions about the importance of judiciary power simply by pointing out that Montesquieu was relatively sparing in his demands on the judiciary. It has been argued, for example, that his principal claim to be 'one of the greatest of liberal thinkers . . . rests not on his famous homage to the English constitution, but on his theory of the criminal law and punishment', because for him '[t]he single most important requirement for the realization of liberty is that only a very few misdeeds should be criminalized at all.'[27]

Yet if this seems to reduce the powers of the *parlement* as a judicial body, its role as an 'intermediate power' rests not simply on its function as a court but on a degree of aristocratic autonomy in *all* functions of the state, not only the judiciary. Montesquieu can advocate a national system of law that challenges France's legal fragmentation, while at the same time calling for the preservation of the *parlements* as both less and more than courts of law. His views on crime and punishment are certainly significant, but the all-too-capacious concept of 'liberalism' should be applied here with caution. If it is taken to imply a 'modern' turn of mind, it may obscure the ways in which his conception of judicial power remains rooted in French absolutism, while 'liberty' is still identified with the remnants of parcellized sovereignty and aristocratic autonomy.

Commerce

The French *parlements* resolve the ambiguities in Montesquieu's 'separation of powers' in a way the English model does not. But there is another feature of the English model that Montesquieu admires with, on the face of it, less ambiguity. *The Spirit of the Laws* devotes a great deal of attention to commerce, remarkably so for a work ostensibly on politics and law – or, to put it more precisely, commerce as he conceives it plays a role no less political than 'economic'. Not only is England, for instance, a prime example of commercial success, but it represents a distinctive blend of liberty with commerce. 'Other nations', he says, 'have made the interests of commerce yield to those of politics; the English, on the contrary, have ever made their political interests give way to those of commerce' (XX.7). It is exceptional, too, in the ways and degrees that the commercial spirit permeates the whole society, as even the nobility engage in commerce. And lest that seem intended as a criticism, Montesquieu assures us that '[t]hey know better than any other people upon earth how to value, at the same time, these three great advantages – religion, commerce, and liberty'.

The English are unique in another way, which is clearly related to the nexus of commerce and liberty: they alone have successfully combined monarchy and 'economic' commerce, as distinct from the commerce of luxury. While monarchies typically devote themselves to procuring 'everything that can contribute to the pride, the pleasure, and the capricious whims of the nation', it is more common in republics to encourage trade that has 'an eye to all the nations of the earth, [bringing] from one what is wanted by another' (XX.4). Monarchies also tend to distrust merchant

---

27   Judith Shklar, *Montesquieu* (Oxford: Oxford University Press, 1987), p. 89.

classes, while republics are inclined to preserve their safety and their security of property. 'Great enterprises, therefore, in commerce are not for monarchical, but for republican, governments.' In all these respects, England represents a notable exception, combining, it seems, monarchical and republican elements in both politics and commerce.

Montesquieu's elaborate discussion of commerce is said to have sparked an interest in political economy among the French; and it would indeed be French thinkers who, not long after, produced groundbreaking work in economic theory, giving new life and meaning to the term 'political economy'. François Quesnay and his physiocratic school, even before the Anglo-Scottish 'classical' political economists, have been credited with a major breakthrough in the evolution of modern economics, on the grounds that they were the first to treat the economy as a systemic totality, in which the processes of production, exchange and consumption were united in an interdependent 'circular flow'; and for them, too, if for somewhat different reasons, England was the model.

Montesquieu was never a 'political economist' in that technical sense, but he did give some credence to the idea that the economy – or the network of commerce – was a self-sustaining mechanism, which, left free to follow its own principles, could promote not only liberty within the state but peace among nations. While he had no illusions about the connections between commerce and war or colonial conquest, he went some distance in questioning the common assumption that trade among nations is a zero-sum game. At least for nations with adequate movable resources to trade, commerce with others possessing more or less equal endowments serves to unite and enrich all parties to the exchange. Those who have little tradeable wealth should stay away from commerce even to obtain the things they do not have: 'it is not those nations who have need of nothing that must lose by trade; it is those who have need of everything' (XX.23).

At the same time, Montesquieu tells us, 'if the spirit of commerce unites nations, it does not in the same manner unite individuals' (XX.2). The commercial spirit displaces all humane and moral virtues, reducing everything to money. Commerce may in some respects do the work of civic virtue, but it cannot by itself serve as the social bond or economic mechanism that automatically converts private vices into public benefits. Yet again, it appears that what is required to harmonize interests and guarantee the common good, or even simple equity, is political authority. The question then may be what form of state can serve this function while maintaining liberty. The English state appears to be the model here; but, in a section disarmingly entitled 'A singular reflection', Montesquieu interjects some comments on France that suggest another option, which resonates with what we already know about his political preferences:

Persons struck with the practice of some states imagine that in France they ought to make laws to engage the nobility to enter into commerce. But these laws would be the means of destroying the nobility, without being of any advantage to trade. The practice of this country is extremely wise; merchants are not nobles, though they may become so. They have hope of obtaining a degree of nobility, unattended with its actual inconveniences. There is no surer way of being advanced above their profession than to manage it well, or with success; the consequence of which is generally an affluent fortune . . .

The possibility of purchasing honor with gold encourages many merchants to put themselves in circumstances by which they may attain it. I do not take it upon me to examine the justice of this bartering for money the price of virtue. There are governments where this may be very useful. (XX.22)

As with Spinoza, then, commerce can work to the public advantage when the lust for money is harnessed to the public good by making wealth a means to achieve the honour of office. But, in accordance with French conditions, the principal agents of the public good for Montesquieu are not republican oligarchs, as in the Dutch Republic, but venal office-holders and specifically those of 'the long robe, which places those who wear it between the great nobility and the people', the *noblesse de robe* that serves as 'the depository of the laws' (XX.22). The wealth derived from commerce can, it would seem, most directly serve the public good when used to purchase office.

A few years later, the physiocrats would invoke the model of English agrarian capitalism to construct their science of political economy. Montesquieu may indeed have been in some respects their forerunner; but the physiocrats systematically developed, in a way that he never did, the principle that the 'economy' has an internal and self-propelling logic of its own. On the strength of that principle, and the slogan *laissez faire, laissez passer,* which they helped to promote, they are commonly regarded as founders not only of political economy but of 'liberal' economics, who influenced the likes of Adam Smith and other classical political economists.

Yet the physiocrats, in a distinctively French context, assigned to the state a role very different from anything envisaged by their Anglo-Scottish equivalents. While they looked to the example of England and its productive agrarian sector in support of their argument that agriculture was the driving force of a 'modern' economy, they acknowledged the fundamental differences between French conditions and the English model – above all, the absence in France of what we have been calling a capitalist landed class. It was, for the physiocrats, up to the state to transform French society, to act in effect as the agent of what Adam Smith would call the 'original accumulation'; and the monarchy still appeared – in the French manner – as the principle of universality in a constellation of particularisms, the principal means of overcoming corporate interests, the fragmentation of both state and economy. In this respect, too, they had something important in common with Montesquieu. But, unlike Montesquieu, for whom 'intermediate bodies' were the guardians of liberty, the physiocrats had their eyes more firmly fixed on economic progress; and this, in their view, required the suppression of fragmented powers by a form of 'legal despotism'. The purpose of the monarchical state was certainly not to impose its own arbitrary will. It was meant to ensure the operation of the 'natural' laws of society and economic mechanisms; but those natural laws had as their condition a strong central state. [28]

Jean-Jacques Rousseau

In the few years between the appearance of Montesquieu's *Spirit of the Laws* and Quesnay's *Tableau économique*, Rousseau produced three of his most important works: the *Discours sur les sciences et les arts* (1750), which first established his reputation as a social thinker; *Discours sur l'origine et les fondements de l'inégalité parmi les hommes*) (1754); and *Discours sur l'économie politique* (1755). His ideas would undergo significant development from one work to the next; but the three discourses have at least one common theme, which would remain at the foundation of all his political thought: a challenge to social doctrines – such as those espoused, Rousseau suggests, by Hobbes and Mandeville – according to which society is bound together above all by the force of personal interest.

It is tempting to avoid any mention of Rousseau's biography. His notoriously difficult personality is certainly important in accounting for the vagaries of his career, his broken friendships with other *philosophes* like Diderot, and his unmistakable vantage point as an 'outsider', which goes beyond his identity as a Genevan in an alien Paris; and, of course, his private life is on dramatic display in his *Confessions* and his *Reveries of a Solitary Walker*, in a way unmatched by almost any other thinker. But his psychological weaknesses have too often permitted a lazy and tendentious dismissal of his political ideas as the neurotic outpourings of a disordered psyche, perhaps an 'authoritarian personality' with a penchant for 'totalitarian democracy'; and we may, as will be argued in what follows, learn less about his work from his personal life than we do from the French historical context which inspired his political ideas.

---

28   On the physiocrats and their conception of the relation between the state and the economy, see David McNally, *Political Economy and the Rise of Capitalism* (Berkeley: University of Californian Press, 1994), Ch. 3.

About his life, it is probably enough to know that he was born the son of a well-educated watchmaker in 1712 in Geneva, which would remain an idealized model for his political reflections; that he fled Geneva at the age of fifteen; that, largely self-educated, he was introduced to French society and intellectual life while under the protection and influence of Mme de Warens, a Catholic lay proselytizer (though he would later return to Calvinism to regain his Genevan citizenship); and that, when he moved to Paris in 1742, he established a close friendship with Diderot and other *philosophes*. His work embraced an astonishingly wide range of subjects, from the philosophy of education in *Émile* to musical theory (which he seems to have regarded as his most important contribution); and his novel, *Julie, or the New Héloise*, is often cited as a founding work of the 'romantic' movement. By the time of his death in 1778, he had established a formidable reputation and also succeeded in breaking with his friends among the *philosophes*, on both personal and intellectual grounds.

Rousseau first made his reputation with the *Discourse on the Arts and Sciences* (which already set him at odds with the 'Enlightenment'). Responding to critics of the *Discourse,* he begins to explain his objections to conceptions of society as held together by the bonds of personal interest, which laid the foundation for his political ideas:

> Our writers like to regard absolutely everything as 'the political master-piece of the century': the sciences, the arts, luxury, commerce, laws – and all other bonds which, in tightening the social knot with the force of personal interest, make men mutually dependent, give them reciprocal needs and common interests, and require that all pursue the happiness of others in order to be able to pursue their own. These ideas are, to be sure, quite attractive, and can be presented in a most favorable light. But . . . [i]s it really such a wonderful thing to have made it impossible for men to live together without mutual bigotry, mutual competition, mutual deceit, mutual treason and mutual destruction? . . . After all, for every two men whose interests converge, there are perhaps one hundred thousand who are adversaries.[29]

Society in Rousseau's time, then, is, in his view, essentially and unavoidably adversarial. The commonality of private interests, whether sustained by force of law or by commercial networks, is largely a sham. In his replies to critics of the first *Discourse* (and there are hints in the *Discourse* itself), he already moves in the direction of singling out private property, with the inequalities that inevitably spring from it, as the principal cause of these

---

29 Jean-Jacques Rousseau, *Narcisse,* Preface, in *Political Theory,* Vol. 6, No. 4, November 1978, p. 549.

adversarial relations. In the second *Discourse* he develops this conception of society, in which men are divided between the rich few and the many who serve them, while the only social ties among them are the deceitful conventions that bind the many to obey and labour for the few, and the networks of commerce that make men rivals to each in the guise of mutual benefit. There can, in such conditions, be no genuine convergence of private interests and a public good; and any invocation of the public welfare or the common good can only be deception in the interests of a few, enforced by state coercion. In circumstances such as these, in other words, there can be no such thing as freedom.

Rousseau was thus from the start at odds with a wide range of thinkers who relied on commerce or the absolutist state, or both together, to sustain the social bond and convert private interests into public goods. At the same time, whatever his nostalgia for some ancient golden age of civic virtue, he denied the possibility of its return, if it ever existed at all. The problem he set himself, which would drive his political ideas from beginning to end, was to find a mechanism for attaining common goods that emanated freely from the individuals who shared them, rather than from some external power of coercion, but did not make unreasonable demands on civic virtue or depend on mutual deception.

In the first *Discourse*, written by Rousseau for a competition staged by the Academy of Dijon, he was replying to a question posed by the Academy: 'Has the restoration of the sciences and arts tended to purify morals?' Rousseau's reply in the negative was not as unusual or provocative as we might think or, indeed, as he himself liked to pretend. There were other contestants who denied the moral benefits of scientific and cultural progress as understood in eighteenth-century Europe; and, for that matter, there existed an important tradition, in the 'quarrel between the ancients and moderns', that questioned the value of modern cultural developments by associating them with Athenian aestheticism as against the civic virtue of ancient Rome or Sparta. Rousseau's departures from this tradition would become far more evident in the second *Discourse*, where his social and political radicalism comes to the fore; but the foundations are laid in the first *Discourse*.

In his reply to critics, Rousseau contemptuously dismisses a conventional reading of his attack on modern culture, which he sums up as follows:

'Knowledge is good for absolutely nothing, bad by nature, it does only ill. It can no more be separated from vice than ignorance from virtue. All literate peoples have been corrupt, all ignorant peoples virtuous. In a word, there is vice only among the learned, while a virtuous man is he alone who knows nothing. There can then be but one way for us to regain honesty; we must move with dispatch to proscribe both learning and the

learned, to burn our libraries, to close our Academies, our colleges and our universities, and to plunge back into the barbarism of earliest times.'
There it is – all of what my adversaries have so effectively refuted.
Except that I never thought, never uttered one single word of any of it.
Nor could anything more contrary to my system be conceived than this absurd doctrine they have had the goodness to attribute to me.[30]

He goes on to say that morals have not, to be sure, been purified by cultural developments as we know them; but there remains the question of causal connections, and here Rousseau appears to suggest that the causes may lie not in learning itself but in its social context:

What a strange and fatal condition – where accumulated riches facilitate still greater riches, but where men with none can acquire none; where the good man knows no way out of his misery; where the most roguish are the most honored and where virtue must be renounced for men to remain honest . . . And so, in the end, my vision is both consoling and useful, for it demonstrates that all these vices belong less to man than to man badly governed.[31]

This passage is significant enough in its attribution of 'vices' not to some universal human nature but to specific modes of organizing social life, but precisely what its author meant by 'man badly governed' would become clearer only in his later works. The first *Discourse*, nonetheless, already gives us some idea of where Rousseau is going. 'Luxury', he tells us,

rarely develops without the sciences and arts, and they never develop without it . . . Granted that luxury is a sure sign of wealth, that it even serves, if you like, to increase wealth. What conclusion must be drawn from this paradox so worthy of our time; and what will become of virtue when one must get rich at any price? Ancient politicians incessantly talked about morals and virtue, those of our time talk only of business and money . . . They evaluate men like herds of cattle. According to them a man is worth no more to the State than the value of his domestic consumption.[32]

It is in the second *Discourse* that Rousseau lays out more precisely what he means when he attributes 'vices' not to human nature but to the social

---

30   *Ibid.*, p. 546.
31   *Ibid.*, p. 550.
32   Rousseau, *First Discourse*, in *The First and Second Discourses*, ed. Roger Masters (New York: St Martin's Press, 1964), p. 51.

contexts in which it manifests itself. At the very heart of the *Discourse on Inequality* is the principle that human beings have a *history* and not an abstract 'human nature'. Rousseau begins by dissociating himself from concepts of the 'state of nature' such as those proposed by Hobbes or Locke. 'The philosophers who have examined the foundations of society', he writes, 'have all felt the necessity of going back to the state of nature, but none of them has reached it.'[33] They have attributed to human beings in the state of nature ideas and practices – conceptions of justice, property and government – that derive from specific social conditions, which have a long history. The philosophers have ascribed to human nature characteristics that could arise only in specific social conditions. Rousseau would later reinforce this social definition of human nature in *Émile*, which, while ostensibly devoted to the development of a uniquely isolated individual, starts from the premise that even the sense of self is produced by relations with others, so that the development of individuality and the direction it takes depend on the nature of relations with others.[34]

What, then, can we say about the original 'nature' of humanity? There are two principles anterior to reason, Rousseau tells us. The first natural instinct is a love of self (*amour de soi*) or, more precisely, an instinct for self-preservation. But we should not, he immediately explains, make Hobbes's fundamental error in defining this natural instinct, which is to assume that the drive for self-preservation necessarily puts us in conflict with others and that 'by virtue of the right [man] claims to the things he needs, he foolishly imagines himself to be the sole proprietor of the whole universe.'[35] Hobbes was right to question all modern definitions of natural right, but he drew conclusions that were no less false. What he should have concluded from his own premises was that, since the state of nature – before the advent of property and government – is the condition in which our own self-preservation is least prejudicial to the self-preservation of others, it was more, not less, conducive to peace. Instead, Hobbes came to the opposite conclusion, because he ascribed to the natural instinct of self-preservation 'the need to satisfy a multitude of passions which are the product of society and which have made laws necessary'. This is not to say that 'savage' human beings are naturally 'good'. It is simply to acknowledge the social conditions that compel self-preservation to take one form rather than another.

The second original instinct is compassion (*pitié*), an 'innate repugnance' in human beings to see their fellows suffer. This instinct is, for example,

---

33   Rousseau, *Second Discourse*, in *ibid.*, p. 102.

34   For a detailed discussion of this point, see Ellen Meiksins Wood, *Mind and Politics: An Approach to the Meaning of Liberal and Socialist Individualism* (Berkeley: University of California Press, 1972).

35   Rousseau, *Second Discourse*, in *ibid.*, pp. 128–9.

recognized by Mandeville; but he fails to see, Rousseau insists, that this is the source of precisely those social virtues Mandeville seeks to deny, those very qualities that make it possible for human beings, in the right conditions, to promote the mutual preservation of the species. If this natural instinct is suppressed or overshadowed in contemporary society, that is, again, a function of social conditions that compel human beings to perceive their interests as mutually antagonistic.

There are, of course, natural differences among human beings, but these cannot by themselves account for the divisions of servitude and domination, or the capacity of some to live on the labour of others. The watershed in the development of humanity was the invention of private property. Rousseau may not be unambiguous about how this revolution came about; but one thing is clear: whatever the first cause of private property, or the social division of labour that seems to have brought it about, the invention of property was decisive in making inequality the principal determinant of social life. Whatever other inequalities there may be among human beings, whether rooted in psychology or innate talent, it is the invention of property that accounts for the divisions between masters and servants, those who labour and those who appropriate the labour of others, and finally the division between rulers and ruled. This also produces the transformation of *amour de soi* into *amour propre*, the conversion of an instinct for self-preservation into active egotism and the antagonisms of self-interest, which other philosophers have mistaken for the natural condition of humanity:

> in a word, competition and rivalry on one hand, opposition of interest on the other; and always the hidden desire to profit at the expense of others. All these evils are the first effect of property and the inseparable consequence of nascent inequality. [36]

It is this account of private property and its consequences that would from then on determine Rousseau's political philosophy. He would in his later work go on to oscillate between the stance of *Émile* (1762), which purports to portray the education of an isolated individual, divorced from a world in which civil society can never be anything but an instrument of the rich against the poor, and, in the same year, the apparently contrary impulse of the *Social Contract*, in which the civic bond is powerful and just. But – and here we should take seriously Rousseau's own contention that all these major works formed a unity – both these classics start from the same premise: that there can be no freedom in society as it now exists, grounded as it is in the inequalities of property and power.

The eponymous hero of *Émile* is educated to withstand all the inevitable

---

36   *Ibid.*, p. 156.

corruptions of a polity like France, with its inequalities of wealth and power, where the few exploit the labour of the many and society is bound together simply by commercial networks or the impositions of the absolutist state. He is, Rousseau seems to suggest, to be educated as a man and not as a citizen. Once Émile's private persona has been shaped, his political education will consist in being sheltered for some time from the real political world while he learns the principles of Rousseau's *Social Contract*, which will, presumably, help to inure him to corruption and maintain his autonomy when once he ventures into civic life.

Émile's arena as a man, before he is a citizen, is the household, not the state. It is in this context that Rousseau elaborates his controversial ideas about the role and education of women. Sometimes dismissed as pure misogyny for emphasizing the differences between women and men and reducing women to mere objects of men's pleasure, his arguments have also been interpreted as in some respects progressive, perhaps a reaction to the culture of the *salon*, which was then regarded as the province of elites guided by the tastes of leisured ladies. In interpretations such as these, Sophie represents a counter to aristocratic sensibilities or the pretensions of the bourgeoisie. What is clear is that, with the specific powers and intelligence Rousseau unquestionably ascribes to women (all great revolutions began with the women, he tells us, and an age when women lose their ascendancy and fail to make men respect their judgment will be the 'last stage of degradation'), Sophie will be the guiding spirit of the household and act as Émile's principal protector from the perversions of corrupt society.[37]

Whatever we make of Rousseau's views on women, with all his characteristic paradoxes, *Émile* must be understood less as a treatise on education – of men or of women – than as a deliberately stark antithesis to the social realities of his time and place. Rousseau denied that *Émile* was ever intended as a blueprint for an ideal education. His presentation of an isolated individual brought up in an artificial environment is an exercise of the imagination that presents a dramatic antithesis to the world as it is. It also amounts to a statement of despair: no good can come of a society constructed on the foundations of property and inequality. The *Social*

---

37   In Chapter 5, in his discussion of Sophie's education, Rousseau makes a significant observation about the difficulties that confront the institution of marriage in the world as it is: 'while social life develops character it differentiates classes, and these two classifications do not correspond, so that the greater the social distinctions, the greater the difficulty of finding the corresponding character. Hence we have ill-assorted marriages and all their accompanying evils; and we find that it follows logically that the further we get from equality, the greater the change in our natural feelings; the wider the distance between great and small, the looser the marriage tie; the deeper the gulf between rich and poor the fewer husbands and fathers. Neither master nor slave belongs to a family, but only to a class.'

Contract makes the leap from that counsel of despair to the portrayal of a civic order in which the social conditions from which *Émile* has withdrawn have somehow been transcended, and civil society can be constructed on a wholly new foundation.

The transition from the first two *Discourses* to the *Social Contract* is impossible to understand without the intervening step of the *Discourse on Political Economy*, where the core of his political thought and many of the key concepts developed in the *Social Contract* – the 'general will', the distinction between 'government' and 'sovereignty' – received their first elaboration. This is a fact of no small significance, and it is a pity that this work is so often neglected. Since the article was written for the *Encyclopédie*, there is every reason to suppose that its primary purpose, like that of many other contributions, was not simply to muse in abstraction about perennial questions but to subject contemporary French institutions to trenchant, if oblique, criticism. The article has a more immediate relation to the urgent issues of his time and place and to the conventional currents of debate than do his other works, and it helps to provide a means of tracing the central ideas of his political theory to their foundations in his specific historical context and in the social struggles of his time.

Rousseau was writing in a tradition of social criticism that decried the corruption of the court, an inflated royal bureaucracy, and an exploitative system of taxation which served not only public purposes but private gain. In these grievances and proposals for reform, the state generally took centre stage, both as the object of complaint and as the proposed agent of reform, often in the same breath. Reformers often presented their cases in the form of claims for the *public* sphere against the essentially *private* character of the feudal principles still embodied in the state and the system of privilege.

It is against this background that Rousseau's political theory must be understood. It has, for example, been said that he was the thinker who 'reduced the *thèse nobiliaire* and the *thèse royale* to insignificance' and who 'put the political problem on an entirely new basis, that of pure democracy.'[38] This may seem an odd and objectionable proposition to those who regard Rousseau's concept of the 'general will' and his provocative formula 'forced to be free' as supremely undemocratic, even 'totalitarian'. But such interpretations seem less plausible when Rousseau's political ideas are grounded in the context of absolutist France. The *Discourse on Political Economy* reveals how his theory of popular sovereignty was shaped by a criticism of specifically French conditions, the French absolutist state and its attendant evils, and how traditional debates surrounding these conditions served to fix the terms in which his argument was cast.

Like Bodin and Montchrétien, Rousseau approaches the issue of the

---

38   Ed. Neumann, introduction to Montesquieu, *Spirit of the Laws*, p. xxix.

French state by first considering the household/state analogy; and he effectively declares his opposition to the prevailing principles of that state by immediately attacking the analogy. In its original French usage, political economy – referring to the management of national resources to increase the nation's prosperity – implied an analogy between the household or family and the state. While the state economy is designated 'political' to distinguish its generality and its public character from the particularity and the private nature of the domestic economy, the distinction presupposes a significant similarity between the art of state management and *oikonomia*, the art of household management. It is this similarity that Rousseau questions in the article on political economy; and, by rejecting the analogy as a basis for redefining the concept of 'political economy', he is making a statement about the set of historical conditions for which that analogy stands.

It is in this context that the 'general will' appears. The concept of the general will is usually treated by commentators – whether hostile or sympathetic to Rousseau – as simply a principle governing the conduct of citizens; but in the *Political Economy*, Rousseau's general will has a different object. Here, his argument is, in the first instance, directed not at the individual citizen but at the 'magistrate' or rulers. His purpose in attacking the household/state analogy is to demonstrate that the magistrate cannot legitimately act in accordance with principles appropriate to the head of a household. 'The principal object of the efforts of the whole house', argues Rousseau, 'is to conserve and increase the patrimony of the father.'[39] This principle of private, domestic 'economy' if applied to the state – treating the state as a means of increasing the 'patrimony' of the magistrate – is fatal to the public interest. The magistrate, therefore, unlike the father who governs the household, cannot rely on his personal, natural inclinations and passions as a standard for governing the state but must follow 'no other rule but public reason, which is the law'.[40] The concept of the general will is introduced to express the uniquely public principle that should regulate the governance of the 'political economy', the management of the state. It is the principle to be followed by the magistrate, the government, whose function is simply to execute the public 'will' which expresses the interests of the community.

At this stage in Rousseau's argument, then, the concept of the general will represents an attempt to define the state as a truly public thing, not a form of private property, and to locate the legitimacy of government in its adherence to the public will and interests of the people, not the private will and interests of the magistrate. Rousseau would later extend the principle of the general will to the community of citizens, especially in the *Social*

39 Rousseau, *A Discourse on Political Economy*, in *The Social Contract and Discourses,* ed. G.D.H. Cole (New York: Dutton, 1950), p. 286.

40 *Ibid.*, p. 288.

Contract. In the Political Economy Rousseau introduces the concepts around which the *Social Contract* is built: sovereignty, the distinction between sovereignty and government, the general will. At least parts of the article seem to have been drawn from the work Rousseau had already done for his projected major study of political institutions, a project he never completed as planned except in the abbreviated form of the *Social Contract,* which he described as an extract from it. The essential unity of the *Discourse on Political Economy* and the *Social Contract* is evident in the first version of the latter work, the so-called Geneva manuscript, where some of the major points of the *Political Economy* – notably some remarks on the household/state analogy – appear almost verbatim. The *Political Economy* and the *Social Contract* belong to the same structure of argumentation, and the logic of the latter work remains incomplete in the absence of ideas contained in the former.

In the *Discourse on Political Economy*, Rousseau first draws a distinction between government and sovereignty and proceeds to outline a theory of *government*, which he treats as synonymous with 'political economy'. In the *Social Contract,* Rousseau develops the theory of *sovereignty*, which is the other side of the coin, only touched upon in the earlier article. In the interim, his interest may actually have shifted from the problem of government to the problem of sovereignty, with a growing conviction that only true popular sovereignty and radical democracy, not simply a reformed and enlightened government, could correct the social ills outlined in his earlier works. In the *Political Economy* the 'general will' is introduced as 'the first principle of public economy and the fundamental rule of government'.[41] The point of this formulation is to identify legitimate government as government in which 'the magistrates belong to the people' and not the reverse, so that the interests it serves are not simply those of the rulers. The *Social Contract* proceeds from here.

Both Bodin and even the less 'absolutist' Montchrétien had constructed the analogy between household and state on the assumption that the king, with the help of his officers, is the appropriate agent of the common good, the representative of universality and the general or public interest, as against the particular and partial interests that comprise the body politic. It is precisely this assumption that Rousseau rejects when he attacks the analogy. His own argument is based on the contrary assumption that rulers are just as likely as are their subjects – indeed, even more likely – to represent a particular or partial interest. For Rousseau, the household/state analogy – in which the state is treated, in effect, as a private estate – simply confirms the reality of the French state and the use of public office, including the office of king, as private property. He insists that a completely different principle – opposed to the private motivations of household management,

---

41   *Ibid.,* p. 292.

with its goal of increasing the patrimony of the master – must guide the management of the state.

Having criticized the analogy on which the notion of political economy is based, he must then go on to redefine 'political economy' itself accordingly, in keeping with the uniquely public purpose of the state. It is here that he introduces the distinction between sovereignty, the supreme legislative power, and government or 'public economy', which merely executes the will of the sovereign.[42] Rousseau was, as we have seen, not the first to draw a distinction between sovereignty and government. Bodin had elaborated that distinction long before. But the differences between Bodin and Rousseau on this score are even more striking than the similarities.

Rousseau's purpose in adopting a similar conceptual device is precisely the opposite of Bodin's. Although, like Bodin, he identifies sovereignty with the power of legislation and maintains the indivisibility of sovereign power, his object in doing so is quite different. Where Bodin's argument is a defence of royal absolutism, Rousseau's is an attack upon it. Rousseau's distinction – again in a sense like Bodin's – is intended to relegate the functions of the magistrate or government to a subordinate position, subject to and dependent upon a higher principle or 'general will'. Yet his intention is not to consolidate but to undermine the power of rulers. The 'Magistrate' stands not only for lesser officials but for all rulers, including kings; and the general will becomes not the will of the ruler, not a manifestation of his supremacy, but an expression of his subordination to the community.

Where Bodin subordinates the particularity of the people to the universality of the ruler, Rousseau subordinates the particularity of the ruler to the universality of the people. For Rousseau, the sovereign will is not something that creates a community out of particular and partial interests by imposing itself from without through royal legislation and the art of public management or 'political economy'. Instead, it is something that emanates from the community itself, expressing its actual common interests, and is imposed on those – the magistrate, the government, the agents of 'public economy' – whose function is merely to execute that will. The logic of this argument demands that it culminate in a radical theory of popular sovereignty, giving full effect to the principle that the sovereign will emanates from the community by actually vesting the sovereign legislative power in a popular assembly. In the *Discourse on Political Economy* Rousseau did not pursue that logic to its conclusion, but he certainly did in the *Social Contract*.

If Rousseau's argument owes a great deal in its form to the idiom of absolutism and to the language of a single, supreme and indivisible public will, he turns that idiom against itself. As many theorists have done, he adopts the form of his adversary's argument to attack its substance. There may be

---

42 *Ibid.*, p. 289.

an element of truth in the proposition that the only French 'tradition of discourse' to which Rousseau was 'not much indebted' was constitutional-ism and that, while 'he was one of the great proponents of the rule of law ... his dedication to that principle was distinct from that of French consti-tutionalists such as Domat or Montesquieu.' In particular:

> In Rousseau's theory, law is identified with the sovereign will, as it was in the absolutist tradition, rather than an external bridle on that will, as it was in the constitutive laws of the French polity. His hostility to intermedi-ate bodies in the state and scorn for representative assemblies, set him off clearly from the constitutionalist tradition.[43]

Yet if Rousseau departed from the constitutionalist tradition, it is in part because the mainstream of French constitutionalism (and arguably even its radical Huguenot form) did not imply a transfer of sovereign legislative power to the 'people' even as embodied in representative institutions. Rousseau's concern is not merely to 'bridle' the absolutist monarchy but to overturn it, not simply to guide sovereign power but to transfer it. But there is another sense in which Rousseau's argument is, after all, best understood in relation to French constitutionalism, at least in its more radical form as exemplified by the Huguenot resistance movement.

The ideological strategy adopted by the Huguenot constitutionalists in their assault on absolutism was, as we have seen, to confront absolutism on its own ground by stressing the particularity of the monarch, attacking his treatment of the state as private property. They insisted instead on the 'people's' proprietary right in the state, asserting that the 'people' constitute the 'majesty' of the king, and transferred the public 'mind' from the king to the 'people', embodied in their officers and representative institutions – 'one mind compounded out of many'. Rousseau's strategy is strikingly similar, except in one decisive respect. He also proceeds by attacking the proprietary character of the absolutist state and the particularity of the ruler, and coun-terposes to them a common public will residing in the community; and he also maintains that the ruler is constituted by the people. At the same time, he perceives a threat not only in the particularity of the monarch but in that of the 'Magistrate' in general. He therefore locates the public will not in the 'public council', in officials and 'intermediate bodies', or in assemblies of estates, but in the people themselves.

Rousseau's attitude towards 'intermediate bodies' is often regarded as one of the more alarming aspects of his thought, an attack on the most cherished principles of liberalism, checks on state power, the freedom of

---

43 Nannerl Keohane, *Philosophy and the State in France: The Renaissance to the Enlightenment* (Princeton: Princeton University Press, 1980), p. 442.

association and opinion, of individual dissent and minority rights, and so on. This is, again, to misread Rousseau's meaning by extracting his argument from its historical setting. Rousseau's refusal to lodge the public will in intermediate institutions does indeed cut him off from the French constitutionalist tradition even in its most radical forms. Yet his rejection of these institutions should not be understood as a ('totalitarian') violation of constitutionalist principles but rather as an attempt to extend and democratize them. Rousseau shares with the radical constitutionalists their concern for transforming the state into a truly 'public' thing which derives its public or general character from the people. That is precisely the message of the *Discourse on Political Economy*.

In the *Social Contract*, if not unequivocally in the earlier article, Rousseau advances from the creation of a truly public magistrate – a magistrate answerable in some unspecified way to the demands of the common good, the 'general will' – to the actual embodiment of that common good and the general will in a functioning popular sovereign. If, in the process, he resumes the language of absolutism in order to vest in the people the powers hitherto lodged in the absolute monarchy, he travels that route not past but through the concerns of constitutionalism and the tradition of popular resistance.

Chapter 1 begins with his famous proposition that 'Man is born free; and everywhere he is in chains.' The 'social contract' as hitherto imagined by philosophers simply represents, in one form or another, a contract of subjection. Rousseau offers an alternative formulation of the principles on which a just and free civic order should be founded. Stripped of inessentials, it comes down to this: 'Each of us puts his person and all his power in common under the supreme direction of the general will, and, in corporate capacity, we receive each member as an indivisible part of the whole.'[44] But to make this undertaking more than just an empty formula, it must be understood to mean that anyone who refuses to obey the general will shall be compelled to do so; and this means nothing less than that 'he will be forced to be free'.[45]

Rousseau might simply have said that civil society, which replaces our liberty in the state of nature with a new kind of civil liberty, including secure proprietorship of our possessions, requires obedience to law; but, instead of making the point that we relinquish certain freedoms in exchange for, and to gain the protection of, others, he chooses to formulate the meaning of his 'social contract' in a deliberately paradoxical and provocative way. We can, up to a point, discount his penchant for paradox and provocation; but there is clearly something more to be said to allay the suspicion that Rousseau is advocating something like 'totalitarian democracy'.

---

44 Rousseau, *Social Contract*, in ed. Cole, *The Social Contract and Discourses*, p. 15.

45 *Ibid.*, p. 18.

Let us first be clear what Rousseau is *not* saying. In invoking the general will, Rousseau is not suggesting that it exists as an abstract 'common good' that can be imposed from without whatever the will of the individuals who constitute the sovereign power. It is, above all, a rule of thumb, the question citizens must ask themselves when they exercise their sovereign power. So, for example, 'the law of public order in assemblies is not so much to maintain in them the general will as to secure that the question be put to it, and the answer always given by it.'[46] A legislative assembly, in other words, should ask itself what decision would promote not this or that private interest but the public good. The general will is not, to be sure, synonymous with the 'will of all'. A majority may choose, and choose knowingly, a course that does not express the general will because it is not conducive to the common good; but no one can claim (as a Robespierre might do) to represent the general will against the will of the majority. When the social bond is broken and there is no common sense of what constitutes the public good, the general will is mute. The principle that the liberty of citizens requires the realization of the general will 'presupposes, indeed, that all the qualities of the general will still reside in the majority: when they cease to do so, whatever side a man may take, liberty is no longer possible.'[47]

Whatever else we can say about Rousseau's general will, it is clear that it can only reside in a sovereign people and can only be effected by at least a majority. It cannot be imposed by a governor who claims to know better. The point is reinforced by Rousseau's account of the distinction between sovereignty and government. While the act of association that establishes the sovereign power can be treated as a contract, the executive power of government cannot be conceived in this way: it is clear, says Rousseau, 'that the institution of government is not a contract, but a law; that the depositories of the executive power are not the people's masters, but its officers; that it can set them up and pull them down when it likes; that for them there is no question of contract, but of obedience'.[48]

But if the people, and not the prince or other magistrates, are truly sovereign, in a way not envisaged by any of Rousseau's Enlightenment compatriots, what checks are there on the sovereign people themselves? It is certainly true to say that Rousseau did not devote his attention to the rights of the minority or to constitutional checks on sovereign power; and it may not be enough to say that, in his time and place, he was preoccupied less by how the sovereign people should conduct themselves than by how their sovereignty could be defended against all other claimants. But the very least that we can say is that his views on 'intermediate bodies', which are commonly regarded as the

---

46   *Ibid.*, p. 104.
47   *Ibid.*, p. 107.
48   *Ibid.*, pp. 99–100.

most telling evidence of a distinctively 'illiberal' turn of mind, have a rather different meaning if we read them in context.

It is again a question of historical perspective. The 'intermediate bodies' that concern the French constitutionalists are not the 'voluntary associations' so important to English liberals, organizations in the private sphere as distinct from – and, at least potentially, against – organs of the state.[49] The French 'intermediate bodies' are the corporate and representative institutions – estates, *parlements,* municipalities, and colleges – which constituted part of *la police,* organs of the polity. It is these institutions whose role in the state constitutionalists proposed to increase, in varying degrees and with varying preferences for some over others. But neither are these bodies legislative assemblies on the model of the English Parliament. These were, in effect, feudal remnants, fragments of the feudal 'parcellized' state. They were recognized, and defended, as such by constitutionalists even as late as Montesquieu, who regarded these elements of 'Gothic' government as essential to the 'moderation' and legitimacy of the French monarchy. This implied, too, that the notion of intermediate bodies was, in the eighteenth century as before, often closely associated with the defence of aristocratic power and might be not only undemocratic but anti-democratic in spirit.

In the eighteenth century, even more explicitly than before, the principle of 'particular' or intermediate powers interposed between king and people was invoked to support the enlargement of power for the nobility, as in the *thèse nobiliaire.* In these formulations the claims of the nobility against the absolutist monarchy were likely to be equally claims against the Third Estate. The notion of constitutional checks and balances thus assumed a clearly aristocratic cast. The theory of intermediate powers was opposed to popular power more unequivocally than were English theories of representation, however undemocratic the intentions of the latter might be. Those who, like Montesquieu, preferred the *parlements* as the model of intermediate powers only partly modified the aristocratic character of the principle by extending it to include the *noblesse de robe*; and their principal claim to autonomy was the venality of office. Even in more radical and anti-absolutist or constitutionalist formulations, as we have seen in the case of the Huguenots, the insistence on intermediate bodies had the deliberate effect

---

49 As for Rousseau's views on voluntary associations, it is worth considering his remarks on the *cercles* of Geneva in the *Lettre à d'Alembert* and his answers to criticisms of these remarks voiced by his friends among the burghers of Geneva who felt that the *cercles* corrupted the republic's artisans and gave them an excessive taste for independence. Rousseau suggests in reply that these *cercles* provide the appropriate education for free citizens, midway between the public education of Greece and the domestic education of monarchies 'where all subjects must remain isolated and must have nothing in common but obedience'. Letter to Theodore Tronchin, 26 November 1758, *Correspondance Complète,* ed. R.A. Leigh (Geneva: Institut et Musée Voltaire, 1965), Vol. V, p. 743.

of limiting not only monarchical but also popular power – for example, by stressing that the right of resistance belonged to the 'people' only as embodied in their officers and corporate representatives. Given the historical meaning and ideological function of these institutions in French political experience, the defence of intermediate bodies did not lend itself so easily to democratic extrapolation and extension, not even to the extent permitted by English theories of parliamentary representation. A democratic argument such as Rousseau's would, in that context, almost inevitably be formulated as an attack on intermediate institutions.

The 'General Will' Redefined

In the end, the question comes down to the particular social interests at stake. For those who felt aggrieved at their inadequate access to the means of extra-economic appropriation provided by the state, for those who, even when they were subject to the state's appropriation through taxation, themselves appropriated the labour of others, constitutional reforms designed to give them a piece of the state might serve very well. But these were not the interests represented by Rousseau. His concern, clearly expressed in the *Discourse on Political Economy*, was for those on whose labour the whole structure of privilege, office, and taxation rested: small producers and notably peasants. Much of the *Political Economy* is devoted to the problem of taxation, and Rousseau's proposals for reforming the fiscal system are explicitly designed to relieve the peasants who bear its brunt. It is here that he provides the clearest insight into his view of the existing state as a system of private appropriation and exploitation; and this is the specific target of his proposals for reform:

> Are not all advantages of society for the powerful and rich? Do they not fill all lucrative posts? Are not all privileges and exemptions reserved for them? . . . [W]hatever the poor pay is lost to them forever, and remains in or returns to the hands of the rich; and, as it is precisely to those men who take part in government, or to their connections, that the proceeds of taxation sooner or later pass, even when they pay their share they have a keen interest in increasing taxes.[50]

The terms of the social contract as it actually exists between the two conditions of men can, Rousseau suggests, be summed up as follows: 'You need me, because I am rich and you are poor; let us therefore make an agreement: I will permit you the honour of serving me, on the condition that you give

---

50 Rousseau, *Political Economy*, in ed. Cole, *The Social Contract and Discourses*, pp. 322–3.

me the little that remains to you for the pains I shall take to command you.'[51] This is the principle on which taxation is now based. Rousseau proposes a system of taxation based on opposing principles, by reforming the state to eliminate the use of taxation as a means of private appropriation and by transferring the tax burden for clearly public purposes to those more able to bear it, in a system of progressive taxation. He dismisses with contempt the idea that the peasant will lapse into idleness if not compelled to work by the demands of taxation: 'Because for him who loses the fruits of his labour, to do nothing is to gain something; and to impose a fine on labour is a very odd way of banishing idleness.'[52]

Rousseau was not, of course, alone in proposing to reform the system of taxation, privilege, and exemption, corrupt administration and venal offices. Similar reforms were part of the Enlightenment agenda in general, with its demands for rationalization of the state and the fiscal apparatus, the unification of law and administration, and a system of office open to merit. All these proposals for reform were in one way or another, directly or indirectly, conditioned by the function of the state as an instrument of appropriation, a private resource, even if some reformers wanted only to extend access to its fruits. And many reformers were convinced of the need to redistribute the burden of taxation in order to stop the drain on the countryside which fed the luxuries of city and court.

Yet Rousseau was alone among the great Enlightenment thinkers to focus on the political structure specifically as a system of exploitation, and to do so not simply from the paternalistic vantage point of enlightened elites but from the perspective of the petty producers whose labour was exploited. He could not be content with reforms that would merely rationalize the apparatus of office that appropriated the fruits of peasant labour. To the extent that his political reforms were intended to attack the state not simply as an inefficient, unequal, or illiberal system of administration and representation but as a system of exploitation, he had eventually to conclude that only absolute popular sovereignty, as the sole means of displacing altogether the proprietary state, would suffice.

Once Rousseau had decided on the necessity of true popular sovereignty if the state and its officers were indeed to be subject to 'public reason', he was obliged to consider how the 'general will' could actually operate, not merely as a notional standard for the behaviour of rulers and citizens but as a practical and active principle of political organization, a 'will' actually emanating from the people and expressed in practice as law. His answer was again shaped by the particular conditions of the existing French state and by the particular ways in which his adopted countrymen had formulated their

---

51 *Ibid.*, pp. 323–4.
52 *Ibid.*, pp. 324–5.

own responses to questions about the common good, how it is to be determined and implemented. The typical French solution, as we have seen, conjured up a single public will, usually embodied in the monarch, or a collection of partial and selfish interests woven together by the king and the officers of the state. None of these solutions, not even those which replaced the monarchical will with 'one mind compounded out of many', simply redefined the common good as a public interest constituted by private interests which would magically coalesce by the workings of an invisible hand, or aggregate themselves in the process of deliberation and legislation by a Parliament representing private interests. That may have been the English model, but it did not conform to French conditions.

When Montesquieu argued that republican government required special virtue, and that monarchy had the advantage of allowing the implementation of the common good with minimal virtue or self-sacrifice on the part of its subjects, he was expressing an assumption common to all these formulations: that while self-interest could serve as the basis of society, perhaps through the networks of commerce, the common good would not naturally emerge out of the interplay of private interests but required either the virtuous suppression of natural self-love or the active intervention of a 'harmonizing' state – not, it must be emphasized, through the medium of representative bodies that assembled all competing interests but as a single unifying will most likely embodied in the absolutist monarch or at least a 'legal despotism'. If the English (and their Scottish spokesmen) in contrast thought – or purported to think – otherwise, especially in the eighteenth century, their optimism did not reflect a greater faith in human nature or an absence of deep divisions in English society. It had more to do with the particular conditions of their economy, a rising capitalism, especially during that brief period when England's commercial empire reigned supreme. It also presupposed the traditionally unitary character of English representative institutions and the relatively secure and united propertied classes whose triumph over both king and people was expressed in the supremacy of Parliament.

French pessimism on this score did not prevent political thinkers from proposing self-love and self-interest as the proper motivating forces of the body politic. Indeed, as we have seen, it became a common theme to suggest that selfish passions translated into interest could be the basis of public well-being, and even that society could fruitfully be conceived as a commercial transaction. Yet this view of society, far from disputing the need for strong monarchical power, generally served to emphasize its necessity. The disruptive and divisive character of commercial transactions, in which all parties pursue their own selfish gain, was as essential to this imagery as were the benefits of commerce. Arguments that, in England, might serve to support a doctrine of limited government might, in France, appear in defence of royal absolutism or even, as in physiocratic doctrine, *laissez faire, laissez passer* enforced by 'legal despotism'. In any case, whether such arguments were marshalled in support of absolutism or 'moderate' constitutional monarchy, the notion of a polity based on the harmony of selfish interests tended to postulate as its necessary condition an alien integrating will.

This is the context in which Rousseau formulated his conception of the general will as an expression of the common good emanating from the sovereign people. Much of his work, even before the *Social Contract*, had been devoted, directly or indirectly, to attacking the conception of society as a commercial transaction in which everyone sought his own gain in the other's loss or enlisted the aid of others only by persuading (or, more likely, deceiving) them to see their own profit in granting it. It is the consequence of property and inequality, he wrote, that each man

> must therefore incessantly seek to interest them in his fate, and to make them find their own profit, in fact or in appearance, in working for his. This makes him deceitful and sly with some, imperious and harsh with others, and makes it necessary for him to abuse all those whom he needs when he cannot make them fear him and not find his interest in serving them usefully.[53]

For Rousseau, such mutual deception was not a cure but a symptom. It was nonsense to suppose that the social bond and the common good could be based on the antagonisms of interest that divided people. Rousseau was bound to be especially hostile to this self-contradictory notion in view of its association with the idea of an external mediating will in the person of a powerful ruler. It clearly seemed to him especially absurd to imagine that a single, monarchical will, or even the will of a plural magistrate, which itself represented a very particular interest, could weld together a common good out of these antagonistic particularisms. At the same time, it was entirely in keeping with his conception of personal autonomy to adopt the view that self-love ought to act as the source of the public good. He therefore set himself the task of discovering how self-love and self-interest could produce a common good without the mediation of 'commercial' transactions or mutual deception and without the intervention of an alien will. His object was to find a form of social organization in which the social bond was based not on what divided people but on what united them, a common interest composed of interests that people really had in common.

It is, then, a mistake to think that in his concept of the general will Rousseau is proposing the suppression of natural instincts and the

---

53   Rousseau, *Discourse on Inequality*, in ed. Masters, *First and Second Discourses*, p. 156.

submergence of self-interest in an abstract 'general will', the individual in the collectivity; nor is it helpful to suggest some kind of antithesis between the 'individualism' of a Diderot and the 'collectivism' of Rousseau.[54] Individual interests are not, for Rousseau, in principle opposed to the general will, any more than *amour de soi* is synonymous with *amour propre*. Interests are 'partial' as opposed to 'general' only when circumstances put them necessarily and essentially in opposition to the interests of others, in the sense that one person's gain is another's loss. Society as it is now constituted forces interests into such mutual antagonism. Rousseau simply acknowledges that no amount of reason or enlightenment will induce these divisive impulses to serve as the basis of social cohesion, at least not without mass delusion or autocratic imposition, both of which are not only undesirable but unreliable. The point is precisely that people cannot be made to will what is against their self-interest. Summarizing the argument of his *Discourse on the Origin of Inequality*, Rousseau writes elsewhere:

> When finally all particular interests conflict with one another, when self-love [*amour de soi*] in ferment becomes egotism [*amour propre*], so that opinion, making the whole universe necessary to each man, makes men born enemies to one another and compels each man to find his advantage only in the other's loss, then conscience, weaker than inflamed passions, is extinguished by them, and remains in the mouths of men only as a word designed for mutual deception. Each one then pretends to wish to sacrifice his own interests to those of the public, and all of them are lying. No one wants the public good unless it accords with his own; thus this accord is the object of true politics which seeks to make people happy and good.[55]

This is far from saying that self-interest is in principle opposed to the common good; indeed, it is to assert that it *must* be the source of the common good. If the 'general will' has any meaning, it is only on the understanding that people actually do have individual self-interests in common, interests that are common not only when mediated by commerce or an external will, but intrinsically; and politics must be built on this common foundation.

The *Social Contract* outlines the political principles appropriate to a society so organized. Though Rousseau is never unequivocally clear about the social pre-conditions for such a political order, his social criticism,

---

54 See Philipp Blom, *A Wicked Company: Freethinkers and Friendship in pre-Revolutionary Paris* (London: Weidenfeld & Nicholson, 2011), where the quarrel between Diderot and Rousseau is characterized in this way.

55 Lettre à Christophe de Beaumont, *Oeuvres Complètes* (Paris: Gallimard, 1964), Vol. IV, p. 937.

especially in the first and second *Discourses*, suggests very strongly that a complete transformation of society would be required. He never tells us how this transformation might be brought about. In the *Social Contract* the best he can do is introduce a kind of *deus ex machina*, the Legislator who lays the foundation for the new society and then withdraws himself. But elsewhere – for example, in his letter to d'Alembert – Rousseau gives indications of how his ideal society might be constituted: a small community of independent petty producers, more or less self-sufficient peasants and artisans. However utopian this picture may be, and however naïve in its understanding of modern economics, it expresses clearly the principle which for Rousseau is the basis of a free society: that no one should be able to appropriate the labour of others or be forced to alienate his own. In the *Social Contract,* he suggests that the fundamental principles of the common good are liberty, the absence of individual dependence, and equality, which is the condition of liberty. These require a distribution of power and wealth in which no citizen can do violence to another and 'no citizen is rich enough to buy another, and none poor enough to be forced to sell himself'.[56]

It is, at the very least, clear that there are conditions without which the social contract cannot exist. For the general will to represent an expression – not an unnaturally (and impossibly) virtuous or forcible violation – of their own self-interest, people must actually, objectively, have interests in common. The common ground shared by interests in society as it is actually constituted is simply too narrow. To widen the scope of commonality requires the removal of those social relations and institutions, most especially inequality, that render people in reality and necessarily enemies by interest. Democratic sovereignty, it appears, is the necessary condition for a state based on 'public reason', rather than on the private interest of the magistrate; and social equality, the breakdown of the division between appropriators and producers, is the condition of democracy.

Rousseau's controversial concept of the 'general will' should, then, be treated not as an idiosyncracy but as an innovation on an old French theme, not as a disturbingly illiberal answer to English questions about the relation between private rights and public interests but as a radically democratic answer to French questions about the source of universality and the public will.

---

56 Rousseau, *Social Contract*, in ed. Cole, *Social Contract and Discourses*, p. 50.

7

THE ENGLISH REVOLUTION

Between late October and early November of 1647, in the midst of civil war, something extraordinary happed at Putney, south of London. Certainly one of the most remarkable episodes in English history, it was and remains a unique historical event. In the course of civil war, the New Model Army, the distinctively well-organized and disciplined military force constructed by Oliver Cromwell and his supporters in their conflict with the royalists, was proving to be not just an effective military machine but a militant political force. Yet deep divisions had emerged between the army 'grandees' and radicals within the rank and file. Against the oligarchic leanings of Cromwell and his allies, and even in fear of a restored monarchy, radicals had drafted a constitution, the first ever in history, intended to establish something like a democratic form of government based on a conception of inalienable rights: 'An Agreement of the People for a Firm and Present Peace, upon Grounds of Common-Right and Freedom; as it was Proposed by the Agents of the Five Regiments of Horse; and Since by the General Approbation of the Army, Offered to the Joint Concurrence of All Free COMMONS of ENGLAND'. This draft constitution was the subject of a thorough debate, which began in St Mary's Church, Putney and continued at the lodgings of the Army's quartermaster general.

That there exists a documentary record in the form of a transcript taken down at the time is a truly astonishing piece of historical luck. It allows us to follow, in the colourful and moving words of the participants themselves, a debate conducted not only in the cool light of reason but also in the heat of passion, about some of the most fundamental questions of social organization and political governance. These debates are being conducted not by philosophers or theologians but by activists and soldiers, speaking in their own language, often the language of the Levellers, political militants and theorists accustomed to addressing not scholars, priests or lawyers but craftsmen, yeoman farmers and the Army rank and file.

The Tudor Era

The remarkable events at Putney no doubt have much to do with personalities and the unpredictable contingencies of civil war; but the issues at stake and the terms in which the ideological battle was joined are inexplicable without reference to a larger historical context, the specific patterns of English economic and political development. In Chapter 1, we considered briefly how the social and political organization of England – in particular, the process of state-formation and the development of agrarian capitalism – differed from that of its neighbours and specifically from what may have appeared, in the seventeenth century, to be the most advanced and powerful kingdom, France. The 'absolutist' state in France was built on a foundation of corporate institutions and competing jurisdictions, while England already had a more strongly unitary state. The French ruling class still depended to a significant extent on 'extra-economic' powers, or 'politically constituted property', which now included office in the monarchical state, giving them access to the fruits of peasant labour in the form of taxes instead of only rents. English landlords, relying more and more on purely 'economic' forms of appropriation, depended on their tenants' profitable production. A vast proportion of land in France remained in the possession of peasants. In England, land was more concentrated in the hands of large proprietors and worked by tenant farmers, increasingly on economic leases, which made them unusually subject to the pressures of economic competition. While French agriculture in the seventeenth century was still largely tied to traditional methods of peasant farming, English landlords and their tenants were already becoming increasingly interested in agricultural 'improvement', finding means to enhance the productivity of labour in response to competitive pressures, especially by innovative use of land, which required redefinition of property rights. This would produce a unique historical dynamic of self-sustaining growth that sharply distinguished England from its neighbours – a difference that would be clearly visible when the English economy alone escaped the general European crisis of the late seventeenth century.

Between the sixteenth and eighteenth centuries, in response to the imperatives of competition and 'improvement', there were mounting assaults on customary rights, assertions of exclusive private ownership against communal rights to common land, challenges to customary tenures and an assortment of use rights to private land, together with various oppressive practices and extortionate rents, accompanied by legal and theoretical efforts to redefine the meaning of property, all of them fiercely contested. These distinctively English patterns in the development of the state and property, not surprisingly, gave rise to specific kinds of conflict, and they defined the major political issues in particular ways. So, for example, where taxation was the major grievance for French peasants, English smallholders were more concerned with protecting their customary rights and warding off expropriation. The developments that produced these specifically English conditions stand out in sharp relief during the sixteenth century. The Tudor monarchy, while continuing the process of state-centralization that had begun long before, consolidated it in particularly visible ways, not least in the establishment of a state Church. At the same time, the realignment of property relations caused major social disruptions. Historians may still disagree about the condition of the English economy in the sixteenth century, whether it was marked by economic growth or declining living standards (or, indeed, both); but, while it may be safe to say that, in the seventeenth century and even perhaps in the latter part of the previous one, living standards for sections of the population were relatively high by European standards (and by the eighteenth century would be more unambiguously so), there is little doubt that many paid a heavy price for it. The sixteenth century was marked by widespread dispossession and distress, causing social upheavals, riots and rebellions of various kinds – as well as the first compulsory system of poor relief, which says much about both England's wealth, the newly consolidated powers of the central state, and the social disruptions it was compelled to confront.

Some historians dispute the extent of eviction by enclosure in the sixteenth century – in particular, enclosure to replace arable with pasture – and there were certainly other economic causes of dispossession and poverty. But there is no mistaking where contemporary observers, not least the Tudor monarchy and its officials, sought to place the blame: a growing propertyless class, which they attributed mainly to enclosure for highly profitable sheep-farming at a time when the economy was not yet ready to absorb a host of dispossessed labourers, was producing a plague of vagrancy and vagabondage. This rabble of 'masterless' men aroused deep trepidation among the ruling classes and spawned a distinctive literature of social criticism, intended not to justify rebellion by disadvantaged classes, nor even necessarily to voice a protest on their behalf, but to articulate the anxieties of their superiors, indeed the Tudor monarchy itself, with a view to bringing the ruling classes to their senses in the face of growing lawlessness, theft, and the danger of civil disorder.[1]

Under the Tudors, one act after another was passed – without much effect – to limit enclosure. It is certainly true that the monarchy had reasons to exaggerate the threat, if only to challenge the power of the landed aristocracy; but there were also critics of enclosure who were more inclined to promote aristocratic power against an overweening monarchy. One such

---

1 On this literature, see Neal Wood, *Foundations of Political Economy: Some Early Tudor Views on State and Society* (Berkeley: University of California Press, 1994).

critic was Thomas Starkey. His *Dialogue Between Pole and Lupset*, apparently written in the 1530s but undiscovered till the nineteenth century, lays out a programme of reform which (though he served as chaplain to Henry VIII) seems intended to balance the powers of the centralizing monarchy with a stronger aristocracy, creating an educated and enlightened ruling class capable of maintaining civil order by improving the conditions of the people. There was also a group of highly placed clerics of Lutheran inclinations in the Church of England – the so-called Commonwealthmen – who, though never openly attacking government or calling for political reform, presented a devastating picture of England's social conditions, spiralling prices, dispossession, poverty, homelessness and growing vagrancy. The blame, it seems, lay largely with 'ungentle gentlemen', those greedy enclosers, landlords and graziers, who, like their sheep, were 'caterpillars of the commonwealth'.[2]

This is the context in which Thomas More's classic, *Utopia,* was composed. It begins with observations on the social consequences of war, which are general to all European powers, and then comments pointedly on a social evil peculiar to England, which can be taken as the underlying theme of the whole book:

The increase of pasture . . . by which your sheep, which are naturally mild, and easily kept in order, may be said now to devour men, and unpeople, not only villages, but towns; for wherever it is found that the sheep of any soil yield a softer and richer wool than ordinary, there the nobility and gentry, and even those holy men the abbots, not contented with the old rents which their farms yielded, nor thinking it enough that they, living at their ease, do no good to the public, resolve to do it hurt instead of good. They stop the course of agriculture, destroying houses and towns, reserving only the churches, and enclose grounds that they may lodge their sheep in them. As if forests and parks had swallowed up too little of the land, those worthy countrymen turn the best inhabited places into solitudes, for when an insatiable wretch, who is a plague to his country, resolves to enclose many thousand acres of ground, the owners as well as tenants are turned out of their possessions, by tricks, or by main force, or being wearied out with ill-usage, they are forced to sell them. By which means those miserable people, both men and women, married and unmarried, old and young, with their poor but numerous families (since country business requires many hands), are all forced to change their seats, not knowing whither to go; and they must sell almost for nothing their household stuff, which could not bring them much money, even though they might stay for a buyer. When that little money

2 Cited in Neal Wood, *Foundations*, p. 176.

is at an end, for it will be soon spent, what is left for them to do, but either to steal and so to be hanged (God knows how justly), or to go about and beg? And if they do this, they are put in prison as idle vaga- bonds; while they would willingly work, but can find none that will hire them; for there is no more occasion for country labor, to which they have been bred, when there is no arable ground left.

More's response to this catastrophe is not an elaborate analysis of England's ills, nor a programme of reform, nor a systematic political theory, but a fantastical fiction portraying 'Utopia' or 'Not-Place', a supremely well-- ordered and happy republic without private property. This masterpiece has been interpreted as everything from pure fantasy, with no political intent, to a founding text of modern socialism. There is, of course, no decisive way of adjudicating these differences of interpretation – though it seems, on the face of it, implausible that More truly believed in a community of property. A man of substantial property, he was himself an encloser; and he showed no sign in his active political life of subscribing to egalitarian, let alone collectivist, principles, nor, for that matter, did he evince much compassion for the lower classes.[3] Even his zealous, not to say bloodthirsty, opposition to the Lutheran heresy – as lord chancellor he took an active part in the persecution of 'heretics' – was inspired in part by his conviction that it was to blame for the peasant revolt in Germany, which aroused the fears of English men of property like More himself. Even in his radical *Utopia*, he outlines a justification of colonization based on a principle that would later serve the English well: that people can be deprived of their land by just war if they fail to make productive use of it. Had More embarked on a programme of practical reform, he might have found himself – at most – not very far from Thomas Starkey (who was influenced by him) in seeking ways to civi- lize the ruling classes. But whatever his conception of the ideal society, it seems likely that his immediate objective, if indeed he had one, was to hold up a mirror to 'ungentle gentlemen', challenging their excesses with a 'utopian' image of their opposite.

For all the turmoil of the sixteenth century, there was, nonetheless, a fundamental unity of purpose and practice between monarchy and landed classes, as partners in a distinctively centralized state. The English aristoc- racy was no longer a militarized feudal nobility, but neither did the Tudor state possess a standing army; and both depended on their partnership to maintain social order. To be sure, the most effective popular rebellions were those supported by local elites; and, in the following century, the landlords would mobilize popular forces in their own conflict with the monarchy. Yet, when in the Civil War the English ruling class came into fatal conflict with

---

3 On More's 'enlightened conservatism', see Wood, *Foundations,* Ch. 6.

the king, it was a battle for control of an already unified English state, and not, as in the French Wars of Religion in the sixteenth century, a struggle between competing jurisdictions or a war between a centralizing monarchy, on the one hand, and, on the other, nobles or municipal authorities protecting their independent powers and privileges, their own little fragments of the state, their 'parcellized sovereignties'.

These historical conditions were reflected in the distinctive patterns of English political thought. In the sixteenth century, for example, the specific development of English society and the English state produced a tradition of political thought in which individuals, without mediation by corporate entities, were conceived as the basic constituents of the state – nicely summed up by Sir Thomas Smith, then Queen Elizabeth's ambassador to France. In a treatise on the English body politic, at least in part intended for the edification of a French audience and therefore assuming no knowledge of English conditions among his readers, he defined a 'commonwealth' or 'societie civill' as 'a societie or common doing of a multitude of free men collected together and united by common accord and covenauntes among themselves, for the conservation of themselves aswell [sic] in peace as in warre.'[4] This represents a telling contrast to the definition of a commonwealth by his contemporary, Jean Bodin, who, reflecting on French conditions, defined it as composed not of free individuals but of 'families, colleges or corporate bodies'.

Smith did not draw any radical conclusions from this definition of the body politic. He took for granted a limited parliamentary franchise, and his conception of representation in Parliament simply assumed that the propertied classes would govern, while other classes would be 'present' in Parliament (as all men, of whatever station, had a right to be), not as members or even as electors but by virtue of the men of property who represent the interests of the commonwealth. The 'sort of men which doe not rule', those who do not enjoy the parliamentary franchise, include

> day labourers, poore husbandmen, yea marchantes or retailers which have no free lande, copiholders, all artificers, as Taylers, Shoomakers, Carpenters,

---

4   Thomas Smith, *De Republica Anglorum*, Ch. 10. It is worth mentioning, too, that Smith already identified the particularities of England's social property relations in his account of the yeomanry: 'these be (for the most part) fermors [i.e., tenants] to gentlemen, and with grasing, frequenting of markettes, and keeping servauntes, not idle servants as the gentleman doth, but such as get both their owne living and parte of their maisters: by these meanes doe come to such wealth, that they are able and daily doe buy the landes of unthriftie gentlemen' (Ch. 23). Smith is here describing what would come to be known as the triadic structure of English agrarian capitalism, the relations among landowners, their capitalist tenants, and the wage labourers employed by capitalist tenant farmers.

Brickemakers, Bricklayers, Masons, &c. These have no voice nor authoritie in our common wealth, and no account is made of them but onelie to be ruled, not to rule other. (Ch. 24)

The 'consent' of Parliament, he adds, 'is taken to be everie mans consent'.

It would be a pupil of Sir Thomas Smith, Bishop John Ponet, often associated with the Commonwealthmen, who would elaborate a justification of violent resistance by private individuals. He produced, in other words, a theory of resistance based on Smith's conception of political society as constituted by a multitude of individuals. In this respect, the contrast between Smith and Bodin is replicated in the difference between Ponet's ideas of resistance and those of the French 'constitutionalists', whose point of departure remained the contest among corporate jurisdictions and a right of resistance as a function of office – precisely the view of resistance that Bodin was seeking to counter.

In Ponet's *Shorte Treatise of Politike Power* (1556), he adopts a conception of the state that might be called 'modern' in its application to an impersonal institutional entity and not simply the personal rule of a monarch; and, for all his religious preoccupations, he emphasizes the secular nature and purpose of the state. The state's objective is the 'wealthe and benefit' of the people; and government is a trust, in which the office-holder acts as a 'proxy', 'attorney' or 'proctor' to the people, who can withdraw the mandate granted to their governors if the government ceases to act in the common interest as defined by the people themselves. While, as we have seen, Protestant doctrine had been used to justify more radical resistance than its canonical founders, Luther and Calvin, had ever been ready to contemplate, Ponet goes beyond existing doctrines in spelling out the right of 'private men' forcibly to resist unlawful or unjust officers and rulers. The difference between Ponet and his 'constitutionalist' counterparts in France or elsewhere on the Continent is sometimes put down to the relative security of Protestants in England (or, indeed, Scotland), which allowed them to risk more radical ideas of individual or 'private' resistance; but Ponet's conception of individual rights surely has structural roots in a distinctively English conception of the polity as constituted not by corporate entities or even a single mystical body, the 'people' as a corporate entity, but in 'a multitude of free men collected together' – an idea that is rooted in a distinct historical reality.

The case of Smith and Ponet illustrates that the idea of a commonwealth constituted by a 'multitude' of individuals, like the conception of the body politic as grounded in corporate entities, could accommodate a fairly wide range of political opinion. The idea of a corporate community did not, to be sure, disappear from English political thought. But, while on the Continent it could operate across a spectrum of opinion from the most unforgiving doctrines of obedience to fairly wide-ranging justifications of resistance, in English conditions it no longer served a useful purpose in resistance theories. Some thinkers would still find it helpful to invoke a mystical corporate community not to justify resistance but to sustain a theory of political obligation and the duty to obey political authority in England. Yet even the most notable defender of royal absolutism, Thomas Hobbes, would feel compelled to counter doctrines of resistance by constructing his argument on a foundation of individual rights and a political society created by a multitude of individuals.

In the sixteenth century, the most noteworthy English exponent of a mystical corporate body as a source of obligation was Richard Hooker. His *Of the Laws of Ecclesiastical Polity,* the first five books of which were published in the 1590s (the last three appeared posthumously in the early seventeenth century), is a classic of Anglican orthodoxy. Aimed against a challenge from Puritan clerics, it was intended to affirm the royal supremacy over the Church. But in the course of his argument, he raises more general political questions and lays out a theory of obligation based on a kind of mystical community to which every individual belongs and whose prior act of submission is binding on future generations. Proceeding from what first appears to be an unambiguous theory of government by consent ('For any prince or potentate to exercise [the power of making laws] not by commission from God or else by authority derived at the first from their consent upon whose persons they impose laws is no better than tyranny.'), he goes on to say that 'to be commanded we do consent when that Society, whereof we be a part, hath at any time before consented, without revoking the same after by the like universal agreement' (I. x). To make the point clearer still, he tells us:

> Wherefore as any man's deed past is good as long as himself continueth; so the act of a public society of men done five hundred years sithence standeth as theirs who presently are of the same societies, because corporations are immortal; we were then alive in our predecessors, and they in their successors do live still.

This means, among other things, that 'In many things assent is given, they that give it not imagining they do so, because the manner of their assenting is not apparent' – an idea of *tacit* consent that would, as we shall see, be taken up by Locke, to somewhat different purposes (though perhaps not as different as some interpreters insist).

Hooker was, it seems, opposed to rule by the arbitrary will of one man, without known laws; but his notion of consent is perfectly compatible with absolute monarchy – as he makes clear when he offers this as his first example of cases in which men give consent not imagining they do: 'when an absolute monarch commandeth his subjects that which seemeth good in his own discretion, hath not his edict the force of law whether they approve or dislike it?' But, however we choose to interpret his theory of consent and the limits it does or does not place on arbitrary power, his notion of the corporate community is striking not only in the ways it differs from Thomas Smith's idea of a commonwealth created by a multitude of individuals but also in the ways it shares with Smith certain common assumptions about the nature of the English body politic.

Hooker takes for granted the absence or weakness of 'intermediary' corporate entities and jurisdictions standing between individual and state. Like Thomas Smith, he assumes the existence of an unusually unified state, a fairly homogeneous and united ruling class and a unitary representative body, which can be said to represent the whole community – in sharp contrast to the French estates, which lie at the heart of Bodin's commonwealth. Hooker's corporate community, in other words, begins to look more like a *national* community, embodied in an English nation state. If the unity of national state and national Church seems less than 'modern', this very particular English unity is possible only because, and to the extent that, the English state – in contrast to 'parcellized sovereignties' and competing jurisdictions elsewhere in Europe – represents a truly sovereign power.

The reality of sovereign power, then, is certainly reflected in English political theory; but the reflection in this period – with the notable exception of Thomas Hobbes – is and remains largely indirect. It is not expressed in a clear idea of indivisible sovereignty. Since in England there was no fundamental conflict of jurisdiction between the monarchy and ruling classes, there was no need to assert the power of one over the other with a conception of indivisible sovereignty. On the contrary, the ancient idea of the 'mixed constitution' was widely held in English political thought, at a time when a French thinker like Bodin was very keen to repudiate such notions and to replace them with one clear and undisputed centre of political authority, a single, indivisible and absolute 'sovereign' power. The English attachment to the idea of the 'mixed constitution', as against the French invention of a clear and systematic idea of sovereignty, did not, as we have seen, mean that France enjoyed a more unified 'sovereign' state. The English 'mixed constitution' expressed the reality of a unitary state, in which monarchy and aristocracy were fundamentally united in joint control of state power. The idea of the 'mixed constitution' was another way of describing, in theoretical terms, the joint control of the state more conventionally expressed in the formula 'the Crown in Parliament', which to this day is used to describe the essence of constitutional power in Britain. Although this state was jointly controlled, it possessed the features of 'sovereignty' far more than did the French state at the time.

The same paradox appears in English and French conceptions of law and the 'sovereign' power of legislation. While Bodin was insisting that the essence of sovereignty was the power to make law and that law was simply the will of the sovereign, the English remained attached to their conception of the common law as the embodiment of age-old custom. They tended to talk about Parliament not so much as making law but as 'discovering' some pre-existing law, perhaps some custom or unwritten constitutional principle that had existed 'time out of mind'. Yet, in reality, the English legal system was already in the sixteenth century far more unified than the French, and Parliament (or the Crown in Parliament) really did have legislative functions more like Bodin's sovereign power. Again, the English conception of law took for granted some long-unchallenged practices, while the conceptual innovations of a thinker like Bodin reflected critical attempts to resolve at least in theory real conflicts over state power, which in practice would remain unresolved until the Revolution.

Crown, Parliament and Multitude

When the Stuarts embarked on their absolutist project, England's ruling classes were still committed to the long-standing partnership between Parliament and Crown, which, despite some moments of tension, had served them very well; but there was neither an inclination nor a social base for a Continental-style absolutism. The propertied classes in general were not in principle opposed to the monarchy. Indeed, they regarded it as a necessary bulwark against social disorder. Both monarchy and aristocracy were strengthened by the bargain in which the demilitarization of the aristocracy, which ceded its traditional coercive powers to the state, was compensated by the state's defence of landed property, underwriting and protecting the aristocracy's purely economic powers of exploitation.

At the same time, the more the propertied classes came to depend on economic exploitation, the less they could tolerate a state that continued to act in the traditional ways of a feudal monarchy. What members of the ruling class wanted was a state that maintained order and sustained their own absolute property rights. They certainly did not want monarchs who themselves behaved like feudal magnates, with their own personal followings, their own economic interests and resources in competition with the landed class. The English ruling class had little to gain from a state which served as just another kind of property, instead of simply serving to protect private property outside the state. So, to the extent that the political development of the monarchical state lagged behind the economic development of the ruling class, conflicts were bound to arise (quite apart from other sources of conflict, such as religious controversies, the complexities and instabilities of Britain's multiple kingdoms, or problems generated by particular royal personalities, which in the case of the stubborn Stuart kings are hard to ignore).

We should not, nonetheless, underestimate the tenacity of the partnership between Parliament and Crown – which was, if anything, strengthened by the long history of social disorder, riots and regional uprisings, religious and political, that preceded the Civil War. However varied the causes, certain social issues were never far from the surface, issues having to do with the realignment and redefinition of property. All this was accompanied by a proliferation of religious sects and open challenges to the authority of the established Church – the national Church which had contributed so much to the centralizing project of the state and which, since the English Reformation, had played an indispensable role in maintaining the state's institutional and ideological authority. On the eve of the Civil War, then, religious and political authority were already in a precarious state; and this certainly predisposed the ruling class to cling to its partnership with the monarchy, in defence of social order.

It is clear from the events leading up to the breach between Parliament and Crown that the propertied classes were willing to go some distance with the king. Still, there were limits, and the Stuarts repeatedly exceeded them – not least, of course, when Charles I ruled for eleven years without convoking Parliament. The imposition of taxes without parliamentary approval, especially in order to support the king's military adventures, was, needless to say, especially unpopular. At any rate, whatever the causes, long-term and immediate, national and local, relations finally broke down and war ensued.

If the landed class had long been united in supporting the partnership between Crown and Parliament, it was no less united in its opposition to the Stuart absolutist project. By far the majority of ruling opinion, inside Parliament no less than in the country outside, fell within the range of opposition to absolute and arbitrary government – at least, monarchical government unaccountable to Parliament. Until late in 1641, parliamentary classes in general remained opposed to what the king was doing; and a substantial majority in Parliament supported the radically anti-absolutist legislative program, including attacks on the Laudian Church, introduced in the preceding months.

Nevertheless, while in 1641 Parliament was all but unanimous in its anti-absolutist programme, historians now repeatedly emphasize that many, indeed most, MPs had no real wish to dispense with monarchy as such. They were generally not, in other words, republicans. We cannot dismiss as mere rhetoric their claims, when they went to war in 1642, to be fighting 'for king and Parliament'. Still, they were equally certain that they could not tolerate – that their own class interests could not sustain – a Continental-style absolutism. There was, besides, no clear division between an old feudal aristocracy defending the king, and a new bourgeoisie, or a capitalist aristocracy, trying to throw off the fetters that impeded its pursuit of progressive economic interests. The landed class was far more homogeneous than that old formula suggests, and little remained of the old-style feudal aristocracy.

Yet by now there were other forces in play that would disrupt this unanimity. The 1620s had marked a turning-point in the political role of the English 'multitude'. Before the king suspended Parliament for eleven years in 1629, his financial problems, among other things, had led to repeated calls for new parliaments to raise the necessary revenues. At the same time, a growing gentry meant that there were more aspirants to membership in Parliament, and elections were more contested than ever before. The electorate was also changing. Inflation alone had the effect of making basic property qualifications less exclusive, widening the social base of the electorate; but expansion of the franchise was also a matter of policy. The gentry were becoming more aware of the political advantages to be gained from mobilizing the people, both in pursuit of their internal rivalries and in disagreements with the Crown. In subsequent decades, there would be retreats (not least by Oliver Cromwell) from this opportunistic commitment to a wider franchise; but between 1621 and 1628, the Commons voted repeatedly to extend the franchise. By 1640, writes one eminent historian of the period, 'the situation in the counties as well as the boroughs had changed out of all recognition from Elizabethan times, and we witness the birth of a political nation, small, partially controlled, but no longer coextensive with the will of the gentry'.[5]

Popular mobilization was not confined to voting. By 1640, the people were taking to the streets with growing regularity. The first acts of the Long Parliament in the autumn of that year were greeted with joyful demonstrations by large crowds in the streets of London. In December, 15,000 people signed the Root and Branch Petition demanding the abolition of episcopacy, and hundreds of them carried the petition to the House of Commons. Archbishop Laud was impeached for treason a week later. The people took to the streets regularly thereafter; from January 1641, there were almost daily popular riots in London. When the Earl of Strafford was executed in May of that year, it was largely under pressure from the 'mob', for whom he had become the chief representative of the absolutist monarchy. At the end of that year, Parliament issued the Grand Remonstrance, listing its grievances – more than two hundred of them – against the king in particularly provocative terms. What made the list especially provocative was that it was clearly intended as an appeal directly to the people outside Parliament, with the objective of mobilizing popular sentiment against the Crown.

This was a new mode of politics, which put the wind up some parliamentarians and suddenly transformed them into royalists. At first, the mobilization of popular forces, especially in London – the hub of the nation

---

5   J.H. Plumb, 'The Growth of the Electorate in England from 1600-1715', *Past and Present* 45 (1969), p. 107.

and disproportionately huge both in its population and in its economic importance – had been the opposition's trump card. But, if riots and popular agitation had been useful instruments of war against the king, they always threatened to exceed the bounds of ruling-class objectives. As the parliamentary debate about the Grand Remonstrance makes clear, it was the calculated appeal to the people, as much as the substance of the document, that some found so alarming and caused them to change sides. We can get a taste of the growing unease from Sir Edward Dering, who had been on the side of the people in the execution of Strafford but was driven into the royalist camp by the Grand Remonstrance. 'Mr. Speaker,' he said,

> when I first heard of a Remonstrance, I presently imagined that like faithful councillors, we should hold up a glass unto his Majesty: I thought to represent unto the King the wicked counsels of pernicious councillors; the restless turbulency of practical Papists . . . I did not dream that we should remonstrate downward, tell stories to the people and talk of the King as of a third person.

The Grand Remonstrance proved to be a major turning-point in the creation of a significant royalist faction. But it was not the first time, nor the last, that anxious members of Parliament expressed their fears of popular mobilization. Before Dering, Sir George Digby, still an active opponent of the king in 1640, had changed sides. Not the least of his worries was the role of the 'multitude' in carrying the Root and Branch Petition to Parliament. He warned the house against the mobilization of

> irregular and tumultuous assemblies of people, be it for never so good an end . . . [T]here is no man of the least insight into nature, or history, but knows the danger, when either true or pretended stimulation, of conscience, hath once given a multitude agitation . . . [W]hat can there be of greater presumption, than for . . . a multitude to teach a parliament, what is, and what is not, the government according to God's word.

The defection of nervous parliamentarians made it possible for the king to rally a substantial force well beyond his personal followers and the relatively small sections of the propertied classes whose interests were inextricably bound up with his – such as the old company merchants who benefited from royal monopolies. At the same time, it meant that the parliamentary cause was now led by those more inclined to popular mobilization. The process of defection, which had begun when some parliamentarians took fright at the impeachment and execution of the Earl of Strafford and at the Grand Remonstrance, would be repeated several times in the following years of civil war, as increasingly radical dangers drove more sections of the opposition away from the parliamentary cause. Even the victorious parliamentarians of the Long Parliament were prepared to negotiate with the king as late as 1648, as, indeed, the leaders of the New Model Army had been in 1647. The next-to-last stage of that peeling-away was the conflict between Cromwell and the Levellers, and the final stage came in the Restoration.

Political Ideas in the English Civil War

The Civil War was not only a time of military conflict but a period of unique intellectual ferment. The breakdown of authority encouraged an unprecedented outpouring of political debate. The population was unusually literate by the standards of the day; and people were regularly exposed not only to the ruling ideologies but to subversive ideas, typically in sermons from their often sectarian parish preachers. A wide range of issues and conflicts were canvassed in a vast profusion of pamphlet literature, addressed not just to the usual elites but to the common man and woman. Yet the breakdown of authority is not enough to account for the airing of grievances and aspirations that might otherwise have remained submerged beneath ruling-class hegemony. The very structure of English society and politics, the specific need of the ruling classes for alliances and popular mobilization, placed radical ideas on the agenda in unprecedented ways.

Let us consider, as it were from the top down, some of the many political ideas that were circulating at this turbulent moment. Before the reign of James I, it was widely accepted that England had a mixed constitution, and this idea continued to play an important part in English political thought across a wide political spectrum. It could be used to defend the rights of Parliament against the Crown; but it certainly did not preclude a major, and in some versions even a dominant, role for the king, as long as it was understood that all rule was ultimately subject to the law as promulgated by the 'Crown in Parliament', which meant the monarch together with the two houses of Parliament.

The erudite King James I himself challenged that idea by claiming, in his book *The Trew Law of Free Monarchies* (1598) and elsewhere, that kings ruled by divine right and were not accountable to any earthly authority. He also famously commissioned a translation of the Bible – the 'Authorized Version' or 'King James Bible', which was intended to displace the English-language Calvinist 'Geneva Bible', not least because of what he took to be its seditious marginal commentaries sanctioning resistance to monarchical authority. Yet even James, while admitting no constitutional limits on his rule, conceded, at least in theory, that the king should rule according to existing law.

Few Englishmen were willing to take a very strong and unambiguous position on the 'absolute' powers of the king, and there was only a short period in the seventeenth century when a small number of royalist thinkers made more absolute claims for royal sovereignty. The most famous of these is Thomas Hobbes, whom we shall discuss in what follows. Another was Sir Robert Filmer, whose major defence of royal absolutism, *Patriarcha*, though written in the 1640s, remained unpublished until long after his death. It was resurrected and, for the first time, printed in 1680 during the renewed conflicts between the king and Parliament, only to be famously and fatally attacked by John Locke, who, as we shall see, singled it out as the main target of his own assault on absolutism.

For the moment, we need only keep in mind that strong absolutist arguments were very unpopular in England. Both Filmer and Hobbes, in their different ways, remained untypical, even among royalists. For that matter, the English never seemed to be much bothered about locating a single, absolute and indivisible sovereign power, residing in the king or in Parliament. They had long grown accustomed to their 'mixed constitution', the joint rule of king and propertied classes in Parliament.

When the time finally came, then, how did the ruling class defend its right to rebel against the king? There were, of course, well-established doctrines of resistance available to them, not least the constitutionalist doctrines of the monarchomachs that had emerged from the French Wars of Religion. In France, the idea of popular sovereignty could readily be invoked to sustain the autonomous jurisdictions of aristocrats and 'lesser magistrates'; but this was not in the first instance the preferred ideological strategy of English parliamentarians. In fact, at least in the early years of the Civil War, the principal theorists of the parliamentary cause actually repudiated doctrines of popular sovereignty. They seemed very reluctant even to claim the sovereignty of Parliament and to replace the Crown in Parliament with an unambiguous parliamentary supremacy.

The battle the English were fighting was different from that of the French. It was not, again, a war of competing jurisdictions and fragmented sovereignties. It was not a matter of particular corporate bodies and privileges defending their autonomy against a monarchical drive to unify the state and replace corporate fragments with one overarching sovereign power. In an already unified sovereign state, which was constituted by king and Parliament together, Parliament was not asserting its own, 'popular' sovereignty against the king's competing claims so much as accusing him of violating their partnership, of breaching their composite sovereignty.

In the period leading up to the Civil War, when tensions between king and ruling class were mounting, Parliament in 1628 produced the Petition of Right, which has come to be regarded as a cornerstone of the English constitution. The distinctive tone of English conflicts between Crown and ruling classes is nicely captured in this document and in the debate surrounding it in Parliament. The petition undoubtedly claimed certain powers for

Parliament, yet it represented itself not as an assertion of parliamentary sovereignty but as a statement about the 'rights and liberties of the subject'. In other words, it is not about competing jurisdictions or sovereignties so much as about the rights of the citizen (or subject) against a state whose unified jurisdiction is taken for granted. It represents a different kind of constitutionalism, which does not concern the rights of one kind of lordship against another, or the claims of lesser lords against greater ones, or 'lesser magistrates' against princes and kings. It has more to do with the relations between individual and state (even if the individuals most immediately concerned are members of the propertied classes).

The debate in Parliament is also telling. When the Commons had accepted the Petition of Right and it went to the Lords, there was a proposal to add a clause 'to leave entire that sovereign power wherewith your Majesty is trusted'. It is perhaps significant enough that those who proposed this amendment saw no incompatibility between the demands of the petition and this assertion of royal power. But even more interesting is the argument advanced by one MP against the proposed clause, in a conference between the two houses of Parliament. In a climate of discontent and anger, argued Sir Henry Marten, the 'vulgar' multitude may not be very friendly to the sacred sovereign power. 'This petition will run through many hands', he said,

> and men will fall to arguing and descanting what sovereign power is . . . what is the latitude? whence the original? where the bounds? etc., with many such curious and captious questions . . . Sovereign power is then best worth when it is held in tacit veneration, not when it is profaned by vulgar hearings or examinations.

For Marten, this may have been a rhetorical ploy, but he understood the mind-set of the ruling class very well: the less said about sovereignty the better. Why raise the issue at all? Why let the 'vulgar' start asking awkward questions about the sources, scope and limits of sovereign power? Let sleeping dogs lie. And so their lordships did, as the Petition of Right was passed without the embarrassing clause.

This whole episode is richly revealing. It tells us much about the disposition of the ruling classes and their relations with the Crown. Grievances they certainly had, but they were apparently confident enough of their partnership with the Crown and their joint role in the state not to feel a strong need to clarify the issue of sovereignty. Besides, whatever issues divided Parliament and Crown, they were united in their common front against the 'vulgar' multitude.

This brings us to another factor that may help to explain the reluctance of parliamentary leaders and thinkers to invoke the doctrine of popular sovereignty. When the French articulated the right of resistance, they had the option of reserving it to 'lesser magistrates' or corporations. But what would happen if the basic constituents of the state were conceived not as 'colleges and corporations' but as a 'multitude of free men'? What implications would it have where corporate powers had largely given way to a centralized state, where the intermediate institutions between the individual and the state had been weakened, and where individuals and their private property had been detached from 'extra-economic' powers and identities? One possibility, of course, was to attach political significance to property, as distinct from prescriptive corporate status or privilege; and this was, of course, done. But the purely quantitative measure of property was more dangerously elastic than qualitative differences of privilege and rank. Would a right of resistance then be claimed by the popular multitude?

The mainstream parliamentary justification of opposition to the king in 1642 tended to be somewhat equivocal. Parliamentarians were inclined to say not so much that the people had a right of rebellion but that the king was the one who was rebelling, so that Parliament had the duty to restore the constitution and the traditional balance between Crown and Parliament. Any true republicans – certainly in today's conventional sense, as genuine opponents of monarchy in principle – stayed largely under cover until 1648, when the conflict had apparently reached a point of no return.

There were, however, a few early attempts to establish a theory of parliamentary sovereignty, the most notable being Henry Parker's *Observations upon some of his Majesties late Answers and Expresses* (1642). Parker claimed that 'power is originally inherent in the people' and that royal authority is derived from that original power through the medium of contracts and agreements. But like French theorists of resistance, Parker still had in mind the 'people' as a corporate entity, on the grounds that it is only as a collectivity that the people were superior to the king, so the people could exercise their powers only through their constitutional representatives. More particularly, he argued that, once having established a Parliament to represent them, the people could not reclaim their original power. It was up to Parliament to guard the interests of the people and to resist the king when he violated their liberties. Parker certainly did not call for the abolition of the monarchy and continued to speak in the language of a mixed constitution, or the King in Parliament; but he did give Parliament, as the people's representative, the last word. Parliament, he argued,

> may not desert the king, but being deserted by the king, when the kingdom is in distress, they may judge of that distress, and relieve it, and are to be accounted, by the virtue of representation, as the whole body of the state.

This argument may have appeared more risky in England than it had in France, because the notion of the people as a corporate entity had already been weakened both in theory and in practice, giving way to the idea of the people as a multitude of individuals. This may help to explain why royalists could counter Parker's argument by claiming that, if Parliament can rebel against the king, there was nothing to prevent the people's similarly rebelling against Parliament.

Parker's defence of parliamentary sovereignty was too extreme even for some prominent parliamentarians. In what appears to be a reply to Parker, the distinguished lawyer, John Selden (1584–1654), long known as a defender of the 'subject's liberties' and the rights of Parliament, argued against Parker's first premise. In his *Table Talk*, written in the early 1640s but unpublished until 1689, Selden, in the entry on 'Contracts', explores the implications of contracts between the people and their rulers. Contracts would mean nothing, he insists, if we could just withdraw from them whenever they cease to be convenient. 'If once we grant we may recede from contracts upon any inconveniency that may afterwards happen, we shall have no bargain kept. If I sell you a horse and do not like my bargain, I will have my horse again.' By the same rules of contract, the principle that the people as a collectivity are greater than the king simply cannot stand up. Just because the people made the king, they are not therefore greater than he, any more than I am greater or richer than you after I have given you my whole fortune and left myself destitute. If I made you greater, greater you remain. Selden's friend Thomas Hobbes was to use related arguments, but in outright defence of royal absolutism.

As for genuine republicanism in the Civil War, some prominent historians insist that republicans never represented more than a small minority against the mainstream of parliamentary thinking. Others point to an important body of 'republican' thought – including political works by the poet John Milton – that had emerged by the late 1640s, which was to have substantial influence in the eighteenth century, not least in the American Revolution. Yet it is not always clear what is meant by 'republicanism'; and the concept is especially ill-suited to capturing the English political experience. The Roman idea of a civic community, to which 'republicanism' is commonly traced, in its original form presupposed a ruling aristocracy that governed itself collectively and in amateur style, with a minimal state. The English context was very different. England had long had an effective central administration; and this political form, the product of distinctive social developments, was unlike any other in Europe or anywhere else. The partnership of monarchy and Parliament was recognized even by so-called republicans, who might argue against absolutism and for a 'mixed constitution' without necessarily advocating abolition of the monarchy.

The term 'republicanism' is often used by historians of political thought in reference not so much to anti-monarchism as to political theories that place strong emphasis on a community of citizens, the importance of 'civic virtue', and the accountability of any political authority to the civic community. But in the English context, a 'republican' emphasis on the civic community, a community of citizens, is often hard to distinguish from other forms of anti-absolutism. The civic community was likely to be identified with Parliament no less by 'republicans' than by more moderate defenders of Parliament against the Crown. This could mean specifically the accountability of any government to a representative institution like Parliament – at which point this 'classical republicanism' shades into less radical forms of mainstream parliamentarism.

In specifically English conditions, what does stand out in sharper relief, as we shall see in a moment, is the division between those for whom the ruling class in Parliament was the rightful embodiment of the civic community or popular power and those for whom the people outside Parliament were truly sovereign. The idea of 'republican liberty' is not very helpful in identifying this division, not least because the Roman Republic was an oligarchy and the original Roman idea of liberty was never democratic. In the concept of 'republicanism', even the distinction between oligarchy and democracy may disappear from view, making it hard to distinguish, for instance, between oligarchic republicans and more radical defenders of the people's liberty against the crown, such as the Levellers. More particularly, the 'people outside Parliament' is a category without meaning in any other context but the English. It has no bearing on the Roman civic community where the 'republican' idea was born, nor on the Italian city-state where it was revived, nor indeed in the Dutch Republic; while in absolutist France, the relevant players in the contest between absolutist kings and those who opposed them were, as we have seen, necessarily different.

It is certainly true that, by the end of the 1640s, there were prominent radicals who favoured an unambiguous parliamentary supremacy and severe restrictions on the power of the Crown and the House of Lords. There were those who even supported the abolition of the monarchy. But some so-called republicanism is not unambiguously opposed to monarchy as such. Republicans in this sense could be advocates of the mixed constitution and could even accept some kind of constitutional monarchy. Even the great republican Algernon Sidney (1622–83), who was to be condemned for treason in 1683 after the failure of the Exclusion programme, continued to speak of a mixed constitution even while calling for revolution in the manuscript that led to his death, the *Discourses Concerning Government*, finally published in 1698.

One thing, at any rate, is clear: even those MPs who were willing to go the whole distance and abolish the monarchy, and to assert some kind of 'popular sovereignty', were likely to take away with one hand what they had given with the other. They generally situated 'popular sovereignty' in Parliament, and not in the 'people' outside – to say nothing of the restrictions they would have placed on the right to elect Parliament. This was true even if they allowed power to revert to the multitude in moments of extreme crisis, as when Cromwell mobilized a popular army whose rank and file he would allow to fight but not to vote. Henry Ireton, Cromwell's son-in-law and the chief spokesman of the 'grandees' in the Putney Debates, was himself a republican of this radical but undemocratic variety. This is exactly the point at which more democratic forces like the Levellers parted company with these oligarchic republicans, claiming sovereignty not just for Parliament but for the multitude, and not just in extreme emergencies but in normal political life.

The body of literature that has come to be known as classical republicanism, of which the most important exponent was James Harrington (1611–77), did produce a distinctive conception of citizenship and civic liberty, which can be said to distinguish it from the traditions of 'liberalism' associated with thinkers like John Locke. The republican conceptions of citizenship and liberty imply something more than the passive enjoyment of individual rights or the 'negative' freedom from external impediments to action. Republican liberty, as Quentin Skinner has argued, is the absence of dependence in any form. The very existence of arbitrary power, however permissively or even benignly it may be exercised, reduces men to servitude, so that free individuals can exist only in free states, governed by a civic community of active citizens. But republicans of this kind seem to have been no less wedded than were less 'republican' parliamentarians to an exclusive political nation. At the very least, their conception of citizenship did not preclude a division between propertied elite and labouring multitude.

Harrington, in the years following the publication of his *Commonwealth of Oceana* (dedicated to Cromwell) in 1656, wrote in opposition to the restoration of the monarchy and was imprisoned in 1661. But even a genuinely radical republican like this was not necessarily a democrat in the sense that we, or even the Levellers, would understand the term. In *Oceana*, Harrington makes some significant observations about the connections between political and economic power. Political power, insofar as it rests on control of the food supply, is grounded in landed property. In some respects, this observation was a double-edged sword. On the one hand, it was the basis of Harrington's claims for the supremacy of representative bodies – at least in places where, as in England, land was no longer in the hands of a feudal nobility but was widely distributed among commoners. This principle could also be taken to mean that property should be more widely and equitably distributed, so that the body of men who are fit to be citizens might be enlarged; or at least landownership should be stabilized by means of the kind of agrarian law he proposed, regulating the acquisition and inheritance of land in order to maintain a relatively wide distribution of political power. This kind of regulation might even be understood as opposing the increasing concentration of landed property that was continuing in England.

On the other hand, on the basis of the same principle, Harrington was very emphatic that citizenship could belong *only* to those who had the 'wherewithal to live of themselves' – that is, it would exclude a substantial number of people without property or dependent for their livelihood on labouring for others. Even in his more or less utopian commonwealth, he never imagined the disappearance of people such as these, though their numbers might be limited. In the real world of his own contemporary England, many people would have been excluded from full rights of citizenship on the basis of such Harringtonian principles.

The Levellers and the Putney Debates

If the main parliamentary leaders were reluctant to invoke the notion of popular sovereignty because they feared its subversive possibilities, their fears were soon to be justified. The war and popular mobilization inevitably opened that Pandora's box. During the revolutionary period, the world was indeed 'turned upside down'. Radical religious sects defied some of the most basic principles of ecclesiastical hierarchy and even conventional social morality. Various groups in which religious and political ideas were inseparable challenged political authority and the dominant system of property, their ideas ranging across a broad spectrum up to and including the most radically democratic doctrines and even the repudiation of private property itself.

By 1647, a wide-ranging programme of political reform was taking root in the New Model Army. Many in the Army rank and file were driven by anger, often generated by Parliament's refusal to pay the soldiers; but many were also motivated by democratic opposition to the parliamentary oligarchy, and even those officers of a less radical disposition were forced to adopt a more militant stance, if only to maintain Army unity and discipline.

The Army itself became a major political issue, its very existence a bone of contention among parliamentarians. When fear of military radicalism and of the 'rabble' of ordinary soldiers drove some parliamentarians to call for the New Model Army to be disbanded, the Army stood firm, refused to accept Parliament's order to disband, and retaliated with a coherent and radical political programme. Largely the work of Henry Ireton, it called for constitutional and religious reforms that went well beyond what Parliament had hitherto demanded, not to mention a purge of Parliament itself to rid it of corrupt MPs and the Army's chief opponents.

The Army was united in defying Parliament's orders to disband, but that unity disguised the divisions within its own ranks and the tenuous control now exercised by Cromwell's officers over the rank and file. There is even debate among historians about whether the Army's seizure of the king in June of 1647 really had the approval of Cromwell or was simply an action by radicals, accepted by Cromwell and Ireton after the fact. These internal divisions had taken shape in the election of regimental Agitators, whose function was to represent the interests and grievances of the rank and file. It was these Agitators who established links with radicals especially in London, and specifically the Levellers. Soon they became the conduits for more wide-ranging discussions, in which not only the nature of the new regime in England but also the most fundamental issues of religion and politics were openly debated in the most democratic way, by officers and ordinary soldiers. The division between the Army grandees and the Levellers represented a substantial divergence between what has been called an 'oligarchic republicanism' and a more democratic radicalism.

The thinkers and activists who have been called 'Levellers' represented a fairly wide range of views. The name itself seems to have appeared earlier in the century to describe people who rose up against practices such as enclosure, 'levelling' hedges, fences or walls; but increasingly the term was used pejoratively to accuse certain radicals of wanting to equalize or 'level', indeed even to abolish, private property.

The man who is commonly regarded as the most important Leveller writer, John Lilburne (1615–57), never showed any inclination to do away with private property. This is perhaps not surprising in a man destined to be a 'middling' merchant himself, apprenticed to a wholesale cloth merchant from 1630 to 1636, though later impeded by monopolies in his attempts to carry on in the same trade. In approximately eighty pamphlets, he consistently defended the rights of the people, generally under the heading of 'life, liberty or estate'. His radicalism consisted above all in his insistence on the power of the people, as against either king or Parliament. One of the leaders of the London crowd when it took to the streets to call for the impeachment of Strafford, he spent the rest of his career defending the 'ancient' rights and liberties of England, the freedom of the people against tyranny and arbitrary rule, the freedom of conscience, the right to due processes of law, and so on. In 1638 he was punished for printing and circulating unlicensed books, and aggravated his situation by denouncing episcopacy. Thereafter, he was to be tried three times for treason, and between 1645 and 1652 imprisoned seven times. In 1652 he was banished for life because of his opposition to corruption and his consistent defence of political and religious liberty, which were evidently no more welcome to Cromwell than they had been to the king and his supporters. Lilburne returned to England in defiance of the banishment order and was tried for treason, acquitted but again imprisoned. He died a few years later, having become a Quaker like many other disappointed radicals. Yet throughout this long and courageous history of struggle in defence of liberty, Lilburne was never a Leveller in the sense intended by those enemies who accused people like him of seeking to abolish all distinctions between rich and poor and promoting common ownership.

Nor was Lilburne exceptional in taking for granted the right of private property. This was typical of the people we now know as Levellers, who were active during the Civil War. In fact, as we shall see, their views on property provoked some even more radical activists – the Diggers – to describe themselves as *True* Levellers, to distinguish themselves from those less inclined really to 'level' property. Still, despite explicit denials, the Levellers continued to be accused – for example, by Ireton in the Putney Debates – of endangering the whole institution of property; and these accusations were not simply tactical. They testify to a real threat posed to ruling-class interests by the Leveller programme.

Even if the mainstream Levellers fell short of advocating communal property, they nonetheless espoused some very radical political ideas which threatened to undermine the rule of the dominant propertied class. At the root of these radical ideas is the notion that the people were sovereign – not Parliament, not some other representatives of the people, not the 'people' in mythical corporate form, but the people as popular 'multitude'. This idea may have made its first explicit appearance in 1645, in *England's Miserie and Remedie*, an anonymous pamphlet in defence of Lilburne attributed at one time or another to various Levellers, including Lilburne himself.

Although in general the Levellers represented small and 'middling' proprietors, craftsmen, traders and yeoman farmers, many of them, including some of their most influential spokesmen, were not only well educated but also fairly prosperous. Even the Putney Debates display a range of views, some more radical than others; but on the whole, we cannot go far wrong if we assume that the Levellers were principally spokesmen for smaller independent proprietors as against large landowners and wealthy merchants, especially the old monopolists. At a time when small proprietors were an increasingly endangered species, as property was becoming increasingly concentrated, they opposed practices such as enclosure and other attacks on customary rights, which accelerated the concentration of property; and they defended the right of the craftsman or farmer to the fruits of his labour.

They were especially opposed to the association of privilege and political rights with large properties. Their programme included reform of taxation, in order to shift the burden to larger proprietors; they strongly opposed taxes that hit the small man hardest, like the excise, and other forms of indirect exploitation of small producers, like the costs of litigation, the laws on debt, church tithes, and so on; they attacked trade monopolies (here they had something in common with many richer parliamentarians) in defence of free trade; they defended customary rights and sought security for customary tenures, which were increasingly being challenged by larger land-owners; and they called for various political reforms such as annual or biennial Parliaments, reform of the legal system (they despised lawyers) and the extension of the franchise. Always bound up with their political programme was an overriding commitment to religious toleration. Perhaps the most radical aspect of their political programme was their emphasis on local self-government, and Levellers not only challenged executive govern-ment but also called for a weaker Parliament, in the interests of stronger local government.

The *Agreement of the People*, which provoked the Putney Debates, ranged over a broad spectrum of constitutional, political and religious issues: regular and frequent election of Parliament but with increasing devo-lution of government to local control (the agreement makes no mention of executive prowess), an extension of the franchise, religious toleration, demo-cratic control of the military, the abolition of tithes and certain other taxes. In the debates, the chief spokesman for the grandees was the outstandingly clever and articulate Commissary-General Henry Ireton, certainly a revolu-tionary if not a democrat, son of the lesser gentry and married to Cromwell's daughter. The most eloquent spokesman for the other side was Colonel Thomas Rainsborough (1610?–48). The issues in dispute drew a sharp line not only between different constitutional positions but divergent class interests.

That part of the Debates that raised the most fundamental political ques-tions turned on the reform of the franchise. The discussion went beyond matters of policy to more fundamental underlying issues, indeed to the very foundations of political order and the system of property. To sustain their political claims, the radicals invoked some revolutionary ideas about the fundamental rights of men (they did indeed mean *men*) and the basis of legitimate government. They argued that every man in England, even the poorest, had a right not to be governed except by his own consent, and that this right was attached to the person and not to property. These ideas were sharply challenged by Ireton and Cromwell, who saw the dangers – not only to government but to property itself – that would follow from taking such arguments to their logical conclusion.

Leveller views on the franchise have been a subject of fierce debate among historians. Part of the problem lies in the tactical retreats of the Levellers in their negotiations with the Army grandees, evidence of which can be found in the Putney Debates and in the various revisions in the *Agreement of the People*. Some historians have argued that the Levellers would have excluded not only 'dependent' people like women, beggars and alms-takers, but also all hired labourers. But the dominant view now is that, while none of the

Levellers ever questioned the exclusion of women (even women, however radically militant they often were in other respects, failed to demand the suffrage for themselves), the starting position of the Leveller leaders – from which they retreated in order to get the agreement of Cromwell and Ireton – was universal adult male suffrage. At the very least, they supported a household suffrage, in which every head of household represented his dependents: women, children and live-in servants. The more radical position was certainly very prominent in the Putney Debates, eloquently articulated by the leading Leveller spokesman, Colonel Rainsborough.

The debate on the franchise revolved especially around the clause in the *Agreement of the People* which demanded: 'That the people of England, being at this day very unequally distributed by counties, cities, and boroughs for the election of their deputies in Parliament, ought to be more indifferently proportioned, according to the number of inhabitants.' There are, to be sure, certain ambiguities in this formulation, and the clever Henry Ireton was very quick to seize on them. The clause could be read as calling simply for correction of anomalies in the current voting system. Not only were there places with a very wide franchise and others with a very limited electorate, but a large town might have no representative at all (because it had not been incorporated prior to some specific date in the past), while some practically depopulated rural areas did. Perhaps, then, the demand for representation apportioned according to population went no further than sorting out these inequities.

Cromwell and Ireton would not have objected to a change of this kind – and they actually did institute such electoral reforms; but Ireton immediately saw in the clause something more. He notes the reference to distribution according to the number of inhabitants, 'the people of England, etc.' and remarks that

> this does make me think, that the meaning is that every man that is an inhabitant is to be equally considered, and to have an equal voice in the election of those represeners . . . and if that be the meaning then I have something to say against it.

Rainsborough makes no effort to disguise that the more democratic construction of this clause is exactly what he has in mind. And here he states, in the most eloquent and moving speech, the principle on which he stakes his claim:

> [F]or really I think that the poorest he that is in England has a life to live as the greatest he; and therefore truly, sir, I think it's clear that every man that is to live under a government ought first by his own consent to put himself under that government; and I do think that the poorest man in

England is not at all bound in a strict sense to that government that he has
not had a voice to put himself under.

Ireton immediately sees the implications of this argument. Rainsborough's
claim that the poorest man in England has the same rights as the greatest
implies that certain rights inhere in men as men (and it is, unfortunately,
always men), just by virtue of their living and breathing: because 'the poorest
he has a life to live', he also possesses the right not to be governed except by
his own consent. 'Give me leave to tell you', Ireton replies, 'that if you make
this the rule, I think you must fly for refuge to an absolute natural right, and
you must deny all civil right.' It can perhaps be argued that, while the Levellers
themselves were still clinging to the rights of 'free-born Englishmen', Ireton
on their behalf constructed a conception of natural right.

At any rate, Ireton's distinction between 'natural' and 'civil' right is a critical one, around which much of the debate revolves. Englishmen, says Ireton,
do have certain rights, but they are rights historically established by English
constitutional traditions and practices. These traditions do not include an
equal franchise, any more than they include equality of property. To establish
the kind of right that Rainsborough demands means circumventing the
English constitution and appealing to some more universal, absolute right,
not based on historical precedents but on the laws of nature itself.

This may be more than some Levellers intended to claim. After all, they
repeatedly talk about the birthrights or 'native rights' of 'free-born
Englishmen', not of mankind in general. In fact, their argument often rests
not so much on an appeal to natural right as on an alternative account of
English history. In answer to Ireton's claim about England's ancient constitution, for example, John Wildman insists that

> Our very laws were made by our conquerors; and whereas it's spoken
> much of chronicles, I conceive there is no credit to be given to any of them;
> and the reason is because those that were our lords, and make us their
> vassals, would suffer nothing else to be chronicled.

So the historical record to which Ireton is appealing records history as the
ruling class has dictated. There is another, suppressed story to be told – and
here Wildman is alluding to a theme widespread among radicals: that the
present constitution of government and property is the legacy of conquest,
the Norman Conquest, and can therefore enjoy no legitimacy.

But if the argument often turns on the popular radical theme of the infamous 'Norman Yoke', there is no doubt that something like a more universal
conception of natural rights keeps emerging from beneath that historical
argument. In fact, the Norman Yoke is illegitimate not just because it has
destroyed a more ancient order in England but apparently also because it

violates certain more basic principles. Those principles may not be systematically laid out in the Putney Debates, but they did get full expression elsewhere, most notably in Richard Overton's *An Arrow Against All Tyrants*, which begins:

> To every individual in nature, is given an individual property by nature, not to be invaded or usurped by any: for every one as he is himselfe, so he hath a selfe propriety, else he could not be himselfe, and on this no second may presume to deprive any of, without manifest violation and affront to the very principles of nature and of the Rules of equity and justice between man and man.

It is on this notion of 'self-propriety', the inviolable property that every man has in his own person, that the Levellers base their claims not only to the franchise and other political rights but to freedom of conscience and religion. This idea was later to be put to different uses by John Locke; but in the hands of the Levellers its radical implications are unmistakable, and Ireton spells them out thus: once you claim this kind of natural right, he argues, 'then I think you must deny all property too'.

Ireton's argument here needs to be looked at more closely. The view that private property itself is a natural right may seem familiar and even commonplace; and John Locke, the political theorist who did most to provide a systematic defence of this view, based it, as we shall see, on something like the Leveller idea of 'self-propriety'. To argue that private property is a natural right may seem the most powerful defence of propertied interests, yet in the Putney Debates we find a defender of the propertied classes like Ireton arguing instead that property is not a natural right but merely a human convention, established by human constitution, grounded in history rather than in nature. But Ireton's view was not at all unusual. It had, as we have seen, long been common in the Western tradition to argue that property is a convention – or, at least, that even if the institution itself is divinely ordained, as Ireton himself concedes, its specific form and distribution are merely conventional.

The idea that property is a right by convention rather than by nature had never in the Western tradition seemed threatening to propertied interests and, in the English context, may even have seemed far less dangerous. Ireton sees that, far from weakening the defence of property, this may indeed be a safer ideological strategy for the propertied classes, because it is not so easy to explain and justify gross inequalities of property on the basis of a natural right vested in the individual. His own argument is simply that the present system has existed as long as anyone can remember, that it belongs to the English constitution, and that any attack on the constitution is a threat to any social order and peace, and hence finally to property itself.

If rights inhere in the person, he argues, why would a man not then also have, by the same right of nature, the right to anything he needs to sustain his person – 'the same right in any goods he sees: meat, drink, clothes, to take and use them for his sustenance' – and indeed a right to make use of land itself in any way he liked? How could any ownership of property, even the most modest, be secure with such an unrestricted and disruptive conception of rights (never mind the more obvious consideration that a majority of poor voters are likely to play havoc with the rights of the rich)? What limits are there to such natural rights? 'I would fain have any man show me their bounds, where you will end, and take away all property.'

Rainsborough, like other Levellers, denies any intention to destroy the institution of property. Many of the people he represents, after all, are proprietors themselves. At the same time, if forced to make a choice, these radicals – or some of them – seem prepared to put aside the sanctity of property. As Major William Rainsborough says, 'the chief end of this government is to preserve persons as well as estates, and if any law shall take hold of my person, it is more dear than my estate'. So the rights of persons prevail over the rights of property – which is precisely what disturbs Henry Ireton.

The position advocated by Ireton is that the franchise should not belong to anyone whose stake or 'interest' in society is only what 'he may carry about with him', who has only – to use Colonel Rainsborough's words – a 'life to live', only the 'interest' of living and breathing, a man who is merely, as Ireton puts it, 'here today and gone tomorrow'. Only those who have a 'fixed' and 'permanent interest' in society, in the form of landed property or the so-called 'freedom' of a corporation, an officially licensed right to conduct trade – only men such as these have a real stake in the state; and so the fate of the community should be in their hands.

When asked directly whether any man can be bound to obey laws to which he has not himself consented (by electing those who make the laws), Ireton says unequivocally, yes – with one proviso: that he can freely leave if he is dissatisfied. A man with a 'permanent interest', one with property 'that does locally fix him in this country', cannot freely leave, while the propertyless, or even those who possess only money, can come and go as they please. In that respect, they are no different from foreigners who visit our shores. We all expect foreign visitors to obey our laws while they are in our country, and to respect those who make the laws, even though they have no right to vote for the legislators.

The Levellers keep insisting on their native rights and ask what the soldiers have fought for in the war, if they are now to be denied those rights. They fought, Edward Sexby declares, 'to recover our birthrights and privileges as Englishmen . . . There are many thousands of us soldiers that have ventured our lives; we have had little property in the kingdom as to our estates, yet we have had a birthright.' To this, Ireton's reply is straightforward: what the Army fought for was the right to be governed by a representative body and a known law rather than by the arbitrary rule of one man. And they fought for the freedom to do business and acquire property. Their true birthright is the English constitution itself, principles of property and government that have stood the test of time, and the security they derive from this constitutional order. To put it another way, the Levellers demanded something closer to democracy in its literal meaning as 'rule by the (common) people'; Ireton offered them constitutional or limited government instead.

The radicals did try to compromise on some of their proposals, in order to reach an accommodation with the grandees; but events were soon to overtake them. The king escaped, a Leveller mutiny was suppressed and army discipline re-established. In December of 1648 came Pride's Purge, when, with or without direct orders from Cromwell, Colonel Thomas Pride drove all opposition to the Army grandees out of Parliament. The king would soon be executed, and Cromwell's commonwealth would truly be in power. Later, Cromwell repudiated his most radical allies and arrested their leaders. Thereafter, the Levellers more or less disappeared from the political scene. But whatever the fate of Leveller thinkers or the availability of their writings, the ideas they represented were already too much a part of the revolutionary culture to disappear with them; and radical ideas such as theirs, to say nothing of the multitude's intrusion into politics, set the agenda for political debate thereafter – not least in the ideas of more 'canonical' theorists like Thomas Hobbes and John Locke.

The Levellers were not the most radical group to emerge during the Civil War.[6] There were others who found their proposed political reforms inadequate and their doctrine of natural right insufficient. There were those, in particular the 'Digger' Gerrard Winstanley, who were willing to acknowledge and accept the dire consequences that Ireton perceived in the concept of natural right, consequences that Levellers like Rainsborough denied, and to insist that there could be no true liberty without destroying the system of property. Yet even the Levellers had proved too radical, and they lost the political battle. Their ideas nonetheless remained a potent force and had a lasting effect on the ideological front. The revolution and their part in it had irrevocably changed the terms of political debate.

One measure of their influence is what happened to the notion of government by consent. The idea of government founded on a contract or the consent of the 'people' had long existed, as we have seen, in various versions,

---

6 For an illuminating contextual discussion of radical ideas in the period, see Geoff Kennedy, *Diggers, Levellers and Agrarian Capitalism: Radical Political Thought in Seventeenth-Century England* (Lanham: Lexington Books, 2008).

from defences of secular authority to justifications of resistance. But not till the Levellers introduced their innovations did the idea of government by consent become the basis of a democratic theory. A definition of the 'people' as consisting of a multitude of individuals may already have established itself; and, in the case of someone like John Ponet, this idea may even have produced a theory of individual resistance. But the Levellers took these ideas much further, while also redefining consent. Here, it was not corporate communities but individuals who would do the consenting, and more than that: the consent would have to be constantly renewed. It is worth noting, too, that the emphasis here is on the original, natural and inviolable rights of the people, not on any sort of mutual agreement or contract which stresses the obligations of subjects as much as their rights. The 'people', furthermore, though it would still leave out at least half the population (women), would come much closer to comprising the popular, labouring multitude, rather than an exclusive political community of propertyholders. And these people would exert their 'popular sovereignty' not just by reclaiming their rights in tyrannical emergencies but regularly and repeatedly, in the normal exercise of their everyday political rights as citizens.

After this theoretical innovation, and after the historic events that brought it into being, English political theory was never the same again. Theorists of a far less radical disposition, including even a defender of royal absolutism like Hobbes, felt obliged to meet the radical argument on its own ground, even to show that their preferred, and less democratic, forms of government met this new test of political legitimacy. In John Locke's time, when the threat from below seemed, to propertied classes, less immediate than the threat from above, Leveller ideas could be selectively mobilized by far less democratic forces in their battles with the Crown (about which more in what follows). The Whig aristocracy, led by Locke's mentor, the first Earl of Shaftesbury, could even associate themselves with the Green Ribbon Club, whose eponymous symbol had been the insignia of the Levellers, worn by mourners in remembrance of the murdered Rainsborough. So the influence of Leveller ideas can be found not only in later radical traditions, in the American Revolution or in the philosophy of the modern British Labour Party and even socialist movements, but in more conservative political ideas which have attempted to appropriate, domesticate and neutralize the radically democratic ideas that emerged in the English Revolution.

Thomas Hobbes

The mobilization of the 'multitude' in Parliament's conflict with the Crown created radicals and royalists together. The English ruling class had a particular need for popular support in pursuit of its struggle against monarchical power; but that need itself divided the propertied classes between those who were willing to take the risk and those who found the king, even with his absolutist aspirations, a safer bet. Just as some MPs were from the beginning more anxious than others about the dangers of popular mobilization, some observers very quickly saw its theoretical as well as its practical implications. No one saw them more clearly than Thomas Hobbes, the man who, despite the almost universal unpopularity of his ideas in his own time and place, is regarded by many as England's greatest political philosopher – if not always for the substance of his arguments, then at least for their rigour, ingenuity and style. Fear of the multitude was very much on his mind.

Already in 1628, in the year of the Petition of Right, he had revealed his political inclinations, translating the *History of the Pelopponesian War* by Thucydides, whose main attraction for Hobbes was that he regarded democracy as, to use Hobbes's own words, 'a foolish thing'. In 1640, Hobbes wrote his first major political work, *The Elements of Law: Natural and Politic* (privately circulated until its publication in 1650), in which he defended absolute sovereignty, in response to the claims of the Short Parliament. A few months later, Hobbes was, as he would later claim, 'the first of all that fled', escaping to France when the Long Parliament convened in November 1640 and began its proceedings against Strafford and Laud. Hobbes evidently feared that Parliament would prosecute him, too, for the subversive (absolutist) ideas expressed in *The Elements of Law*. In self-imposed exile in France, he wrote *De Cive*, at a time when mobs at home were demanding the abolition of episcopacy, and when the House of Commons was giving formal expression to its appeal for popular support in the Grand Remonstrance.

In *De Cive*, Hobbes developed the principles outlined in *The Elements of Law*, elaborating an argument that effectively denied the political legitimacy of the multitude and those who claimed its support. This work, written in Latin and published a decade later in English as *Philosophical Rudiments Concerning Government and Society*, would also form (with some significant and telling variations in response to intervening events) the basis of his great classic, *Leviathan*, written at the end of his exile and published in 1651, after which he returned from France.

Hobbes was a remarkable and in many ways contradictory figure. In an autobiographical poem he describes himself as born a twin with fear in 1588, the year of the Spanish Armada, and fear was certainly to figure prominently in his life and his work. Yet there is nothing cautious about his provocative ideas. The son of a lowly cleric, he was not a wealthy man himself; but throughout his life, after his education at Oxford, he associated with and faithfully served aristocracy, especially as tutor and secretary to William, second Earl of Cavendish, and later to William Cavendish, third Earl of Devonshire. Yet his work displays a consistent, if paradoxical, egalitarianism which seems genuine and deeply rooted despite the reactionary political purposes to which it is applied. There can be no doubt of his commitment to royal absolutism; and while in France, he even served as mathematics tutor to the exiled Prince of Wales. Yet his arguments in favour of absolutism were so unorthodox, indeed so clearly inspired by radical ideas, that even royalists found him dangerous. Some even accused him of being democratic, to say nothing of those who attacked his views on religion as little short of atheism. In 1666, after the Restoration, the House of Commons cited Hobbes's atheism as a cause of the fire and plague of London, and only intervention by influential friends (including, possibly, the king, his former pupil) saved him from being punished for heresy.

Not only did Hobbes's defence of absolutism start from what looked like dangerously radical premises, but it also treated with contempt all more traditional justifications of monarchical rule. Not for him the divine right of kings or reliance on biblical precedent. Hobbes chose to found his argument on the latest and most advanced principles of science and mathematics – as might be expected from someone who was acquainted with Galileo and who even (apparently) served as secretary for a short time to Francis Bacon, besides carrying on a scientific correspondence with Descartes. Nor was his defence of absolutism incompatible with the execution of the king and his replacement by the 'Protectorate'. Hobbes's argument in *Leviathan* could, as we shall see, just as well legitimize an Oliver Cromwell as a Charles or James Stuart – and, in fact, it has been suggested that his classic work was written as part of the so-called Engagement controversy of 1649–52, in which people debated the propriety of taking an oath acknowledging the legitimacy of the existing Cromwellian regime. Finally, this purveyor of some very unappealing and misanthropic political ideas seems to have been a rather attractive, humorous and lively personality, a brilliant conversationalist, and a generous man (charitable to the poor, for instance, in a way that his famous successor John Locke – ostensibly more democratic, more kindly disposed to human nature, and certainly richer – never was). And whatever else we may say about him, he is without doubt one of the greatest prose stylists among English philosophers.

In the early 1640s Hobbes put his genius, and his taste for paradox, to work on the new ideological and theoretical problems thrown up by the politics of this turbulent moment in English history. The most obvious problem he confronted was how to defend absolute monarchy in the face of powerful and almost universal opposition to it. *The Elements of Law*, composed when Parliament was assembled for the first time in eleven years and the tensions leading to civil war were coming to a head, already laid out his defence of absolute sovereignty. Here, his main objective was to defend the king against the claims of Parliament. The role of the 'multitude' in this work was simply to transfer its powers unconditionally to an absolute sovereign. In *De Cive*, Hobbes elaborates this argument in a way that indicates a preoccupation with another, more far-reaching problem than the rights of Parliament against the Crown. Among the most difficult questions for a man of his persuasion had to do not just with Parliament but with the political role of the 'multitude' outside Parliament. This is an aspect of Hobbes's thought that commentators have neglected. Yet it was Hobbes who translated into theoretical terms the opposition, from both royalist and parliamentarian camps, to the multitude's invasion of the political domain. Parliament's reliance on popular support gave a new political function to people who up to now had lacked an acknowledged presence in the political arena, a recognized role as active citizens. Not only did the parliamentary opponents of the king claim legitimacy for their cause on the basis of the multitude's support, they also seemed to be moving in the direction of empowering the multitude itself. The gentry had shown itself at times willing to expand the franchise; and in moments of crisis, parliamentary leaders were ready to include in the political nation, at least temporarily, an even wider body of people, if not as electors then as agents of resistance to tyrannical rule. Eventually, the political personality of the 'multitude' as revolutionary agents would be given dramatic expression by the mobilization of the New Model Army; and finally, their spokesmen would demand full rights of normal citizenship.

In *The Elements of Law*, Hobbes confronted this process of political inclusion in its earlier stages. In his later work, he would face its more extreme and radical manifestations. We need to remember, too, that any political rights claimed by the multitude in England would belong not to Jean Bodin's 'colleges and corporate bodies' but to Sir Thomas Smith's 'multitude of free men collected together'. This could be taken to mean – as the Levellers insisted it did mean – that political rights belonged not just to some corporate entity or its official representatives but to each and every man just by virtue of being alive. Hobbes took on this challenge, too, and met these claims on their own terms.

The Elements of Law and De Cive

Both *The Elements of Law* and *De Cive* have the effect of denying the political role of the multitude – or, to put it more accurately, in these texts Hobbes finds a way of redefining and neutralizing that role. Where there had been other defenders of obedience to secular authorities who had relied on ascribing consent to a corporate body of the 'people', Hobbes adopts a more difficult solution, ascribing consent to a multitude of free and equal individuals, each endowed with natural rights unmediated by any corporate body or representative. He then sets out to demonstrate that the political task of the multitude is to create an absolute sovereign power; and it does this by handing over its own powers, wholly and unconditionally. The multitude expresses its political personality not by resisting tyrannical rule but by giving up its right to resist.

Hobbes's argument, especially in *De Cive*, is ingeniously constructed. He

starts with certain propositions about what human life would be like without government, in the so-called state of nature, depicting human nature in
the starkest and most dismal terms and bringing into sharp relief just those
qualities in human nature that make 'civil society', society with government,
necessary and desirable. Since all men seek glory and profit in comparison
with others, they would normally be inclined to strive for domination over
others more than simply for their company. So the principal feeling they
have for one another is not goodwill but fear. The main reason for this
mutual fear is that men are naturally equal (the great inequalities among
human beings are not natural but 'civil', that is, created in and by civil society and its laws). More specifically, they are equal enough to be able to kill
one another. Driven by the natural desire to avoid evil, their chief motivation
is the fear of death, the greatest evil in nature. This inclination to avoid evil
in general and death in particular is as natural and inevitable as the motion
by which a stone is impelled to roll downward.

Hobbes here introduces the idea of natural rights, but in his own
distinctive way. If self-preservation, or the avoidance of death, is a natural
impulse, it is reasonable for human beings to do everything necessary to
preserve themselves. When we speak of 'rights', we mean nothing more
than 'that liberty which every man hath to make use of his naturall faculties according to right reason' (I.7). So the foundation of natural right is
that every man must do his utmost 'to protect his life and members'. But,
of course, since every other man has the same right, the end result is that
no one is secure, and the state of nature is a state of war 'of all men
against all men'. The exercise of natural right proves to be self-defeating,
and some way must be found out of this impasse. Natural law dictates that
a way must be found to provide the security lacking in the state of nature.
The answer is civil society, where every person is protected against every
other by the coercive force of government.

There are, argues Hobbes, two ways for men to join together in civil society: either by coercion or by consent, that is, by conquest or by agreeing to
help one another. Government by conquest is perfectly legitimate and even
in a sense consensual (so much for the illegitimacy of the 'Norman Yoke'),
and those subjected to it are bound to obey their masters, unless they choose
to die. As for government established by direct consent, people may agree to
pursue the same goals and the common good; but there will inevitably be
constant disagreement and conflict among them, and constant dissent when
their private interests seem to diverge from the common good.

Human beings, in other words, have many and divergent individual or
particular wills; so the secret of civil society is to unite their wills into one
single will, to submit their own individual wills voluntarily to some single
person or council. The object is to create a kind of civil person, an artificial entity with a will of its own, apart from the individual people who

compose it. This entity, to which 'each particular man hath subjected his will' – whether that entity is embodied in a single person (as Hobbes clearly prefers, since a single person can more easily embody a single will) or in an assembly – 'is said to have the Supreme Power, or Chiefe Command, or Dominion; which power, and Right of commanding, consists in this, that each Citizen has conveyed all his strength and power to that man, or Counsell; which to have done . . . is nothing else than to have parted with his Right of resisting' (V.11).

Hobbes stresses that this supreme or sovereign power is absolute, unlimited by laws or constitutional restrictions. For power to be limited, it would have to be limited by some other power, which would then become sovereign. So in every state, whatever illusions people may have about it, there exists some ultimate authority which is sovereign and absolute. There is no 'mixed constitution' for Hobbes.

Here is a carefully elaborated defence of absolute rule, which provides a persuasive case for the kind of absolute power sought by Charles I, and against Parliament's demands for its rightful place in the mixed constitution. Yet, on the face of it, an absolute parliamentary sovereignty would do just well as an absolute monarchy. It would, at any rate, satisfy Hobbes's definition of sovereign power, if not his real preferences. But there is more to his argument than this; and its significance, in his historical context, is clear enough. At least as interesting and significant as Hobbes's definition of sovereignty is what he has to say about the multitude.

Hobbes has painstakingly constructed a theory of government by consent, created by a multitude of individual men voluntarily, in pursuit of their own self-interest. This much is consistent with the distinctive English idea of a commonwealth constituted by the 'people' as individuals rather than as a corporate body or a collection of corporate entities. So far, what he says might even be consistent with the views of the Levellers. Yet, for Hobbes, this multitude of individuals can and must establish an absolute sovereign power in order to constitute a political society, and this same multitude cannot by its own volition simply dissolve the sovereign power it has itself created.

Hobbes is very insistent about what a 'multitude of men' is and is not, what it can and cannot do. The multitude is many individuals, not one. As a single collectivity, it does not exist, except insofar as the individual wills and powers of which it is composed are transferred to some single artificial entity: 'a multitude of men (gathering themselves of their owne free wills into society) . . . is not any one body, but many men, whereof each one has his owne will, and his peculiar judgment' (VI.1). The multitude as a collection of individuals has no collective identity, no legal status. It 'cannot promise, contract, acquire Right, conveigh Right, act, have, possesse, and the like, unlesse it be every one apart, and Man by Man; so as there must be as many promises, compacts, rights, and actions as Men' (VI.1 note). Nor can anyone claim legitimacy for an act of rebellion on the grounds of support by the multitude. Since only individuals can act or consent, no one can claim the support of the 'multitude', nor can the 'multitude' claim any status apart from those – and only those – individuals who compose it.

In *The Elements of Law*, Hobbes showed that the rights claimed by Parliament belonged to the sovereign, in this case the king, by arguing that civil society and the sovereign power had been created by a transfer of power from the people to the sovereign. In *De Cive*, he finds it necessary to emphasize that, once civil society and the sovereign power have been established, the people or 'multitude' has no further political role. Where there is a sovereign monarch, that monarch acts for the 'people'. Where the sovereign power consists of more than one person, the 'people' can act only in the form of an assembly, such as Parliament. There are clearly no circumstances in which the people outside Parliament, in the streets or anywhere else, can act as a political body:

> When we say the People, or Multitude, wills, commands, or doth any thing, it is understood that the City [i.e., the state] which Commands, Wills and acts by the will of one, or the concurring will of more, which cannot be done, but in an Assembly. (VI.1 note)

If in *Elements* Hobbes was challenging the claims of Parliament against the Crown, in *De Cive* he is forced to turn his attention not only to a recalcitrant Parliament but, even worse, to the mob in the streets.

In *De Cive*, Hobbes is clearly preoccupied with 'sedition' and the prospects of civil war:

> Neither must we ascribe any action to the multitude, as it's one, but (if all or more of them doe agree) it will not be an Action, but as many actions, as Men. For although in some great Sedition, it's commonly said, That the People of that City have taken up Armes; yet is it true of those onely who are in Armes, or who consent to them. For the City [the state], which is one Person, cannot take up Armes against itselfe. (VI.1)

But why, then, cannot each individual withdraw his consent and overthrow the sovereign by means of many such individual acts combined (or perhaps, *in extremis*, an individual act of tyrannicide)? Even if, answers Hobbes, it were true that the sovereign power is merely the product of each man's agreement with every other to join in mutual self-help, the dissolution of that agreement would require every single individual to withdraw his consent – something that seems very unlikely. Furthermore, even if a rebellion were supported by a majority, that majority itself would have no standing. No such majority can claim to be acting on behalf of the whole multitude, because the principle of majority rule – the principle that everyone is bound by the majority's decision – is itself a product of civil society and cannot apply outside it or against an established government. The contract that establishes civil society is not just an agreement among individuals in a compact of mutual self-help. The sovereign power is certainly established by their mutual agreement, but it is an agreement to transfer their powers to someone else. So they are obligated not only to each other but to the sovereign power to whom they conveyed their powers and rights. 'Wherefore no subjects, how many soever they be, can with any Right despoyle him who bears the chiefe Rule, of his authority, even [i.e., especially] without his own consent' (VI.20).

It is hard not to admire the skill with which Hobbes has gone about his task. He not only accepts that the English state is a 'multitude of free men collected together' but even insists on giving that proposition its most radical construction: the commonwealth is a multitude of free and equal individuals, each possessing the same natural rights as all others – rights inherent in the individual person, not in his corporate status or in his property. Hobbes then constructs an absolutist argument on premises of which no Leveller would be ashamed.

Hobbes makes use of the proposition that the multitude is a collection of individuals rather than a corporate entity not in order to stress the political rights of the multitude but, on the contrary, to deprive the multitude of its political personality. To put it more precisely, in his theory the political function of the multitude is to cancel itself. The very act that establishes the multitude as a political entity is the act by which people give up their right of resistance. And he has turned the idea of individual rights on its head: yes indeed, every man possesses certain rights by nature, but he cannot enjoy his natural rights without effectively giving them up to a sovereign power.

It is worth pausing here to summarize again the ways in which Hobbes's argument is conditioned by the specific historical circumstances he is confronting. The immediate context is clear: Parliament, in its challenge to the absolutist aspirations of the king, has not only claimed its rightful share of the 'Crown in Parliament'. It has also mobilized the multitude outside Parliament and justified its own resistance by claiming the support of the many. Hobbes has undermined Parliament's case by repudiating both the mixed constitution and the political status of the multitude.

But there are also more fundamental, so to speak structural, reasons for this concerted attack on the rights of the multitude, rooted in specifically English conditions. In France, as we have seen, Bodin's groundbreaking theory of sovereignty had countered doctrines of resistance that vested the right to resist in corporate bodies and their representatives, by claiming that such bodies had no autonomous powers. All such lesser powers derived from the higher, ultimate, absolute and sovereign power. Bodin makes no attempt to argue that these corporate bodies somehow consented to an absolute monarch. Taking for granted that the state is a patchwork of fragmented jurisdictions, he simply argues that, among all the apparently independent powers and entities which represent merely particular or regional interests, there must be some superior power that unites them into one and represents the interests of the whole.

Hobbes, too, invokes such a sovereign power, but he does so in a different context. He is not dealing with a French state in which a growing absolute monarchy both supports and competes with a ruling class that claims its own autonomous powers and privileges. Hobbes's context is a unified English state, in which the ruling class has forfeited its independent powers to the state, accepting and even sharing in that unified state. This ruling class depends on private property and economic exploitation more than on the independent powers of jurisdiction or corporate privilege. This much is obviously clear to Hobbes, even if we do not accept the arguments of commentators who call him a 'bourgeois' thinker or attribute to him a precocious understanding of England's growing capitalism. It is also clear that the English ruling class, economically strong as it is in its control of land, and politically powerful as it is in its control of Parliament, does not enjoy the kind of independent jurisdictional and military power that would permit a successful challenge to the Crown without the support of the popular multitude.

So Hobbes has to cope not with Bodin's 'colleges and corporate bodies' but with Sir Thomas Smith's 'multitude of free men collected together'. If that multitude is, as Smith suggests, 'united by common accord and convenauntes among themselves, for the conservation of themselves aswell in peace as in warre', if individuals are united in a commonwealth by 'common and mutual consent for their conservation', Hobbes now has to show that their conservation requires an absolute sovereign power and that such a power is itself established by their 'common and mutual consent'. And now, in the midst of civil war, he has to confront the 'multitude' not only as a theoretical abstraction or as a passive mass but as a real political agent, a multitude of common folk whose political role is growing every day. His task is to acknowledge this reality while removing its sting.

Leviathan

When Hobbes was writing *De Cive*, the Civil War was just beginning. By the time he wrote *Leviathan*, events had moved far and fast. The New Model Army had been mobilized, the king had been executed, Parliament had passed acts to abolish the monarchy and the House of Lords, and Cromwell had established the Commonwealth. These events were accompanied by fierce debates, at every level, inside and outside Parliament, in broadsides, pamphlets and philosophical treatises – debates about the legitimacy of regicide, about the authority of Cromwell's regime and whether it was right to take the oath of 'engagement' to be faithful to it, about the extent and limits of political reform. And, of course, a wide range of radical ideas and movements had emerged, forcing onto the agenda much more far-reaching political programmes than even Cromwell had in mind.

In this new context, Hobbes revived, elaborated and modified the arguments of *De Cive*. By this time, he not only had to come to terms with the intervening dramatic events but with significant changes in his own circumstances. His earlier work had provoked violent reactions, especially among theologians, and he apparently lost his position in the exiled royal household thanks to their interventions. The hostility felt by Hobbes for critics of this kind is vividly evident in the ideas on religion outlined in *Leviathan*. That hostility, together with his willingness, or need, now to reconcile himself to Cromwell, gives that work much of its distinctive flavour.

Leviathan is, to be sure, a self-conscious effort to elaborate a science of politics with the same kind of certainty enjoyed by physics and mathematics. Its philosophical foundations are carefully and systematically constructed, in explicit or implicit debate with other philosophers as far back as Aristotle, with the most ostentatious applications of the latest scientific principles. Yet if all this makes *Leviathan* seem less like a political tract written for a specific occasion than a treatise designed for all times and all seasons, there can be little doubt of its political and personal urgency, to say nothing of its burning anger.

The argument of *Leviathan* is generally the same as that of *De Cive*, and much of the text is little more than repetition or paraphrase of the earlier work. But the few substantive divergences between the two books are significant. One of the most striking features of *Leviathan* is the space Hobbes devotes to religion. Something like half the book deals with the 'Christian Commonwealth'. This preoccupation reflects not only his anger at his theological critics but, above all, his conviction that religion has been a major cause of civil war. In his history of the Civil War, *Behemoth*, written after the Restoration, the corruption of the people by ministers, papists, and sectarians would head his list of reasons for that great disorder. There can be no doubt that religious liberty had been a principal objective in the revolutionary programme, and more particularly, religion had played a central role in legitimating rebellion against the king.

In *Leviathan*, Hobbes's main objective in the discussion of religion was to demonstrate that true Christianity requires obedience to secular authority. There can be no conflict between Church and state. A man cannot serve two masters, and there is no universal Church that can claim precedence over every particular secular power. The Church in every commonwealth is subject to its own civil sovereign. In this respect, Hobbes's views on religion merely sustain his absolutist political argument. Yet it is one of the many paradoxes in Hobbes's thought that the theological arguments he mobilized to make this absolutist case – materialist and secularist arguments inimical to orthodox brands of Christianity, whether Catholic, Anglican or Presbyterian – seemed to his critics to have more in common with the religion of radicals like Winstanley than with the theology of royalists like Archbishop Laud.

As for the main political argument, *Leviathan*, like *De Cive*, starts with the natural condition of humanity. This time, Hobbes spells out in greater detail the characteristics of human nature which make civil society necessary. Applying the principles of physics and its laws of motion, he tries to reduce human motivations to their most basic, as it were atomic, components, treating human passions – notably, of course, the impulse to avoid pain, the instinct of self-preservation, and the fear of death – as instances of matter in motion, the principles of attraction and repulsion. The result of this exploration is an account of the state of nature much the same as that depicted in *De Cive*: a state of war, 'of all against all'. This might not mean constant fighting, but it would generate a state of fear and uncertainty during which there would be no assurance that open war would not break out. Life would be, in Hobbes's most famous phrase, 'solitary, poore, nasty, brutish, and short'. And again he spells out the laws and rights of nature that must lead to the establishment of civil society. Without it, there can be no security of the person or property, let alone comfort and 'commodious living'. In the state of nature, there is no proper distinction between *mine* and *thine*, since every man gets what he can; so the right of property is a civil right which depends on the sovereign power.

Here, too, all men are naturally free and equal, all endowed with the same rights of nature, yet those natural rights are self-defeating without a sovereign power; and here, too, the state of war is ended by mutual agreement among individuals to transfer their powers to an absolute sovereign. Starting with the most extreme premises about natural equality, he ends with an equally extreme absolutism. His starting premises about natural equality, which imply that there is no systematic and universal inequality among human beings that could account for domination and subjection, even extends to the relations between men and women. Hobbes goes further than most political theorists in acknowledging the equality of women; but just as his convictions about the equality among men does not prevent him from justifying absolute rule by some over others, he can find reasons for the almost universal dominion of men over women. It is men who generally found commonwealths, probably because they are generally stronger and monopolize coercive force; and so civil law almost universally gives men dominion over their families. But the subjection of women to men, like the subjection of men to a sovereign power, is in principle consensual. In both cases, the basic reason for consent appears to be fear, either fear of the conqueror himself or fear of others from whom the subject person is seeking protection.

In *Leviathan*, as in *De Cive*, Hobbes is fighting his battle on several fronts. He is, at least implicitly, challenging various available anti-absolutist arguments, such as those of the monarchomachs in France; but he is also taking issue with existing absolutist theories, if only to fill loopholes in them and to make them more airtight against new and unprecedented challenges. A conception of sovereignty such as that of Bodin would certainly serve some of Hobbes's purposes. For example, it challenges the notion of a mixed constitution, and Hobbes is able to use something like Bodin's conception to argue against the claims of Parliament by demonstrating that power must be absolute and indivisible. Bodin's definition of law as simply the will of the sovereign is also useful to Hobbes. In the English context, it can be used against the common law tradition and against Parliament's claim to be the paramount interpreter of common law. But if the French doctrine of sovereignty is capable of serving many of Hobbes's purposes, there is one major thing it cannot do: it cannot cope with a multitude of free individuals who claim the right of resistance and even more active and continuous political rights.

Some commentators have argued that the individualism of Hobbes's argument was forced on him by monarchomach theories of resistance (as well as by his scientific aspirations, the thought experiment of breaking down the civil order into its atomic particles). These French theories of resistance were based on the idea that the royal power ultimately derived from the people as a collective entity. The people, though individually inferior to the king, were collectively superior to him. Therefore, as a corporate community they had a collective right to resist through the medium of their representatives. So Hobbes, it has been argued, set out to deny that such a corporate community existed in the first place. Outside civil society, he maintained, there exists only a multitude of individuals. Only a sovereign power can transform such a motley collection of individuals into a community. So the sovereign power is not created by or answerable to some pre-existing community. On the contrary, the sovereign power creates the community itself.

Now Hobbes was certainly thinking of the monarchomachs in some of his arguments. But it still remains unclear why it would not have sufficed simply to take over Bodin's argument against the monarchomachs. Why was it not enough just to say, as Bodin did, that the unity of the commonwealth can be created only by a sovereign power, without which there exists only a collection of disunited, fragmented and particular interests which cannot represent a single overarching common good? Why was Hobbes compelled to think in terms of individuals endowed with natural rights, and to defend absolutism by starting with a multitude of free and equal individuals?

Hobbes's argument about the multitude, as we have already observed, addressed some very specific conditions in England, conditions which French thinkers like Bodin were not compelled to confront. The monarchomachs, for example, asserted not the rights of individual citizens but the autonomous powers of nobles and various corporate bodies. The issue, in other words, was not so much the rights of persons as the rights of office, or, to put it another way, it was not so much a question of rights at all so much as a question of powers and privileges. If anything, resistance was a duty attached to public office, not an individual right inherent in humanity.

These French doctrines of resistance assigned no political role to the multitude; and in countering them, an absolutist thinker like Bodin did not have to deal with either a theory of individual rights or with the multitude's claims to political agency. The problem he faced was not so much popular activism as the pretensions of lesser nobles and municipal officials and their claims to own a fragment of the state. His task, then, was to challenge the autonomy of these corporate powers and privileges, which continued to play such an important part in the French polity. He simply had to deny their independence and to demonstrate that they ultimately derived from the sovereign power. In the fragmented polity of France, he was also able to counter their claims by invoking a larger, more comprehensive corporate entity, the kingdom as a whole, represented by the sovereign power.

Hobbes, as we have seen, faced a wholly different set of problems when he wrote *De Cive*. The structure of the English state and English property relations in general, as well as the immediate conditions of England in 1640 in particular, meant that the monarch, faced not with a host of fragmented jurisdictions but with a unitary representative and legislative body, had no greater claim than did Parliament to represent the body politic in its entirety, in the way the French king could claim to represent a larger corporate entity than did the estates or 'lesser magistrates'. English conditions also compelled Hobbes to deal with the 'multitude', and with the rights of citizens, in completely new ways. The intervening developments between *De Cive* and *Leviathan* obliged him to take the argument one step further.

In *De Cive*, Hobbes imagines a multitude of free individuals who contract with one another to transfer their powers, once and for all, to an absolute sovereign. From then on, the sovereign represents them and they have no right to call back the powers they have given away. Even in the unlikely case that every individual were to agree with every other to withdraw the powers they have granted to the sovereign, they still could not dissolve the sovereign power, because their mutual agreement to transfer their powers to someone else means that they have an obligation not only to each other but to the sovereign power they created and which they cannot remove without its consent.

In *Leviathan*, the argument undergoes some subtle but significant changes. One of them, emphasized by Quentin Skinner, is a modified definition of liberty. In *Elements*, Skinner points out, Hobbes never clearly defined freedom or liberty, while in *De Cive*, in order to counter 'republican' arguments that the very existence of absolute or arbitrary government reduces men to servitude, he offers a clear and simple definition of liberty as 'nothing other than *the absence of impediments to motion*'. However absolute the sovereign power may be, our subjection to it cannot be equated with servitude. Finally, in *Leviathan*, Hobbes defines liberty not simply as the absence of impediments to motion but the absence of *external* impediments. This is, for Skinner, 'a moment of great historical significance'.[7] Hobbes can now distinguish between liberty and power, the absence of impediments to action, on the one hand, and, on the other, the capacity to act. Intrinsic limitations or constraints – such as the fear that leads to submission – may take away our power, but only external obstacles can take away our liberty. This represents a landmark in the modern theory of liberty because Hobbes is here 'the first to answer the republican theorists by proferring an alternative definition in which the presence of freedom is construed entirely as absence of impediments rather than absence of dependence'.[8] In this way, Skinner argues, Hobbes sets in train the divergence between republican and liberal conceptions of liberty.

Hobbes also modifies his account of the agreement that creates the sovereign power. In *De Cive*, the agreement to establish a sovereign power was formulated like this: 'I conveigh my Right on this Party, upon condition that you passe yours to the same' (VI.20). In *Leviathan*, the wording is different: 'I Authorise and give up my Right of Governing my selfe, to this Man, or to this assembly of men, on this condition, that thou give up thy Right to him, and Authorise all his Actions in like manner' (XVII). The new element here is the idea of authorization: people create a sovereign to represent them not simply by transferring their powers to him but by authorizing him to act on their behalf, making themselves the authors of the sovereign's every action.

What is the effect of this apparently minor change of wording, and why did Hobbes feel obliged to introduce it? On the one hand, the new formulation appears to make the powers of the sovereign even more absolute or unlimited. In the earlier version, although there is no agreement between people and sovereign but only an agreement among the people to transfer their powers, Hobbes may have felt that there was still some hint of a compact with the sovereign when he suggested that the original agreement creates a 'double obligation', a bond not only between each subject and

7   Quentin Skinner, *Hobbes and Republican Liberty* (Cambridge: Cambridge University Press, 2008), p. 131.
8   *Ibid.*, p. 157.

every other but also between each subject and the sovereign. In the new formulation, Hobbes emphatically denies any suggestion of a mutual bond or obligation between subject and sovereign. He insists that the sovereign is party to no compact or covenant, has no contractual obligation to his subjects, is subject to no contractual conditions and therefore can be guilty of no breach of any covenant. The argument is strengthened by the claim that the sovereign's every act is not only his own but that of its 'authors', the subjects who 'authorized' him and whom he represents. So having been authorized to maintain peace and preserve the lives of his subjects, he has an unlimited right to determine the means to achieve those ends, without conditions and without interference from his subjects. He can, indeed must, even control the public expression of opinion. And he can do all these things as tyrannically as he likes without breaking any rules of justice. Hobbes expects his sovereign to rule by means of law that is known to his subjects, but there is no real check against the ruler's tyrannical behaviour except his own rationality. If every act of the sovereign is 'authorized', to accuse him of injustice would be to accuse the 'author' of committing an injustice against himself.

On the other hand, the very same formulation has another, apparently contrary meaning. The transfer of powers in *De Cive* is performed once and for all. The people have permanently alienated their powers and cannot under any circumstances take them back or bestow them elsewhere. In *Leviathan*, by contrast, subjects do not simply give away the power to act but always remain the 'authors' of the sovereign's acts. So the act of authorization may imply some limiting conditions after all. If subjects simply give away their powers, what the sovereign does with those powers is, in a sense, no longer their business. But if every subject remains the author of the sovereign's actions, those actions must, in the end, be consistent with the authors' purposes. If the authors authorized a sovereign power to preserve their lives and their security, the sovereign may have unlimited rights to decide how to do this; but the one thing the authors cannot have authorized him to do is to fail at this task.

And so, Hobbes tells us:

The Obligation of Subjects to the Soveraign, is understood to last as long, and no longer, than the power lasteth, by which he is able to protect them. For the right men have by Nature to protect themselves, when none else can protect them, can by no Covenant be relinquished . . . The end [goal] of Obedience is Protection; which, wheresoever a man seeth it, either in his own, or in anothers sword, Nature applyeth his obedience to it, and his endeavour to maintaine it. (XXI)

And clearly, any sovereign power – with its capacity to keep the peace – is subject to violent death, in foreign wars or in 'Intestine Discord'. When the sovereign power can no longer keep the peace or protect its subjects it no longer exists, and obligation ends (which may bring Hobbes closer to Spinoza). In the face of Hobbes's insistence on the unlimited and absolute nature of sovereign power, this concession may seem empty. It certainly does not mean that he is imposing 'liberal' standards of legitimacy upon the sovereign power, entitling subjects to resist a ruler that exceeds the limits of legitimate authority. At best, it means that rulers who fail to maintain their power have, *ipso facto*, lost their authority to rule. Yet in its historical context, this principle is significant enough; for one of its main consequences – and perhaps its main purpose – is to legitimate the power of Oliver Cromwell. In the earlier formulation, the sovereign authority no longer belongs to the people after the original agreement. Even a defeated Stuart king would continue to possess that authority once it had been granted and passed on to him by its original recipient. But now, in *Leviathan*, since the people's authority has never been truly alienated, it does not belong to the fallen king or his successors but still to the people. At least, authority passes, if not directly to the people themselves, then to whoever can preserve the peace, whoever can fulfil the purpose for which they created the sovereign power. By definition, it belongs to the victorious man or men whose sword can guarantee the 'protection' which compels obedience, in this case Cromwell, who would become the 'Lord Protector'.

With his concept of authorization, then, Hobbes has perfected his defence of absolutism built on radical premises. On the face of it, his conclusion is deeply anti-democratic: any de facto government, any government capable of maintaining order, no matter how tyrannical, must be regarded as legitimate. It must even be regarded as based on consent, authorized by its subjects. Yet Hobbes's absolutist theory of authorization has the effect of legitimating a revolutionary regime. As one intepreter of Hobbes's work has argued, 'The first modern revolution had taken place, and Hobbes believed it would be wrong to seek to reverse it.'[9]

While his conclusions were anything but democratic, Hobbes reached them by appropriating some of the most radically democratic ideas of his day. The Levellers had accomplished a revolution in political thought by insisting that consent to government must be given by a multitude of individuals rather than by some corporate body that claims to represent them, and that such consent must be given continuously – not just by reserving the right of resistance *in extremis* but in the form of the vote – and not in one act of submission that binds them indefinitely. Hobbes met the Leveller challenge with his theory of authorization, a theory of continuing consent

---

9 Introduction to *Divine Right and Democracy: An Anthology of Political Writing in Stuart England*, ed. David Wooton (Harmondsworth: Penguin, 1986), p. 58.

without voting. With that theory, he put the finishing touches on a justification of absolutism built on the premise that men are free and equal in the state of nature, that they are endowed with certain natural rights, and that they cannot be bound to obey any government to which they have not, as a multitude of individuals, given their continuous consent.

John Locke

Although radicals like the Levellers effected a revolution in political theory and set the agenda of political debate in England from then on, in practice they were roundly defeated, as Cromwell turned against the radical alliance which had brought him to power while frightening away the bulk of the parliamentary classes. With that betrayal, the Commonwealth lost the wider social base that might have sustained the republican revolution; but the irony is that even this was not enough to reassure less radical parliamentarians. The experience of the Civil War, with the revolutionary forces it had unleashed, ended by reuniting the propertied class, not behind the parliamentary project that had driven them to conflict with the king but, on the contrary, behind the restoration of the Stuart monarchy. Anything, even a renewal of the absolutist threat, was evidently better than a 'world turned upside down'.

The Restoration was not, of course, the end of the matter. It simply postponed until 1688 the realization of the parliamentary project begun in 1641. The years between 1660 and 1688 saw renewed and growing conflicts not so very different from the ones that had brought about the Civil War. By the late 1670s, there had emerged parliamentary opposition ready to take on the king yet again, and another decade of crisis finally ended in success. The so-called Glorious Revolution ended Stuart rule, bringing William and Mary of Orange to the throne, and with them, or so historical convention informs us, the kind of constitutional monarchy and parliamentary supremacy that remains in place today – the kind of political order, in other words, that the ruling class in Parliament had sought in 1641.

In the renewed conflicts between Parliament and Crown, there was yet another recurring theme. Among the aristocrats who led the parliamentary opposition in the 1670s and early 1680s, there were, again, some who were prepared to further their cause by forging alliances with radical forces, especially in London. Between 1679 and 1681, there was what amounted to a revolutionary crisis – the Exclusion Crisis – sparked by (ultimately failed) attempts to exclude from the royal succession Charles I's presumptive heir, his brother James, on the grounds that he was a Roman Catholic and, it was feared, likely to revive the Stuart's absolutist project. The most important leader of these radical Whigs, as they came to be called, was Anthony Ashley Cooper (1622–83), first Earl of Shaftesbury, a wealthy and 'improving' landowner who was also deeply involved in colonial trade, employer, patron and friend of the philosopher John Locke. The association between the two men was very close, and Locke appears to have been actively involved in Shaftesbury's political activities. Their dealings with radicals have persuaded some commentators that Locke's true sympathies lay with the radicals; and they have interpreted his political writings, specifically his famous *Two Treatises of Government*, on that assumption. But Locke's relationship with radical ideas is more complicated than that and requires closer scrutiny.

Locke, born in 1632 the son of a country attorney and small landowner on the fringes of the lesser gentry, began his career as an Oxford don. Although he started as a lecturer in Greek, rhetoric and moral philosophy, he began to study medicine informally. In 1666 he met Shaftesbury and soon joined his household as secretary, family tutor and physician – in which capacity he saved his employer's life by removing an abscess of the liver. Before and after his mentor's death in 1683, Locke held various government posts having to do with the colonies, plantations and trade, matters in which Shaftesbury, Lord Chancellor for a time in the 1670s, was keenly interested. Locke managed to amass a tidy, if moderate, fortune from his inheritance, his government salaries and various investments in lucrative commercial ventures. Because of his – or at least his patron's – involvement in subversive activities, he cautiously removed himself to Holland for a time in the 1680s, returning after the 'Glorious Revolution' and serving the new government.

Locke's intellectual interests were many and varied. He published significant works on economics and theology; an influential work on education, *Some Thoughts Concerning Education* (1693); and the ground-breaking *Letter on Toleration* (1689), a powerful plea for religious toleration. He was keenly interested in agriculture; and this interest, as we shall see, is reflected in his theory of property. Probably his most famous work, which became one of the most widely read books of the eighteenth century and a major influence in the Enlightenment, was *An Essay Concerning Human Understanding* (1690), a treatise on the origins and nature of human knowledge.

The *Essay* was addressed in part to the rejuvenation of the gentry which Locke believed was in decline: self-indulgent, extravagant and slothful. Among his aims was to show how ordinary literate people might become more 'industrious and rational' – in the words of his *Second Treatise of Government*. Locke was writing a kind of 'natural history' of the human psyche, in the tradition of Francis Bacon's 'natural histories' of plants, animals and various human practices and institutions. Like Bacon, Locke urges his readers to purify their minds by freeing themselves from the yoke of custom, fashion and received opinion. Then, as autonomous, self-directed individuals, they should reason about their own ideas and those of others.

Gentlemen are warned that without self-improvement, they will eventually be replaced by those of lower condition who surpass them in knowledge.[10]

Locke's argument is based on the by now familiar concept of the mind as a *tabula rasa*, a blank slate, at birth, on which sensations from the natural and social environment are imprinted. His view that knowledge derives from sense experience is the basis of 'empiricist' theories of knowledge, but it also implies that most human differences are due not to heredity but to different circumstances and education. At the same time, throughout his works, though cherishing the self-made man, he is convinced that the rich and poor will always be with us and that the former will always dominate the latter. Not only does he take for granted the relations between 'master' and 'servant', he even justifies slavery. Still, the ruling class, if only out of prudent self-interest, must govern in an enlightened and rational way, resisting tyranny while upholding political institutions limited by law and accountable to some kind of electorate, in a pluralistic society enjoying freedom of speech, association and religion. He stresses the value of labour, industry, thrift, sobriety and moderation, in sharp contrast, for example, to Hobbes's fondness for the classic heroic (and aristocratic?) virtues of courage, nobility, magnanimity, honour and glory.

Locke's most important intervention in political debate, the *Two Treatises*, was published anonymously in 1690; and he always denied authorship throughout his life, acknowledging it only in a codicil to his will. There has even been much debate about exactly when the *Treatises* (which, for all practical purposes, represent a single work) was written. It used to be thought that it was written not long before its publication, and thus represented a justification of the Glorious Revolution after the fact. It is now more generally accepted that the *Treatises* was written a decade earlier, probably in 1679–81 – that is, around the time of the Exclusion Crisis. This makes it not a retrospective justification of a revolution already safely completed but a subversive call to revolutionary action. If this is so, it certainly explains Locke's reluctance to admit authorship, especially since the Revolution never looked absolutely secure to its participants. Whatever Locke's motivations in writing this work, it was to have great influence in later centuries, across a wide political spectrum, not least in the American Revolution and in other revolutions thereafter.

One thing – and perhaps only one – is clear and uncontroversial about Locke's *Two Treatises of Government*. It is a powerful attack on absolute monarchy, a call for 'limited', constitutional, parliamentary government and the rule of law. These are the qualities that people have in mind when they

---

10 For a comprehensive discussion of these points, see Neal Wood, *The Politics of Locke's Philosophy: A Social Study of 'An Essay Concerning Human Understanding'* (Berkeley: University of California Press, 1983).

describe it as a founding text of 'liberalism'. Beyond that, the interpretation of Locke's political ideas remains a subject of fierce controversy. In particular, commentators are divided about how radically democratic Locke was – whether, for example, his political ideas came close to those of the Levellers or, on the contrary, represented the interests of the Whig aristocracy. Another major subject of debate has to do with Locke's position in relation to the 'rise of capitalism' – whether 'capitalism' is a meaningful category at all in discussions of the seventeenth century and, if it is, whether Locke can be considered a commentator on, or even an advocate of, those social and political changes we associate with capitalism in its early stages.

It will by now to be clear to readers of this book that its author regards the 'rise of capitalism' as a useful idea, for reasons laid out especially in Chapter 1 and earlier in this chapter.[11] It should also be blindingly obvious that to speak of the 'rise of capitalism', or to situate Locke in that historical context, in no way suggests that he or his contemporaries had any notion of 'capitalism' or any prescience about future historical developments. It simply means, as we have seen, that he lived at a time of significant changes in relations and conceptions of property, which were always fiercely contested, and that Locke was very conscious of the issues at stake in both practice and theory. He was, as will be argued in what follows, on the side of the 'improving' landlords; and his argument was ideally suited to the interests of a progressive landed aristocracy engaged in capitalist agriculture and colonial trade: in short, to the interests of men like Shaftesbury.

This is not to deny that Locke was, in the context of his time and place, some kind of 'radical'; but his radicalism, as we shall see, had more politically in common with Cromwell or Ireton than with the Levellers. What makes his political theory especially complex and interesting is that he arrives at Ireton's conclusions (though without any hint of repudiating monarchy) while starting from Leveller premises. He adopts radical ideas to make the strongest possible case against absolutism but is always careful to limit their most democratic implications.

The *Two Treatises of Government*

The *First Treatise*, less commonly read than the *Second*, is a detailed refutation of the case for royal absolutism in *Patriarcha*, written by Robert Filmer decades earlier but resurrected and published by supporters of the

---

11 For more detailed arguments on this score, and on Locke's political theory in general, see my articles 'Locke Against Democracy: Representation, Consent and Suffrage in the *Two Treatises*', *History of Political Thought* XIII.4, Winter 1992, pp. 657–89; and 'Radicalism, Capitalism and Historical Contexts: Not Only a Reply to Richard Ashcraft on John Locke', *History of Political Thought* XV.3, Autumn 1994, pp. 323–72.

king in the monarchy's new conflicts with Parliament. In painstaking detail, in language dripping with irony and ill-disguised contempt, Locke takes apart Filmer's ingenious and idiosyncratic argument that royal power descends from Adam and the patriarchal power bestowed on him by God. Locke's efforts here are devoted less to laying out a coherent political theory of his own than to challenging Filmer's logic, as well as his biblical scholarship, by demonstrating (sometimes unfairly) the absurdities and inconsistencies in *Patriarcha*; but the fundamental premises of the *First Treatise*, though spelled out more systematically in the *Second*, are clear: men are naturally free and equal, and no free man can be bound to obey a government without his own consent, so that no absolute government can be regarded as legitimate.

In the *Second Treatise* Locke is no longer just debating with one specific author, and he constructs a systematic and more or less coherent political theory. Like Hobbes, he begins with a 'state of nature' and outlines the conditions that make civil society necessary and desirable. But where Hobbes concludes that any government capable of maintaining order – and, more particularly, an absolute government – is better than the 'state of war' which would exist in its absence, Locke's purpose is precisely to deny the legitimacy of the kind of government Hobbes advocates. For Locke, a government's capacity to keep the peace is not enough to compel obedience to it, and something more is required to explain how men, born free and equal, acquire an obligation to obey.

Locke's argument is not always easy to follow. His concept of the state of nature is especially ambiguous. He is, to begin with, very keen to dissociate his conception of the state of nature from Hobbes's state of war. The state of nature, he insists, is a condition governed by certain laws of nature, certain divinely ordained moral precepts, which human reason can discover. Locke's account of human nature also seems far less grim than that of Hobbes. Human beings, it seems, are capable of living together without government, and they even take pleasure in each other's company. If Hobbes bases civil society on the worst in human nature, Locke founds it on the best of human qualities, reason and the capacity to live by moral rules. Yet this version of the state of nature appears to be less an account of some historical reality than a kind of moral ideal. Its main purpose is to serve as a standard against which to judge what counts as a legitimate government, a true civil society. Just as Hobbes's worst case scenario was designed to emphasize the necessity of absolute government, Locke's optimistic portrait is meant to rule out all absolutist forms as contrary to natural liberty, equality and reason.

At the same time, there seems to be another state of nature in Locke's theory, not just a moral ideal but something like a historical condition – if not an actual historical stage in human development then at least what the world would really be like without government. Here, the emphasis seems to be on human selfishness, perhaps based on a belief in original sin. If men really could live together governed only by their own reason and by the laws of nature, Locke now makes clear, civil society would be unnecessary. In the end, Locke's 'real' state of nature is not a million miles away from the condition of uncertainty that is Hobbes's state of war. Society without government is fraught with uncertainties and 'inconveniencies'. In particular, in the state of nature, where the only laws are natural laws, and where every man must execute the laws himself, there is no impartial judge to whom people can appeal in case of conflict, so each man must be judge in his own case. Such conditions are inevitably unstable, and no one can be certain that the smallest conflict will not end in war. Since Locke, as we shall see, imagines the (historical) state of nature as a form of social organization in which private property already exists, the likelihood of conflict is, of course, that much greater. So men (and it is indeed men) have found it useful, even necessary, to establish civil society.

Locke's account of the state of nature may not be as clear and consistent as it could be, but his message here is reasonably unambiguous: free, equal and rational men agree to establish civil society in order to avoid the inconveniences of the natural state, as they do in Hobbes's version of the story. But since rational men can never be understood as having agreed to something that would worsen their condition, much depends on how their 'natural' condition is presented. For Hobbes, any form of government capable of maintaining peace and order is better than the state of war. In Locke's case, what men are trying to avoid is not – or not simply – a state of war but a condition in which their obedience to natural law is made too uncertain and unsafe by the absence of a common and impartial judge.

This has important implications in establishing the criteria of legitimate government. Against the background of Locke's state of nature, free men can never be understood as having agreed to absolute government, a government not subject to the rule of law. In relation to a ruler who is above the law, people would still be in the state of nature, comparable to their relations with other men at a time when there was no impartial judge to settle conflicts between them. The ruler would here be judge in his own case. In fact, in such circumstances the government's use of its coercive powers on its own subjects – the use of its official powers of enforcement and punishment – would be 'force without right', and therefore nothing better than a state of war.

Locke's civil society, too, is established by agreement among free individuals, but unlike Hobbes's government founded by consent, the agreement to establish civil society is not simultaneously a transfer of power. Men, according to Locke, first agree to form a society and then, in a separate act, establish some form of government, not by unconditionally handing over their powers but as a kind of trust. Government, in other words, is entrusted, but only on certain conditions, with the powers each man enjoyed in the state of nature. If those conditions are violated, power returns to the people. They do not, however, thereby return to the state of nature. The dissolution of government does not, as seems to be the case for Hobbes, mean the disintegration of society. This account of the state of nature and the formation of civil society for Locke means, among other things, that men do have a right of revolution, a right to resist and overthrow a tyrannical or unlawful government; and they can do so without fear of dissolving society itself.

In the end, the differences between Hobbes and Locke have less to do with fundamental disagreements about human nature, or about what the world would be like without government, than with very immediate political considerations. Hobbes's objective is to legitimize absolute government, whether in the hands of a Stuart king or a Cromwellian 'Protector'. Locke is seeking to justify resistance to a Stuart king and the establishment of parliamentary supremacy. Both men make use of radical ideas and arguments, Hobbes to turn them on their head in defence of absolutism, Locke to strengthen his anti-absolutist case. But if Locke's anti-absolutist argument is more consistent with radical principles than is Hobbes's absolutism – more consistent, for example, with the Leveller view of 'self-propriety' and rights – his use of radical ideas is, in its own way, no less complex and ambiguous than Hobbes's.

Locke's political theory as outlined in the *Second Treatise* might be understood as a theoretical expression of the alliance between the Whig aristocracy and London radicals, a mobilization of radical ideas in order to advance the interests of the propertied classes. It is also useful to keep in mind that when Locke was writing, England was no longer in the throes of civil war, popular radicalism had been effectively suppressed and the threat from below was less immediate than the threat from above. This may have given him the confidence to appropriate revolutionary ideas which radical parliamentarians in the 1640s – men like Cromwell and Ireton – had rejected and feared. But the fact that Locke adopts the very Leveller concepts that Ireton, in the Putney Debates, so forcefully refuted does not by itself make Locke a Leveller. A major part of Locke's theoretical strategy is to adapt such radical ideas for the sole purpose of making the strongest case for Parliament against the king, and for the right of revolution, while at the same time depriving those ideas of their most democratic implications.

Readers will remember that, during the Putney Debates, Ireton warned against the consequences of adopting a conception of natural right. Followed to its logical conclusion, he insisted, it would end by endangering all property. Yet Locke adopts precisely such an idea of natural right. He even bases it on the Leveller principle that every man has a property in his own person, from which follow certain inalienable rights. Locke cannot have been familiar with the transcript of the Putney Debates, even if he knew about Leveller ideas; but such ideas were in the air, and his argument proceeds uncannily as if his object were to demonstrate that Ireton's fears (like Filmer's warnings) were unfounded. He seems to be saying that a doctrine of natural right, based on the Leveller concept of 'self-propriety', can be construed in such a way as to argue for a right of revolution against an absolute monarch but without any 'levelling' consequences, any danger to property, or any threat of popular democracy.

Ireton (like Hobbes and many others) took it for granted that the surest way to sustain the interests of the propertied classes was to insist that property, or at least its existing form and distribution, was simply a human convention, not derived from natural right but upheld by constitution and tradition. Locke, by contrast, sets out to demonstrate that property itself does indeed exist by right of nature, and he not only denies that the notion of natural right represents a threat to the existing social order but even finds a way of turning the concept of natural right to the defence of property and inequality.

We shall return to Locke's theory of property in a moment. But there are also other ways in which he adapts something like Leveller ideas to something like Ireton's politics. At the heart of Locke's political theory is his doctrine of consent. Again, no free man can be obliged to obey a government to which he has not consented. Much, then, depends on what is meant by consent – and, as we have seen, it could, in seventeenth-century England, mean almost anything. For the Levellers it meant that free men must have the right to vote. For Hobbes it meant that men have effectively consented to absolute monarchy or at least any existing government capable of staying in power and keeping the peace. What, then, does it mean for Locke?

Locke cites with approval Hooker's notion of consent which, though it meant something less extreme than it did for Hobbes, implied that men were bound by agreements made in the distant past. But Locke is far more concerned than Hooker to rule out absolute government, so there is obviously more to be said about his doctrine of consent.[12] We can probably learn more about Locke, again, by reading the *Second Treatise* against the background of the Putney Debates.

In response to the Leveller question of whether any free man can be obligated to a government to which he has not given his individual consent – a consent requiring constant renewal in the form of the franchise – Ireton replied that of course there are cases in which people are obliged to obey without consenting by means of the vote: foreigners, who certainly do not enjoy the right to vote, are expected to obey the law. They are free to leave the country if they choose not to obey. By contrast, men with a 'fixed,

---

12 For more on Locke's relation to Hooker, see my 'Locke Against Democracy', pp. 664–7; and 'Radicalism, Capitalism and Historical Contexts', pp. 331–3.

permanent' interest in the form of property cannot easily depart and leave everything behind; so their political obligation must be based on consent. Those without property, who merely have the 'interest of breathing', are more like foreigners in this respect. They are 'here today and gone tomorrow' and require no special rights apart from the right to depart.

Locke, at first glance, appears to be on the Levellers' side, with his insistence on the universal right of all free men to be governed by their own consent. Yet he finds an ingenious way of making universal consent consistent with Ireton's less democratic conclusion. Locke, like Ireton, cites the example of the foreigner who visits our shores. Locke, like Ireton, points out that such a person, indeed anyone who uses our highways and breathes our air, is expected to obey our laws. But there is one significant difference between Ireton and Locke: while Ireton cites this as a case of obligation without consent, Locke suggests that, even in such cases, consent has actually been given after all. The point is simply that there are two kinds of consent, 'express' and 'tacit', the latter probably derived from Hooker's notion of a 'secret' consent and the idea that people can give their consent even without knowing that they do so. Anyone who lives and breathes within our borders has given tacit consent to our government and has thus accepted the obligation to obey.

Locke has shown how, even with Leveller premises, we need not arrive at Leveller conclusions or suffer the consequences feared by Ireton. Ireton and the Levellers both argued on the basis that consent meant the franchise, so Ireton was compelled to demonstrate that obligation did not require consent. Locke adopts a different strategy: obligation does require consent but consent does not require the franchise. For that matter, Locke's argument is not inconsistent with the view that an individual can be 'represented' in Parliament without the right to vote, just as propertyless men could, according to Thomas Smith or Richard Hooker, be 'present' in Parliament or (as later thinkers would describe it) 'virtually' represented.

Locke never tells us in so many words what he thinks about the franchise, except for one passage (§158) that appears to propose nothing more than the correction of the notorious anomalies in the voting system, in much the same way that Ireton himself had suggested. We need to remember, too, that throughout the seventeenth century, regulations on the franchise fluctuated constantly, as the ruling class shamelessly manipulated the right to vote, its generosity growing whenever it needed popular support against the Crown, as was the case during the Exclusion Crisis. It is possible that Locke would have advocated this tactical expansion of the franchise at such a critical moment. But it remains significant that, with the doctrine of tacit consent, he neatly severed the connection between consent and the franchise, which both Ireton and the Levellers had taken for granted.

Locke seems to have a more elastic idea of consent than does Ireton. Had he not already laid a foundation for excluding absolutism as a legitimate form of government, his 'tacit' consent might come dangerously close to Hobbes's view that the mere existence of a functioning government implies consent. But however easily, even unconsciously, people may give their consent, according to Locke, there are, again, only certain kinds of government to which free men can be understood as having consented, and these do not include absolute monarchy, because such a government defeats the very purpose for which civil society was established in the first place.

When a ruler acts not according to the law but by his own arbitrary will, or when he interferes with a properly constituted legislative body or tries to change the means of electing it, when government subjects the state to a foreign power (all of which Stuart kings could be accused of doing), or when government, including legislative bodies, violates the trust reposed in it by invading the liberties and properties of the subjects, government is dissolved and the people have a right to constitute a new one. In general, as long as a properly constituted legislative power – Parliament in England – exists and is allowed to go about its business without undue interference, it can be assumed that no right of revolution exists, though there may be times when even legislators act contrary to their trust. In any case, if the normal processes of changing government have been denied to the people, they have a right to rebel and set up a new one by extra-parliamentary means.

It should be emphasized here again that granting people the right of 'revolution' need not entail granting them more normal, everyday political rights, as we already know from Cromwell and Ireton, who granted some people the right to take up arms against a government but not the right to vote for one. We also know that even the most radical convictions about *natural* equality need not be expressed in equally radical views of *political* equality. The view that men are naturally free and equal was, in the seventeenth century, consistent with everything from radical democracy to royal absolutism, everything from Winstanley to Hobbes – and Locke seems to stand somewhere between these extremes.

The disconnection between natural and political equality is even more vividly demonstrated in what Locke has to say about women. He may not go as far as Hobbes in explicitly granting the equality of women; but in his argument against Filmer's patriarchal defence of royal absolutism, Locke goes quite far in asserting joint parental or even maternal powers in the family against the kind of absolute paternal right on which Filmer bases his case for the absolute power of kings. Locke does not deny the superiority of fathers, or the 'foundation in nature' of the husband's authority over his wife. But he goes some distance in denying a divine command that subjected Eve to Adam, or women to men, and accuses Filmer of substituting his own 'fancies' for divine truths. Yet none of this has implications for the political rights of women. So much does Locke, like virtually all his contemporaries

– including, apparently, women themselves – take for granted the exclusion of women from the political sphere, that in giving them a more exalted role in the household he senses no political danger, no possibility of being misunderstood as proposing to admit women into the realm of politics.

Locke, beginning with the Leveller idea of 'self-propriety' and natural right, ends in a political position perfectly consistent with Ireton's more oligarchic stance. He does, to be sure, seem to hold a fairly radical view on the right of revolution in extreme emergencies, a right he is prepared to grant to the 'people' in general (that is, perhaps, to all free male heads of households), and not just to their representatives in Parliament. This was a view shared only by the most radical Whigs. But, as the examples of Cromwell and Ireton dramatically demonstrate, even a more radical view of revolution did not, in seventeenth-century England, necessarily rule out the exclusion of many free men from more normal political rights. After all, the rank and file of the New Model Army had been accorded a right of revolution in no uncertain terms, but the very same Army grandees who had mobilized them insisted on denying them the simple right to vote for their representatives in Parliament. When asked why the Army had fought, if they were to be denied political rights, Ireton replied that they had won enough by gaining the right to be governed by a representative body and a known law rather than by the arbitrary rule of one man, and the freedom to do business and acquire property. This, too, is what it means to be a member of political society; but to be an 'elector', endowed with the franchise, is another matter altogether.[13]

Locke's Theory of Property

Although the chapter on property seems to have been added to the *Second Treatise* after its original completion, it certainly plays a significant part in Locke's political theory. It is here that he fleshes out the theory of natural right which forms the basis of his anti-absolutist argument. He does so by elaborating the principle that every man has a property in his own person from which other rights follow. But if, for Locke as for the Levellers, the property that men have in their persons entails certain inalienable natural rights, it does not, as we have seen, necessarily entail all those political rights envisaged by the Levellers. A closer look at Locke's distinctive elaboration of 'self-propriety' and how it differs from that of the Levellers reveals a great deal about both his theory of property and his politics.

God, says Locke, 'hath given the World to Men in common' (§26). Yet the view that the world began as a common *dominium* was, as we have seen, fairly conventional in the Western tradition and could accommodate

---

13   For more on this point, see 'Locke Against Democracy', pp. 688–9.

everything from a strong defence of private property to Winstanley's radical repudiation of property. Locke sets out to demonstrate not only that men's common ownership of the earth is compatible with private property but that such property is grounded in natural right. Here he puts to brilliant use the idea of 'self-propriety'. 'Though the Earth, and all inferior Creatures be common to all Men', Locke begins, 'yet every Man has a Property in his own Person. This no Body has any Right to but himself. The Labour of his Body and the Work of his Hands, we may say, are properly his' (§27). Self-ownership, and the property that every man has in his own labour, then becomes the source of property in things and land. Anything in which a man 'mixes his labour', anything which, through his labour, he removes or changes from its natural state, anything to which he has added something by his labour, becomes his property and excludes the rights of other men. This is how private property grows out of common ownership, not by common consent but by natural right – as an extension of a man's person and his labour, in which he has an exclusive right by nature. In any case, although God did give the earth to men in common, he did not give it to them in order to waste it. He gave it to the 'industrious and rational' for the sake of 'improvement', to add to its value, usefulness and productivity by means of labour.

Locke does, to be sure, maintain that there are certain limits on accumulation established by natural law. The most obvious – apart from the physical limits of the capacity to labour – is that no man should accumulate so much that he cannot consume it and lets it go to waste or spoil. Nor should he accumulate so much that he damages the interests of his fellows. He must leave enough, and good enough, to respect everyone else's right to subsistence. These 'spoilage' and 'sufficiency' limitations seem to mean that a man's own capacity for labour together with that of his family, and his own capacity for consumption together with that of his household, set strict natural – and moral – limits on what he can accumulate. So it is hard to imagine how large accumulations and vast inequalities of wealth can be consistent with natural law.

Locke has a simple answer. There is one development in human society that changes everything: the invention of money. Money makes it possible for people to accumulate more than they themselves can consume without violating the natural law of prohibition against spoilage. The decision to attach some kind of value to gold or silver as a medium of exchange means that wealth can be accumulated in a form that keeps indefinitely. It also permits exchange and profitable commerce, which in turn create an incentive for increasing productivity and wealth. Without money and commerce, there would be neither possibility nor motivation for 'improvement' and accumulation.

The improvement of land encouraged by money and commerce also means that less land can support more people. On the one hand, this might be taken to mean that, although people now can accumulate more without violating the spoilage limitation, they have no need to do so in order to live well. They can produce more wealth, and they can therefore leave more for others. Locke has indeed been interpreted as opposing large concentrations of property in this way. On the other hand, Locke suggests that money, commerce and 'improvement', by making land more productive and giving it more value, actually add to the 'common stock' of humanity. This means that people can accumulate more without depriving others and without violating the 'sufficiency' limitation. A man who accumulates and improves large holdings, far from violating the rights of others, actually enhances their well-being.

In such conditions, furthermore, many people can even live without any property at all, because they can exchange their labour for a wage. It turns out that the labour which gives a man a right to property may be someone else's labour. Locke clearly takes for granted that some will have large properties and others none at all. Indeed some will create the wealth of others by working for them. 'Master and Servant', he writes, 'are Names as old as History' (§85), and servants (a term that, in the seventeenth century, included many wage labourers) can sell their labour without losing their natural liberty, as long as the relation between master and servant is a contractual one, not an unconditional and permanent alienation but a sale of labour for a certain time. (Locke also justifies slavery, but on different grounds: a man who loses his liberty by conquest in a lawful war may be spared his life in exchange for his permanent servitude.) And where land is 'improved' and profitably utilized, even the servant may be better off than the owners of unimproved land.

Nor does Locke stop there, for the invention of money has yet another implication. Since money has value only because men have consented to it, this also implies that they have consented to its consequences: 'it is plain, that Men have agreed to disproportionate and unequal Possession of the Earth, they having by a tacit and voluntary consent found out a way, how a man may fairly possess more land than he himself can use the product of' (§50). Although specific laws and constitutions regulate specific systems of property, the inequality to which men have consented is not dependent on any such specific laws. It applies wherever money exists. This appears to mean that no government can override that agreement by seeking to alter the conditions of inequality to which men have agreed. The invention of money and everything that follows from it changes conditions so radically that natural law, together with man's natural freedom, equality and common possession of the earth, become consistent not only with private property but also with gross inequalities. And all of this has the legitimacy that comes from free consent.

Locke was not the only, or even the first, to suggest that property originates in labour; but he was certainly the first to elaborate this principle so
systematically, both as a theory of property and as a theory of natural
right. He also, as we shall see, gives a very specific twist to the idea that
property originates in labour, which sets him decisively apart from his
predecessors. Locke's conception of natural right is central to his argument against absolutism; but the implications of his theory of property go
well beyond his anti-absolutist politics. Here, again, we can learn a great
deal about Locke by considering his theory against the background of the
Putney Debates.

Readers may recall Major William Rainsborough's remark at Putney that
'the chief end of this government is to preserve persons as well as estates,
and if any law shall take hold of my person, it is more dear than my estate'.
The Levellers certainly believed in the right of private property, but Major
Rainsborough was here giving the *person* priority over property, and this
was precisely the principle Ireton most feared. Here, as elsewhere, Locke
finds a way of circumventing this consequence of Leveller doctrine.

Locke states unequivocally that the 'chief end' of civil society 'is the preservation of Property' (§85). This seems unambiguous enough, and at first
glance appears to leave no room for rights that inhere in the person as
distinct from property. Yet when, in his controversial chapter on property, he
defines property itself, Locke often uses a broad definition which includes
'life, liberty and estates'. Formulae such as 'life, liberty and property', or
'persons, liberties and estates' had become conventional in asserting the
rights of the subject since the Petition of Right, appearing, for example, in
the Grand Remonstrance; and Lilburne had asserted the 'ancient' fundamental right of every Englishman to be protected from arbitrary and illegal
intrusions on his 'life, liberty or estate'. Locke's inclusion of all these rights
in the single category 'property' certainly implies that the purpose of
government is, as Major Rainsborough insists, 'to preserve persons as well
as estates', that every man, even one without 'estates', possesses something
that government is obliged to preserve, and that therefore such a person has
certain basic rights. It is on the basis that rights inhere in the person, with or
without a 'fixed interest' in the form of property, that Colonel Thomas
Rainsborough demands an extension of the franchise even to the 'poorest
he'. Ireton sees the danger of invoking rights that inhere in the person just
by virtue of living and breathing, which implies that such rights exist by
nature and not by convention or the English constitution. But Locke has
found a way of ascribing natural rights to the person while avoiding the
hazard foreseen by Ireton and has, yet again, made Leveller principles
consistent with Ireton's politics. His doctrine of consent, for instance,
makes it possible to speak of such natural rights without requiring anything
more than what Ireton is willing to concede: that the rights of every person

are adequately protected by the existence of a representative body and a known law rather than by the arbitrary rule of one man.

As for property, when Locke describes it as a natural right, he seems to mean something rather different from what the Levellers intended, or more particularly, he is answering a different question. In the debate between Rainsborough and Ireton, both parties seem to agree that the institution of private property is divinely ordained (though this does not preclude the belief that in the beginning the earth was given to men in common). For example, in response to the accusation that the doctrine of natural right endangers all property, Rainsborough insists that he has no such intention and that the demand for a voice in government certainly does not imply the destruction of property. Property, in fact, exists by divine law: 'The law of God says it, else why God made that law, thou shalt not steal?' Although Ireton repudiates the idea of natural right as the basis of property, he does not deny this divine commandment, nor does he suggest that property as such has no divine authority. But this, for him, is not the main issue. The question is whether the existing distribution of property and, more particularly, the distribution of political rights that goes with it are legitimate.

Ireton argues that the institution of property in general may exist by divine law, but the particular right of any individual to any particular property is no more divinely ordained than is the right to elect Parliament. 'Divine law', he says, 'extends not to particular things.' It 'does not determine particulars but generals, in relation to man and man, and to property, and all things else'. Any connection between divine law and a particular man's property is very remote, and 'our property descends from other things'. Particular rights to property, no less than political rights, derive from convention and historical precedent. If we challenge those conventions and precedents by appealing to some transhistorical natural right, we shall endanger all property. After all, if every man has a natural right to whatever he needs for his subsistence, then surely no private property can be secure.

Colonel Rainsborough does indeed invoke some kind of natural right, though he denies any intention of endangering private property. But the significant point is that neither he nor the other Levellers invoke natural right as a way of explaining how people come to have a property in some particular thing. Certainly, the Levellers dispute the legitimacy of the historical and constitutional precedents invoked by Ireton to support the existing distribution of property and political rights. The Levellers offer different historical precedents, and they claim certain 'native' rights which have been violated by the Norman Conquest. They do call on a notion of natural right or self-propriety to support their historical claims; but the main object of that notion is liberty, not private property.

The Leveller argument was most clearly laid out by Richard Overton in his pamphlet *An Arrow Against All Tyrants*, whose eloquent and frequently cited definition of 'self-propriety' was quoted earlier. Overton certainly insists that 'mine and thine' could not exist if men had no inviolable property in their own selves, but he simply means that no man can securely enjoy what he possesses if his natural freedom is subject to usurpation and his person to arbitrary violation. As to the origin of material property itself, Overton says nothing; but we can get some sense of what he thinks from his reference to the principles of Magna Carta, repeated in the Petition of Right, and his quotation from Sir Edward Coke's commentaries:

> No man shall be disseised, that is, put out of seisin [have taken from him], or dispossessed of his free-hold, that is, lands or livelyhood, or of his liberties or free customes, that is, of such franchises and freedomes, and free customes, as belong to him by his free birth-right; unlesse it be by the lawfull judgements, that is verdict of his equals (that is of men of his own condition) or by the Law of the land . . . by the due course and processes of law.

The relevant property rights here are various civil and customary rights, recognized by statute or customary law (freehold tenures, the 'freedom' of corporations, 'franchises' or licences to conduct business, and so on). Overton says nothing about the natural origin of property. He only insists that a man's natural freedom gives him an inalienable right to 'the due course and processes of law' and that no interference with his property is legitimate without such processes. The emphasis, again, is not on property as such but on liberty and the illegitimacy of arbitrary power.

The Leveller argument seems to be something like this: every man has a property in his own person. From this follow certain liberties: the liberty not to be subject to anyone else's authority without consent, the liberty to follow one's own religious beliefs, and, indeed, the liberty to enjoy one's possessions without unlawful interference, that is, without interference by any power not properly constituted, accountable and acting according to the due processes of law.

Certainly, the Levellers undoubtedly dispute the legitimacy of the historical and constitutional precedents invoked by Ireton, and they do so by claiming 'native' rights which have been violated by the Norman Conquest. The argument based on self-propriety makes clear what the Levellers think about legitimate power, but it does not explain how some people come to have legitimate possessions. It does mean that political rights cannot be based on property in the sense of 'estates'. These rights belong to the person. And it also means that the existing distribution of property represents little more than theft, acquired by conquest and preserved by illegitimate power. The Levellers want to dissociate political power from wealth and privilege, and they want to protect small property from unjust and oppressive interference.

But there is nothing in their arguments that would be inconsistent with Ireton's principle that particular properties exist by convention. The point is simply that some conventions are legitimate and others not, depending on whether they respect or violate natural liberty.

If demonstrating the natural origin of particular properties was not the objective of radicals like the Levellers, John Locke's purpose is rather more complicated, though the issue has been somewhat confused by commentators who emphasize the continuity between Leveller ideas of self-propriety and the Lockean theory of property. Locke sets out precisely to answer the difficult question of particulars: 'how any one should ever come to have a Property in any thing' (§25). His reasons are complex, but one clear objective is to strengthen the inviolability of property by making it independent of, and prior to, civil society: if men have a right to property before and apart from civil society, which belongs to them by nature and not by grant from government or the community, that simply reinforces the principle that no government can interfere with property unlawfully.

Locke is also undoubtedly trying to meet, yet again, a challenge from Filmer. In support of his claim that political power and property descended by grant from God to Adam, Filmer takes issue with all those who claim – and this, in one way or another, includes thinkers as diverse as Hobbes and Ireton, and perhaps even the Levellers – that property exists by the consent of men, because this implies that possession of the earth was originally common. Filmer simply argues that, if this were so, private property would be an unimaginable sin against God's will; and, at the very least, it would have required the universal consent of mankind, of which there is absolutely no evidence. Locke, in his refutation of absolutist theory in general and Filmer in particular, takes on this argument too. He demonstrates how it is possible for private property to be consistent with God's grant of the earth to men in common, 'how Men might come to have a property in several parts of that which God gave to Mankind in common, and that without any express Compact of all the commoners' (§25).

But there is more to Locke's conception of natural right than its role in his case against absolutism, as becomes evident when we compare him, again, to the Levellers. We may begin to understand the differences between Locke and the Levellers by considering one simple fact: the Levellers had no strong incentive to accept Ireton's argument that natural right was an enemy to custom and convention. They certainly wanted to repudiate some conventions and customs, those that established the current system of power and privilege. But one of their main objectives was to *protect* certain customs, the customary rights and tenures of ordinary 'free-born' Englishmen, which were being attacked by the dominant classes. So the Levellers were not really interested in demonstrating that natural right took precedence over custom in general. What they wanted to show was that certain customary rights had the support of more universal, even natural, principles, and that the extinction of these rights without due processes of law and by an illegitimate government was a violation of natural liberty. Locke appears to have no comparable attachment to customary rights. His theory of natural right does indeed endanger custom and convention, but not in the sense feared by Ireton. Locke's theory of natural right threatens not the properties of landlords like Shaftesbury but the customary rights of commoners. At any rate, Locke adapted and modified the Leveller idea of 'self-propriety' in an ingenious way, again preserving the delicate balance which is characteristic of his political theory in general: on the one hand, a radical anti-absolutism, and on the other, a careful limitation of its democratic implications.

Locke's theory of property gives substance to the notion of natural right which he deploys so powerfully in his attack on absolutism. To invoke a natural and inalienable right to 'life, liberty and estate', which no government is entitled to violate, certainly adds strength to the case against absolutism. The argument that property is rooted in an individual right which belongs to every man was also designed, again, to counter Filmer's claim that all political power and property are derived from God's grant to Adam and not from some universal (male) human right.

There may be other political reasons for Locke's argument too. It has, for instance, been suggested that the chapter on property, and the importance Locke attaches to labour as the source of property, represents a gesture to the 'industrious' classes whom Shaftesbury's party was courting in its attempts to forge an oppositional alliance during the Exclusion Crisis (though we shall see in a moment that 'labour' has a rather flexible meaning in Locke's theory of property, which fits the 'improving' landlord no less than the 'industrious' classes who work with their own hands). At the same time, the chapter on property also helps to neutralize some of the more democratic possibilities inherent in the radical conception of natural right. The theory of property includes a neat justification of gross inequality, which makes Locke's revolutionary theory compatible with the existing distribution of property in England.

In all these ways, the chapter on property has an important political meaning for Locke, but it also has implications that go far beyond its consequences for his theory of politics. The chapter represents a major rethinking of property in principle, which has to do with distinctively English historical developments.

Improvement

Locke's argument on property turns on the notion of 'improvement'. The theme running throughout the chapter is that the earth is there to be made productive and that this is why private property, which emanates from labour, trumps common possession. The very word 'improve', it is worth noting, in its original sense (derived from the Anglo-French *emprouwer*) means to 'turn to profit' or to 'manage for profit'; and this is clearly the sense in which Locke and his contemporaries used it. Locke repeatedly insists that most of the value inherent in land comes not from nature but from labour and improvement: 'tis *Labour* indeed that *puts the difference of value* on everything' (§40). It is clear, too, that the 'value' he has in mind is exchange or commercial value. He even offers specific calculations of value contributed by labour as against nature. 'I think', he suggests, 'it will be but a very modest Computation to say, that of the *Products* of the Earth useful to the Life of Man, $9/10$ are the *effects of labour*', and then immediately corrects himself: it would be more accurate to say that 99/100 should be attributed to labour rather than to nature (§40). An acre of land in unimproved America, which may be as naturally fertile as an acre in England, is not worth 1/1000 of the English acre, 'if all the Profit an *Indian* received from it were to be valued and sold here' (§43). Unimproved land is waste, so that a man who takes it out of common ownership and appropriates it to himself – he who removes land from the common and encloses it – in order to improve it has given something to humanity, not taken it away.

We already know that, for Locke, there is no direct correspondence between labour and property, because one man can appropriate the labour of another. It now appears that the issue for Locke has less to do with the activity of labour as such than with its profitable use. In calculating the value of the acre in America, for instance, he refers not to the Indian's labour, his expenditure of effort, but to the (lack of) profit he receives, in the absence of a well-developed commerce. The issue, in other words, is not the labour of a human being but the productivity of property and its application to commercial profit.

In a famous and much-debated passage, Locke writes that 'the Grass my Horse has bit; the Turfs my Servant has cut; and the Ore I have digg'd in any place where I have a right to them in common with others, become my *Property*' (§28). Much ink has been spilled on this passage and what it tells us, for example, about Locke's views on wage labour (the labour of the servant who cuts the turfs). But what is truly striking about this 'turfs' passage is that Locke treats 'the Turfs my Servant has cut' as equivalent to 'the Ore I have digg'd'. This means not only that I, the master, have appropriated the labour of my servant, but that this appropriation is in principle no different from the servant's labouring activity itself. My own digging and my appropriating the fruits of my servant's cutting are, for all intents and purposes, the same. But Locke is not interested in simply passive appropriation. The point is rather that the landlord who puts his land to productive use, who improves it, even if it is by means of someone else's labour, is being industrious, no less – perhaps more – than the labouring servant.

We have become so accustomed to the identification of 'producers' with the employers of labour (as in 'automobile producers' in conflict with trade unions) that we fail to see its implications, but it is important to keep in mind that certain very specific historical conditions were required to make it possible. Traditional ruling classes in pre-capitalist societies, passively appropriating rents from dependent peasants, would never think of themselves as 'producers'. The kind of appropriation that can be called 'productive' is distinctively capitalist. It implies that property is used actively, not for 'conspicuous consumption', nor simply to obtain the means of 'extra-economic' coercion, but for investment and increasing profit. Wealth is acquired not simply by using coercive force to extract more surplus labour from direct producers, in the manner of rentier aristocrats, but nor is it acquired by 'buying cheap and selling dear' in the manner of pre-capitalist merchants. Wealth is created by increasing labour productivity (output per unit of work), to produce profits that are realized in market transactions.

By conflating 'labour' with the production of profit, Locke becomes perhaps the first thinker to construct a systematic theory of property based on something like these capitalist principles. He is certainly not a theorist of a mature, industrial capitalism; but his view of property, with its emphasis on productivity for profit, already sets him apart from his predecessors. His idea that value is actively created in production is already vastly different from traditional views which focus simply on the process of exchange, the 'sphere of circulation'. (Only William Petty, often called the founder of political economy, had suggested anything like this 'labour theory of value' in the seventeenth century.) Locke in his economic works is critical of those landed aristocrats who passively collect rents without improving their land, and he is equally critical of merchants who simply act as middlemen, buying cheap in one market and selling at a higher price in another, or hoarding goods to raise their price, or cornering a market to increase the profits of sale. Both types of proprietor are, in his view, parasitic. They are anything but 'producers'. Yet his attack on proprietors of this kind should not be misread as a defence of working people against the dominant classes. He certainly praises industrious artisans and tradesmen, but his ideal seems to be the great improving landlord, whom he regards as the ultimate source of wealth in the community, what he calls the 'first producer' – a man like Shaftesbury, capitalist landlord and investor in colonial trade, a man who is not only 'industrious' but whose vast property contributes greatly to the wealth of the community.

Locke's view of property is very well suited to the conditions of England in the early days of agrarian capitalism. It clearly reflects a condition in which highly concentrated landownership and large holdings were associated with a uniquely productive agriculture (productive not just in the sense of total output but output per unit of work). He also, like Sir Thomas Smith, takes for granted the triadic structure of English agriculture, the triad of landlord, tenant, and 'servant' or wage labourer, which, though not widespread throughout the country was well established in the southern and south-western parts of England that Locke knew best. His language of 'improvement' echoes the scientific literature devoted to the techniques of agriculture which flourished in England at this time, especially emanating from the Royal Society and the groups of learned men with whom Locke and Shaftesbury were closely connected. More particularly, his constant references to common land as waste, his praise for the removal of land from the common, and indeed for enclosure, had very powerful resonances in that time and place.[14]

We need to be reminded that the definition of property was, in Locke's day, a very immediate practical issue. A new definition of property was in the process of establishing itself, challenging traditional forms not just in theory but in practice. It was constantly arising, for example, in disputes over common and customary rights. Increasingly, the principle of 'improvement' for profitable exchange was taking precedence over other principles and other claims to property, whether those claims were based on custom or on some fundamental right of subsistence. Enhancing productivity itself became a reason for excluding other rights.[15]

There are in the seventeenth century already examples of legal decisions, in conflicts over land, where judges invoke principles very much like those outlined by Locke, in order to give exclusive property precedence over common and customary rights. Such arguments were used to support the landlord seeking to extinguish the customary rights of commoners, to

---

14 At one point in his argument, Locke acknowledges that there may be, as in England, common land recognized by law, and in such circumstances, it cannot be enclosed without consent (§35). But this qualification is not as restrictive as it may seem at first sight. As I argue in 'Locke Against Democracy': 'Even if we leave aside the kinds of co-ercion that were available to larger landowners in relation to vulnerable poor men, which could compel the latter to consent . . . [t]here were, of course, already massive concentrations of land outside the reach of communal rights, and there were also many cases in which common rights on land already legally owned, often by a large landlord, existed by custom but without unambiguous legal standing. The extinction of such customary rights was, above all, what enclosure was about and the reason for the conflicts it generated. There is nothing in the *Second Treatise* that would tend towards the protection of these customary rights, and a great deal, having to do with the benefits of enclosure and its contribution to the wealth of the community, that would argue in favour of their extinction, in the interests of the commonwealth. In fact, as we have seen, it was precisely the kind of argument from improvement employed by Locke that was increasingly being used as a legal challenge to customary rights' (pp. 681–2).

15 E.P. Thompson charts the transformation in the idea of property rights as it manifested itself in practice in 'Custom, Law and Common Right', in his *Customs in Common* (London: Merlin, 1991).

exclude them from common land, to turn common land into exclusive private property by means of enclosure. Enclosure, exclusion and improvement, as Locke had said, enhanced the wealth of the community and added more to the 'common stock' than it subtracted. In the eighteenth century, when enclosure would rapidly accelerate with the active involvement of Parliament, reasons of 'improvement' would be cited systematically as the basis of title to property and as grounds for extinguishing traditional rights. This is not the only way in which Locke's theory of property supported the interests of landlords like Shaftesbury. We have already alluded to Locke's justification of slavery. His views on improvement could also be easily mobilized in defence of colonial expansion and the expropriation of indigenous peoples, as his remarks on America and its native peoples make painfully obvious. If the unimproved lands of the Americas represented nothing but 'waste', it was a divinely ordained duty for Europeans to enclose and improve them, just as 'industrious' and 'rational' men had done in the original state of nature. 'In the beginning all the World was *America*' (§49), with no money, no commerce, no improvement. If the world – or some of it – had been removed from that natural state at the behest of God, anything that remained in such a primitive condition must surely go the same way. Locke may not have been alone in devising a justification of empire that had less to do with jurisdiction than with property, but he went far beyond the simple principle of *res nullius* invoked by other defenders of colonial appropriation. The issue for him was not simply vacant or unused land but rather land left unimproved for profitable commerce. Nor was he simply arguing, as Grotius had done, that things become property when and because they are used and transformed. The right of property – and that includes colonial appropriation – for Locke derived from the creation of value.[16]

John Locke constructed a powerful defence of parliamentary, 'limited' government, but without embracing democracy. It would take a very long time, and a great deal of struggle, before parliamentary government was democratized even to the point of universal male suffrage of a kind approaching what the Levellers had demanded, to say nothing of the vote for women. When these victories were won at last, they were certainly worth winning; but by that time, the franchise could no longer make the kind of difference that the Levellers had hoped it would. The issue had by then been settled in favour of capitalist property. The old political struggles over common and customary rights had been lost, and many spheres of social life were subject

---

16 Something like Locke's argument was used decades earlier to justify the English colonization of Irish lands. Sir John Davies, one of the architects of English policy in Ireland, justifies expropriation and settlement in strikingly Lockean terms, precisely by measuring the value created by improvement. I discuss these points at greater length in my *Empire of Capital*, chs 4 and 5.

not to the requirements of democratic accountability but to the imperatives of capitalist competition and profit-maximization.

The Lockean Paradigm in Eighteenth-Century England

Much of the scholarly debate about eighteenth-century Western political thought, and Anglo-American thought in particular, has for some time now revolved around the relation between virtue and commerce, a debate in which John Pocock is the major reference point.[17] Pocock's narrative as it concerns eighteenth-century England goes something like this:

In the mid-1690s there was a financial revolution that produced a 'sudden and traumatic discovery of capital', in the form of public credit and with it the growth of government patronage. The critical and emblematic moment was the establishment of the Bank of England. This represented nothing less than a revolution in the nature and idea of property. The essential shifts in the structure and ideology of English property which some people see earlier in the seventeenth century, or even in the sixteenth, were, it would seem, of little consequence. The *real* transformation of property, the transformation of its structure and morality, occurred with 'spectacular abruptness' in the mid-1690s and was accompanied by sudden changes in the psychology of politics. This revolutionary shift marked the beginning of commercial society. It was the moment when relations among citizens, and between them and government, began to take the form of capitalist relations – which, in Pocock's terms, means relations between creditors and debtors.[18]

Political discourse, says Pocock, had to find ways of dealing with this transformation, to contest or justify a new commercial, oligarchic and imperial Britain. The vocabulary of classical republicanism was mobilized to deal with a revitalized conflict between landed and 'monied interests', preceded and shaped by a conflict between real property and government

---

17 See Pocock's collection of essays, *Virtue, Commerce and History: Essays on Political Thought and History, Chiefly in the Eighteenth Century* (Cambridge: Cambridge University Press, 1985).

18 Pocock has suggested that his approach to history is more 'diachronic' than 'synchronic' in the manner of Skinner. Skinner's 'historical intelligence', says Pocock, is focused on 'the synchronic, the detailed reconstruction of language situations as they exist at a given time', in contrast to Pocock's own approach, which, he says, 'leans to the diachronic, the study of what happens when languages change or texts migrate from one historical situation to another' (*Rethinking the Foundations of Modern Political Thought*, eds A. Brett and J. Tully, Cambridge: Cambridge University Press, 2006, p. 45). But it cannot be said that historical *process* figures very prominently in Pocock's account of eighteenth-century England. His revolutionary moment does indeed occur with 'spectacular abruptness', with no apparent grounding in the social transformations of the previous centuries.

patronage; and here we can find the origins of commercial ideology, in the controversy between 'virtue' and 'corruption'. One of the main ideological requirements for the new commercial ideology in its defence against opposition was to finesse the antithesis of virtue and commerce. It had to challenge the counterposition of an independent landed interest and a more or less corrupt – or at any rate corrupting – monied interest. The answers provided by ideologues of commercial society generally had to do with the civilizing effects of commerce, which eliminates the need for civic virtue by taming the passions or harnessing them to the public good. So the main axis of controversy in eighteenth-century political discourse concerns the opposition between a conception of property which stresses possession and civic virtue, and one that stresses exchange and its civilizing of the passions.

This narrative also has the effect of displacing Locke from the centre of the modern revolution in property and the theorization of an emergent capitalism. Locke is, according to this argument, irrelevant to the ways in which capitalist or commercial society was reflected on, criticized or legitimated. He is irrelevant both in the sense that commercial society did not yet exist and was not yet an issue in his period, and in the sense that the categories, the vocabularies, used to conceptualize commercial society in the eighteenth century were different from and often opposed to Locke's.

There is, to be sure, considerable controversy about Pocock's narrative and his assumptions about the relations between virtue and commerce in early modern European discourse. There are those who object not only to his analysis of Britain but to his analytic categories in general. After all, civic humanism in Italian city-states linked commerce, liberty and virtue; and commerce was readily embraced by Dutch republicans. Others insist that the importance of republican discourse in eighteenth-century England has been grossly exaggerated, and still others that American thinkers, building on both English and other European traditions of discourse, were perfectly capable of combining liberal and republican discourses, or, indeed, civic virtue and commerce. But, even when questions are raised about the nature and extent of civic humanism or republicanism, or about the relation between virtue and commerce in political discourse, the fundamental terms of the debate remain unchallenged.

It has already been suggested here that the idea of 'republicanism' is a rather blunt instrument, which is particularly ill adapted to the specificities of English politics. Much the same can be said about 'commerce', whether or not it is conceived as antithetical to, or as a substitute for, virtue. The very idea of 'commerce', to say nothing of 'commercial society', conceals as much as it reveals. The distinctive development of capitalism set England apart from other commercial societies. The commercial, oligarchic and imperial order of the eighteenth century was grounded in agrarian capitalism and its very specific property regime; and any opposition between landed and monied interests presupposed a more fundamental commonality among the propertied classes. Both country gentlemen and merchants, whether Tories or Whigs, belonged to the capitalist property regime.

The so-called commercial revolution did not just materialize from nowhere, nor was it simply a linguistic transformation. It was the end of a long process of development – the development of what we are calling agrarian capitalism. This was a process that created a powerful capitalist landed class, which, having defeated absolutism, came out of the revolution of 1688–9 effectively in command of England and in strong position to consolidate the property regime they had been establishing throughout the previous century. The foundation of the Bank of England – Pocock's revolutionary moment – was a result of their victory, particularly the greatest among them, the Whigs who had led the Revolution of 1688 and were its main beneficiaries.

The fact that the Bank of England emerged in response to the needs of an emergent landlord capitalist class made it different from any other public bank in Europe and tells us much about the specificities of English history. The Bank was a uniquely English institution; and this difference has a history, because banking in England had already developed in distinctively English ways. The Bank of England was the culmination of developments that had been in process since at least the sixteenth century. Banking on the Continent had developed largely to finance and facilitate long-distance trade or arbitrage among separate markets. The English system was fairly weak in those respects in the early days, but it developed ways to meet its own specific needs. In particular, it developed forms of banking which catered to investment by the landed class; this was something completely new, with no parallels on the Continent, and clearly an expression of England's agrarian capitalism.

Long before the Bank of England, the English agrarian economy had already developed in distinctive ways. The particular relations between large landowners and tenants who were capital farmers meant that English agriculture was responding to new requirements of competition and profit-maximization with no historical precedent. This created new needs for investment capital in ways unknown to capital-starved Continental peasants or even rentier landlords; and English banks developed as providers of investment capital to facilitate production in unique and historically unprecedented ways.

The English banking system, more than any other, dealt with transactions among producers – not just among commercial agents, or even producers and consumers, but among producers themselves in an increasingly specialized network of production. This was not a function of some late commercial or industrial economy. It was born in the English countryside, in particular with the specialization of English farming countries, which meant producers were obliged to deal with each other in distinctive ways very different from, say, the peasant economy and local peasant markets in France. English banking developed to meet the needs of an increasingly integrated domestic market, and a metropolitan market centred on London. This was not just a matter of geographic scope, the difference between short- and long-distance trade. It had to do with fundamental features of English society and the English economy which set England apart from its European neighbours.

The immediate forerunners of the Bank of England were the goldsmith bankers. Their object was not just to facilitate old forms of trade, profit on alienation or buying cheap and selling dear, but to encourage investment in profitable production. What distinguished the Bank of England was not that it was a public bank but almost the opposite: that the public bank in England was an extension of private banking in its specific English form. It is true that it acquired the right to conduct its private business by offering to provide public credit, especially to finance war, but its principles and its general banking functions continued already existing English private banking practices.

The Bank of England did not, then, represent the sudden emergence of a thoroughly novel commercial regime. It was an extension of long-developing social property relations, the property relations of agrarian capitalism. These developments had set in motion a new and unprecedented historical dynamic, one major feature of which was an unprecedented self-sustaining economic growth – unlike anything anywhere else in Europe, including the highly commercialized Dutch Republic. The commercial capitalism of the eighteenth century in England was firmly rooted in these distinctive developments and would have been impossible without them. Whatever novelties emerged in eighteenth-century England, the revolutionary transformation in the property regime preceded them and was their precondition.

What, then, of the growth of government patronage enabled by the emergence of public credit? The apparatus of patronage, which would in the eighteenth century grow into what William Cobbett famously called 'Old Corruption', was a parasitic growth that fed on wealth created as much by capitalist agriculture as by mercantile activity. If landed wealth, in other words, was, by definition, 'real' rather than 'mobile', it was no less 'commercial' for that. If anything, the agrarian interest conformed to the capitalist logic more than did the monopolistic trading companies which survived as a pre-capitalist relic. The Tory country squire engaged in productive and improving agriculture was more capitalist than the old East India Company merchant; and the squire's wealth was more capitalist than the fortunes of the privileged few who grew rich on state patronage and public corruption.

There was, of course, nothing new about the use of state office, privilege or patronage in pursuit of personal wealth. This was, as we have seen, as much the rule as the exception throughout Europe. What distinguished the English mode of 'extra-economic' appropriation from, for example, the French, was that in eighteenth-century England it was a secondary, parasitic growth. French office-holders lined their pockets above all by directly taxing the productive classes, in particular the peasants. When the Land Tax was instituted in England in the 1690s, at the very moment that Parliament firmly established its control of taxation, the English propertied classes in Parliament were taxing themselves, transferring to the state wealth they had already appropriated from producers in the form of rent or profit. Old Corruption was a bone of contention not only among radicals like Cobbett but also among propertied elites, not because it represented a new commercial or capitalist order pitted against an antagonistic landed interest but, on the contrary, because it was parasitic on capitalist wealth that was at least as much landed as mercantile. The problem was not capitalist property. It was that a few corrupt and parasitic types were creaming off the profits of productive capital.

There certainly existed a strand of criticism that counterposed the moral qualities of landed property to the values of commercial profit; but even the most uncompromising critics testify to the realities of agrarian capitalism. The target of criticism was likely to be precisely a capitalist landlord who put profit above duty and responsibility, the obligations of hierarchy, rank and deference. Such critics might scorn the fruits of 'improvement' or imperial expansion; but, for the most part, if there was an opposition between virtue and commerce in eighteenth-century political discourse, it was a conflict within a ruling class generally agreed on England's novel property regime, even if some were more opposed than others to its excesses. If there was, for such critics, an opposition between the values of commerce and the virtues of landed property, it was not about an antithesis between agriculture and profit. It was about commerce unrestrained by moral values or class duties, about the excesses of Whig expansionism, about the abdication of traditional responsibilities by landowners who subordinated all their duties, the obligations of rank, to their commercial profits, about the ostentation of country parks and landscape gardens as against the productivity of agricultural improvement.

What divided critics like this from defenders of 'commercial society' like Joseph Addison or Daniel Defoe (Pocock's examples) was not a conflict over capitalist property. It had to do with the uses to which capitalist wealth was being put. Addison, for instance, was all in favour of large landed estates combining pleasure with profit, agricultural improvement with luxurious landscape gardens. Defoe's admiration for England's distinctive planted gardens lay along the same lines, a tribute to profit and rural aesthetics at the same time. But to critics, agricultural improvement and profitable production were one thing, ostentatious display and luxurious excess quite another.[19]

---

19 I discuss the very specifically English rural aesthetic that joined beauty with productivity and profit, in the manner of Addison and Defoe, in Ellen Meiksins Wood, *The Pristine Culture of Capitalism: A Historical Essay on Old Regimes and Modern States* (London: Verso, 1991), pp. 109–113.

Even when the virtues of the landed classes were held up against the vices of merchants, that opposition was likely to be deployed not against but in favour of the capitalist property regime. The fear that commerce could endanger virtue was an important theme even in the classics of political economy – nowhere more than in the work of Adam Smith. But it surely tells us something about the specificities of British capitalism that Smith, in the *Wealth of Nations*, sought a solution to the moral conundrum of commerce and virtue, which had troubled him throughout his career, by turning more, not less, to the commercial disciplines of competition and looking to the state not to impose a civic virtue alien to commercial transactions but rather to ensure that commercial disciplines would truly operate, against the inclinations of merchants and manufacturers. Even his friend Adam Ferguson, who continued to be plagued by the tensions between commerce and virtue (and even if we ascribe to him some kind of 'republicanism'), nonetheless regarded market mechanisms as the engine of progress (about which a little more in the next chapter). More particularly, neither one of them, whatever they may have thought about the corrupting effects of commerce or the vices of merchants, advocated a form of landed property that was not subject to the economic imperatives of 'improvement'; and nor did many other less equivocal critics of 'commercial society'.

Both advocates and critics took for granted agrarian capitalism, the product of transformations that had happened long before; and their discourse was accordingly distinctive. England certainly was not the only European state to have a powerful interest in commerce; and nor, as we have seen, did English thinkers first make commerce do the work of civic virtue. What was unique to England was that commerce itself was conceived in new ways in both theory and practice, a capitalist commerce with a dynamic of its own and, indeed, a new morality.

It seems perverse to define political discourse in eighteenth-century England in the terms of a dispute among propertied classes whose agreements on the existing property regime far outweighed their disagreements, or to magnify ill-tempered disputes among gentlemen into conflicts of revolutionary moment. Debate there certainly was; but, seen against the background of the turbulence and violence of other, truly fundamental oppositions in the history of England, the eighteenth century seems more remarkable for its settled consensus among men of property. The property regime that governed England during that century resulted from a long history of conflicts, all of them involving a great deal of force. It was established in struggles against threats from above and below – ranging from the defeat of rebellions by small proprietors in the sixteenth and early seventeenth centuries, to the destruction of unparliamentary taxation; from the suppression of popular threats which had emerged so dramatically during the Civil War, to the final suppression of the threats to property posed by royal absolutism, decisively defeated in

1688–9. In the eighteenth century, there were significant developments that followed from that history: for instance, parliamentary enclosures and a forceful redefinition of property rights by means of what has been called judicial terror, the criminalization of customary rights and introduction of the death penalty for many new offences against property.

There would, of course, be major changes in British society with the advance of industrial capitalism; but the transformative moments in the history of England's distinctive 'commercial society' belong more to the seventeenth, and even the sixteenth, century than to the eighteenth. These transformations laid the foundations of capitalist industrialization, generating an economic system that not only made agricultural producers uniquely subject to market imperatives and the requirements of competitive production but also propelled the mass dispossession that created both a labour force and a new kind of consumer market for wholly new forms of industrial production.[20] It is certainly true that seventeenth-century thinkers could hardly have imagined a market mechanism in the eighteenth-century manner, but they could and did conceptualize the property regime that was its essential condition. Whatever innovations occurred in eighteenth-century 'discourse', they did not represent an abrupt transformation but the consolidation of already established principles. Parliament and the courts, for instance, could increasingly be relied on to put into practice the conception of property which had come to the fore in the seventeenth century; and resistance to those principles did not come from propertied classes but from below. Nothing reveals more effectively the connection between the earlier transformation and what followed than the fact that after the settlement of 1688, which consolidated the property regime in Parliament, the state no longer opposed landed interests by interfering with enclosure in the way it often had before. Parliament itself became the enclosers' principal agent.

Locke did not, of course, invent this property regime; nor did he invent a wholly new discourse to capture it. In less systematic form, the idea of claims to property deriving from 'improvement' and the creation of value had been at work for some time, both in domestic property disputes and in justifications of empire. It was certainly visible in seventeenth-century improvement literature, as well as in disputes between landlords or capitalist tenants and those whose use rights impeded improvement and capital accumulation. The same idea appears early in the seventeenth century, as we have seen, in defence of English imperial policy, particularly the colonial settlement of Ireland. But Locke gave the conception its first systematic elaboration, and in that sense his theory gave conceptual expression to the revolution in the English property regime. What we observe in the eighteenth century are the consequences of that regime still playing themselves out.

---

20   For more on this, see my 'Question of Market-Dependence', esp. pp. 80–84.

The Lockean paradigm was, in this sense, very much still present – indeed, came fully into its own – in eighteenth-century England. What, then, should we make of the fact that the greatest British philosopher of the century (considered by many the greatest philosopher ever to have written in the English language) was a thinker whose principal contribution to philosophy had the effect of denying the very possibility of political theory in the manner of Locke? David Hume was not a political theorist; but he had much to say about what kind of theorizing about politics is *not* possible, and that included Locke's political ideas. Starting from an 'empiricist' premise apparently akin to Locke's, that all knowledge ultimately derives from sense experience, Hume ends with a philosophical scepticism that challenges precisely the pretensions of human reason that are central to traditional ideas of natural law, natural right and social contract.

Reason, Hume tells us, can do no more than establish connections among ideas, which themselves are feeble derivations from original sense impressions. It cannot reach beyond original perceptions to any kind of ultimate truth. We can trace connections between premises and conclusions, but we can never be certain about the truth of the premises themselves. This means that our beliefs, even about such basic principles as cause and effect, to say nothing of our moral and political judgments, cannot claim to be grounded in necessary truths or universal, immutable natural laws. There is, to be sure, a human nature, which, among other things, inclines human beings to recognize that their interests require political communities, property and the security of agreements needed to maintain them, which we can call the principles of justice. But there is no basis for judging forms of government on the grounds of abstract 'rational' principles or natural law.

Hume, somewhat paradoxically, attributes to human nature a propensity to 'sympathy', which, on the face of it, seems very like Rousseau's *pitié*, a projection of our sense of self to others, which is the basis of human sociality and even morality. A natural benevolence or a feeling for humanity even form the basis of justice, although that emerges through the mediations of convention, particularly in circumstances of scarcity that require the security of property. But Hume finds himself unable consistently to sustain the idea of sympathy without challenging his own philosophy, which allows for no conception of the self beyond the simple awareness that accompanies each of our sense impressions. Yet rather than relinquish the idea of sympathy, he eventually ends by putting in question his own philosophical system and embraces a scepticism even more profound than before, no longer seeking to explain sympathy as a projection of the self.[21]

---

21   For a discussion of this point, see my *Mind and Politics* (Berkeley and Los Angeles: University of California, 1972), esp. pp. 66–73.

Hume's philosophy seems to represent a striking challenge to Locke's political theory, but his work in the end confirms the depth of the settled consensus and the persistence of what we are calling the Lockean paradigm. If his epistemology puts in question the very possibility of Locke's political philosophy, his classic *History of England,* which during his lifetime remained his greatest success, tells us something more about his views on politics and property. It is true that, in Hume's account of English history since Roman times, he makes no unambiguous claims for the superiority of England's 'mixed constitution' and remains true to his philosophical scepticism: it seems that any form of government that operates according to some kind of regular and settled laws should probably be supported. But what may tell us more about the Lockean consensus is that Hume appears to take for granted the distinctly English property regime of agrarian capitalism. When he associates commercial society with progress, as do the classical political economists, he does not oppose the virtues of real property to commerce. It is not just that, for him, commerce promotes prosperity, liberty and even politeness. He also sings the praises of the 'rising gentry', a dynamic agrarian class quite unlike the 'ancient barons'. This new landed class, instead of dissipating its fortunes, 'endeavoured to turn their lands to best account with regard to profit'; and in the process, they increased the cities and enhanced the wealth and power of 'the middle rank of men'.[22]

Hume's friend Adam Smith was no less committed to the idea of 'sympathy', though his convictions about 'moral sentiments' and a natural 'feeling of humanity' may seem to run counter to the *Wealth of Nations,* where the pursuit of self-interest appears to overtake benevolence as the driving force of social interaction. Despite his distrust of mercantile classes and their selfish inclinations, Smith is able to advocate the advancement of 'commercial society' and to reconcile the moral demands of sympathy and justice with self-interest; but he can do so because, and perhaps only because, he is convinced (however mistakenly) that market disciplines will enhance equity, indeed equality, as well as 'opulence'. This conviction may have come more easily to him because of specifically English conditions. England not only

---

22   David Hume, *History of England*, Vol. 3, Appendix 3 (London: T. Cadell, 1773), pp. 488–9. Much the same could be said about another major figure of the eighteenth century, Edmund Burke. A discussion of his political thought will have to await another volume that encompasses the American and French revolutions, which, for better or worse, inspired so much of his political thinking. For now, it is worth simply noting that when he launched the attack on the empire in India which was perhaps his most notable political act, his chief complaint, as head of a parliamentary committee, was that the empire had become 'completely corrupted by turning it into a vehicle for tribute', when it should instead 'fix its commerce upon a commercial basis'; 'Ninth Report of the Select Committee', in ed. Peter Marshall, *The Writings and Speeches of Edmund Burke* (Oxford: Oxford University Press, 1985), p. 241.

had an unusually integrated market and an unusually integrated state. It also came closer than other trading nations to his model of 'the natural progress of opulence', in which commercial success is driven less by mercantile interests than by a productive agriculture. Adapting physiocratic ideas to English conditions may have encouraged Smith to be more sanguine about the self-sustaining integrative power of the market and its spontaneous capacity to forge a common good.

'Commercial society', then, was rooted in the transformations of the previous century; and in the eighteenth century the property regime captured by Locke's theory of property was very much alive. Locke's political discourse may not have been the language of Addison or Defoe – though they certainly shared the ethic of improvement. It may not have been the philosophical language of David Hume. Locke's language of contract and natural right may not have been the language of eighteenth-century political or economic theory. But the discourse of this property regime was more than ever the language of Parliament in defining crimes against property, in property disputes and in deliberations on enclosure. If the Lockean paradigm was more or less invisible, it was because it represented a settled consensus within the ruling elites. They may have had less use in the eighteenth century for arguments based on natural rights or on contracts than did their seventeenth-century forebears defending Parliament against the Crown. They also increasingly had reason, in an age of revolution, to avoid any language that could be turned against them from below. But on certain very basic principles they were agreed, and these were principles that Locke had spelled out more systematically than had any other political thinker.

These principles constituted a very particular conception of property, including a commitment to its productive and profitable use, especially in the form of agricultural improvement, and the primacy of its purely economic value over common and customary rights. This was a conception of property that favoured capitalist production and appropriation as against non-capitalist forms, including the kind of political appropriation still favoured by the French and other Continental elites. Disputes within the English ruling elements, about virtue and commerce or real and mobile property, could be conducted in the secure knowledge that, when all was said and done, the antagonists stood together on the same solid ground. There was no longer any need to talk about it, at least not in polite company.

8

ENLIGHTENMENT OR CAPITALISM?

Their goal was not mainly to gain a greater understanding of the physical world, but to bring reason to bear on man's place within it – that is, among other things, to bring morality and politics wholly within the scope of rational inquiry. On the face of it, these ambitions were realised. The ideas of the Enlightenment changed the world. Their legacy was western modernity . . . The West's inheritance from the intellectual battles of the 18th century was liberalism and capitalism. These have made the West, for good or ill, what it is.

This characterization of the Enlightenment assumes that, whatever national variations there may have been in Western history, 'the West' came together in the Enlightenment to form a common liberal and capitalist 'modernity'. That account comes not from a scholarly source but from an article in *The Economist* published in the 1990s.[1] Yet its portrayal of 'western modernity' – in which liberalism, capitalism and the intellectual project of the Enlightenment together represent a single cultural formation whose first principle is rationalism – could have been written, with this or that stylistic adjustment, by a wide range of historians and social thinkers, supporters or critics of the Enlightenment (or both together), from Max Weber, or indeed Hegel long before him, to anti-Enlightenment postmodernists today. From passionate advocates to unrelenting critics, commentators have portrayed modernity, for evil or for good, in much the same way. This has been so whether the Enlightenment is regarded as the pinnacle of human emancipation or as an abject failure that at best has been unable to forestall the tragedies of modern times (the 'dialectic of Enlightenment') and at worst has been their source, the cause of genocide and threats of nuclear annihilation. If there is today a conventional idea of 'modernity', it remains a composite of the capitalist market, formal democracy, and technological progress, rooted in the 'rationalism' of the Enlightenment.

---

1   'Crimes of Reason', *The Economist*, 16 March 1996, p. 97.

There have, of course, been various refinements in historical accounts of 'the Enlightenment'. We now have not just one Enlightenment but many, produced by many national cultures; and we have a 'Radical Enlightenment', with roots in the seventeenth century and especially Spinoza, which preceded the more moderate variety typically acknowledged by historical convention and would continue to influence more radical and democratic forces. The proliferation of 'Enlightenments' may even put in question whether there was ever any definable moment or movement deserving of the name 'the Enlightenment' or any other special designation of its own. 'The Enlightenment is beginning to be everything', writes one distinguished scholar, 'and therefore nothing.'[2] But none of this has displaced the portrait of modernity in which the various threads of 'rationalization', cultural, political and economic, are inextricably connected, even if they have reached their full realization in some places more than in others.

The argument that follows here is intended to disentangle some of these disparate threads. More particularly, it is intended to disentangle the 'Enlightenment project' from the culture of capitalism. It is not here simply a question of the many differences among national and local cultures that mark the particular Enlightenments of, say, France, the Netherlands, or Germany. What is at issue here is the connection – or the lack of it – between the intellectual and political themes most commonly associated with the 'Enlightenment(s)' and the distinctive culture of capitalism.

Modernity and the 'Bourgeois Paradigm'

'Neither the historian nor the philosopher', Jonathan Israel tells us, 'is likely to get very far with discussing "modernity" unless he or she starts by differentiating Radical Enlightenment from conservative [or] moderate mainstream Enlightenment.' Anyone seeking to investigate the rise of modernity 'as a system of democratic values and individual liberties', he continues, must pay closer attention than is normally given to 'the crucible in which those values originated and developed – the Radical Enlightenment'.[3]

Since our objective here is precisely to investigate 'modernity', and especially its values of democracy and liberty, let us start with Israel's distinction between the two competing strands of the Enlightenment. The critical distinction is 'the difference between reason alone and reason combined with faith and tradition [which] was a ubiquitous and absolute difference.' On the one hand, the 'moderate mainstream' associated with Newton and Locke

---

2   Darnton, 'Washington's False Teeth', 27 March 1997.

3   Jonathan Israel, *Radical Enlightenment: Philosophy and the Making of Modernity 1650–1750* (Oxford: Oxford University Press, 2002), pp. 11, 13.

aspired to conquer ignorance and superstition, establish toleration, and revolutionize ideas, education, and attitudes by means of philosophy but in such a way as to preserve and safeguard what were judged essential elements of the older structures, effecting a viable synthesis of old and new, and of reason and faith.

On the other hand, the Radical Enlightenment, with its most important roots in Spinoza,

> whether on an atheistic or deistic basis, rejected all compromise with the past and sought to sweep away existing structures entirely, rejecting the Creation as traditionally understood in Judaeo-Christian civilization, and the intervention of a providential God in human affairs, denying the possibility of miracles, and reward and punishment in an afterlife, scorning all forms of ecclesiastical authority, and refusing to accept that there is any God-ordained social hierarchy, concentration of privilege or land-ownership in noble hands, or religious sanction for monarchy. From its origins in the 1650s and 1660s the philosophical radicalism of the European Early Enlightenment characteristically combined immense reverence for science, and for mathematical logic, with some form of non-providential deism, if not outright materialism and atheism along with unmistakably republican, even democratic tendencies.[4]

It would be reasonable to ask how far Israel's distinction between the two 'Enlightenments' can take us in understanding modern ideas of democracy and liberty. This distinction, whatever its other strengths (and weaknesses), considerably overstates the gulf between the conservatism of the 'moderate mainstream' and the 'democratic tendencies' of the 'Radical' Enlightenment. Spinoza himself was certainly more radical than Locke in his approach to religion and ecclesiastical authority; but, on the political spectrum from Locke to, say, the Levellers (to say nothing of other, more radical forces), the Dutch philosopher's oligarchic republic may seem closer in spirit to Locke's parliamentary government (even while the two philosophers seem closer to each other in their philosophical radicalism, or, for that matter, in their attitudes to religion, than either one would be to radically democratic religious sects in the English Revolution).

But even if we set aside all the complexities in the relations among philosophical, religious and political radicalisms (and even if we pass over a conception of 'democratic tendencies' so restricted that it places a 'radical' Spinoza in diametric opposition to a 'conservative' Locke), it is still worth asking how much we can learn about 'modernity' and 'democratic values'

---

4 *Ibid.*, pp. 11–12.

by concentrating on the 'Radical Enlightenment'. The problem is not only that, when placed along such a limited spectrum, the differences between 'radical' and 'moderate' may seem greater than they are. The point is that even when there seems to be substantial philosophical agreement on the subject of equality or liberty, there are limits to what that can tell us about modern democratic values if we ignore contextual divergences that may give very diverse meanings to conceptions of democracy, equality and liberty. It is not, again, simply a question of national differences. We may speak, with caution, of a 'European Enlightenment' ranging 'from Portugal to Russia and from Ireland to Sicily', all of them 'preoccupied not only with the same intellectual problems but often even the very same books'.[5] But even if we do allow for an inclusive 'European' culture of Enlightenment, this cannot dispose of major contextual differences, such as those between (French) absolutism and (English) capitalism, which engendered different conceptions of equality and liberty and left very different political legacies.

It may after all be useful to begin, as Robert Darnton has suggested, by 'deflating' the Enlightenment – not belittling its importance, nor even underestimating the commonalities of European culture, but considering at least one 'Enlightenment' as a concrete historical phenomenon, a 'movement, a cause, a campaign to change minds and reform institutions', in a specific time and place. This movement, which began in early eighteenth-century France, Darnton tells us, certainly had origins that can be traced to intellectual developments in other parts of Europe, in the previous century or even before; and it certainly had affinities with cultural trends elsewhere. But the educative and reforming mission of the French Enlightenment remains distinct.

In eighteenth-century France, and specifically in Paris, there was an explosion of activity among intellectuals and men of letters, who, whatever their other similarities and differences, self-consciously identified themselves with

> a new spirit, the sense of participation in a secular crusade. It began with derision, as an attempt to laugh bigots out of polite society, and it ended with the occupation of the moral high ground, as a campaign for the liberation of mankind, including the enserfed and enslaved, Protestants, Jews, blacks, and (in the case of Condorcet) women . . . [It] grew out of a crisis during the last years of the reign of Louis XIV [and] came to a head while France suffered through a series of demographic, economic, and

---

5 *Ibid.*, p. v. Israel is rather too insistent on dismissing national differences – even when, for example, he acknowledges that the interests of the English landed gentry produced 'appreciably different' cultural effects than those of 'urban and commercial' classes in the Dutch Republic (p. 22).

military disasters [during which, with the state] on the verge of collapse, men of letters attached to the court . . . questioned the basis of Bourbon absolutism and the religious orthodoxy it enforced.[6]

This 'secular crusade' soon moved well beyond a conversation among courtly men of letters. The *philosophes*, as we have seen, took on a mission far more ambitious and inclusive than the subjection of bigots in polite society to ridicule; and this mission would have influences far beyond French borders. The writings of the *philosophes* would plant their seeds in everything from Kantian philosophy to revolutionary doctrines in America. But Darnton's judicious account of a 'movement' with clear geographic and temporal boundaries and a more or less explicit practical objective places it in perspective in a way that more grandiose and capacious conceptions of 'Enlightenment', even those that distinguish between 'moderate' and 'radical' Enlightenments, do not.

There may be a difference between speaking, on the one hand, of *the* Enlightenment as a trans-European, even global, phenomenon without a specific historical referent, or, on the other, of many particular Enlightenments with very specific locations and times. But both presuppose a common denominator, a culture of 'reason'; and, even when they acknowledge the many different ways and degrees in which that culture challenged superstition or faith in, say, England, France, Germany, Italy, Russia or Romania, they are likely – when not explicitly, then often by default – to leave intact a model of modernity that lumps together scientific, political and economic 'rationality', or liberal democracy and the capitalist market.

In this model, the Enlightenment, for many the pivotal moment in the onset of modernity, is typically bound up with capitalism. This is so not only in the most simplistic forms of Marxism, in which the Enlightenment is a bourgeois – and hence, in common usage, capitalist – class ideology. The Enlightenment and capitalism are also intertwined in the Weberian notion of 'rationalization', in which the rise of the 'rational' (bureaucratic) state and the 'rational' (capitalist) organization of production belong, for better or worse, to the same historical process as the Enlightenment elevation of reason over ignorance and superstition. Whether that process is a cause for celebration or lament, whether it constitutes the liberation of the individual or the 'iron cage' or both together in the ambiguities of 'disenchantment', these economic, political and cultural manifestations represent the many facets of a single historical tendency. The bourgeois here too is the principal agent, the undifferentiated bearer of economic, political and cultural rationalization.

Conventional ways of thinking about capitalism and its history tend to

---

6 *Ibid.*, p. 35.

obscure its specificity, taking it for granted and naturalizing it, as if its principles and laws of motion were universal, natural laws.[7] Either capitalism has always existed in one form or another, at least in embryo or in the depths of human nature, or it is the natural destination of history. Even if it is the final outcome of a long historical process, that destination seems to have been reached by historical movements that were themselves already driven by essentially capitalist laws of motion, like the need for constant technological progress to increase labour productivity. The implication is that there really is no need to explain the origin of capitalism. Since historians first started writing about the emergence of capitalism, with very rare exceptions, there has scarcely existed an explanation that did not begin by assuming the very thing that needed to be explained. Accounts of the origin of capitalism have been fundamentally circular: they have assumed the prior existence of capitalism in order to explain its coming into being. Capitalism comes about by means of already capitalist processes, an already existing capitalist rationality. It is just a maturation of age-old commercial practices and their liberation from political and cultural constraints. All that historians are obliged to do in explaining the development of capitalism is to account for the removal of obstacles to the free development of an age-old, eternal historical dynamic, not the emergence of a radically new one.

This conception of capitalism is deeply embedded in Western culture. It is manifest in the conventional conflation of 'bourgeois' and 'capitalist', together with conceptions of modernity – and now postmodernity – that are based, explicitly or implicitly, on that conflation. Underlying the identification of bourgeois and capitalist is a model of Western historical development – which I call the 'bourgeois paradigm'[8] – that represents capitalism as a natural product of commercialization, the growth of cities and the expansion of trade. The same model underlies some familiar dichotomies, which tend to be closely linked: rural v. urban, agriculture v. commerce and industry, status v. contract, aristocracy v. bourgeoisie, feudalism v. capitalism, and, of course, superstition (or magic, or religion) v. reason. In these accounts the burgher or bourgeois – by definition a town-dweller – is the principal agent of progress, whether he achieves his ends by means of bourgeois revolution or by some less cataclysmic means.

The argument here proceeds from a different conception of capitalism and the historical process that brought it about. It also departs, of course, from accounts of 'commercial society' that evade the historical issue by

---

7 The work of Robert Brenner represents the most important departure from this tendency, especially in his contributions to *The Brenner Debate*. I discuss the historiography of capitalism and its origin at greater length in *The Origin of Capitalism: A Longer View* (London: Verso, 2002), chs 1–3.

8 I first suggested this phrase in my *Pristine Culture*, pp. 2–11.

treating the emergence of capitalism not as a social transformation but as a sudden shift of language. The argument here insists on the specificity of capitalism as a system with unique imperatives, a system distinctively driven to improve the productivity of labour by technical means, in order to meet the requirements of competition and profit-maximization. It has nothing to do with the distinction between urban and rural, or agriculture and commerce or industry. Just as agriculture and landlords can be capitalist (and the presupposition of the present argument is that capitalism was born in the English countryside), so too can cities, commerce, industry and the bourgeoisie be non-capitalist. This means that bourgeois modernity and the Enlightenment are one thing, while capitalism is something else altogether.

To make the distinction between English capitalism and the historical context of the French Enlightenment is not to deny that they shared certain common historical preconditions nor that the culture of capitalism displayed certain traits that we associate with the Enlightenment – such as an interest in science and technology. The point is rather that capitalism's distinctive economic logic has been accompanied by its own very specific cultural and ideological formations which set it apart from others, which depart in significant ways from the cultural pattern associated with the Enlightenment, and which are even sometimes diametrically opposed to Enlightenment principles.

Bourgeois but Not Capitalist

If there is a kernel of truth in the crude proposition that the ideas of the French Enlightenment were somehow 'bourgeois', it is certainly not in the sense that they were capitalist. The relevant context here is not capitalism but absolutism. The absolutist state, as we have seen in earlier chapters, constituted both a political and an economic system in the sense that the state was a primary economic resource, a form of 'politically constituted property'. Office in the state was a form of private property, not only in the sense that many offices were venal but more generally in the sense that it gave its possessors access to peasant-produced surpluses through the medium of taxation, which was a source of private wealth no less than of public revenues. There also were other, decentralized forms of politically constituted property, not only the remnants of feudal lordship but various other corporate powers and privileges. The role of corporate autonomy, rights and privileges as means of appropriation helps to account for the strength of corporate principles in France, in theory and practice.

The eighteenth-century French bourgeoisie was not a capitalist class, or even, in large part, a commercial class of any kind. A typical French bourgeois, the kind of person who would, for example, constitute the revolutionary bourgeoisie of 1789, was likely to be an office-holder, a professional, even an intellectual (about which more in a moment). The material interests of the French bourgeois were likely to be bound up with the state. This could be either directly through office or stipends from the state, or indirectly, negatively, through opposition to exclusion from privilege, to exclusion from higher offices reserved for birth or wealth, and to the aristocracy's most precious privilege, exemption from the taxes that so burdened the Third Estate.

How did these material interests find expression in Enlightenment principles? The interests of such non-capitalist bourgeois were typically expressed in the commitment to civil equality, for example, in principles that would be embodied in the slogan 'careers open to talent' – which meant, in particular, access to state office. The same interests were also expressed in the assertion of universalism against particularism, specifically the universalism of the *nation* or *citizenship*, and ultimately humanity itself, against the structure of corporate privilege, against special status, private law, exclusive rights, and so on – in other words, inclusive against exclusive principles, universality against privilege.

This is not to say that bourgeois class interests by themselves created the preoccupation with equality, or even that Enlightenment ideas belonged exclusively to the bourgeoisie. After all, enlightened aristocrats played a prominent role. But bourgeois class interests, in a society structured by corporate hierarchy, help to explain the salience of equality and universalism in Enlightenment culture.

There is, nonetheless, something more specific to be said about the relevant bourgeois culture. The culture of the Enlightenment is not some undifferentiated bourgeois ideology but a much more particular expression of one specific section of the bourgeoisie, the intellectuals. The particular character of the French Enlightenment in many ways derives from the mentality, the corporate consciousness, the *esprit de corps*, even the caste-consciousness, and indeed the material interests, of a new type of professional intellectual. But it also needs to be emphasized that the professionalization of the intellectual in France was less a symptom of 'modernity' than a feature of the ancien régime and the corporate structure of the absolutist state. It was very much a part of a system in which the state and office were primary economic resources. What is at issue here, then, is the professionalization of the intellectual as a kind of office-holder in a society where office was a form of appropriation. It was also a society organized on corporatist principles, and that too has a great deal to do with the mentality of Enlightenment intellectuals in France. In the context of France's corporatist organization, the intellectual profession assumed some of the character of the 'intermediary bodies' that were so much a part of the French polity and French political thought, with its own corporate solidarity and consciousness, and even a certain corporate autonomy, or at least an aspiration to that kind of autonomy.

The clearest and most important illustration of this formation is the Paris Academy. Here, first, is how Voltaire, in his *Lettres philosophiques*, compares the *académies* in France with the Royal Society in England. We can discount the heavy irony with which these little essays are written because, on the main point, Voltaire's account is accurate and goes right to the heart of the matter:

> The English have had an Academy of Sciences much longer than we, but it is not as well organized as ours . . . The Royal Society of London lacks the two things most necessary to men, payment and rules. A place in the [French] Académie is a small but certain fortune for a geometrist, or a chemist. In London, on the contrary, it costs them to belong to the Royal Society.[9]

Voltaire goes on to make a distinction between the amateurs who belong to the Royal Society, and the experts who belong to the Académie in Paris; and he draws an analogy between well-disciplined and well-paid soldiers, on the one hand, and volunteers on the other. This epigrammatic comparison points to some real and significant differences between English and French intellectuals, and also to more fundamental social, economic and political divergences between England and France. It should be emphasized that the difference between the two academies is not that one was more interested in applied and the other more in pure or theoretical science. Both engaged in 'pure' science, and both are also notable for the degree to which their conception of science was utilitarian; but their utilitarian objectives were different and, more particularly, they were responding to different needs.

The members of the Paris Académie before the Revolution were agents of the absolutist state, and the Académie itself was part of the absolutist project to centralize culture around the king. It performed essential functions for the state, and its research projects were often directly dictated by the needs of the state – such as, in its early days, long-term projects having to do with navigation, mapping French territory, military mechanics, and (this is exquisitely emblematic) developing a hydraulic theory for the construction of fountains. The Académie also increasingly became the official arbiter of technological matters, judging inventions presented to the king. By contrast, the Royal Society, effectively founded in 1660 (though it received its first charter in 1662), deliberately set itself apart from the state. Instead of choosing another contemporary model, Samuel Hartlib's 'Agency of Universal Learning', which would have been supported by the state, the

---

9 Voltaire, *Lettres philosophiques, ou Lettres anglaises*, ed. Réne Pomeau (Paris: Garnier Frères, 1964), Letter 24, p. 154 (the translation of the passage is my own).

Royal Society deliberately chose to derive its income from members' subscriptions.

'The Royal Society', writes the historian of science Charles Webster, 'purposely avoided entanglement with national policy. Accordingly the Royal Society was freed from state regulation, but it was also divested of a large element of the humanitarianism and utopianism of the "Agency of Universal Learning".[10] The Society was characterized, as he puts it, by an 'absence of public responsibility'. It is worth adding that, in this respect, the differences between the Paris Académie and the Royal Society correspond to a fundamental difference between pre-capitalist and capitalist societies: while pre-capitalist powers of appropriation are typically inseparable from the performance of certain communal or public functions – jurisdictional, military, political – capitalist property is unique in the degree to which appropriation is separate from the performance of such public functions – in other words, it is notable exactly for 'the absence of public responsibility'.

At any rate, although we should clearly not be misled by Voltaire's observation that the Royal Society was full of amateurs and dilettantes (it had among its active members some of the foremost scientists of their or any other day, from Boyle to Newton), there is an important truth in his observation. The general (not, to be sure, necessarily active) membership of the Royal Society came in large part from the landed classes, especially the gentry: men who did not regard their intellectual pursuits as a kind of professional activity.[11] The active core, including those who would by any standard be called scientists, would certainly not have regarded their scientific pursuits as a form of salaried service, let alone a type of office-holding. Their collective consciousness, if they could be said to have one, was clearly something very different from the corporate consciousness of professional

---

10   Charles Webster, *The Great Instauration: Science, Medicine and Reform, 1626–1660* (London: Duckworth, 1975), p. 97.

11   On the social composition of the Society in its early years, see, for instance, Lotte Mulligan, 'Civil War Politics, Religion and the Royal Society', in *The Intellectual Revolution of the Seventeenth Century*, ed. Charles Webster (London and Boston: Routledge & Kegan Paul, 1974), pp. 317–46. Mulligan looks at members of the Royal Society who were old enough to have been involved in the Civil War and breaks them down according to such factors as their social rank and occupation as well as political and religious leanings. See, in particular, the table on p. 340, which indicates that 55 per cent of these members came from the gentry and another 18 per cent from the nobility (with those of merchant or artisan background at 14 per cent). In his introduction, the editor points out the flaws in such a purely statistical approach in any attempt to determine the social, political and religious origins of English science – partly on the grounds that only a very small proportion of members of the Royal Society were active. But the figures remain significant, and, as will be suggested in what follows, there were some fundamental commonalities of interest between the grandees of the Society and their less active amateur co-members.

intellectuals in France. More particularly, their different status, and their very different relation to the state, were expressed in the very specific preoccupations of the Society.

This is not to deny that there were many common concerns among academicians in England and France. But in at least one respect the English were distinctive, indeed unique. If, for instance, we consider the concerns of the founders of the Royal Society – distinguished figures, both scientists and non-scientists, such as Robert Boyle, John Evelyn, Robert Hooke, William Petty, Christopher Wren, and the first co-secretaries of the Society, Henry Oldenburg and John Wilkins, not to mention members such as Lord Shaftesbury and Locke – one of the things that stands out is their shared preoccupation with agriculture, and specifically its 'improvement', the enhancement of its *productivity*. One of the Society's earliest projects was a county-by-county survey of English farming, based on what may be the first ever systematic questionnaire on a technical subject – probably compiled by Robert Boyle. This preoccupation was part of a larger trend: the explosion in the seventeenth century of a body of literature devoted to improving agricultural practices.[12] In that respect, even the most active core of the Society

---

12   The study was conducted by the 'Georgical' committee of the Society. Among its members and those associated with its work were not only such dignitaries as Boyle, Evelyn and Wilkins, but also Shaftesbury, Locke's patron, the very model of the early capitalist landlord, whose farms were situated in the heart of agrarian capitalism (see Neal Wood, *John Locke and Agrarian Capitalism*, Berkeley: University of California Press, 1984, pp. 21–2, 26). This gives at least an indication of the convergence between the interests of landlords and the scientific preoccupations of the Society's core members. It is worth noting, too, that founders of the Royal Society such as Boyle, Evelyn, Oldenburg, Petty and Wilkins had in common their earlier involvement in Hartlib's Agency of Universal Learning (Webster, *Great Instauration*, p. 99). As Webster points out: 'Husbandry more than any other subject was used by Hartlib to demonstrate the aims of his Agency to "do good, in love to the Publick"' (p. 472).

One final remark: some commentators have pointed out that the Royal Society underwent a significant transformation, even a decline, in the decades following its foundation. Margaret Espinasse's 'The Decline and Fall of Restoration Science', in ed. Webster, *Intellectual Revolution*, pp. 347–68, associates this 'decline' with the dominance of an aristocratic outlook and the loss of interest in trades and industry in favour of arts more suitable to gentlemen. But there is, perhaps, in this judgment a bit too much of the 'bourgeois paradigm'. There was, to begin with, a significant continuity between the preoccupations of the Society in its golden age and the gentlemanly pursuits of the subsequent century. In any case, the notion of 'improvement' demonstrates that a shift from 'bourgeois' interests in trades or industry to 'gentlemanly' or 'aristocratic' pursuits like farming is no indication of declining interest in productivity or profit. The following century may have been less scientifically distinguished than the first decade or two of the Royal Society, but it was certainly the age in which the culture of improvement came into its own. In that sense (as in others), the scientific preoccupations of the Royal Society in the seventeenth century, and indeed the 'aristocratic' interests of that time, came to fruition in the eighteenth century.

had fundamental interests in common with the less active amateurs from the aristocracy and gentry.

There is nothing in France, even in the eighteenth century, like the 'improvement' literature of seventeenth-century England, and that cultural fact conforms to a material reality. Although it is sometimes said that in the eighteenth century the productivity of French agriculture was more or less the same as it was in England at the time, this simply means that total output or land productivity was roughly the same. But it took a larger labour force in France than in England to produce that total output. What the English had that the French did not was an imperative to improve labour productivity (output per unit of work), that imperative derived from a system of social and economic relations very different from those prevailing in France, a system that already in the seventeenth century subjected English agricultural producers to the requirements of a competitive market – in other words, agrarian capitalism.

To sum up the comparison between England and France simply and crudely: where French science in the eighteenth century typically answered the needs of the state, English science, even a century earlier, was already answering the needs of property, and property in an increasingly capitalist form.

The principal differences can be brought into sharper relief by means of an interesting paradox – or something that may look paradoxical from the vantage point of the bourgeois paradigm and the conception of modernity that goes with it. If we were to compare the French academicians of the eighteenth century with English scientists of the seventeenth using our conventional criteria of modernity, even discounting the time difference, the French would undoubtedly emerge as the more 'modern': they were the professionals, in a so-called rational, bureaucratic organization. The English were amateurs and dilettantes in a more formally irrational system. The French were by definition largely bourgeois. The membership of the Royal Society was overwhelmingly landed, mainly from the gentry but also the nobility.

Yet, seen from a different angle, which one is more 'modern': the corporatist French bourgeois professional academician serving the absolutist state, or the English improving landlord, member of the Royal Society with an 'amateurish' scientific interest in a capitalist-style enhancement of labour productivity?

Progress and the Republic of Letters

The example of the Paris Académie may give us some clues about the ways in which the material and institutional interests of intellectuals shaped the culture of the Enlightenment. First, in a society where access to the state, to the lucrative resources of state salaries, pensions and privileges, was a primary material concern and where access to high office depended on birth or wealth, the question of qualification for office was a very live issue. It might not be too much to say that a significant part of French Enlightenment culture had to do with redefining the qualifications for office. This redefinition took the form of an ideology that sought to replace an aristocracy of birth or wealth with an aristocracy of talent and intellect. No doubt, intellectuals in general have a material interest in so-called meritocracy, but this would be especially so in a society in which life chances were so closely bound up with the state and public office.

The symbiosis between intellectuals and the absolutist state is visible in other ways too. The bureaucratization of culture in the absolutist state encouraged some distinctive cultural patterns – in particular, the standardization of language that was a favourite project of the absolutist state, or French classicism, with its precise and formal aesthetic and philosophical rules.[13] This cultural configuration helped to promote the sense of intellectuals as a corporate community, with their own internal laws and culture. Under these conditions, where intellectuals had a very self-conscious corporate consciousness, and where that consciousness had very specific institutional expressions, the idea of an intellectual community, a Republic of Letters, acquired a very concrete meaning. It is not at all difficult to see how the idea of a Republic of Letters worked itself out in the Enlightenment, especially in the concept of progress.

The most obvious point about the Enlightenment concept of progress is that its source and its model is scientific knowledge, the cumulative, directional quality of that particular form of knowledge. In the end, that is what the idea of progress comes down to: whatever other evils, reverses and moral lapses have punctuated human history, the mind, especially in the form of scientific knowledge, is, according to this view, the one thing we can count on to advance, however slowly and painfully and however much the perfection of any kind of knowledge is projected into an indefinite future.

Now, in itself, the idea of progress as the advance of knowledge may not be particularly distinctive. It is certainly not enough to distinguish England from France, or the Enlightenment of either one from all the other 'Enlightenments'. Nor would it be true to say that the French had no interest in material progress. For instance, the idea that human civilization has gone through various stages of material organization, or the idea that human history has been characterized by several successive modes of subsistence, from hunting to pastoral through agricultural to

---

13 In my *Pristine Culture*, I contrast these French cultural patterns with the English culture of capitalism – expressed in various domains, from language to gardening.

'commercial' society, owes as much to French thinkers as it does to Englishmen or indeed to the Scottish political economists who theorized the experience of English capitalism. But the corporate consciousness of French intellectuals gives this concept of progress a special flavour. It is not surprising that the notion of progress that we associate with the French Enlightenment in particular conceives of the history of civilization as, above all else, the history of the Republic of Letters. It misses the point completely just to conflate this with the notion of technological progress in the sense we associate with capitalism and the enhancement of labour productivity by technological means.

The culmination of the Enlightenment conception of progress, in a way its last gasp, is Condorcet's *Sketch for a Historical Picture of the Progress of the Human Mind* – published in 1795, after the ideas of the Enlightenment had already been enlisted in two major revolutions, and written while he was hiding from the Jacobins in fear of his life. It can, of course, be argued that Condorcet was not a representative figure; that his optimism, no less than his universalism and egalitarianism (at least in anticipation of progress), was exceptional even among the great Enlightenment thinkers. Optimism was in any case only one side of the Enlightenment picture. The secular view of history that distinguishes this concept of progress from religious millennialism is necessarily two-sided: it does not simply make assumptions about human perfectibility or the historical possibilities available to human agency. It is also, and for the same reasons, shot through with pessimism about the dark side of human life; and the tension between these two is a constant theme in the Enlightenment.

But if Condorcet is exceptional, the very qualities that make him so also make him perhaps the most revealing example. His notion of progress as the universal triumph of human reason over ignorance and superstition may be more uncompromising than others of his time; but it does represent a crystallization, without ambiguities, of the themes that bind all Enlightenment figures together and give the concept of 'Enlightenment' whatever meaning it has. Precisely because his optimism about the beneficence of human reason is so uncompromising, because his universalism is so wide-ranging and cosmopolitan – because, in other words, he takes Enlightenment principles to what critics would regard as their extremes – his *Sketch* provides a clear and simple measure against which to test the standard accusations levelled at the 'Enlightenment project', about the inherent oppressiveness of its rationalism and the imperialism of its universalist principles.

Here, first, is how Condorcet sums up the goal of human progress: 'Our hopes for the future condition of the human race can be subsumed under three important heads: the abolition of inequality between nations, the progress of equality within each nation, and the true perfection of mankind.'

'The final end of the social art', Condorcet says in the most unambiguous terms, is 'real equality'.[14]

Here are his views on imperialism:

> Survey the history of our settlements and commercial undertakings in Africa or in Asia and you will see how our trade monopolies, our treachery, our murderous contempt for men of another colour or creed, the insolence of our usurpations, the intrigues or the exaggerated proselytic zeal of our priests, have destroyed the respect and goodwill that the superiority of our knowledge and the benefits of our commerce at first won for us in the eyes of the inhabitants.[15]

And on sexual oppression:

> Among the causes of the progress of the human mind that are of the utmost importance to the general happiness, we must number the complete annihilation of the prejudices that have brought about an inequality of rights between the sexes, an inequality fatal even to the party in whose favour it works. It is vain for us to look for a justification of this principle in any differences of physical organization, intellect or moral sensibility between men and women. This inequality has its origin solely in an abuse of strength.[16]

Condorcet may not be typical in the degree to which he holds such views, but even postmodernist critics of the Enlightenment may have some difficulty in deconstructing this discourse of equality or transforming it into something evil and oppressive. Nor can we dismiss the many ambiguities in the Enlightenment legacy, or the dangers inherent in excessive optimism about the perfection of humanity, not to mention the evils perpetrated in the name of progress. But it remains significant that here, in the *locus classicus* of Enlightenment optimism, equality within and between nations, races and sexes emerges not in opposition to, or in uneasy juxtaposition with, rationalism and universalism but as their logical conclusion, the final destination of progress.

Condorcet illustrates to perfection how the French preoccupation with the narrative of mind and the Republic of Letters is related to a kind of

14   Antoine-Nicolas de Condorcet, *Sketch for a Historical Picture of the Progress of the Human Mind*, trans. June Baraclough (London: Weidenfeld & Nicholson, 1955), pp. 172, 173.

15   *Ibid.*, pp. 175–6.

16   *Ibid.*, p. 193.

universalism and (to a greater or lesser extent) egalitarianism. There is no doubt that French intellectuals (with notable exceptions like Diderot – the Genevan Rousseau is something else altogether) envisaged themselves as an aristocracy of intellect, an elite, which consciously distanced itself from artisans and more vulgar kinds of professionals. Yet in this very particular and fairly short historical conjuncture, intellectual elitism, and even the material interests of intellectuals, had certain interesting and paradoxical effects. In the first place, in its own historical context, this meritocracy, in its commitment to the ideal of 'careers open to talent', had mildly democratic implications. But there were also other, wider implications. These thinkers saw it as their special mission to disseminate knowledge, which is the most distinctive and important feature of the French Enlightenment.

Condorcet, for instance, called for mass education – and he actually devised a plan for the Académie as the institution that would preside over a system of mass education. The kind of egalitarianism he espoused, his insistence on defining progress in terms of increasing equality and social inclusion, was inseparable from his view of the intellectual's mission. In a sense, his egalitarianism and his elitism were two sides of one coin. For him, as for other Enlightenment figures, the intellectuals' special claim to status and authority was their role in educating the world.

There is no intention here of exaggerating the Enlightenment commitment to equality. There were obviously strict limits to the equality envisaged even by thinkers like Condorcet, let alone, say, Voltaire, and much of it was in any case deferred to an indefinite future. But it is still significant as an aspiration, and it is significant how, in these very particular historical conditions, the logic of intellectual elitism impelled Enlightenment thinkers in that direction, into ideas that could be, and were, appropriated by far more radical and revolutionary forces.

No one can doubt that Enlightenment universalism could and did have oppressive, racist and imperialist manifestations; but it is also important to keep in mind something that postmodernist critics systematically forget: the connection between Enlightenment universalism and a critical temper that subjected European knowledge, European authority and European culture to more trenchant critique than any other. Even the conception of progress, which is supposed to be the essence of Enlightenment Eurocentrism, had anti-imperialist implications. The conception of progress as the progress of the human mind and knowledge takes for granted that the advance of knowledge is a very long-term cumulative process, projecting if not into infinity at least into the indefinite future. This conception, to be sure, implies that at some point, if not in the foreseeable future, certain truths can and will be discovered; and it further implies that some cultures are more advanced and therefore superior to others. But it also implies – perhaps even more fundamentally – that any given knowledge is open to question, that all authority is subject to challenge, that no one has a monopoly on truth.

The appropriation of history by intellectuals certainly evinces a far-reaching hubris. But at the same time that these intellectuals are arrogating history unto themselves, they are also taking on the burden of human fallibility and the whole dark history of human error and evil. A deep pessimism is never very far away from Enlightenment optimism. It is, in fact, just the other side of the same coin. If Enlightenment conceptions of knowledge and progress are founded on a kind of universalism, then it is a universalism that implies open-endedness, flexibility, scepticism. For all its dangers, Enlightenment universalism has provided a theoretical underpinning for emancipatory projects much more effective than anything postmodernists have been able to devise. So, indeed, has the concept of progress. For that matter, it gives us something that postmodernist celebrations of diversity and difference do not and cannot: a *reason* for recognizing and respecting otherness – if only on the grounds that the cumulative and open-ended quality of human knowledge and the progress of the human mind require us to be careful about closing any doors.

Condorcet may not have been typical in the degree to which he took the emancipatory logic of the Enlightenment seriously, but it says something about the complexity of the Enlightenment – and about the vacuity of many criticisms today – that this most classic example of Enlightenment optimism and universalism is also the one that most explicitly attacks the very evils ascribed to that Enlightenment optimism by critics today: racism, sexism, imperialism. Nor is this an accidental or contradictory juxtaposition: Condorcet's universalism and his optimism about human progress rest on the same foundation as his commitment to equality, his respect for the authenticity and integrity of other cultures, his attack on imperialism.

The Ideology of Capitalism

In the French Enlightenment we are approaching the end of a long history in which the inextricable unity of political and economic power is a central preoccupation of Western political thought. In the specific conditions of French absolutism, this preoccupation centred on privilege and access to high office, which gave a special salience to ideas of equality. It is true that, with few notable exceptions, the great Enlightenment figures were generally elitist and took hierarchy for granted – not to mention their own position, or aspirations, in that hierarchy. This was true even of Condorcet. Yet, for very concrete historical, even material, reasons, eighteenth-century France produced an ideology of universalism with more or less democratic and egalitarian implications. The Revolution would take that ideology much further than most *philosophes* intended; and the revolutionary legacy, with wide-ranging implications far beyond French borders, would certainly survive. But in the mainstream of Western political discourse, the Enlightenment 'project' would be overtaken by a different cultural formation, producing different notions of equality and shaping modern conceptions of democracy, the roots of which are traceable to early English capitalism.

England, needless to say, shared much with its European neighbours; but it had something specifically its own, a distinctively *capitalist* culture. English culture had certainly inherited some of the same universalistic legacies as had the French – for instance, the universalisms of Christianity and natural law. It was an Englishman, Isaac Newton, who practically invented the idea that the world was governed by certain universal, mathematical laws. As for equality, the English certainly took second place to no one in formulating ideas about the natural equality of men; and, of course, ideas of equality, at least of an ambiguous and qualified sort, did play a part in the ideology of England's ruling class in its battles against monarchical excesses, as in Locke's political theory. For that matter, the whole Enlightenment concept of progress owes a great deal to Locke – though it could be argued that the French conception of progress owes more to his epistemology, while the Anglo-Scottish conception has a greater affinity with his theory of property. But the point here is that, for all this common cultural legacy, English capitalism produced its own very specific ideological requirements. The interesting question is what happened when these universalistic and egalitarian ideas came within the orbit of capitalism.

We have seen how the social structure of France – its forms of appropriation by means of 'politically constituted property', the related importance of corporate principles – gave a particular salience to equality as an oppositional principle. The English situation was very different. In sharp contrast to France, corporate principles were already very weak in the seventeenth century, and they never had been as strong. The development of capitalist property forms was undermining the old extra-economic principles of hierarchy, and old conceptions of natural or prescriptive inequality were already seriously undermined. This made it harder to construct a theoretical case for inequality grounded in classic justifications of corporate hierarchy or appeals to a 'great chain of being'.

There is another point too. The old conception of bourgeois revolution as applied to the French is flawed in many ways, but the flaws have more to do with the conflation of bourgeois with capitalist than with the antithesis of bourgeoisie and aristocracy. There was indeed a conflict between 'bourgeoisie' and aristocracy, and that conflict did have material implications, which certainly would figure centrally in revolutionary ideology. But the bourgeois interests at stake in the conflict had less to do with capitalism than with the system of privilege and access to higher state office. This gave the aspiration to equality a special force. In England, the case was again very different. There was indeed a capitalist interest, but it was no less 'aristocratic' than 'bourgeois'; and in its struggles to maintain its own supremacy, equality was obviously not the objective. In fact, the idea of equality could become a real liability, as it did in the form of seventeenth-century English radicalism. If the theory of natural or prescriptive inequality, of corporate hierarchy and privilege, was the main problem facing the French bourgeoisie, for the English capitalist class the problem was, on the contrary, a theory of natural equality. In the absence of the old corporate principles and hierarchies, they were obliged to find wholly new ways of justifying domination that were compatible with natural equality. The English – although they were, as we have seen, building on a long tradition of Western political thought in combining ideas of natural equality with vast political and social inequalities – were especially creative in constructing a theoretical justification of inequality on a foundation of natural equality.

Here the most instructive example comes from John Locke. What makes him such a revealing object of comparison is the common ground he shares with his Enlightenment successors, which brings their divergences into sharp relief. Locke was certainly a major influence on the Enlightenment, especially through his epistemology. While he never went as far as Condorcet would later go, he had some reasonably enlightened attitudes about natural equality, as well as toleration and opposition to tyrannical government. But he also had some very distinctive ideas which set him apart from the main figures of the French Enlightenment and which are uniquely characteristic of capitalism. In fact, it is striking that, though Locke is writing a century before Condorcet at an early stage of capitalist development, some of his seventeenth-century attitudes have a more familiar ring to those of us who live in advanced capitalist societies.

The central issue for capitalist landlords was something rather different from the questions that confronted a non-capitalist bourgeoisie. In particular, they had to establish a certain kind of right to property, a historically unprecedented kind of right, which excluded and extinguished all other use rights, customary and common. They had to establish the primacy of profit and the market over rights of subsistence. All this created a very distinctive ideological pattern, which emerged in both theory and practice. The culture of 'improvement', which was such a striking feature of the Royal Society, appears not only in Locke's political theory but increasingly in English property law and in court decisions about property rights; in the new science of political economy; in the dispossession of small producers. 'Improvement', in the sense of productivity for profit, trumped all other goods. It would increasingly be cited in favour of exclusive private property: that is, property that excluded not only other individuals' rights to use it, but also communal regulation of production of a kind that would prevail for much longer in

France. Improvement could, in other words, as Locke makes very clear, turn even the most egalitarian ideas into justifications of dispossession.

Let us consider again Locke's famous observation, in the *Second Treatise*, that 'in the beginning, all the World was *America*' (§II.49). America here stands for the quintessentially primitive condition of humanity in the continuum of human development, and it provides a standard against which to judge a more advanced condition. Locke is here making the point that the earliest, and the natural, condition of the earth was effectively 'waste', and that human beings have a divine obligation to remove the earth from the waste, to make the earth *productive*, to *improve* it. His measure of improvement or productivity, as we have seen, is 'profit', not in the older meaning of advantage, whether material or otherwise, but quite simply as exchange value or commercial gain. As we saw in Chapter 7, Locke makes it clear that the issue is not labour as such but the productive – and, more particularly, the profitable – use of property.

This argument has many implications – for instance, that improvement, or productivity and profit, trump any other claims, such as the customary rights of English commoners, or the rights of indigenous peoples. For all the natural equality of men, on which Locke emphatically insists, the requirements of productivity and profit trump that, too. This is, put simply, a warrant for capitalist property. It is also a warrant for appropriating 'waste' land, and so for settler 'plantations'. Locke can even reconcile slavery with his assertion of men's natural freedom and equality: although no one can enslave himself by contract or consent, people can be legitimately enslaved as captives in a just war. This more or less traditional justification of slavery, apparently as a punishment for violation of natural law, would apply to any time and place.[17] Here again Locke's view contrasts sharply with Condorcet's, for whom the abolition of slavery would be a sign of progress.

Having begun his case against absolutism, then, with the unambiguous premise that men are free and equal in the state of nature, Locke goes on to cover his flank by finding ingenious and historically novel ways to justify inequality, deploying radical arguments against absolutism while taking great care to denude them of their most democratic and egalitarian implications. His approach to natural law in the *Second Treatise* – spelling out, with dialectical ingenuity, the conditions in which natural-law restrictions on accumulation of property can be overcome without violating natural law – also nicely illustrates how this supremely universalistic principle could be subordinated, or at least harnessed, to the requirements of private property and capital accumulation. In both cases, 'improvement' is the overriding principle.

We get a fairly clear picture of what constitutes progress for Locke, and

---

17   See Locke, *Second Treatise*, § 23.

the contrast with Condorcet is striking. Consider the main axis along which
each thinker divides the advanced from the undeveloped state of humanity:
for Condorcet it is rationality v. ignorance and superstition, equality v.
inequality; for Locke it is profit v. waste. Locke certainly identifies rationality as a superior condition, but while for Condorcet the progress of reason
is inextricably bound up with the advance of equality, for Locke rationality
is paired with 'industriousness' and is very hard to dissociate from productivity and profit. In fact, beginning with the proposition that all men are
naturally equal, he turns these principles of productivity and profit into a
new and historically unprecedented kind of validation of inequality.

The contrasts between Locke and Condorcet bring into sharp relief the
differences between the ideologies of capitalism and enlightenment. For
all their qualifications, Condorcet's egalitarian aspirations are striking,
and they are in sharp contrast to Locke. If, for Condorcet, equality is an
objective for the indefinite future, for Locke it is a reality in an unrecover-
able past or, at best, a moral principle conceived as easily compatible with
gross inequalities in the real world. Locke's theory of knowledge and his
views on education may suggest a fundamental egalitarianism, which
attributes differences among human beings in large part not to nature but
to experience; and he certainly ascribes to 'industriousness' a greater
weight than, say, to aristocratic birth. But he shows little sign of any aspiration like Condorcet's hope for 'the abolition of inequality between
nations, the progress of equality within each nation, and the true perfection of mankind'. If for Condorcet the objective is the improvement of
humanity, for Locke the objective is the 'improvement' of property. The
progress of humanity is subordinated to, or at least subsumed under, the
advance of productivity and profit.

In the eighteenth century the 'Scottish Enlightenment' would produce
ideas of progress and equality very much akin to those in France, which on
the face of it have more in common with Condorcet than with Locke. Yet
even here, there are significant divergences. In the French versions, even
when they are at their most materialist, the story of progress is the story of
the human mind, as a development from barbarism and superstition to
reason and Enlightenment. Condorcet's *Sketch*, for instance, presents all
kinds of economic, social and political advances as the development of
mind and reason. An even more striking example comes from Turgot. His
Discourse on the Successive Progress of the Human Mind was delivered in
1750, and though he never wrote the universal history he was planning, his
ideas on the subject seem to have been influential, not least on his friend
Condorcet. The case of Turgot is significant not only because commentators treat him as a pivotal figure in the Enlightenment idea of progress, and
even of the socio-economic theory of progress, but also because he is mainly
known as an economist, both as a theorist and a state administrator, who

might be expected to tell the story in its most materialist or economistic form. Yet for him, too, the principal issue is the 'steps taken by the human mind' in the progress 'from barbarism to refinement', from ignorance to knowledge, from superstition to reason and enlightenment. The principal agents of history are learned men and scholars, even academicians, the kind of people who constitute the Republic of Letters.

On the other side of the Channel, it was Scottish more than English political economists who developed something analogous to the French conception of progress, but they did so against the immediate background of English capitalism. The Scots, in fact, theorized English capitalism more effectively than did English theorists, no doubt because they were more conscious of its difference, its otherness, seen from the vantage point of the Scottish experience. The great Scottish intellectuals were very conscious of the contrast between English prosperity and Scottish poverty at the time of Union in 1707 and the hopes of economic improvement that had motivated many of its supporters. While the Scots more than the English wrote from an intellectual perspective with certain self-conscious affinities to the French, the example of England's material wealth was ever present in their conceptions of history and human development. At the heart of Adam Smith's political economy, like David Hume's history of England, is the English model of progress.

The Scottish Enlightenment was no less interested than the French in the whole range of progress – advances in knowledge, culture, politics, morality – but the distinctive development of the English economy was always at the core. One of the classics of the anglophone literature on progress, Adam Ferguson's *Essay on the History of Civil Society*, is, for example, a very wide-ranging story of progress, with many different aspects, social, political, cultural, as well as economic. The critical turning-point is identified in Part II, 'Of the History of Rude Nations', where Ferguson draws a line between 'Rude Nations prior to the Establishment of Property' and 'Rude Nations, under the Impressions of Property and Interest'. Beyond the invention of property that constitutes the dividing line between savagery and barbarism among 'rude' nations, the minimal condition for moving beyond rudeness to refinement is the division of labour; but it is the advent of commercial society that sets in train a distinctive capacity to sustain progress by directing the pursuit of individual self-interest to progressive development.

Commerce does, to be sure, endanger civic virtue, and political wisdom is required to preserve it; but the mechanisms of the market, and precisely those imperatives of competition that threaten virtue, are for Ferguson the only conceivable engine of self-sustaining progress. He does not attribute to the market quite the same role in integrating selfish motivations as does his friend Adam Smith, who eventually sought a solution in the disciplines of competition; and Ferguson still assigns to the political domain a greater role in preserving social bonds and moral order. But there is no mistaking his conviction, shared by Smith and Hume, that whatever may have been accomplished by the evolution of the human mind, it is commercial mechanisms and the enhancement of productivity for profit that set in motion progress as a self-sustaining process.

The advance of scientific knowledge as the engine of progress seems, then, to be displaced by a different kind of historical mechanism, a self-sustaining economic growth that, in historical reality, existed at that time only in England. Much the same idea of progress appears in the work of Adam Smith, and it is here that we can see the implications of such an argument for conceptions of equality. It may be true that Smith shared Condorcet's commitment to equality, as well as liberty and justice;[18] but for the Scot the burden of progressive development falls unambiguously on the market. The desirable effects of equitable distribution are, above all, a consequence of market mechanisms. The natural outcome of economic growth will be not only to raise the living standards of the poor but also to rebalance the distribution between profit and wages, on the grounds that the greater the amount of 'stock' or capital, the lower the rate of profit in relation to wages.

This is not the place to consider the flaws in Smith's economic argument. Suffice it to say that any mistakes he may have made about the relation between the growth of 'opulence' and the distribution of wealth among classes only made it easier for some of his successors to factor out the benevolence of his intentions and reduce his economics to the ruthless operations of the market. What is significant for our purposes is that, even if we reject conventional interpretations of Smith as a 'free market' theorist in the manner of a Friedrich Hayek or a Milton Friedman, even if we insist on his unrelenting commitment to the 'moral sentiments' and equitable distribution or the role of the state in achieving those ends, even if his advocacy of a 'free' market presumes its contribution to justice and equity, to make the economic mechanisms of a capitalist market the engine of historical advance inevitably risks allowing market imperatives to trump other social goods. In the manner of the Lockean paradigm, the advance of productivity for profit seems to overtake the improvement of humanity as the main criterion of progress.

---

18 For a compelling case that Smith and Condorcet, whatever their differences, shared common ground in their commitment to such ethical and political principles, contrary to conventional caricatures of a coldly unfeeling and rationalist 'Enlightenment', see Emma Rothschild, *Economic Sentiments: Adam Smith, Condorcet, and the Enlightenment* (Cambridge, Mass: Harvard University Press, 2001).

Capitalism and Democracy

The elevation of market mechanisms to moral imperatives was clearly an important development in Western social thought. But capitalism would have even more far-reaching effects in recasting the political terrain. The social map was completely redrawn by capitalism's distinctive configuration of political and economic power; and ways of thinking about rule and domination, about liberty and equality, were accordingly transformed.

We can gain some perspective on these transformations by looking back briefly at the notions of freedom and equality as they had evolved in the history of Western political theory. It had become fairly common to defend the right to rule while acknowledging and even stressing the universal freedom and equality of men (and, of course, it has generally been men). What makes Western political theory particularly interesting and even puzzling in this respect is that it invented a defence of domination not simply combined with, but even based on, a notion of equality, which specifically denies any natural division between ruler and ruled, or any justification of domination on the grounds of natural inequality. Hobbes, who defends an absolutist monarchy on the grounds of a very radical notion of natural equality and a denial that there exists any natural division between ruler and ruled, may be the most extreme and paradoxical example; but he certainly was not alone in combining equality with domination. That paradox has been a staple of Western political thought. This is not to say that ideas of equality and universal human community are exclusive to the culture of what, for lack of a better term, we call the West; and neither is it unusual for such ideas to coexist more or less happily with the realities of inequality and domination. But the Western canon is distinctive in its systematic mobilization of egalitarian doctrines and ideas of a universal human community in the *justification* of both class and imperial domination.

As long as the principle of domination is accepted on its own terms – whether as the 'mandate of heaven' or even simply on the basis of tradition or perhaps hereditary principles, the dynastic principles of royal bloodlines or descent from the Prophet – it can be perfectly compatible with the idea of general human equality. But Western political theory, at least at certain seminal moments in its history, confronted a very specific problem in explicating the juxtaposition of equality and domination. It had to find ways of explaining and justifying domination *on the basis* of equality. Or, to put it another way, it had to find new ways of systematically explaining and justifying domination itself.

The idea of natural equality became a troublesome issue when and because it was coupled with a notion of political equality, a fundamental challenge to the very idea of rule. Before the ancient Greeks invented a wholly new civic sphere and the new identity of citizenship, it had always been clear that the state represented domination, even, or especially, where men were assumed to be naturally equal. But now, the state itself – in fact, the state above all – represented equality. Equality, in other words, was not a simple fact of nature that had no bearing on the right to rule. Equality resided in the political sphere itself, expressed in the political identity of citizenship.

In societies where wealth and dominance depended fundamentally on privileged access to political rights, where economic power was so closely bound up with legal, political and military status, the concept of civic equality posed serious risks to dominant classes. In the case of ancient Greek democracy, the invention of citizenship and civic equality, while it certainly did not eliminate economic and social inequalities, had real practical effects on disparities of economic power, limiting the possibilities of 'extra-economic' exploitation. The citizenship enjoyed by peasants, for instance, spared them the kinds of dependence on lords or a tax-hungry state that have plagued most peasants throughout history.[19]

Yet if the civic ideal seemed a threat to rulers and propertied elites, once the idea had taken root it was difficult to eradicate; and it became necessary to find new ways of justifying domination within a civic community. Hellenistic and Roman emperors preserved the ancient civic principles but found ways of adapting them to serve imperial purposes. Alexander the Great and his successors, for instance, appropriated the principal themes that had emerged from the life of the polis, its notions of citizenship, law, freedom and equality. They then deprived these ideas of their subversive force by transplanting them from polis to 'cosmopolis', the universal polis of the Empire. On the elevated plane of the imperial cosmopolis, all men were equal under the skin; but in the real world of everyday life, some were rich and some were poor, and the emperor ruled over all his imperial subjects. The Roman Empire that followed would perfect this strategy of displacing the civic idea to a less dangerous sphere.

The idea of the cosmopolis did have its own egalitarian possibilities. Hellenistic Stoic philosophy, for example, produced the idea of a universal cosmic order governed by principles of natural reason, a kind of natural law, accessible to all human beings.[20] But Roman Stoics would take the sting out of this idea. Elaborating their own conception of a universal empire, a single world empire ruled by one absolute ruler, the Romans found their own ways of converting the old principles of the polis into imperial ideas. In the Roman concept of citizenship, the ancient civic principles of active political agency were replaced by an increasingly passive conception of citizenship. At the same time, Roman thinkers (like Cicero) put their own distinctive stamp on the idea of natural law, neatly combining a notion of universal moral equality

---

19 The ancient Greeks are discussed at some length in my *Citizens to Lords*.
20 For more on this, see *ibid.*, esp. pp. 103–14.

with an explicit commitment to social and political inequality and domination. The old Greek civic community, with its principles of freedom and equality, was removed to a still higher level of abstraction, still more detached from the realities of social inequality and political hierarchy.

This elaboration of natural law owed a great deal to the characteristically Roman duality of state and property, political power and ownership. The idea of two modes of authority, each with its own distinctive domain, would be readily adapted not only to asserting the *imperium* of Caesar while preserving his subjects' *dominium*, their exclusive claims to private property, but also to acknowledging the dominance of gods while preserving the authority of Caesar. Even when the lines between property and jurisdiction were blurred by the parcellization of sovereignty, the Roman legacy survived. The Romans produced a way of thinking about property and spheres of authority that made it possible to insist on one universal cosmic *logos,* a universal and common natural law, the equality of all human beings, and even a supreme divine authority, while still declaring the sanctity of private property, the legitimacy of social inequality and the absolute authority of earthly governments – and that included the authority of governments that by any reasonable standard defied the ethical principles of divine or natural law. It was only a short conceptual step to Western Christianity and its distinctive division of labour between Caesar and God.[21] The Western Christian tradition, especially its dissenting sects, would, to be sure, produce its own kinds of radical egalitarianism; but its official orthodoxies took the final step in relegating human equality to a sphere beyond this world: from polis to cosmopolis to heaven.

In the Middle Ages, it became more difficult to manage the delicate balance between equality in one sphere and domination in another. Even the old Christian dualism could not suffice. Feudal lordship depended unequivocally on a legal and political hierarchy embodied in formal status differences, and economic exploitation depended directly on that

---

21   The philosopher Seneca (ca. 3 BC–AD 65) nicely illustrates the conceptual sequence. Explicating Stoic doctrine, he demonstrates how all things can be considered common, at least to wise men, while still remaining individual and private property. He draws a significant analogy with the rights of the emperor: 'all things are [Caesar's] by right of his authority [*imperio*]', yet at the same time the sense in which everything is his by right of *imperium* must be distinguished from the way things belong to him as his own personal property by right of inheritance, 'by actual right and ownership', or *dominium*. Seneca then goes on to apply the analogy to the gods: 'while it is true that all things belong to the gods, all things are not consecrated to the gods, and . . . only in the case of the things that religion has assigned to a divinity is it possible to discover sacrilege' (*On Benefits,* VII.vi–vii). In other words, just as Caesar's *imperium* does not preclude the property of others, the *dominium* of the gods over all things does not preclude the authority of earthly powers in this world.

extra-economic hierarchy. The capacity of landlords to exploit the labour of peasants required a monopoly of political and military power, and a legally formalized structure of lordship and dependence. Feudal ideologies of domination tended to be quite explicit about their inegalitarian foundations, which meant that Christian brotherhood and equality before God were obliged to coexist not only with earthly inequality but with ideas of a divinely ordained cosmic hierarchy, a 'Great Chain of Being'.

The idea of a universal moral equality and government based on the consent of naturally free men would, nonetheless, remain deeply rooted in the Western tradition; and thinkers worked out elaborate conceptions of natural freedom and equality that did not endanger ideas of unaccountable and virtually unconditional rule. Ideas of natural freedom, equality and government by consent could even be mobilized in defence of absolute monarchical power. Still, the strategy was not without its risks, which could be exploited by doctrines of resistance.

There would be a brief moment in the 'Age of Enlightenment' when the structure of privilege and office in the absolutist state gave earthly equality a special salience among intellectual elites. But this would soon be overtaken by a different, specifically capitalist culture, with its own conceptions of equality. With the advent of capitalism, the ideological possibilities and the needs of dominant classes would change radically. Once economic power no longer depended on extra-economic status or privilege, the civic ideal of political equality could be brought back to earth in wholly new ways. For the first time in history, the rhetoric of democracy could become the preferred and systematic ideological strategy of domination, both class domination and imperialism. In the 'early modern' period covered by this book, that ideological strategy was not yet fully viable, but nor was it necessary or even possible completely to suppress the civic ideal. Ruling ideas were increasingly challenged by more democratic aspirations, and new ways were found to renegotiate, in new historical conditions, the relation between civic equality and social inequalities.

Locke's conception of property is a milestone in Western political thought not simply because it represents a novel theory of property rights but because it points to a redefinition of the political sphere. There were, in Locke's time and thereafter, significant political conflicts over the meaning of property; and principles very much like the ones Locke was invoking were being used to underwrite new legal conceptions of property, to say nothing of colonial expansion. The capacity to mobilize the law for such purposes, and to gain the support of the state in redefining property, of course presupposes control of political processes. Privileged access to the political domain gave propertied classes in England huge advantages in shaping the law to their requirements. Yet the effect of redefining property in this way was to shift relations of domination away from politics and into a separate economic sphere. It would be a long time before political rights were more equally distributed; and the state would continue to be used by propertied classes, often with great force, to discipline their labouring subordinates. But by the time democratic rights were finally extended, the disciplines of the market and capital's control of production had made direct coercion by the state less important to the dominant classes: political equality would no longer have the same direct effects on social domination and economic inequality.

In eighteenth-century England, that extension of democratic rights was still a distant prospect, but the formation of an 'economic' sphere distinct from the political domain was well advanced; and with it would come a new conception of politics and democratic rights. The 'economy' became the subject of a new mode of theorizing, the 'science' of economics. The classical political economists were not the first in history to reflect on the processes of production, appropriation and distribution that are the primary subjects of the economic discipline; nor were the English or the Scots the first to theorize about self-propelling economic 'circuits'. But never before the advent of capitalism had it been possible to conceive of economic processes as abstracted from 'non-economic' relations and practices, operating according to their own distinct laws, the purely 'economic' laws of the market, and without the integration imposed by a 'legal despotism' in the physiocratic manner. It had never before been possible to conceptualize an 'economy' with its own forms of coercion, to which political categories seemed not to apply. The 'laws' of supply and demand, the production and distribution of goods, or the formation of wages and prices could, for the purposes of economic 'science', be treated as impersonal mechanisms; and human beings in the economic sphere could be perceived as abstract factors of production, whose relations to each other were very different from the relations of power, domination and subordination that defined the political sphere, the sphere of rulers and subjects or citizens and states.

This new kind of 'economy' would redefine the political sphere. The development of capitalism was making it possible for the first time in history to conceive of political rights as having little bearing on the distribution of social and economic power; and it was becoming possible to imagine a distinct political sphere in which all citizens were formally equal, a political sphere abstracted from the inequalities of wealth and economic power outside the political domain. Political progress, or even the progress of democracy, could be conceived in terms that were socially indifferent, with an emphasis on political and civil rights that regulated the relations between citizen and state, not the maldistribution of social and economic power among citizens, who in the abstract sphere of politics were equal.

If in the 'Age of Enlightenment' intellectual elites, and not only popular forces, had just begun to challenge the long Western tradition of transforming ideas of natural equality into justifications of inequality and domination, capitalism neatly circumvented that challenge by abstracting the political sphere from economic hierarchies and coercion. It made possible not only a neat division of labour between discrete and autonomous 'sciences', which is reflected in both classical political economy and liberal political philosophy, but also a view of the world in which 'economic' forms of power and coercion are not recognized as power and coercion at all. In the political domain, it may be necessary to limit excesses of power or to safeguard democratic liberties; but the political principles of liberty and checks on power do not belong in the 'economy'. Indeed, a free economy is one in which economic imperatives are given free rein. The essence of the capitalist 'economy' is that a very wide range of human activities, which in other times and places were subject to the state or to communal regulation of various kinds, have been transferred to the economic domain. In that ever-expanding domain, human beings are governed not only by the hierarchies of the workplace but also by the compulsions of the market, the relentless requirements of profit-maximization and constant capital accumulation, none of which are subject to democratic freedom or accountability.

INDEX